THIRD   EDITION

CASES IN STRATEGIC MANAGEMENT

Thomas L. Wheelen
University of South Florida

J. David Hunger
Iowa State University

THIRD   EDITION

CASES IN STRATEGIC MANAGEMENT

Thomas L. Wheelen
University of South Florida

J. David Hunger
Iowa State University

ADDISON-WESLEY PUBLISHING COMPANY

Reading, Massachusetts • Menlo Park, California
New York • Don Mills, Ontario • Wokingham, England
Amsterdam • Bonn • Sydney • Singapore • Tokyo
Madrid • San Juan

Sponsoring Editor: Mary Fischer
Managing Editor: Mary Clare McEwing
Production Supervisor: Peggy J. Flanagan
Software Production Supervisor: Mary J. Coffey
Production Services: The Book Department, Inc.
Text Designer: Deborah Schneck
Cover Designer: Marshall Henrichs
Copyeditor: Fannie Toldi
Permissions Editor: Mary Dyer
Manufacturing Media Supervisor: Lu Anne Piskadlo

Library of Congress Cataloging-in-Publication Data

Wheelen, Thomas L.
    Cases in strategic management/Thomas L. Wheelen and J. David Hunger.,—3rd ed.
      p.   cm.
    ISBN 0–201–50826–5
    1. Strategic planning—Case studies. I. Hunger, J. David, 1941–   . II. Title.
HD30.28.W428   1990
658.4′012—dc20   89–17667
                                                           CIP

ABCDEFGHIJ-DO-943210

DEDICATED TO

THE WHEELEN FAMILY

- My parents, Thomas L. and Kathryn E.
- My children
  Kathryn E.
  Thomas L., II
  Richard D.

THE HUNGER FAMILY

- My parents, Jackson S. and Elizabeth C.
- My wife, Betty
- My children
  Karen C.
  Susan S.
  Laura E.
  Merry K.

Preface

This book contains 31 current, comprehensive cases of actual business corporations and industries in the midst of strategic change. Eight time-tested cases have been included from *Strategic Management and Business Policy*, Third Edition (1989). The other 23 cases are completely new. This balance provides some of the most popular cases already published, and the latest, most current cases available today. This casebook may be used with the paperback text *Strategic Management*, Third Edition (1990) by Wheelen and Hunger or with other texts or books of readings at either the undergraduate or graduate level.

The companies described in these cases vary in size from the small, local **JJ's—Women's Clothing Store (25)** to the large, worldwide **Xerox Corporation (6)**. Some of them, such as **Piper Aircraft (29)**, are units of even larger corporations, like Lear Siegler. Others, like **Harcourt, Brace, Jovanovich (31)** and **Federated Department Stores (24)**, are independent firms that are in serious danger of being bought by another corporation. In contrast, **Polaroid Corporation (5)**, **Anheuser-Busch (9)**, and **Harley-Davidson (27)** are examples of companies that are actively acquiring new businesses either to diversify into new product lines or to increase their competitive advantage in their current businesses. A few, however, are like **General Mills (11)** and **Hershey Foods (12)**, who must decide which businesses to keep and which to de-emphasize or sell. The cases vary from the fairly low-tech operations of **Ying May Garment Factory (19)** and **Plastic Suppliers (17)** to the high-tech systems houses of **Applied CAD Knowledge (20)**, **Fared Robot Systems (22)**, and **Hogan Systems (7)**. They profile companies like **Johnson Products (2)**, which chooses to compete by focusing on specific product lines for a particular market niche, as well as companies like the fast-growing **Limited (23)**, which is trying through differentiation to replace traditional department stores as the dominant merchandiser of clothing and other soft goods in the United States. The cases range in emphasis from the **Golden Gate Brewing Company (8)**, which is focusing on the San Francisco area, to **Bombardier (28)** of Quebec, which is working to dominate not only the North American but also the international snowmobile market. **Ying May Garment Factory (19)** and **Caishikou Barbershop (18)** are examples of cases highlighting business activities in the fast-developing Pacific Rim area of the world.

The organizations highlighted in these cases may provide services for nearby customers, like the **University Pharmacy (26)** and **Caishikou Barbershop (18)**, or they may globally manufacture and market mass-produced products, like **Reebok International (3)** and **Liz Claiborne, Inc (1)**. The corporation's image may be one of middle-American family values, such as **Hardee's (14)** and **Wendy's**

(13) fast-food restaurants, or it may be very different, like **Bally's (30)** involvement in pinball machines and gambling casinos. All in all, the cases in this book provide some examples of highly publicized firms—such as **Apple Computer (4)**—in "glamorous" industries like personal computers, as well as the less publicized corporations—such as **Pioneer Hi-Bred International (15)**—in the more "down-to-earth" agribusiness industry. (But watch out for the impact that biotechnology research at companies like Pioneer is likely to have on the future of the world!)

The cases in this book cover a wide range of issues that are discussed in a typical business policy/strategic management course. Given the multifaceted nature of complex and comprehensive policy cases, no attempt has been made in this book to categorize or to arrange the cases by issue or by strategic management elements such as formulation, implementation, or evaluation and control. We strongly believe that the reader should be left free to roam through each case situation without any preconceptions of what is or is not important. The reader should be willing to search for any and all relevant issues, regardless of what the case authors may have originally believed was *the* issue. As writers of cases, both of us have learned through experience that a well-written policy case is like a polished diamond. It provides many different facets to the viewer, depending upon the intensity and direction of the light.

Each case has been class-tested in a business policy/strategic management course. Except for the four favorite cases of Xerox, Piper Aircraft, Pioneer Hi-Bred, and Hershey Foods, all the cases are very recent and take place between 1986 and 1989. Most include in-depth information on the industry involved as well as a complete set of financial statements over a three- to five-year period for the corporation under discussion. In addition, complete notes on the **Food Service Industry (10)** and on **Maquiladora Operations (16)** (joint U.S.–Mexico manufacturing facilities to be used with Case 17–**Plastic Suppliers**) are provided. The **Note on the Food Service Industry (10)** may be used not only with the **General Mills (11)** and **Hershey Foods (12)** cases, but also with the **Wendy's (13)** and **Hardee's (14)** cases. The cases are grouped into eleven industry categories of fashion, information technology, brewing, food, restaurant/fast food, agribusiness, international manufacturing and services, manufacturing technology: systems houses, retailing, personal transportation, and entertainment.

Each case is about the real problems of a real organization. These cases help the student bridge the gap between the theories of the ivory tower and the practices of the real world. The high quality of these cases is shown by the fact that the majority of them have been critiqued at workshops conducted by the North American Case Research Association and the Midwest Society for Case Research and/or accepted for publication in leading case journals such as *Case Research Journal, Journal of Management Case Studies,* and *Annual Advances in Business Cases.*

The 31 cases presented in this book are followed by an appendix chapter that explains the *case method* and the *strategic audit.* It suggests the strategic audit as a helpful checklist to use in analyzing complex and comprehensive business policy/strategic management cases. The appendix also provides information on researching a company and on presenting case analysis. Financial ratios are summarized, and tables detailing changes over time in the consumer price index and prime interest rate are included.

DECISION SUPPORT DISKETTES

The decision support software Strategic Financial Analyzer (ST. FAN™), packaged with this book was specially developed for students of strategic management and business policy. This software allows the instructor to introduce students to meaningful *computer-assisted strategic and financial analysis* from cases in the book. The software is used with the Lotus® 1-2-3® program on IBM-compatible (MS-DOS) personal computers with two disk drives. The software is "user friendly" and requires minimal knowledge of Lotus 1-2-3, programming, or microcomputers beyond the basic knowledge of "booting up." The student can learn to use the software in less than one hour, from the instructions provided, so that the instructor need not be involved.

This software, the most comprehensive software package available for students of strategic management, will enhance the student's knowledge of financial and strategic management analytical techniques. The Strategic Audit Worksheet allows the student to quickly organize and print out his/her strategic audit. This software links the classroom with the methods that strategic managers use in their companies.

The software helps students to complete *on their own*, quickly and easily, the financial analysis of complex strategy/policy cases. It uses historical financial information (*not* the constant dollar format used in previous software) in the form of balance sheets and income statements from the cases to generate:

- 27 financial ratios (see Appendix).
- Common-size balance sheets and income statements (see Appendix).
- Scenario construction box, which enables the students to develop *pro forma* projected financial statements to accompany their recommendations. *A special feature of this box is that it interacts directly with Lotus 1-2-3 for ease of operation.*
- A strategic audit worksheet enabling students to do a complete S.W.O.T. analysis on the personal computer (see Figure 3 in Appendix).

In addition, as a special feature, the program automatically calculates financial ratios and develops common-size balance sheets and income statements for the *pro forma* projections generated by the students in their scenario construction. This enables the student to check to see if the recommendation is feasible and in general agreement with the historical ratios and relationships.

Available separately from Addison-Wesley is a full-function *Student Edition of Lotus® 1-2-3®*. The Lotus® Student Edition is compatible with the decision support disks included with this book.

INSTRUCTOR'S MANUAL

A comprehensive Instructor's Manual has been carefully constructed to accompany this book. A standardized format is provided for each case: (1) case abstract, (2) case issues and subjects, (3) steps covered in the strategic decision-making process (see Figure 2 in Appendix), (4) case objectives, (5) suggested classroom approaches, (6) discussion questions, (7) student paper, (8) case author's teaching note, (9) student strategic audit, and (10) financial analysis—27 ratios plus common-size statements for the 16 cases that are on the Strategic Financial Analyzer (ST. FAN™) software.

The Instructor's Manual also contains two additional cases to be used as follow-up cases to extend class discussion and analysis. These are *Applied CAD Knowledge* (*C*) and *Harley-Davidson* (*B*). The instructor at his or her discretion may copy these to hand out to students in class.

ACKNOWL-EDGMENTS

Our special thanks go to editors Mary Fischer and John Weimeister of Addison-Wesley Publishing Company for their support of this third edition. We are extremely grateful to Mary Clare McEwing and Peggy Flanagan of Addison-Wesley and to Mary Day Fewlass of The Book Department, Inc. for their supervision of the production process, and to Fannie Toldi for her careful copyediting. The valuable contributions of the people at Addison-Wesley are reflected in the overall quality of the book and in the fact that it was published on time—every time!

We thank Betty Hunger for her typing of the Preface and June Blonde for her typing of the Instructor's Manual. We are very thankful to the many students who tried out the cases we chose to include in this book. Their comments helped us find any flaws in the cases before the book went to the printer. A special note of thanks goes to Glenn Wilt and Gilbert Gonzalez for their original development of our decision support software and to David Tansic of the University of Arizona for his helpful suggestions. We are especially grateful to Gilbert Gonzalez for his development of our new improved decision support software, Strategic Financial Analyzer (ST. FAN™). A note of thanks is also given to Mark Monsour for his development of the student instructions for the software.

In addition, we express our appreciation to Dr. Charles Handy and Dr. David Shrock, past and present Deans, respectively, and to Dr. John Wacker, Management Department Chair, of Iowa State University's College of Business Administration, for their provision of the resources so necessary to produce a casebook. We also thank Kathy Wheelen for her assistance in the preparation of the book, Instructor's Manual, and software.

Finally, we thank the many people who have sent us cases for possible inclusion in this book. We appreciate your interest in our efforts and thank you for your willingness to write quality comprehensive cases. It would be extremely difficult to teach a course in business policy/strategic management without your efforts. We acknowledge our dept to you—the people who write and use cases in the classroom. This book is yours.

Tampa, Florida   T.L.W.
Ames, Iowa   J.D.H.

Contents

About the Contributors

Moustafa H. Abdelsamad, D.B.A. (George Washington University), is Dean of the College of Business and Industry at Southeastern Massachusetts University. He previously served as Professor of Finance and Associate Dean for Graduate Studies in Business at Virginia Commonwealth University. He is Editor-in-Chief, *SAM Advanced Management Journal* and past International President of the Society for Advancement of Management. He is the author of *A Guide to Capital Expenditure Analysis*, and two chapters in the *Dow Jones-Irwin Capital Budgeting Handbook*. He is the author or coauthor of numerous articles in various publications.

Sexton Adams, Ph.D., is Professor of Management at North Texas State University. He has also taught at the University of Northern Colorado and Pepperdine University. He is actively engaged as consultant to various organizations in strategic planning and management development. He is the author of *Administrative Policy and Strategy* and *Personnel Management* and is coauthor of *The Corporate Promotables* and *Modern Personnel Management*. He has published business policy cases in over 20 case books.

Virginia L. Blackburn, D.B.A. (University of Kentucky), is Assistant Professor of Management at Iowa State University. She is the 1989 Random House award winner for outstanding case development and is the author of several articles on corporate governance and diversification strategy and company performance.

James W. Clinton, Ph.D. (St. Louis University), is Professor of Management, University of Northern Colorado. Previously, he was a research analyst and project leader with the Department of Defense. He has authored six business policy cases, several of which appear in strategic management texts, as well as articles in *Computerworld* and *SAM Advanced Management Journal*.

Thomas Conquest, M.S. (Iowa State University), is an electrical engineer with Lear Siegler, Inc., Grand Rapids, Michigan. Previously, he was with the Collins Group of Rockwell International.

David B. Croll, Ph.D. (Pennsylvania State University), is Associate Professor of Accounting, University of Virginia. He was a visiting professor at the University of Michigan. He is co-author of *Behavioral Accounting—A Reader*. His cases have appeared in over 10 management and accounting textbooks as well as in the *Journal of Management Case Studies*. He is currently con-

sultant to the U.S. Navy, the Institute of Textile Technology, and the Institute of Chartered Financial Analysts.

Steven M. Dawson, Ph.D. (University of Michigan), is Professor of Finance, University of Hawaii, and formerly Visiting Professor at the University of International Business and Economics (Beijing), the National University of Singapore, the Chinese University of Hong Kong, and the University of Michigan. He is the author of over 65 articles and has 10 cases published in textbooks.

Phyllis Feddeler, M.B.A. (University of South Florida), is with Barnett Bank and was formerly a teaching assistant for strategic management at the University of South Florida.

Janiece L. Gallagher, M.B.A. (University of South Florida), is Vice-President of Finance for Medcare, a large medical development/management company headquartered in Brandon, Florida. Previously, she was a partner in a medical consulting firm specializing in strategic planning and strategic management of high-tech medical facilities. She was also an instructor of Strategic Management and Business Policy at the University of South Florida.

Lynda L. Goulet, M.B.A. (University of Northern Iowa), is Instructor of Management, University of Northern Iowa. She has taught courses in strategic planning, management fundamentals, and quantitative methods for the last 12 years. She has written or coauthored numerous papers and case studies, which have appeared in *Annual Advances in Business Cases* and more than 10 different management and policy textbooks. She is currently editor of *Annual Advances in Business Cases* and is coauthoring a policy text.

Walter E. Greene is Professor of Management and Business Policy at Pan American University (which became UT-Pan American on September 1, 1989). He was formerly a USAF Commissioned officer and has worked with industry prior to entering the teaching profession. He has written several articles, and his cases have appeared in over 10 textbooks. He has served on the Board of Directors of SWDSI, SWSBI and is presently Vice-President of Programs, SWSBI.

Adelaide Griffin, Ph.D., is Professor of Management at Texas Woman's University, and has served as Visiting Professor to the University of Texas at Arlington. She has published articles in the field of strategic planning with special emphasis on the health care industry, a monograph on the special problems and successful strategies used by executive women, as well as numerous cases and papers. She is coauthor of the textbook, *Modern Personnel Management*, and the monograph, *Executive Women in the Dallas/Ft. Worth Metroplex: Significant Problems and Successful Strategies*.

Ward D. Harder, M.B.A. (Middle Tennessee State University), C.P.A. (State of Tennessee), is Associate Professor of Accounting, Motlow State Community College. He received the 1988 Public Service Award from the Tennessee Society of C.P.A.s for his efforts in education, industry, government, and public service. He has presented papers at the meetings of the American Accounting Association and the Midwest Society for Case Research. He is the author of 15 cases, which have appeared in several publications. He has been selected as the winner of the Teaching Excellence Award at Motlow State.

Stuart C. Hinrichs, M.S. (Iowa State University), is an airline pilot with Pan American Airlines. He was formerly an officer in the United States Navy serving on the faculty of Iowa State University as a NROTC instructor.

Alan N. Hoffman, D.B.A. (Indiana University), is Associate Professor of Management, Bentley College, Waltham, Massachusetts. He has published articles in the *Academy of Management Journal, Journal of Business Strategies, Business Forum*, and *Human Relations*.

J. David Hunger, Ph.D. (Ohio State University), is Professor of Strategic Management at Iowa State University. Previously, he was with George Mason University and the University of Virginia. His research interests lie in strategic management, conflict management, and leadership. He has worked in management positions for Procter & Gamble, Lazarus Department Store, and the U.S. Army. He has been active as consultant and trainer to business corporations, as well as to state and federal government agencies. He has written numerous articles and cases appearing in the *Academy of Management Journal, Journal of Management, Case Research Journal, International Journal of Management, Journal of Management Case Studies, Human Resource Management, SAM Advanced Management Journal*, and the *Handbook of Business Strategy*, among others. Dr. Hunger is a member of the Academy of Management, Midwest Society for Case Research, North American Case Research Association, and Strategic Management Society. He presently serves as President of the Midwest Society for Case Research and on the Board of Directors of the Midwest Management Society and on the editorial review boards of the *SAM Advanced Management Journal* and the *Journal of Management Case Studies*. He is coauthor of *Strategic Management and Business Policy* and *Strategic Management*.

Raymond M. Kinnunen, D.B.A. (Louisiana State University), is Associate Professor of Management and Chairman of the Management Department at Northeastern University. In addition to teaching at Northeastern, he has taught in advanced management programs at INCAE in Central America and IMEDE in Lausanne, Switzerland. Before joining the faculty of the College of Business at Northeastern University, he was employed as a production engineer and analyst with E. I. duPont deNemours and Company. His research interests are in the areas of corporate strategy and management control systems. Professor Kinnunen is the author of numerous articles in such periodicals as *Academy of Management Review, Journal of General Management, University of Michigan Business Review, Management Accounting, Transportation Journal, IEEE Transactions on Engineering Management*, and cases published in the *Case Research Journal* and numerous textbooks.

Joseph Lampel, Ph.D. (McGill University), is Assistant Professor at New York University in the area of business strategy and policy. He has published articles on the subject of technological innovation as well as cases dealing with strategic management. He is currently conducting research on the development of strategies in industries characterized by large and infrequent transactions.

Richard I. Levin, Ph.D. (University of North Carolina at Chapel Hill), is the Phillip Hettleman Professor of Business Administration at the Graduate School of Business Administration, University of North Carolina, Chapel Hill. Professor Levin was formerly Associate Dean of the Graduate School of Business Administration at that institution. He served as President of the Southern Management Association for two years. He is the author of 16 books in statistics, operations research, planning, and financial management, including *Statistics for Management*, 4th edition, *Quantitative Approaches to Management*, 7th edition, *Buy Low Sell High Collect Early and Pay Late*, and *The Executives Illustrated Primer of Long Range Planning*. Mr. Levin has authored over 40 articles and approximately 50 cases. He is the founder of four companies and took one of them public in the late 1960s.

Larry Maxwell is a financial analyst with the 3M company, St. Paul, Minnesota.

Charles E. Michaels, Jr., Ph.D. (University of South Florida), is Assistant Professor of Management at the University of South Florida. He has served on the Editorial Review Board for *SAM Advanced Management Journal* and has authored articles and papers in the fields of business management and industrial psychology.

William Miller, M.S. (Iowa State University), is an industrial engineer specialist in the Process Development Department of the Collins Transmission Systems Division of Rockwell International, Dallas, Texas.

Robert L. Nixon, Ph.D. (Cornell University), is Associate Professor of Management and Organizational Behavior and Theory at the University of South Florida. His publications focus on the effects of information systems in the organization. He is the author of numerous papers and articles.

Deborah Reading, M.S. (Iowa State University), is a program coordinator with the Office of International Educational Services, Iowa State University.

David Saveraid, M.S. (Iowa State University), is a project specialist with the Farm Information Management Services Division of Pioneer Hi-Bred, International, Johnston, Iowa.

JoAnn K. L. Schwinghammer, Ph.D. (University of Arkansas), is Professor of Marketing, Mankato State University, Mankato, Minnesota. She was formerly on the marketing faculty at North Texas State University. She is the author of several cases, which have appeared in the *Case Research Journal* and numerous marketing, management, and small business textbooks. She serves as a reviewer for the *Case Research Journal* and the *Midwest Journal of Business and Economics.*

John A. Seeger, D.B.A. (Harvard University), served as a consultant, Chief Executive Officer of two small businesses, and an administrator at M.I.T., spending 16 years in industry before returning to academia. At Northeastern University he was awarded the University Certificate of Excellence in Teaching; he is now Professor of Management at Bentley College. His papers have appeared in a variety of journals and books, including the *Academy of Management Journal,* the *Strategic Management Journal, Entrepreneurship Theory and Practice,* and the *Case Research Journal* (of which he serves as Associate Editor). His cases appear in 40 texts in strategic management, marketing, organization behavior, and human resource management. He serves as Eastern Regional Director of the North American Case Research Association, and as Chair of the Eastern Casewriters' Association. He has lectured widely in Europe and South America, and consults in strategic management and organizational design.

Jamal Shamsie, Ph.D. (McGill University), is coordinator of McGill's undergraduate course in business strategy and policy. He has published several articles and cases in strategic management, some of which are based upon field studies. He is presently engaged in research on the development of sustainable competitive advantages in various types of industries.

Charles B. Shrader, Ph.D. (Indiana University), is Assistant Professor of Management, Iowa State University. He is the 1989 Random House award winner for outstanding case development and is the author or coauthor of several articles and professional papers on strategic planning, organization structure, and organization performance.

Joyce P. Vincelette, D.B.A. (Indiana University), is Professor of Business Administration at Trenton State College. She was previously a faculty member at the University of South Florida. She has served on the Editorial Review Board for the *SAM Advanced Management Journal* and has authored articles and professional papers in the areas of human resource management and organizational behavior.

Charles R. Wagner, Ph.D. (University of Nebraska, Lincoln), is Emeritus Professor of Accounting at Mankato State University, Mankato, Minnesota, and was formerly on the faculty at Creigh- ton University, the University of South Dakota, Gustavus Adolphus College, and St. Cloud State University. He has authored numerous cases made available through the International Case Clearing House at Harvard Business School. His articles have appeared in *Management Accounting* and *Internal Auditor.* Professor Wagner served as a National Director of Education for the National Association of Accountants, as well as a member of the Regional Council, President, and Vice President of the South Central Minnesota Chapter of the NAA.

Kathryn E. Wheelen is a student at St. Petersburg Community College and works as a research assistant in case development.

Thomas L. Wheelen, D.B.A. (George Washington University), is Professor of Strategic Management, University of South Florida, and was formally the Ralph A. Beeton Professor of Free Enterprise at the McIntire School of Commerce, University of Virginia. He was Visiting Professor at both the University of Arizona and Northeastern University. He has worked in management positions for General Electric and the U.S. Navy. He has been active as a consultant and trainer to business corporations, as well as to federal and state government agencies. He serves on the Board of Directors of Lazer Surgical Software, Inc. He served on the editorial boards of the *Journal of Management* and serves on the editorial boards of *Journal of Management Case Studies* and *SAM Advanced Management Journal.* He is coauthor of *Strategic Management and Business Policy* and *Strategic Management,* as well as coeditor of *Developments in Management Information Systems* and *Collective Bargaining in the Public Sector,* and codeveloper of the Software, *Financial Analyzer (FAN).* He has authored 37 articles appearing in such journals as *Journal of Management, Business Quarterly, Personnel Journal, SAM Advanced Management Journal, Journal of Retailing, International Journal of Management,* and the *Handbook of Business Strategy.* His cases appear in 27 management textbooks as well as the *Journal of Management Case Studies* and *Case Research Journal.* He has served on the Board of Directors of the Southern Management Association, as Vice President at Large for the Society for the Advancement of Management, and as President of the North American Case Research Association. He is a member of the Academy of Management, Southern Management Association, North American Case Research Association, Society for Advancement of Management, Institute for Decision Science, Midwest Society for Case Research, Strategic Management Association, and Strategic Planning Society. He is currently Vice-President of Strategic Management with the Society for the Advancement of Management.

Other Contributing Authors:

Brent Calinicos
Christine Specter
Marrett Varghese
Xenia Wong

C A S E 1

Liz Claiborne, Inc.

SEXTON ADAMS • ADELAIDE GRIFFIN

An upbeat soundtrack, very similar to the one used on the television program "Lifestyles of the Rich and Famous," introduced a parade of well-proportioned, attractive young models who carried on a steady stream of fashionable outfits for half an hour. The outfits varied from contrasting black and white ensembles to colorful pastel knits to khaki safari outfits to denim skirts, jackets, and jeans.[1] The skirt length, hovering to just above the knee, leads experts within the fashion industry to wonder if this was to be the trend. The fashion industry was locked in a debate over what the length for women's skirts should be. This debate resulted in many women shoppers being reluctant to purchase skirts and dresses, for fear the length would soon be out of style. As the show proceeded, photographers, eager to snap a picture of each new arrival, clustered around the runway. At the close, the sound of resounding applause filled the room for several moments. Liz Claiborne's 1987 pre-fall line of clothing had arrived!

BACKGROUND AND HISTORY

In 1976 Elisabeth Claiborne Ortenberg started a small sportswear company with her husband, Art. She was 47 years old and had been designing clothes since the age of 21. She and her husband formed the company with $250,000 in capital, $200,000 of which was a loan from family and friends. At first the operation was deliberately kept small because Claiborne Ortenberg wanted to design all the clothes herself. In 1985 Liz Claiborne, Inc. was named as a Fortune 500 company. *Fortune* declared it "the second most admired corporation in the United States."[2] In 1988, Liz Claiborne, Inc. became a leader in the apparel industry: sales reached one billion dollars in 1987.

The company was formed with the business and professional woman in mind at a time when this market was on the verge of phenomenal growth.[3] Claiborne

---

This case was prepared by Suzanne King, Terri Klein, Richard Waller, and Charlie Wong under the supervision of Professor Sexton Adams, North Texas State University and Professor Adelaide Griffin, Texas Woman's University. Copyright © 1988 by Sexton Adams and Adelaide Griffin. Reprinted by permission.

Ortenberg relied on the assumption that there were women in the corporate environment who wanted to go to work in something other than a female version of the clothes being worn by male executives.[4] When women first entered the work force, designers simply took the typical man's business suit and changed it a little so it could be worn by a woman.[5] Claiborne Ortenberg correctly reasoned that most working women had jobs that didn't necessarily require them to dress in formal executive wear. Rather, they could go to work dressed casually in a broad range of styles. However, dressing daily for a job called for a wardrobe with not only depth but also versatility and affordability. Claiborne Ortenberg managed to address each one of these concerns with her fashions and was, for a while, alone in her endeavors. She correctly identified a market void and filled it—by identifying the consumer and her needs. In this way, said Brenda Gall, a Vice-President of Merrill Lynch, Liz Claiborne quickly became a jump ahead of the competition.[6]

The fashion show described previously is somewhat deceptive because of the shapeliness of the models. The success of the fashions was due in part to the way in which Liz Claiborne's clothes fit the typical woman, whose figure most often deviated from that of the models used in the fashion shows. Claiborne Ortenberg included herself in the category of women "who want to look thinner than they really are."[7] Despite the fact that women were generally thought to be in better shape than they used to be, clothing sales showed that 30% of them were overweight.[8] Liz Claiborne's fashions were designed to enhance flawless figures, while also camouflaging imperfect ones.

Jerome A. Chazen, Vice-Chairman of Liz Claiborne, Inc. attributed the company's success to two factors. One was the increasing number of women entering the work force. Chazen felt that the difference in women going to work was "billions of dollars a year in clothes."[9] The other factor in the company's success, Chazen felt, was Liz herself. According to him, "She has an eye (for fashion) as finely tuned as a musician with absolute pitch."[10] The company was formed with the strategy of carving out a market niche between the world of the pants suit and the world of high fashion.[11] This niche turned out to be much bigger than anyone expected—big enough to "park a truck in," according to one industry analyst.[12]

ORGANIZATION AND MANAGEMENT

Industry analysts believed that the strength of the management team was the key to the success of Liz Claiborne, Inc. This view was shared by retailers. Mark Shulman, Senior Vice-President and General Merchandise Manager for I. Magnin, a group of San Francisco-based specialty stores, agreed that the company "is probably the best-run apparel company on Seventh Avenue today."[13] Gall noted the rarity of finding a start-up company with "four key individuals with complementary strengths in various areas of the business."[14] Liz Claiborne, Inc., however, proved to be an exception. Claiborne Ortenberg's background was in design. She served as an apprentice to designers Tina Lesser, Ben Rieg, and Omar Khayam, and was a designer at Jonathan Logan for 16 years.[15] Arthur Ortenberg's expertise was in planning and administration, while Chazen's strength was the retail side of the business. Leonard Boxer's background was in production and sourcing.[16] Boxer retired at the end of 1985 to serve on the company's Board of Directors.

Management gave close attention to every detail of the company's operations from design to manufacturing. "They planned their business from day one, and they're still planning," observed Gall.[17] Management was also cautious in dealing with the press. The company's founders refused to be interviewed for an October, 1986, story that appeared in *Madison Avenue*.[18] Claiborne Ortenberg and Ortenberg were interviewed in January, 1988, for a two-part article in *The New Yorker*. Before he consented to the interview, however, Ortenberg "had been at some pains to establish that he and his wife did not talk to the press much."[19] The reason for their reluctance to appear in the limelight was that the company was founded on a team basis. Harvey L. Falk, Executive Vice-President—Operations and Corporate Planning, explained this idea as follows: "We really try not to give notoriety to any one person, unless that person is Liz. Once we go beyond Liz, we then talk team. The company is put forward on a team basis because that's what we believe in here. . . ."[20] Liz Claiborne, Inc. went one step beyond the claim that people are one of a company's most valuable resources. The company believed that "people are a company's one indispensable asset."[21]

The company's founders were not afraid to delegate authority. Unlike other buyers, Jack Listanowsky, Senior Vice-President—Knitwear Production, did not have to get clearance from New York before making a decision when he was negotiating with factory people. Listanowsky had the following comment about Ortenberg's management style: "That's one of the things I admire about Art. He gives people full latitude."[22] Although she no longer designed the clothes herself, Claiborne Ortenberg kept a discerning eye on that side of the business.

To gauge consumers' response to the company's apparel offerings, Liz Claiborne, Inc. monitored retail sales. Management studied weekly Systematic Updated Retail Feedback (SURF) reports from a representative sample of sixteen stores.[23] Chazen dismissed the practice that most apparel manufacturers followed of identifying best-selling items by retailers' purchases of the products, adding "I like to think we use the cash register as the primary tool for market research."[24]

In November, 1987, the responsibilities of several of the company's executives were expanded. President Claiborne Ortenberg was also named Chairman and Chief Executive Officer, and Co-Chairmen Ortenberg and Chazen were elected Vice-Chairmen.[25] The company also established a policy committee to report directly to the Board of Directors. The members of this committee included Claiborne Ortenberg, Ortenberg, Chazen, Jay Margolis, and Falk.[26] The policy committee assumed responsibility for the day-to-day operations of the company.

Gall predicted that passage of control from the original managers to their successors will present the biggest challenge to the company in the future.[27] Liz Claiborne, Inc. prepared for this transition in 1987. The company created a strategy planning committee and three new executive positions "to provide for the perpetuation of the Company and of the Claiborne spirit long after its founding officers have retired."[28] The responsibilities of the strategy planning committee included "evaluating new business opportunities—monitoring market share and identifying areas within our current businesses where we can modify and grow."[29] The members of this committee are described in Exhibit 1.1.

The three new executive positions were Executive Vice President—Operations and Corporate Planning, Senior Vice President—Corporate Sales and Marketing, and President—Liz Claiborne Sportswear Group. All production planning, raw materials acquisition, and manufacturing and distribution activities were consolidated within the position of Executive Vice President—Operations and Corporate Planning.[30] The responsibility for coordinating sales and marketing activities among the company's various divisions was given to the Senior Vice President—Corporate Sales and Marketing.[31] The company be-

EXHIBIT 1.1   **Strategy Planning Committee, Liz Claiborne, Inc.**

MEMBER	PRESENT TITLE	POSITIONS HELD PRIOR TO JOINING COMPANY
Robert Bernard	Senior Vice-President—Corporate Sales and Marketing	Various managerial and executive capacities at R. H. Macy's (California)
Jo Miller	Senior Vice-President—First Issue Retail Division, Co-President	Merchandise manager of the Limited, Inc.
Allen McNeary	Senior Vice President—Dress Division, President	President of Alexander Julian Womenswear, a subsidiary of Levi Strauss; several executive merchandising positions; and a vice-president at Saks Fifth Avenue
Terry S. Feldman	Senior Vice President—Operations	Merchandiser for Nygard International, an apparel manufacturer; purchasing agent for Judy Bond, Inc., an apparel manufacturer; and vice-president of merchandising for Jones New York, Inc., an apparel company
Dennis Gay	Senior Vice President—Collection Division, Division Head	Divisional vice president and merchandise manager for Bergdorf Goodman (New York), a specialty retailer; divisional merchandise manager for Bullocks Department Stores (California)

SOURCE: Liz Claiborne, Inc., 1987 *Form 10-K*.

lieved that bringing the Collection, Lizsport, and Lizwear divisions under the control of a single president would enable them "to better manage their phenomenal growth."[32] The last position was held by Margolis, who previously served in various managerial and executive capacities within the Menswear Division. Prior to joining the company, Margolis was Division President of Ron Chereskin, Inc., a division of Cluett Peabody, Inc., a sportswear manufacturer.[33]

The company's rapid growth and diversification placed great demands on management. Additional management personnel were needed to keep pace with the company's expanding product line. Exhibit 1.2 shows the company's organizational structure. Each of the company's divisions had a separate management team. Top management believed that this organization structure enabled the company to respond quickly to changes in the environment.[34]

DIVERSIFICATION

The company pursued a strategy of related diversification. Liz Claiborne, Inc. broadened its product line through new product development, licensing agreements, and acquisitions. Many market segments within the apparel industry were identified and targeted by the company.

Women's sportswear was segmented into Collection, Lizsport, and Lizwear. Collection was the most sophisticated of the three lines, while Lizwear was the most casual.[35] The product line was expanded with the additions of two new sportswear labels, each occupying a different price zone. In the latter half of 1987, the Dana Buchman Division introduced "bridge" sportswear to fill the niche between the "better apparel" and "designer" price levels.[36] The First Issue sportswear label was launched in 1988 and was sold at company-operated stores of the same name. The concentration of apparel offerings at each end of the price zone was also a factor in the company's decision to add dresses to its product line. The company filled the void between the less expensive wrapper dresses and the more expensive dresses designed for special occasions.[37]

The concept of component dressing was introduced in girls' wear and menswear in the hopes of duplicating the success the company enjoyed in women's apparel. Girls' wear, originally marketed under the Lizkids label, was redefined in 1986 and sold under the Lizwear label. In 1987 the company announced plans to "phase out this business for the present time."[38] The product line of the Menswear Division was expanded in 1987; dress shirts, neckwear, hosiery, and underwear were added to the casual apparel already offered.[39]

Another opportunity the company pursued was the special-size market. Sportswear and dresses in petite sizes were introduced. The creation of specialty stores catering to petite customers and a national chain of petite stores was a boon for this business.[40] Several internal changes were made in 1987 to strengthen the petite business. These changes included "new, enlarged showrooms and office space, the hiring of a special Petite designer, and a new reporting responsibility within our Sportswear Group."[41]

Licensing agreements also contributed to the company's growth. Such an agreement allowed another firm to manufacture and market a product under

EXHIBIT 1.2   **Organizational Structure, Liz Claiborne, Inc.**

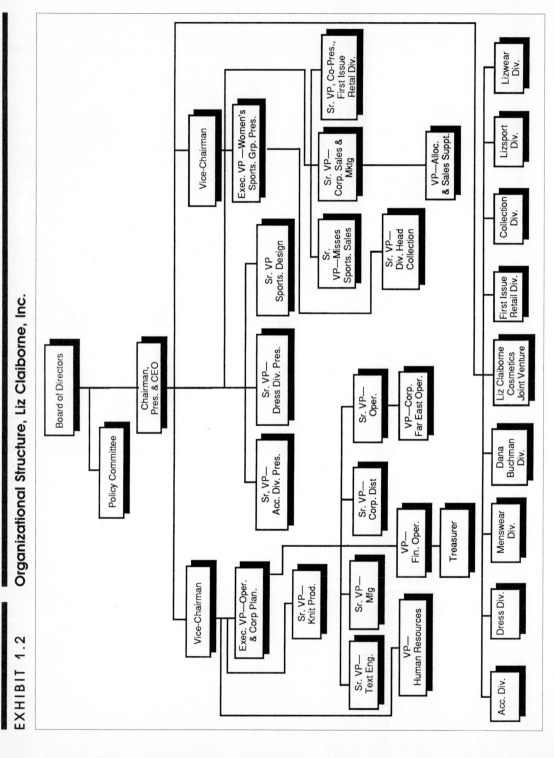

SOURCE: Liz Claiborne, Inc., 1987 Annual Report.

the Liz Claiborne name. In return for the use of its name, the company received royalty income. The payment received by the company was the greater of a certain percentage (generally 4 to 8%) of net sales or a guaranteed minimum royalty that generally increased over the term of the licensing agreement.[42] Products covered by licensing agreements included women's shoes (Marx and Newman division of U.S. Shoe Corporation); women's hosiery (Kayser–Roth); sunglasses; frames for prescription eyewear; bedsheets, pillowcases, quilt covers, and bath towels (Burlington Industries); fragrances and related products (Liz Claiborne Cosmetics); women's sportswear and dresses in Japan; and women's accessories in Canada.[43] The guideline followed by the company in assessing licensing opportunities was whether or not there was a valid need for the product.[44]

In January, 1986, the company purchased from a former licensee the Kayser–Roth Accessories Division of Wickes Companies, Inc., for approximately $8.5 million.[45] The Accessories Division produced and distributed handbags, small leather goods, belts, scarves, and knitted accessories. Liz Claiborne believed that this acquisition would improve the performance of the accessories business because the company could gain more design control and achieve a greater coordination of the marketing effort between accessories and apparel.[46] Liz Claiborne was now prepared to dress her customer from head to toe.

In 1985 the company formed Liz Claiborne Cosmetics, a joint venture with Avon Products, Inc., to produce and distribute fragrances and cosmetics.[47] The company had high hopes for this venture. Chazen described the potential benefits of Liz Claiborne's association with Avon as follows: "Avon has fabulous research, development, and manufacturing facilities. Beyond that, it has expertise in 26 foreign countries. If there are foreign sales in our future, Avon will make a good practical partner for us."[48] Liz Claiborne Cosmetics achieved sales of $26 million in its first five months in the marketplace in 1986.[49] The company earned royalty income of $1.6 million in 1987 and $1.0 million in 1986 under a licensing agreement with the joint venture.[50]

The relationship with Avon, however, was not to be a happy one. In December, 1987, Liz Claiborne, Inc. initiated negotiations to acquire Avon's 50% interest in the venture; the company claimed that Avon's purchase of Parfums Stern in September, 1987, violated an agreement not to compete with the joint venture.[51] Avon valued its share of the venture at $20 to $25 million, considerably higher than Liz Claiborne, Inc.'s offer of $3 million.[52] Disagreement over a buyout price resulted in Avon's threat not to fill orders for the venture. Liz Claiborne, Inc. countered by filing suit in the State Supreme Court in Manhattan. The company alleged that Avon's refusal to fill orders for the "crucial 1988 Fall/Christmas seasons, which together account for over 70 percent of annual sales," would "irreparably harm and likely destroy the business."[53] Avon was ordered to fill orders for the venture through the end of August. Further litigation to resolve this dispute might be required.

Exhibit 1.3 shows each product category as a percentage of sales for 1985–1987. Sportswear accounted for 65% of sales in 1987 as compared to 80% in 1985. Sales for the Dana Buchman label were in excess of $5 million for its initial

EXHIBIT 1.3

Product Categories as a Percentage of Sales, Liz Claiborne, Inc.

	1987	1986	1985
Misses sportswear	53%	54%	64%
Petite sportswear	12	13	16
Sportswear total	65	67	80
Dresses	14	16	16
Accessories	13	10	—
Menswear	7	5	2
Girls	1	2	2
Total	100%	100%	100%

SOURCE: Liz Claiborne, Inc., 1987 *Form 10-K.*

four-month shipping period.[54] Dresses declined from 16% of sales in 1985 to 14% in 1987. Accessories accounted for 13% of sales in 1987 as compared to 10% in 1986. Prior to 1986 the company earned royalty income from accessory sales. Menswear grew from 2% of sales in 1985 to 7% in 1987. (Menswear was first shipped in September, 1985.) Sales of girls' wear as a percentage of total sales remained relatively stable from 1985 to 1987.

Exhibit 1.4 lists various rates of growth for Liz Claiborne, Inc. for 1981–1986. Industry analysts believed that the company would have to test new waters to maintain these phenomenal rates of growth. As Gall observed, Liz Claiborne "doesn't rest on its laurels. They're open to anything that seems right for them."[55] In early 1988 the company announced plans to enter the special-size market once again with a line of half-sizes to be sold under a new label. The targeted shipping date was the latter half of 1989.[56] The company was also considering the additions of intimate wear and costume jewelry to its product line in 1989.[57]

EXHIBIT 1.4

Rates of Growth for 1981–1986, Liz Claiborne, Inc.

Sales	46.0%
Cash Flow	54.5%
Earnings	53.5%
Dividends	99.5%
Book Value	62.5%

SOURCE: Value Line, 4 December 1987.

SALES AND MARKETING

Almost all of Liz Claiborne, Inc.'s sales were made to approximately 3,500 customer accounts in the United States, operating approximately 9,000 department and specialty store locations. Sales were also made to direct-mail catalogue companies and foreign customers. In 1987 the company targeted several foreign markets for an increase in the distribution of Liz Claiborne products. The company invaded the Canadian market and opened a Toronto distribution facility for use in this connection.[58] The next forays would be into West Germany and other European markets.[59]

Approximately 25% of Liz Claiborne, Inc.'s 1987 sales was made by the company's 10 largest customers, and approximately 76% of 1987 sales was made to the company's 100 largest customers. The largest store group customer in 1987 was Federated Department Stores, Inc., which accounted for 11% of Liz Claiborne, Inc.'s 1987 net sales.[60]

The sales of Liz Claiborne, Inc.'s widely diversified product line were supported by 80 to 90 salespeople.[61] The sales force represented a deviation from industry norms in that salespeople did not travel. Although the Accessories Division retained the outside sales force it had when the company acquired the business in 1986 and there was a road force for Liz Claiborne Cosmetics, the company's apparel salespeople could always be found in the company's New York City showrooms, where virtually all sales were consummated. Instead of calling on stores' buyers, salespeople waited for them to come and place the orders. This approach proved to be a big plus for Liz Claiborne, Inc. Not only did it save traveling costs and improve control of the company's sales operations, but this approach also enabled a relationship to be established at a higher level almost immediately. "On the road, a salesman is lucky if he sees the buyer. He almost never sees anyone above the buyer level because those people are busy. But when retailers come to New York, top management often comes to see the market. So there's a much greater opportunity to meet these people," explained Chazen.[62]

Liz Claiborne, Inc.'s salespeople were not like those of a typical apparel manufacturer. They were not pushy so as to get an order at any cost. "They don't oversell; they keep the customers a wee bit hungry," noted one industry analyst.[63] Though not pushy, Liz Claiborne, Inc.'s salespeople were demanding. Buyers were not allowed to pick and choose among garments shown but were required to take an entire line.[64]

Liz Claiborne, Inc. was geared to selling to large retailers whose executives visited the company's New York City showrooms several times a year.[65] According to Julie Richard, Assistant Manager of the Liz Claiborne showroom at the Dallas Apparel Mart, buyers had to purchase at least $200,000 a year to get the Liz Claiborne line. This requirement eliminated, as well as alienated, many small store chains that had supported Liz Claiborne from the time the company was formed.[66]

Frequent visits to stores were made by a group of 15 traveling consultants who supported retail salespeople; these consultants conducted seminars and clinics to help retailers combat in-store problems. Liz Claiborne, Inc.'s goals and fashion point of view were communicated to the stores' salespeople to give them a better understanding of the company. "The most important thing they get across," Chazen said, "is that we care about them and the consumers and we expect them to care in turn."[67]

In late 1987 the company announced the initiation of "Project Consumer." The goal of this program was to reinforce and further strengthen the bond that existed between Liz Claiborne, Inc. and its customers. One part of this project was to increase the number of in-store product specialists who were trained by the company and who, along with the company's traveling consultants, were responsible for training retail salespeople and the setting up of Liz Claiborne displays.[68]

Promotion for Liz Claiborne merchandise was limited in the sense of advertising. Approximately $16.1 million was attributed to advertising costs in 1987.[69] Not until 1985 did the company begin contributing to the cost of the advertising licensees were required to run.[70] Liz Claiborne, Inc. also established a cooperative advertising program in which the customer's advertising expenditures were matched, up to a maximum of 2% of the customer's apparel purchases and up to a maximum of 3% of the customer's accessories purchases.[71]

In September, 1986, when the company introduced fragrances under the joint venture with Avon, Liz Claiborne, Inc. kicked off its first national advertising campaign, engineered by DDB Needham Worldwide.[72] The company stubbornly refused to offer gift-with-purchase, purchase-with-purchases, or any of the other promotional gimmicks so common to the fragrance industry. Instead, Liz Claiborne, Inc. preferred to rely on high quality and unique packaging to sell the product.[73]

One interesting form of promotion used by Liz Claiborne, Inc. was "Claiboards," booklets that listed the name and style numbers, by style groups, as well as pictures of every item in the company's product line. Claiboards were "a road map of the way we put the line together," said Chazen.[74] Later when the booklets somehow found their way into competitors' hands, Claiboards were replaced by "Claiboards Receiving Guides," which contained basically the same information but no photographs. According to one retail store manager, Claiboards Receiving Guides were well received by retailers in helping them put the goods together.[75] Another subtle form of promotion was the eye-catching Liz Claiborne displays that the company helped retailers set up in department stores. Items that could be mixed and matched to create several different outfits were displayed together, so that the shopper was saved time.[76]

Liz Claiborne products were conceived and marketed as "designer" items. A consistent approach to design and quality was followed. Although Liz Claiborne, Inc. maintained a "designer" image, the company's products generally were priced in the "better apparel" range, which is less expensive than many "designer" lines. Exhibit 1.5 shows the price ranges of the company's products in 1987.

When pricing clothes, Claiborne Ortenberg put herself in her customer's position and asked herself, "How much would I want to pay for that piece?"[77] By

EXHIBIT 1.5	**1987 Suggested Retail Prices**	
	Liz Claiborne Collections	
	Women's sportswear	$11–$196
	Dresses	$66–$290
	Accessories	$12–$140
	Claiborne Menswear	
	Sportswear and furnishings	$ 5–$275
	Dana Buchman	
	"Bridge" sportswear	$76–$296
	First Issue	
	Sportswear and accessories	$ 5–$158

SOURCE: 1987 Liz Claiborne, Inc., *Form 10-K.*

knowing well what the customers needed and how much they were able to afford, Liz Claiborne, Inc. successfully achieved recognition and loyalty across product lines and attracted the attention of competitors in the process. However, sources close to the company expressed concern that the low price tags might bring about a loss of status for the merchandise. Soon, they felt, everyone would be able to afford the fashions, and the clothes would slowly lose their "designer" appeal.[78]

RETAILING

In a further step to satisfy customers, Liz Claiborne, Inc. announced plans to expand into the retail business in 1986. The company had always felt that one of the biggest problems facing department stores was the lack of trained people on the sales floor. There was a missing link between the apparel makers, buyers, and the salespeople. The apparel makers' ideas of how sales should be handled were often miscommunicated by the buyers to the salespeople. "The problem is especially acute in "branch stores," claimed Chazen. "Buyers never even visit some of their branches, so people operate with blinders on. Stores pay the price in lost sales and in turning off the customer who is looking for help."[79]

The company formalized "Project Consumer" in 1987 to provide an example of courtesy and service while attracting new customers. In addition to increasing the number of in-store product specialists, a facet of Project Consumer was the successful opening of the first of a limited number of Liz Claiborne "boutiques" at Jordan Marsh in Boston in September, 1987.[80] Twelve clerks were posted in the 6,000-square-foot area, five at the cashier's counter, and seven on the floor. The number of clerks was twice that generally found in similar department store sales areas.[81] This created a "store-within-a-store" where the customers would find a complete and fully coordinated array of Liz Claiborne fashions, accessories, shoes, and fragrances. This "personalized selling space" featured fixtures and displays built to the company's own specifications and was staffed by specially trained personnel to help shoppers find just the right Liz Claiborne products they needed to complete their wardrobes.[82] The next of these stores was scheduled to open at Marshall Field in Chicago in the spring of 1988.[83]

In November, 1987, the company decided to evaluate and introduce a limited number of Liz Claiborne prototype and presentational specialty shops in key United States markets. According to the company, this was the most significant part of "Project Consumer" in terms of staying close to the consumer. Management believed that these stores would enable the company to track sales, style, colors, and other product information more closely and to respond more quickly to consumers' changing desires.[84] As of April, 1988, no definite plans had been made as to the types, location, size, or merchandising approach of these stores.[85]

The company-operated First Issue stores carried a collection of women's casual sportswear and accessories under a new label independent from the other Liz Claiborne labels. The first of these stores opened at the Americana in Manhasset, New York, in February, 1983, and was followed by three additional stores in Georgetown Park, Washington, D.C., and Woodridge Mall and Paramus Park Mall in New Jersey. With sportswear priced just below the Liz Claiborne collection, the marketing strategy for these stores called for shipments of new merchandise at least once a month. If everything went as planned, the company would add seven to ten First Issue stores during 1988; these would primarily be located on the East Coast and would eventually go nationwide.[86] With First Issue, the company was admitted into a new market and had established a new label to develop and expand.[87]

The company also operated six Liz Claiborne outlet stores. Located within East Coast "outlet centers" comprised primarily of manufacturer-operated stores, these outlet stores were where excess merchandise was moved in the hopes of making a final sale. The company planned to open ten additional outlet stores during 1988.[88]

Liz Claiborne, Inc.'s retail operations were working out nicely and results had generally exceeded expectations, according to *Value Line*.[89] However, some industry observers were still cautious in endorsing the company's move into the retail marketplace. After all, Liz Claiborne, Inc.'s establishment of a retail business represented an entry into a new market, accompanied by the risks inherent in any new business. Furthermore, the company had no extensive experience in the operation and marketing of the retail business. Finally, the competition in this field included firms with which the company had not competed before, including a number of the company's customers at that time. Apparel designer Ralph Lauren had angered New York City department stores when he expanded into retail with his own stores in 1986. The area retailers believed that his stores would be in direct competition with their department stores. Industry observers wondered whether Liz Claiborne, Inc. also would alienate department store customers who feared that some of their sales would be siphoned off.[90]

FINANCE

From a financial point of view, Liz Claiborne, Inc. appeared to represent an investor's dream. In recent years market researchers had given the company rave reviews, calling it "probably the best stock I've ever recommended."[91] The company went public in 1981, trading on the over-the-counter exchange. Since that time, the stock price has increased tremendously—sometimes as much as 25 times its original value.[92] While other apparel merchandisers were struggling just to break even, Liz Claiborne, Inc. was growing every year by phenomenal percentages.[93]

Despite its continuous growth and expansion over the years, the company was able to maintain a strong financial position. In fact, financial success was no longer news to the company. Record sales and net income had been achieved every year since the company went public.[94] The company's consolidated balance sheets and statements of income are presented in Exhibits 1.6 and 1.7.

EXHIBIT 1.6

Consolidated Balance Sheets, Liz Claiborne, Inc.
(Dollar Amounts in Thousands)

	DECEMBER 26, 1987	DECEMBER 26, 1986
Assets		
Current assets		
Cash	$ 2,704	$ 2,628
Short-term investments	157,762	101,441
Accounts receivable	80,591	57,718
Inventories	156,375	114,879
Deferred income tax benefits	6,563	2,861
Other current assets	19,994	14,860
Total current assets	423,989	294,387
Property and equipment		
Building	15,002	13,702
Machinery and equipment	22,085	13,599
Furniture and fixtures	8,916	6,007
Leasehold improvements	23,900	14,608
Total property and equipment	69,903	47,916
Less—Accumulated depreciation and amortization	16,763	11,118
	53,140	36,798
Investment in joint venture	3,767	3,392
Other assets	1,473	925
Total assets	$482,369	$335,502

(Continued)

EXHIBIT 1.6   **(Continued)**

	DECEMBER 26, 1987	DECEMBER 26, 1986
Liabilities and Stockholders' Equity		
Current liabilities		
Long-term debt due within one year	$ 357	$ —
Note payable	—	4,900
Advances from developer	—	2,409
Accounts payable	53,044	39,820
Accrued expenses	43,374	26,166
Income taxes payable	6,412	7,921
Total current liabilities	103,187	81,216
Long-term debt	14,464	—
Deferred Income Taxes	7,762	6,499
Stockholders' equity		
Preferred stock, $.01 par value, authorized shares—50,000,000 in 1987 and 1,500,000 in 1986, outstanding shares—none	—	—
Common stock, $1 par value, authorized shares—250,000,000 in 1987 and 125,000,000 in 1986, outstanding shares—87,135,873 in 1987 and 43,279,361 in 1986	87,136	43,279
Capital in excess of par value	29,889	21,404
Retained earnings	239,931	183,104
Total stockholders' equity	356,956	247,787
Total liabilities and stockholders' equity	$482,369	$335,502

SOURCE: Liz Claiborne, Inc., 1987 *Annual Report.*

A tremendous amount of working capital was required to sustain the company's continuous growth. The traditional source of funds for capital expenditures was retained earnings. Anticipating $28 million in capital expenditures in 1988, Liz Claiborne, Inc. increased its lines of credit to $180 million in 1987.[95]

In spite of the drop in the company's stock price caused by the October, 1987, stock market crash, the company was still able to maintain a 12% cash dividend-payout ratio in 1987. In addition, the company had declared two-for-one stock splits in each of the years 1984, 1986, and 1987. Market analysts saw this as a means to keep cash inside the company and to make Liz Claiborne, Inc.'s stock more affordable to investors.

The financial forecast for the company was somewhat mixed. Liz Claiborne, Inc. would benefit from a lower tax rate, gains in established apparel lines, and

EXHIBIT 1.7

Consolidated Statements of Income, Liz Claiborne, Inc.
(Dollar Amounts in Thousands Except per Share Data)

	FISCAL YEAR ENDED	
	December 26, 1987	December 26, 1986
Net Sales	$1,053,324	$813,497
Costs and expenses		
Cost of sales	655,569	502,247
Selling, general and administrative expenses	194,686	146,289
Interest expense	670	1,122
Interest and other income—net	(5, 626)	(5,463)
Total costs and expenses	845,299	644,195
Income before provision for income taxes	208,025	169,302
Provision for income taxes	93,611	83,108
Net income	$ 114,414	$ 86,194
Earnings per common share	$ 1.32	$ 1.00
Dividends declared per common share	$ .16	$ .12

SOURCE: Liz Claiborne, Inc., 1987 *Annual Report.*

contributions from new divisions and ventures. However, newly incurred costs related to the expansion into retail and the company's own pessimistic admission of a sub-par future could spell trouble. Operating in a highly market-sensitive industry, the company needed a strong economy to sustain its aggressive expansion program. *Beta* is a measure of the volatility of a particular stock relative to the market. The beta for Liz Claiborne, Inc. was 1.55 in March, 1988.[96] In other words, if the market goes up or down 10%, Liz Claiborne's stock would increase or decrease 15.5%.

In light of the uncertain economic outlook, most stock analysts were not recommending Liz Claiborne, Inc.'s stock to investors.[97] After maintaining a high ranking for most of its existence as a public company, Liz Claiborne, Inc.'s stock was rated as below average for timeliness with an average degree of safety by *Value Line* as of March, 1988.[98]

MANUFACTURING AND PRODUCTION

All of Liz Claiborne, Inc.'s products were designed by house staffs, under the overseeing eye of Liz herself, and were manufactured through arrangements with independent suppliers.[99] Eighty-eight percent of production was contracted to foreign manufacturers.[100] Foreign manufacturers were located mainly in the Far East in countries such as Taiwan, Hong Kong, South Korea, Sri Lanka, and the

Philippines.[101] By finding production sources overseas, Liz Claiborne, Inc. had successfully avoided the overhead burden of manufacturing its own products. This enabled the company's return on equity to reach almost 50% in some years. Production costs were lowered tremendously by producing overseas, which allowed Liz Claiborne, Inc. to fulfill its goal of offering designer clothing without the designer price.[102] The underlying reason for the price difference between foreign and domestic manufacturing appeared to be the difference in labor costs. Foreign labor was traditionally much less expensive than domestic labor. Richard Goldman, one of three brothers who ran Ricke Knitting Mills (a large American knitwear factory), said that his factory may have to pay $7.00–$8.00 per hour for labor, while foreign countries may pay as little as $.22 per hour.[103]

For imported clothing, there was usually a five- or six-to-one ratio between the retail price and the manufacturer's price. For example, if an item was expected to sell in a retail store for $60, the manufacturer's price should have been around $10 or $12. The ratio was largely dependent on tariff levels, which could vary according to the type of garment.[104] Goldman reported that his American-made sweaters were sold for $50–$70 in retail stores but gave no indication of the manufacturing cost of each item.[105]

Neither Claiborne Ortenberg nor her husband were involved with imports before they formed the company. Apparently, what got them to be involved was the fact that it was so difficult to find domestic suppliers willing and able to provide Claiborne Ortenberg with the variety of fabrics and quality of tailoring she wanted when she began to design under her own name.[106] Dana Buchman, Chief Knitwear Designer of the company, said she had been to several American knitwear companies "where they would hardly give me the time of day."[107] The staff of Liz Claiborne, Inc., including Liz herself, felt that the quality of foreign manufacturing best fit the needs of the company. On the other hand, Goldman, the American manufacturer, claimed that there was no difference in the quality of American products—only the price. He went on to say that "we've demonstrated to them that we're willing to drop whatever we're doing to satisfy them (Liz Claiborne, Inc.), as long as they give us the same lead time they do overseas."[108] To do business with foreign manufacturers, Liz Claiborne, Inc. had to pay for the production eighteen months in advance of shipment to the U.S.[109]

One of Liz Claiborne, Inc.'s top innovations was to break the fashion year into six seasons rather than four: extra fall and spring lines were added. This kept production rates steady and relaxed the inventory loads for stores. Shoppers always had a fresh selection of designs to choose from.[110] However, New York City was the only city with six fashion "markets" in which designs for each fashion season were previewed. Other major cities traditionally had four markets, which meant that two of Liz Claiborne's fashion seasons missed being previewed.[111] The company normally based the quantity of production on the number of garments expected to sell within the two-month period that each season stayed in the stores. Most items sold out, some of them very quickly. However, there was no provision for increasing production in response to demand. In addition, no garment was ever repeated in a later season, but a successful garment could serve as inspiration for a similar, subsequent design.[112] Because Liz Claiborne, Inc. had to pay the foreign manufacturers eighteen months in advance of shipment, it was impossible for the company to increase production of a popular item. Likewise, it could not cancel a production order for an item that was not selling.[113]

Liz Claiborne, Inc. had seven different lines of clothing. For each season, within each line, the clothes were grouped according to the use of common yarns and colors. A typical group might have consisted of a sweater, a skirt, a pair of pants, and a T-shirt. Because emphasis on "coordinated dressing" was a feature of the company, retailers were urged to display Liz Claiborne clothing in a designated spot by itself, arranged in chosen groups. The company felt that the clothing sold better that way because the customer was encouraged to buy the whole group at once.[114]

Because Liz Claiborne, Inc. did most of its manufacturing in the Far East, it was extremely vulnerable to the effects of the falling value of the U.S. dollar. When the dollar became weakened, it was less cost effective to manufacture outside the U.S. In 1987, the value of the dollar was slipping steadily.[115] Liz Claiborne, Inc.'s manufacturing plans for 1988 included a big push into Canada, where a new distribution center that exclusively served the Canadian market was opened.[116] The company has expanded its offices overseas, with 1986 additions in Singapore and Israel and a 1987 addition in Florence, Italy. The company increased its emphasis on diversifying and solidifying its manufacturing base, as it supported a Far East supplier in the development of a modern stitching factory in the Chinatown area of New York City. To meet the increased demands on the distribution systems, a new custom-engineered distribution center was constructed in New Jersey.[117]

Because Liz Claiborne, Inc. did its manufacturing outside the U.S., it could suffer considerably if particular tariff and quota legislation for foreign manufacturers were passed. The quota system, which limited the right of various foreign countries to export goods to the U.S., was one of the most formidable obstacles that the clothing importer faced. Liz Claiborne had been successful by establishing relationships with factories that possessed large quota holdings.[118] The proposed Textile and Apparel Trade Enforcement Act (the Jenkins bill) had posed the most recent threat to Liz Claiborne. If the bill had become law, it would have reduced textile and apparel imports from Hong Kong, Taiwan, and South Korea by between 25%–30%. The bill was passed by both the House and the Senate but, fortunately for Liz Claiborne, was vetoed by President Reagan. However, the bill's supporters refused to give up and were still trying to get a veto override from Congress.[119]

INDUSTRY AND COMPETITORS

The apparel industry was one of the largest and most competitive of all industries in the United States. There were three basic types of operations within the apparel industry—manufacturers, jobbers, and contractors. Manufacturers purchased materials, cut, sewed, and sold the finished product. Jobbers also purchased raw materials and sold the finished product. However, the jobber had the processing of the product done on contract to an outside factory. The contractor received the raw materials from the outside party and manufactured the product to its specifications.[120]

Liz Claiborne, Inc. was "organized to design, contract for the manufacture of, and market clothes for the business and professional woman."[121] One of Liz Claiborne, Inc.'s competitors was Bernard Chaus, Inc. Both companies had almost all of their merchandise manufactured for them in the Far East, and this allowed Bernard Chaus to compete with Liz Claiborne, Inc. on a price basis.[122] There were several problems associated with manufacturing overseas. Long lead times were needed to process orders, and the quota system could be poorly managed. In 1986, U.S. Customs embargoed Bernard Chaus merchandise worth $11.6 million because inaccurate record keeping by a Chinese supplier resulted in shipments that exceeded the quota.[123]

The success of Liz Claiborne opened up the market for clothes designed for the professional woman. Other manufacturers who competed for the professional woman included Evan Picone, Donna Karan, Ralph Lauren, and Adrienne Vittadini. It was rather difficult to pinpoint the exact competition for Liz Claiborne, Inc. The company was convinced that the concept of designer clothes at nondesigner prices separated Liz Claiborne, Inc. from the rest of the market. Industry observer Peter Oberlink remarked, "exactly who is the competition is difficult to say. Claiborne still seems to occupy a zone to herself."[124] Liz Claiborne, Inc.'s management believed that it was the "largest women's sportswear manufacturer in the United States" and "the largest better dress company in America."[125]

Apparel makers, including Liz Claiborne Inc., were beginning to take a more active role on the sales floor. The goal was to improve the quality of service and increase efficiency. Evan Picone planned to increase the size of its staff of traveling consultants from eight to sixteen. Other apparel companies agreed to share the cost of a salesperson with department stores. Although apparel makers would not disclose the costs involved, the stores in which these programs were introduced showed 20%–40% increases in sales. Bernard Chaus, Chairman of Bernard Chaus, Inc. objected to this practice because he believed that apparel makers would engage in a bidding war, with the winners receiving the prime locations on the sales floor.[126]

The United States Department of Commerce reported that real disposable income reached its best year-to-year gain of the '80s in February, 1984, and two months later apparel and accessories reached their best year-to-year increase of 14%.[127] (See Exhibit 1.8.) The close correlation between real disposable income and sales of apparel and accessories was one of the problems affecting the market. "The consumer's reluctance—or inability—to buy results from the weak growth in income combined with these factors:

1. A long prior period of meager savings
2. An installment-debt rate higher than it's been in decades

EXHIBIT 1.8   **Consumer Apparel Expenditures**

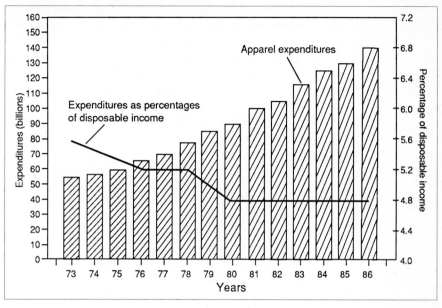

SOURCE: Department of Commerce.

3. The insecurity and loss of confidence stemming from October's Black Monday and Terrible Tuesday

4. The loss of real purchasing power coming from the marked increase in apparel prices, one result of the sharp decline in the exchange value of the dollar."[128]

Apparel prices climbed a record 2% in March, 1988, after a 0.1% increase in January and a 0.3% drop in February. Because of the slowdown in consumer spending for apparel and accessories, the retailer was passing a major portion of the problem at the store level back to the apparel maker. In the last several seasons, most retailers were unable to sell at list prices and were forced to discount as never before, and they forced the manufacturers to reduce prices also. Liz Claiborne, Inc. felt the effects of the contracting market much less than did the average manufacturer. However, management believed that merchandise might have to be sold below regular mark-up to move excess inventory. Liz Claiborne, Inc. combined product, price, and service to retailers into a successful package. Industry analysts noted that "while the rest of the apparel industry is locked in the doldrums, Liz Claiborne grows by an insane 70 percent annually."[129]

Because the economy had been expanding since October, 1982, many consumers and industry analysts were led to fear that times would soon turn bad. Deborah Bronston of Prudential-Bache predicted that "only good brands with consumer loyalty that offer stores good service will do well in 1988."[130] Accessory sales, however, might not be adversely affected by a recession. Laurence Leeds, Jr., Chairman of Manhattan Industries, noted that "accessories always do better in bad times. A man won't pay $500 for a suit, but he will pay $30 for a dress shirt or $15 for a bright pair of suspenders to spruce up his wardrobe."[131]

Liz Claiborne, Inc.'s entry into retail with the opening of the First Issue stores meant that the company was competing on that level as well. First Issue stores were owned and operated by Liz Claiborne, Inc. to "sell only its own merchandise, priced and designed to compete with casual clothing stores like the Gap and the Limited."[132] Retailers that carried imported merchandise were hurt by the falling dollar. Retailers' only options were to pass the increased manufacturing costs on to the consumer or let their profit margins suffer. The decline in the value of the dollar allowed domestic apparel manufacturers to be more competitive with foreign suppliers. Consequently, the Limited, Inc. was trying to find domestic production sources. Industry analysts believed that saturation of the market would hurt the business of specialty apparel chains such as the Gap.[133]

Major retailers suffered sales declines for April, 1988, relative to the same month for the previous year. Stacy Ruchalmer, an industry analyst with Shearson Lehman Hutton, Inc., attributed the poor results to "a lack of fashion (in women's apparel). . . . There's nothing new and exciting yet in the stores."[134] The Limited reported a decrease in sales of 8%; same-store sales (stores open for a year or more) fell 16%.[135] The Gap had net income of $76.1 million and the Limited reported a profit of $259.4 million in 1987.[136] (See Exhibit 1.9.)

EXHIBIT 1.9

1987 Comparative Financial Statistics
(In Millions of Dollars)

	SALES	PROFIT	RETURN ON EQUITY
Manufacturers			
Liz Claiborne	$1,053	$114.4	33.9%
Bernard Chaus	334	13.3	33.8%
Nike	954	59.4	16.8%
Reebok Int.	1,389	165.2	30.1%
Retailers			
The Limited	$3,499.5	$259.4	34.2%
The Gap	1,000.9	76.1	30.4%

SOURCE: *Business Week*, 15 April 1988; *Business Week*, 14 March 1988.

FUTURE   Liz Claiborne, Inc.'s 1987 earnings release reported good news and bad news. The good news was record earnings for the year and quarter ended December 26, 1987. The bad news was that management expected only a marginal increase in earnings in 1988.[137] The reasons given for management's pessimism were slackening consumer spending following the October, 1987, stock market crash and uncertainty regarding skirt lengths.[138] Chazen commented, "If I were a woman, I would throw up my hands and say, 'I won't buy anything until you guys make up your minds.'"[139] After the announcement, the company's stock fell $2.50 or 15% to $16.50 on 6,000,000 shares.[140]

The same downbeat forecast accompanied the company's first quarter earnings release in April, 1988. Sales were $327.5 million for the first quarter of 1988 as compared to $275 million for the same period of 1987.[141] Net income increased from $32.2 million to $33.8 million, while cost of sales and selling, general, and administrative expense rose 26% and 23%, respectively.[142] The company predicted a slight drop in earnings for the first six months of 1988. The outlook for the economy and for the apparel industry was highly uncertain. Was Liz Claiborne, Inc. headed for hard times or would the success story continue?

NOTES

1. Peter Oberlink, "Liz Is Big Biz," *Madison Avenue*, October 1986, p. 30.

2. James Lardner, "The Sweater Trade—II," *The New Yorker*, January 18, 1988, p. 61.

3. Rayna Skolnik, "Liz the Wiz," *Sales and Marketing Management*, September 9, 1985, p. 50.

4. Oberlink, "Liz Is Big Biz," p. 28.

5. Adam Smith, "How Liz Claiborne Designed an Empire," *Esquire*, January 1986, p. 79.

6. Oberlink, "Liz Is Big Biz," p. 29.

7. *Ibid.*, p. 30.

8. Smith, "How Liz Claiborne Designed an Empire," p. 79.

9. *Ibid.*, p. 78.

10. *Ibid.*

11. Lardner, "The Sweater Trade—II," p. 62.

12. Peter Traub, and Marvin E. Newman, "Behind All of That Glitz and Glitter, the Garment District Means Business," *Smithsonian*, August 1985, p. 37.

13. Skolnik, "Liz the Wiz," p. 50.

14. Oberlink, "Liz Is Big Biz," p. 29.

15. William Hoffer, "Businesswomen: Equal But Different," *Nation's Business*, August 1987, p. 47.

16. Oberlink, "Liz Is Big Biz," p. 29.

17. *Ibid.*

18. *Ibid.*

19. Lardner, "The Sweater Trade—II," p. 61.

20. Oberlink, "Liz Is Big Biz," p. 31.

21. Liz Claiborne, Inc., *1984 Annual Report*, p. 4.

22. James Lardner, "The Sweater Trade—I," *The New Yorker*, January 11, 1988, p. 48.

23. Skolnik, "Liz the Wiz," p. 52.

24. *Ibid.*

25. "Liz Claiborne, Inc. Reorganizes Duties of Senior Officials," *Wall Street Journal*, November 12, 1987, p. 46.

26. *Ibid.*

27. Oberlink, "Liz Is Big Biz," p. 31.

28. Liz Claiborne, Inc., *1987 Annual Report*, p. 5.

29. *Ibid.*

30. *Ibid.*, pp. 5–6.

31. *Ibid.*, p. 6.

32. *Ibid.*, p. 9.

33. Liz Claiborne, Inc., *1987 Form 10-K*, p. 15.

34. Liz Claiborne, Inc., *1983 Annual Report*, p. 2.

35. Liz Claiborne, Inc., *1985 Annual Report*, p. 4; Liz Claiborne, Inc., *1987 Form 10-K*, p. 3.

36. Liz Claiborne, Inc., *1986 Annual Report*, p. 10.

37. Liz Claiborne, Inc., *1983 Annual Report*, p. 6.

38. Liz Claiborne, Inc., *1987 Annual Report*, p. 9.

39. Liz Claiborne, Inc., *1986 Annual Report*, p. 10.

40. Liz Claiborne, Inc., *1984 Annual Report*, p. 2.

41. Liz Claiborne, Inc., *1987 Annual Report*, p. 10.

42. Liz Claiborne, Inc., *1987 Form 10-K*, p. 11.

43. Liz Claiborne, Inc., *1984 Annual Report*, p. 6; Liz Claiborne, Inc., *1985 Annual Report*, p. 4; Liz Claiborne, Inc., *1987 Form 10-K*, p. 11.

44. Liz Claiborne, Inc., *1984 Annual Report*, p. 6.

45. Liz Claiborne, Inc., *1986 Annual Report*, p. 22.

46. Liz Claiborne, Inc., *1985 Annual Report*, p. 6.

47. *Ibid.*

48. Skolnik, "Liz the Wiz," p. 52.

49. Liz Claiborne, Inc., *1987 Annual Report*, p. 9.

50. *Ibid.*, p. 21.

51. "Avon Is Told to Fill Liz Claiborne Orders Until End of August," *Wall Street Journal*, March 16, 1988, p. 46.

52. *Ibid.*

53. *Ibid.*

54. Liz Claiborne, Inc., *1987 Annual Report*, p. 10.

55. Skolnik, "Liz the Wiz," p. 52.

56. Liz Claiborne, Inc., *1987 Form 10-K*, p. 2.

57. *Value Line*, March 4, 1988.

58. Liz Claiborne, Inc., *1987 Form 10-K*, p. 6.

59. *Value Line*, March 4, 1988.

60. Liz Claiborne, Inc., *1987 Form 10-K*, p. 7.

61. "Liz Claiborne's Pattern for Success," *Sales and Marketing Management*, June 1987, p. 54.

62. Skolnik, "Liz the Wiz," p. 51.

63. "Liz Claiborne's Pattern for Success," p. 54.

64. *Ibid.*

65. *Ibid.*

66. Interview with Julie Richard, Assistant Manager of the Liz Claiborne Showroom at the Dallas Apparel Mart, April 13, 1988.

67. Skolnik, "Liz the Wiz," p. 51.

68. Liz Claiborne, Inc., *1987 Annual Report*, p. 12.

69. Liz Claiborne, Inc., *1987 Form 10-K*, p. 8.

70. Skolnik, "Liz the Wiz," p. 52.

71. Liz Claiborne, Inc., *1987 Form 10-K*, p. 8.

72. Oberlink, "Liz Is Big Biz," p. 30.

73. Liz Claiborne, Inc., *1987 Annual Report*, pp. 2–4.

74. Skolnik, "Liz the Wiz," p. 51.

75. *Ibid.*, pp. 51–52.

76. Skolnik, "Liz the Wiz," p. 51.

77. Oberlink, "Liz Is Big Biz," p. 30.

78. Interview with Julie Richard.

79. Skolnik, "Liz the Wiz," p. 51.

80. Liz Claiborne, Inc., *1987 Annual Report*, p. 12.

81. Ann Hagedorn, "Apparel Makers Play Bigger Part on Sales Floor, *Wall Street Journal*, March 2, 1988, p. 25.

82. Liz Claiborne, Inc., *1987 Annual Report*, p. 12.

83. *Value Line*, March 4, 1988.

84. Liz Claiborne, Inc., *1987 Annual Report*, p. 12.

85. Liz Claiborne, Inc., *1987 Form 10-K*, p. 6.

86. *Ibid.*, p. 5.

87. Liz Claiborne, Inc., *1987 Annual Report*, p. 12.

88. Liz Claiborne, Inc., *1987 Form 10-K*, p. 8.

89. *Value Line*, March 4, 1988.

90. "Store Wars," *Forbes*, January 11, 1988, p. 75.

91. Oberlink, "Liz Is Big Biz," p. 29.

92. *Ibid.*

93. James Traub and Marvin E. Newman, "Behind All of That Glitz and Glitter, the Garment District Means Business," p. 37.

94. Liz Claiborne, Inc., *1981–1987 Annual Reports*, p. 17.

95. Liz Claiborne, Inc., *1987 Annual Report*, p. 15.

96. *Value Line*, March 4, 1988.

97. Interview with Stockbroker, AG Edwards & Sons, Inc., Denton, Texas, February 18, 1988.

98. *Value Line*, March 4, 1988.

99. *Standard & Poor's OTC Stock Reports.*

100. *Value Line*, March 4, 1988.

101. Smith, "How Liz Claiborne Designed an Empire," p. 79.

102. Oberlink, "Liz Is Big Biz," p. 29.

103. Lardner, "The Sweater Trade—II," p. 58.

104. Lardner, "The Sweater Trade—I," p. 44.

105. Lardner, "The Sweater Trade—II," p. 58.

106. *Ibid.*, p. 61.

107. *Ibid.*, p. 62.

108. *Ibid.*, p. 58.

109. Interview with Julie Richard.

110. Oberlink, "Liz Is Big Biz," p. 29.

111. Interview with Julie Richard.

112. Lardner, "The Sweater Trade—I," p. 45.

113. Interview with Julie Richard.

114. Lardner, "The Sweater Trade—I," p. 44.

115. Sanford L. Jacobs, "Claiborne Says Miniskirts May Mean Mini-Increase in Earnings for 1988," *Wall Street Journal*, February 26, 1988, p. 28.

116. *Value Line*, March 4, 1988.

117. Liz Claiborne, Inc., *1986 Annual Report*, p. 4.

118. Lardner, "The Sweater Trade—II," p. 63.

119. *Ibid.*, p. 59.

120. U.S. Department of Commerce Bureau of the Census, *Current Industrial Reports—Apparel*, July 1987, p. 29.

121. *Value Line*, December 4, 1987.

122. *Standard & Poor's Industry Survey*, August 27, 1987, p. 83.

123. *Ibid.*, pp. 83–84.

124. Oberlink, "Liz Is Big Biz," p. 29.

125. Liz Claiborne, Inc., *1987 Annual Report*, pp. 9–10.

126. Hagedorn, "Apparel Makers Play Bigger Part on Sales Floor," p. 25.

127. *Value Line*, December 4, 1987.

128. *Ibid.*

129. Peter Traub and Marvin E. Newman, "Behind All of That Glitz and Glitter, the Garment District Means Business," p. 37.

130. Gail Bronson, "Apparel, Shoes, and Textiles," *Forbes*, January 11, 1988, p. 74.

131. *Ibid.*, p. 76.

132. "Store Wars," p. 75.

133. Amy Dunkin, "Shopkeepers Brace for the End of a Buying Spree, "*Business Week*, January 11, 1988, p. 99.

134. Teri Agins, "Major Retailers Report Declines in Sales for April," *Wall Street Journal*, May 6, 1988, p. 4.

135. *Ibid.*

136. "Corporate Scoreboard," *Business Week*, March 14, 1988, p. 136–137.

137. Priscilla Ann Smith, "Largest Issues Tumble on Interest-Rate, Dollar Action, but Composite Index Rises," *Wall Street Journal*, February 26, 1988, p. 23.

138. Jacobs, "Claiborne Says Miniskirts May Mean Mini-Increase in Earnings for 1988," p. 28.

139. *Ibid.*

140. *Ibid.*

141. "Liz Claiborne's Profit Rose 5% in 1st Period; Leslie Fay's Fell 37%," *Wall Street Journal*, April 28, 1988, p. 40.

142. *Ibid.*

Johnson Products Company, Inc., A Turnaround Strategy

THOMAS L. WHEELEN • CHARLES E. MICHAELS, JR. • ROBERT L. NIXON • JANIECE L. GALLAGHER

GEORGE E. JOHNSON— ENTREPRENEUR

In 1954, George E. Johnson estimated it would take $500 to get his new product, Ultra Wave Hair Culture, a hair straightener for black men, to the marketplace. The first loan officer that he approached was not impressed with his new product. The loan officer said, "You've got a good job, you've been there ten years, why blow it? If your boss finds out that you're in business, you might lose your job and then you can't pay us back." Mr. Johnson was very disappointed, but he did not give up. He went to another bank and told the loan officer that he wanted to go to California on vacation and needed a $250 loan. The loan was granted. With this loan, Johnson, his wife, Joan, his brother, John, and a friend, Dr. Herbert Martini, a chemist, started Johnson Products on February 15, 1954. The company was organized as an Illinois corporation in 1957, but in 1969, its state of incorporation was changed to Delaware. On December 10, 1969, it became the first black-owned company to be publicly held.

George E. Johnson began his career as a door-to-door salesman in Chicago for Fuller Products, which made cosmetics for blacks. Some time later, he had an opportunity to work as an assistant chemist with Dr. Herbert Martini in the lab at Fuller Products. During the ten years Johnson worked with Martini, he learned the foundations upon which he built his own cosmetics business.

Johnson started the Johnson Products Company after he became aware that many blacks were unhappy with their naturally coarse, thick hair. These blacks wanted their hair straightened so that they could have more flexibility in their hair styling. The beginning of Johnson Products can be traced back to a particular day on which Johnson met a barber who had visited the managers at Fuller Products and sought help in formulating an improved hair straightener. Fuller Products was not interested, but Johnson was.

A special note of thanks to Professor Neil H. Snyder of the McIntire School of Commerce at the University of Virginia. Dr. Snyder authored "Johnson Products Company, Inc.," and co-authored "Johnson Products, Inc. . . . The Challenges of the 1980s." The first case appears in *Strategic Management and Business Policy*, first edition, and the second case appears in the second edition of that book.

This case was prepared by Professor Thomas L. Wheelen, Charles E. Michaels, Jr., Robert L. Nixon, and Ms. Janiece L. Gallagher, MBA student of the University of South Florida. This case was presented at the North American Case Research Association Meeting, 1988. Abstracted in the *Proceedings of the North American Case Research Association, 1988*. Reprinted by permission of the authors and the North American Case Research Association. Copyright © 1987 by Thomas L. Wheelen.

Johnson spoke with the barber, Orville Nelson, about his problem and, to explore the matter further, later visited his shop. At the shop, Johnson found customers standing in line to have their hair straightened, but the straightener being used simply did not work. Johnson and Nelson formed a short-lived partnership by putting up $250 each in capital, and Johnson sought Dr. Martini's assistance in identifying the problem with existing hair straighteners.

To obtain as much information as he could about the demand for hair straighteners, Johnson visited many owners of beauty shops with black clientele; there he hoped to discover "their perceptions of the market." He found that the problem was universal: blacks wanted a hair straightener that worked. Mr. Johnson was quoted as saying, "Black beauticians used a hot comb and grease on the hair of black women. Dr. Martini and I agreed that the smoke was bad for the health and the grease was no good for the hair, so we worked on a process to eliminate the smoke and grease and came up with a cream press permanent, cream shampoo and Ultra-Sheen that could be applied at home between visits to the beauty shop." Using a hot comb technique, a client had to redo the hairstyle constantly, because rain or moisture would destroy the arrangement.

Although Johnson was not the first to enter the market for black hair care products, his company became a leading firm because of his efforts to satisfy the needs of the black consumer. However, the "black revolution" of the 1960s brought the Afro and a dilemma. Mr. Johnson said, "I didn't know if it was a fad or not, so I took a wait-and-see attitude until I was sure it was a trend. Then we developed Afro Sheen for the natural. But, I always felt the natural wouldn't last. It's too monotonous, and sure enough, women are moving from it."

Historically a vigorous, competitive manufacturer of hair care products and cosmetics, Johnson Products also became an important black institution and a growing American business. In 1971, Johnson Products Company, Inc. became the first black-owned firm to be listed on the American Stock Exchange. Through innovative product development and promotional techniques, it rapidly became one of the success stories of American business in the 1960s and early 1970s.

The Johnson story might have ended one day in October 1964 when a devastating fire swept through the plant on Green Street in Chicago and virtually destroyed all of the production facilities. Instead of abandoning the business, George E. Johnson and his employees salvaged what they could and, with the help of suppliers and Fuller Products Company, the company was operating from temporary headquarters within a week.

Growth of the company was steady but certainly not spectacular until product innovations in 1965 ushered in a period of rapid sales growth. In four years (1971–1975) gross sales increased from $13 million to $39 million. However, since 1975 the firm has experienced a series of setbacks.

Its first attempt to move beyond the ethnic market through an expensive men's cologne, "Black Tie," was a diaster. This failure was attributed to improper distribution channels, and poor shelf space and displays at retail establishments. Coinciding with this setback was the mounting pressure exerted by

EXHIBIT 2.1

Excerpts of Remarks Made to Shareholders at the Annual Meeting, by President George E. Johnson, December 10, 1986

I feel somewhat better today about where we are as a company than I did last year at this time. I don't mean to imply that we are out of the woods by any stretch of the imagination. What I am saying is that we made some genuine advances last year in several key areas and that the road before us is perhaps a little less rocky than a year ago.

I said last year that we would be biting many bullets to achieve "must" goals, that we were guardedly optimistic about being able to push forward and that we would do so by taking carefully measured steps. In a nutshell, that was pretty much the scenario for fiscal 1986. One significant measure of our progress is that our basic hair care products business turned profitable in the fourth quarter compared with a sizeable loss in the same quarter a year earlier.

Reaching that point took a great deal of soul searching as we tried to figure out how to curtail even further the outflow of cash so vitally needed for day-to-day operations. Although expenses had been reduced sharply in the previous year, it wasn't enough. We needed to cut at least $3 million more.

To accomplish this we took the extremely difficult step last April to eliminate 20% of the work force, and followed that with 10%–20% across-the-board salary reductions. These actions, together with others, resulted in annualized savings of approximately $3.5 million. Some of this is reflected in the 56% drop in our fiscal 1986 loss compared with fiscal 1985.

There was deep concern that cutting more staff would tend to impede operational efficiency. But just the opposite happened. We were able to tighten many functions, eliminate others and become a more cohesive organization, thanks to the responsive attitudes of all of our people.

The most encouraging aspect of this $3.5 million savings is that we will continue to benefit by approximately that amount in the current year, which means that hair care products operations should be profitable even if sales remain at fiscal 1986 levels. We are anticipating better than that.

In working out our turnaround strategy, we had objective input from Buccino & Associates, Inc., a management consulting firm with excellent credentials for aiding companies in situations such as ours. They started with us last April and completed their assignment last month.

Another area of urgency last year that took a great amount of management time was the replacement of our short-term debt with a flexible long-term financing arrangement that also would include more dollars for working capital. The additional money was critical if we were to generate and maintain forward momentum.

It was with considerable satisfaction that we concluded, late last October, a fully secured three-year credit agreement, including renewal options, with a national financing institution that provided us with a total of $10 million in the form of a $4-million term loan and a $6-million revolving credit. Approximately $6 million of the loan proceeds were used immediately to repay existing bank debt. The balance will be available for us to draw on as needed to operate the business.

To increase further our cash resources, we entered into an agreement with a real estate developer to sell approximately eleven acres of unneeded Chicago headquarters property, including a 200,000-square-foot office and warehouse building for $2.7 million. To date, we have received two non-refundable deposits amounting to $500,000. We expect to net $2.5 million from the sale and immediately use $1.6 million to reduce our term debt. The balance will be available for working capital.

The major factor affecting our hair care products sales continues to be intensive competition. There has been no let up. In fact, general market companies have been making noises that they expect to gobble up our industry. I don't foresee that ever happening, but the infighting could get even rougher, which might lead to a small shakeout in the industry.

Changing hair fashions, to some extent, also have had an effect on our business. Until about two years ago, curly hair was the rage and our Classy Curl hair curl kits generated good sales. But as most of you well know, fashion can be fickle. What is in vogue one day can become old hat the next, and that is what happened in most parts of the country to the curly hair look. This of course, has been eating into our hair curl kit sales.

But the bright side is that the fashion pendulum has swung back to relaxed hair stylings, and that can be good for Johnson Products because relaxer and conditioner and hair dress products traditionally have been our strengths. Ultra Sheen brand, long our mainstay, is widely known and through the years has generated considerable loyalty among users. And we continually have added attractive products to the line such as Ultra Sheen Light Conditioner and Hair Dress, which is just going into distribution.

Gentle-Treatment No-Lye Conditioning Relaxer is our best seller as well as one of the leaders among all products in the retail marketplace. A testimony to its quality is its consistent growth in popularity since its introduction in 1981. Moreover, we have been taking full advantage of the selling power of the brand name by marketing a variety of products under the Gentle-Treatment label. Extending the line even more with quality terms is an ongoing priority.

Because of Gentle-Treatment's success, we moved to expand the brand's base of customers with the introduction last August of Gentle-Treatment Xtra, which is a stronger formulation that should have great appeal to the large percentage of potential users with hard-to-relax hair. I'm delighted to report that up to this time, sales of both the regular and Xtra formulas have been exceeding expectations. Even more encouraging is that we already have received a number of reorders for Xtra, and it appears that these sales have not been at the expense of the original product.

Our sights this year are set on improving business with the professional beautician. This group is very important to us not only because of the products they buy but because they can be instrumental in motivating consumers to buy our products in their salons or at other retail outlets. Our premium-priced Ultra Sheen's Precise brand is a staple in hair salons, and we are moving to make our more modest-priced Bantu products even more attractive by offering the brand as a hair care system.

In order to achieve sales goals we will need a consistently strong performance from our sales force, and we believe that in its current form it can deliver what we expect. The restructuring of the entire sales organization in fiscal 1986, when

(Continued)

EXHIBIT 2.1   **(Continued)**

we established profit centers and began concentrating in geographic areas representing our main marketplaces, gave us a realistic operating concept. Moreover, we improved the caliber of individual sales representatives last year and initiated intensive ongoing sales training programs designed to help each one deal more effectively with and sell to both the retail and professional markets.

At the management level, we made a move that should enable the field staff to understand its role more clearly as it relates to the marketing process. Essentially, we combined the marketing and sales functions under the direction of a single officer. These were individual responsibilities before, and we found that there often were communication breakdowns between the two that taxed efficiency. Under the new arrangements, sales and marketing activities, which are closely interrelated, are being carried out with a greater understanding by all concerned of the potential ramifications each of these vital functions has on the other.

As for advertising and promotion, our plans mainly include pushing important brands and using carefully selected media that experience has shown to be especially effective for us. The advertising and promotion budget this year will be about 21 percent higher than last year's expenditure.

Last year we entered the private-label manufacturing business as a way of putting our expertise and excess plant capacity to profitable use. Although we made a variety of products for several large companies, our volume was disappointing. However, we continue to be enthused about the potential for developing this kind of business and we are working hard to do so. A number of proposals are currently under review by prospective customers. We believe that some will result in contracts.

A management change in our international division augurs well for its future. Plans to improve these operations include more European promotions and the establishment of more distributors or licensers in the Caribbean, Central and South America, and in selected African countries.

The Debbie's School of Beauty Culture subsidiary also contributed to fourth quarter profitability, and its losses for the full year were lower than for the previous year. Although enrollments trended slightly downward, collection action against students' accounts previously written off contributed to our increase in total revenue. At this point enrollments appear to be relatively stable.

In summary, our position and prospects today certainly are slightly better than a year ago for the following reasons: our break-even point has been reduced substantially, we have sorely needed working capital, the hair care fashion trend is favoring our relaxer products, several new products could do very well, our sales organization is stronger and better trained, coordination between sales and marketing has improved, and every individual in the company is striving to accelerate a complete turnaround.

But even with all these positives, the yellow caution light still signals brightly, telling us we must continue to act prudently and take carefully measured steps as we inch forward to achieve our goals.

Thank you.

major competing firms, primarily Revlon, which viewed the fast-growing ethnic market as an untapped well.

In February of 1975, the firm's public image was seriously damaged when it felt obligated to sign a consent order issued by the Federal Trade Commission requiring that warning labels be placed on its best-selling hair straightener, Ultra Sheen Permanent Creme Relaxer. Although its competitors also used the damaging chemical, sodium hydroxide, in their products, they were not compelled to take similar action until twenty months later.

Compounding these problems were the generally poor state of the economy and the high level of black unemployment in the late 1970s and early 1980s. The company experienced its first operating loss in 1980, and has sustained losses of $14,839,000 on sales of $254,585,000 over the past seven fiscal years (1980–1986). Only in 1981 and 1983 did the company post a profit (see Exhibit 2.9).

On April 4, 1986, the company hired a management consulting firm, Buccino & Associates, to help develop and implement a turnaround strategic plan. Some of the consultants' recommendations resulted in immediate retrenchment tactics—that is, the work force was cut back from 558 to 431 employees, and the salaries of the remaining employees were cut 10%–20%. These actions, combined with others, resulted in annualized savings of approximately $3.5 million.

Would the stockholders be pleased with this news? On December 1, 1986, George E. Johnson and his staff were finalizing his remarks to the shareholders for the Annual Meeting on December 10, 1986. Excerpts from those remarks are presented in Exhibit 2.1.

Company Highlights

1954	Company founded with one product, Ultra Wave Hair Culture
1957	Ultra Sheen Conditioner and Hair Dress introduced
1958	Ultra Sheen line entered professional beauticians' market
1960	Ultra Sheen line introduced in retail market
1964	Fire destroys production facilities
1965	Ultra Sheen No-Base Creme Relaxer introduced
1966	Completed first phase of new headquarters
1968	Afro Sheen products introduced
	Established The George E. Johnson Foundation
1969	Sponsored its first nationwide TV special, ". . . and Beautiful"
1969	First black-owned company to become publicly held
1970	Ultra Sheen cosmetics introduced
1971	Began sponsorship of "Soul Train," nationally syndicated TV show
	First black-owned company listed on American Stock Exchange
1972	Established The George E. Johnson Educational Fund

Company Highlights	
1973	Completed third phase of new headquarters
1975	Entered men's fragrance market with "Black Tie" cologne and splash-on
	Started exporting to Nigeria
	Acquired the Debbie's School of Beauty Culture—5 salons
1979	Cosmetics lines were reformulated
	Acquired Freedom Distributors, which distributed the company's and competitors' products on the eastern seaboard
1980	Established Johnson Products of Nigeria as a manufacturing subsidiary, with a 40% interest
	Introduced Ultra Sheen Precise, first of 42 innovative product lines
1981	Overseas expansion by establishing a sales and service center in Eastbourne, England
	Introduced new products Gentle Treatment, Tender Treatment and Bantu Curl
1982	Established Debbie Howell Cosmetics, direct sales line in key black market areas
	Introduced 19 new products
	Formed Mello Touch Labs, Inc. to manufacture, market and distribute a line of consumer products
1983	Introduced two lines of cosmetics, Ultra Sheen and Moisture Formula
	Sold Freedom Distributors
1984	Introduced Metra Star Curls for men
	Two additional Debbie Schools of Beauty Culture were opened in Texas and Georgia
1985	Restructured the marketing and sales organization
	Two new products were introduced—a unique exothermus hair curling system and deep penetrating conditioner. They were sold to both the professional and retail markets
	Signed Michael Jordan of the Chicago Bulls to a multi-year endorsement contract
1986	Excel Manufacturing Company, Inc. was formed as a private label arm of the company

STRATEGIC MANAGERS

George E. Johnson (age 59) serves as the Chairman of the Board and President. Mr. Johnson's business affiliations include board positions with Commonwealth Edison Company, Metropolitan Life Insurance Company, American Health and Beauty Aids Institute (Chairman) and the Cosmetic, Toiletry and Fragrance Association. He is also a member of a number of civic, charitable, professional, and social organizations.

Dorothy McConner (age 57) serves as the Executive Vice-President; Vice-President, Administration; and Corporate Secretary. She was elected a Director of the company in 1979. Mrs. McConner has been with the company for approximately twenty-five years and was selected *Blackbook*'s 1975 Business-woman of the Year.

David N. Corner (age 56) joined the company in December, 1979 as Vice-President, Finance; and Chief Financial Officer. Before joining this company, he was with Libby, McNeil & Libby, Inc., most recently as Vice-President, Finance; and Treasurer.

Marilynn J. Cason (age 43) was elected Vice-President in 1977 and was promoted to Vice-President, International, in 1986. She also served as Corporate Counsel. She has been responsible for the Nigerian operations for the past three and one-half years. Before joining the company in 1975, she spent three years as an attorney for Kraft, Inc., and three years as an associate attorney with the Denver law firm of Dawson, Nagel, Sherman and Horwald.

Tehsel S. Dhaliwal (age 45), with the company since 1973, served previously as Director of Manufacturing Operations. He was promoted to Vice-President of Operations in 1983.

Joan B. Johnson (age 57), wife of George E. Johnson, shared in the founding of the company in 1954. She presently serves as Treasurer and Director.

Danny O. Clarke (age 37) serves as Vice-President and Controller, a position he has held since 1984. He has served as Internal Auditor, Assistant Controller, and Controller since joining the company in 1977. Prior to joining the company, he was General Accounting Manager for a division of Container Corporation of America.

Sylvia J. Wynn (age 45) was promoted to Vice-President, Marketing and Sales in 1986. Having held similar positions with major brand products for Avon, Gillette, and Playtex, she joined the company as a marketing manager in 1983. A year later she was appointed Marketing Director.

Each executive officer was last elected as such on August 31, 1986, and shall serve until a successor is appointed and qualified. Mr. Clarke was appointed as Vice-President in March 1984 and Ms. Wynn in March 1986. Deborah A. Howell serves as President of Debbie's School of Beauty Culture, which has been a wholly owned subsidiary since 1975.

The three internal directors are George E. and Joan B. Johnson and Dorothy McConner. The outside directors are the following persons.

Alvin J. Boatte (age 57) has served as President of the Independence Bank of Chicago, Illinois, and became its Chairman of the Board in 1980. He has served as a Director of this company since 1969.

Melvin D. Jefferson (age 63) is owner and President of Superior Beauty and Barber Supply (Detroit, Michigan), a full-service distributor of beauty and hair care products. He has served as a Director of this company since 1969.

Jesse L. Howell (age 58) serves as Executive Vice-President of Debbie's School of Beauty Culture, Inc. (a wholly-owned subsidiary of the company since 1975). He has served as a Director of the company since 1977.

John T. Schriver, a Director of the company, resigned in 1986.

EXHIBIT 2.2   Stock Ownership

TITLE OF CLASS	NAMES AND ADDRESSES OF BENEFICIAL OWNERS	NUMBER OF SHARES BENEFICIALLY OWNED	% OF CLASS
Common stock	George E. Johnson, Trustee of personal trust[1] 95 Brentwood Drive Glencoe, Illinois 60022	1,989,475	49.9
Common stock	Joan B. Johnson, Trustee of personal trust[2] 95 Brentwood Drive Glencoe, Illinois 60022	180,000	4.5
Common stock	Joan B. Johnson, Trustee for children[1,2]	254,000	6.4
Common stock	Total shares owned by George E. and Joan B. Johnson	2,423,475	60.8

As of November 3, 1986, directors and officers of the company (eleven persons in all) beneficially owned the following shares:

Common stock		2,456,950[3]	61.6

[1] Mrs. Johnson disclaims beneficial ownership in these shares.

[2] Mr. Johnson disclaims beneficial ownership in these shares.

[3] Includes 1,800 shares under options exercisable within 60 days.

OWNERSHIP

Because of their direct and indirect ownership of shares of the company's stock, Mr. George E. Johnson and Mrs. Joan B. Johnson may be deemed to be controlling persons of the company for the purposes of the federal securities law. As shown in Exhibit 2.2, the Johnson family controls 60.8% of the company.

EXECUTIVE COMPENSATION

The eleven officers and directors were paid a total of $1,061,697 in cash compensation in 1985. In 1986, the fourteen officers and directors received $751,833 in cash compensation. The outside directors were paid a fee of $5,000 in 1985 and $2,500 in 1986. Below are the 1985 and 1986 salaries of the key company executives.

	Cash Compensation	
	1985	1986
George E. Johnson	$195,200	$177,750
Dorothy McConner	95,400	86,961
David N. Corner	97,886	89,227
Tehsel S. Dhaliwal	N/A	80,685
Jesse L. Howell	144,846	100,539

SUBSIDIARIES AND FACILITIES

The company's corporate offices and manufacturing facilities are located in a building held by it in fee; this building is on a twelve-acre tract at 8522 South Lafayette Avenue, Chicago, Illinois. The building encompasses approximately 64,000 square feet of office space and 176,000 square feet for manufacturing and warehousing purposes.

To support its continued growth, the company acquired additional property adjacent to the South Lafayette facilities at 87th Street and Dan Ryan Expressway in November 1974, at a cost of $1,100,000. This property consists of approximately eleven acres of land (compared to the twelve-acre tract of the old facility) and a 200,000 square foot building. This building currently houses warehousing, selected administrative offices of the company, and the administrative offices of Johnson's subsidiary, Debbie's School of Beauty Culture, Inc. The remainder of the building is under lease.

Johnson Products distributes its retail products mostly through national and regional drug, grocery, and mass merchandising chains. In 1979, it acquired Freedom Distributors, which distributed both the company's and its competitors' products on the eastern seaboard. It sold Freedom in 1983.

Its professional product lines are sold to beauty salons and barber shops. The company's wholly-owned subsidiary, Debbie's School of Beauty Culture, operates thirteen beautician-training facilities throughout the country. In 1977, Johnson Products Company purchased a Chicago building of 12,000 square feet. This facility now houses one of Debbie's schools. The other twelve locations are leased. The locations and terms of the leases are outlined in Exhibit 2.3.

The school's staff currently includes approximately 100 administrative personnel and instructors who direct a 1500-hour course completed over nine and one half months. The curriculum includes these subjects: anatomy, hairdressing, hair weaving, personal appearance, skin and nail care, shop management, and product education.

Since its acquisition in 1975, Debbie's has operated profitably each year with the exception of fiscal 1982 and 1985. Its poor performance in 1982 was attributed to the economic recession and curtailment in federal funding for certain types of education. In 1983, Debbie's graduated a record 1000 students, compared to the previous class of 455 students. Revenues and profits increased substantially. Fiscal year 1984 was another excellent year as enrollments increased by 25% over those of the previous year and generated an equal percentage increase in both revenues and income. In 1985, however, Debbie's revenues were off about $1.5 million from the $5.5 million of fiscal 1984, and it suffered a net loss for the year. The decline was attributed to the reduction in the number of students entering and completing the school's programs.

Competition from other schools providing the same course of study has increased sharply. To combat a sharp drop in enrollments, top management was freed from many administrative functions in 1986 so that they could concentrate on attracting new students. Although enrollment still trended slightly downward, aggressive collection against students' accounts previously written off in

EXHIBIT 2.3

Facilities of Johnson Products

LOCATION	APPROXIMATE SQUARE FOOTAGE	LEASE EXPIRES[2]
Chicago, Illinois	25,000	December 31, 1986[1]
Chicago, Illinois	15,000	December 31, 1986[1]
Chicago, Illinois	5,000	December 31, 1986[1]
Harvey, Illinois	9,000	December 31, 1986
East St. Louis, Illinois	12,000	December 31, 1986
Detroit, Michigan	7,200	December 31, 1986
Birmingham, Alabama	28,000	October 31, 1988
Indianapolis, Indiana	10,000	December 31, 1986
Atlanta, Georgia	5,000	July 31, 1989
Houston, Texas	10,000	January 31, 1987
St. Louis, Missouri	6,100	July 31, 1987
Houston, Texas	8,100	July 10, 1990

[1] The Chicago leases that expire in December, 1986 are renewable at the option of Debbie's. In addition, Debbie's operates one Ultra Precise Beauty Boutique in Chicago with approximately 2000 ft[2]. Although the lease expired on September 30, 1986, the Company expects that the new lease will be negotiated on terms comparable to those for similar situations.

[2] Total operating expense for leases in fiscal years ended August 31, 1986, 1985, and 1984 was $457,000, $347,000 and $229,000, respectively.

1985 ($1.4 million) contributed to an increase in total revenue. Enrollments seem to have stabilized, and Debbie's loss in 1986 was less than it had been the previous year.

Debbie's also operates a salon division, which consists of three Ultra Precise Beauty Boutiques in Chicago, one of which is situated in a Sears department store. All of Debbie's schools and salons use Johnson Products predominately.

In 1982, Debbie's established Debbie Howell Cosmetics, a direct-sales organization to promote Johnson's new line of cosmetics. This division currently employs consultants in about thirty cities that the firm believes to be key black-consumer markets. Losses in its first year of operation (approximately $147,000) were due primarily to start-up costs. The parent company is optimistic about the future of the direct sales endeavor because it believes that this sales technique has proven to be successful for companies such as Avon and Mary Kay Cosmetics. There are plans to expand further in existing markets, and in other key black-consumer market areas, but this organization still remains relatively small.

In October, 1983, Mellow Touch Labs, Inc. was formed to manufacture, market, and distribute a line of consumer products. Mello Touch shares common manufacturing, marketing, and distribution facilities, as well as resources, with the parent company.

In March, 1986, Excel Manufacturing Company, Inc. was formed as a private label arm of the company. It manufactures to the customers' specifications a broad base of products, ranging from medicated gels to lotions, to hair, skin and baby care products. Like Mellow Touch it shares common facilities and resources with the parent company.

INDUSTRY AND COMPETITION

In 1986, consumers spent $8.615 billion on toiletries and cosmetics. (See Exhibit 2.4.) While continued gains are expected for years ahead, the industry's real growth rate is expected to fall to an annual increase of 2%–3%. This growth is well below that experienced in the 1960s and 1970s. The decline is attributed to the fact that the rate of women entering the labor force is now lower, indicating that the trend of the 1960s and 1970s for multi-income families may have run its course and stabilized.

One of the fastest growing market segments in the toiletries and cosmetics industry is the ethnic market, consisting of an estimated 40 million blacks, Hispanics, and other minorities. Minority women are estimated to spend three times more per person on cosmetics than white women, and it is estimated that 30% of Johnson's sales are accounted for by minorities other than blacks. The market for ethnic hair care products has become a $1 billion industry growing by approximately 11% annually, while the ethnic toiletries and cosmetics market is growing at an annual rate of 20%.

In the 1984 U.S. Census, the black population was approximately 28.9 million with a median age of 27.8. Although in 1979 the 25–34 age group had accounted for 14.1% of the black population, by 1987, this had increased to 17.7% (see Exhibit 2.5). With these shifts in population, black consumers are experiencing an increase in their disposable incomes greater than that of the population at large. Between 1972 and 1979, blacks' aggregate income expanded 194%, from $30 billion to $88.2 billion, and in 1983, it almost doubled again to $170.3 billion. With statistics like these the ethnic consumer is being sought after as never before.

As the disposable income of the ethnic consumer increases, competition in the industry has become fierce. Johnson Products' large competitors include Revlon, with Realistic hair straightener and Polished Amber lines; Avon with its Shades of Beauty and Earth & Fire lines of makeup products for black women; Cosmair's L'Oreal of Paris, which has a product line called Radience that consists of hair colors and formula hair relaxers; and Alberto Culver.

By 1984, the market penetration of the larger national companies may have peaked, but Johnson Products was still in fierce competition with 50 or more black-owned regional firms, most of which made only one or two brands. Examples of these companies are M & M Products Company with its product Sta-Sof-Fro; and Pro-Line, a small but innovative black hair care firm that has introduced new products such as Perm Repair and Cherry Fragrance Oil Shampoo. Fueling the competitive fires is the fact that the innovative product offerings of the 1960s and 1970s have seemed harder to develop in the 1980s

EXHIBIT 2.4   Selected Financial Information on Competitors

COMPANY	SALES[1]				
	1986	1985	1984	1983	1982
Alberto-Culver	$ 435.4	368.6	348.6	313.7	320.4
Avon Products	2,883.1	2,470.1	3,141.3	3,000.1	3,000.6
Gillette	2,818.3	2,400.0	2,288.6	2,183.3	2,239.0
Helene Curtis	400.1	360.8	370.3	330.4	243.2
Noxell Corp.	438.8	382.1	349.5	304.3	261.9
Redkin Labs	103.2	108.5	101.4	86.3	84.6
Industry total	8,615.0	7,388.0	7,789.2	7,305.0	7,111.1

COMPANY	PROFIT[1]				
	1986	1985	1984	1983	1982
Alberto-Culver	13.3	7.9	4.5	3.9	6.6
Avon Products	158.7	128.2	181.7	164.4	196.6
Gillette	184.7	159.9	159.3	145.9	135.1
Helene Curtis	10.3	8.9	2.7	10.4	3.6
Noxell Corp.	37.1	32.4	28.3	23.2	18.5
Redkin Labs	2.0	8.4	8.3	6.4	6.5
Industry total	540.0	466.9	490.4	448.9	440.0

COMPANY	NET PROFIT MARGIN (%)				
	1986	1985	1984	1983	1982
Alberto-Culver	3.1%	2.1%	1.3%	1.3%	2.1%
Avon Products	5.5	5.2	5.5	5.5	6.6
Gillette	6.4	6.7	7.0	6.7	6.0
Helene Curtis	2.6	2.5	0.7	3.2	1.5
Noxell Corp.	8.5	8.5	8.1	7.6	7.1
Redkin Labs	1.9	7.7	8.2	7.4	7.6
Industry total	6.3	6.3	6.3	6.2	6.2

COMPANY	OPERATING MARGIN (%)				
	1986	1985	1984	1983	1982
Alberto-Culver	8.3%	7.8%	5.0%	5.1%	6.0%
Avon Products	13.8	12.6	14.7	13.6	15.7
Gillette	18.4	19.5	18.7	18.1	17.7
Helene Curtis	8.0	7.8	3.1	8.3	5.2
Noxell Corp.	17.3	17.5	16.0	14.5	13.7
Redkin Labs	7.0	16.2	16.8	15.7	16.2
Industry total	16.0	15.7	15.4	14.9	15.4

[1] These figures are stated in million of dollars.

EXHIBIT 2.5		**Demographics of the Black Population**					
AGE	1978	1979	1980	1981	1982	1983	1984	1985

AGE	1978	1979	1980	1981	1982	1983	1984	1985
Labor Force by % of U.S. Population								
16–19	8.8	8.4	8.0	7.5	7.3	6.6	7.6	6.8
20–24	16.0	16.1	15.8	16.0	16.3	15.4	16.7	14.7
25–34	28.0	28.6	29.5	31.0	30.8	32.8	31.4	31.8
35–44	19.4	19.5	19.7	20.0	20.3	21.3	20.7	22.3
45–54	15.8	15.7	15.6	14.5	14.2	13.8	13.8	14.0
55–64	9.2	9.1	9.0	9.0	9.0	8.7	8.2	8.4
65+	2.8	2.6	2.4	2.0	2.1	1.8	1.4	2.1
Mean Income of U.S. Blacks								
14–24	$ 6,673	$ 7,738	$ 7,898[1]	$10,350[1]	$10,487[1]	$ 2,111[1]	$10,387[1]	N/A
25–34	11,815	12,916	14,018	15,079	16,256	16,092	16,956	N/A
35–44	14,021	15,277	16,788	18,350	19,172	21,385	22,459	N/A
45–54	14,983	16,933	18,013	19,286	19,812	25,809	28,215	N/A
55–64	11,976	14,741	16,301	17,089	18,093	19,527	18,135	N/A
65+	8,363	8,713	10,472	10,650	11,566	14,161	12,042	N/A
Number of Blacks as % Total of U.S. Population								
16–19	9.3[2]	9.1[2]	11.3[3]	10.8[4]	10.5[4]	9.0[4]	9.3[4]	9.6[4]
20–24	14.4[3]	13.5[3]	10.3	10.5	10.5	9.7	9.8	9.9
25–34	14.5	15.0	17.1	16.6	17.0	18.0	17.7	17.8
35–44	10.3	10.4	10.2	10.3	10.6	11.9	11.7	11.5
45–54	9.0	9.0	8.6	8.4	8.3	8.0	8.6	8.3
55–64	7.1	7.1	7.2	7.1	7.1	7.6	7.6	7.2
65+	7.8	7.9	7.9	7.9	8.0	9.2	9.2	8.1

SOURCE: Statistical Abstracts of U.S., 1984, 1985, 1986 and 1987.

[1] These figures represent the age category of 15–24.

[2] These figures represent the age category of 14–17.

[3] These figures represent the age category of 18–24.

[4] These figures represent the age category of 15–19.

(see Exhibit 2.6). A few imaginative products producing above-average growth have been introduced, but the sales advances are closely tied to the increase in consumers' disposable income.

A major shift in the industry occurred when computerized inventory-management techniques were introduced at the retail level. Use of this technique permanently reduced the amount of stock needed on hand to sustain the particular dollar-level of sales, and resulted in a fierce battle for market share and shelf space. Because the production of innovative products is expensive and risky, companies have been forced to defend their traditional offerings.

EXHIBIT 2.6   **Major Product Lines Introduced Since 1980**

	YEAR INTRODUCED
Professional Lines	
Ultra Sheen brand	
Precise Conditioning Relaxer	1980
Precise Curl System	1980
Precise No-Lye Relaxer	1983
Bantu Curl brand (8 products)	1981
Ultra Sheen II	1983
New shampoo	1985
Retail Lines	
Afro Sheen brand	1980
Ultra Sheen brand	
Natural Body Formula	1980
Ultra Sheen No-Lye Relaxer	1983
Pump-dispensed conditioner and hair dress	1985
Classy Curl brand	1980
Tender Treatment brand	1980
Gentle Treatment brand	1981
Gentle Treatment Instant Conditioner	1983
Super Setting Lotion	1983
No-Lye Condition Relaxer	1983
Extra-No-Lye Conditioning Creme Relaxer	1985

Therefore, to increase their sales, the personal health care manufacturers were increasing their advertising and promotional budgets on a yearly basis.

INTERNATIONAL SUBSIDIARIES

After ten and one-half years with the company, Marilynn Cason was elected Vice-President, International in 1986. She had been serving as Vice-President and Corporate Counsel, yet for much of her time in the past several years she was deeply involved with international operations.

In 1980, the executives of the company made the strategic decision to establish Johnson Products of Nigeria as the first American company to manufacture hair care products in Nigeria. The company holds a 40% interest in this business venture with Nigerian partners representing various segments of the nation's business community. Mr. Johnson said of the Nigerian investment:

> We have been exporting to Nigeria since 1975, but actually our products have been sold there since the 1960s. Consequently, we have excellent corporate and product name recognition. . . . By manufacturing in Nigeria we are taking what

we believe is the best approach to building on our well-established reputation and maximizing the opportunities available in a developing country.

The company's investment in Nigeria was $1.6 million. The facilities include a 36,000 square foot manufacturing and warehousing building located just outside the capital of Lagos. An additional 18,000 square foot facility is available if expansion is deemed necessary.

Optimism about the potential profitability of this venture waned as major losses were incurred. First-year losses totalled $380,000. These were attributed to extremely heavy living costs in accommodating a team of Johnson Products representatives from headquarters who supervised the setting up of the plant and the early stages of operations. Ms. Cason was a member of the team and managed the operation for three and one-half years. Total losses in fiscal 1981 were $466,000. In fiscal 1982 losses were $1,802,000, which included a $1,557,000 write-down of investment and advances to this subsidiary. However, in 1985 and 1986 it was a profitable operation.

Many difficulties have plagued the operation from the start. Problems first stemmed from smuggling activities, which forced Johnson Products of Nigeria, Ltd. to compete with its own product being sold on the black market at prices well below retail. Then in 1981, in an effort to stave off illegal imports, the Nigerian government severely restricted the flow of goods entering the country. The Nigerian plant, manufacturing more than 30 different products under Ultra Sheen and Afro Sheen brands, was forced to suspend operations on several occasions because of difficulties in receiving shipments of raw materials and other goods.

In 1983, Nigeria remained the largest market in black Africa, as well as the one most likely to provide business opportunities for American firms in the medium- and long-term. One of the main problems for the past few years centers around the Nigerian government's lack of foreign exchange. This causes prolonged delays in the acquisition of raw materials even when import licenses have been granted. Although it is believed that the basic raw-materials problem will not be resolved in the immediate future, the company will maintain some degree of production in the country. Basically, Nigeria is an untapped ethnic consumer market with approximately 100 million people and an annual growth rate in excess of 3%.

In continuing its overseas expansion, Johnson Products established a sales and service center in Eastbourne, England (40 miles south of London) in October, 1981. It is essentially a low-overhead central distribution center for the Great Britain and Western European markets, primarily France, Germany, Belgium, and Holland. This 3,000 square foot facility has allowed the company to offer a broader range of its professional and retail products to that area. In fiscal 1983, this distribution center "made a positive contribution" toward profit, according to corporate records. Personal income in England experienced an increase in 1985 that prompted an approximate 2% growth in personal consumption. These markets are to be supported by an expanding advertising and promotion campaign.

Although competition is very intense throughout the Caribbean markets, the company has distributors in Haiti and in Puerto Rico, Johnson's biggest market in the Caribbean area. In 1981, the company entered into its first licensing agreement with a Jamaican manufacturer. Johnson Products supplies the raw materials as well as technical and marketing support, and in turn it receives a royalty for services. The company is waiting for approval of a similar licensing agreement in Trinidad.

The company's future emphasis will be on opening new markets in those Central and South American countries that have the fewest import restrictions. Management is also exploring the business opportunities in several other African countries.

Despite continued expansion, international sales in 1986 decreased by 10.5%. Below is the breakdown of sales in the United States and international markets.

	Sales (Millions of Dollars)					
	1986	**1985**	**1984**	**1983**	**1982**	**1981**
United States	$32,956	$36,069	$39,366	$43,624	$40,933	$40,933
International	1,586	1,772	2,161	2,151	1,514	2,690

PRODUCTS

Johnson Products currently manufactures over 100 different products, more than 50 of which have been developed since January 1980. Most of these have been matched by similar new products from Johnson's competitors. Before the introduction of Ultra Sheen Precise in 1980, the company admits, it had not offered a single innovative new product in over 15 years. Because of this lack of innovation, the firm's public image had waned and its reputation among professional beauty operators had faltered. Each product introduction in the following four years was designed to portray the firm as an industry innovator, "personally concerned with solving the beauty problems of black consumers."

According to Mr. Johnson, "In assessing why our business [1980] had slacked we learned several things. For one, we were no longer thought of as an innovative, sophisticated organization. We found also a low level of loyalty from professional beauticians and salon operators. In addition, there was an apparent lack of understanding among large retail buyers that Johnson Products is a large, substantial organization."

He also cited other problems, including:

1. Increased competition from large and small regional competitors.

2. Competition for shelf-space allocations.

3. Changes in the buying habits of the consumer, due to economic conditions.

4. Bad times in the economy caused retailers to carry smaller inventories, causing higher frequencies of stock-out conditions and loss of customer goodwill.

Johnson's product lines fall into two categories, those marketed to the professional industry and those sold to the general public. (See Exhibit 2.6.) Hair care products accounted for 86%, 89%, and 86% of net sales and other operating revenue in 1984, 1985 and 1986, respectively. The firm also manufactures two lines of cosmetics, Ultra Sheen and Moisture Formula. Retail sales to the general public is the company's largest segment.

MARKETING AND SALES

In March, 1986, Ms. Sylvia J. Wynn was named Vice-President, Marketing and Sales, and the two functions of marketing and sales that were previously directed by two individuals were combined. Mr. Johnson said, "Combining the two areas was a practical move because they were closely related. . . . Decisions now are being made with a full awareness of their overall ramification on both areas. An important by-product of this change has been a paring down and better utilization of our sales force, along with a keener understanding among the field staff of marketing and promotional strategies." In the past, the company found that often there were communication breakdowns between the two officers who directed marketing and sales and these breakdowns caused inefficiencies in these areas.

A restructuring of the entire sales force was accomplished in fiscal 1986. Three sales zones were established as profit centers. A support system to provide marketing and other support services to each zone was developed. According to management this should facilitate the selling process.

A top priority in 1985 was to get more shelf space by getting closer to the individual who decides which products get what shelf space. To do this the company initiated an intensive, ongoing sales-training program designed to help each sales person to deal more effectively with and sell to both the retail and professional markets. Utilizing a salesperson to call on both markets was a departure from previous practices; sales representatives have stronger retail selling backgrounds. This training program also promotes the careful monitoring of each salesperson's results.

On September 1, 1986, the company initiated a new sales commission program that would enable salaries to double when specific sales goals are met. Response to the plan by the staff has been positive and encouraging.

Marketing strategies have also been redirected to a more intense concentration on key customer groups. In addition to focusing on the company's broad national needs, marketing will be doing even more to develop attractive promotions directed specifically toward distributors and major retailers, and to provide support to the three zone offices, which are "closer to our customers and have a better understanding of their customers."

The company has experimented with several extensive promotional campaigns. The "Win A Date" contest, offering a male and female winner each a weekend date in Jamaica with the two Classy Curl models, was used in the Classy Curl campaign. In promoting the Gentle Treatment Conditioning Creme Relaxer the "Great Model Search" was conducted. More than 7000 consumers entered this contest, and the winners were used as models in promotional campaigns in 1983. The 1983 tour also featured the Gap Band.

Soon after these promotions, an A. C. Nielson audit survey was conducted; it showed an increase of market share in both product categories. The "Great Model Search" program, now entitled "Gentle-Treatment Model Search," draws thousands of entries annually. Each contestant must show proof of product purchase. The highlight of the 1986 contest will be a 17-city promotional tour by the 1986 winner.

In 1985, Michael Jordan, the Chicago Bulls basketball team's superstar, was signed to a multi-year contract for his endorsement of selected products. At this time, the company is working to develop a suitable program in which he can participate effectively.

One of the company's product development goals for the 1980s was to increase professional market share. The professional-sales market segment currently constitutes about 15% of the firm's total hair care business, and this decade has seen sales in this segment increase between 15% and 20% annually. The first market introduction in 1983 was the Precise No-Lye Relaxer. This has been followed each year by improved versions of earlier lines Ultra Sheen II and Bantu. Special promotions and training programs are being aimed at the professional market segment with this goal in mind.

In 1982, Johnson Products commissioned a study to research consumer opinions and/or perceptions of the company. The study showed that there were (1) a high level of name recognition (93%), (2) a feeling that its products guarantee quality (68%), and (3) a belief that the firm is reliable and trustworthy (70%).

EXHIBIT 2.7   **Advertising and Promotion Expenditures, 1975–1986**

YEAR	DOLLARS	PERCENTAGE OF NET SALES
1986	$ 5,384,000	18
1985	5,986,000	18
1984	10,031,000	20
1983	7,226,000	16
1982	7,467,000	18
1981	8,076,000	17
1980	7,243,000	21
1979	6,019,000	18
1978	6,211,000	17
1977	5,731,000	18
1976	5,608,000	14
1975	4,498,000	12

Drastic cuts in advertising expenditures were made in 1985 and 1986, as shown in Exhibit 2.7. The company has found that even though reports indicate that its advertising is still being well received and effective in attracting customers to its products, quite often, when customers go to buy, the item they want is out of stock.

The frequent lack of retail shelf space for the large number of black hair care products is a major problem for the industry. It is further complicated as new companies enter the regional markets. The competition from large companies such as Revlon, Avon, and Fashion Fair, still in pursuit of the ethnic dollar, has added a new facet to the problem. It is further complicated by competition from 50 small regional manufacturers, who enter into the regional markets with a restricted product line yet compete for the same shelf space.

RESEARCH AND DEVELOPMENT

Since January 1980, the Johnson Products Research Center has introduced, for both the retail and professional markets, more than 50 new products and line extensions. These new products accounted for more than 80% of sales in 1985, compared to 60%, 48%, and 36% in 1983, 1982, and 1981, respectively.

One significant aspect of the company is its capability to perform basic scientific research; this capability has enabled Johnson Products to develop unique technologies for the production of a variety of beauty products. During the past few years the company has received several patents for products presently on the market and several other patents are pending.

The Johnson Products Research Center is considered to be the largest laboratory of its kind devoted exclusively to the research and development of beauty care products for black consumers. In 1984, a staff of thirty-four technicians and scientists, representing a variety of scientific disciplines, worked with the latest sophisticated equipment in a 7,000 square foot research laboratory. By 1986, the staff had been reduced to 20, and expenditures for research and development were the lowest since those of 1976. (See Exhibit 2.8.) Approximately one third of the research and development manhours are spent on quality control; the rest are spent on new product development and the improvement of existing products. In-house capabilities are supplemented through the use of outside consultants and technical services, in the developing of concepts, designing of packages, and researching the characteristics of ethnic skin and hair.

FINANCE

During the seven fiscal years 1980–1986 the company's losses in seventeen of the twenty-eight quarters totalled $14,839,000 on sales of $254,585,000. Johnson Products was profitable only in 1981 and 1983. During the last three of those years, the company lost money in nine out of twelve quarters.

To reduce expenditures and costs in the past seven years, several cost cutting programs have been implemented. In 1982, total staff was reduced by approximately 10% through an increase in employee productivity and the elimination

EXHIBIT 2.8

R & D Expenditures

YEAR	R & D EXPENDITURES
1986	$693,000
1985	840,000
1984	818,000
1983	799,000
1982	868,000
1981	870,000
1980	782,000
1979	690,000
1978	763,000
1977	739,000
1976	525,000
1975	467,000

of certain job functions. The turnaround strategic plan for 1986 has resulted in a reduction in the number of employees by approximately 20%, to 431 employees. Salaries of the remaining employees were cut by 10%–20%. The company also started to perform some previously contracted services (e.g., building maintenance and silk-screening of plastic bottles) in-house.

During the last quarter of 1986 the company lost $2,154,000. George E. Johnson told the shareholders, "Fiscal 1986 could mark the end of a series of substantial losses. Our cautious optimism is based on a number of actions that lifted a great amount of pressure from management, enabling us to concentrate fully on building profitable sales." He went on to say, "Our primary objective last year was to find new ways to stem the outflow of sorely needed cash in our hair care products business without affecting our ability to produce and sell quality products." The company was able to reduce its losses by 56% over those of 1985, but sales for 1986 were reduced by $3,769,000 or 11.2%. The impact of the company's financial condition is reflected in the company's stock price. It has varied from a high of $20.625 in 1976 to a low of $1.75 in 1986 (see Exhibit 2.9).

The company owns a 40% interest in Johnson Products of Nigeria, Ltd. Because of the significant operating losses at Johnson Products of Nigeria, Ltd. and other external factors, the Johnson investment and advances to the Nigerian operation were written down in 1982. Previously, Johnson's 40% interest in this venture was carried at acquisition cost adjusted for equity in losses through July 31 of each year. Fiscal year 1986 was a profitable year for the Nigerian operation. Because this affiliate is still in operation, Johnson may be required in the future to advance significant amounts of working capital to this venture.

EXHIBIT 2.9

Johnson Products Company: Financial Review, 1978–1986

(In Thousands of Dollars Except Per Share Data, Percentages, and Employee Data)

Years Ended August 31	1986	1985	1984	1983	1982	1981	1980	1979	1978
Summary of Operations									
Net sales	$29,811	$33,580	$35,589	$40,937	$39,177	$43,197	$32,294	$31,337	$37,246
Other operating revenue	4,731	4,261	5,938	4,838	3,270	3,710	2,842	1,801	1,416
Total net sales and other operating revenue	34,542	37,841	41,527	45,775	42,447	46,907	35,136	33,138	38,662
Cost of sales	13,243	15,169	15,419	16,649	18,191	19,528	15,250	12,291	14,854
Selling, general and administrative (exclusive of advertising and promotion)	17,028	20,283	21,055	18,490	19,122	17,866	16,773	14,657	13,776
Advertising and promotion	5,384	5,986	10,031	7,226	7,467	8,076	7,243	6,019	6,211
Equity in losses and write-down of investment in Nigerian affiliate	—	—	—	—	1,802	466	380	—	—
Interest expense (income), net	870	917	624	424	414	48	(270)	(450)	(416)
Income (loss) before income taxes	(1,983)	(4,514)	(5,602)	2,986	(4,549)	923	(4,240)	621	4,237
Income taxes (benefit)	—	—	(1,519)	1,358	(926)	538	(1,861)	300	2,000
Net income (loss)	(1,983)	(4,514)	(4,083)	1,628	(3,623)	385	(2,379)	321	2,237
Net income (loss) per share	(.50)	(1.13)	(1.03)	.41	(.91)	.10	(.60)	.08	.56
Dividends per share	—	—	—	—	—	—	.18	.36	.36
Other Financial Data									
Research and development expenses	693	840	818	799	868	870	782	690	763
Current assets	14,915	16,768	19,694	19,894	20,082	20,112	18,573	18,658	22,632
Current liabilities	8,584	13,369	11,983	7,186	9,022	6,683	5,396	2,989	5,510
Working capital	6,331	3,399	7,711	12,708	11,060	13,429	13,177	15,669	17,122

(Continued)

EXHIBIT 2.9 (Continued)

Years Ended August 31	1986	1985	1984	1983	1982	1981	1980	1979	1978
Property, net	8,068	8,891	9,120	9,210	9,133	8,988	9,062	9,400	9,346
Total assets	23,517	26,598	29,850	29,785	29,659	30,860	29,205	29,886	33,505
Capital lease obligations	16	111	221	299	—	—	—	—	—
Shareholders' equity	11,150	13,118	17,646	21,715	20,062	23,660	23,257	26,355	27,433
Shareholders' equity per share	2.80	3.29	4.43	5.46	5.05	5.96	5.86	6.63	6.87
Capital expenditures	302	754	803	987	1,076	791	528	1,008	864
Ratios									
Income (loss) before income taxes to net sales and other operating revenue	(5.7%)	(11.9%)	(13.5%)	6.5%	(10.7%)	2.0%	(12.1%)	1.9%	11.0%
Net income (loss) to net sales and other operating revenue	(5.7%)	(11.9%)	(9.8%)	3.6%	(8.5%)	.8%	(6.8%)	1.0%	5.8%
Return on average shareholders' equity	(16.3%)	(29.3%)	(20.7%)	7.8%	(16.6%)	1.6%	(9.6%)	1.2%	8.2%
Advertising and promotion to net sales and other operating revenue	15.6%	15.8%	24.2%	15.8%	17.6%	17.2%	20.6%	18.2%	16.1%
Average common and common equivalent shares outstanding (000s)[1]	3,987	3,984	3,982	3,980	3,973	3,972	3,972	3,976	3,995
Stock price range (high)	4	6½	11	11⅜	3½	5⅛	5⅜	6¾	11¼
Stock price range (low)	1¾	2¼	3	3⅛	2	2⅛	2⅛	3½	8⅞
Sales per share (dollars)	7.35	8.28	6.78	11.50	10.68	11.81	8.85	8.34	9.73
Number of employees	431	558	540	550	540	568	563	516	553

SOURCE: 1986 *Annual Report*, and *Value Line Investment Survey*, April 19, 1985, p. 821.

[1] Common equivalent shares consist of Class B common shares for the years 1974 through 1976.

EXHIBIT 2.10

Johnson Products Company: Consolidated Balance Sheets

Years Ended August 31	1986	1985
Assets		
Current assets:		
Cash	$ 996,000	$ 455,000
Receivables:		
Trade, less allowance for doubtful accounts of $425,000 in 1986 and $300,000 in 1985	9,112,000	9,118,000
Other	120,000	502,000
Refundable income taxes	—	30,000
Inventories	4,112,000	5,897,000
Prepaid expenses	575,000	766,000
Total current assets	14,915,000	16,768,000
Property, plant and equipment	19,052,000	19,147,000
Less accumulated depreciation and amortization	10,984,000	10,256,000
	8,068,000	8,891,000
Other assets:		
Cash value, officers' life insurance	166,000	435,000
Investments	244,000	244,000
Miscellaneous receivables	124,000	260,000
	534,000	939,000
Total assets	23,517,000	26,598,000
Liabilities and Shareholders' Equity		
Current liabilities:		
Short-term loans	2,269,000	6,293,000
Accounts payable	3,082,000	4,403,000
Current maturities of long-term debt and capital lease obligations	329,000	113,000
Accrued expenses	2,200,000	2,064,000
Income taxes	248,000	371,000
Deferred income	456,000	125,000
Total current liabilities	8,584,000	13,369,000
Long-term debt	3,767,000	—
Capital lease obligations	16,000	111,000
Shareholders' equity		
Capital stock:		
Preferred stock, no par; authorized 300,000 shares; none issued	—	—
Common stock, $.50 par; authorized 7,504,400 shares; issued 4,052,722 shares	2,027,000	2,027,000
Additional paid-in capital	628,000	627,000

(Continued)

EXHIBIT 2.10 **(Continued)**

Years Ended August 31	1986	1985
Liabilities and Shareholders' Equity (Continued)		
Retained earnings	8,849,000	10,832,000
Treasury stock, 65,560 shares in 1986 and 68,140 shares in 1985, at cost	(354,000)	(368,000)
	11,150,000	13,118,000
Total liabilities and shareholders' equity	$23,517,000	$26,598,000

EXHIBIT 2.11 **Johnson Products Company: Consolidated Statements of Operations, 1984–1986**

Years Ended August 31	1986	1985	1984
Net sales	29,811,000	33,580,000	35,589,000
Other operating revenue	4,731,000	4,261,000	5,938,000
	34,542,000	37,841,000	41,527,000
Cost and expenses:			
Cost of sales	13,243,000	15,169,000	15,419,000
Selling, general and administrative expenses	22,412,000	26,269,000	31,086,000
	35,655,000	41,438,000	46,505,000
Loss from operations	(1,113,000)	(3,597,000)	(4,978,000)
Interest expense, net	870,000	917,000	624,000
Loss before income taxes	(1,983,000)	(4,514,000)	(5,602,000)
Income taxes	—	—	(1,519,000)
Net loss	(1,983,000)	(4,514,000)	(4,083,000)
Net loss per common and common equivalent share	$ (.50)	$ (1.13)	$ (1.03)

EXHIBIT 2.12   **Johnson Products Company: Consolidated Statements of Shareholders' Equity**

Years Ended August 31, 1986, 1985, and 1984	COMMON STOCK	ADDITIONAL PAID-IN CAPITAL	RETAINED EARNINGS	TREASURY STOCK	TOTAL SHAREHOLDERS' EQUITY
Balance, August 31, 1983	$2,027,000	$649,000	$19,430,000	$(391,000)	$21,715,000
Net loss			(4,083,000)		(4,083,000)
Compensation arising from restricted stock plan		11,000			11,000
Exercise of stock options		(7,000)		11,000	4,000
Other			(1,000)		(1,000)
Balance, August 31, 1984	$2,027,000	$653,000	$15,346,000	$(380,000)	$17,646,000
Net loss			(4,514,000)		(4,514,000)
Compensation arising from restricted stock plan		(15,000)			(15,000)
Exercise of stock options		(11,000)		12,000	1,000
Balance, August 31, 1985	$2,027,000	$627,000	$10,832,000	$(368,000)	$13,118,000
Net loss			(1,983,000)		(1,983,000)
Compensation arising from restricted stock plan		(14,000)			(14,000)
Exercise of stock options		(13,000)		14,000	1,000
Other		28,000			28,000
Balance, August 31, 1986	$2,027,000	$628,000	$ 8,849,000	$(354,000)	$11,150,000

The company's total export shipments to twenty-two foreign countries, including Canada, provided less than 10% of consolidated revenue for 1986.

To strengthen its financial position, the company negotiated a fully secured $10 million refinancing package with a national financial institution. The arrangement provided the company a $4 million term loan and revolving credit of up to $6 million, based on available collateral. The company also has a firm offer to buy eleven acres and 200,000 square feet of Johnson Products' office and plant space at the 87th Street and Dan Ryan Expressway facility, for $2.7 million. Management expects to net $2.5 million and use $1.5 million to reduce the company's $38 million long-term debt. The remainder would be used for working capital.

The company's financial information is shown in Exhibits 2.9–2.12.

Reebok International, Ltd.

SEXTON ADAMS • ADELAIDE GRIFFIN

It was summer 1988. The students' riots in Seoul, South Korea had subsided. Athletes from around the world were gathering in Seoul for the 1988 Summer Olympics. American athletes were eager to improve on their poor performance in the Winter Olympics held earlier in Calgary, Canada. As most Americans could not be in Seoul, they would be watching the games on the NBC television stations.

"We will be back after this commercial break," said Bryant Gumbel, the NBC host, after explaining how a Korean boxer won by a "walk-over" because his American opponent showed up late for his bout. Then came a commercial that featured a group of oddly individualistic characters in Reebok shoes going about their business: a fairy-godmother type in a crowd emerging from a subway, all white and bouffant with a crown; a bevy of wood nymphs tiptoeing through a forest glade; and a three-legged man in baseball cap and raincoat. All were wearing brightly colored Reeboks.

This was Reebok's new avant-garde, abstract and controversial "U.B.U." commercial.

BACKGROUND AND HISTORY

In 1979, Paul Fireman first saw Reebok shoes at a Chicago trade show while shopping for his family's business, an outdoor equipment distributorship. Immediately he and his buddy, Jim Barclay, who is now Executive Vice-President, purchased the exclusive North American license from Reebok International, Ltd. In 1979, Reebok USA's entire line was represented by three different running shoes, each handmade in England and carrying a substantial price tag. By December 1987, the line consisted of 250 models in 12 categories, all competitively priced.[1]

The history of Reebok, named after the African gazelle, goes much deeper. In the early 1890s, Joseph William Foster, of Bolton, England, made the first pair of cleated track shoes. By 1895, the idea was so popular that J. W. Foster & Sons became the world's first athletic-shoe company. The mainstay of the business was hand-stitched shoes for Britain's most elite runners, including the 1924 Great Britain Olympic track team, made famous in the movie *Chariots of Fire*. In 1958, Joseph and Jeffrey Foster (grandsons of the founder) started a companion firm, Reebok International, Ltd., which eventually absorbed the parent company.

This case was prepared by Terri Hamby, Tony Oweh, Al Sowry, and Kathy Weiss under the supervision of Professor Sexton Adams, University of North Texas and Professor Adelaide Griffin, Texas Woman's University. Copyright © 1988 by Sexton Adams and Adelaide Griffin. Reprinted by permission.

Fireman encountered limited success in marketing the high-priced running shoes in the U.S., and in 1981, he approached Pentland Industries, a British shoe distributor, for financial help. Pentland agreed to provide the monetary backing for Reebok, USA because, as Chairman Stephen Rubin recalled, "We felt it would be quite a good brand."[2] And indeed it was! Pentland provided Fireman with $77,500 cash in exchange for 56% of Reebok, USA.

By 1981, sales exceeded $1.3 million, but the big success story continued to elude Reebok, USA. However, the experience was not completely wasted. "One thing we learned very early on was to watch the consumers," remembered Barclay.[3] And in 1981, Barclay returned from a California road trip convinced of the upcoming aerobics craze.

"As we did our research," Fireman recalled, "we discovered no one was making a shoe that was right for this market. In fact, no one even thought the market existed."[4] Thus Reebok designed the first women's aerobic shoe—a ballet type with a heavily cushioned sole, a soft, supple garment leather upper, and wrinkles at the toe. Ironically, the wrinkled toe was originally a manufacturing mistake. According to Fireman, "The shoe, when they lasted (stitched) it, actually ended up wrinkled all in the front toe of the shoe. . . . We fell in love with them and so did the consumer. What happened was, we went back immediately and told them to order the samples and they had sent us a telegram with terrible apologies, explaining that they had never put wrinkles in a shoe before and they would straighten it out immediately. The essence was, they straightened it out. It took us months to figure out how to manufacture them with wrinkles."[5]

Finally, in September 1982, the aerobic Freestyle and Energizer lines were introduced with their wrinkled toes. Very few shoes were sold in the first three months and Fireman began to contemplate the destiny of "thousands of pairs of shoes."[6] But in the fourth month, the shoes suddenly sold out and the rest, as they say, was history. In 1982, U.S. sales climbed to $3.5 million.

Reebok, USA and Reebok International merged in July 1985 to form Reebok International, Ltd. A public offering of 4 million shares was made to finance the company's phenomenal growth. Fireman continued in the company as its Chairman and CEO.

Through multiple line extensions and acquisitions, Reebok International, Ltd. has sustained five years of rapid growth and expansion. (See Exhibit 3.1.) Between 1983 and 1987, the company's sales expanded at an average annual rate of 155%.[7] In fact, Reebok's growth pattern has been so incredible that the January 11, 1988 issue of *Forbes* reported that the company had the highest five-year growth rate in net sales and net income of any company surveyed. Additionally, *Forbes* ranked Reebok as the #1 return on investment over the five years ended 1987.[8]

However, industry analysts agreed that growth of this magnitude in the Reebok footwear market could not continue, and this fact was not lost on Reebok's chairman. "The excitement has peaked already," conceded Fireman.[9]

EXHIBIT 3.1

Financial Growth 1983–1987, Reebok International, Ltd.

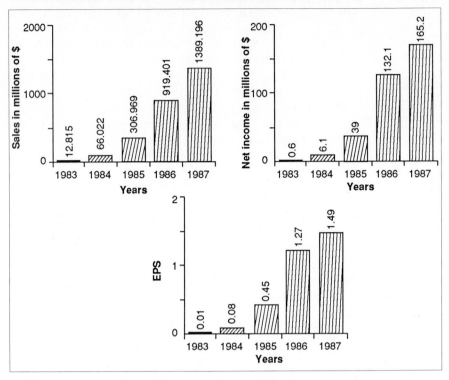

SOURCE: *1987 Annual Report.* Reebok International, Ltd.

In his strategy to carry Reebok into maturity, Fireman planned to diversify the company into a $2 billion international organization by 1990.

MANAGEMENT

Reebok's success was founded on management's belief that it was, above all, a consumer marketing company. Stated Brenda Gall, a Merrill Lynch textiles and apparel analyst, "Reebok's management recognized that most purchases of athletic footwear are for comfort and fashion, not performance. And they marketed the product accordingly."[10]

Management also contended that the growth of the Reebok brand itself would be dictated by the consumer, and they were determined not to put undue pressure on the Reebok brand. This philosophy led the company to its current three-fold strategy: acquisitions, internal development/product differentiation, and international expansion. Consequently, Reebok was no longer involved in just the $3.5 billion U.S. athletic footwear business. The total market in which it had become a player was valued at over $25 billion.[11] Reebok's market shares for its products are given in Exhibit 3.2. Industry observers believed that guid-

EXHIBIT 3.2

Reebok's Total Market
(in billions of dollars)

Market	TOTAL MARKET VALUE	REEBOK VALUE
U.S. athletic shoes	$ 3.5	$1.11 = 31.7%
U.S. sportwear/apparel	5.0	.50 = 1.0%
U.S. casual dress shoes	12.0	.15 = 1.25%
International athletic shoes	4.5	.20 = 4.4%
Total Market	25.0	1.389 = 5.56%

SOURCE: Reebok International, Ltd., *1987 Annual Report*, p. 11.

ing Reebok from a domestic, one-product company to a multi-national, multi-brand enterprise would require the expertise of skilled professional management at every level.

Fireman strengthened Reebok's management ranks by bringing in several executives from the outside (see Exhibit 3.3). In March 1987, Fireman hired C. Joseph LaBonte, an acquisitions specialist, as the company's new President and Chief Operating Officer. Douglas Arbetman, formerly of Calvin Klein, joined the company in September 1986 to take control of the faltering Reebok apparel line. Charles Lauer was hired away from the Papagallo division of U.S. Shoe Corp. to head up the Metaphors division.[12] The new management team was definitely young, with an average age of 28. "This is the first time in my life I've been the old man in an organization," quipped the 47-year-old LaBonte.[13]

In 1981, the Reebok organization was run by twelve employees. Seven years later, in 1988, the company employed approximately 2400 workers, including employees of its subsidiaries. Yet Reebok continued to rely on oral communication, rather than memos and carbon copies, for the free flow of ideas and information. Even the doors of top management remained open to all. "No one says that we do it better than anyone else, but you have to create in an organization a comfort zone for your people to be able to make mistakes," explained LaBonte.[14] Thus, Reebok attracted a group of bright, dynamic professionals who were encouraged to take risks.

At the top was the biggest speculator of all, Chairman and CEO Paul Fireman. It was Fireman who decided to place the first big orders for tennis shoes with the manufacturer before they were even sold to retailers. "He's a gambler. He rolled 'em and it paid off," said Tom Ellis of Prince.[15] Mr. Fireman was described as aggressive, stimulating to his co-workers, and a perfectionist. "In some ways he is the glue that holds a lot of things together, and in other ways he is just a disruption that keeps you always questioning," explained Betsy Richardson, Reebok's Tennis Product Manager.[16]

Fireman was a self-made millionaire and yet remained unpretentious, at times even flustered, at the heights of his success. In 1987, he received a base salary of $357,200; but a bonus equal to 5% of the company's pre-tax earnings

EXHIBIT 3.3   **Reebok International, Ltd. Executive Officers**

NAME	AGE	OFFICE HELD	PREVIOUS EXPERIENCE
Paul Fireman	44	Chief Executive Officer Chairman of the Board of Directors	
C. Joseph LaBonte	48	President and Chief Operating Officer	Vantage Group, Inc.—CEO; 20th Century Fox Film Corp.— President and COO
James E. Barclay	47	Executive Vice-President	Reebok—VP, Sales & Marketing; Pres., Reebok Footwear
John B. Douglas, III	34	Vice-President & General Counsel	Stanhome Inc.—Int'l. Counsel; Xerox Corp.—Legal Dept.
Paul R. Duncan	47	Sr. Vice-President, Treasurer and Chief Financial Officer	Towle Mfg. Co.—Vice-Chairman; Sr. VP, Finance CFO
Joseph F. Foster	52	President, Reebok International; Corporate VP	Reebok—Managing Director of UK Subsidiary
David D. Harshbarger	50	Sr. Vice-President, Human Resources	Sealy, Inc.—VP, Human Resources
Stanley I. Kravetz	55	Pres., The Rockport Company; Corporate Vice-President	John A. Frye Co.—President; Timberland Co.—Exec. VP, Director
Frank O'Connell	44	Pres., Reebok North America; Corporate Vice-President	HBO Video Inc.—CEO; Shaun Software Inc.—Chairman, Pres. & CEO; Fox Video Games Inc.—Pres. & CEO
Douglas R. Arbetman	40	Pres., Reebok Apparel Division; Corporate Vice-President	Calvin Klein Industries—VP Cole of California—VP

SOURCE: Reebok International, Ltd., *1987 Form 10-K*, pp. 11–12.

in excess of $20 million made him the nation's second highest paid executive in 1986 (behind Lee Iacocca).[17] Fireman's pay was strictly structured from the beginning, when Pentland Industries provided the first cash infusion for the then struggling Reebok. According to Pentland's Stephen Rubin, "Paul would have been perfectly happy to have a high salary, but we wanted to minimize our risk as well as create a potential for unlimited incentive."[18] Thus Fireman's original compensation package called for a base salary of $65,000 plus 10% of pre-tax earnings over $100,000. However, when Reebok's stock went public in 1985, the board adopted the current formula because Kidder Peabody, the company's investment banker, foresaw difficulty selling the issue. Fireman's salary and bonus structure were up for review again in 1990.[19]

This bonus structure led industry observers to speculate whether Reebok's use of equity rather than the use of less costly debt for its expansion was truly to the benefit of the shareholders. In fact, a few shareholders have actually written to Fireman to say they think it outrageous for anyone to take that much money out of the company. Fireman simply wrote back that he agreed with them but then added, "I'm not goint to give it back."[20]

By relinquishing his presidency in March 1987 to Joseph LaBonte, Fireman relieved himself of the day-to-day decisions. He remained the spokesman to the financial world and, supported by an extensive staff of respected designers, equipped with state-of-the-art R&D facilities, became more involved with his first love, the product. Reebok's research facilities were modern, high-tech, and filled with many machines and computers. It was not uncommon to find a man running on a treadmill, testing new products and designs. Reebok's R&D staff had developed their Energy Return System to counter Nike's "visible air" concept.[21]

ORGANIZATION

Reebok was divided into five main operating units: Reebok North America, Reebok International, Rockport, Avia, and Ellesse. All units were relatively autonomous, but were responsible to a three-man top management team: Fireman, LaBonte, and Duncan. (See Exhibit 3.4.) According to Fireman, "Each group has its own needs and if we apply formula thinking, we'll lose the ability to react quickly to the market."[22] Additionally, internal competition was a common theme among the subsidiaries. "We told Avia to hit all our soft spots. If they don't, someone else will," said LaBonte.[23]

Reebok North America

Five independent divisions operated within Reebok N.A. The Reebok Footwear Division marketed footwear for aerobics, fitness, basketball, walking, tennis and running. Controlling 32% of the market, the Reebok Footwear Division exhibited a 17.8% increase in sales to $991 million in 1987.[24] The Division also maintained a before-tax operating profit of 28%, due to controlled overhead costs, fast inventory turnover, and a limited number of distribution channels.

The Reebok Apparel Division was established in late 1985 with a three-year strategic plan. Sales in 1986 of $39 million greatly exceeded the anticipated $5–10 million volume.[25] However, the internal support system for this level of sales was not in place, and this lack of organization nearly led to disaster. According to LaBonte, "The brand was so damn hot that anything we put on the racks just blew out of there." But product quality and distribution were poor. "The good news was that our distribution was so bad that we didn't ruin ourselves. Most of the clothes never reached the shelves in time for the holiday sales," he continued.[26] In 1987, the Division was refocused: the spread of the apparel line was reduced, the footwear and apparel salesforces were consolidated, and new management was hired. The 1987 sales for the Reebok Apparel Division totalled $47 million, accounting for less than 1% total market share.[27] Operating margins were not available for Reebok apparel.

EXHIBIT 3.4   **Reebok Executive Organization Chart**

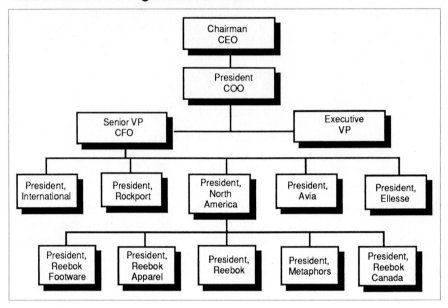

The Weebok Division was established in 1987 to market athletic shoes for infants and children. The Metaphors Division was also started in 1987 to design and market a line of casual women's footwear. Reebok's Canadian distributor, ESE Sports Co. Ltd., was acquired in June 1987 and has since operated under the name of Reebok Canada. The division distributed the Reebok, Weebok, and Rockport brands throughout Canada. Sales and earnings figures were not available for these divisions and were presumed minimal by industry analysts.

Reebok International

The responsibility of the International Division was the marketing of Reebok products outside the U.S. and Canada. This function was accomplished via a network of wholly owned subsidiaries in France, West Germany, Holland, and Austria. Other distributors were also employed in more than fifty countries. (The International Division holds partial ownership in seven of these.) Approximately 7.8 million pairs of Reebok shoes were sold outside the U.S. in 1987, with a wholesale value of $200 million (compared to 817,000 pairs in 1985).[28]

International sales revenues increased by 400% in 1987 over the prior year and the company held a 4.5% share in the overseas market. Revenue from international operations included royalties on sales to foreign distributors and thus profit margins were not applicable. Joseph W. Foster has been in charge of Reebok International since March 1986.

Rockport

The Rockport Company, the largest U.S. walking shoe manufacturer, was well known for its quality products. It was purchased in 1986. The Rockport subsidiary designed, developed, and marketed casual dress and fitness walking shoes for both men and women. Since its acquisition in May 1987, the John A. Frye Company has operated as a Rockport subsidiary. Frye was involved in the production and marketing of high quality dress and casual shoes and boots and possessed its own domestic production facilities. The Rockport Division had a $150 million share (1.25%) of the $12 billion U.S. casual shoe market. Rockport sales grew by 65% in 1987.[29] The Rockport Division operated on a 14% pre-tax profit margin. Stanley I. Kravetz, former President of John A. Frye Co., served as President of the Rockport subsidiary.

Avia

In expanding within the U.S. athletic footwear market with its 1987 purchase of Avia, not only did Reebok acquire an additional 3% market share (which doubled to 6% by late 1988), but it also entered a market whose consumers were more concerned with performance than with fashion. *Sports Ink*, an industry newsletter, estimated that 80% of Reeboks were worn for street wear, but Avia's shoes were worn almost exclusively for sports. "People buy Avia for the function," confirmed Avia's Vice-President of Marketing James Solomon. "Avia is concerned with technology first, fashion second."[30] Avia holds several important patents including a cantilever sole on its aerobic shoes. In addition, the strong management team that built Avia was viewed as an extremely valuable asset. Reebok got a lot for its $181 million! Avia operated autonomously as a wholly owned subsidiary with its management team in place and Dean Croft remaining as Avia's president. Avia also continued to market its Donner Mountain line which consisted of walking shoes, casual footwear, and hiking boots. Avia sales grew by 118% to $153 million in 1987, and the pre-tax operating margin was 11%.[31]

Ellesse

On January 20, 1988, Reebok International, Ltd. completed its purchase of Ellesse, USA, Inc. (an Italian maker of high-end sportswear and athletic shoes) and the exclusive rights to use the Ellesse trademark in the U.S. and Canada.

The company planned to operate Ellesse USA as an autonomous, wholly owned subsidiary. Ellesse had widespread recognition and was represented on the international tennis circuit by Chris Evert, who had been an Ellesse athlete since 1978.[32] Financial operating information was not available for Ellesse because of its recent acquisition.

MANUFACTURING AND PRODUCTION

The majority of Reebok's products were produced by foreign independent manufacturers, the exceptions being certain items of apparel and Frye footwear.[33] Each of the operating units contracted with these manufacturers on an individual basis and provided detailed specifications for production and quality control. South Korean manufacturers produced 77% of Reebok's footwear, with the largest of these responsible for 36% of the total production. Rockport did not depend on any single country for more than 25% of its production; Avia's products were manufactured predominantly in Taiwan.[34]

Political upheaval and terroristic outbreaks in South Korea led to extensive labor unrest in late 1987. Consequently, Reebok experienced third-quarter 1987 production problems, which resulted in the Reebok Footwear Division's inability to meet customer orders. The company has taken steps to build up the 1988 inventory to meet the heavy back-to-school demand. Reebok made an effort to diversify its production capacities, in both the number of factories and countries utilized. Additionally, a three year contract has been negotiated with the company's largest manufacturer in South Korea, calling for the production of at least 2.3 million pairs of shoes per month.[35]

When the company was ready to undertake manufacturing in China in 1985, rival Nike Inc. had already spent five years training Chinese management. Reebok was able to take advantage of Nike's learning curve. Thus, when Reebok chose a factory previously used by Nike, cleanliness and quality were already ingrained in the Chinese managers. Between August and October 1987, Reebok produced 50,000 pairs of shoes in China and was gearing up to make 3 million pairs in 1988. Within two years of production, Reebok will be turning out as many shoes as Nike is after six.[36]

Since 1981, a servicing fee was paid to a wholly owned subsidiary of Pentland Industries for assistance in the production efforts of Reebok North America and Reebok International in the Far East. This fee amounted to $13.5 billion in 1987. Among the services provided were inspection of finished goods prior to shipment and arrangement for issuance of letters of credit from foreign banks to pay manufacturers for finished goods.

Reebok's footwear products were manufactured primarily from leather, nylon, rubber, ethylvinyl acetate, polyurethane and pigskin.[37] Materials were obtained from a number of sources. Materials costs should abate in the 1988–1989 season as leather costs drop because of the large number of cattle killed in the U.S. summer's drought. Industry experts were uncertain of the impact of this development.

Footwear imported by Reebok into the U.S. for sale was subject to U.S. Customs duties, ranging from 8.5% to 37.5%. The charges varied depending on whether the principal component of the shoe was leather or another material.[38]

INDUSTRY SITUATION

According to Standard & Poor, the sluggishness in the retailing environment continued to plague the shoe industry. As a result, heavy discounting at the consumer level has negatively affected many shoe retailers.

The industry also faced uncertainty in trade legislation designed to restrict importation of footwear and textiles. U.S. imports of textiles, apparel, and footwear had increased due to the labor cost savings that foreign production provided (see Exhibit 3.5). Domestic apparel workers, of whom over 50% were represented by a union, earned $5.85 per hour in 1986, compared to wage rates in the Far East that ranged from $0.20 to $2.00 per hour.[39] Because labor was the single largest component of apparel and footwear products, foreign manufacturers maintained a competitive advantage.

EXHIBIT 3.5   **U.S. Imports of Textiles, Apparel, and Footwear**

Country	IMPORTS (Millions of dollars)				% OF TOTAL IMPORTS		
	1982	1983	1984	1985	1982	1985	% CHANGE 82–85
Mexico	207.4	233.2	295.2	377.5	31.9	32.2	+82.0
Dom. Republic	117.9	138.1	168.0	209.4	18.2	17.9	+77.6
Haiti	70.7	81.9	91.5	118.3	10.9	10.1	+67.2
Costa Rica	45.4	62.5	73.7	86.3	7.0	7.4	+90.1
Korea	10.2	14.7	23.7	49.7	1.5	4.2	+386.3
Philippines	29.9	31.0	36.5	46.1	4.5	3.9	+54.2
Jamaica	11.0	12.8	23.2	39.5	1.6	3.4	+258.9
Colombia	27.7	29.7	36.2	32.5	4.2	2.8	+17.4
Hong Kong	23.8	21.2	31.0	30.8	3.6	2.6	+29.3
Barbados	18.7	24.3	16.2	29.9	2.9	2.5	+59.4
Honduras	21.7	20.0	22.1	23.5	3.3	2.0	+8.2
Belize	4.9	6.4	13.8	14.3	1.0	1.2	+193.4
Canada	12.7	18.1	21.6	13.7	1.9	1.2	+8.3
Taiwan	5.1	4.2	7.7	13.3	1.0	1.1	+161.1
All other	42.5	47.0	66.0	87.6	6.6	7.5	+106.1
Total	649.6	745.0	926.4	1172.4	100.0	100.0	+80.5

SOURCE: Standard & Poor's industry surveys, *Textiles, Apparel and Home Furnishings*, Page T99, August 2, 1987.

Import quotas could create a problem for Reebok if the proposed Textile and Apparel Trade Enforcement Act of 1987 is revived in the next session of Congress in 1989. The bill was designed to reduce textile and apparel imports from Hong Kong, Taiwan, and South Korea by 25–30%. Though this bill was passed by both the House and the Senate, President Reagan vetoed it in 1987. Reebok's management believed that if this bill became law, it would impose quotas on footwear also, and that such quotas could adversely affect the company.[40] Analysts believed, however, that the quotas would not affect the higher price brands, i.e., Reebok and Nike, as much as it would the smaller firms. Because of their big profit margins, as high as 30%, the industry leaders would be favored by foreign manufacturers.[41]

Analysts for the National Sporting Goods Association (NSGA) forecasted a moderate rise in consumer spending for sporting goods in 1988. The NSGA also noted that because 1988 was an Olympic year, the public's interest in sporting activities could be heightened.[42] According to NSGA, within the athletic footwear category, aerobic and golf shoes were expected to show the fastest growth in 1988.

EXHIBIT 3.6   **Pairs of Athletic Shoes Sold in the U.S.**

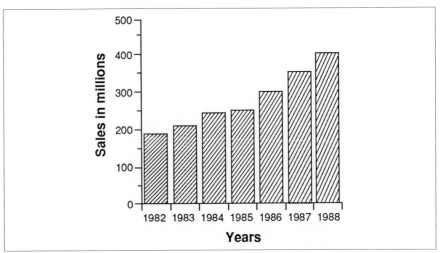

SOURCE: Converse Inc.

COMPETITION

The athletic shoe industry was extremely competitive in virtually every segment. The same was true for the athletic apparel industry. Total sales for the athletic shoe industry were expected to total $9.7 billion in 1988, a figure more than twice that of sales in 1982.[43] (See Exhibit 3.6.) Reebok's major competitors included Nike, Converse, and Adidas. In well-established market segments, such as tennis, running, and basketball shoes, competition was especially intense. The market share of each competitor is shown in Exhibit 3.7. Competition in each of the markets for Reebok's products was manifested in different forms: price, quality, brand image, promotion, and ability to meet delivery commitments to retailers.[44]

Reebok would spend about $70 million in total advertising in 1988, including $44 million for the Reebok brand alone, up 46% from 1987. Nike, on the other hand, intended to fan the competitive flames in 1989. After spending $34 million in 1988, Nike would hike its ad budget to about $45 million in 1989.[45]

As of November 1988, Nike had picked up some market share, moving from 18.6% in 1987, to 25%; Reebok was believed to have fallen from 37% to 32%.[46]

EXHIBIT 3.7   **Market Share in the U.S. Athletic Footware Market**

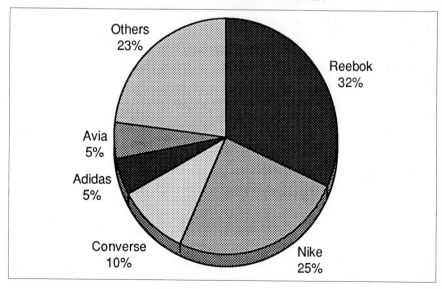

SOURCE: P. Sloan, "Reebok Rethinks 'U.B.U.,'" *Advertising Age,* September 26, 1988, p. 1.

Until 1986, Nike led Reebok but was later overtaken. Now it may be Nike's turn again.

Traditionally, Nike has had a stronger following in the fitness-conscious segment of the market whereas Reebok was more popular among the fashion conscious. Reebok faced several challenges in an industry where fads could fade fast. Even though sales had exploded, Reebok faced an uncertain future outside the fashion market. As Converse Chairman Richard B. Loynd said, "Reebok got its start as a women's fashion shoe; they're going to find it much tougher to move into other markets than their traditional strength."[47]

According to industry analysts, the war between Nike and Reebok was now being waged on big-city playgrounds for the youth market. Though consumers in this segment (15–22 years old) constituted only 15% of the U.S. population, they bought 30% of the sneakers and influenced another 10% of sales by example and word of mouth.[48] On the average, according to analysts, teens purchased about four pairs of sneakers yearly. In 1987, according to analysts, Nike, Reebok, and Converse each had a 24% share of the predominantly youth-oriented basketball shoe market. In September, 1988 however, Nike's share had jumped to 35% whereas Reebok and Converse saw a decline in their market share.[49]

Nike was said to have "slam-dunked" Reebok in early 1988 with an advertising blitz that featured tough-looking teens emerging from a subway in Nikes. Industry watchers thought Nike was winning the playground war. Nike recorded sales growth of 81% in fiscal 1988, compared to the 15–17% expected for Reebok in the same period.[50]

MARKETING

What more could a marketing manager ask for than the likes of Mick Jagger, Bruce Springsteen, and Lionel Richie seen in their music videos in Reebok shoes, unsolicited? Even Cybill Shepherd appeared in a stylish black evening gown with her orange Reebok shoes at the Emmy awards in 1986.[51]

Industry observers believed that Reebok owed its sizzling success to market savvy, innovation, and lucky timing. Pete Janssen, general merchandising manager for Athlete's Foot Marketing Associates, Inc., a 500-store chain, said, "Reebok's such a hot name that we have trouble selling anything else."[52] Paul Fireman described the demand for his company's shoes as "outrageous." The bright colors and soft leather made the shoes an overnight smash, particularly among women, who had not been major buyers of expensive athletic shoes. Reebok got women to spend an unheard-of $40 on a pair of athletic shoes.

The Reebok brand was targeted at people with active lifestyles, from age 15–39 years. The company's 1988 expenditure of $44 million for advertising this brand alone reflected management's belief in the importance of customer awareness of the company's tradename and trademarks.[53] Reebok's marketing efforts included consumer and trade advertising, point-of-sale material, creative design techniques, and in-store promotion.

The Reebok Apparel Division developed and marketed men's, women's, and children's sportswear, performance wear, and accessories directed at the moderate- to higher-priced market segment. Performance wear included clothes designed for aerobics, tennis, fitness and running, while Reebok sportswear was casual apparel with athletic inspiration.

Metaphors shoes were intended to be lightweight and comfortable, yet stylish. These shoes were targeted at the moderate- to upper-moderate market and were sold through a network of independent sales representatives whose only line was Metaphors.

Rockport brands were lightweight and comfortable casual, dress, and fitness walking shoes for men and women. The Rockport division was a leader in the development of biomechanically designed shoes that were structured for the walking motion of the foot. The Rockport Walking Institute, established in 1985, was devoted to scientific research in the physiological benefit and biomechanical aspects of fitness walking.[54] This division's marketing activities included sales training clinics, technical brochures, the sponsorship of educational and medical programs on walking, and walking events. A particular focus was the promotion of walking as a form of exercise. Rockport had sponsored three books and a movie on the subject.

Avia, like Rockport, placed strong emphasis on design technology. The Avia brand was marketed as athletic footwear for aerobics, basketball, fitness, tennis, exercise walking, and volleyball. Avia brands were primarily purchased by active athletic participants who valued functionality and performance as key features.

All of Reebok's brands were sold in upscale specialty, sporting goods and department stores. Foot Locker, a specialty athletic chain, accounted for 12.8% of the company's 1987 net sales.[55] "I believe the consumer judges the quality of the brand today by the quality of its distribution," said Fireman. "A department store can sell a Reebok product for 25% off and it won't do any damage to the cachet. But if a mass merchandiser sold it for 25% above retail, it would be considered cheap."[56]

ADVERTISING

Some industry analysts thought Reebok had problems deciding how to position itself. In May 1987, Ammirati & Puris, Inc., the company's ad agency in New York, resigned the multi-million dollar account after only two months because Reebok officials continuously changed their minds on the direction their advertising should go. "We were cranking out new work everyday," said Ed Vick, a top official at the ad agency. "I don't mind working nights and weekends, but they wanted to change direction every week. We would do things that we would get approved on up through the ranks," continued Mr. Vick, "the chairman would like it, and then he would call the product manager, who didn't like it. . . . Then we'd start with the product manager . . . and he would call the chairman and the chairman didn't like it."[57] Reebok quickly gave the account to Chiat/Day in New York, a former Nike agency.

Chiat/Day created the "U.B.U." campaign for Reebok. This was the first umbrella campaign for Reebok brands. The ad portrayed a crowd as a collection of free spirits who believed in themselves. "U.B.U." was created to counter

Nike's highly successful "Just Do It" campaign. Both campaigns targeted the youth market; while "U.B.U.," in its TV sports ads, featured a group of oddly individualistic characters in Reeboks going about their business, Nike's "Just Do It" spotlighted serious-faced athletes puffing and perspiring during workouts.

"U.B.U." had been popular with department stores, but not with sporting goods outlets. With 80% of sales from sporting goods outlets and only 20% from department stores, Reebok should be worried. A standing joke in the buying office of one sporting-goods chain was, "Let them be U.B.U. We be Nike."[58] Jim Hines, Vice-President of Merchandise, Oshman Sporting Goods Stores, Houston, said, "Reebok's ads don't hit the mark for us. They may be award-winning and they may even sell a lot of shoes, but they don't say to the athlete, 'This is what we stand for.' . . . I'm not sure I understand them."[59]

Reebok management remained divided in their opinions of the "U.B.U." campaign. Inside sources claimed that Fireman, once described as having been ambivalent about "U.B.U.," had put out marching orders to move the campaign along. President and Chief Operating Officer LaBonte claimed that the "U.B.U." strategy was on target, but lacking in execution. However, when asked his feelings on the funky ads, Mark Goldston, Reebok's new Chief Marketing Officer, replied, "My personal opinions are not important at this point."[60]

It was rumored that Reebok was reassessing the new "U.B.U." campaign as the company grappled with the need to convey a performance message equal to that of its major rival, Nike. Rumors also had it that Reebok's executives had contacted other ad agencies and that "U.B.U." and its creator were in danger of being axed.[61] The company had probably realized that the "U.B.U." campaign must go beyond funky imagery to more hard-hitting execution.

Unlike its major rivals such as Nike and Converse, Reebok did not use major sports celebrity endorsers. This was because Reebok was a latecomer to the athletic scene. Most major National Basketball Association (NBA) stars were already tied up in long-term contracts with Reebok's competitors. According to *Advertising Age*, Reebok was about to sign the NBA's Number One draft choice for 1988, Danny Manning, as a celebrity endorser.[62]

PERFORMANCE

With its yuppy and preppy image, Reebok's real Achilles' heel was performance. "Reebok made its reputation in soft leather shoes, but if you use those shoes for rigorous activity, they will fall apart," said William A. Lawliss, Vice-President of Marketing at Smart, Inc., a sporting good consulting firm.[63] Experts said just as consumers got tired of designer jeans and returned to reliable brands such as Levis, they would again choose shoes that can withstand the rigor of sport. Comfort and style might not be everything; Reebok had a higher return rate than other major companies, according to Stephen Faust, president of Athlete's Foot.[64]

Few fads have been hotter than Reebok's athletic shoes and few companies have run to the $1 billion sales mark as fast as Reebok did in just eight years. "The big question for Reebok has been: 'What do they do for an encore?'" said

Charlotte F. Hughes, a footwear analyst for Montgomery Securities. "Their growth has been phenomenal, but it's not sustainable."[65]

FINANCE

The year 1987 was the first in Reebok's history that triple-digit sales and profit gains were not reported.[66] Net income, as a percentage of sales, had been decreasing since 1986. The reasons for this decline were three-fold: (1) a higher proportion of sales from Rockport, Frye, Avia, and Reebok Canada, where margins were lower than the domestic Reebok brands; (2) markdowns related to apparel operations; and (3) amortization expense related to recent acquisitions.[67] Selling, general, and administrative expenses increased as a percentage of sales in the same period, because of the inclusion of Rockport and Avia's expenses. The company's balance sheet and income statement are presented in Exhibits 3.8 and 3.9.

Second quarter 1988 results showed strong sales, up 28.8%, including a 14.8% increase in the domestic Reebok brand alone. However, the management acknowledged in November 1988 that the increased competition had been harmful

EXHIBIT 3.8   **Consolidated Balance Sheets, Reebok International Ltd.**
(Dollar Amounts in Thousands except Per Share Data)

Six months ended June 30	1988	1987	1986[1]
Assets			
Current assets:			
Cash	$ 15,528	$ 60,167	$ 66,077
Accounts receivable, net of allowance for doubtful accounts (1987, $9,232; 1986, $4,783)	332,294	204,676	120,075
Inventory	365,989	240,898	122,522
Deferred income taxes	23,189	19,534	5,589
Prepaid expenses		10,821	2,324
Total current assets		536,096	316,587
Property and equipment	72,350	73,477	21,198
Less accumulated depreciation and amortization		8,968	1,980
Net property		4,509	19,218
Non-current assets:			
Intangibles, net amortization	299,262	251,490	102,956
Cash, restricted		11,583	1,504
Other		4,688	115
Total Non-current assets		267,761	104,575
Total assets	$1,108,612	$868,366	$440,380

(Continued)

EXHIBIT 3.8   (Continued)

Six months ended June 30	1988	1987	1986[1]
Liabilities and Stockholders' Equity			
Current liabilities:			
Notes payable	$ 142,156	$ 54,626	$ 22,111
Current portion of capital lease obligations		399	24
Interest-bearing accounts payable	138,762	57,255	16,486
Accounts payable and accrued expenses	102,170	117,817	67,865
Income taxes payable	40,003	38,272	34,384
Dividends payable[2]	8,464		
Total current liabilities	431,555	268,369	140,870
Long-term debt	11,105	10,570	—
Capital lease obligations, net of current portion		2,042	664
Deferred income taxes		2,622	1,245
Other liabilities[2]	4,866		
Commitments			
Stockholders' equality			
Common stock, par value $.01; authorized 250,000,000 shares; issued and outstanding 1987, 112,561,047; 1986, 52,835,540		1,125	528
Additional paid in capital		263,877	119,433
Retained earnings		320,886	177,844
Unearned compensation		(5,371)	(1,650)
Foreign currency translation adjustment		4,246	1,446
Total stockholders' equity	661,086	584,763	297,601
Total liabilities and stockholders' equity	$1,108,612	$868,366	$440,380

[1] 1988 figures are unaudited.

[2] 1988 statements only.

SOURCE: Reebok International, Ltd., *1987 Annual Report* and *Form 10-K*.

and that they expected an 80% drop in profit for the fourth quarter.[68] Selling expenses were up, reflecting a near doubling in advertising expenses, with the new "U.B.U." campaign. Inventories, valued at $366 million, were higher than management would have liked; but because Reebok was primarily a second-half business, these levels were not really out of line.[69]

Reebok's stock was first made public in 1985 with an offering of 4 million shares. As of December, 1987, 112,561,047 shares of common stock were issued and outstanding.[70] Despite the rapid increase in the number of shares, return on equity and EPS remained high through the first half of 1988, because of high earnings, rapid inventory turnover, and the company's low level of invest-

EXHIBIT 3.9   **Consolidated Statements of Income, Reebok International Ltd.**
(Dollars Amounts in thousands, except per share data)

Six months ended June 30	1988	1987	1986	1985
Net sales	$916,010	$1,389,196	$919,401	$306,969
Other income	3,693	10,240	4,472	1,834
	919,703	1,399,436	923,873	308.803
Costs and expenses:				
Cost of sales	557,411	808,991	521,978	176,462
Selling expenses	116,026	164,896	83,294	31,846
General and administrative expenses	76,265	102,191	54,470	21,631
Amortization of intangibles	7,078	12,453	2,280	—
Interest expense	5,409	4,771	694	755
Total costs and expenses	762,189	1,093,302	662,716	230,694
Income before income taxes	157,514	306,134	261,157	78,109
Income taxes	64,304	140,934	129,023	39,147
Net income	$ 93,210	$ 165,200	$132,134	$ 38,962
Net income per common share	$ 0.82	$ 1.49	$ 1.27	$ .45
Weighted average common shares outstanding	113,976	111,234	103,784	85,896

SOURCE: Reebok International, Ltd., *1987 Annual Report* and *Form 10-K*.

ment in fixed assets. As of September 1988, Pentland Industries owned 32.1% of the common stock, Fireman owned 20%, and other insiders, 9.3%.[71]

Analysts continued to recommend Reebok's common stock. Citing a strong balance sheet and an established consumer franchise, they believed that the stock had much to offer investors who were willing to tolerate the risks associated with any consumer products company.[72]

As mentioned previously, *Forbes* ranked Reebok first in return on investment over the five years ended 1987, a distinction which normally favored highly leveraged firms. But Reebok was particularly unusual in that the company consistently operated with minimal debt. Funds resulting from operations were sufficient to meet the cash requirements for increases in working capital. Even more surprising was that Reebok's acquisitions had been purchased primarily with cash from retained earnings and stock issuances. (See Exhibit 3.10.) According to company records, management expected this trend to continue.

FUTURE MARKETS   In addition to Reebok's acquistion strategy, the company planned to expand international sales. In 1987, Reebok marketed its products in 45 countries, with its most recent expansions into Singapore, Malaysia, and the Philippines.[73]

EXHIBIT 3.10

Acquisitions, Reebok International, Ltd.

DATE	ACQUISITION	PRICE
9/3/86	Rockport	$118.5 million cash
4/2/87	Avia	$181.0 million cash and
		194,000 shares Reebok common stock
5/8/87	Frye	$10.0 million cash
6/12/87	ESE Sports	$18.0 million cash
1/20/88	Ellesse, USA	$25.0 million cash

SOURCE: Reebok International, LTD., *1987 Annual Report* and *Form 10-K.*

International revenues accounted for 4.5% of Reebok's total sales. Joseph Foster, President of the International Division, planned to increase this contribution substantially in 1988, with an ultimate goal of 50%.[74] However, industry analysts felt that Reebok was bound to encounter serious competition with such well-entrenched international brands as Adidas and Puma.

According to industry observers, Reebok was well qualified to pursue this expansion strategy because Foster had extensive international experience. Also, the company's ties with British shoe distributor Pentland Industries would provide some advantages in the foreign markets.[75]

Analysts believed that the foreign athletic shoe market was more than three times the size of that in the U.S. and three to four years behind in maturation. Fireman himself claimed the aerobics boom was just beginning overseas and the women's athletic shoe market, Reebok's major strength, was virtually untapped.[76]

Additionally, the company viewed growth outside the United States as a hedge against the declining U.S. dollar. Reebok's products were denominated in U.S. dollars and thus the cost of sales declined for their wholly owned subsidiaries when the dollar dropped against foreign currencies.[77]

EPILOGUE

Without a doubt, Reebok International Ltd. has experienced a meteoric rise to fame since its founding in 1979. Through the years, Paul Fireman has led this organization to dominance in the U.S. athletic footwear market. However, some industry insiders expected Fireman to fall flat on his face as the company faced stiff competition, potential production and supply problems, and a growth question regarding the company's self-image.

As if these controversies weren't enough, *The Wall Street Journal* reported on November 3, 1988, that "Reebok's Stock Rises Sharply on Rumors of Leveraged Buyout That Firm Denies." Although company sources flatly denied these rumors, industry observers noted that this was the third time such stories had surfaced on Wall Street in 1988. The company's denials notwithstanding,

Reebok's stock closed at $14.25 a share, up $1.25 on November 2, 1988 in NYSE composite trading.[78]

For Reebok, 1989 may prove to be a pivotal year. Quoting George Walker, Vice President of Hermans Sporting Goods, "Our children and our children's children will be reading about Reebok as a case study at Harvard Business School."[79] But will they be wearing Reeboks to class?

NOTES

1. Louise Ackerman, "Reebok: Tennis' Billion-Dollar Superstar," *Tennis*, December 1987, p. 46.

2. Robert Heller, "Pentland Industries Vision," *Management Today*, June 1987, p. 52.

3. Ackerman, "Reebok: Tennis' Superstar," p. 48.

4. *Reebok News*, "Backgrounder," press release, date not given, p. 4.

5. "Sneaker Wars," Interview from ABC's *20/20*, August 19, 1988, transcript p. 7.

6. *Reebok News*, "Backgrounder," p. 4.

7. Stuart Gannes, "America's Fastest-Growing Companies," *Fortune*, May 23, 1988, p. 31.

8. Reebok International, Ltd., *1987 Annual Report*, p. 12.

9. Aimee L. Stern, "Reebok: In for the Distance," *Business Month*, August 1987, p. 22.

10. "Reebok International +152.7%," *Institutional Investor*, March 1987, p. 78.

11. Reebok International, Ltd., *1987 Annual Report*, p. 11.

12. Stern, "In for the Distance," p. 22.

13. *Ibid.*, p. 22.

14. Ackerman, "Tennis' Superstar," p. 49.

15. *Ibid.*, p. 49.

16. *Ibid.*, p. 49.

17. Stern, "In for the Distance," p. 24.

18. Anthony Ramirez, "Meet One Big Bonus Baby," *Fortune*, December 19, 1988, p. 66.

19. *Ibid.*, p. 66.

20. *Ibid.*, p. 66.

21. "Sneaker Wars," transcript p. 8.

22. Stern, "In for the Distance," p. 24.

23. Leslie Helm, "Reebok's Recent Blisters Seem to Be Healing," *Business Week*, August 3, 1987, p. 62.

24. Reebok International, Ltd., *1987 Annual Report*, p. 15.

25. *Ibid.*, p. 23.

26. Gannes, "Fastest Growing Companies," p. 32.

27. Reebok International, Ltd., *1987 Annual Report*, p. 23.

28. Reebok International, Ltd., *1987 Form 10-K*, p. 4.

29. Reebok International, Ltd., *1987 Annual Report*, p. 20.

30. Marcy Magiera, "Avia Buy Puts Reebok on Nike Turf," *Advertising Age*, March 16, 1987, p. 12.

31. Reebok International, Ltd., *1987 Annual Report*, pp. 16 & 19.

32. *Ibid.*, p. 7.

33. Reebok International, Ltd., *1987 Form 10-K*, p. 7.

34. *Ibid.*, p. 7.

35. *Ibid.*, p. 7.

36. Dori Jones Yang, "Setting Up Shop in China: Three Paths to Success," *Business Week*, October 19, 1987, p. 74.

37. Reebok International, Ltd., *1987 Form 10-K*, p. 8.

38. *Ibid.*, p. 8.

39. Karen J. Sack, "Textiles, Apparel and Home Furnishings," *Standard & Poor's Industry Surveys*, August 27, 1987, p. T83.

40. Reebok International, Ltd., *1987 Form 10-K*, p. 8.

41. Stern, "In for the Distance," p. 25.

42. "Sporting Goods: Modest Industry Growth Expected," *Standard & Poor's Industry Surveys*, March 10, 1988, p. L38.

43. Joseph Pereira, "Pricey Sneakers Worn in Inner City Help Set Nation's Fashion Trend," *Wall Street Journal*, December 1, 1988, p. 1.

44. Reebok International, Ltd., *1987 Form 10-K*, p. 10.

45. Pat Sloan, "Reebok Rethinks 'U.B.U.'," *Advertising Age* September 26, 1988, p. 1.

46. *Ibid.*, p. 90.

47. Lois Therrien, "Reeboks: How Far Can a Fad Run?" *Business Week*, February 24, 1986, p. 90.

48. Joseph Pereira, "Reebok Trails Nike in Fight for Teens' Hearts and Feet," *Wall Street Journal*, September 23, 1988, p. 3.

49. *Ibid.*, p. 3.

50. *Ibid.*, p. 3.

51. Therrien, "How Far Can A Fad Run?" p. 90.

52. *Ibid.*, p. 90.

53. Sloan, "Reebok Rethinks 'U.B.U.'," p. 90.

54. Reebok International, Ltd., *1987 Form 10-K*, p. 5.

55. *Ibid.*, p. 9.

56. Stern, "In for the Distance," p. 23.

57. Alan Radding and Brian Moran, "Reebok Rebound," *Advertising Age*, May 4, 1987, p. 4.

58. Sloan, "Reebok Rethinks 'U.B.U.'," p. 1.

59. *Ibid.*, p. 90.

60. *Ibid.*, p. 90.

61. *Ibid.*, p. 90.

62. *Ibid.*, p. 1.

63. Helm, "Recent Blisters Seem to Be Healing," p. 62.

64. Therrien, "How Far Can a Fad Run?" p. 90.

65. Lois Therrien, "Can Reebok Sprint Even Faster?" *Business Week*, October 6, 1986, pp. 74–75.

66. Reebok International, Ltd., *1987 Annual Report*, p. 2.

67. *Ibid.*, p. 30.

68. Pereira, "Pricey Sneakers Set Nation's Fashion Trend," p. 1.

69. Margaret A. Gilliam, "Reebok International," *First Boston Equity Research*, July 28, 1988, p. 1.

70. Reebok International, Ltd., *1987 Annual Report*, p. 32.

71. H. B. Udis, "Reebok International," *Value Line*, September 2, 1988, p. 1672.

72. *Ibid.*, p. 1672.

73. Stern, "In for the Distance," p. 25.

74. *Ibid.*, p. 25.

75. *Ibid.*, p. 25.

76. *Ibid.*, p. 25.

77. Reebok International, Ltd., *1987 Annual Report*, p. 27.

78. Joseph Pereira, "Reebok's Stock Rises Sharply on Rumors of Leveraged Buy-Out That Firm Denies," *Wall Street Journal*, November 3, 1988, p. A3.

79. Ackerman, "Tennis' Billion-Dollar Superstar," p. 50.

CASE 4

Apple Computer, Inc., 1987 . . . The Second Decade

Phyllis Feddeler • Thomas L. Wheelen • David B. Croll

On July 20, 1987, John Sculley, the CEO of Apple Computer Inc., is mulling over a report prepared for him by his marketing department. This strategic-analysis report focuses on the computer industry's outlook for the late 1980s, with special emphasis on the recently announced IBM Personal System 2 or PS/2, and Intel's new 80386 microchip.

Apple is a $1.9 billion company that designs, manufactures, sells, and services personal computers (PCs) and related software and peripheral products. The major sources of Apple's customers are homes, businesses, and educational in-stitutions. Although the company is best established in the education segment with the Apple II, it is trying, through its Macintosh product line, to become a more significant competitor in the business markets. Apple also competes internationally, and 26% of its revenues come from outside of the United States. The principal methods of distribution are the independent retail dealer, national retail accounts, and direct sales.

Until recently, experts questioned whether Apple would survive, because of the general slump in the computer industry and Apple's lackluster sales. Even though the company was successfully reorganized in 1985 into a leaner, more profitable organization, some pointed out that cutting costs is not a growth strategy, especially in an innovation-driven industry. Furthermore, it was doubt-ful that Apple could coexist with IBM, the dominant competitor, in the business market. In 1986, the first "open" Macintosh, designed to provide owners with ease in modification, was introduced. IBM PCs had always been "open."

This case was prepared by Ms. Phyllis Feddeler, MBA student, Professor Thomas L. Wheelen of the University of South Florida, and Professor David B. Croll of the McIntire School of Commerce at the University of Virginia. It was presented at the *North American Case Research Association Meeting, 1988.* All rights are reserved to the case authors and the North American Case Research Association. Copyright © 1987 and 1989 by Thomas L. Wheelen. Revised in 1989. Reprinted by permission.

HISTORICAL BACKGROUND

The company was founded in 1976 by Steven P. Jobs, who was then 21, and Stephen Wozniak, 26. With only $1,350, raised by the sale of a VW van and an HP programmable calculator, and an order for fifty computers with a selling price of less than $700, the two young men began their business by manufacturing the Apple I in Jobs' garage.

Not long afterward, a mutual friend helped recruit A. D. "Mike" Markkula to help market the company and give it a million-dollar image. Markkula had successfully managed the marketing departments of two semiconductor com-

EXHIBIT 4.1

Mike Markkula's Original Business Plan: Strategies and Objectives {November 18, 1976}

MAJOR OBJECTIVES

1. Obtain a market share greater than or equal to two (2) times that of the nearest competitor.
2. Realize equal or greater than 20% pretax profit.
3. Grow to $500 million annual sales in 10 years.
4. Establish and maintain an operating environment conducive to human growth and development.
5. Continue to make significant technological contributions to the home computer industry.
6. (Possible) Structure company for easy exit of founders within-five years.

KEY STRATEGIES

1. It is extremely important for Apple to be the first recognized leader in the home computer marketplace.
2. Continually market peripheral products for the basic computer, thereby generating sales equal to or greater than the initial computer purchase.
3. Allocate sufficient funds to R&D to guarantee technological leadership consistent with market demands.
4. Attract and retain absolutely outstanding personnel.
5. Rifle-shoot the hobby market as the first stepping stone to the major market.
6. Maintain significant effort in manufacturing, to continually reduce cost of production.
7. Grow at the same rate that the market grows.
8. Design and market the computer to be more economical than a dedicated system in specific applications, even though all features of the Apple are not used.

SOURCE: John Sculley, Odyssey (New York: Harper & Row Publishers, 1987), pp. 387–388.

panies, Fairchild Semiconductor and Intel Corporation, that had experienced dynamic growth. Markkula's original business plan for Apple was the founders' dream and vision for the future of the new company (see Exhibit 4.1).[1] On January 3, 1977, when Apple Computer was incorporated, there were fewer than 50,000 computers in the world. A decade later, more than 50,000 computers were built and sold every day.[2] In December 1980 the company went public with an offering of 4.6 million shares of common stock. In May 1981 there was a secondary offering of 2.6 million shares of common stock by approximately 100 selling stockholders, all of whom had acquired their shares through the employee stock plan or private placement.

In the high-growth industry of personal computers, Apple did grow quickly, despite increasing numbers of business failures among competitors. In 1986, Apple was the second-largest competitor, next to IBM, in the U.S. PC industry. (See Exhibit 4.2.)

During the years of high growth, the company suffered internal turmoil because of disagreements as to the company's direction, especially in terms of product development (see Exhibit 4.3). Jobs' pet project, the Macintosh, was consuming an amount of funds disproportionate to the revenues it was bringing in. Internal rivalry grew between the Apple product department and the Mac product department. First Wozniak resigned (he now works as a consultant to Apple) and, in September 1985, Jobs resigned and took with him five key managers. Jobs intended to begin another company called Next, Inc. In a lawsuit filed against Jobs, Apple accused him of "misappropriating Apple secrets and of breaching his fiduciary responsibility by plotting to form a new company and recruiting selected employees while still Chairman of Apple . . ."[3]

When John Sculley (a former CEO of Pepsi-Cola Company, who started working at Apple in May 1983) took over full control, Apple had just suffered its first loss as a public company and had undergone a reorganization that

---

EXHIBIT 4.2   **Market Share of PC Sales**

	1986 (% OF TOTAL SALES)	1985 (% OF TOTAL SALES)
1. IBM	29.5	40.5
2. Apple	7.3	10.3
3. Compaq	7.0	5.2
4. Zenith	4.2	2.4
5. Tandy	3.4	4.6
6. Commodore	1.9	3.8
7. Other	46.7	33.2

SOURCE: Dataquest Inc.

EXHIBIT 4.3   The Rise of John Sculley and the Fall of Steven Jobs

Steve Jobs personally recruited John Sculley to be CEO of Apple. The initial job contact was between Gerry Roche, Chairman of Heidrick and Struggles, Inc., and John Sculley. Sculley asked, "How does Jobs feel about this?" Roche responded, "He wants to find someone who is really great who he can learn from. The chief executive will report directly to the board. Steve is focused largely on product development."[1] This meeting took place over the Thanksgiving Day holidays in 1982. The negotiations between Apple and Sculley lasted for approximately five months. Sculley joined the company in May, 1983. Jobs at one meeting told Sculley that "You can sell sugared water to children the rest of your career or you can change the world a little."[2] Sculley's original employment called for $1 million in annual pay (half in salary and half in bonus), $1 million up front to join Apple, and $1 million in severance pay if things did not work out. The contract also had a housing clause that cost Apple an additional million dollars. Sculley was also awarded stock options on 350,000 shares.[3]

At the hiring time, Sculley said of Jobs: "Steve is a great visionary." Jobs responded that "Sculley is someone I can learn from."[4] Sculley was hired to help Apple maintain its market share in the personal computer market. Since 1981, Apple's market share had been declining. The hiring also marked the beginning of the transition for Apple from an entrepreneurial corporate culture to a professional corporate culture. Jobs (age 28) and Sculley (age 44) quickly developed a remarkably close friendship. The relationship was part brotherly, part father–son. Sculley said, "Steve and I became soul mates and near-constant companions. We spoke with each other for hours throughout every day. . . . We had an unwritten understanding that either one could interrupt the other in whatever he was doing."[5] Their closeness provoked resentment among other top management executives at Apple. Sculley said of Jobs and himself, "Apple has one leader, Steve and me."[6]

In 1983, Sculley had consolidated the company's nine highly decentralized divisions organized along products lines into three divisions. The new organization had one division for the production of the Apple II family of products, another division for the development and production of the Macintosh (MAC) and the third division for sales of all Apple products. Jobs was named manager of the newly formed Macintosh Division.

In October 1984, the alliance between Jobs and Sculley started to deteriorate. Jobs had dual roles as Chairman of the Board and General Manager of the MAC division. He and Sculley, CEO, were faced with conflicting authority relationships—each was a subordinate to each other yet they both had authority over each other. This organizational structure caused many conflicts and much stress in their management partnership and friendship. The MAC division was not performing up to expectations, but Sculley felt awkward demanding better performance from Jobs because of his dual management roles. Some of Macintosh's major problems were (1) lagging sales—an automated plant to turn out 80,000 Macintoshes per month was built, but demand never exceeded 30,000; (2) Lisa (business version) had low acceptance by business corporations; (3) the closed architecture did not allow add-on options; (4) target market focused on business instead of Apple's traditional buyers in homes and schools, and (5) they were not delivering on a promised option that would make the Macintosh IBM compatible.[7]

Jobs treated the MAC division employees as the elite group of Apple employees. They were given special perks—free fruit juice and a masseur on call.[8] Steve felt that the Macintosh people represented the best of Apple. The company now consisted of two groups—Macintosh employees and others. The MAC people referred to everyone else in the company as "bozos." It got to the point that MAC people wore buttons with a line running through the face of Bozo the clown.[9]

In February 1985, Steven Wozniak severed all ties with Apple. He owned about 4% of the company's stock valued at approximately $70 million. Mr. Wozniak said that the Apple II division ". . . had been ignored in the hope that it will die and go away. . . ." He left to establish a new company.[10]

In early 1985, Sculley concluded that he had to remove Jobs as the General Manager. Sculley anguished for days over this problem. Finally, his responsibilities to the stockholders, the board, and the employees won out over strong friendship with Jobs. He went to Steve's office to inform him of his decision. He was going to present his decision at the next board meeting. What followed was a violent disagreement between Jobs and Sculley. At the April 10 board meeting, Sculley told the board,

> I'm asking Steve to step down and you can back me on it and I will take responsibility for running the company, or we can do nothing and you're going to have to find yourself a new CEO. . . . We've got enough problems and we've got to solve them right now.[11]

Sculley was fully prepared to resign. The board meeting was spread over two days. The board unanimously agreed to ask Steve to step down as executive vice-president, but continue as the chairman. It gave Sculley the authority to implement the reorganization.[12]

The next six weeks was a period of a bitter power struggle, as Sculley wrested control of the company from Jobs. There were many discussions between Jobs and Sculley. Jobs wanted to retain some day-to-day operating responsibilities. It was a time of power politics. Jobs lobbied informally with other executives and board members to ascertain if he could remove Sculley from the company. Sculley was advised by an Apple executive not to take a scheduled trip to China, because Jobs was planning to overthrow him while he was in China. It all came to a head at the executive committee meeting on May 24. Sculley reiterated that he was the one running Apple. The round-table meeting lasted for three hours. The committee tried to find a future role for Jobs but failed. Jobs volunteered to take his scheduled vacation and return after the company reorganization was completed.

On May 31, Sculley signed the paperwork removing Jobs as Executive Vice President. It was also announced that the company had been reorganized along functional lines. Promotions and job responsibilities were also announced.[13] In a conversation with Mike Markkula, Sculley said, "When I got the board's authority to remove Steve, I shouldn't have waited around. I should have acted immediately. I was trying to make it easier on Steve and what I did was create a big mess. That was my mistake."[14] This year of chaos cost Mike almost $200 million in the value of his stock holdings.[15]

(Continued)

EXHIBIT 4.3 **(Continued)**

From the end of May to the middle of June, Sculley reorganized the company. On June 14, Sculley announced a cut in the permanent workforce by 20% (1,200 employees), eliminated almost all of the temporary workforce, and closed three factories; Apple produced its first-ever quarterly loss ($17.2 million). Later, the advertising budget of the company was reduced.

Jobs returned to the company. His new office was in an auxiliary building that he called "Siberia." Jobs held 7 million shares or 11.3% of the company's outstanding stock. His holdings were worth more than $400 million in 1983 and dropped to $120 million in June, 1984. He resigned in September 17, 1985.[16] About his new company, Next, Jobs said, "I have a certain degree of confidence that I can do it again." He is pretty certain that he can have another spectacular product and company. "I did it in the garage when Apple started, and I did it in the metaphorical garage when MAC started."[17]

SOURCES: J. Sculley, Odyssey (New York: Harper & Row Publishers, 1987)—cites: (1) p. 60; (3) p. 107; (5) p. 155; (6) p. 198; (7) pp. 227–297; (9) p. 241; (11) p. 242; (12) pp. 241–243; (13) pp. 245–261; (14) p. 275; (15) p. 272; and (16) p. 317.

(2) and (4). J. Dreyfuss, "John Sculley Rises in the West," *Fortune*, July 9, 1984, p. 183.

(8) B. Uttal, "Behind the Fall of Steven Jobs," *Fortune*, August 5, 1985, p. 22.

(10) P.A. Bellew, "Apple Computer Co-Founder Wozniak will Leave Firm, Citing Disagreements," *Wall Street Journal*, February 7, 1985, p. 38.

(17) "Showdown in Silicon Valley," *Newsweek*, September 30, 1985, p. 50.

included laying off 20% of its employees. Shipments of Macintosh PCs were only 10,000 per month but the manufacturing capacity was 80,000 per month. Although the Macintosh was easy to use, it was criticized in the business world for being underpowered and overpriced. Sculley, who had no prior experience in the computer industry, knew marketing and personally pitched the Macintosh to large corporations such as GE and Eastman Kodak and to software manufacturers, before the improved Macintosh was introduced in January 1986.

MANAGEMENT

Apple is trying to centralize its operations and involve its senior management in day-to-day decisions. In 1985, Sculley turned over responsibility of these decisions to Delbert Yocam, the Chief Operating Officer; Sculley could then spend his time on long-term planning. (See Exhibits 4.4 and 4.5 for the Board of Directors and top management.) New high-level management positions included Vice-President of Advanced Technology and Vice-President of U.S. Sales and Marketing. Between September 1986 and the end of 1986, the number of employees had grown from approximately 5600 to 5940.

In January 1986, an out-of-court settlement was reached with Steven P. Jobs. It allowed Apple to preview the first product from Job's new company, Next,

EXHIBIT 4.4   **Board of Directors and Officers of Apple, Inc.**

BOARD OF DIRECTORS

Peter D. Crisp
General Partner—Venrock
Associates; venture capital
investments

Albert A. Eisenstat
Senior Vice-President, Secretary,
and General Counsel—Apple
Computer, Inc.

A. C. Markkula, Jr.
Chairman—ADM Aviation, Inc.;
private flight service

Arthur Rock
Principal—Arthur Rock & Co.;
venture capital investments

Philip Schlein
Partner—U.S. Venture Partners;
venture capital investments

John Sculley
Chairman, President, and Chief
Executive Officer—Apple
Computer, Inc.

Henry Singleton
Chairman—Teledyne, Inc.;
diversified manufacturing company

OFFICERS

John Sculley
Chairman, President, and Chief
Executive Officer

Delbert W. Yocam
Executive Vice-President and Chief
Operating Officer

Albert A. Eisenstat
Senior Vice-President and General
Counsel

William V. Campbell
Executive Vice-President—U.S. Sales
and Marketing

Michael H. Spindler
Senior Vice-President—International
Sales and Marketing

David J. Barram
Vice-President—Finance, and Chief
Financial Officer

Charles W. Berger
Vice-President—Business
Development

Deborah A. Coleman
Vice-President—Operations

Jean-Louis Gassée
Vice-President—Product
Development

Lawrence G. Tesler
Vice-President—Advanced
Technology

Roy Weaver, Jr.
Vice President—Distribution

Robert W. Saltmarsh
Treasurer

SOURCE: Apple Computer, Inc., *Annual Report 1986.*

for a specified period of time. It also restricted the hiring of additional Apple employees for at least six months.[4]

MICRO-COMPUTER INDUSTRY

There are two types of computer companies, those that follow and those that lead. Leaders are established by their developing and producing the best selling products. The followers wait for the leaders to build their products and then copy or "clone" them.

EXHIBIT 4.5 **Executive Officers of Apple, Inc.**

The following information was compiled December 15, 1986.

John Sculley (age 47) joined Apple as President and Chief Executive Officer and a Director in May 1983, and was named Chairman of the Board of Directors in January 1986. Prior to joining Apple, Mr. Sculley was President and Chief Executive Officer of Pepsi-Cola Company, a producer and distributor of soft drink products, from 1977 to 1983. Pepsi-Cola Company is a division of PepsiCo, Inc. of which Mr. Sculley was also a Senior Vice-President. Mr. Sculley is also a director of Communications Satellite Corporation.

Delbert W. Yocam (age 42) joined Apple in November 1979 as Director of Materials, was promoted to Vice-President and General Manager of Manufacturing in August 1981, to Vice-President and General Manager of Operations in September 1982, and in December 1983, was appointed Executive Vice-President and General Manager, Apple II Division. In May 1985, Mr. Yocam was named Executive Vice-President, Group Executive of Product Operations, and in July 1985, he was appointed Executive Vice-President and Chief Operating Officer.

Albert A. Eisenstat (age 56) joined Apple in July 1980 as Vice-President and General Counsel; he has also served as Secretary of Apple since September 1980. In November 1985, Mr. Eisenstat was promoted to Senior Vice-President and was elected to the Board of Directors to fill the vacancy created by the resignation of Steven P. Jobs. Mr. Eisenstat is also a director of Adobe Systems, Inc. of Commercial Metals Company, and of Computer Task Group, Inc.

William V. Campbell (age 46) joined Apple as Vice-President of Marketing in June 1983; was appointed Vice-President, U.S. Sales, in January 1984; was appointed Executive Vice-President, Sales, in September 1984; and became Executive Vice-President, U.S. Sales and Marketing in June 1985. Before joining Apple, Mr. Campbell served as Director of Marketing for Eastman Kodak Company (a photographic equipment and supplies manufacturer) from May 1982 to June 1983, and as Account Director for J. Walter Thompson Advertising from January 1980 to May 1982. Mr. Campbell is also a director of Champion Parts Rebuilders.

Michael H. Spindler (age 44) joined Apple as European Marketing Manager in September 1980; was promoted to Vice-President and General Manager, Europe, in January 1984; was named Vice-President, International, in February 1985; and was promoted to Senior Vice-President of International Sales and Marketing in September 1986.

David J. Barram (age 42) joined Apple in April 1985 as Vice-President of Finance and Chief Financial Officer. Prior to his employment with Apple, he was the Vice-President of Finance and Administration and Chief Financial Officer of Silicon Graphics, Inc., a manufacturer of high-performance engineering workstations, from April 1983 to April 1985. From January 1970 to April 1983, Mr. Barram held various positions at Hewlett–Packard Company, a diversified electronics measurement and computer equipment manufacturer; his most recent position there was Group Controller of the Technical Computer Division.

Charles W. Berger (age 32) joined Apple in April 1982 as Treasurer and was appointed Director of Strategic Sales in June 1985. In September 1986, Mr. Berger was appointed Vice-President of Business Development. Prior to joining Apple,

Mr. Berger served as Assistant Treasurer at Rolm Corporation, a wholly-owned subsidiary of IBM Corporation that manufactures computerized telephone switches and digital telephones, and President of Rolm Credit Corporation.

Deborah A. Coleman (age 33) joined Apple in November 1981, initially as Controller and subsequently as Director of Operations of the Macintosh Division. Ms. Coleman was promoted to Director of Manufacturing in June 1985, to Vice-President of Manufacturing in November 1985, and to Vice-President of Operations in October 1986. Before joining Apple, Ms. Coleman served as a financial manager and cost-accounting supervisor at Hewlett–Packard Company.

Jean-Louis Gassée (age 42) joined Apple in February 1981 as General Manager of Seedrin S.A.F.L., a wholly owned subsidiary of the company. In May 1985, Mr. Gassée became Director of Marketing of the Macintosh Division, and in June 1985, he was named Vice-President, Product Development.

Lawrence G. Tesler (age 41) joined Apple in July 1980 as a senior member of the technical staff. Beginning in October 1980, he was appointed Project Supervisor, Lisa Applications Software; in August 1981, Section Manager, Lisa Applications Software; in February 1983, Consulting Engineering and Manager of Object-Oriented Systems. Prior to Mr. Tesler' s promotion to Vice-President of Advanced Technology in October 1986, Mr. Tesler served as Director of Advanced Development from July 1986 to October 1986.

Roy H. Weaver, Jr. (age 54) joined Apple in September 1980 as U.S. Distribution Manager. In April 1981, he was Director of Distribution and Service Operations, and in April 1982, he was promoted to General Manager of Distribution and Service. In September 1982, he was appointed Vice-President and General Manager of the Distribution, Service, and Support Division; in September 1984, Vice-President, Field Operations; and in June 1985, Vice-President, Distribution.

Robert W. Saltmarsh (age 36) joined Apple as Assistant Treasurer in November 1982 and was promoted to Treasurer in October 1985. Between November 1978 and November 1982, Mr. Saltmarsh worked for Data General Corporation, a minicomputer manufacturer, first as European Treasury Manager and then as Corporate Treasury Manager.

SOURCE: Apple Computer, Inc., *1986 10-K Report.*

Since IBM first introduced its PC in 1981, many computer manufacturers have followed their lead. Marketing an innovative computer before IBM has presented its version is risky. If IBM later introduces a comparable machine with proprietary features, the earlier versions may be rendered obsolete and have to be redesigned.

For the past several years the microcomputer industry has been in a slump, but increased sales for the first quarter of 1987 (see Exhibit 4.6) might indicate that the entire industry is coming out of its recession. Dealer sales rose by 15% in the first two months of 1987 and PC shipments to computer stores rose 19% during the first quarter of 1987. Analysts believe that these strong first-quarter earnings, which contributed to the increases in the stock prices of companies

EXHIBIT 4.6   **1987 First-Quarter Sales**

	SALES (MILLIONS OF DOLLARS)		PERCENT CHANGE
	1986	1987	
Apple	$ 409	$ 575	+41.0
Digital	1,928	2,410	+25.0
IBM	10,127	10,682	+5.5
Intel	280	395	+41.0
National Semiconductor	324	398	+23.0
NCR	961	1,122	+17.0

SOURCE: Quarterly reports of these companies.

such as IBM, Wang, Prime Computer, Inc., and Apple, also mean that sales will continue to increase.[5]

Important new developments in the personal computer industry include desktop publishing and the recent use of Intel Corporation's 80386 microchip. In desktop publishing, a PC is used to produce low-cost, high-quality printed documents in-house. It was Apple's innovation with the Macintosh. Since the introduction of the Macintosh, however, software developers have been creating desktop publishing programs for the IBM PC, and other companies will be soon to follow. The 80386 microchip, referred to as the 386, offers to increase the speed, memory, and multitasking capabilities of microcomputers.

In the summer of 1986, Compaq became the first company to market a personal computer with a 386; IBM began marketing its 386 models in April 1987. Both of these computers are proving to be quite popular. For instance, by December 1986, Compaq had shipped 10,000 Deskpro 386s and was having trouble keeping up with orders. It is expected that 386 machines will make up around 10% of the entire PC market by the end of 1987, and 25% of the market by 1990. However, one problem with machines using the 80386 microchip is that the machines cannot take full advantage of its capabilities until software catches up with the new technology, which might take several years.[6]

Other than the microprocessor itself, software is becoming one of the most important parts of the computer. Companies such as Lotus and Microsoft develop software programs specifically for a particular computer model.

In April of 1987, IBM came out with its new product line, called the Personal System 2, or PS/2. Designed in part to discourage clonemakers, IBM incorporated custom microchips, and doubled the amount of software that will have to be written to make clone machines 100% compatible with PS/2. Those companies that use the Micro Channel to connect personal computers to mainframes (in other words IBM's top mainframe customers, or about half of the market) are expected to purchase the PS/2. However, sales of IBM compatibles were up more than 10% in the first five months of 1987, so many customers might not be inclined to switch over to the PS/2.[7]

FORECAST OF DEMAND

Overall computer sales are expected to grow in 1987. Some experts predict that the growth rate of microcomputer sales will range from 7% to 10%. Others expect the microcomputer market to grow by only 3% because of indecision in the business markets about IBM's new products. For example, PC unit growth in major corporations was 100% from 1981–1984, but this growth could slow to only 48% in 1987 because companies are waiting to see how good the IBM PS/2 products are.[8]

Currently, the hot topic in the personal computer market is the 80386 microchip, which is manufactured by Intel Corporation.

The second hot issue, desktop publishing, is becoming so popular that dozens of companies are finding ways to adapt PCs to provide this option. It is expected that the sales of publishing systems for machines that are based on IBM and IBM-compatible computers will exceed the sales of the Macintosh in 1987. The market is growing very quickly, though, and Macintosh sales will probably grow by 70%.[9]

Corporate capital-equipment spending in the U.S. is projected to increase at an average annual rate of 8.8% in the last three quarters of 1987 compared to just 4.2% in 1986. However, the demand for Apple computers in the business environment depends on Apple's ability to convince its customer corporations' MIS managers and the people who actually buy computers, that the Macintosh line offers more than any competing machines can offer. In corporations, large multiple-computer sales are not awarded on price alone, but also on value and performance. Many business people think that Apple does not provide the necessary support to corporations, but the company plans to improve its support before 1988. Buyers of large computers will also require a 25% increase in computing capacity in 1987.

The home computer market is projected to reach $34.5 billion wholesale in 1987. Twenty percent of consumers plan to purchase a computer in 1987 or 1988, and half of those intend to spend less than $1,000. Currently, there are approximately 2.5–3 million units of IBM computers in homes. Many people, try as they might, cannot yet justify the purchase of a home computer, as evidenced by a 1985 survey that found that 76.7% of shoppers did not know what they would do with a home computer if they purchased one.

Networking is becoming increasingly important in the business market. Computer customers are being drawn to networks at an accelerating pace as software improves and technical difficulties subside. Access to a Local Area Network (LAN) makes computing easier for the average customer and places the complex issues on the shoulders of somebody more technically competent. Currently,

---

EXHIBIT 4.7

Projected World-Wide Sales
(in Billions of Dollars)

BUSINESS COMPUTERS		MICRO SALES		LAN EQUIPMENT	
Year	Sales	Year	Sales	Year	Sales
1990	50.0	1990	47.9	1991	3.02
1988	45.7	1988	38.9	1990	2.49
1986	40.6	1986	32.0	1989	2.05
1984	37.6	1984	24.4	1988	1.64
1982	28.1	1982	6.8	1986	.92

SOURCE: Kimball Brown, Dataquest.

only about 6% of the 13 million PCs installed in U.S. corporate offices are or were connected to a LAN. That percentage is expected to more than double by 1990. The number of networks installed worldwide is expected to be 220,000 by the end of 1987, up from 52,000 in 1984. As shown in Exhibit 4.7, worldwide sales of networks could hit $3.02 billion by 1990. The leaders in networking shipments in 1986 are shown below.

1986 Shipments

TERMINAL NETWORK, UNITS		PC NETWORK, UNITS	
Digital Equipment	3,750	Boyell	8,200
Proteon	1,220	3 Com	8,200
Wang	850	IBM PC Net	7,500
Xerox	750	Fox	3,800
Ungermann–Bass	450	Orchid	3,150
		IBM Token-Ring	1,200

DEC was the first computer giant to capitalize on network demand when it set up dozens of three-member teams, with representatives from sales, service, and software, to push local networking. Many computer companies are now working on expanding their product lines to include networking. For example, in the past year DEC, AT&T, Hewlett–Packard, and Apple have all introduced new network products and regrouped their sales forces to go after the business market. Major computer makers are moving into this $1.5-billion market, which had been dominated by such independents as Ungermann–Bass, Novell, 3 Com, and Fox Research. Future network wars are possible. Tandem Computers, Inc., for example, has teamed with Boeing Company's computer services division, to sell factory networks. IBM also has joined with Microsoft Corporation, a software company, which is designing software to link the new PS/2 computers together. IBM's top corporate priority of late has been the networking market.

MARKET SEGMENTS

Apple's objectives are to excel in the business markets, where computer sales are growing fastest, but not to get dragged into the low-priced end of the computer industry. To achieve these objectives, it plans to exploit and develop the communications talents of the Macintosh family.

There are three types of companies that use Apple computers. First are the technical and aerospace corporations, such as DuPont, Hughes Company, Chevron, Motorola, General Dynamics, and Plessey–British telecommunications, which use the Macintosh for computer-aided design and other technical uses. Second, there are service companies such as Arthur Young; Peat, Marwick, Mitchell; and Seafirst Bank's Seattle branches, which have many employees who are computer illiterate. In these companies, use of the Macintosh reduces training costs. Third are the groups such as Knight–Ridder and marketing departments of GE that need the desktop-publishing capabilities provided by the Macintosh and the LaserWriter.

Two-thirds of the one million Macintoshes that have been sold are in the business marketplace, and 27% of these units are in companies having fewer than 100 employees, 37% are in companies having 100–999 employees, and the remaining 36% are in companies with more than 1000 employees.[10]

International markets are becoming more important, as the computer revolution is just beginning in many countries. Apple's goal is to become multi-local by providing products tailored to each market, wherever it may be. In the United Kingdom, for example, Apples Centres, satellite stores dedicated exclusively to selling Apple desktop solutions, provide business dealers with showcase locations in high-traffic areas. In Japan, Kanjitalk systems of software give Macintosh the three traditional Japanese alphabets, in addition to English, so Japanese users are provided immediate access to a powerful library of Macintosh software.

In the consumer segment, Apple has historically experienced increased sales during the Christmas season, especially with the Apple IIc.

At this time no one customer of Apple accounts for 10% of net sales.

Apple currently has no significant U.S. government contracts, but plans to expand its sales efforts to the government. It has a separate thirty-person sales group that hopes to snare some of the estimated $1.6 billion federal microcomputer market.

COMPETITION

The market for the design, manufacture, sale, and servicing of personal computers and their related software and peripheral products is highly competitive. It has been characterized by rapid technological advances in both hardware and software development—advances that have substantially increased the capabilities and applications of personal computers. The principal competitive factors in this market are the product's quality and reliability, the relation of its price to its performance, the manufacturer's marketing and distribution capabilities, the quality of service and support, the availability of hardware and software accessories, and corporate reputation.

Many companies, such as IBM Corporation, Compaq Computer Corporation, AT&T Company, Tandy Corporation, Hewlett–Packard Company, Commodore Corporation, Atari Corporation, and various Japanese and Asian manufacturers, some of which have considerably greater financial resources than those of Apple, are very active in the personal computer market. In office automation and information processing, Apple competes directly with the companies mentioned and with other large domestic and foreign manufacturers, such as Digital Equipment Corporation and Wang Corporation.

IBM

Approximately 10 million IBM PCs and compatibles are in the business world, but for the first time since the IBM PC was hatched in an obscure lab in Florida six years ago, the company is focusing its full technological and marketing expertise on its PCs. This focus could pose a critical threat to Apple. Before the introduction of the IBM PS/2, IBM's various PCs outsold the Macintosh by a 5:1 ratio in all businesses. In the largest corporations, IBM and IBM-compatible machines accounted for more than 75% of the PCs in use. If corporations perceive the new IBM PCs to be similar to the Macintosh, then the distinctive quality of the Macintosh will be reduced.

With its new PCs, IBM is aggressively attempting to regain its momentum in the PC industry. Evidence of its strong marketing approach is seen in the name "Personal Systems," which underscore the PCs' role as partners with IBM mainframes and midrange computers in corporate networks. Some competitors complain that in its marketing of the PS/2, IBM has implied that only they will perform such tasks as sharing complex software with IBM mainframes across companywide networks. IBM's commitment is also seen in research and development. About half of the technology being put into the new machines is being developed by IBM (vs. one-fifth in 1981). On the new 32-bit machine, 80% is IBM technology.

IBM's market share went below 30% in 1986 because of the PC clonemakers, such as Compaq, Tandy, and Korea's Daewoo. For the PS/2, IBM did not switch to totally proprietary hardware and software, which would have made it harder for its competition to clone the products, because it would have made it harder for customers to tailor the new PCs to their businesses and so would have limited PC sales. In an effort to stave off clonemakers, IBM did design a new way of sending graphic images to a screen and embedded that software in custom microchips. The machines's design also doubles the amount of software needed to make a clone 100% compatible with a new IBM PC. Thus, in the time it takes cloners to duplicate the PS/2, IBM will have put $50 million in ads behind its new machines and will keep the clones from reaching IBM's best corporate customers. Another competitive edge for the new PS/2 will be the efficiency of its manufacture. IBM PS/2 machines are based on circuit boards designed to be assembled at IBM's Austin, Texas factory, a model of advanced automation, and are very cheap to make. Final assembly takes less than one minute.

The company introduced four new machines: two replacements for its PC/AT and one for its basic PC, plus a 32-bit machine that is as powerful as a small minicomputer. At the low end of IBM's new line is the Model 30, which in 1987 sold for $1,695. Like Apple's Macintosh, the Model 30 creates elaborate graphics, synthesizes music, and stores data on disks only $3\frac{1}{2}$ inches across. The new system, in fact, looks like a ringing endorsement of Apple's designs. But the price is no lower than that of a Macintosh and far above that of the Macintosh-like Apple IIGS. Experts feel that if IBM had priced the Model 30 at $1,000 or less that it would undoubtedly be successful. Higher up in the line are three machines, Models 50, 60, and 80, which cost from $3,600 to $11,000. All eventually will use new software and hardware accessories for easy communication with IBM mainframes. The best-received PS/2 appears to be the Model 50, which is a desktop system that is twice as fast as IBM's older, top-end PC/AT and, at $3,845, is regarded as competitively priced with the most powerful AT-compatibles.[11]

Some disadvantages of the new IBM Personal System/2 are that (1) it uses a different kind of floppy disk so it is difficult to transfer programs and files from previous IBMs to the new machines; (2) it can't use the add-in circuit cards designed for existing PCs (a new feature, called the Micro Channel, is used for connecting circuit cards and accepts only add-ons designed specifically for it, so existing PC circuit cards are obsolete); and (3) powerful software that will let the new PC use its power won't exist for a year after introduction.

The software for both the PC/AT and the new PS/2 is not sophisticated enough to take full advantage of the power of their chips—or to deliver the productivity that is promised with the new operating systems. Once these promised capabilities are realized, the machines will be able to perform several tasks at once and handle the voluminous software instructions and graphics needed to make PCs nearly as easy to use as typewriters.

Microsoft's new operating system for the 3-year-old IBM PC/AT should be ready by 1988. Also ready in 1988 should be another operating system for a new generation of extremely powerful, 32-bit personal computers. Based on Intel's new 386 microchip, they are now being introduced by IBM and others.

Windows, a Microsoft software program to be built into new operating systems, will be sold with every new IBM PC, except the most basic model. Windows uses graphics similar to those of Apple's Macintosh and will simplify the commands needed to operate the new PCs and therefore make them much easier to use.

Another software company, Lotus, will produce a spreadsheet, called 1-2-3/M, for use with IBM microcomputers and mainframes. Over the next decade, Lotus and IBM will jointly develop and market products for a full range of computers.

Dealers have complained that not only do they have to upgrade sales and support staffs (in the computer stores), but they are also required to invest the time and money needed for their staff members to gain expertise in at least one specialized computer application, such as accounting. Dealers can't offset such costs by selling the high-profit hardware upgrades that went with older IBM PCs. Many additional functions are built into the new PS/2 models, and there is very little opportunity to add disk drives or monitors, which formerly were a major source of revenue.[12]

In May 1987, 15% of PC sales in U.S. computer stores were PS/2 models, but two-thirds of those were the PS/2 Model 30, which does not include the advanced PS/2 features.

International Data Corporation surveys show that 52% of corporate computer buyers delayed making major purchasing decisions immediately after the PS/2 introduction.[13]

AT&T

Another competitor in the PC business is AT&T, which has not been extremely successful of late. It has even been rumored that the $36 billion telephone giant might make its computer business a separate company to be jointly owned by its Italian computer partner, Olivetti. AT&T owns 23.5% of Olivetti, which supplies AT&T with its PCs and relies on the phone giant for its U.S. distribution. Although AT&T supposedly lost $800 million on its computer business in 1986, its strategy is to become a full-blown information-networking company. The company dominates phone networking, but is the underdog in computers. The company's marketing presence has faded after an early success with Olivetti-built PCs. AT&T didn't keep up with industry-wide price cuts in 1986, but has more recently cut prices to stay competitive. Dataquest estimates that AT&T PC shipments fell 25% to 172,000 units in 1987. The company will probably buy more products from outside vendors and spend development money on building computers with distinct advantages. One of AT&T's marketing tactics is called Selected International Accounts. In this approach, one team is sent to major multinational corporations and sells the entire product line for the office. New products to be launched in September 1987 include a new PC based on Intel Corp's 80386 microprocessor, which is claimed to not mimic the new IBM PS/2. Development money is being spent on operating systems and environment for the machine.[14]

Compaq

Compaq, founded in the early 1980's, is second only to IBM in the number of office PC units it has sold. In 1986, its inexpensive clones sliced IBM's share of the worldwide PC market from 52% to 32%, while Compaq's share doubled from 7.5% to 15%. Compaq has a market valuation of $1.6 billion, and it got there by building IBM-compatible computers that cost about the same as IBM PCs but outperformed them or offered something extra. In 1986, Compaq's earnings were $43 million with sales of $625 million. In 1987 its first-quarter earnings rose 142% to $20.2 million, while sales rose $210.94 million. Large companies accounted for 45% of Compaq's sales in 1986. Estimates for 1987 earnings are $98 million, or $2.50 per share on sales of $931 million, and estimates for 1988 earnings run from $3.00 to $3.50 per share. Analysts expect revenues for 1988 to reach $1.2 billion.

The company claims to have no plans to clone IBM's new product line, the PS/2, unless it becomes a widely accepted standard. Compaq sees an opportunity to succeed with potential purchasers who aren't delaying their purchasing decisions because of IBM's PS/2. Because customers have already sunk an estimated $80 billion into IBM PCs, PC clones, and the hardware options and software that work with them, and because there are some disadvantages to the PS/2 itself, the company is betting that even IBM will not be able to quickly get previous owners to trade up to the PS/2 line. Industry watchers, on the other hand, think that Compaq probably is cloning PS/2 as quickly as possible.

Compaq is, however, starting to assume more of a leadership role. For instance, in the end of summer 1986, it brought out the first IBM-compatible PC to use Intel's 386, a microchip with more than twice the power of the chips then used in IBM's most powerful model. In its PS/2 line, IBM did not introduce a product to compete directly with the Compaq model, the $6,500 Deskpro 386, and analysts say it will take some time for the company to fill that gap. About 20,000 Deskpro 386s were sold in the last quarter of 1986 and 25,000 in the first quarter of 1987. These sales added about $225 million to revenues. In fact, the company's desktop models are so popular that it hasn't been possible to fill all of the orders. Demand for Compaq's newest portable, the Portable III, is so strong, the company says, that it will be unable to fill all the orders until the fall of 1987.

With the international markets becoming so important in terms of potential sales, Compaq has made a goal to increase its sales outside the U.S. from 19% to 45% of revenues.[15]

Digital Equipment Corporation (DEC)

DEC is a full-line competitor with IBM. With its superior networking products, the company has been able to penetrate some of IBM's largest commercial accounts. DEC's net income increased approximately 80% to $1.1 billion in the year ending June 30, 1987. As a large company, DEC could pose an increasingly large threat to Apple in the years to come.

In 1986 DEC introduced an engineering workstation that directly competes with the Macintosh II and the IBM PS/2 Model 80, which both double as engineering workstations. DEC has reduced the price of its basic workstation by 50% to $4,600.

Other Competitors

Industry watchers feel that it should only take around six months for IBM PS/2 clones to start appearing. IBM's market share fell in 1986 because of the success of clonemakers such as Compaq, Tandy, and Korea's Daewoo. IBM is not the only company hurt by clonemakers. One can be sure that if IBM's success is impeded, then other less powerful companies in the industry are vulnerable, too. The biggest problem for rival computer makers may lie in the future. If IBM begins to upgrade its products more rapidly to take timely advantage of technological improvements, its rivals will be placed on a treadmill of shortened production cycles and increased capital investment.

Potential competition comes from the international arena, too. An example is Korea-based Daewoo Telecom Co. Daewoo kicked off the lastest round in the low-priced computer battle in 1986; its Leading Edge model already has snared a 5% share of the home computer market. Another example is Multitech Industrial Corporation, a Taiwan-based firm that has been making computers for years and could become a legitimate rival to Japanese, Korean, and U.S. multinational corporations. The company's most recent offering is an IBM PC/AT compatible computer using Intel Corp's new 32-bit 80386 microchip. The machine hit the U.S. and European markets months before IBM brought out its first 80386-based machine. To successfully expand overseas, Multitech has adopted the name of Acer Technologies for its products and is launching a $5 million ad campaign to sell the name to consumers and computer distributors.[16]

Other companies that offer competition, especially in the less-than-$1,000 market, include Blue Chip, United Kingdom-based Amstrad (PC 1512), Commodore International (PC 10-1 and PC 10-2), Atari (PC), and Franklin Computer (PC 8000).[17]

PRODUCTION

The raw materials essential to Apple's business are generally available from multiple sources. Some components, such as power supplies, integrated circuits, and plastic housings, are obtained from single sources, although Apple believes that other sources for such parts are available. New products often utilize custom components that are available only from a single source upon initial introduction of the product. Although Apple generally qualifies other sources after the product is introduced, the inability to obtain components fast enough to satisfy demand for the new product can cause significant delays in product delivery. The Apple IIGS encountered such delays during the fourth quarter of 1986.

Apple's foreign operations consist of three manufacturing facilities in Ireland and Singapore. In the United States, the company has four manufacturing facilities.

In general, Apple sells its products directly to customers, who typically purchase products on an as-needed basis and frequently change delivery schedules and order rates. For this reason, Apple's backlog of orders at any particular date might not represent its actual sales for any succeeding period.

MARKETING

William V. Campbell, Apple's Executive Vice-President for U.S. sales and Marketing, says, "We've been dragged to our mission kicking and screaming. We've put together a business advisory panel. No longer do we put out technology for technology's sake." Marketing and distribution expenses were $477 million or 25% of sales in 1986. In 1986 more was spent in sales and marketing programs than in advertising and merchandising (excluding increases related to the Apple IIGS rollout and a new television campaign).

One goal is to increase international sales from 26% of total sales. There has been strong growth in newer markets, including Spain, Sweden, Holland, and Belgium. Sales in Japan are also rising, to reflect the initial success with Kanjitalk. The largest international markets are France, Canada, and Australia.[18]

PRODUCTS

Apple has two computer families, the Apple II and Macintosh families. The Apple II, the company's original line, has a large customer base in the education and home markets. There are three Apple II models, the IIC, IIE, and the IIGS. The Macintosh line has four models, the Macintosh 512K, Macintosh Plus, Macintosh SE, and Macintosh II. Macintosh is targeted towards the business markets.[19]

The Apple Line

Apple IIC

Introduced late in the 1986 fiscal year, the updated IIC can provide up to one megabyte of memory, which enables users to work with sophisticated software programs.

Apple IIGS and Apple IIE

The IIGS was introduced in September 1986 and is a high-end model, featuring a 16-bit microprocessor, high-resolution color graphics, advanced sound capabilities, and up to one megabyte of internal memory. Although the IIGS is praised for its speed and graphics, production problems slowed sales during the Christmas quarter of 1986, when the company usually earns more than one-third of its annual profit. Some experts complain that what is being done on the GS can be accomplished just as well on a II Plus, IIE, or IIC. They say that about the only thing that can't be done with the old Apple II that can be done with the new GS is high-resolution color graphics. Color graphics are a bonus, but for routine, everyday tasks, they aren't really necessary. Apple IIE users can buy an upgrade kit that will give their computers all Apple IIGS capabilities.

The Macintosh Line

The Macintosh is an extremely user-friendly computer that makes use of graphic icons (pictorial representatives of function) and a mouse devise, which allows a user to enter commands without touching the keyboard. Apple relies on the Macintosh for more than half of its revenues and earnings. In 1985, Apple sold 100,000 Macintoshes to businesses with annual revenues of more than $100 million. Sales of 175,000 surpassed Apple II sales for the first time in 1986. The prediction for 1987 is 325,000. As of 1986, the Macintosh had about 7% of total sales to the business market. Shipments of the Macintosh doubled in 1986, while worldwide PC shipments rose only 9%. Approximately one million Macintoshes have been sold; nearly two-thirds of those sales were in the business marketplace. Companies with fewer than 100 employees comprise 27% of sales, 37% are in companies with 100–999 employees, and 36% in companies with more than 1,000 employees.

Desktop publishing, which Macintosh pioneered, is a method for printing typeset-quality documents. Approximately 50,000 Macintosh publishing systems were sold in 1986 and sales of accompanying printers grossed around $150 million.

Microsoft's Excel, a spreadsheet program, enables the Macintosh to go head-to-head with an IBM PC running Lotus's 1-2-3. In large companies, desktop-publishing enthusiasts have helped Apple sell the Macintosh for other uses. Since people began trying other Macintosh software, including their Excel spreadsheet, a lot of Lotus users have transferred their files. Some claim that the Macintosh increases productivity faster than do other computers because it is easier to use. Apple makes software developers conform to a single set of commands, so that once an operator has mastered those commands, it is relatively easy to learn another Macintosh software package.

Apple still owns the rights to Macintosh's built-in programs, so it can't be cloned the way the IBM PC can.

Macintosh Plus

Introduced in January 1986, the Mac Plus has a high-speed socket that limits the means by which hardware options can be connected. Thus Apple is courting companies whose add-on options can help sell the Macintosh—companies such as Radius Inc., whose 15-inch screen for the Macintosh Plus has scored big. Along with the LaserWriter Plus printer, this model opened the door for Apple in business. In fact, the two are seen as the standard for the rapidly growing desktop publishing market.

Macintosh 512K Enhanced

The 512K Enhanced was introduced in the early spring of 1986 and is a more affordable version of the Macintosh Plus. Now that the Macintosh Plus is selling to corporations and Apple has introduced a new model of the Macintosh, prices on the 512K Enhanced are falling to around $4,100. That makes it less expensive than the new IIGS and about the same price as the Atari 1040ST.

Macintosh SE

To get into corporate MIS departments, Apple has created Macintosh II and the Macintosh SE, which embrace MS/DOS, Unix, Ethernet, token ring, and all else dear to the heart of the corporate PC user. The new "open" Macintosh is designed to be flexible enough that its owners can customize it, and thus this Macintosh will eliminate one of business customers' largest objections to the old "closed" Macintosh. For instance, the machine has several card slots, so owners can customize a machine simply by plugging in circuit cards to give it new functions, such as high-resolution graphics.

The Macintosh SE, with prices ranging from $2,898 to $4,500, is intended to become the Macintosh line's staple for office use. It is an enhanced version of the flagship Macintosh Plus and uses the same, relatively slower Motorola 68000 microprocessor, but has room for the add-on features, such as extra speed or memory, demanded by customers.

SE stands for System Expansion. The Macintosh SE is equipped with an internal slot for add-in cards and with two internal disks, one of which can be a 20-megabyte SCSI (Small Computer System Interface) hard drive. With Dayna's DaynaFile, a disk drive that connects directly to the Macintosh via a SCSI port and acts as an external 5-$\frac{1}{4}$-inch drive, it is possible to access such IBM compatible files as Lotus 1-2-3, dBase III, or WordPerfect as though they had been created on a Macintosh disk.

Macintosh II

The Macintosh II costs up to $12,000 and has a 13-inch color screen, four megabytes of internal memory, and an 80-megabyte hard disk. It combines advanced color graphics with computational muscle rivaling machines with three times the price. With this machine, Apple beat IBM to the 32-bit generation, because it features Motorola Corp.'s 68020 chip and thereby presents a direct challenge to the high-powered 386 PCs. Larry Magid, Senior Analyst at Seybold, San Jose, California says, "There no longer is an excuse for not buying a Mac. Now it's a matter of which machine is more suited to your application, to your environment. The Mac II is a credible second standard computer in the corporate area."

Other Products

The *AppleTalk* local-area network can link as many as thirty-two computers and peripheral devices. The company claims that *AppleTalk*, one of Apple's most successful new products in 1986, is the first and only network solution that is as easy to learn and use as Macintosh itself. There is an *AppleTalk* network connection built into every new Macintosh and Apple IIGS. This network "configures" itself so that linking computers, printers, and other peripherals becomes extremely simple and economical. As of 1986 there are over 200,000 *AppleTalk* networks in place. However, some people see LANs as the next bottleneck for Apple in the corporate world. *AppleTalk* is fine for small groups (eight or fewer machines) but might not be adequate if hundreds of machines need to be connected.

The *LaserWriter* and *LaserWriter Plus*, introduced January 1986, are high-resolution laser printers.

New peripherals include Hard Disc 20SC, Apple II-compatible UniDisk 3.5-inch 800K disk drive, ImageWriter II printer, and Apple Personal Modem.

The company announced in 1986 that it is creating a new software subsidiary to develop critical programs for its Apple II and Macintosh computers. This new subsidiary should also open up new areas of exploration for small vendors. William V. Campbell, who will be President of the new company, denies an anti-Microsoft strategy, but a highly placed Apple insider says one goal was to make Apple less dependent on Microsoft, which sells 50% of the software bought each year for Apple's Macintosh. Like IBM, Apple sees Microsoft aiding the enemy, because Microsoft's Windows program can turn another PC into a Mac look-alike. In 1986, the world-wide software sales were $27 billion.

One future worry about Apple's product line is that the Macintosh won't be unique for long. Graphics options for the IBM PC are moving fast, and dozens of companies are finding ways in which PCs can be adapted for desktop publishing. It is predicted that sometime in 1987, sales of desktop publishing systems based on IBM and IBM-compatible computers will start to exceed sales on the Macintosh. Even though the market is growing so quickly that Apple's own desktop publishing sales will increase by 70% in 1987, the Macintosh may lose some of its edge.

RESEARCH AND DEVELOPMENT

Apple's design principle is, "No matter how powerful or sophisticated the system, keep it simple to set up and operate." R&D expenses in 1986 increased to $128 million or 6.7% of sales, from $73 million or 3.8% of sales in 1985. The company plans to increase its research budget by 30%, to $166 million, or about 7% of projected sales in fiscal 1987. These funds went to significant additions to the engineering staff, to increases in prototype materials and tooling, and to the purchases of other equipment and proprietary design software that can shorten product development cycles. In March 1986, the company installed a $15.5 million Cray X-MP/48 supercomputer from Cray Research Inc. One of the largest and most powerful scientific supercomputers in the world, the Cray can simulate new computer architectures and operating systems in three months to one year less than was ever before possible.

Current programs include a collaborative effort with the National Geographic Society and LucasFilm Ltd. to explore the effective use of optical technologies (video and compact disks) for the Apple II line in education. These devices can store vast amounts of information, including still and moving images and stereo sound, and still allow easy interaction.

Apple University Consortium brings universities and countries together to share and explore the integration of technology and education. The United States has thirty-two consortium members.

Apple's Office of Special Education represents the company's commitment to work with educational institutions and human services organizations, to identify and assist the computer-related needs of disabled persons.

PROMOTIONS

For the fiscal year 1986, advertising expenditures were $157,833,000. This figure is down from $187,457,000 in 1985 and $179,739,000 in 1984. This total includes both salaries and other costs of in-house advertising, graphic design, and public relations departments, as well as the costs of advertising in various media and employing outside advertising agencies.

Recent ads call the Macintosh "The computer for the rest of us." Another slogan, "The Power to Be Your Best," focuses on people and how Apple products help them realize their full potential. Consumers who are a bit more educated about computers now want to know precisely how a computer will solve real problems in their work and their lives. In response to these consumers, image ads are no longer being used.

DISTRIBUTION

Apple has distribution facilities in the U.S., Europe, Canada, and Australia. In 1986 the U.S. dealer organization was trimmed by 25% and sales per dealer location increased by 15%. A field sales force gave the best service to those dealers with the best performance.[20]

Apple's strategy is to carefully select its dealers and restrict distribution of the more complex products to the most sophisticated outlets, which will attract business customers. For example, Businessland, Inc. sells both IBM and Apple products to large corporations. The dealer's most important characteristic is that it markets Apple machines effectively.

However, Apple is up against the direct-sales forces of IBM and DEC, and many experts think that it's not possible to sell in the business market without a direct-sales force. Through a national accounts program, Apple has been trying to convince the heads of information services and data processing departments how Apple products differ and why those differences are important to business. Between 1985 and 1987, more than twenty companies have put Apple on their approved vendor list.

Mass merchants, such as Target Stores, The Wiz, Toys 'R' Us, Wal-Mart, K-Mart, and Jamesway Corp., which have been selling home computers since the late 70s and early 80s, ushered in Commodore's 64 and Atari's 600 XL and 130 XE. This competition may cause some concern to Apple's retailers. It is most likely, though, that the middle-market outlets such as Radio Shack will suffer more than will the specialty retailer at the hands of the discounters selling clones, because the specialty retailers are geared toward businesses.[21]

EXHIBIT 4.8 **Consolidated Statements of Income—Nine-Year Summary, Apple Computer**

(Dollars and Shares in Thousands, Except Per Share Amounts)

	1986	1985	1984	1983	1982	1981	1980	1979	1978
Net Sales	$1,901,898	$1,918,280	$1,515,876	$982,769	$583,061	$334,763	$117,126	$47,867	$ 7,883
Costs and expenses:									
Cost of sales	891,112	1,117,864	878,586	505,765	288,001	170,124	66,490	27,450	3,960
Research and development	127,758	72,526	71,136	60,040	37,979	20,956	7,282	3,601	597
Marketing and distribution	476,685	478,079	398,463	229,961	119,945	55,369	12,619	8,802	1,170
General and administrative	132,812	110,077	81,840	57,364	34,927	22,191	7,150	2,080	609
Total costs and expenses	1,628,367	1,778,546	1,430,025	853,130	480,852	268,640	93,541	41,933	6,336
Operating income	273,531	102,768	85,851	129,639	102,209	66,143	23,585	5,933	1,547
Interest and other income, net	36,187	17,277	23,334	16,483	14,563	10,400	567	0	0
Income before taxes on income	309,718	120,045	109,185	146,122	116,772	76,543	24,152	5,933	1,547
Provision for income taxes	155,755	58,822	45,130	69,408	55,466	37,123	12,454	860	754
Net income	$ 153,963	$ 61,223	$ 64,055	$ 76,714	$ 61,306	$ 39,420	$ 11,698	$ 5,073	$ 793
Earnings per common and common equivalent share	$ 2.39	$ .99	$ 1.05	1.28	1.06	.70	.24	.12	.03
Common and common equivalent shares used in the calculations of earnings per share	64,315	61,895	60,887	59,867	57,798	56,181	48,412	43,620	31,544

SOURCE: Apple Computer, Inc., *Annual Report*, 1986, p. 38; *Annual Report*, 1984, p. 38; *Annual Report*, 1983, p. 16; and *Annual Report*, 1981, p. 16.

NOTE: The financial data was expanded to include the years 1981–1978.

Approximately 4500 dealers sell computers. During 1985, about 7% dropped out of the business because their profit margins were down. Apple and IBM (51% of computer store sales) requalify their dealers to be sure that only the best carry products such as the Macintosh II and the most powerful models of the new IBM PS/2 line. Of Apple's 2000 dealers, 300 have been chosen to carry the top-of-the-line Macintosh II. Apple is expected to allow 800 more to carry the Macintosh II. Apple feels that the fewer the stores carrying the product, the higher the profit margins. Dealers who aren't allowed to carry the best products will have to compete in the high-volume discount business—almost a guarantee of thin margins for these retailers.

FINANCIAL POSITION

Apple relies on funds from operations ($273 million in 1986; $102 million in 1985) to meet its liquidity needs. It also uses proceeds from the sale of common stock ($46 million in 1986 vs. $22 million in 1985) under the company's stock-option and employee stock-purchase plans, and related tax benefits ($9 million in 1986 vs. $3 million in 1985). In 1986, Apple had $576,215,000 in cash and no debt. See Exhibits 4.8 and 4.9 for detailed information.

EXHIBIT 4.9

Consolidated Balance Sheets, Apple Computer, Inc.
(Dollar Amounts in Thousands)

	SEPT. 26, 1986	SEPT. 25, 1985	SEPT. 28, 1984
Assets			
Current assets:			
Cash and temporary cash investments	$ 576,215	$337,013	$114,888
Accounts receivable	263,126	220,157	258,238
Inventories	108,680	166,951	264,619
Prepaid income taxes	53,029	70,375	26,751
Other current assets	39,884	27,569	23,055
Total current assets	1,040,934	822,065	687,551
Net Property, plant and equipment	107,315	90,446	75,868
Other assets	11,879	23,666	25,367
Total assets	1,160,128	936,177	788,786
Liabilities and Shareholders' Equity			
Current liabilities	328,535	295,425	255,184
Deferred income taxes	137,506	90,265	69,037
Shareholders' equity	694,087	550,177	464,565
Total liabilities and shareholders' equity	1,160,128	935,867	788,786

SOURCE: Apple Computer, Inc., *Annual Report*, 1986.

Apple stock was the most active OTC issue of 1986; it rose $18\frac{1}{2}$ points on $7.71 billion of volume and finished the year at $40\frac{1}{2}$. Prior to 1987 its record price was $63\frac{1}{4}$—that level was reached in 1983 after its all-time low of $10\frac{3}{4}$ only a year earlier. Apple's stock traded over the counter on the NASDAQ. Officers and directors control about 11% of the outstanding common, while institutions hold approximately 60%. The largest investor (as of December, 1986) is Citicorp with 4.7 million shares, followed by Atlanta/Sosnoff Capital, which has 2.2 million. There are about 35,000 shareholders of record. As of 1986 there were about 65 million shares outstanding. Apple stock has risen to close to $80 in 1987.

On April 23, 1987, Apple announced its first-ever quarterly dividend of $.12 per share. The company also announced a 2-for-1 stock split. This makes Apple one of the first Silicon-Valley-based computer and electronics concerns to pay a dividend. Mr. Sculley called the dividend "an expression of confidence" in Apple's long-term future. Apple plans to continue paying this dividend quarterly.

NOTES

1. J. Sculley, *Odyssey*, (New York: Harper & Row, 1987), p. 388.

2. *Ibid*, pp. 387–388.

3. "Jobs Calls Apple's Suit 'Absurd, Shock,'" *Tampa Tribune*, September 26, 1985, p. 2F.

4. P. Watt, "Out-of-Court-Settlement Allows Apple to Preview Next Products," *Computerworld*, January 27, 1986, pp. 100, 123.

5. G. Lewis, "The First Sign of Spring for IBM and Its Rivals," *Business Week*, April 27, 1987, pp. 35–36.

6. J. Steinberg, "Computer Marketing: Technology Drives Industry Down a New Path," *Advertising Age*, April 6, 1987, pp. S-3–S-10.

7. "Who's Afraid of IBM?" *Business Week*, June 29, 1987, pp. 68–74.

8. J. Steinberg, p. S-5.

9. K. M. Hafner, "Apple's Comeback," *Business Week*, January 19, 1987, pp. 84–89.

10. E. D. Meyer, "Waiting Impatiently at the Gates of MIS Kindgom," *Datamation*, April 15, 1987, pp. 37–38.

11. P. Nulty, "IBM, Clonebuster," *Fortune*, April 27, 1987, p. 225; and R. Brandt, "The Billion-Dollar Whiz Kid," *Business Week*, April 13, 1987, pp. 68–76.

12. Brandt, "The Billion-Dollar Whiz Kid," pp. 68–76; and "Computer Retailers: Things Have Gone from Worse to Bad," *Business Week*, June 8, 1987, pp. 104–109.

13. "Who's Afraid of IBM," p. 69.

14. "AT&T May Be Ready to Cut Its Losses in Computers," *Business Week*, June 6, 1987, p. 30.

15. "Who's Afraid of IBM," pp. 68–74.

16. C. Wilder, "IBM, Industry Clouds Break Away," *Computerworld*, April 20, 1981, p. 125.

17. F. Brookman, "Clones Tap into Mass Retail with Mixed Results," *Advertising Age*, June 6, 1987, p. 5.

18. Apple Computer, Inc., *1986 Annual Report*, p. 8.

19. Hafner, "Apple's Comeback." pp. 84–98; 1986 *Annual Report* pp. 1–12; C. H. Gajeway, "Machine Specifics: Apple," *Family Computing*, April 1987, p. 28; J. Schwartz, "Apple's Big Mac Attack," *Newsweek*, March 19, 1987, p. 48; and Meyer, "Waiting Impatiently at the Gates of MIS Kingdom," pp. 37–38.

20. Apple Computer, Inc., *1986 Annual Report*, p. 10.

21. Brookman, "Clones Tap into Mass Retail with Mixed Results," p. 5.

Polaroid Corporation

SEXTON ADAMS • ADELAIDE GRIFFIN

"What a turnaround," thought Ian McAlister Booth, as he sat alone in his Cambridge, Massachusetts, office. As Polaroid's President and CEO, he had undertaken a massive challenge of reversing the company from a serious midlife crisis. The dramatic success of the new camera system Spectra had boosted not only the company earnings, but also the morale at Polaroid. Revenues for 1986 grew 26% to $1.63 billion, and profits had almost tripled to $103.5 million. Polaroid's stock had jumped 55% over the past twelve months to a price of $71, in May 1987. Polaroid meanwhile had to devise methods to sustain the consumers' interest in instant photography, rekindled by Spectra's success, as competition from the compact cameras continued to be a major threat. Booth was convinced that the electronic camera would be the product of the future, but it was still in the developmental stage and would require five to ten years before it could enter the mass market. Polaroid's diversification attempts to expand its industrial photography and magnetic media business seemed to be in the right direction, although the results had so far been mixed.

INDUSTRY

The photographic equipment industry covered a wide variety of products, including cameras, sensitized film and paper, photocopier and micrographics equipment. Demand for traditional photographic products had continued to be soft in recent years because of domestic market saturation, competition from other leisure goods, and sluggish foreign markets. In addition, the challenge of electronic imaging systems had caused many producers to restructure their operations and adopt new manufacturing plans, which included diversified products and technologies that complemented their silver–halide-based products.[1]

Current Situation

The photographic equipment and supplies industry had an average annual growth rate of 4.5% between 1972 and 1984, after inflation adjustments. (See Exhibit 5.1.) Increased purchases of consumer electronic products, manufacturers' diversification into complementary products, and original equipment manufacturing agreements between U.S. and foreign firms all had depressed

This case was prepared by Simon Feng, Joannie Jianto and Shibani Paul under the supervision of Professor Sexton Adams, North Texas State University, and Professor Adelaide Griffin, Texas Woman's University. Copyright © 1988 by Sexton Adams and Adelaide Griffin. Reprinted by permission.

EXHIBIT 5.1

Historical Trends: Photographic Equipment and Supplies

(Dollar Amounts in Millions Except as Noted)

	1972	1973	1974	1975	1976	1977
Industry Data						
Value of shipments[1]	5,624	6,435	7,493	7,627	8,845	9,947
Value of shipments (1982$)	10,692	11,856	12,974	11,996	13,259	14,418
Total employment (000)	96	101	109	99.9	107	112
Production workers (000)	56.0	58.4	62.1	53.8	58.3	61.7

[1] Value of all products and services sold by the Photographic Equipment & Supplies industry.
SOURCE: U.S. Industrial Outlook 1987, pp. 35–42.

U.S. production. Shipments dropped 4% (in constant dollars) in 1985 and approximately 1% in 1986 (See Exhibit 5.2).

Containment of operating costs continued to be a major concern to manufacturers of photographic products. Workforce reductions had been an important contributor towards lowering costs. During 1986, industry employment declined 2%, to 100,000 workers. The number of production workers, who accounted for about half of the total, dropped 4%, to 50,000. Employment declined for four consecutive years at an average rate of 4%, to reach its lowest level in 1986 since 1975 (see Exhibit 5.2).

Stable raw material prices also helped keep manufacturing costs down. The average producer price index for photographic equipment and supplies rose only 1% in 1986. The price index for equipment alone remained flat. Photographic supply prices increased only 1.5%, largely because the price index for silver, one of the more expensive inputs for sensitized photographic supplies, was 10% below the 1985 average.[2]

Consumer Photography

Polaroid won a ten-year patent infringement case against Kodak in January 1986 and once again became the sole producer, distributor and maker of instant photographic cameras and film.[3]

Demand for amateur instant photographic products had remained soft, and camera sales had declined each year since the peak year, 1978. In an effort to revive consumer interest, Polaroid introduced a new camera system called Spectra in 1986, the first in fourteen years. The success of this system was expected to result in the first upturn in instant camera sales in eight years. New medical, technical, and industrial applications of instant products continued to be developed, so that these markets showed steady growth.[4]

Sales of disc cameras were held down during 1986, primarily by the increased popularity of compact, automatic, non-SLR 35mm cameras. Sales of the 110

1978	1979	1980	1981	1982	1983	1984
11,536	13,410	15,867	16,927	17,038	17,366	18.702
16,072	17,698	16,399	16,905	17,038	17,191	18.150
112	114	114	114	119	110	104
64.3	64.6	62.6	62.7	64.1	57.6	53.7

cartridge camera, which was superseded by the disc camera in 1982, continued to decline. In 1986, sales were down 20%, to about 1.6 million units. Sales of the 126 cartridge camera were virtually nonexistent.

The introduction of autofocus SLR (single lens reflex) 35mm cameras helped to renew consumer interest in this previously stagnant product group. SLR imports declined 12% in 1985, but rose 5%, to 3.5 million units, in 1986. Sales of moderately priced non-SLR 35mm cameras continued to increase. Unit imports rose 30%, to 3.7 million units, during 1986. The import value of both SLR and non-SLR 35mm cameras exceeded $600 million in 1986.[5]

EXHIBIT 5.2   **Recent Performance and Forecast: Photographic Equipment and Supplies**

(Dollar Amounts in Millions Except as Noted)

	1984	1985[1]	1986[2]	1987[3]
Industry Data				
Value of shipments[4]	18,702	18,000	18,000	—
Value of shipments (1982$)	18,150	17,400	17,300	17,300
Total employment (000)	104	102	100	98
Production workers (000)	53.7	52.0	50.0	49.0

SOURCE: U.S. Industrial Outlook 1987, pp. 35–42.

[1] Estimated except for exports and imports.

[2] Estimated.

[3] Forecast.

[4] Value of all products and services sold by the Photographic Equipment and supplies industry.

Recent advancements in electronic imaging were based on a blend of technologies from the semiconductor, computer, and photographic industries. The formal introduction of an all-electronic still camera/video system took place in 1986. The system was targeted for the professional market and was priced near $40,000. Although several manufacturers were developing similar products, which included refinements in picture resolution, industry analysts did not expect the price of the electronic still camera to fall below $10,000 before the mid-1990s.[6]

Photofinishing

Between 1981 and 1985, the retail market for amateur photofinishing grew at a compound annual rate of 11%. The continued quality and performance improvements and increased variety of photographic films were factors that contributed to the steady growth in recent years. In 1986, the market grew by 8%, to $3.8 billion.[7]

HISTORY OF THE COMPANY

Founded in 1937 by scientist-entrepreneur, Edwin H. Land, Polaroid's chief product was sunglasses. But Land's major aim was to convince Detroit to put polarized filters on every automobile. After a refusal from the auto makers, Polaroid switched to the manufacture of the picture-in-a-minute camera, an invention of Land's, which started the firm's success story in 1947.

From 1947 to the end of the 70s, Polaroid had focused on its product development to realize Dr. Land's concept of absolute one-step photography. Several products were introduced, which included Swinger, SX-70, and OneStep Land cameras. Its OneStep Land camera, introduced in 1977, became the best selling camera in the United States for five consecutive years.[8]

The signs of maturity, however, became apparent in the early 1980s. Although Polaroid still sold slightly more than two-thirds of all instant cameras, the challenge worldwide was to stop the decline of the instant share of the total camera market. In 1981, Polaroid's share of the total U.S. camera market was 20.6%, but by 1983, it was only 15.9%. By 1982, profit from operations had sagged to $50 million from its previous high of $175 million in 1978.[9]

Polaroid, in fact, had to take some big steps away from its traditional focus on consumer instant photography. Much of this started in 1982, when Dr. Edwin H. Land left the company to pursue private research and development. At that time, William J. McCune, Jr., then President and Chairman and CEO, believed that the company had to put together a plan to merge its current emphasis on chemical imaging with the electronic-imaging opportunities of the future. Since that time, Polaroid intensified its efforts toward developing products for its technical and industrial photographic markets.[10]

In 1983 Polaroid for the first time began marketing film products in conventional film format for use in existing 35mm cameras and instruments. At the same time Polaroid was reorganizing the company into three profit centers (consumer, industrial, and magnetics) to deal effectively with the expansion of its business. To increase productivity, the company also launched programs to reduce manufacturing costs through design changes, improved yields, and new manufacturing techniques and practices. Through cost cutting and cutbacks— from 21,000 employees in 1978 to 14,000 in the end of 1983—Polaroid began to see a steady though not dramatic recovery in operating profits. Results of 1983 showed profit from operations had increased from $23.5 million in 1982 to $129.7 million.[11]

In 1984, as Polaroid entered the magnetic media market with floppy disks and video cassettes (both VHS and BETA formats), it was clearly acting on its strategic vision.[12]

Meanwhile, R&D efforts were branching into fiber optic communication, ink jet printers, and semiconductors; the first two efforts stemmed from the 1983 acquisitions of two small firms, and the latter included a new microelectronics R&D facility estimated to cost $10–$15 million.[13]

Early in 1986, Polaroid's victory in a patent suit forced Eastman Kodak out of the instant camera business. A Federal Appeals Court affirmed earlier judgments that Kodak had made unauthorized use of seven patents belonging to Polaroid. The parties were still attempting to reach a settlement in 1987, regarding the damages which could range from $500 million to $1 billion. If Polaroid could prove that Kodak had "willfully and deliberately" infringed on its patents it could get treble damages approximating $1 billion.[14] The falling dollar in 1986 also gave a hefty boost to Polaroid's profits from abroad, a big part of its business. Most important, in April 1986 the company introduced Spectra as previously mentioned, a new camera that reignited interest in instant photography.[15]

MANAGEMENT STYLE

Under its founder, entrepreneur Edwin H. Land, Polaroid Corporation was perceived as a meeting place for talented technologists to exchange ideas and invent innovative products. Land once retorted, "We're not here to make profits. . . . We're here to make innovation."[16] A brilliant inventor with more than 500 patents, Land closely linked his product philosophy and attitude towards research. Polaroid under him carried out pure research on a broad base, but concentrated its application on relatively few products. This narrow product line policy had been consistent throughout Polaroid's history. With each new series of cameras, older models were discontinued. Land also believed that a product should meet the "test of uniqueness" before it was brought to market. Land hoped to continuously develop new products for consumers even though there was no clear demand for some of them in the market. It has been observed that in Polaroid "the corporate philosophy was to invent a new camera, and then roll out a big ad campaign to sell consumers on the merits of the technology."[17]

Land was also characterized as being aloof and authoritarian in the manner in which he presided over Polaroid from its founding in 1937, until his retirement in 1982.[18] He chose William J. McCune, Jr., one of his principal research collaborators, to be his successor. McAlister Booth, who had been Chief Operating Officer since January 1982 and President since December 1983, was elected President and CEO in January 1986 and McCune remained the Chairman. "There is a clear change since Dr. Land retired," according to Eugene Glazer, an analyst for Dean Witter Reynolds. "Dr. Land went for what he felt were the big products, whether there was a market for them or not. Now Polaroid is marketing versus product directed. It is trying to find out what the consumer wants, to do market research as it never did before."[19] The new marketing orientation became clearly evident when Booth assumed the position of CEO at Polaroid, marking a clear break with the Land era. He was described as being a manager first and a technologist second. Unlike McCune, who established his reputation by working in the laboratory, Booth achieved recognition by managing in the field. He successfully built a pioneering color film factory, by completing the three year project on time and within budget.[20] "Booth is very vocal about return on equity and improving our earnings," said one staffer. "McCune likes to talk about technical things."[21]

The two men also had distinct management styles. McCune generally kept away from the workers, largely in the paternalistic tradition that dominated Polaroid during the Land era. Attempting to break down the barriers, Booth wandered the halls of Polaroid's Cambridge headquarters, and asked questions and showed a willingness to listen to new ideas.[22] Morale was on the upswing under Booth and according to one Polaroid staffer, "There's a feeling that the company's back on track."[23]

McCune and Booth spent the past few years reorganizing the company to make it more innovative in the new environment of global competition. Polaroid had to learn to be "fast innovators" according to Booth, because of the fact that, "the protective umbrella of patents is a little more porous than it used to be. People are inventing around patents."[24] At the organizational level, Booth realized that the existing monolithic management and decision making apparatus had to be broken into smaller pieces. In the past it had inhibited creativity and put a heavy burden on decision making at the higher levels; this combination had led to inefficiencies and costly mistakes.[25] The first major step was to reorganize the company into three major business units—consumer, industrial, and magnetic—with plans to eventually make them all function in matrix fashion with R&D, engineering, manufacturing, and marketing. Booth used an organizational scale of *one* to *ten* to explain the changes he desired. *Ten* was made up of autonomous groups each with its own manufacturing, engineering and marketing, and *one* was a totally functional organization with a single marketing, and a single manufacturing division for the whole company. Although Polaroid according to Booth had initially been a *one*, it was currently between *two* and *three*, and he hoped to get it to *six* or *seven* in the organizational scale.[26] (See Exhibit 5.3.)

At the level of personnel, there was a sharp cutback from 20,000 in 1978 to 12,932 in December 1985. Project focus, a year-long internal study of Polaroid

EXHIBIT 5.3   **Table of Organization, Polaroid Corporation**

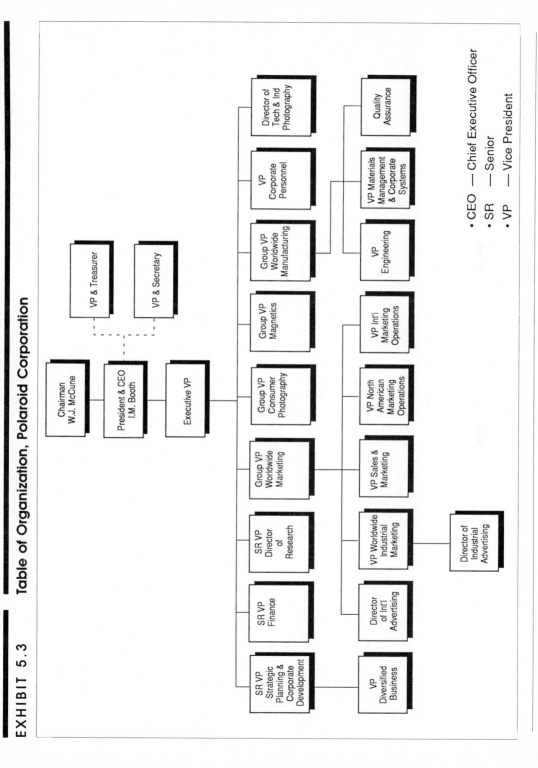

SOURCE: Company records.

employees' performance and attitudes, had revealed that "employees were overpaid and undermotivated and had little understanding of Polaroid's long term goals."[27] As a result of the study, a $30 million severance program was introduced in April 1985 to shrink the salaried work force, and a new campaign to dispense with the company's "civil service mentality" was initiated."[28] Further, Polaroid attempted to create an entrepreneurial atmosphere: it started a performance-based compensation plan for salaried members, established work groups to oversee job design and recommend workplace innovations, and set up a system for reviewing key personnel policies and practices. In creating a new organization and new rules, Polaroid got heavy input from its workers, who were not unionized. In addition, Polaroid's Chairman and President hosted employee events, to communicate personally the company's business strategies and strategies for change in the workplace. Although Booth was aware that change often created anxiety, he emphasized that, "If you are going to be agile and productive and innovative, you have to have an environment that is boiling. . . . In the long term maybe the greatest stability you could have in a company is the ability to continually change."[29]

Polaroid's top management realized that technology and the environment changed fast, often in paths outside the company's traditional field of expertise. In expanding into commercial markets and new products, the new CEO and Chairman demonstrated a willingness to use methods such as joint ventures and acquisitions, which Land had clearly distrusted.[30] According to Booth, "There are no free lunches. You weigh the giving up of some control against the benefit of being there more quickly."[31] To help Polaroid to look beyond its traditional technologies, it was buying into other companies and contracting research.[32]

Some analysts believe that Polaroid's diversification into new high tech areas represented an aggressive positive step for a company, once satisfied with resting on its instant-photo laurels. A spokesman for Polaroid indicated, "Our best bet for the future is to take our lumps now and make our investments to pay off at the end of the decade. That might mean sacrificing short term (profits) to get us back on track in 1990."[33] Some of Booth's critics believed that Land's seemingly cavalier attitude towards the bottom line had not been fully exorcised.[34] Other observers questioned whether a management team hired by Land, and nurtured in the no-competition years of instant photography, could succeed in the existing market conditions, which were highly competitive. According to one insider, "They want to get into new industries, but they just don't have the executives to take them there."[35] Some other critics have viewed Polaroid's current diversification strategies as a betrayal of Land's legacy.[36] Even Land, who no longer had official ties to Polaroid, had expressed his dissatisfaction with the diversification efforts.[37] He was the largest shareholder with 8.3% of stock, which he decided to sell in May 1985 as he felt that Polaroid's 4% yield was "not safely adequate" to fund the operations of the non-profit research institute he had started.[38]

**PRODUCT
DEVELOPMENT
AND RESEARCH**

During the past years, Polaroid Corporation's contributions to the field of instant imaging were numerous. The product development and research efforts can be classified into the following categories: consumer photography, industrial and professional photography, magnetic media and others.[39] (See Exhibit 5.4.)

EXHIBIT 5.4

Major Development and Research, Polaroid Corporation

I. Consumer Photography
Automatic 100 (1963)
Swinger (1965)
Big Swinger (1968)
300 Series; ColorPack II (1969)
SX-70 (1973)
Time Zero Supercolor Film (1979)
Sun 600 Light Management System (1981)
Spectra (1986)

II. Industrial and Professional Photography
ID-2 Land Identification System (1960)
Extended Range Polacolor Film
Instant color transparency for overhead projection
Tabletop slide copier for instant color and black and white prints from 35mm slides
Pack film for medical diagnostic imaging
Instant industrial radiographic film
SX-70 system adapter used in photomicrography
35mm Instant Slide System (1983)
Professional Chrome (1985)
Colorgraph Type 691 Film (1985)
Palette computer image recorder (1985)
Chromajet 4000 high performance ink jet printer (1986)
FreezeFrame (1986)

III. Magnetic Media
Floppy diskette (1983)
$5\frac{1}{4}$ HD DS diskette; $3\frac{1}{2}$ micro HD DS diskette (1985)
High-density floppy research
Video tapes—VHS, Beta, and 8mm (1983)
Hi-Fi VHS T120 video cassette—VHS, Beta (1985)

IV. Other Business Development
DMP-128 (1985)
Polaform hologram (1985)
Plastic LCD (1985)
Convertibles (1985)
Solar cell research
Medical diagnostic systems

SOURCE: Company records.

Consumer Photography

Available in 1973, the SX-70 was the first fully automatic camera, using digital logic functions to automate all controls needed to take a picture, except focusing. All its mechanical and electrical operations were powered by a wafer-thin battery supplied in each film pack.[40]

In 1981 a new concept was introduced, the Polaroid Sun 600 Light Management System. The new 600 cameras, through electronically mixing of ambient light with strobe light for an optimum exposure, made it possible for consumers to obtain high quality pictures over a much broader range of circumstances than was previously possible.[41]

On April 2, 1986, Polaroid introduced Spectra, an advanced photographic system designed to set new standards of quality in instant photography. The new Spectra System was a folding, wedge-shaped, electronically controlled camera with automatic focus and exposure control that used a new rectangular-format instant film. The film combined two imaging chemistries for rich, faithful color photographs of great brightness and clarity.[42]

The Spectra System also consisted of a range of accessories for extended photographic creativity and a new laser print service that provided computer-enhanced copies and enlargements.

Industrial and Professional Photography

The four established sectors of Polaroid's industrial and professional business were professional and commercial photography, visual presentation products, identification systems, and medical and scientific data recording.[43]

In 1985, Polaroid's technical and industrial photographic business, which accounted for approximately 40% of the company's revenues, continued to focus on making Polaroid instant photography a key component of the growing number of imaging systems being used in the visual communications environment. Polaroid's unique capacity to transform data from a wide variety of sources—35mm cameras, on-line computer displays, scientific and medical diagnostic systems, video tape, electronic imaging peripherals, and many other traditional and specialized photographic devices—into instant, high quality hardcopy prints suitable to particular applications was a major asset of this growing business segment for Polaroid.[44]

Its 35mm Instant Slide System produced ready-to-project slides without a darkroom, wet chemicals, or expensive equipment; it thereby combined the versatility of 35mm camera systems with the immediate results of instant photography. Other technical and industrial products included an economically priced direct-screen instant CRT camera and a nonphotographic overhead transparency material for use with color ink jet printers.

In 1985, the company continued to develop and market new peripheral devices designed to make instant hardcopy records in conjunction with a wide range of electronic imaging systems. The Polaroid Palette computer image recorder, which produced presentation-quality instant photographic hardcopy from computer graphics images, was compatible with 90% of personal computers used in business.[45]

A new instant video film recorder, FreezeFrame, which delivered high quality instant prints or slides from video images, was distributed through industrial video dealers in the fall of 1986.[46]

Magnetic Media

Polaroid's magnetic media business continued to expand with the introduction of new products and services, and the intensification of research projects in high-density information storage products.

With the introduction of a super high grade, high-fidelity VHS T120 video cassette, as well as four 8mm video cassettes, Polaroid offered a full line of premium quality video tapes in VHS and Beta, and 8mm formats. Other products designed to expand the current line of high-fidelity video cassettes were also expected to be introduced.

Two professional quality diskettes were introduced in 1985: a $5\frac{1}{4}$-inch high-density, double-sided diskette and a $3\frac{1}{2}$-inch micro high-density, double-sided diskette. These joined Polaroid's line of 8-inch and $5\frac{1}{4}$-inch diskettes. Polaroid also was working on a high-density floppy disk for personal computers that would hold more information than hard disks could.[47]

Other Business Developments

Polaroid continued to pursue the development of non-photographic products and services based on innovative applications or extensions of its core technologies, and, in some cases, research partnerships with other companies whose technologies complemented Polaroid's.

Major activities included these: Data Recovery Service, which provided users of Polaroid diskettes with a unique opportunity to recover, free of charge, data that had been lost accidentally; a unique photopolymer film, DMP-128, which facilitated the rapid mass production of reflection holograms of exceptional clarity, brightness, and realism; a new plastic liquid crystal display (LCD) material which could be used to replace conventional glass LCDs; and a new sunglass system for wearers of prescription eyeglasses.

The team of researchers assembled by Polaroid and Spire were working to commercialize solar cell research: they sought to develop amorphous silicon devices of higher efficiency and performance than photovoltaic cells. Another major effort was aimed at developing a new generation of simple, cost-effective, and rapid medical diagnostic systems that could perform reliably on blood or other fluid samples without the need for complicated laboratory equipment or technical staff.[48]

EXHIBIT 5.5   **Ten Year Financial Summary (Unaudited), Polaroid Corporation and Subsidiary Companies**

(Dollar Amounts in Millions, Except Per Share Data)

Years ended December 31	1986	1985	1984
Consolidated Statement of Earnings			
Net sales			
United States	$ 964.3	$ 779.3	$ 743.5
International	664.9	515.9	528.0
Total net sales	1,629.2	1,295.2	1,271.5
Cost of goods sold	921.7	756.0	735.2
Marketing, research, engineering, and administrative expenses	571.8	505.6	492.6
Total costs	1,493.5	1,261.6	1,227.8
Profit from operations	135.7	33.6	43.7
Other income	18.1	28.9	39.5
Interest expense	18.6	22.3	20.9
Earnings before income taxes	135.2	40.2	62.3
Federal, state and foreign income taxes (credit)	31.7	3.3	36.6
Net earnings	$ 103.5	$ 36.9	$ 25.7
Earnings per share	$ 3.34	$ 1.19	$ .83
Cash dividends per share	$ 1.00	$ 1.00	$ 1.00
Average shares outstanding (in thousands)	30,959	30,959	30,959
Selected Balance Sheet Information			
Working capital	$ 637.0	$ 697.8	$ 734.2
Net property, plant and equipment	357.7	349.0	306.6
Total assets	1,479.2	1,384.7	1,346.0
Long-term debt	—	124.6	124.5
Stockholders' equity	994.7	922.2	916.3
Other Statistical Data			
Additions to property, plant and equipment	$ 82.9	$ 104.5	$ 82.7
Depreciation	$ 71.2	$ 56.9	$ 50.8
Payroll and benefits	$ 548.2	$ 510.2	$ 475.4
Number of employees, end of year	14,765[1]	12,932	13,402
Return on average stockholders' equity	10.8%	4.0%	2.8%

SOURCE: Polaroid Corp., *1986 Annual Report.*

[1] Includes approximately 1,900 worldwide temporary employees.

FINANCE/ ACCOUNTING   As the market for instant photography went into a decline, Polaroid's profits decreased dramatically from $194.5 million in 1978 to $61.7 million in 1982. Return on equity fell steeply from a ten year high of 13.8% in 1978 to 2.5% in

1983	1982	1981	1980	1979	1978	1977
$ 730.1	$ 752.5	$ 817.8	$ 791.8	$ 757.2	$ 817.4	$ 645.8
524.4	541.4	601.8	659.0	604.3	559.2	416.1
1,254.5	1,293.9	1,419.6	1,450.8	1,361.5	1,376.6	1,061.9
698.3	769.6	855.4	831.1	876.8	778.3	575.7
462.1	472.6	520.8	483.9	449.4	418.2	337.3
1,160.4	1,242.2	1,376.2	1,315.0	1,326.2	1,196.5	913.0
94.1	51.7	43.4	135.8	35.3	180.1	148.9
32.5	45.5	49.2	25.4	13.3	20.3	19.0
26.5	35.5	29.9	17.0	12.8	5.9	6.4
100.1	61.7	62.7	144.2	35.8	194.5	161.5
50.4	38.2	31.6	58.8	(.3)	76.1	69.2
$ 49.7	$ 23.5	$ 31.1	$ 85.4	$ 36.1	$ 118.4	$ 92.3
$ 1.61	$ .73	$ .95	$ 2.60	$ 1.10	$ 3.60	$ 2.81
$ 1.00	$ 1.00	$ 1.00	$ 1.00	$ 1.00	$ .90	$ .65
30,959	32,144	32,855	32,855	32,855	32,855	32,855
$ 769.0	$ 745.4	$ 749.5	$ 721.9	$ 535.9	$ 609.5	$ 589.6
277.0	281.8	332.9	362.2	371.6	294.8	225.9
1,319.1	1,323.6	1,434.7	1,404.0	1,253.7	1,276.0	1,076.7
124.4	124.3	124.2	124.1	—	—	—
921.6	902.9	958.2	960.0	907.5	904.3	815.5
$ 50.1	$ 31.5	$ 42.5	$ 68.1	$ 134.6	$ 115.0	$ 68.7
$ 51.8	$ 62.2	$ 69.2	$ 62.7	$ 51.7	$ 43.0	$ 39.5
$ 474.5	$ 487.0	$ 550.5	$ 497.3	$ 464.1	$ 421.4	$ 332.2
13,871	14,540	16,784	17,454	18,416	20,884	16,394
5.4%	2.5%	3.2%	9.1%	4.0%	13.8%	11.8%

1982. (See Exhibit 5.5.) Reorganization of the company in 1982, which was aimed at building the non-consumer business, helped Polaroid reverse the declining trend in its earnings.[49]

In 1985, Polaroid began a major restructuring and streamlining of its twenty-three operating divisions, to boost the Company's sagging profits.[50] The first

EXHIBIT 5.6

Net Earnings, Polaroid Corporation
(Dollar Amounts in Millions)

1986	$103.5	1983	$49.7
1985	$36.9	1982	$23.5
1984	$25.7	1981	$31.1

SOURCE: Polaroid Corp., *1986 Annual Report*, pp. 46–47.

step of the reorganization was a severance program to reduce the company's payroll costs. Worldwide sales of Polaroid Corporation and its subsidiaries in 1985 increased slightly to $1.3 billion. Sales in the United States increased 5% to $779.3 million in 1985 from $743.5 million in 1984; this increase resulted primarily from the sale of magnetic products. International sales were 2% lower in 1985 compared to 1984, primarily because of the strength of the U.S. dollar throughout most of the year. Profit from operations decreased to $33.6 million in 1985 after a $39 million pre-tax charge for the Polaroid Severance Program. Research and development expenses decreased from $134.9 million in 1984 to $118.7 million in 1985. The combination of higher sales and savings from ongoing cost reduction programs, designed to improve efficiencies in the company's operations, more than offset increased costs associated with new products and programs.[51]

Experiencing rapid growth in 1986, Polaroid reported sales of $1.63 billion, which was attributed to the introduction of Spectra, which reignited interest in instant photography. Net income advanced to $103.5 million from $36.9 million in 1985 and earnings per share also increased to $3.34 in 1986 from $1.19 in 1985. (See Exhibits 5.6, 5.7, 5.8, 5.9.) The weaker dollar helped by increasing the value of the company's $665 million in overseas sales.[52] The net after-tax foreign currency exchange gain from balance sheet translations in 1986 amounted to $0.36 per share compared with a gain of $0.35 in 1985. Capital expenditures for 1986 were $83 million compared to $105 million in 1985.[53] Cost cutting, including a 6% staff reduction over 1985 and 1986, dramatically reduced expenses.[54]

EXHIBIT 5.7

Earnings Per Share, Polaroid Corporation
(In Dollars)

1986	$3.34	1983	$1.61
1985	$1.19	1982	$ .73
1984	$ .83	1981	$ .95

SOURCE: Polaroid Corp., *1986 Annual Report*, pp. 46–47.

EXHIBIT 5.8

Consolidated Statement of Earnings and Retained Earnings, Polaroid Corporation and Subsidiary Companies

(Dollar Amounts in Millions, Except Per Share Data)

Years ended December 31	1986	1985	1984
Net sales			
United States	$ 964.3	$ 779.3	$ 743.5
International	664.9	515.9	528.0
Total net sales	1,629.2	1,295.2	1,271.5
Cost of goods sold	921.7	756.0	735.2
Marketing, research, engineering and administrative expenses	571.8	505.6	492.6
Total costs	1,493.5	1,261.6	1,227.8
Profit from operations	135.7	33.6	43.7
Other income			
Interest income	20.6	31.2	37.3
Other	(2.5)	(2.3)	2.2
Total other income	18.1	28.9	39.5
Interest expense	18.6	22.3	20.9
Earnings before income taxes	135.2	40.2	62.3
Federal, state and foreign income taxes	31.7	3.3	36.6
Net earnings	103.5	36.9	25.7
Retained earnings at beginning of year	814.2	808.3	813.6
Less cash dividends	31.0	31.0	31.0
Retained earnings at end of year	$ 886.7	$ 814.2	$ 808.3
Earnings per share	$ 3.34	$ 1.19	$ .83
Cash dividends per share	$ 1.00	$ 1.00	$ 1.00
Average shares outstanding (in thousands)	30,959	30,959	30,959

SOURCE: Polaroid Corp., *1986 Annual Report*, p. 38.

Historically Polaroid has been conservative in its financial affairs, and has carried limited long-term debt.[55] Polaroid repaid all its long-term debt of $120 million in August 1985 and had been financing its growth out of cash flow.[56] The company's clean balance sheet with assets of approximately $1,479 million made it a potential takeover candidate and Polaroid adopted an anti-takeover plan in September 1986 to deal with that problem.[57] The company also began an extensive program to reduce its working capital. In 1986 Booth reaffirmed his commitment to a goal of achieving a 10% return on shareholders' equity in the next few years.[58]

Polaroid has been described as the quintessential glamour stock during the go-go years of the late 60s and early 70s when it sold at a price as high as $140.

EXHIBIT 5.9

Consolidated Balance Sheet, Polaroid Corporation and Subsidiary Companies

(Dollar Amounts in Millions)

December 31, 1986 and 1985	1986	1985
Assets		
Current assets		
Cash and short-term investments	$ 166.8	$ 314.5
Receivables, less allowances of $11.5 ($12.3 in 1985)	434.3	300.4
Inventories	425.0	335.0
Prepaid expenses	95.4	85.8
Total current assets	1,121.5	1,035.7
Property, plant and equipment		
Land	12.2	11.9
Buildings	217.8	213.4
Machinery and equipment	779.3	727.9
Construction in process	33.1	41.4
Gross property, plant and equipment	1,042.4	994.6
Less accumulated depreciation	684.7	645.6
Net property, plant and equipment	357.7	349.0
Total assets	$1,479.2	$1,384.7
Liabilities and stockholders' equity		
Current liabilities		
Short-term debt	$ 171.3	$ 77.9
Payables and accruals	170.7	139.1
Compensation and benefits	109.3	107.1
Federal, state and foreign income taxes	33.2	13.8
Total current liabilities	484.5	337.9
Long-term debt	—	124.6
Stockholders' equity		
Preferred stock, 20,000,000 shares authorized and unissued	—	—
Common stock, $1 par value, authorized 60,000,000 shares, issued 32,855,475 shares	32.9	32.9
Additional paid-in capital	122.0	122.0
Retained earnings	886.7	814.2
	1,041.6	969.1
Less treasury stock, at cost, 1,896,300 shares	46.9	46.9
Total stockholders' equity	994.7	922.2
Total liabilities and stockholders' equity	$1,479.2	$1,384.7

SOURCE: Polaroid Corp., *1986 Annual Report*, p. 39

It then collapsed to a low of $15 in 1975 and remained at the low range for several years. A few analysts felt that the stock was undervalued in the "cash rich, overstaffed, free spending company" with unrecognized assets.[59] Following the success of Spectra, Polaroid's stock increased dramatically by 55% over a twelve-month period and was selling at a price of $71 in February 1987.[60] Despite the optimism of Polaroid's management, Eugene Glazer of Dean Witter Reynolds Inc. believed that the market had already factored Spectra's prospects into Polaroid's stock price.[61]

Polaroid's victory in the patent infringement suit against Eastman Kodak in January 1986 could win it as much as $1 billion in damages, plus cost and other relief from Kodak, which would infuse large amounts of cash into the company. With assets of $12.15 billion, Kodak was not expected to be totally devastated. It has been suggested that it might be cheaper for Kodak to take over Polaroid, a company much smaller in size. Kodak's president, however, said, "I'm not sure we'd want Polaroid, but we'll have to see what the damages are."[62]

MARKETING

Spectra

When sales of Polaroid instant cameras dropped rapidly from its peak of 9.6 million in 1978 to only 3.8 million in 1982, Polaroid realized that American consumers had increasingly grown disenchanted with instant photography. They seemed to prefer the Japanese-made 35mm cameras which began flooding the U.S. market in the late 1970s and early 1980s. Prints from 35mm film were considered by consumers to be sharper, brighter, and bigger than instant photographs. The rapid expansion of one-hour print developing stores also undermined the benefits of instant photography, which was viewed by consumers as being bulky, expensive, and inconvenient.[63]

In spite of the decline, Polaroid executives firmly believed that new camera technology and aggressive promotion could revive the instant market. For the first time, they let marketing and not R&D drive their new product attempt. So in 1982, the first strategic business group for consumer products was created. That group was entrusted with the task of developing an exciting camera that would attract consumers back to instant photography. The Spectra instant photography system was the product of the close cooperation between the marketing and the engineering department at Polaroid.[64]

Polaroid undertook the largest consumer research program in its history, conducting 300 market studies and more than 2,000 personal interviews. The marketing team then developed the camera specifications and transferred their list to research and engineering. To convey newness, the shape of the housing had to be completely different from previous Polaroid cameras.

By 1984 Polaroid had a prototype to test among its most critical target audience: upscale families and 35mm photographers who did not own instant cameras or did not use them. Results from the consumer tests were used to develop the picture's size, shape, and color, as well as accessories for the camera. Spectra was finally launched in 1986 with an enormous $40 million ad budget for that year alone.[65] According to CEO Booth "Spectra is essential to the financial growth of Polaroid. We expect to see bottom line results in a matter of months."

Spectra indeed turned out to be an instant success for Polaroid. Brenda Landry, an industry analyst at Morgan Stanley, estimated that 800,000 Spectra cameras were sold in 1986.[66] Further, Kodak's departure from the instant camera business meant that part of the $1 billion instant photography business in the U.S. would pass to Polaroid. Kodak had about 25% of market share in 1985 and half of that was expected to go to Polaroid, according to a Value Line investment survey in December 1986.

The major elements behind Spectra's success had been technical innovation, astute marketing, and lucky timing, according to analysts. Its upscale marketing campaign had emphasized how Spectra provided better quality pictures, with sharper images and better colors, than its instant-photo predecessors. It also had the state-of-the-art electronic accessories and offered a copying service that featured laser technology.[67]

Since the 1960s the company had sold mostly low price cameras to blue collar people. Polaroids old 600 series cameras sold for $25 to $80. Spectra carried a suggested price of $225 but it retailed for $130 to $249 depending on the accessories, which could be purchased separately or as part of the package. It had a high tech feel that one photo retailer described as "the Porsche look." The company was redesigning the Spectra film for use in its cheaper cameras, and was scheduled to introduce Spectra ONYX in April 1987, its first line extension of the Spectra instant photography system. The new model would be sold only through specialty photography dealers in two versions—with and without accessories—at suggested retail prices of $280 and $350.

Despite the relatively high price, demand for Spectra had boomed in the market in 1986. According to Peter Eichorn, Vice President of the North American Marketing operation, Spectra sales had been "substantially ahead of our forecasts and way beyond any products in our history."[68] Polaroid had been producing cameras and film, seven days a week on three shifts, to meet demand.[69] The company's only U.S. manufacturing facility in Norwood, Massachusetts had been running "flat out to meet the exceedingly high demand" said Brian O'Connor, Vice President of Sales and Marketing. Despite such full capacity production, some dealers had complained initially about distribution delays and forced film rationing. There were also indications of potential trouble ahead, in Polaroid's retailer network: discounters were selling cameras at cost, at the expense of smaller camera stores. "Spectra is being sold at cost by discounters as soon as its introduced," said Mike Howard general manager of St. Louis Photo Supply. He felt he could not compete with the price offered by Dolgins, a local discount chain and had to cancel his orders. Similar problems were encountered in other places in the southern region.[70]

EXHIBIT 5.10

Consumer Instant Camera Sales, Polaroid Corporation
(Dollar Amounts in Millions)

1986	$4.3	1982	$3.8
1985	$3.5	⋮	
1984	$3.6	1978	$9.4
1983	$3.8		

SOURCE: Polaroid *Fact Book & Financial Summary 1973–1983*, and *1986 Annual Report*.

Polaroid's current marketing strategy in consumer photography targeted new parents, extended families, and young adults.[71] One promotion tied Kimberly-Clark's Huggies disposable diapers with a free Polaroid camera offer.[72] The Spectra ad campaign created a "halo effect" that sparked interest in Polaroid's other consumer product line, Sun 600 series cameras, which sold 20% more units in 1986 than it had the year before. According to William J. O'Neill Jr., Polaroid's Vice President for Consumer Photography, "Spectra has rekindled consumers' interest in instant photography."[73] Demand for Polaroid's entire instant camera line increased by 23% in 1986 over the previous year.[74] (See Exhibit 5.10.)

Distribution

Domestic distribution of imaging products for consumer markets was made by Polaroid through photographic stores; retail food, drug, discount and department store outlets; and selected wholesalers. Polaroid sold to its premium customers directly through its own premium department and through independent agents. Domestic distribution of photographic products for industrial, advanced amateur, scientific and medical applications were made directly through its industrial and technical sales department and through independent industrial agents.[75]

Domestic distribution of magnetic products had varied. Traditional outlets had been utilized for distributing videocassettes. Polaroid market research indicated that mass merchandisers and discount stores accounted for 42% of video cassette sales in 1985, compared with 30% in 1984.[76] In 1985, a separate sales force was established to market diskettes to retail and end user accounts, distributors and through catalogues.[77] Foreign distribution of imaging products was made through wholly owned subsidiaries in 21 countries and through selected unrelated distributors in more than 100 other countries.[78]

Advertising

Different advertising agencies handled the accounts for consumer photography and the industrial products at Polaroid. Midway through Spectra's development, Polaroid parted with its agency of thirty years, Doyle Dane Bernbach, New York. Preliminary work that DDB prepared for the Spectra failed to impress Polaroid and in mid '84 the company moved its entire $50 million consumer advertising account to Ally and Gargano.[79] Despite their creativity, it has been suggested that Polaroid, a strong believer in consumer recall tests, disagreed on the weight of the test scores shown in evaluating the success of a campaign. Ally resigned the account in December 1985. BBDO of New York, which had earlier been handling Polaroid's sales promotion and direct response activities, was assigned the consumer photography account in the U.S. Ogilvy and Mather Worldwide replaced DDB as Polaroid's major international agency for its $20 million advertising in Europe and the Middle East.[80]

Polaroid was aware that the company had to find innovative ways to communicate the intrinsic benefits of instant photography. In the past, it had done so through award-winning advertising ranging from the 1960s "Meet the Swinger" to the highly successful James Garner–Marriette Hartley campaign. BBDO's current Spectra campaign with the theme "we take your pictures seriously" proved extremely successful.[81] The agency launched its $40 million

---

EXHIBIT 5.11

Advertising Expenditures, Polaroid Corporation
(Dollar Amounts in Thousands)

	1985	1984
Magazine	$ 3,565	$ 6,746
Newspaper	538	1,253
Newspaper supply	0	28
Business publishing	1,635	888
Network T.V	20,049	17,337
Spot T.V	2,727	2,980
Network radio	160	0
Spot radio	483	1,387
Network cable	383	887
Outdoor	14	0
Total measured	9,555	31,506
Unmeasured[1]	40,000	42,641
Total	69,555	74,148

SOURCE: *Advertising Age*, November 3, 1986, p. S-49.

[1] Unmeasured figures are estimates from direct mail, promotion, company, cooperative contribution, trade show activity, and interactive.

multimedia promotion at an elaborate press event in April 1986, which over-shadowed Kodak's $25 million campaign for its new VR-35 cameras. Spectra's advertising campaign featured heavy prime time network T.V. spending and also heavy print schedules in all major consumer magazines and direct mail catalogs. For the first time, a twenty-five–market outdoor board campaign and heavy sales promotion at shopping malls had also been undertaken.[82]

Over the past several years, Polaroid had augmented the importance of market research and high test scores in evaluations of advertising merit and effectiveness. The company increased its marketing research staff in addition to its use of outside consultants in that area. It has been suggested that long review processes and the number of people making suggestions had probably made the job of agencies such as DDB more difficult. However, the decision-making vacuum may have been remedied by the creation of the position of Vice President of Worldwide Advertising. While analysts have welcomed Polaroid's marketing orientation and open mindedness to acquisitions and partnerships, some are worried that "all the flash, fun and cutting edge innovation will leave Polaroid; that its creativity will flounder."[83]

Advertising expenditures for Polaroid in 1985 and 1984 are shown in Exhibit 5.11. Advertising spending by the major photography equipment companies in 1985 is shown in Exhibit 5.12. Polaroid's advertising expenditure as a percentage of U.S. sales was the highest among its competitors. Polaroid's total measured advertising budget for 1986 was $40 million. It will be increasing its 1987 ad budget by about 25% to $50 million. The new ad campaign would be promoting Spectra ONYX, the first line extension of the Spectra instant photography system. Polaroid spent about $2 to $3 million annually advertising its industrial and technical products. Polaroid's third business unit, magnetic media, was a little more than two years old. By relying on name and package recognition, advertising support for video cassette tapes fell from $870,000 in 1984 to just $54,000 in 1985.[84]

EXHIBIT 5.12   **Photographic Equipment Company Advertising Spending, Polaroid Corporation**

(Dollar Amounts in Thousands)

COMPANY	U.S. ADVERTISING SPENDING		U.S. SALES		ADVERTISING AS % OF U.S. SALE	
	1985	1984	1985	1984	1985	1984
Canon Inc.	81,201	102,721	1,500,600	1,260,000	5.4	8.2
Eastman Kodak	247,300	329,066	7,392,000	7,414,000	3.3	4.4
Minolta Co.	56,734	33,541	N/A	N/A	N/A	N/A
Polaroid Corp.	69,555	74,148	779,300	743,500	8.9	10.0

SOURCE: *Advertising Age*, November 3, 1986, p. S-63.

International Marketing

Polaroid's overseas sales growth in Europe, Asia, Pacific and the Western Hemisphere can be seen in Exhibit 5.13.[85] International sales in 1986 constituted $664.9 million from total worldwide sales of $1,629.2 million. The weakening of the U.S. dollar further increased the value of the company's international sales.[86] The export marketing division had twenty-three staff members at Polaroid's U.K. headquarters in St. Albans, England. The division managed the export of Polaroid's products which included twenty cameras, forty types of films, sunglasses, videotapes, and computer graphics equipment to forty-six countries. Half the division's annual $5 million marketing expenditures were focused on sixteen Middle Eastern countries. When Polaroid entered this market in the mid-1960s, its instant cameras had a special appeal. It helped to break down religious taboos against taking pictures of women in the Arab world, which could henceforth be done in the privacy of the home. With the oil boom in the 60s and 70s no marketing expertise was needed to service those markets. However, Kodak started a major marketing effort in that area in the early 80s. "Competition with Kodak forced our prices down, and for a while it was tough," according to David Everard, managing director of Polaroid's Export Marketing Division.[87] With falling oil prices, the economies slowed down, and many people preferred the less expensive Kodak instant cameras and film. Kodak was able to acquire one-fourth of the instant photography market in the Middle East. The exit of Kodak in January 1986 from this market, due to patent violation, removed the major threat facing Polaroid. Yet the export division initiated a new marketing strategy in that period to penetrate those foreign markets more effectively.

Polaroid adapted its marketing mix to harmonize with a country's culture in its international operations. For example, camera boxes worldwide carried a photograph of a swimsuit-clad woman, whereas the ones sold in the Middle East featured flowers. A photography contest and the first large outdoor bill-

EXHIBIT 5.13

Sales by Geographic Area, Polaroid Corporation
(Dollar Amounts in Millions)

	INTERNATIONAL	UNITED STATES
1986	$664.9	$964.3
1985	515.9	779.3
1984	528.0	779.3
1983	524.4	730.1
1982	541.4	752.5
1981	601.8	817.8

SOURCE: Polaroid Corp., *1986 Annual Report*, pp. 46–47.

board in Saudi Arabia were some of the devices used in Polaroid's new marketing strategy. Its major international agency, Ogilvy & Mather, generally operated through a local agency in each country. The use of local T.V. in countries where T.V. advertising was permitted had been the most cost effective way of advertising in a large portion of the Arab world. The Pan-Arabic Press, which published magazines mainly in London and Paris, had been another useful medium for advertising both consumer and non-consumer goods for Polaroid. In fact, products such as diagnostics, graphics and security identification card systems had increased from less than 10% of Polaroid's business in the Middle East to 50%.[88]

COMPETITION	### Consumer Photography

With the introduction of Spectra in April 1986 and Spectra ONYX, its first line extension, in April 1987, Polaroid hoped to get a larger share away from the $860 million compact camera business. With 35mm cameras becoming the fastest growing segment of the photography industry (25% annual growth), Polaroid faced intense competition not only from Kodak but also from a large number of Japanese camera manufacturers, notably Nikon, Canon, and Minolta.[89]

Industry analyst Eugene Glazer at Dean Witter described ONYX as "evolutionary but not dramatically different from the earlier Spectra."[90] He expected additional models of Spectra to be introduced in 1987 at lower price points. In January 1986, Kodak introduced its VR-35 cameras, made for it in Japan, which retailed at prices lower than the Spectra system, and were aimed at replacing the loss of its Instamatic business. However, Elerbert Keppler, publisher of *Modern Photography* magazine, is of the opinion "The new camera doesn't have the features to propel it to the top of the heap."[91]

The popularity of Spectra had increased sales of instant film, and according to Brenda Landry of Morgan Stanley, "that's where the real profits are."[92] But to keep film profits rising it was felt that Polaroid would need to match 35mm in quality, or cut the price of its film. Consumers paid approximately $0.80 each for instant photographs whereas conventional ones cost $0.40. William O'Neill Jr., head of consumer photography products, believed that in the long run, Polaroid could not impose more than a 20% premium for instant film. But Booth stated his feelings clearly when he said "... innovation is the way to go, not price."[93] Meanwhile, Polaroid had to face indirect competition, mainly from Kodak, Fuji, and Konica, in the realm of film. Kodak controlled as much as 85% of the U.S. market in color film, but Fuji had seized most of the growth in recent years by keeping its prices 10% below Kodak's.[94] Although the laser-technology reprint service for Spectra had produced some of the flexibility of 35mm prints, according to Eugene Glazer, an analyst at Dean Witter Reynolds, "everything about the system (Spectra) is going to be expensive."[95]

With the technology of the computer displacing the chemistry of film, electronic cameras were expected to revolutionize photography. About a dozen companies had developed prototypes, and Canon introduced a model for sale in 1986, priced steeply at $6,000. Polaroid had developed components for the electronic camera in early 1987, but it did not have a prototype at that period. The development of this product had placed Polaroid in direct competition with not only Kodak, but also against electronic giants such as Sony and Matsushita. The quality of the prints of the existing model was still poor, and Polaroid was optimistic about developing a superior product using its instant photograph technology. According to Booth, "I think it will be five to ten years until an electronic camera hits the mass market, but we're going at it like it might happen tomorrow."[96] Peter Enderlin, analyst at Smith Barney, was of the opinion that although Polaroid was attempting to add enhanced electronics in the instant cameras, it would probably wait until 1988 to introduce such sophisticated technology.[97]

Technical and Industrial Photography

In the technical applications of instant photography, Polaroid had the business all to itself after Kodak was forced to withdraw because of the patent suit. According to Peter Enderlin, "It's a very important and growing business; Polaroid could do very well there over the long run."[98]

Polaroid has attempted to transform itself into a major industrial electronics supplier. The Palette Computer Image Recorder, introduced in 1983, dominated the market in 1986 for making color prints from monochrome computer display.[99] Its industrial and professional type films numbered forty-five in 1986. Medical ultrasonic instrumentation was perhaps one of the most important markets targeted by Polaroid instant film.[100] To secure long-term growth, the company had taken on various aspects of electronic imaging, fiber optics, and medical diagnostics.[101] "It's important that we change perceptions about the sort of products Polaroid has" said Robert Delahunt, Polaroid's Vice-President of Worldwide Industrial Marketing. "What really counts is that the marketplace perceives and understands that we will support these products. We'll be plotting a course to grow our industrial market to a healthy one-third of sales."[102]

Magnetic Media

When Polaroid decided to enter the magnetic imaging business in videotapes and floppy discs, it had acted clearly on its strategic vision: the technology involved solving the same kind of problems it had encountered in its film-making operation.[103] Booth considered both the products as "two explosive growth markets" and relied on Polaroid's name recognition to draw market share. Because of unforseen difficulties in competing in unfamiliar commodity businesses, those ventures had, however, yielded mixed results.[104]

Polaroid's videocassettes were estimated to occupy a 10% share of the approximate $1 billion U.S. videocassette market in 1986.[105] Its competitors included 3M, TDK, and Sony, which were each estimated to hold between a 15% and 20% market share. Polaroid offered a full line of premium quality tapes manufactured by JVC (VHS format), Sony (Beta format) and Toshiba (8mm format) to Polaroid specifications. "The Polaroid name has translated well into the videocassette category," according to Peter Enderlin, photo marketing analyst with Smith Barney, Harnes Upham & Company.[106] In February, 1985, Polaroid also began marketing an 8mm video camera recorder made by Toshiba Corporation, the Japanese electronics giant.[107]

However, Polaroid had not been very successful in the super-competitive $600 million to $700 million U.S. floppy-disc market. The market, which was established to be growing at a rate of 40% annually, was divided among fifty-two firms, most of them small veterans except for Kodak, Hitachi, 3M and Fuji.[108] Price was a weapon being used by some manufacturers in the crowded marketplace, even though Polaroid believed that buyers would not "jeopardize quality by shopping cost."[109] Nevertheless, Polaroid had lost money and according to Booth, "We're still struggling in the floppy disc area. We have to get our marketing act together."[110] Polaroid was developing a high density floppy disk and if it was able to deliver on time and at the right price, it could become the first significant product outside of photography. Expressing his enthusiasm about the product, Booth said, "High-density floppy disks could very quickly become a $50-million-a-year business for us."[111] In 1985, Polaroid purchased a major portion of Verbatim Corporation's Data Encore division, which included disc duplication systems and proprietary data protection systems. Polaroid also established a proprietary Data Rescue Service, which recovered data lost by Polaroid disc users.[112]

FUTURE DIRECTIONS

Revenues were expected to continue rising in 1987, even though they were not expected to grow at a rate higher than 20%, possibly because of a higher tax rate. The emphasis currently was on the sale of cameras, where the markup was far lower than it was on film. According to Value Line projections, the Spectra mix could cause a shift to a higher percentage of more profitable film in 1987. Polaroid was expected to enjoy another year of extra sales as a direct outcome of Kodak's departure from the instant scene.[113] Earnings for 1987 were projected at $3.65 per share versus 1986's calculated at $3.34. The estimated earning for 1987, however, did not include the potentially large damage award from Eastman Kodak resulting from the successful patent infringement suit.[114]

The immediate issue facing Polaroid was how to keep consumers' enthusiasm for the Spectra system high, until Polaroid was able to develop the electronic camera using its instant photographic technology, for mass market introduction. The electronic camera was a big gamble considering the competition it would face from electronic giants such as Sony, Matsushita, and its traditional rival Kodak. For the short term Polaroid had little choice but to proceed with instant photography. Practically all its assets were invested in manufacturing and marketing instant products, and 60% of its sales came from consumer photography. Recent diversifications into magnetic media products had been modest in scale and in success.[115] Polaroid's goal of entering the high-density floppy disk business and being successful was dependent on how soon it could develop the product and at what price.

Outlining corporate strategy for the next several years, Booth emphasized that instant imaging would continue to be the major focus; however, Polaroid would devote a significant portion of its creative resources to fiber optics, medical diagnostics, photovoltaics, memory system, and flexible-liquid-crystal display, for long-term growth. He reaffirmed his commitment to a goal of attaining 10% return on shareholders' equity in the next few years.[116]

NOTES

1. U.S. Department of Commerce, Domestic & International Business Administration: *U.S. Industrial Outlook 1987*, (Washington, D.C.: U.S. Government Printing Office, 1987), p. 35-1.

2. *Ibid.*, p. 35-1.

3. *Ibid.*, p. 35-1

4. *Ibid.*, p. 35-1.

5. *Ibid.*, p. 35-1.

6. *Ibid.*, p. 35-2.

7. *Ibid.*, p. 35-2.

8. Polaroid Corporation, *Fact Book & Financial Summary: 1973–1983*, 1984, p. 4.

9. John Teresko, "Snap, Snap: It's a New Picture at Polaroid," *Industry Week*, October 1, 1984, p. 65.

10. *Ibid.*

11. *Ibid.*

12. *Ibid.*, p. 68.

13. Mark Mehler, "Focusing in on Polaroid's Future," *Financial World*, November 28–December 11, 1984, p. 41.

14. Alex Taylor III, "Kodak Scrambles to Refocus," *Fortune*, March 3, 1987, p. 36.

15. Brian Dumaine, "How Polaroid Flashed Back," *Fortune*, February 16, 1987, p. 72.

16. Alex Beam, "A Troubled Polaroid Is Tearing Down the House That Land Built," *Business Week*, April 29, 1985, p. 51.

17. Dumaine, "How Polaroid Flashed Back," p. 72.

18. *Ibid.*

19. Gay Jervey, "Polaroid Develops Marketing Orientation," *Advertising Age*, January 30, 1984, p. 4.

20. Dumaine, "How Polaroid Flashed Back," p. 72.

21. Alex Beam, "Is Polaroid Playing to a Market That Just Isn't There," *Business Week*, April 7, 1986, p. 83.

22. *Ibid.*

23. Clem Morgelle, "Booth: Creating a New Polaroid," *Dun's Business Month*, August 1985, p. 51.

24. Beam, "Is Polaroid Playing to a Market That Just Isn't There," p. 83.

25. Morgelle, "Booth: Creating a New Polaroid," p. 51.

26. *Ibid.*

27. Beam, "A Troubled Polaroid Is Tearing Down the House That Land Built," p. 51.

28. *Ibid.*

29. Morgelle, "Booth: Creating a New Polaroid," p. 52.

30. Beam, "A Troubled Polaroid Is Tearing Down the House That Land Build," p. 51.

31. Morgelle, "Booth: Creating a New Polaroid," p. 52.

32. Teresko, "Snap, Snap: It's a New Picture at Polaroid," p. 68.

33. Mehler, "Focusing in on Polaroid's Future," p. 40.

34. Beam, "Is Polaroid Playing to a Market That Just Isn't There," p. 83.

35. Beam, "A Troubled Polaroid Is Tearing Down the House That Land Built," p. 51.

36. Beam, "Is Polaroid Playing to a Market That Just Isn't There," p. 83.

37. Beam, "A Troubled Polaroid Is Tearing Down the House That Land Built," p. 51.

38. *Business Week*, May 13, 1985, p. 36.

39. Polaroid Corporation, *1985 Annual Report*, p. 6.

40. *Fact Book & Financial Summary: 1973–1983*, p. 4.

41. *Ibid.*, p. 5.

42. Polaroid Corporation, *1986 First Quarter Financial Report*, p. 18.

43. Polaroid Corporation, *1985 Annual Report*, p. 8.

44. *Ibid.*

45. *Ibid.*, p. 10.

46. Polaroid Corporation, *1986 Fourth Quarter Sales & Earnings Report*, p. 3.

47. Polaroid Corporation, *1985 Annual Report*, p. 14.

48. *Ibid.*, p. 14.

49. Beam, "A Troubled Polaroid Is Tearing Down the House That Land Built," p. 51.

50. *Business Week*, April 15, 1985, p. 52.

51. Polaroid Corporation, *1985 Annual Report*, pp. 48–50.

52. Alex Beam, "Spectra Instant Success Gives Polaroid a Shot in the Arm," *Business Week*, November 3, 1986, p. 32.

53. Polaroid Corporation, *1986 Fourth Quarter Sales & Earnings Report*, p. 4.

54. Beam, "Spectra Instant Success Gives Polaroid a Shot in the Arm," p. 32.

55. Mehler, "Focusing in on Polaroid's Future," p. 41.

56. Dumaine, "How Polaroid Flashed Back," p. 72.

57. *Wall Street Journal—Western Edition*, September 10, 1986, p. 43, col. 3.

58. Polaroid Corporation, *1986 First Quarter Financial Report*, p. 18.

59. *Business Week*, June 24, 1985, p. 98.

60. Dumaine, "How Polaroid Flashed Back," p. 72.

61. Timothy Harper, "Spectra Clicks Instantly in Moslem Market," *Advertising Age*, November 3, 1986, p. 12.

62. Taylor, "Kodak Scrambles to Refocus," pp. 34–36.

63. Lisa E. Phillips, "Spectra Unites Polaroid's Family," *Advertising Age*, October 6, 1986, p. 4.

64. *Ibid.*, p. 100.

65. *Ibid.*

66. Dumaine, "How Polaroid Flashed Back," p. 72.

67. Beam, "Spectra Instant Success Gives Polaroid a Shot in the Arm," p. 32.

68. Phillips, "Spectra Unites Polaroid's Family," p. 4.

69. Alex Taylor III, "Spectra Not Clicking—Yet," *Advertising Age*, June 2, 1986, p. 3.

70. *Ibid.*, p. 89.

71. Polaroid Corporation, *1985 Annual Report*, p. 6.

72. Harper, "Spectra Clicks Instantly in Moslem Market," p. 12.

73. Beam, "Spectra Instant Success Gives Polaroid a Shot in the Arm," p. 32.

74. Polaroid Corporation, *1986 Fourth Quarter Sales & Earnings Report*, p. 3.

75. Polaroid Corporation, *1985 10-K Form*, p. 3.

76. *1985 Annual Report*, p. 12.

77. *Ibid.*

78. Polaroid Corporation, *10-K Form*, p. 4.

79. Phillips, "Spectra Unites Polaroid's Family," p. 100.

80. Harper, "Spectra Clicks Instantly in Moslem Market," p. 12.

81. Jervey, "Polaroid Develops Marketing Orientation," p. 4.

82. Phillips, "Spectra Unites Polaroid's Family," p. 100.

83. *Ibid.*

84. Harper, "Spectra Clicks Instantly in Moslem Market," p. 12.

85. Polaroid Corporation, *1985 Annual Report*, p. 46.

86. Beam, "Is Polaroid Playing to a Market That Just Isn't There," p. 83.

87. Jervey, "Polaroid Develops Marketing Orientation," p. 4.

88. Harper, "Polaroid Clicks Instantly in Moslem Market," p. 12.

89. Taylor, "Kodak Scrambles to Refocus," pp. 34–36.

90. *Advertising Age*, September 3, 1986, p. 76.

91. *Ibid.*, p. 36.

92. Dumaine, "How Polaroid Flashed Back," p. 73.

93. *Ibid.*

94. Taylor, "Kodak Scrambles to Refocus," p. 36.

95. Lisa Phillips, "Specter of Spectra Hangs over Kodak; Can Polaroid Stem Slide," *Advertising Age*, March 24, 1986, p. 3.

96. Dumaine, "How Polaroid Flashed Back," p. 76.

97. *Advertising Age*, September 3, 1986, p. 76.

98. Taylor, "Kodak Scrambles to Refocus," pp. 34–36.

99. Gail Bronson, "Watching the Wrong Birdie," *Forbes*, April 28, 1986, p. 96.

100. Mehler, "Focusing in on Polaroid's Future," p. 41.

101. Harper, "Spectra Clicks Instantly in Moslem Market," p. 12.

102. Teresko, "Snap, Snap: It's a New Picture at Polaroid," p. 68.

103. *Ibid.*

104. Bronson, "Watching the Wrong Birdie," p. 100.

105. Polaroid Corporation, *1986 Fourth Quarter Sales & Earnings Report*, p. 3.

106. Harper, "Spectra Clicks Instantly in Moslem Market," p. 12.

107. Beam, "A Troubled Polaroid Is Tearing Down the House That Land Built," p. 51.

108. Harper, "Spectra Clicks Instantly in Moslem Market," p. 12.

109. Teresko, "Snap, Snap: It's a New Picture at Polaroid," p. 68.

110. Bronson, "Watching the Wrong Birdie," p. 100.

111. Dumaine, "How Polaroid Flashed Back," p. 76.

112. Harper, "Spectra Clicks Instantly in Moslem Market," p. 12.

113. *Standard & Poor's Corporation Descriptions*, Standard & Poor's Corporation Publishers, November 6, 1986.

114. *Ibid.*

115. Beam, "Is Polaroid Playing to a Market That Just Isn't There," p. 83.

116. Polaroid Corporation, *1986 First Quarter Financial Report*, pp. 12–13.

Xerox Corporation: Proposed Diversification

J. DAVID HUNGER ● THOMAS CONQUEST ● WILLIAM MILLER

In the autumn of 1982, David Kearns was facing some difficult problems as the new Chief Executive Officer of the Xerox Corporation. His company had recently posted a 39% drop in third quarter earnings. This was Xerox's fourth quarterly decline in a row and the picture didn't appear any brighter for the current quarter. Much of the profit decline had been attributed to narrow profit margins brought on by steep price-cutting on many copier models in response to increasing competition, especially from the Japanese. In addition, profits had been reduced by the severance costs of trimming its work force; by the strength of the dollar, which eroded the dollar values of sales made abroad; and particularly, by the sluggish economy. Xerox had been forced to reduce its work force by 2,174 in 1981, down to 120,981 people worldwide. This was the first such reduction in the company's history. Further reductions occurred in 1982 and more were predicted for the coming year. Kearns had watched Xerox's share of the plain paper copier market slip from 95% in the early 1970s to about 45% in 1982. In addition, Xerox stock, which had traded for as high as $172 in 1972, was selling for less than $40 in 1982.

Xerox's attempt to lessen its dependence on the competitive copier market, by moving into the broader office-automation arena, had proved less than spectacular. The Office Products Division has had only one profitable quarter in its seven-year history and racked up losses last year totaling approximately $90 million. Kearns recently admitted to analysts that he did not expect the unit to be profitable until 1984.[1] The division had recently been reorganized in an attempt to more effectively deal with some of these problems. Shortly after the reorganization, however, two of the key executives of the Office Products Division resigned to form their own company. Industry reaction to these resignations and Xerox's proposed acquisition of an insurance company have given rise to reports that Xerox may be somewhat less than enthusiastic about the office-automation marketplace and its strategies to garner a piece of the market.

Wall Street analysts were puzzled over Xerox's recent offer to acquire Crum & Forster, an insurance holding company, for about $1.65 billion in cash and

---

This case was prepared by Professor J. David Hunger, Thomas Conquest, and William Miller of the College of Business, Iowa State University, Ames, Iowa as a basis for class discussion rather than to illustrate either effective or ineffective organizational practices. Copyright © 1984 by J. David Hunger. Presented at the 1984 Workshop of the Midwest Society for Case Research. This case also appears in C. F. Douds (ed.), *Annual Advances in Business Cases, 1984* (Chicago: Midwest Case Writers Association, 1983), pp. 203–242 and *Journal of Management Case Studies*, Vol. I, No. 1 (Spring 1985), pp. 13–35. Reprinted by permission.

securities. The proposed acquisition thrusts Xerox, with a mixed record in diversification efforts, into the property-casualty insurance field, where it has no experience. Kearns has defended the proposed acquisition by saying that it could eventually produce a lot of cash, which Xerox needs to support its vigorous research efforts in its core businesses. He maintained that Xerox's entry into the insurance business would not alter its commitment to the office-automation market, nor would it sap resources from Xerox's basic business.[2] Some analysts felt, however, that the acquisition might have been a defensive move to counter a rumored offer by GTE in late summer 1982 to acquire Xerox Corporation. The offer had apparently been made on a very quiet, friendly basis. The mere presence of such an offer, nevertheless, might have prompted top management to more seriously consider making itself less attractive to an acquiring firm by diversifying out of the high-tech industry and by taking on more debt.[3]

HISTORY

Xerography, from the Greek words for "dry" and "writing," is basically a process that uses static electricity to make copies instantly on plain paper. Every office worker today takes it for granted, but it took Chester Carlson, a patent attorney and amateur physicist, several years of dabbling in his kitchen to discover the fundamental principles of what he called "electrophotography." By 1927 he had enough of a process to patent it, and he set up a small lab behind a beauty parlor in Astoria, Long Island, to pursue his experiments. His breakthrough came on October 22, 1938, when he duplicated a glass slide on which he had written: "10-22-38 ASTORIA."

Selling his process was more difficult and frustrating than inventing it. During the next six years Carlson was turned down by more than twenty companies, including such notables as IBM, RCA, and General Electric. Finally, in 1944, the Battelle Memorial Institute, a nonprofit research organization in Columbus, Ohio, became interested. It signed a royalty-sharing contract with Carlson and began to develop the process. In 1947 Battelle entered into an agreement with a small photographic paper company in Rochester, New York, called Haloid, giving the company the right to develop an "electrophotography" machine. Chester Carlson joined Haloid as a consultant.

Haloid's president, Joseph C. Wilson, had grown up with the business. His grandfather had been one of the company's founders in 1906, and his father had worked for the firm from the start. As Haloid and Battelle continued to develop electrophotography, Wilson decided that the process needed a more distinctive name. A Greek scholar from Ohio State University suggested "xeros" (dry) and "graphien" (writing) to form the word "xerography." The machine itself, they decided, would be called Xerox.

Haloid introduced its first copier in 1949, but it was slow and complicated. Haloid found the early models to be better for making lithography masters than for copying documents, but management was sure they were on the right track. In 1958, they changed the name of the company to Haloid Xerox, and in 1959 the firm marketed the first dependable, easy-to-use document copier.

The 914 copier, so named because it could copy sheets as large as 9 × 14 inches, was very successful, and within three years the company was ranked among the FORTUNE 500. In 1961, management changed the name of the company to Xerox.

Between 1959, when Xerox introduced the world's first convenient office copier, and 1974, its sales exploded from $33 million a year to $3.6 billion; its profits mushroomed from $2 million to $331 million; and the price of its stock soared from $2 a share to $172. The company had grown by 100 times in fifteen years. In that same short period, photocopying machines dramatically transformed the nature of office work. Xerography made carbon paper and mimeograph machines obsolete and drastically reduced typing time. By year-end 1970, Xerox held a dominant position in the world-wide office plain-paper copier marketplace with more than a 95% share of the market.

This monopolistic market share was seriously eroded in the 1970s because of increased competition from many sources. Xerox had built its business by creating the plain-paper copier market and then protecting it with a solid wall of patents, a classic entry barrier to keep out competition. In 1975, however, the company signed a consent decree with the Federal Trade Commission. The decree forced Xerox to license other companies wanting to use its process. The seventeen-year patent protection was also expiring and Xerox's technology could be used by anyone. Recognizing the mature state of the reprographics industry, Xerox has positioned itself, through both horizontal and vertical integration, to become a major competitor in the *Office of the Future* marketplace. In 1981, Xerox executives stated to stockholders in the company's annual report that the overriding corporate objective over the next decade is to be one of the leading companies in providing productivity to the office. "In order to accomplish this," asserted top management, "Xerox must maintain and strengthen its position of leadership in reprographics—as we refer to our total copying and duplicating business—*and* emerge from the 1980's as a leading systems company that is a major factor in automating the office."[4]

MANAGEMENT

David T. Kearns, who had served previously as President and Chief Operating Officer of Xerox, succeeded C. Peter McColough as Chief Executive Officer in May 1982. McColough, who had joined Xerox in 1954 and served as chief executive since 1968, continued as Chairman of the Board. Other key executives and related information are shown in Exhibit 6.1. Xerox's top management has generally been promoted from within. Outside help has been recruited when the company has had to deal with significant changes in strategy or the introduction of new products.

There are nineteen directors on the Xerox board, eight of whom are officers of the corporation. The eleven outside directors include a retired Executive Vice-President of Xerox, two university professors (one from Europe), the Chairman of the Board of Prudential Insurance, a retired Chairman of American Express, the President of the Children's Television Workshop, a Managing Director of

EXHIBIT 6.1 **1982 Top Management, Xerox Corporation**

NAME	TITLE	YEARS WITH XEROX	JOBS PRIOR TO XEROX	EXPERTISE
D. T. Kearns*	Chief Executive Officer	11	IBM: Vice-President of Data Processing	Marketing
W. F. Glavin*	Executive Vice-President	12	IBM: Vice-President Operations	Operations
W. F. Souders*	Executive Vice-President	18		Marketing
J. V. Titsworth*	Executive Vice-President	3	Control Data: Executive Vice-President, Systems	
M. H. Antonini	Group Vice-President	7	Eltra Corp.: Group Vice-President	Operations
			Kaiser Jeep International: Vice-President	
R. D. Firth	Group Vice-President	13	IBM: Various Positions	Personnel
M. Howard*	Senior Vice-President, Chief Financial Officer	12	Shoe Corp. of America: Vice-President	Finance
F. J. Pipp	Group Vice-President	11	Ford Motor Co.	Manufacturing
R. M. Pippitt*	Senior Vice-President	21		Marketing
R. S. Banks	Vice-President & General Counsel	15	E. I. Dupont: Attorney	Legal Affairs
E. K. Damon	Vice-President & Secretary	33		Accounting
S. B. Ross	Vice-President & Controller	16	Macmillan Publishing Co.; C.P.A. Harris, Kerr & Forster: Accountant	Finance
J. S. Crowley*	Executive Vice-President	5	McKinsey & Co.: Sr. Partner and Director	Administration
J. E. Goldman*	Senior Vice-President	14	Ford Motor Co.	Engineering

SOURCE: Xerox *Form 10-K Annual Report*, 1981.

* Also serve on the Board of Directors.

Deutsch Bank AG, the Chairman of an investment firm, a President of a university, and two partners in a Washington-based law firm. Together, the corporation's directors and officers own about 1% of the common stock of the firm.

The corporation introduced an executive long-term incentive plan in 1976 under which approximately 5.4 million shares of common stock have been reserved for issue. In December 1981, the Board of Directors amended the plan to provide for the issuance of incentive stock options as defined in the Economic Recovery Tax Act of 1981. Under the plan, eligible employees may be granted incentive stock rights, incentive stock options, non-qualified stock options, stock appreciation rights, and performance unit rights. Performance rights entitle the employee to receive the value of the performance unit in cash, in shares of common stock, or a combination of the two at the company's discretion. The value of a performance unit is determined by a formula based upon the achievement of specific performance goals. Performance unit rights are payable at the end of a five-year award period.

BUSINESS SEGMENTS	Although Xerox Corporation is organized around a set of groups and divisions, it primarily defines itself in terms of its various businesses. Xerox's principal business segment is reprographics, consisting of the development, manufacture, and marketing of xerographic copiers and duplicators, electronic printing systems, and providing related service. Another significant segment is paper, consisting primarily of the distribution of paper related to reprographic products. The other business segments include electric typewriters, word processors, small computers, facsimile transceivers, toner and other supplies, and publishing education-related materials. Estimated revenues and profits for each product line are shown in Exhibit 6.2.

Reprographics

Xerox manufactures and markets reprographic equipment for lease or purchase. Leasing accounted for over 55% of the company's revenues in 1981. The revenues and profits from this segment depend principally on the number of units of xerographic equipment leased and the usage of these units. In 1981, the Reprographics segment accounted for 72% of revenues.

Copiers

Copying machines have been and still are the largest segment of Xerox's business. However, Xerox has experienced problems in this segment over the past few years. Increased competition from IBM and Kodak in the medium-volume market and Japan in the lower-volume market has significantly decreased Xerox's market share. Competing now with 40 companies selling at least 240 different models, Xerox's share of the plain-paper copier industry in the United States has dropped from 67% to 43% over the past five years. The market, however, has grown in terms of total revenues, from $2.8 billion in 1976 to $7.5 billion in 1981. Competitors imported more than a million units into the country in 1981. Analysts expected this number to increase by 50% in 1982.[5] Xerox faces similar competition worldwide. Current estimates of market share data are presented in Exhibit 6.3.

"We really should have been thinking about the market on a much broader basis," says Kearns.[6] Xerox ignored the low-cost, coated-paper copier that dominated the world copier market before Xerox introduced the first plain-paper copier. But the coated-paper copiers served a market much larger than anyone knew. Xerox has clearly fought back to regain some of its lost market

EXHIBIT 6.2

Estimated Revenues, Operating Profit, and Operating Margins by Product Line, 1981, Xerox Corporation

(Dollar Amounts In Millions)

PRODUCT LINE	REVENUES	OPERATING PROFIT	OPERATING MARGIN (%)
Copiers			
Rentals	$4,805	$ —	—
Sales	1,135	—	—
Paper & supplies	795	—	—
Total	6,735	1,400	20.8
Office products			
Word processing & small computers	310	(22)	—
Facsimile	95	11	11.6
Total	405	(11)	—
Peripherals			
Printing	125	(15)	—
Xerox Computer Services	90	10	11.1
Shugart	200	25	12.5
Century Data	110	10	9.1
Diablo	130	13	10.0
Versatec	75	7	9.3
Kurzweil	5	0.5	10.0
Total	735	50.5	6.9
Other products			
Publishing	320	30	9.4
WUI	175	26	14.9
Other	310	25	8.1
Total	805	81	10.1
TOTAL	$8,680	1,520.5	17.5

SOURCE: *Xerox: A Strategic Analysis* (New York: Northern Business Information, Inc., 1982), p. 6.

share. It has cut prices on its lower-volume models, concentrating on cutting costs to improve profit margins, and decentralizing the management of the reprographics group to enable managers more timely and market-oriented decision-making. Two desktop copiers, the 2350 and 2830, were introduced in 1982 with a selling price of around $3,500 each. A new line of low- and medium-volume copiers will be introduced in January 1983 labeled the "10" series. These copiers will be imported from Fuji Xerox Co. in Japan. "If you can't beat 'em,

EXHIBIT 6.3

Estimated Copier Revenues and Market Share by Geographic Area, 1981, Xerox Corporation

AREA	MARKET SIZE	XEROX REVENUES (MILLIONS OF $)	XEROX MARKET SHARE
U.S.	7,350	$3,160	43%
Europe	4,900	2,200	45%
Japan	1,510	620	41%
Canada	725	410	56%
Other	—	525	—

SOURCE: *Xerox: A Strategic Analysis* (New York: Northern Business Information, Inc., 1982), p. 79.

join 'em," states Peter McColough.[7] To help lower costs, Xerox will also bring in parts and subassemblies from the Japanese affiliate. Production of the new 10 series costs between 40% and 50% less than earlier machines.

Another technique used by Xerox to stay competitive is called *competitive benchmarking*. This means looking carefully at the lowest priced competing copier, determining exactly how it is being produced for less, and developing a plan to make and sell a competitive product.

In large copiers, Xerox still dominates the industry with a 70% market share. This is due mainly to Xerox's large and experienced sales and service staff. Japanese companies currently lack extensive service support and are not seen to offer Xerox much competition in the high-priced copier market in the near future. Xerox has many models in this market with high output rates and sorting capabilities. Prices range from $25,000 to $125,000.

In a maturing market with high competition, Xerox management realizes that the copier segment will not provide growing profits in the long run as the company would like. This realization underlies the company's diversification into office automation. Eugene C. Glazer of Dean Witter Reynolds states, "Eventually the company won't make it if they have to depend only on copiers."[8] In the company's annual report, David Kearns notes, "To continue to succeed in the face of strong competition, Xerox must undergo major and lasting change." Robert D. Firth, however, President of the Reprographics group, maintains, "Our copier business is and will remain the main business of Xerox for the projectable future."[9]

Electronic Printing

Listed under Peripherals in Exhibit 6.2, this segment became a dominant product line in 1977, with the introduction of the 9700 electronic printer. Until March 1982, the electronic-printing segment reported to U.S. copier operations in Rochester. Now established as the Printing Systems Division, it reports directly to corporate headquarters in Stamford, Connecticut. The traditional computer-printout method has been impact printing, with ink ribbons and mechanical printing heads on 11 × 17-inch fan-fold computer paper. Although this printing serves many purposes, Xerox management believes that for periodic reports, forms, proposals, or other information stored on electronic computer data files, non-bulky and clear printouts would be a better alternative. With its electronic printer, Xerox has combined computer technology, lasers, and xerography to design a printer that can print exceptionally clear text on standard $8\frac{1}{2}$ × 11-inch paper. In addition, this printer can print graphics, which cannot be done on most traditional printers, and it has multiple copy and sorting capabilities as well. Xerox management sees electronic printing as playing a large role in the company's future. Customers seem to agree. Jack Jones, Vice-President of the Southern Railway System, states that "the quality of the print is such that everybody is enthusiastic about the smaller page."[10]

In 1980 Xerox developed the 5700 printing system. Priced at $66,000, this unit is designed to be used in an office environment, whereas the 9700 is geared more toward a computer room. The 5700 has the same basic technology as the 9700, but is extremely easy to use and has a touch-control screen to eliminate operator confusion. It can also be connected to Xerox's Ethernet network system, which can link a printer to various word processors or computer terminals on the network. A lower-priced model with many of the same features as the 9700 and 5700 has been released on a limited basis. The 2700, priced at $19,000, is marketed for the small business that can't afford some of the more expensive models.

Xerox has approximately 40% of the global market for electronic printing—slightly behind IBM, with Honeywell a distant third in market share. The market in electronic printing may soon be crowded with heavy competition from Japanese companies, such as Canon and Fujitsu. It is also a market in which new technology can change things drastically. Ink-jet printing and heat-transfer processes are already being considered as printing alternatives.

Currently, electronic printing accounts for only 15% of the $8.7 billion computer-printing market. Predictions for electronic printing are for a $5.8 billion market by 1986. According to Robert Adams, president of Xerox's Printing Systems Division, "The majority of information generated from host computers and word processors will someday be produced by electronic printers."[11] Although Xerox revenues in 1981 from electronic printing were estimated at $125 million by Northern Business Information, Inc., a New York-based research firm, the newly established Printing Systems Division was hoping for $300 million in revenues in 1982 and $2 billion annually in revenues by 1987.[12]

Office Products

The Office Products Division (responsible for electronic typewriters, word processors, and facsimile telecopiers) and the Office Systems Division manufacture and market information processing equipment for use in the *Office of the Future*.

EXHIBIT 6.4

Estimated Office Products Revenues and Market Share by Geographic Area, 1981, Xerox Corporation

(Dollar Amounts in Millions)

SEGMENT	U.S. MARKET SIZE	U.S. XEROX SHARE	XEROX REVENUES		
			U.S.	International	Total
Word processing	1,385	13%	180	115	295
Facsimile telecopiers	165	30%	50	45	95
Small business systems	1,300	1%	10	5	15

SOURCE: *Xerox: A Strategic Analysis* (New York: Northern Business Information, Inc., 1982), p. 115.

Although office products accounted for only 10% of the company's revenues in 1981, the commitment was made several years ago to steer Xerox away from a copier-only company to an information company capable of supplying many types of office information and equipment. Current estimates of market share data for both divisions are provided in Exhibit 6.4.

The 860 Information Processing System, first marketed in 1979, is a word-processing workstation with full text-editing capability. It is medium priced and designed for use by professional and clerical personnel. It has limited programming capability. Xerox introduced its 8010 Star Professional work-station in 1981 for a price of $17,000. It is designed for use by managers and professionals to perform word and data processing tasks with a minimum of training. Its ease of use makes it very desirable for the preparation of presentations and reports.

In 1981, the 820 Information Processor was developed to service a broad range of needs. It can be used as a limited professional workstation for small businesses that cannot afford the Star. It can also be used as a business or personal computer or a word processor. Prices for the microcomputer system start at $3,000 and options for word processing capability bring the price up to $6,500. These prices make the model very competitive with the Apple II or Radio Shack TRS Model III personal computer and also with the IBM Displaywriter and Wang Wangwriter word processors. Xerox also introduced in 1981 a new line of electronic typewriters, called Memorywriters, and an inexpensive (under $1,000) personal computer.

Probably the biggest gamble that Xerox is taking in the office product segment is its *Ethernet* concept. Ethernet is a communication network, designed for short physical distances (intra-building), that will connect many pieces of office equipment by coaxial cable together into one information system. This concept allows several word processors or professional workstations to use common databanks or printing facilities that are in different physical locations within the building. Xerox's marketing strategy is to force its Ethernet network as an industry standard so that all manufacturers of office equipment will be pressured to make their equipment compatible.

Peter McColough describes the development this way: "We can go into your company and tell you that you don't have to stick with Xerox. You can go to DEC, Intel, or anybody else. The IBM approach says: 'We'll put our system in there with IBM equipment, but you won't be able to get much else.'"[13] This compatibility argument is an extremely effective marketing tool for customers leery of total commitment. The automated office product market is highly competitive and expanding. Major competitors include IBM, Wang, Exxon, Hewlett-Packard, and dozens of smaller companies.

Many problems currently face Xerox's office product divisions. Contributions to profits have been nonexistent for the last several years. Although Xerox has intentionally sacrificed profits to get a jump on competitors, the new products are not selling as management had hoped they would by this time. Of the 300 Ethernet system installations planned for 1981, only 45 were completed. Marketing may be to blame. The company acknowledged that the 820 had met with little success in the retail sales environment because many had perceived the machine as an entry into the home computer market, not the office. Software development problems created delays for the full-scale production of the 8010 Star. In addition, the country's prolonged recession has prevented companies from making commitments in office automation.

Disagreements between top management and division management resulted in the resignations of Donald Massaro, President of Xerox Office Systems, and David E. Liddle, Vice-President. The 39-year-old Massaro had founded Shugart Associates, a leading computer-memory manufacturer that had been acquired by Xerox in 1977. Liddle, a 10-year Xerox veteran, had worked closely with Massaro to develop the Star and Ethernet. In an interview with *Business Week*, Massaro asserted that he resigned because he wanted complete control of Xerox's office systems effort. He conceded, however, that in a corporation like Xerox in which 75% of the revenues and almost all the profits came from copiers and duplicators, "it was frustrating trying to get the attention of top management."[14] Analysts felt that Massaro's resignation was an expected result of the battle between the "old Xerox," epitomized by the conservative East Coast copier group, and the "new Xerox," epitomized by the freewheeling California-type entrepreneurial Massaro. A consultant who had worked extensively with Xerox suggested that a real schism had developed. "The copier people didn't like the idea they were being used as a cash cow and Xerox's office systems people could spend all this money without making any."[15]

In a report from Strategic, Inc., before the Office Products Division was split, the company's President, Michael Killen, boldly predicted, "Xerox will fail because the Office Products Division will fail; and the Office Products Division will fail because Ethernet will fail."[16] Killen's rationale is that Ethernet is built on base-band modulation techniques, which limit information over the network to interactive data. Broad-band modulation techniques, on the other hand, although more complex with which to interface components, allow video and voice communications as well as interactive data.

Ethernet may not become the formal industry standard supported by the Institute of Electrical and Electronics Engineers. Much squabbling is still going on over this issue. Hewlett-Packard, for example, has dropped its support of Ethernet in favor of the slightly different IEEE 802 proposed local-area-net-working (LAN) standard. Nevertheless, Xerox's management plans to continue working to get Ethernet accepted by the industry as an informal standard even though IBM is said to be working on its own version of Ethernet.

Many people continue to believe that Ethernet is a viable system. John W. King, an industry analyst, says, "Ethernet is alive and well and has excellent prospects through the 1980s." King sees Ethernet and broad band networks working together.[17] Many new electronic components have been developed to simplify connecting equipment to Ethernet. Digital Equipment Corporation (DEC) and Intel agreed to a joint venture with Xerox in May 1980. DEC's role was to provide design expertise in the area of communication transceivers and computer networks. Intel provided expertise in integrated circuits for communications functions. Because Xerox has based all its products in the office segment around Ethernet, its future is of vital strategic importance.

Other Segments

Xerox is one of the largest distributors in the world of standard-cut sheet paper used for writing, typing, copying, and other office needs. In addition, it also distributes many types of office chemicals for use with its machines.

Xerox's peripheral subsidiaries are generally composed of acquisitions that helped to vertically integrate the company. Shugart Associates manufactures floppy disk drives, Diablo Systems, Inc. manufactures daisy wheel printers (a substitute technology for IBM's famous typewriter ball), Century Data Systems manufactures rigid disk drives, Versatec manufactures electrostatic printers and plotters, and Kurzweil makes optical scanners. Xerox Computer Services was established in 1970 as an outgrowth of its Scientific Data Systems acquisition and offers timesharing and software packages. Other products and services include published materials, information services, medical systems, and a credit service.

MARKETING

In the past, Xerox has traditionally been a single-product company, selling copiers to large businesses through its own sales and service force. This has changed over the past several years as it has diversified its product lines and redefined its customers. All the company's product lines have been revamped to offer a wide range of products, not only to larger companies, but to smaller businesses as well. With the advent of Ethernet, a systems approach to marketing has become necessary.

To better meet the distribution problems associated with the company's new concepts, Xerox is experimenting with new distribution techniques. Independent distributors and dealers have been contracted to sell products not only to end users, but also to Original Equipment Manufacturers (OEMs) who resell the products as part of a larger system. These distribution channels reduce the company's expenses, thereby increasing profit margins while unburdening the company's own sales force. Xerox also plans to use retail chains as well as its own retail stores to reach small business people. It has already opened approximately thirty retail stores throughout the United States and management has plans to open more nationwide. All outlets are named *The Xerox Store* and are designed to make the small business person comfortable in a store with a familiar name and reputation. In addition to selling Xerox's equipment, these retail outlets also carry brand name equipment of other manufacturers (including competitors) for home and office use. Most of this other equipment complements Xerox's own product line. This supermarket approach includes the selling of Apple Computers, Hewlett-Packard calculators, Matsushita dictating machines, as well as a host of other products.[18]

Xerox is also using new promotions as part of its marketing strategy. To better compete with Japanese firms for the small business person's dollar, management has cut prices on many products. Mail order and telephone campaigns are also being used to reach smaller firms. For the larger customers, Xerox has been offering quantity discounts as an incentive to buy total systems.

According to industry analysts, Xerox has three major marketing strengths. First, its sales and service staff is the largest in the industry. These people have excellent sales skills and are well known in most major companies. Second, the company has large financial resources to fund challenging new product developments. No other company, with the possible exception of IBM, could have tackled the highly complex Star workstation project. Third, the Xerox name is a household word, and gives the business person a feeling of confidence when it comes to getting the product serviced.

If there is any weakness in the company's marketing department, analysts agree it is its lack of expertise in marketing complex office products and systems. There is apparently a world of difference between marketing stand-alone copying machines and marketing technically more involved information handling and processing systems. In addition, retailing is a new field for Xerox and one in which it has no previous experience. There appears to be some confusion among customers as to the purpose of several particular products. For example, Xerox's efforts to sell the 820 to the retail market through Xerox stores as well as distributors has been costly and somewhat ineffective. Jack Darcy, Senior Vice-President of Kierulff Distributors, an independent distributor that sells equipment from many manufacturers to industrial users, says, "There is such a difference in the mentality to run a successful retail operation and to run a successful industrial business. At Kierulff, we're pointing our effort totally toward the industrial. Xerox, as I understand it, is a consumer product. We're not interested."[19]

FINANCIAL

Consolidated income statements and balance sheets for the five-year period of 1977–1981 are shown in Exhibits 6.5, 6.6, and 6.7. Although Xerox's management considers the firm to be strong financially, it can be seen that both revenues and profits have been increasing at a decreasing rate. From 1964 to 1974, net income had grown 24% per year on 30% annual revenue gains. From 1975 to 1981, revenues increased 15%, compounded annually, while earnings for the same period increased by slightly over 12% per year. In the first nine months of 1982, Xerox's net income was $370 million, down 24% from the same period the year earlier. Revenues were $6.24 billion, slightly down from $6.28 billion during the same period in 1981.

Data outlining Xerox's common-stock performance is given in Exhibit 6.8. The company's stock, which made millionaires of several early investors, has

EXHIBIT 6.5

Consolidated Income Statements 1977–1981, Xerox Corporation

(Dollar Amounts in Millions, Except Per-Share Data)

	1981	1980	1979	1978	1977
Operating revenues					
Rentals and services	$5,279.6	$5,151.6	$4,606.3	$4,130.5	$3,713.8
Sales	3,411.4	3,044.9	2,390.1	1,887.5	1,368.2
Total operating revenues	8,691.0	8,196.5	6,996.4	6,018.0	5,082.0
Costs and expenses					
Cost of rentals & services	2,269.5	2,167.5	1,905.0	1,691.6	1,477.1
Cost of sales	1,570.8	1,435.6	1,075.1	770.6	579.8
Research & development	526.3	435.8	378.1	311.0	269.0
Selling, administrative, & general	3,095.0	2,882.1	2,432.9	2,089.0	1,760.9
Total costs & expenses	7,461.6	6,921.0	5,791.1	4,862.2	4,086.8
Operating income	1,229.4	1,275.5	1,205.3	1,155.8	995.2
Other income less interest expense	(49.5)	3.6	1.7	(64.6)	(82.4)
Income before income taxes	1,179.9	1,279.1	1,207.0	1,091.2	912.8
Income taxes	454.4	611.8	587.2	528.0	440.5
Income before outside shareholders' interests	725.5	667.3	619.8	563.2	472.3
Outside shareholders' interests	127.3	102.4	104.8	86.7	68.3
Net income	$ 598.2	$ 564.9	$ 515.0	$ 476.5	$ 404.0
Average common shares outstanding	84.5	84.4	84.1	84.1	83.9
Net income per common share	$ 7.08	$ 6.69	$ 6.12	$ 5.91	$ 5.15

SOURCE: *Moody's 1982 Industrial Manual*, p. 4672 and *1981 Annual Report*, Xerox Corporation, p. 29.

EXHIBIT 6.6

Consolidated Balance Sheets 1977–1981, Xerox Corporation

(Dollar Amounts in Millions)

	1981	1980	1979	1978	1977
Assets					
Current assets					
Cash	$ 45.2	$ 86.8	$ 42.2	$ 57.7	$ 73.3
Bank time deposits	234.0	228.8	267.7	412.0	338.4
Marketable securities	148.0	207.3	447.7	269.8	280.3
Trade receivables	1,245.3	1,163.8	1,120.4	927.5	731.0
Receivable from Xerox Credit Corp.	178.2	196.3	—	—	—
Accrued revenues	403.3	376.8	259.3	211.3	191.6
Inventories	1,131.9	1,090.2	785.8	601.8	525.3
Other current assets	230.2	210.0	180.5	158.7	128.7
Total current assets	3,616.1	3,560.0	3,103.6	2,638.8	2,268.6
Trade receivables due after one year	245.5	199.4	274.2	216.2	104.9
Rental equipment & related inventories	1,905.1	1,966.8	1,736.4	1,501.2	1,397.7
Land, buildings, & equipment	1,438.7	1,410.4	1,222.3	1,111.3	1,029.2
Investments, at equity	319.6	226.6	105.7	67.9	63.2
Other assets	149.4	150.6	111.4	230.3	183.0
Total assets	$7,674.4	$7,513.8	$6,553.6	$5,765.7	$5,046.6
Liabilities and Shareholders' Equity					
Current liabilities					
Notes payable	$ 224.2	$ 208.4	$ 96.3	$ 64.5	$ 109.6
Current portion of long-term debt	96.3	80.0	40.2	52.4	57.5
Accounts payable	340.2	315.8	325.1	273.2	209.4
Salaries, profit-sharing, other accruals	909.9	907.3	689.5	600.7	475.1
Income taxes	346.5	425.4	426.0	328.8	232.3
Other current liabilities	163.7	147.8	102.2	81.3	61.7
Total current liabilities	2,080.8	2,084.7	1,679.3	1,400.9	1,145.6
Long-term debt	869.5	898.3	913.0	938.3	1,020.0
Other noncurrent liabilities	145.0	133.0	127.9	97.2	46.1
Deferred income taxes	247.0	142.7	110.4	62.7	—
Deferred investment tax credits	108.9	85.6	70.1	63.2	59.6
Outside shareholders' interests in equity of subsidiaries	495.6	539.5	431.5	349.0	315.2
Shareholders' equity					
Common stock, $1 par value authorized 100,000 shares	84.3	84.3	83.9	83.8	80.1
Class B stock, $1 par value authorized $600,000 shares	.2	.2	.2	.3	.3
Additional paid-in capital	306.0	304.9	286.8	286.0	257.3

	1981	1980	1979	1978	1977
Retained earnings	3,500.1	3,155.4	2,866.2	2,501.3	2,142.0
Cumulative translation adjustments	(150.1)	98.8	—	—	—
Total	3,740.5	3,643.6	3,237.1	2,871.4	2,479.7
Deduct class B stock receivables	12.9	13.6	15.7	17.0	19.6
Total shareholders' equity	3,727.6	3,630.0	3,221.4	2,854.4	2,460.1
Total liabilities and shareholders' equity	$7,674.4	$7,513.8	$6,553.6	$5,765.7	$5,046.6

SOURCE: *Moody's 1982 Industrial Manual*, p. 4673 and *1981 Annual Report*, Xerox Corporation, pp. 30–31.

EXHIBIT 6.7

Business Segment Data, 1979–1981*, Xerox Corporation
(Dollar Amounts in Millions)

	1981	1980	1979
Reprographics			
Rentals and services	$4,974.2	$4,840.9	$4,313.1
Sales	1,419.2	1,224.1	990.6
Total operating revenues	6,393.4	6,065.0	5,303.7
Operating profit	1,355.6	1,326.1	1,243.0
Identifiable assets	5,172.2	5,212.4	4,544.9
Depreciation	717.9	718.6	664.6
Capital expenditures	1,202.3	1,108.0	1,004.0
Paper			
Operating revenues (sales)	554.5	573.6	446.4
Operating profit	34.9	44.2	34.9
Identifiable assets	202.6	220.9	185.5
Depreciation	8.0	8.3	7.7
Capital expenditures	11.0	13.1	11.3
Other Businesses			
Rentals and services	449.3	409.1	357.1
Sales	1,437.7	1,247.2	953.1
Transfers between segments	37.4	34.0	16.6
Total operating revenues	1,924.4	1,690.3	1,326.8
Operating profit	107.8	124.7	106.1
Identifiable assets	1,511.2	1,398.0	1,171.5
Depreciation	96.8	98.3	90.3
Capital expenditures	188.1	192.4	179.7

SOURCE: *1981 Annual Report*, Xerox Corporation, p. 36.

* Figures do not sum to data in consolidated income statements because of various adjustments and expenses due to foreign currency gains and losses and general expense items not included in this exhibit.

EXHIBIT 6.8   **Stock Performance, 1973–1982, Xerox Corporation**

	1982	1981	1980	1979	1978
High price ($)	41.8	64.0	71.8	69.1	64.0
Low price ($)	27.1	37.4	48.6	52.6	40.5
Book value ($)	46.45	44.11	42.90	38.29	34.72
Earnings per share ($)	—	7.08	7.33	6.69	5.77
P/E ratio	—	7.1	8.2	9.0	8.9
Dividends per share ($)	3.00	3.00	2.80	2.40	2.00
Earnings yield (%)	—	14.1	12.2	11.1	11.2
Dividend yield (%)	—	5.9	4.7	4.0	3.9
Common shares (million)	84.55	84.51	84.48	84.14	80.24

SOURCE: *Value Line Investment Survey*, November 12, 1982.

recently traded as low as $27 per share, bringing its P/E ratio to an all-time low. In addition, Xerox stock reacted negatively, falling over $3 per share, to the news of the proposed acquisition of Crum & Forster. Investment analysts have recently advised customers to postpone purchases of Xerox stock "until current operations show some sign of life."[20]

Xerox attributes much of the earnings decline to greatly reduced profit margins, as shown in Exhibit 6.9. The company's after-tax profit margin in the third quarter of 1982 was equal to 4.7% of sales, down from 7.9% a year earlier. In the first nine months of 1982, the profit margin was 5.9% compared with 7.7% in 1981. Xerox top management attributes the squeeze on profit margins to several factors:

1. Increased competition has forced price reductions on many copier models, especially in the low-volume segment where competition has been the fiercest. Reductions of up to 27% have been seen on many models.

2. Increased revenues have occurred in the low-volume copier segment, in which margins are traditionally lower. (See Exhibit 6.10.)

3. There have been increasing expenditures for research and development, and capital expenditures. In 1981, Xerox spent $526 million and $1.4 billion for these items, respectively. Of the 1981 total for capital expenditures, $1.1 billion was for additions to rental equipment and related inventories, and the balance was for additions to land, buildings, and equipment.

4. Revenues and net income from foreign operations represented 44% and 41%, respectively, of the company's 1981 total. Because of the strong dollar, it is estimated that foreign-currency translations created a $64.5 million loss to Xerox in 1981. If unfavorable currency impacts were excluded, international revenue growth would have been 13% in 1981 over 1980, slightly higher than domestic growth.

1977	1976	1975	1974	1973
58.8	68.4	87.6	127.1	170.0
43.1	48.8	46.4	49.0	114.8
30.76	27.30	23.97	22.14	18.89
5.06	4.51	3.07	4.18	3.80
9.9	13.2	20.8	22.3	39.0
1.50	1.10	1.00	1.00	.90
10.1	7.6	4.8	4.5	2.6
3.0	1.9	1.6	1.1	.6
80.37	79.83	79.57	79.24	27.17

EXHIBIT 6.9   **After-Tax Margins, 1967–1982, Xerox Corporation**

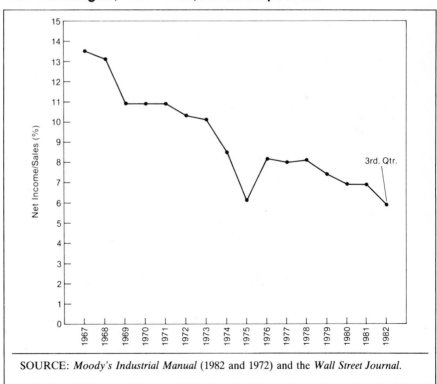

SOURCE: *Moody's Industrial Manual* (1982 and 1972) and the *Wall Street Journal.*

SOURCE: Moody's Industrial Manual (1982 and 1972) *and the Wall Street Journal.*

EXHIBIT 6.10

Copier Revenues and Operating Profit by Market Segment, 1981, Xerox Corporation

(Dollar Amounts in Millions)

SEGMENT	REVENUE ($)	OPERATING PROFIT ($)	OPERATING MARGINS (%)
Low volume	2,020	300	14.9
Medium volume	2,265	700	30.9
High volume	1,835	365	19.9
Paper & supplies	795	70	8.8
TOTAL	6,915	1,435	20.8

SOURCE: *Xerox: A Strategic Analysis* (New York: Northern Business Information, Inc., 1982), p. 80.

5. The reduction of overhead cost the company $63 million in severance costs in 1981.

RESEARCH AND DEVELOPMENT

The Xerox research and development program is directed mostly to the development of new and improved copying and duplicating equipment and supplies, facsimile and digital communications equipment, computer peripheral equipment and services, as well as to the development of new products and capabilities in other areas related to the broad field of information systems.

The company's Palo Alto Research Center (PARC), established in Palo Alto, California, in 1969 by then-President Peter McColough, was to provide the technology Xerox needed to become "an architect of information" in the office. Flourishing under a hands-off policy by corporate headquarters, PARC soon developed an excellent reputation within the research community. The Center developed technology in computer-aided design, artificial intelligence, and laser printers. Xerox's ability to design custom chips for use in future copiers comes largely from PARC. Nevertheless, analysts contend that Xerox has been unable to really take advantage of PARC's research on computerized office systems, its original reason for being. Arguing that Xerox's sheer size slows decision-making, analysts state that the corporation has trouble translating first-rate research into profitable products. It is simply unable to move quickly into small, fast-changing markets.

Loose management by headquarters also may have encouraged PARC to go into the development of products that were not necessarily in line with the corporation's needs. For example, PARC worked in the mid-1970s to develop the Alto, a computer with some of the attributes of a personal computer, which was supposed to serve as a research prototype. Alto and its software became so popular inside Xerox that some researchers began to develop it as a commercial product. This put PARC into direct conflict with Xerox's product development group, which was developing a rival machine called the Star. Because the Star was in line with the company's expressed product strategy of developing complete office systems, the Alto was ignored by top management and emphasis was placed on the Star and the Ethernet concept. The conflict between PARC and Xerox's top management has resulted in a number of researchers leaving PARC for firms such as Atari and Apple.

Jack Goldman, Xerox's former research chief, suggests that a big company like Xerox wants every product to be a "home run" in order to justify the costs of marketing and development. Another former employee says that top management "followed the big-bang strategy. They wanted to build absolutely the best office system instead of taking things bit by bit."[21]

In 1981, Xerox incurred $526 million in research and development expenses, approximately 6% of total revenues. Less than $35 million went to PARC. The 6% of total revenues represents less than the average percentage of research and development to sales of some of Xerox's major competitors (Hewlett-Packard, 9.7%; Apple Computer, 6.3%; Burroughs, 6.5%; Commodore, 5.9%; Digital Equipment Corp., 9.0%; Honeywell, 7.0%; IBM, 5.5%; Wang, 7.5%, CPT, 5.0%).[22]

OPERATIONS AND INTERNATIONAL

Xerox's principal xerographic facilities are located on a 1,047-acre site owned in Webster, New York, a suburb of Rochester. Corporate headquarters were moved to Stamford, Connecticut, in 1969 in order that corporate attention would be given not only to xerography, but to xerography overseas, to computers, data processing, education and other extensions of activity generated by acquisitions, mergers, and related research. The Office Products Division, recently reorganized into Office Products and Office Systems, is located in Dallas, Texas. The Office Systems Division, located in Palo Alto, California, is responsible for marketing local, network-based office systems to end users. In forming these two divisions, Xerox retained centralized marketing, sales, and manufacturing functions with the Office Products Division in Dallas.

Xerox's largest interests outside the United States are the Rank Xerox Companies—composed of Rank Xerox Limited of London, England, Rank Xerox Holding B.V. of the Netherlands, and their respective subsidiaries— and the other subsidiaries jointly owned by Xerox and the Rank Organization. Approximately 51% of the voting power of Rank Xerox Limited and Rank Xerox Holding B.V. is owned directly or indirectly by Xerox and 49% is owned directly or indirectly by the Rank Organization Limited. The earnings of the Rank Xerox Companies are allocated according to an agreement between Xerox and the Rank Organization. For 1981, approximately 66% of the earnings of Rank Xerox was allocated to Xerox. Rank Xerox Limited manufactures and markets most xerographic copier/duplicator products developed by Xerox. Its manufacturing operations are located principally in the United Kingdom.

Fuji Xerox Co., Ltd., of Tokyo, Japan, equally owned by Fuji Photo Film Co., Ltd., of Japan and by Rank Xerox Limited, manufactures in Japan various copiers, duplicators, and supplies, which are marketed in Japan and in other areas of the Far East. They are also marketed by Xerox in the United States and by Rank Xerox Limited in Europe.

THE PROPOSED CRUM & FORSTER ACQUISITION

In September 1982, Xerox announced an agreement to acquire Crum & Forster, an insurance holding company, for about $1.65 billion in cash and securities. Crum & Forster, the nation's fifteenth largest property-casualty insurer with a 1981 premium volume of $1.6 billion, is largely involved in writing insurance for businesses. In 1981, it drew 83% of its premiums from commercial insurance lines. Its biggest line is workers' compensation insurance, which generated 28% of premiums last year. Other lines include commercial casualty, commercial automobile, multiple-peril and fire insurance. In 1981, its operating income was $171 million, up 17% over 1980. Its net income of $176 million increased 24 percent over 1980. (See Exhibits 6.11 and 6.12.) This increase in net income,

EXHIBIT 6.11

Consolidated Statement of Income, Crum & Forster and Subsidiaries

Years Ended December 31 (Dollar Amounts in Thousands, Except Per Share Data)

	1981	1980	1979	1978	1977
Income					
Net premiums written	$1,624,614	$1,660,636	$1,585,022	$1,436,061	$1,283,149
Increase (decrease) in unearned premiums	15,522	(4,473)	50,742	69,891	60,210
Premiums earned	1,609,092	1,665,109	1,534,280	1,366,170	1,222,939
Net investment income	270,199	220,957	171,967	132,526	103,400
Commission income	45,203	44,306	38,280	26,564	11,870
Rental income on operating properties	591	627	541	876	566
Total income	1,925,085	1,930,999	1,745,068	1,526,136	1,338,775
Expenses					
Losses	954,844	988,041	881,070	769,907	722,228
Loss expenses	173,907	187,377	183,995	144,423	131,252

	1981	1980	1979	1978	1977
Acquisition costs	496,328	507,847	450,936	400,257	339,075
General expenses	65,505	46,315	39,843	26,102	17,509
Dividends to policyholders	62,940	55,371	26,866	24,622	21,895
Total expenses	1,753,524	1,784,951	1,582,710	1,365,311	1,231,959
Operating income before federal and foreign income taxes	171,561	146,048	162,358	160,825	106,816
Provision for (recovery of) federal and foreign income taxes:					
Current	593	3,497	1,032	11,991	1,107
Deferred	(5,185)	(8,911)	13,275	22,912	20,615
Operating income	176,153	151,462	148,051	125,922	85,094
Net realized capital (losses) gains	(160)	(19,790)	(5,968)	(6,627)	4,385
Discontinued operations		9,886	1,265	979	1,135
Net income	$ 175,993	$ 141,558	$ 143,348	$ 120,274	$ 90,614

Earnings Per Common Share
Primary:

	1981	1980	1979	1978	1977
Operating income	$6.16	$5.39	$5.36	$4.69	$3.23
Net realized capital (losses) gains	(.01)	(.70)	(.22)	(.25)	.17
Discontinued operations		.35	.04	.04	.04
Net income	6.15	5.04	5.18	4.48	3.44
Fully Diluted:					
Operating income	6.02	5.26	5.20	4.52	3.11
Net realized capital (losses) gains	(.01)	(.68)	(.21)	(.24)	.16
Discontinued operations		.34	.04	.04	.04
Net income	6.01	4.92	5.03	4.32	3.31

Cash and Accrued Dividends Per Share

	1981	1980	1979	1978	1977
Preferred Series A	2.40	2.40	2.40	2.40	2.40
Common	1.54	1.35	1.15	.905	.80

SOURCE: Crum & Forster, *1981 Annual Report*, p. 19.

EXHIBIT 6.12 **Consolidated Balance Sheet at December 31, Crum & Forster and Subsidiaries**

(Dollar Amounts in Thousands)

	1981	1980
Assets		
Fixed maturities		
Bonds, at amortized cost (market $1,648,849 and $1,575,439, respectively)	$2,376,859	$2,118,257
Preferred stocks, at amortized cost (market $87,705 and $93,895, respectively)	120,344	119,976
Equity securities		
Preferred stocks, at market (cost $28,486 and $36,383, respectively)	21,486	29,746
Common stocks, at market (cost $350,119 and $286,841, respectively)	413,016	455,070
Short-term investments, at cost (market $270,139 and $361,459, respectively)	270,136	361,472
Investment in real estate (net of accumulated depreciation of $13,702)	—	15,417
Cash	11,689	9,740
Receivables:		
Premiums (net of allowance for uncollectible accounts of $6,245 and $6,019, respectively)	439,356	372,904
Other	192,008	99,294
Equity in assets of insurance associations	5,204	8,339
Acquisition costs applicable to unearned premiums	144,939	146,919
Land, buildings, and equipment used in operations (net of accumulated depreciation of $40,832 and $38,492, respectively)	75,591	65,249
Other assets	89,480	60,602
Total assets	4,160,108	3,862,985
Liabilities		
Unearned premiums	661,759	646,237
Unpaid losses	1,672,510	1,510,458
Unpaid loss expenses	402,978	360,645
Dividends to policyholders	65,189	54,320
Accounts payable and accrued liabilities	314,981	295,496
Mortgages payable	19,372	12,104
Deferred federal and foreign income taxes		
Unrealized appreciation of equity investments	16,984	46,571
Other	60,945	65,338
Other liabilities	22,000	12,312
Total liabilities	3,236,718	3,003,481

	1981	1980
Stockholders' Equity		
Preferred stock (liquidating value $4,804 and $5,467, respectively)	480	547
Common stock (issued 28,487,085 and 28,071,639 shares, respectively)	17,804	17,545
Additional paid-in capital	39,175	31,858
Retained earnings	827,084	694,911
Net unrealized appreciation of equity investments	38,913	115,021
Less treasury stock at cost (4,000 and 16,000 shares, respectively)	(66)	(378)
Total stockholders' equity	923,390	859,504
Total liabilities and stockholders' equity	$4,160,108	$3,862,985

SOURCE: Crum & Forster, *1981 Annual Report*, p. 20.

however, was due almost entirely to an increase in net investment income of $270 million. Pre-tax underwriting losses of over $70 million were somewhat larger than in 1980. (See Exhibit 6.13.) In effect, although insurance premiums were insufficient to cover claims and expenses, interest from the investment of these premiums enabled the firm to make a profit. In the first half of 1982, Crum & Forster's operating profit was down 30% to $64.8 million ($2.25 per share) from $92.1 million ($3.24 per share) a year earlier.

Xerox offered $55 for each Crum & Forster share, and gave holders the choice of receiving either cash or a combination of Xerox common and a new Xerox preferred stock. At $55 per share, Crum & Forster shareholders will receive about 1.7 times book value, which was $32.33 per share in June, 1982. The Xerox offer is double the pre-offer price and 40% above the stock's fifteen-year high price.

Xerox plans to finance the cash part of the acquisition, about $800 million, through existing revolving-credit agreements and short-term bank loans, and will not touch any cash holdings set aside for its office-products businesses. Xerox claims that the acquisition will be self-funding, in that interest costs associated with the takeover will be covered by Crum & Forster's earnings.[23]

Responding to industry puzzlement over Xerox's choice of diversification, Kearns has cited the following reasons for the acquisition:

- Xerox believes that the property-casualty insurance lines offer the best growth opportunities in the insurance business. Crum & Forster's lines aren't heavily dominated by a few industries, as in auto coverage.

- Xerox perceives the acquisition to be an expansion of Xerox's commercial financial services, pioneered by Xerox Credit Corporation. Formed in 1979, Xerox Credit is expecting to report a profit of about $35 million in 1982, about double 1981's profits.

- The acquisition will provide investment income that Xerox needs to support its vigorous research efforts in copiers, duplicators, electronic typewriters, and other office equipment.

EXHIBIT 6.13

Business Segments, Crum & Forster and Subsidiaries
(Dollar Amounts in Thousands)

	1981	1980	1979
Revenues			
Workers' compensation	$ 443,086	$ 431,257	$ 376,349
Casualty	304,454	358,882	357,622
Automobile—commercial	171,586	175,714	161,874
Automobile—personal	167,493	166,699	137,989
Commercial multiple-peril	218,389	217,564	208,049
Fire and allied	133,056	171,154	164,255
Homeowners'	95,246	85,532	77,722
Marine	95,169	79,781	69,743
Fidelity and surety	25,816	23,666	18,957
Investments	277,931	229,383	178,064
Other	591	627	541
Total	1,932,817	1,940,259	1,751,165
Operating Profit (Loss)			
Workers' compensation	14,241	2,796	(1,935)
Casualty	9,615	(10,431)	12,386
Automobile—commercial	(17,342)	(12,602)	1,760
Automobile—personal	(20,671)	(15,568)	(11,842)
Commercial multiple-peril	(44,775)	(7,303)	3,141
Fire and allied	(6,912)	(5,952)	6,084
Homeowners'	(8,265)	(9,291)	(3,284)
Marine	(1,324)	(6,978)	(8,781)
Fidelity and surety	2,937	2,919	3,148
Investments	270,199	220,957	171,967
Other	591	627	541
Total	198,294	159,174	173,185
General corporate expenses	(26,733)	(13,126)	(10,827)
Operating income before federal and foreign income taxes	$ 171,561	$ 146,048	$ 162,358

SOURCE: Crum & Forster, *1981 Annual Report*, p. 29.

- Xerox foresees a reduction of its tax rate during the down phase of the insurance cycle. Crum & Forster's current underwriting losses, which totaled $110 million before taxes in the first half of 1982, offer potential tax benefits to Xerox. The insurer currently pays relatively little in taxes and says its effective federal income tax rate has ranged from 12% to 14% of operating profit.[24]

Xerox watchers, however, wonder whether the company has lost confidence in its office automation business. Amy Wohl, president of Advanced Office Concepts Corp., responded to the announcement by saying, "This says Xerox doesn't feel its current set of investments gives enough return."[25] "My hunch," says office automation analyst Patricia Seybold, "is that office products may never be profitable for them. They've lost momentum."[26] Kearns, however, disagrees: "This is a very aggressive strategy to grow this business more rapidly with two market segments very different from each other." As he explains it, Xerox management believes that they can maintain their total commitment to office automation and still diversify into a self-funding, high-growth area. "We concluded we could leverage the balance sheet at this time to branch out to other areas for a better return to our shareholders."[27]

Xerox, however, has had a mixed record in previous diversification attempts. In 1969, for example, the company purchased Scientific Data Systems (SDS), a manufacturer of mainframe computers, for 10 million shares of Xerox stock worth approximately $908 million. Hoping to compete with IBM, Xerox management hoped that SDS's expertise in computers would be worth giving the SDS stockholders a 73% premium over the stock's market price. Renamed Xerox Data Systems (XDS), the new division's sales fell below $100 million in 1970 and failed to show a profit. By 1972, XDS had lost $100 million before taxes. Losses ranging from $25 to $44 million annually continued until 1975 when the company wrote off the division at an $84 million loss. After six years of effort, XDS still had less than 1% of the mainframe computer market. Analysts reported that Xerox management had been surprised by the lack of R&D capability in Scientific Data Systems.[28]

In 1979, Xerox purchased Western Union International (WUI), an international communications carrier, for $212 million. This represented Xerox's first entry into telecommunications and operations in a regulated environment. Before it purchased WUI, Xerox already had a proposal before the Federal Communications Commission for a domestic data-communications network called XTEN. This project was subsequently canceled because Xerox felt that the funds could be better used elsewhere. In December 1981, Xerox announced that it had reached an agreement to sell WUI to MCI Communications Corp. for $185 million, a $27 million loss. Other recent acquisitions, such as Shugart Associates, have been of a smaller nature, less than $50 million, and represent Xerox's attempt to diversify, both horizontally and vertically, in the information-processing industry in order to bolster its position in the office-automation marketplace.

Just as the current recession has had a negative impact on Xerox's business, the weak economic climate has hurt the insurance industry. Pressures on pricing have cut underwriting profits for property and casualty insurance companies and, with interest rates declining, investment profits may drop. In the last quarter of 1982, the industry looked forward to record underwriting losses offset by record income from investments. Insurers in recent years have been willing to cut their rates and write policies at a loss in order to generate policyholders' premiums for investment activities. Analysts fear, however, that the industry's underwriting losses may be growing faster than its investment income.[29]

On the other hand, declining interest rates have several positive effects on the insurance business. First, the bonds that comprise the bulk of the companies' portfolios are worth more when rates come down. Second, the insurers' reserves for future claims liabilities are likely to be adequate when interest rates (and by association, inflation) are low. Third, low interest rates raise the prospect of an end to the destructive three-year price war still raging in the industry. Finally, with rates coming down, general economic prospects might brighten enough to increase demand for insurers' services.

Once a turnaround in pricing occurs, industry analysts expect profits to show strong growth over the next three to five years. Between 1975 and 1979, after the last recession, industry profits increased almost eight times. The rebound is not expected to be as strong this time, but considerable growth is predicted. Lower inflation, reduced interest rates, and generally improved economic conditions are predicted to boost the demand for insurance by the mid-1980s.[30]

In reaction to the announcement of the proposed acquisition of Crum & Forster by Xerox, Moody's Investors Service lowered its ratings of several debt issues of Xerox. Moody's said its action "reflects the anticipated additional claim on existing cash flow in support of debt to be issued to acquire Crum & Forster, and the effect of competitive conditions in the company's key markets."[31]

THE OFFICE OF THE FUTURE

The high costs of management, professional, and clerical workers, in combination with continued favorable trends for electronic systems capabilities and costs, establishes Office Automation as a major growth market in the 1980s. The powerful, basic reason for automating offices is that white-collar salaries are a huge and intractable cost of doing business. In 1980, 60% of the $1.3 trillion paid out for wages, salaries, and benefits in the United States went to office workers. Meanwhile the prices of electronics have been falling. Computer memory has become cheaper at a compound annual rate of 42% over the last five years, and the price of the logic chips that give computers their intelligence has dropped about 28% a year.

Although in theory office automation makes sense, the market has not developed as quickly as vendors had hoped. According to Wang Laboratories, only 60 or so of the largest industrial corporations have acquired as many as 100 office workstations. A much smaller number have linked them into pervasive networks. Demand has simply developed more slowly than anyone thought it would a few years ago. The current market is so narrow that profits might not appear for years.[32]

Vendors give many reasons for the slow growth of this market. First of all, the recession has cut back capital-spending plans of many organizations. Second, the lack of convincing studies on the savings associated with office automation has heightened customers' reluctance to purchase. Third, in developing

EXHIBIT 6.14

The U.S. Market for Office Automation Equipment
(Dollar Amounts in Millions)

	1981	1986
Word processors	$2,200	$6,000
Electronic typewriters	275	1,200
Professional workstations	5	250
Intelligent copiers	185	900
Digital PBX's	220	4,100

SOURCE: "Dataquest, Inc.," *Fortune*, May 3, 1982, p. 184.

automation for managers and professionals, there is a problem in specifying exactly what steps or processes these individuals go through in doing their jobs. Fourth, top management does not yet feel comfortable with a computer terminal on their desks. Fifth, the confusion over which networking system, broad-band or base-band, will prevail, has made buyers slower to purchase networks. Finally, despite the universal desire of business people to find better ways of doing work, office automation remains poorly understood.[33]

Dataquest, Inc., a California-based market research firm, estimates that U.S. shipments of equipment that can be linked to form electronic offices should grow 34% a year through 1986. Total revenues are predicted to grow between $12 and $15 billion by 1986.[34] Exhibit 6.14 describes the predicted growth in the U.S. market for office automation equipment.

This anticipation of a "booming" market for office automation has brought dozens of companies into the competition. AT&T, IBM, and Xerox have declared the market a key to their futures. In 1981, the top three mini-computer companies—Digital Equipment, Hewlett-Packard, and Data General—launched office automation systems within 30 days of one another. The most successful vendors court the end user and are actually encouraged to do so by most corporate customers. Buyers will designate "preferred" vendors, but leave the final decisions to the line managers and secretaries who have to use the gear. Analysts see IBM, Wang, Digital Equipment, and Xerox as being in the best position to capture large pieces of the growing market. Yet there appear to be enough profitable niches to reward any company that can fill a particular customer's need.

Xerox's thrust in office automation has been in directing its equipment to professionals and managers, and in selling complete systems. Its strategy in gaining a share of this market has the following characteristics:

• sacrifice profits for market share until the mid-1980s;
• aim automation at the executive rather than at clerical workers;
• design machines with a multitude of uses;

- provide buyers with the opportunity to use the best available equipment from a range of suppliers;
- be the first to enter new markets;
- make products easy and nonfatiguing to use.

Although the traditionally routine tasks have been automated so far, manufacturers of this equipment must reach beyond the secretary to managers and professionals, for office automation to reach its true potential. These individuals account for 80% of the white-collar salaries. The more complex products, such as professional workstations and intelligent copiers, may not come into their own for some time. Analysts estimate that in 1985 only 6% of managers and professionals are likely to be using sophisticated workstations.[35]

NOTES

1. *Electronic News*, October 4, 1982, p. 22.

2. *Time*, November 1, 1982, p. 67, and *Wall Street Journal*, September 22, 1982, p. 3.

3. *Datamation*, February 1983, pp. 90–98.

4. Xerox Corporation, *1981 Annual Report*, p. 3.

5. *Sales and Marketing Management*, February 8, 1982, p. 24.

6. *Forbes*, July 7, 1980, pp. 40–41.

7. *Ibid.*

8. *Sales and Marketing Management*, February 8, 1982, p. 24.

9. *Ibid.*

10. *Infosystems*, January 1981.

11. *Ibid.*

12. *Business Week*, August 23, 1982, p. 80, and *Xerox: A Strategic Analysis* by Northern Business Information, Inc., New York, NY: January 1982, p. 156.

13. *Forbes*, July 7, 1980, pp. 40–41.

14. *Business Week*, October 18, 1982, p. 134M.

15. *Datamation*, February 1983, p. 92.

16. *Infosystems*, February 1982, p. 26.

17. *Mini-Micro Systems*, February 1982, p. 18.

18. *Business Week*, April 21, 1980, p. 130.

19. *Electronic News*, December 7, 1981, p. 18.

20. *Value Line*, November 12, 1982, p. 1128.

21. *Fortune*, September 5, 1983, pp. 97–102.

22. *Value Line*, November 12, 1982, pp. 1055, 1085, 1087, 1089, 1098, 1102, 1103, 1113, and 1115.

23. *Wall Street Journal*, September 22, 1982, p. 24.

24. *Ibid.*

25. *Business Week*, October 4, 1982, p. 52.

26. *Ibid.*

27. *Ibid.*

28. *Electronics*, March 29, 1981, p. 86.

29. *Wall Street Journal*, December 30, 1982, p. 20.

30. *Value Line*, October 22, 1982, p. 637.

31. *Wall Street Journal*, October 1982.

32. *Fortune*, May 3, 1982, p. 176.

33. *Ibid.*

34. *Ibid.*

35. *Ibid.*

Hogan Systems, Inc.

SEXTON ADAMS • ADELAIDE GRIFFIN

In 1977, former commercial bank officer Bernie Hogan realized that a need existed for banking software products that could be accessed from terminals and modified easily. As an entrepreneur, Hogan raised $250,000 in venture capital and incorporated Hogan Systems, Inc., in California.[1,2,3]

The firm became a leading provider of on-line, integrated banking application software packages that were primarily used on large scale IBM and IBM plug-compatible computer systems. Hogan's products were marketed to commercial banks, thrift institutions, and other organizations that offered deposit and lending services, in the United States, Canada, Great Britain, Australia, New Zealand, and elsewhere in the world.[4,5]

The company delivered its first software product in 1980 but posted losses of $558,000. The following year, Bernie Hogan sold out despite software sales of $3 million and earnings of $601,000. Richard Streller, co-founder of the company, succeeded Hogan as President and Chief Executive Officer.[6] By 1982, Hogan's products were installed at fifty-five sites and sales peaked at $9 million. After the firm went public in December, 1982, an observer noted that

> The right image and the right product have made Hogan one of the hottest stocks in a hot market. . . . Of one thing there is little doubt: Hogan's greatest long-term strength lies in its product, which is well matched to its market. Historically, big banks have built and maintained their own computer systems. But deregulation, permitting new computer-based services, and the rapid advance of technology have overwhelmed bankers. Now they're looking outside for new systems and systems designers. And Hogan offers them an off-the-shelf system that can be easily adapted for individual bank requirements, sometimes at less than half what it would cost a bank to install a similar system on its own.[7]

A financial analyst observed that "Hogan has no real competition, its management is talented, and its product is top-flight."[8] By March, 1984, sales had reached $36 million with earnings of $7 million and 120 customers had licensed the firm's 360 products.[9]

In February, 1984, Hogan introduced the Integrated Loans Processing System. Under development for three years, the system included 771 programs, 243 batch and 66 online reports, nearly 2,400 total librarian members, 46 hierarchical data bases and 54 sequential data bases.[10] An order backlog in excess of $6 million existed for the $500,000 system, which was installed in forty client sites. With more than 500,000 COBOL source statements, the systems

This case was prepared by C. Bates, R. Kincaid, D. Lindsay, and T. Pezanosky under the supervision of Professor Sexton Adams, North Texas State University and Professor Adelaide Griffin, Texas Woman's University. Copyright © 1988 by Sexton Adams and Adelaide Griffin. Reprinted by permission.

integrated consumer, mortgage, and commercial loan processing capabilities in what was described as "the most complex loan system ever developed."[11]

Unfortunately, the system had not been thoroughly tested and did not work reliably. According to one of Hogan's vice-presidents, the premature release of the loan system had been "suicidal" and led to enormous financial damage and loss of credibility for Hogan.[12] Another source reported that Hogan had paid $28 million related to litigation that had arisen from the release of the product.[13]

As revenues continued to drop and losses mounted in the wake of the disastrous installation of the malfunctioning loan package, Streller moved up to Chairman of the Board in September, 1984. George L. "Larry" McTavish, 43, became the first President and Chief Operating Officer who had been brought in from the outside. In McTavish's estimation, Hogan failed to provide a full package of customer services, including installation and maintenance of their products at the client's site; Hogan's software had to be installed either by the bank's MIS department or a third-party vendor. After learning that Hogan's clients paid outside contractors more than $30 million per year to install software packages purchased from Hogan, McTavish moved quickly to remedy this situation. He realized that increasing customer service would not only improve customer satisfaction but would also provide an opportunity for the company to generate additional revenues.[14]

McTavish also restructured license fees to ensure that client banks could not supply newly acquired subsidiaries with copies of Hogan's software without paying Hogan. Hogan's Preferred Client Services system was introduced to capitalize on the trend toward upscale banking: it provided special fee-based services for larger depositors. This new system generated combined financial statements that allowed banks to report and manage a depositor's assets in an integrated manner.[15]

In spite of a 23% drop in sales to $28 million and pre-tax losses of $19 million in the year ended March 31, 1985, Streller was optimistic that the company would recover fully. The company's other products were successfully installed at seventy-six sites as of June, 1985, and continued to perform customer banks' accounting functions on a daily basis.[16]

Streller subsequently resigned and George Peterson was named as Chairman of the Board. In October, 1985, the revised system for consumer loans was reintroduced, and a version adding commercial loans was introduced in June, 1986.[17]

A NEW ERA

In May, 1986, Hogan entered into a landmark agreement with IBM. Industry analysts described the twenty-year pact as "the most ironclad" agreement that IBM had ever made with a major vendor of vertical market application products.[18] In addition to increasing Hogan's sales revenue, the agreement with IBM was seen as a means to allow Hogan to increase its revenue from software maintenance while cutting its advertising costs.[19] Under the terms of the agreement, IBM was given exclusive rights to market Hogan products in North

America for five years.[20] In addition, IBM was given first right of refusal on Hogan's future products. Hogan was to phase out its fourteen-member direct sales force and IBM was to form a seventy-two–member sales group to market Hogan's products nationwide. IBM assumed responsibility for providing product installation and telephone hotline services, while Hogan was responsible for providing backup diagnostic support.[21]

McTavish noted that one of the major benefits of the agreement was that Hogan was to be made privy to certain areas of IBM's technology and planning, thereby implying that Hogan's strategic planning for product development would be more accurate. McTavish acknowledged that the loss of Hogan's distribution capability put the company in a precarious position.[22] One industry observer suggested that the terms of the contract allowed Hogan to terminate the marketing agreement after five years if they were not satisfied with IBM's performance.[23]

Industry analysts agreed that IBM's alliance with Hogan would substantially boost Hogan's credibility in the industry. Some observers had previously believed that "it was only a matter of time before Hogan slid into Chapter 11," but the IBM agreement virtually guaranteed Hogan's continued existence. Bank management information systems officers who had invested hundreds of thousands of dollars in Hogan software breathed a collective sigh of relief, but Hogan's competitors had mixed reactions.[24]

Although IBM's name and sales force were seen as a potential threat by some competitors, Uccel Corporation, one of Hogan's major rivals, claimed that they were not unduly worried about the IBM–Hogan combination. Donald Steel, Vice President and General Manager of Uccel's Financial Systems Division, noted that they had gone head to head with Hogan four times in the four months prior to the IBM–Hogan agreement and had sold their product to all four clients.[25] Key observers noted that hardware vendors had not had much success in selling applications software, especially in the banking industry. Donald Adkinson, former IBM sales manager and consultant for both IBM and Hogan, said that "a software package like Hogan's is hard to understand and sell" and that software companies that specialized in marketing to the banking industry would be able to outsell the IBM sales staff. According to Adkinson, the agreement with IBM could be beneficial to Hogan if IBM provided technical support and tinkered with Hogan's software to make it run more efficiently.[26]

It soon became obvious that the agreement with IBM was to have subtle repercussions for Hogan. Very soon after signing the agreement with IBM, Hogan announced it had entered into a three-year joint venture with Midland Bank of Sheffield, England. With deposits in excess of $93 billion, Midland was the eighteenth largest bank in the world. This deal, valued at more than $10 million, marked Hogan's first attempt to enter the high end of the banking software market. Previously, the megabank market had been all but closed to Hogan because the world's largest financial institutions tended to develop their own software. In addition to supplying Midland with its entire product line,

Hogan made a commitment to develop an integrated software package that would give megabanks (with deposits in excess of $75 billion) the same capabilities as medium-sized banks. Because most of the world's approximately 150 megabanks were located in North America, IBM's exclusive right of first refusal for all future Hogan products sold in North America guaranteed that it would also benefit from Hogan's new venture.[27]

By February, 1987, the firm had reissued the mortgage loan software (Phase 3 of the fully rewritten Integrated Loans Processing System). More than sixty financial institutions were eagerly awaiting the release, despite the fact that the complete package was priced at $2.5 million.[28] To address the lack of integrated loan processing systems for mortgage banking, Hogan's enhanced system allowed lenders "to monitor their 'pipeline' of applications and commitments to best take advantage of selling their loans in the fast-growing secondary market."[29]

CHANGE OF FOCUS

Until 1987, the core of Hogan's banking software products had been marketed to mid-sized retail and commercial banks with assets from $750 million to $75 billion. Hogan broadened its target market, however, through the acquisition of two subsidiaries. In March, 1987, Hogan acquired Systems 4, a vendor of integrated software for community banks with assets less than $200 million. System 4's software package was marketed under the name BankVision.[30] Hogan believed that the acquisition had "filled in the small end of the market" and hired James J. Murphy as the Senior Vice President for Community Banking.[31]

Hogan's second acquisition was GDK Systems, Inc., in May, 1987. GDK marketed an International Money Management System (IMMS) which supported international banking concerns such as foreign exchange, money market trading, international loans, customer information, multicurrency accounting, and global positions and exposures.[32]

The products of Hogan's newly acquired subsidiaries were not subject to IBM's exclusive marketing franchise. However, each had a relationship with IBM in which they participated in IBM's Industry Marketing Assistance Program (IMAP).[33]

Following his successful acquisition of the two subsidiaries, McTavish was promoted to Chairman of the Board and Chief Executive Officer in June, 1987. Richard Aldridge assumed the position of President and Chief Operating Officer and George Peterson, former Chairman, remained on the Board of Directors.

The software industry was stunned when McTavish resigned five weeks later because of "philosophical differences" with the company's board of directors.[34] McTavish's sudden departure was especially surprising to the numerous industry observers who had credited him with "masterminding the strategy that enabled the once-floundering company to regain profitability and creditability."[35] Although McTavish and the board of directors agreed to not reveal the nature of their differences, numerous theories abounded. An interested spectator noted that "Hogan's board has been more actively involved in running the company than most boards are."[36] One source suggested that "McTavish's resignation may have resulted from a power struggle with former Chairman Peterson, who remains on the board. There may have been some professional jealously between Peterson and McTavish, since McTavish is credited with turning around the company."[37]

Others speculated that Hogan's board of directors might have chafed under the loss of independence that resulted from the IBM marketing alliance engineered by McTavish. Gary W. Fiedler, who was named to replace McTavish, claimed that his predecessor's resignation was "a private matter" and denied rumors that Hogan was having difficulty with IBM.[38]

A projected loss of $2.5 to $3 million in the fiscal quarter ending September 30, 1987, was attributed to a decline in software sales both internationally and domestically. Hogan also noted that "severance pay of Mr. McTavish and options granted Mr. Fiedler came to about $700,000."[39] Observers noted that, sixteen months after signing the exclusive marketing agreement with IBM, "Hogan's growth prospects remain an enigma. IBM's exclusive North American sales rights have not borne the fruit originally expected."[40]

Hogan was struck another blow in September, 1987, when Midland Bank announced its decision to drop its joint development project with Hogan. Although Midland planned to continue using Hogan's integrated software, the bank's new management and internal restructuring was cited as the reason for discontinuing participation in the project.[41] In response, Hogan announced its plans to incorporate the high performance capabilities of the megabank product into its existing integrated banking applications rather than complete development of a separate megabank product.[42]

| THE BANKING/ FINANCIAL SOFTWARE INDUSTRY | Competition in the realm of software development actually began in 1969 when IBM unbundled its software (this allowed software to be sold separately from hardware) in response to growing pressure from critics and antitrust suits filed by Applied Data Research, Inc., and other software developers. By 1986, more than a dozen software firms had annual revenues in the range of $80 to $120 million, and a smaller group had revenues in the $180 to $220 million range.[43] |

In the mid-1980's, the banking/finance segment was the largest and fastest-growing segment of the computer services business. Banking had always been the staple of the computer services industry, and banking's importance to the industry was predicted to increase. Total computer services revenues increased 24% in 1984 to $40 billion; 10% of the increase came from banks and other financial institutions; no other group contributed as large a share.[44]

Banks, well able to purchase computer services, provided a large and attractive market to computer service vendors. In 1983, there were 15,000 banks in the U.S. and they had $1.7 trillion on deposit. Commercial banks, the largest purchaser of computer services, bought more than 60% of the services sold to banks and other financial institutions. The increased use of computer services was attributed to deregulation of the banking industry; to competition with retailers, brokers, and insurance firms; and to a host of new applications such as automated teller machines, sweep accounts, and consolidated customer accounts.[45]

Understanding the complexity of the needs of a financial institution required thinking of the technical environment at a typical financial institution as a quilt. Each patch on the quilt represented a different product delivery system bounded on all sides by seams that represented differences in the way each system handled the same data. When an attempt was made to move information from one system to another, a seam was encountered.[46] What most banks sought was a software product that would do the whole job for them, covering all internal applications; they wanted a superpackage.[47]

The solution to the problem lay with integrated systems, which allowed various application systems to be used together with the data flowing smoothly from one system to another. The computer services companies that dominated the financial/banking computer services industry did so through the development of integrated banking systems. To remove seams, integrated systems standardized the way the product systems manipulated and stored information. Hogan, the biggest vendor of primary applications systems for the largest banks, provided an integrated, on-line, real-time system.[48]

The financial/banking industry realized the important ties that bound their future with that of the computer services industry. Possible technological developments were a major consideration in the financial/banking industry's future. By 1988, electronic technology played a key role in the industry, and the progression of sophisticated links between data processing and communications hinted at future possibilities that almost defied imagination.[49] One source said,

> Artificial intelligence and expert systems are becoming part of the technological menu of the largest financial services companies.... A mid-1987 study by the Bank Administration Institute of the 100 largest banks, holding companies, and savings and loans about use of artificial intelligence and expert systems shows an increasing interest in the technology. Forty-five percent said they were exploring, developing, or using artificial intelligence. Twenty-seven percent said their AI systems had reached the utilization stage.[50]

Hogan Systems intended to play a major role in the future of the financial/banking industry. James J. Murphy, Senior Vice-President of Hogan, said, "We have the domestic community bank product. We intend to have that communicate with the money center bank which has the Hogan/IBM product. It will connect to GDK software for international banking. The net of all that (is) you end up with an international financial connection that runs across all IBM hardware."[51]

THE ENVIRONMENT

Hogan's success was directly dependent on the success of the financial institutions it served. Unfortunately, 1987 and 1988 were not good years for banks. In 1987, the Federal Deposit Insurance Corporation closed 184 banks, the most in a single year since the Great Depression. The banks closed by the FDIC had $37.6 million in average assets. By March 1, 1988, eleven banks in Texas had failed and the number of banks that had failed nationwide totaled twenty-eight.[52] The U.S. Comptroller of the Currency analyzed national bank failures since 1979 and reported that most of the banks had failed due to incompetent management, director weakness, or insider abuse, rather than because of economic weakness.[53]

In 1987, the nation's 200 largest banks had swallowed a combined loss of $2.1 billion, with losses of more than $7.2 billion posted by the top 25 banks. This followed lackluster performance in 1986 with after-tax earnings of $12.9 billion.[54] One observer commented that

> Review of environmental factors suggests that a quick turnaround is not in store.... The expected slowdown in population growth will mean more competition for consumer business. The average age of the U.S. population will continue to rise, leading banks and other businesses to reassess their mix of financial services. Slower expansion of the labor force will intensify competition for technologically proficient workers.... Many smaller banks that want to maintain their local orientation while diversifying their sources of income will make greater use of fee-based services. These banks also will sell more services that are "manufactured" by other institutions.... Banks face an increasing regulatory and public policy burden. Changing societal values seem likely to increase that burden.... The result of these various factors will be that banks will be asked more often to act as policemen, tax collectors, credit allocators, and instruments of foreign aid and domestic welfare policies.... A marketing orientation seems to be missing at the top levels of many banking organizations.... Competitive pressures will make it necessary for commercial banks to become aggressive in minimizing costs and putting advanced technology to work.[55]

However, the prognosis had improved by early 1988. One source reported that if the economy eluded recession and there was no deterioration in credit quality a 14% increase was expected in bank earnings in 1988.[56]

GOVERNMENT AND LEGAL ISSUES

The introduction of computer technology forced the legal system in the 1980s to address a number of issues that had not been envisioned twenty years previously. A multitude of legal questions arose, ranging from the fundamental copyrightability of computer programs to the question of state and federal jurisdiction over copyright laws.[57] In 1976, a new copyright law was enacted by the Congress to replace the one that had been in effect since 1909. The 1976 law established federal preemption of all state and common law copyright laws and made explicit that copyright protection extended only to the expression of an idea, not to the idea itself. However, the law did not include computer programs.[58]

The Computer Software Copyright Act was passed by the U.S. Congress in 1980. In amending the 1976 law, it added a provision that defined computer programs but did not elaborate on the scope of software copyright protection.[59] By 1988, conflicting rulings by circuit courts in different areas of the country had failed to clarify software copyright liability, and it was uncertain when and if the Supreme Court would consider the scope of copyright protection. Therefore, the software industry was left to cope with a great deal of legal uncertainty.[60]

Another issue related to computer technology dealt with the growing concern in the U.S. in the 1980s about the right to privacy. A nationwide controversy grew regarding the potential for employers to obtain details of the private lives of employees by delving into electronic data bases in which information was stored by individual Social Security numbers. One source suggested that "after health care, privacy in the workplace may be the most important social issue in the 1990's."[61] Another source stated that

> Two forces threaten our privacy. One is the growth of information technology, with its enhanced capacity for surveillance, communication, computation, storage, and retrieval. A second, and more insidious threat, is the increased value of information in decision-making. Information is increasingly valuable to policy makers; they covet it even if acquiring it invades another's privacy.[62]

In addition to the privacy risk were identified six other risks related to data processing that might result in a loss for companies. These included risks due to selling/leasing computer hardware and software, defective software, inaccurate data, security risks, loss of the data system itself, and the providing of data processing services to others.[63]

Internationally, a wide diversity existed in the number and severity of laws governing the transborder flow of data. These regulations impacted the operations of any multinational firm.

Because Hogan's clients were financial institutions, any regulations that affected the banking industry also affected Hogan. After the Stock Market Crash of 1929 and the Great Depression, the U.S. government had moved to regulate the banking industry more closely. In 1933, Congress passed the Banking Act, which contained three major provisions: (1) separation of commercial and investment banking, (2) regulation by the Fed of the amount of interest that banks could pay on time deposits, and (3) creation of the Federal Deposit Insurance Corporation.[64]

Rapidly rising market interest rates, in combination with major technological innovations in communications and data processing, caused a number of regulations to have harmful effects on depository institutions. Although regulations put all depository institutions at a competitive disadvantage, they threatened the very existence of thrift institutions. Therefore, two major acts were passed in the early 1980s: the Depository Institutions Deregulation and Monetary

Control Act of 1980, and the Garn–St. Germain Depository Institutions Act of 1982. These laws reversed the trend toward even stricter regulations.[65]

In 1988, discussion centered on further deregulation as, for the first time, Congress seriously considered repealing key portions of the 1933 act which separated commercial and investment banking.[66] Analysts felt these developments had and would continue to increase the competitive pressures facing commercial banks, thereby providing companies such as Hogan with additional opportunities to profit from providing technologically sophisticated information systems to the banking/financial industry.[67]

MANAGEMENT

On February 8, 1988, Richard Aldridge resigned as President and Chief Operating Officer. Although no reason was given for his departure, disagreements with Gary Fiedler and the board of directors were rumored to have led to Aldridge's resignation.[68] Specifically, Fiedler was alleged to be unhappy with Hogan's sales and held Aldridge responsible.[69] Major internal restructuring occurred after Aldridge's departure. (See Exhibit 7.1.) According to Fiedler, the new organizational structure "will facilitate a customer and market approach to managing the business. We are focusing our attention on realizing the full potential of our current business and expanding our product offering to the financial services industry."[70]

Elected to the board of directors of Hogan Systems in September, 1986, Gary W. Fiedler was named Chairman of the Board and Chief Executive Officer in July, 1987. After Aldridge's resignation in February, 1988, Fiedler also became the company's President and Chief Operating Officer.[71]

Prior to taking the helm at Hogan, Fiedler had served as Chairman and CEO at First Interstate Bank of Nevada since January, 1985. He had previously been Executive Vice President and Manager, Operations Group, at First Interstate Bank of California and had served as Manager of the California Banking Group, a position in which he was responsible for 335 First Interstate retail branches.[72]

Before joining the First Interstate system in 1982, Fiedler was a Senior Vice President at Wells Fargo Bank of San Francisco. At Wells Fargo, he spent a year as General Manager of the bank's London Branch Group and later ran the bank's Cash Management Services Division in San Francisco. From 1969 to 1981, Fiedler was employed by Mellon Bank of Pittsburgh, where he held various corporate lending positions and at one time managed the bank's Los Angeles office.[73]

Hogan's top executive served in many voluntary capacities in the financial world. Fiedler was a member of the Government Relations Council of the American Banker's Association and was President-elect of the Nevada Bankers Association prior to his appointment at Hogan. A member of the Young President's Organization, Fiedler had graduated from Carnegie-Mellon University in Pittsburgh with a business degree in Administration and Management.[74]

EXHIBIT 7.1 **Organization Chart, Hogan Systems, Inc.**
February 8, 1988

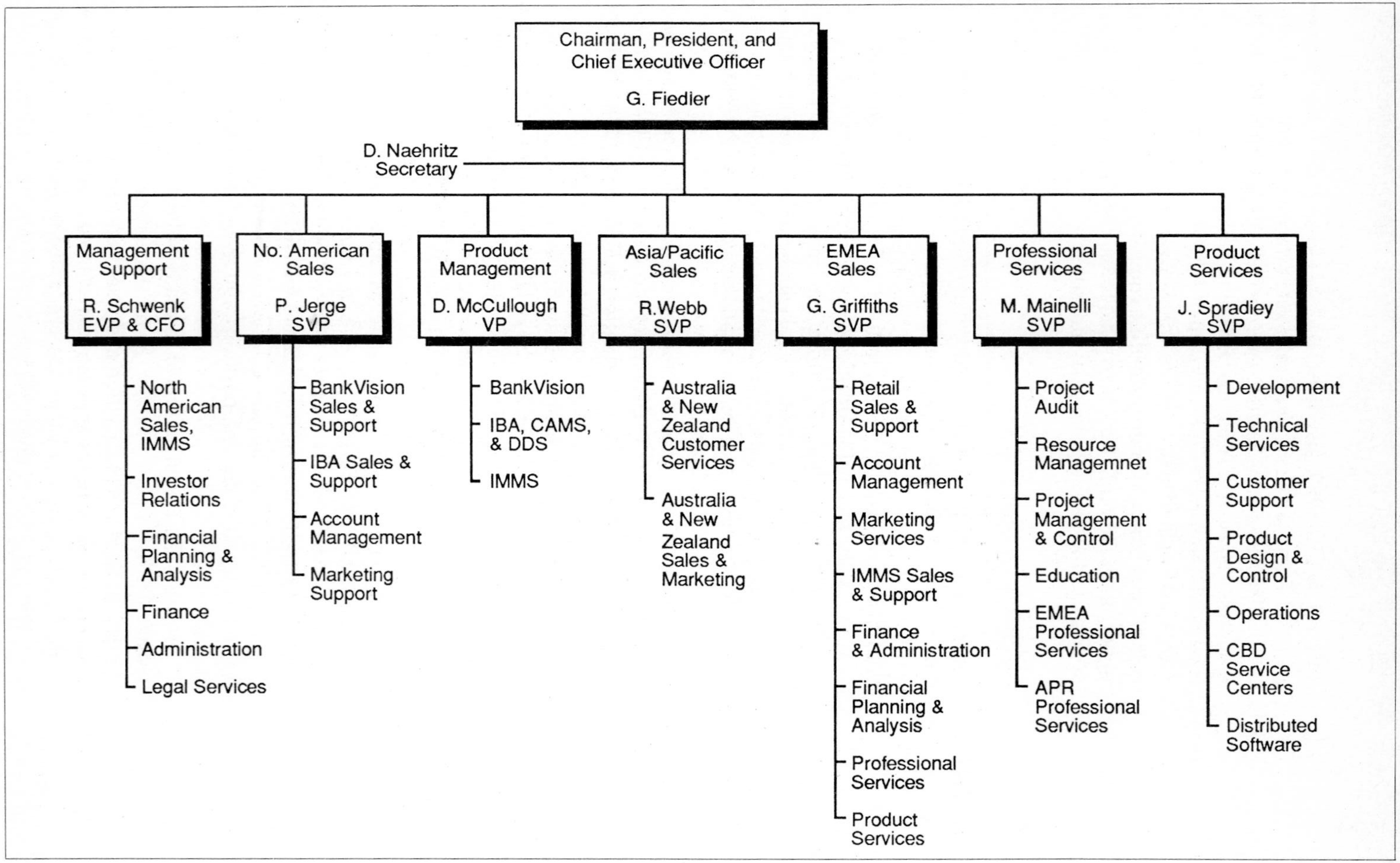

Organization chart with the following structure:

Chairman, President, and Chief Executive Officer — G. Fiedler

D. Naehritz, Secretary

Management Support — R. Schwenk, EVP & CFO
- North American Sales, IMMS
- Investor Relations
- Financial Planning & Analysis
- Finance
- Administration
- Legal Services

No. American Sales — P. Jerge, SVP
- BankVision Sales & Support
- IBA Sales & Support
- Account Management
- Marketing Support

Product Management — D. McCullough, VP
- BankVision
- IBA, CAMS, & DDS
- IMMS

Asia/Pacific Sales — R. Webb, SVP
- Australia & New Zealand Customer Services
- Australia & New Zealand Sales & Marketing

EMEA Sales — G. Griffiths, SVP
- Retail Sales & Support
- Account Management
- Marketing Services
- IMMS Sales & Support
- Finance & Administration
- Financial Planning & Analysis
- Professional Services
- Product Services

Professional Services — M. Mainelli, SVP
- Project Audit
- Resource Managemnet
- Project Management & Control
- Education
- EMEA Professional Services
- APR Professional Services

Product Services — J. Spradiey, SVP
- Development
- Technical Services
- Customer Support
- Product Design & Control
- Operations
- CBD Service Centers
- Distributed Software

SOURCE: Hogan Systems Company records.

Users and industry analysts applauded Fiedler's appointment as Chairman of the Board, even though he had not previously worked for a software company. His many years of experience as a banker were considered to be a critical success factor in the financial software industry.[75]

After the reorganization of the corporate structure in February, 1988, Geoff Griffiths retained the role of Senior Vice-President of Sales and Marketing for IBA and IMMS in the Europe, Middle East, and Africa marketplace, and Richard B. Webb remained as Senior Vice-President of Sales and Marketing for IBA and IMMS in the Australia and Asia/Pacific marketplace. Hogan's Executive Vice-President and Chief Financial Officer, Richard C. Schwenk, was appointed to the Board of Directors and also assumed the responsibility for IMMS sales and marketing in North America.[76]

C. Donald McCullough, Jr., joined Hogan as Vice-President of Product Planning in February, 1985, and also served as the chief liaison to the Hogan Users Group. He was appointed Vice-President of Product Management for all products on a worldwide basis in February, 1988, and assumed responsibility for market analysis, planning, and strategy for all products. During his career, McCullough gained more than twenty years of diverse management experience in manufacturing, services, and government industry sectors, including ten years at Martin Marietta Data Systems with sales and product management duties.[77]

Patric J. Jerge joined Hogan in November, 1978, and was one of the company's first ten employees. He served as Vice-President of Western Region Sales and as Vice-President of Product Development before being appointed Senior Vice-President of the Field Operations Group. In February, 1988, Jerge was appointed Senior Vice-President of Sales and Marketing for Retail Banking Products in North America and assumed responsibility for market support for the IBA product under the IBM marketing agreement, as well as sales and marketing responsibility for the BankVision product in the community bank segment. Previously, Jerge was with University Computing Company for five years.[78]

Michael R. Mainelli became Hogan's Vice-President of Management Services in March, 1985. He was promoted to Senior Vice-President of Product Services in July, 1985, and was subsequently appointed as Senior Vice-President of special projects. He assumed the role of Senior Vice-President of Professional Services for all products on a worldwide basis in February, 1988, with responsibility for customer consulting, education, installation, and implementation support for all products. Prior to 1985, Mainelli was with Martin Marietta Data Systems for fourteen years, most recently as Executive Director for Middle East Operations.[79]

After his appointment in February, 1988, as Senior Vice-President of Product Services for all products on a worldwide basis, Jack R. Spradley assumed responsibility for product development, product maintenance, and customer support for all products. Previously, Spradley had been Hogan's Senior Vice-President of Product Services for IBA products in North America. He began his career with Hogan in 1986 as Executive Vice-President of Hogan Services Corporation, which provided support for the implementation and use of all Hogan products. Prior to joining Hogan, Spradley was Corporate Vice-President with the SEI Corporation, and he had been with Martin Marietta Data Systems for twenty-three years, during which time he was co-founder and Executive Director of the Data Systems Division.[80]

Senior Vice-President of the Community Bank Division, James J. Murphy joined Hogan in June, 1987. As the Community Bank Division's top executive, he was responsible for all activities pertaining to the development, support, and sale of Hogan's community and correspondent banking products. A seasoned computer industry executive, Murphy came to Hogan after twenty-four years with International Business Machines. During his tenure with IBM, he held various sales, sales management, and product management positions. As an IBM Product Manager, he was responsible for IBM's application software programs for the financial services industry.[81]

Donald F. Campbell, Hogan's Group Vice-President of Sales, was responsible for all of the company's sales consulting activities which supported IBM sales of IBA products. Prior to joining Hogan in August, 1985, Campbell spent eight years with Cincom Systems, Inc., as Director of Marketing and Product Planning. He was also Manager of European Marketing for Cincom Systems International in Brussels, Belgium.[82]

In July, 1987, Stuart K. "Keith" Williams joined Hogan as Senior Vice-President and Chief Executive of GDK Systems with responsibility for all activities pertaining to the development, support, and sale of Hogan's IMMS product. Williams had previously been with BIS Banking Systems, Ltd., for six years as Director of International Operations for the company's banking software. Earlier, Williams had spent eight years with IBM in the United Kingdom in sales and as product manager for IBM's System/36 and System/38 computer lines.[83]

MARKETING

The three main product groups sold by Hogan Systems, Inc., were each marketed in a unique manner. The Integrated Banking Application (IBA) was marketed directly by IBM in North America and by Hogan elsewhere in the world. Hogan was responsible for supporting IBM's sales force through its Sales Support Group, Marketing Support Group, and Direct Sales Function. IBM's strengths were with the technical community in the bank, while Hogan's strengths were with the end-user community. Hogan's provision of support for the IBM sales force was considered to be a limited one-year agreement, but Patric J. Jerge, Senior Vice-President of North American Sales for Hogan, expected the arrangement to continue for an indefinite time.[84]

The community banking product BankVision was supported by a six-person direct-sales force that called upon markets targeted for the product. The sales force formerly concentrated its marketing efforts for the community bank product in Colorado, New Mexico, and Montana, but their efforts were redirected to include Texas, Oklahoma, and Louisiana, after the acquisition of Systems 4 by Dallas-based Hogan.[85]

The International Money Management System (IMMS) was marketed directly by a group out of a New York office. Hogan acquired IMMS when it bought out GDK Systems. The three-person IMMS sales force called on prospects in New York (where the main money center banks were located), as well as in Chicago, San Francisco, and Toronto.[86]

Supporting efforts in all of these areas was Hogan's Marketing Support Group. They took care of advertising campaigns for the products using direct mail to bankers, and they also produced sales collateral materials and quarterly newsletters that contained interviews with the customer base on how they were using Hogan's products.[87]

Three or four of the top executives of a financial institution were targeted for IBA marketing efforts, including the CEO, the executive in charge of operations, the senior MIS executive, and the marketing executive. Usually only the CEO was targeted for community bank marketing efforts for the BankVision product because those banks were usually so small that the CEO was active in daily operations. For IMMS, Hogan usually targeted the person responsible for the international area of the bank's operations.[88]

The main marketing and pricing strategies that Hogan followed were based on the particular product and market segments being targeted. The IBA market price was set by IBM, but they mirrored the pricing structure utilized by Hogan. This followed a value-added pricing strategy because of the flexibility that the IBM/Hogan combination brought to the banking industry.[89]

In the community banking market, banks were looking for turnkey solutions and Hogan was price-competitive. Hogan's systems were generally marketed according to the asset size of the bank. A large community bank ($250 million) generally required more computing services than did a small community bank ($25 million).[90]

A value-added pricing strategy was used by Hogan for the IMMS market because of the one-of-a-kind products provided for global risk management. In addition to providing the basic IMMS software license, Hogan contracted to provide a multitude of additional services to customize the base product to the needs of the particular institution being serviced.[91]

The opportunities for Hogan's future growth were dependent on the product being offered. The IBA market was thought to consist of approximately 600 prospects in North America; this included banks, savings and loan institutions, and large servicers of multiple banks. By 1988, Hogan had licensed 130 of these prospects. Patric J. Jerge expected this market to disappear or need replacement products. The product being offered in 1988 was assessed by Jerge as being viable for the next five or six years. Jerge felt that IBM's involvement would help Hogan to plan for the future and develop replacement products. A possibility for expansion in this market segment remained because geographical barriers were coming down in the banking industry, as banks began crossing state lines, and the number of mergers and acquisitions rose to new heights.

Also, banking deregulation in Europe was just beginning in 1988, and this was expected to create additional demand for Hogan's IBA product.[92]

Hogan's management believed that about 13,000 prospects existed for Hogan's community banking product and had just begun to address this market segment in 1988. These community banks tended to be family-owned and were well known and respected in their local communities; they ranged in size from $10 million "Mom and Pop" banks to $500-million holding companies. Jerge felt that this was a viable market in the long term because, in his estimation, banks in this segment would not be "gobbled up" in mergers.[93]

The market for Hogan's IMMS product was finite in the U.S.; the main growth potential was overseas. The on-going services and additional applications of the product provided a good potential for long-term growth for the IMMS software package.[94]

Jerge suggested that, in order for Hogan to continue to grow in all markets, additional products would have to be offered and that these products would be obtained through Hogan's continued acquisition of products or companies. Jerge also revealed that Hogan had an opportunity to contract for marketing rights for products that met Hogan's quality standards.[95]

According to Jerge, Hogan was the definite leader in the mid-sized bank market; none of the competition approached the 15–16% market share held by Hogan's IBA product. In this market segment, the primary competitors were Systematics, Cullinet, Uccel, MTech, and numerous small companies with single applications. It was noted that fully integrated products such as those provided by Hogan were not always viable for banks that sought a way to solve a problem in a single area.[96]

One source claimed that Systematics, Inc., was Hogan's only real competition in terms of providing a package that could truly be identified as an integrated system.[97] However, by early 1988, Cullinet Software, Inc., had entered the banking software market with a $2-million on-line real-time consumer banking system that was described by one expert as "a vastly superior design."[98] As a cooperative marketing partner of Digital Equipment Corporation, Cullinet was the only major banking software company with products that could run on either IBM or DEC equipment.[99] Furthermore, Uccel Corporation and MTech were also rumored to be developing integrated systems but were several years behind Hogan.[100]

MTech was a Dallas-based data processing service firm that earned about 75% of its revenue from processing data for 1,400 financial institutions in eighteen states. Early in 1988, Electronic Data Systems, a major Dallas-based data processor for credit unions, began actions to acquire MTech. With regard to the EDS–MTech merger, one observer said that "the surviving company will be the undisputed biggest in the market with combined revenues (in 1987) of more than $400 million from data processing for banks, thrifts, and credit unions."[101]

In the community banking market, Hogan was a small player because they had just begun to market their BankVision product on a regional basis in

1988. NCR and Burroughs, who sold both hardware and software products to the community banks, were Hogan's primary competitors in this market. Low-cost service bureaus were another source of competition. However, there was no single dominant player within the market.[102]

A product comparable to Hogan's International Money Management System was not being offered by any other source in the first half of 1988. The nearest competitors were mini-computer systems that did not provide features comparable to Hogan's IMMS system. In early 1988, Jerge noted that Hogan had contracts with 12 customers out of approximately 200 prospects in this segment of the market.[103]

The marketing environment facing Hogan in 1988 was one of considerable challenge. Although the banks in Texas and in other energy-dependent states were struggling, Patric Jerge believed that the outcome would be beneficial to Hogan's interests in the long run. Jerge said that banks that had previously focused on oil and real estate opportunities would need the flexibility and competitive edge provided by Hogan's products to reorient themselves in consumer banking. However, he acknowledged that many of the banks felt they could not afford the technology even though they recognized their need for it.[104]

Internationally, the world continued to shrink in the 1980s as the number of international corporations grew and international transactions multiplied. Furthermore, the increasing number of people in the foreign exchange market created additional demand for computerized systems that could deal with the complexities of international finance. By 1988, 39% of Hogan's business was with financial institutions that were not located in North America.[105]

FINANCE

For Hogan, operating income peaked in 1984 at $9.56 million (Exhibit 7.2).[106] After incurring losses of $16.37 and $5.74 million during the next two years (see Exhibit 7.3), Hogan again showed an operating income of $8.83 million in fiscal 1987.[107]

In 1982, software product revenues accounted for 80% of total revenues but had declined to 42% by 1987 (see Exhibit 7.4). This disturbing trend continued in fiscal 1988 when Hogan reported software revenues of $3.5 million in the first quarter, down from $4.9 million in the same period in 1987 (see Exhibit 7.5). At the same time, the company's net profit was $1.9 million.[108]

Software product revenues continued to decline during the second quarter of 1988, falling by $1.1 million compared to the same period in 1987. General and administrative costs increased by $3.3 million over the prior year's second quarter, primarily as a result of a $2-million increase in allowances for doubtful accounts receivable and customers' claims, as well as hiring and severance costs for several executives (Exhibit 7.5). Hogan also began a stock repurchase program during the second quarter of 1988 whereby the company planned to purchase up to one million shares of its common stock to be used in connection with an employee stock incentive program.[109]

EXHIBIT 7.2

Statements of Operations, Hogan Systems, Inc.
(Dollar Amounts in Thousands)

Year Ended March 31	1984	1983	1982
Revenues			
Software products	$30,073	$14,230	$6,663
Maintenance fees	3,374	1,655	675
Customer service fees	2,975	1,197	977
Total revenues	36,422	17,082	8,315
Costs and expenses			
Software development	8,356	4,605	2,114
Customer service	4,123	1,838	1,048
Selling and marketing	8,657	2,973	1,100
General and administrative	4,762	1,580	1,751
Depreciation of purchased software	967	670	539
Total costs and expenses	26,865	11,666	6,552
Operating income	9,557	5,416	1,763
Interest income	1,891	460	8
Interest (expense)		(226)	(361)
Income before income taxes	11,448	5,650	1,410
Provision for income taxes	4,350	1,908	
Net income	$ 7,098	$ 3,742	$1,410
Net income per share	$ 0.55	$ 0.36	
Net income, as above			$1,410
Pro forma provision for income taxes			303
Pro forma net income			$1,107
Pro forma net income per share			$ 0.12
Weighted average number of shares outstanding	12,896	10,421	9,215

SOURCE: Hogan Systems, Inc., *1984 Annual Report*.

By December 31, 1987, Hogan's profits had fallen 37% despite a 10% increase in revenue (Exhibit 7.5). Hogan said that its third-quarter results in fiscal 1988 were aided by a $600,000-software sale to the National Australia Bank and a $3.6-million contract settlement with Midland Bank.[110,111,112]

Hogan had an executive bonus plan that included all officers of the company. For the years ended March 31, 1987, 1986, and 1985, executive bonuses totaled $570,000, $230,000, and $721,000, respectively.[113,114]

Effective May 1, 1985, the company discontinued the marketing development of its Management Systems for International Banking (MISB) software prod-

EXHIBIT 7.3

Consolidated Statements of Operations, Hogan Systems, Inc.

(Amounts in Thousands, Except Per Share Data)

Year Ended March 31	1987	1986	1985
Revenue			
Software products	$18,547	$12,234	$ 17,120
Maintenance fees	13,292	7,840	6,173
Customer service fees	12,252	6,939	4,952
Total revenues	44,091	27,013	28,245
Expenses			
Software development	9,163	9,377	15,520
Customer service	13,327	10,088	10,139
Selling and marketing	4,505	6,159	7,934
General and administrative	8,268	7,131	11,019
Total expenses	35,263	32,755	44,612
Operating income (loss)	8,828	(5,742)	(16,367)
Interest income	1,405	1,660	2,764
Provision for loss on discontinued product	(721)	(2,770)	(7,000)
Income (loss) before income taxes and extraordinary item	9,512	(6,852)	(20,603)
Provision (benefit) for income taxes	4,185		(6,755)
Income (loss) before extraordinary item	5,327	(6,852)	(13,848)
Realization of operating loss carryforward	4,185		
Net income (loss)	$ 9,512	$ (6,852)	$(13,848)
Per share data			
Income (loss) before extraordinary item	$ 0.37	$ (0.52)	$ (1.06)
Extraordinary item	0.29	—	—
Net income (loss)	$ 0.66	$ (0.52)	$ (1.06)
Weighted average number of common shares	14,331	13,167	13,019

SOURCE: Hogan Systems, Inc., *1987 Annual Report*.

ucts. The company recorded costs associated with this discontinuance aggregating $721,000, $2,770,000, and $7,000,000 during fiscal years 1987, 1986, and 1985 respectively.[115]

On the balance-sheet side of the financial statements, trade receivables were identified by one analyst as being a key indicator. In 1983, the balance was $593,000. After the failure of the Integrated Loans Processing System in 1984, the balance had nearly doubled to $1,175,000. By 1987, the balance had grown

EXHIBIT 7.4

Revenue from Software Sales, Hogan Systems, Inc.

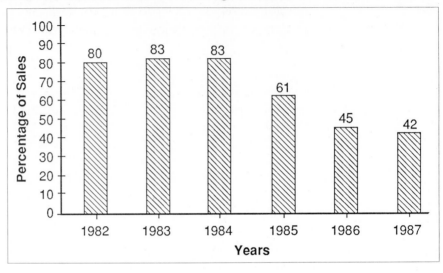

SOURCE: Hogan Systems, Inc., *1984* and *1987 Annual Reports.*

to $4.1 million (see Exhibit 7.6). The analyst felt that increases in this account reflected Hogan's inability to deliver promised products for which cash advances had been received.[116]

According to one source, Hogan received either $2.5 million or a 45% royalty fee per quarter, whichever was greater, from IBM as a result of the 1986 agreement.[117] As of December, 1987, Hogan's royalty receipts had not exceeded the minimum of $2.5 million per quarter.[118].

The company's principal sources of liquidity were cash flow from operations and the sale of common stock. At the end of fiscal 1987, Hogan planned to reinvest its earnings in operations and did not plan to pay cash dividends to common stockholders in the foreseeable future. (See Exhibits 7.7, 7.8, and 7.9.)[119]

OPERATIONS

Hogan phased out its sales force because of the agreement with IBM and subsequently discovered that IBM's sales personnel had no idea how to sell Hogan's product. Hogan was then faced with the lengthy and expensive task of recruiting and training a new sales force. Because of this, Hogan failed to generate revenue from the sale of its products for more than a year.[120]

Internally, products were developed in an unstructured manner. Hogan's programming staff consisted of some of the most technically competent personnel in the industry. Creative and highly independent, these computer "techies" were artisans who actively resisted any efforts to force them to conform to any

EXHIBIT 7.5   **Consolidated Statements of Operations For Three Quarters Ended December 31, 1987, Hogan Systems, Inc.**

(Amounts in Thousands of Dollars Except Per Share Data)

	Three Months Ended December 31		Three Months Ended September 30		Three Months Ended June 30	
	1987	1986	1987	1986	1987	1986
Revenues						
Software products	$ 3,336	$ 4,244	$ 2,901	$ 4,001	$ 3,511	$ 4,975
Maintenance fees	3,241	3,018	2,556	2,998	3,372	2,956
Customer service fees	4,412	3,657	4,909	3,762	4,503	4,201
Contract settlement and related fees	3,603	—	—	—	—	—
Deferred maintenance adjustment	(2,495)	—	—	—	—	—
Total revenues	$12,097	$10,919	$10,366	$10,761	$11,386	$12,132
Expenses						
Software development	$ 2,827	$ 1,929	$ 2,832	$ 2,268	$ 2,495	$ 2,834
Customer service	4,739	3,687	4,753	3,743	4,585	4,009
Selling and marketing	838	638	687	1,124	675	2,008
General and administrative	2,491	2,044	5,264	1,960	2,090	2,454
Total expenses	$10,895	$ 8,298	$13,536	$ 9,095	$ 9,845	$11,305
Operating income (loss)	$ 1,202	$ 2,621	$ (3,170)	$ 1,666	$ 1,541	$ 827
Interest income	662	336	363	302	377	398
Income (loss) before income taxes and extraordinary item	$ 1,864	$ 2,957	$ (2,807)	$ 1,968	$ 1,918	$ 1,225
Provision for income taxes	950	1,297	(887)	857	887	558
Income (loss) before extraordinary item	$ 914	$ 1,660	$ (1,920)	$ 1,111	$ 1,031	$ 667
Realization of operating loss carryforward	$ 950	1,279	(887)	849	887	450
Net income (loss)	$ 1,864	$ 2,939	$ (2,807)	$ 1,960	$ 1,918	$ 1,117
Per share data						
Income (loss) before extraordinary item	$ .06	$ .11	$ (.13)	$ .07	.07	$ .05
Net income (loss)	—	—	$ (.19)	$ .13	.13	.08
Earnings per share	$ .13	$ .20	$ —	$ —	$ —	$ —
Weighted average number of shares	14,200	14,900	14,500	14,800	15,259	14,680

SOURCE: Hogan Systems company records.

EXHIBIT 7.6

Trade Receivables Due after One Year, Hogan Systems, Inc.

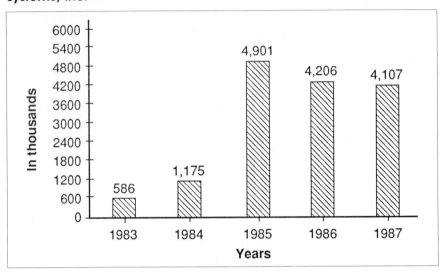

SOURCE: Hogan Systems, Inc., *1984–1987 Annual Reports.*

type of standardization. New product development was largely unplanned and was not coordinated with the objectives and activities of the rest of the organization. Apparently there were no initial reviews of the designs of proposed projects; instead, changes were made to correct obvious design errors after projects were completed.[121]

Each of Hogan's clients required computer software that was customized to meet their special requirements. Therefore, some of Hogan's staff members were assigned to install and modify Hogan's standard products as required by the client. Upon learning of a successful modification to one of the basic products, Hogan's board members reputedly instructed the marketing department to notify prospective clients that a new enhancement to the product was available. Unfortunately, attempting to transfer modifications from one customized system to another created substantial technical problems.[122]

Some industry observers felt that the company was selling new products before the products had been fully developed and tested. It was rumored that, upon being informed that the release of a new product was to be announced on the following Monday, the product development staff was required to work around the clock to finish and test the product on Saturday and Sunday. It was not unusual for programmers to work at least sixty hours a week. Although Hogan's salaries were reputed to have been 30% higher than the rest of the industry, some personnel believed the financial compensation was not equitable

EXHIBIT 7.7   **Consolidated Balance Sheets, 1987, Hogan Systems, Inc.**
(Dollar Amounts in Thousands of Dollars)

	MARCH 31	
	1987	1986
Assets		
Current assets:		
Cash and short-term investments	$21,239	$17,252
Accounts receivable, net of allowance for doubtful accounts of $999,000 and $512,000	14,677	14,322
Prepaid expenses and other current assets	554	623
Total current assets	36,470	32,197
Cash pledged under escrow agreement	2,400	
Installment receivables collectible after one year, net of allowance for doubtful accounts of $1,867,000 at March 31, 1986	4,107	4,206
Furniture, equipment and leasehold improvements, at cost, net of accumulated depreciation of $7,495,000 and $5,172,000	4,657	6,347
Software, at cost, net of accumulated amortization of $3,963,000 and $3,554,000	3,163	1,056
Other assets	593	378
Total assets	$51,390	$44,184
Liabilities and Shareholders' Equity		
Current liabilities		
Accounts payable	$ 1,189	$ 1,885
Accrued payroll	945	1,218
Deferred maintenance and training revenue	5,560	8,411
Accrual for discontinued product	2,166	2,797
Other	3,228	3,340
Total current liabilities	13,088	17,651
Customer deposits on software systems	451	651
Accrual for discontinued product	975	1,139
Other liabilities	742	591
Total liabilities	15,256	20,032
Shareholders' equity:		
Common stock, par value $.01—authorized 50,000,000 shares—outstanding 13,852,000 at March 31, 1987 and 13,364,000 at March 31, 1986	139	134
Capital in excess of par value	37,867	35,469
Accumulated deficit	(1,872)	(11,451)
Total shareholders' equity	36,134	24,152
Total liabilities and shareholders' equity	$51,390	$44,184

SOURCE: Hogan Systems, Inc., *1987 Annual Report.*

EXHIBIT 7.8

Consolidated Balance Sheets For Three Quarters Ended December 31, 1987, Hogan Systems, Inc.

(Dollar Amounts in Thousands)

	DECEMBER 31, 1987	SEPTEMBER 30, 1987	JUNE 30, 1987
Assets			
Current assets			
Cash and short-term investments	$30,520	$24,413	$23,132
Accounts receivable, net	9,812	21,421	14,924
Prepaid expenses and other current assets	948	676	757
Total current assets	$41,280	$46,510	$38,813
Cash pledged under escrow agreement	—	—	2,400
Installment receivables due after one year	932	919	4,004
Fixed assets, software, and other assets	9,509	—	—
Furniture, equipment and leasehold improvements, at cost, net of accumulated depreciation of $8,641,000 and $8,093,000	—	4,214	4,401
Software, at cost, net of accumulated amortization of $4,167,000 and $4,064,000	—	3,980	3,601
Other assets	—	698	660
Total assets	$51,721	$56,321	$53,879
Liabilities			
Current liabilities:			
Accounts payable and accrued expenses	$ 3,707	$ 3,093	$ 1,662
Deferred maintenance and training revenue	6,976	4,609	5,022
Deferred customer service revenue	—	2,512	—
Accrual for discontinued product	—	—	377
Other	5,809	5,734	4,607
Total current liabilities	$16,492	$15,948	$11,668
Deferred software revenue	1,005	1,370	—
Deferred customer service revenue	—	1,803	993
Customer deposits on software systems	—	—	1,245
Accrual for discontinued product	—	—	945
Other liabilities	968	1,056	79
Total liabilities	$18,465	$20,177	$14,930
Shareholders' equity	33,256	—	—
Common stock, par value $.01–50,000,000 shares authorized; 14,482,000 outstanding at September 30, 1987 and 14,476,000 outstanding at June 30, 1987	—	145	145
Capital in excess of par value	—	38,146	38,126
Accumulated earnings (deficit)	—	(2,147)	678
Total shareholders' equity	$33,256	$36,144	$38,949
Total liabilities and shareholders' equity	$51,721	$56,321	$53,879

SOURCE: Hogan Systems company records

EXHIBIT 7.9

Profits, Revenues, and Income, Hogan Systems, Inc.

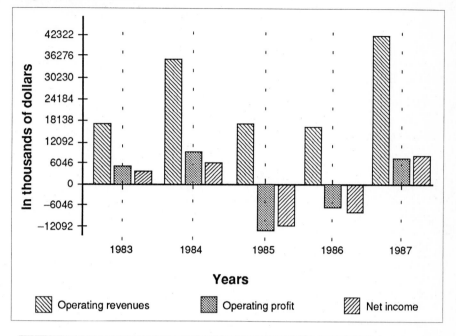

SOURCE: Hogan Systems company records.

in terms of the number of hours the programmers were required to work. In addition, the "family" atmosphere that had prevailed in the pre-IBM days disappeared and was replaced by a "pressure cooker" environment. It was not surprising, therefore, that Hogan had a high turnover rate among its programmers and management staff.[123]

THE FUTURE

Gary Fiedler, Hogan's President and Chairman of the Board, stated that, in his estimation, the company's main problem was "lumpy sales" that caused a discontinuous revenue stream.[124] However, an industry analyst remarked that "Hogan's not in financial trouble, but its problem is marketing. They have to come to grips with how to sell their packages."[125] The same analyst also suggested that Hogan's interests might best be served by becoming independent from IBM and seeking other marketing alternatives.[126] Other informed observers noted that the Cullinet/DEC alliance may have made it infeasible for Hogan to break away from IBM.

By mid-1988, it was obvious that many issues needed to be resolved to ensure the long-term success of Hogan Systems, Inc. Whether the company's management team fully realized the extent of the problems facing them remained to be seen.

A FINAL COMMENT

In mid-1988, a newspaper article provided a synopsis of the financial crises, layoffs, and management upheaval that had plagued Hogan Systems since 1984, and concluded

In the fiscal year ended March 31, Hogan earned $2.1 million or $0.15/share on revenues of $46.7 million, numbers that Fiedler describes as "unsatisfactory."

"There were some events that we consider to be positioning events that depressed our profitability," said Fiedler. "We are spending heavily on development and will continue to spend heavily this year."

"What we have got to do is stabilize that growth. It has got to be sustainable growth. That I think is something that has not been handled well in the past. . . . I think it is sustainable."[127]

NOTES

1. "Aldridge Resigns As COO, President of Hogan Systems," *Dallas Morning News*, February 9, 1988, p. 7D.

2. Tom Lawton, "A Banking Software Story," *Datamation*, November 1, 1985, p. 100.

3. Thomas O'Donnell, "Software's Solid Citizen," *Forbes*, August 29, 1983, p. 71.

4. "Hogan Systems, Inc.," *Rotan Mosle Guide— Texas/Oklahoma* (Deerfield, Illinois: Scholl Communications Incorporated, 1985), p. 104.

5. Robert H. Stovall, "Vigorous Growth At a Discount," *Financial World*, (November 28–December 11, 1984), p. 53.

6. O'Donnell, "Software's Solid Citizen," p. 71.

7. *Ibid.*, p. 70.

8. *Ibid.*, p. 70.

9. Lawton, "A Banking Software Story," p. 100.

10. Paul, Gillin, "Loans Processing System Out for IBM CPUs," *Computerworld*, April 9, 1984, p. 77.

11. Lawton, "A Banking Software Story," p. 100.

12. *Ibid.*, p. 100.

13. Interview with Gary W. Fiedler, President and Chairman of the Board—Hogan Systems, Inc., February 8, 1988.

14. Robert J. Crutchfield, "Yankee Down South," *Datamation*, January 1, 1985, p. 129.

15. *Ibid.*, p. 129.

16. Lawton, "A Banking Software Story," p. 100.

17. David O. Tyson, "Hogan Starts Delivering Rewritten Loans System," *American Banker*, February 11, 1987, p. 6.

18. Charles Babcock, "IBM Partnership a Boon to Trouble-Plagued Hogan," *Computerworld*, May 19, 1986, p. 146.

19. *Ibid.*, p. 146.

20. Robert J. Crutchfield, "Banking on Big Blue," *Datamation*, July 15, 1986, p. 34.

21. Babcock, "IBM Partnership a Boon to Trouble-Plagued Hogan," p. 144.

22. Crutchfield, "Banking on Big Blue," p. 38.

23. Interview with Jim Poyner, Technical Analyst— Rauscher Pierce Refsnes, Inc., February 19, 1988.

24. "Will IBM Agreement Rescue Hogan?" *ABA Banking Journal*, August, 1986, p. 22.

25. Babcock, "IBM Partnership a Boon to Trouble-Plagued Hogan," p. 144.

26. "Will IBM Agreement Rescue Hogan?" p. 24.

27. Crutchfield, "Banking on Big Blue," p. 32.

28. Tyson, "Hogan Starts Delivering Rewritten Loans System," p. 6.

29. David LaGesse, "Hogan Enhances Loan Soft-

ware for Mortgage Banking Clients," *American Banker*, March 13, 1987, p. 6.

30. David O. Tyson, "Hogan Takes Aim at Community Banks with New Integrated Software," *American Banker*, October 5, 1987, p. 14.

31. David O. Tyson, "Hogan Plans to Appeal to Community Banks, Build International System with BankVision," *American Banker*, September 30, 1987, p. 8.

32. Yvette D. Kantrow, "Hogan Buys Marketer of International Software," *American Banker*, (May 8, 1987), p. 2.

33. David O. Tyson, "Hogan Executives Disclaim IBM Link in Abrupt McTavish Exit," *American Banker*, July 12, 1987, p. 5.

34. *Ibid.*, p. 5.

35. Alan Alper, "Hogan Chairman Resigns," *Computerworld*, July 20, 1987, p. 74.

36. *Ibid.*, p. 74.

37. *Ibid.*, p. 74.

38. Tyson, "Hogan Executives Disclaim IBM Link in Abrupt McTavish Exit," p. 5.

39. *Ibid.*, p. 5.

40. Clinton Wilder, "Hogan–IBM Pact Fails to Deliver," *Computerworld*, September 28, 1987, p. 95.

41. David O. Tyson, "Midland Bank to Continue with Hogan," *American Banker*, September 10, 1987, p. 13.

42. Hogan News Release, "Hogan Systems Reports Profit for Third Quarter of Fiscal Year 1988," January 26, 1988, pp. 1–4.

43. Charles Babcock, "Hungry Giant Looms over Software Marketplace," *Computerworld*, November 3, 1986, p. 209.

44. Lawton, "A Banking Software Story," p. 98.

45. *Ibid.*, p. 98.

46. Scott C. Miller, "Unraveling Seams between Computer Systems," *American Banker*, September 9, 1987, p. 10.

47. Lawton, "A Banking Software Story," p. 98.

48. Miller, "Unraveling Seams between Computer Systems," p. 10.

49. John A. Pearce, II, Richard B. Robinson, Jr., and Larry D. Alexander, *Company and Industry Cases in Strategy and Policy* (Homewood, Illinois: Richard D. Irwin, 1986), p. 136.

50. Michael P. Sullivan. "Expert Marketers Put Expert Systems to Use," *American Banker*, March 3, 1988, p. 4.

51. Tyson, "Hogan Takes Aim at Community Banks with New Integrated Software," p. 14.

52. "3 Texas Bank Failures Boost US Total to 28," *American Banker*, March 1, 1988, p. 14.

53. "The Bruisers Took a Beating in 1987," *Business Week*, April 4, 1988, p. 90.

54. *Ibid.*, p. 90.

55. Thomas P. Rideout. "First the Bad News . . . ," *ABA Banking Journal*, October, 1987, p. 38.

56. "The Bruisers Took a Beating in 1987," p. 90.

57. Mehdi Beheshtian. "Computer Copyright Law," *Journal of Systems Management*, September, 1986, pp. 6–11.

58. Esther Roditti Schachter, "Software Protection in the Throes of a Legal Morass," *Datamation*, June 1, 1987, pp. 49–58.

59. *Ibid.*, p. 50.

60. *Ibid.*, p. 53.

61. "Privacy," *Business Week*, March 28, 1988, pp. 61–68.

62. Richard O. Mason, "Four Ethical Issues of the Information Age," *MIS Quarterly*, March, 1986, p. 5.

63. Arthur E. Parry, "Seven Exposures CFO's Should Know About," *Healthcare Financial Management*, June, 1983, pp. 24–30.

64. Nicholas A. Lash, *Banking Laws and Regulations* (Englewood Cliffs, N. J.: Prentice-Hall, 1987), pp. 15–20.

65. *Ibid.*

66. "Banks Are on the Brink of Breaking Loose," *Business Week*, March 7, 1988, p. 99.

67. Interview with Jim Poyner.

68. Clinton Wilder, "Hogan Exec Resigns; Firm Faces Struggle," *Computerworld*, February 15, 1988, p. 105.

69. David O. Tyson, "Hogan Systems President Quits as Software Sales Disappoint," *American Banker*, February 10, 1988, p. 2.

70. Hogan News Release, "Hogan Announces Organizational Changes," February 8, 1988, p. 2.

71. *Ibid.*, p. 1.

72. Hogan Systems company records: Gary W. Fiedler.

73. *Ibid.*

74. *Ibid.*

75. Rosemary Hamilton, "Bank Experience Valuable Asset for Hogan CEO," *Computerworld*, August 31, 1987, p. 69.

76. Hogan News Release. "Hogan Announces . . . Changes."

77. Hogan Systems company records: C. Donald McCullough, Jr.

78. Hogan Systems company records: Patric J. Jerge.

79. Hogan Systems company records: Michael R. Mainelli.

80. Hogan Systems company records: Jack R. Spradley.

81. Hogan Systems company records: James J. Murphy.

82. Hogan Systems company records: Donald F. Campbell.

83. Hogan Systems company records: Stuart K. Williams.

84. Interview with Patric J. Jerge, Senior Vice-President of Sales and Marketing—Hogan System, Inc., March 14, 1988.

85. *Ibid.*

86. *Ibid.*

87. *Ibid.*

88. *Ibid.*

89. *Ibid.*

90. *Ibid.*

91. *Ibid.*

92. *Ibid.*

93. *Ibid.*

94. *Ibid.*

95. *Ibid.*

96. *Ibid.*

97. Edith Myers, "Hard Time for Bank Software," *Datamation*, March 15, 1985, p. 66.

98. Nell Margolis and Rosemary Hamilton, "Cullinet Braces for Battle of Its Life," *Computerworld*, March 28, 1988, p. 1.

99. *Ibid.*, p. 112.

100. Interview with Fiedler.

101. David O. Tyson. "EDS, MTech Merger Expected by End of March," *American Banker*, March 14, 1988, p. 2.

102. Interview with Jerge.

103. *Ibid.*

104. Interview with Jerge.

105. *Ibid.*

106. Hogan Systems, Inc., *1984* Annual Report, p. 18.

107. Hogan Systems, Inc., *1985* Annual Report, p. 16.

108. Hogan Systems company records, *First Quarter Report*, 1988.

109. Hogan Systems company records, *Second Quarter Report*, 1988.

110. Hogan News Release, "Hogan Systems Reports Profit for Third Quarter of Fiscal Year 1988," pp. 3–4.

111. David O. Tyson, "Hogan Projects Big Loss, To Analysts' Surprise," *American Banker*, September 8, 1987, p. 3.

112. "Profit At Hogan Systems Declines 37%," *Dallas Morning News*, January 27, 1988, p. 4D.

113. Hogan Systems, Inc., *1986 Annual Report*, p. 19.

114. Hogan Systems, Inc., *1987 Annual Report*, p. 14.

115. *Ibid.*

116. Interview with Jim Poyner.

117. *Ibid.*

118. Hogan Systems, Inc., *1987 Annual Report*.

119. *Ibid.*

120. Interview with reputable confidential informant, April 15, 1988.

121. *Ibid.*

122. *Ibid.*

123. *Ibid.*

124. Interview with Gary Fiedler.

125. Wilder, "Hogan Exec Resigns . . . ," p. 105.

126. Interview with Jim Poyner.

127. Jim Mitchell, "All Systems Go," *Dallas Morning News*, May 7, 1988, p. 1F.

CASE 8

The Golden Gate Brewing Company

BRENT CALLINICOS ● RICHARD I. LEVIN

At a booth in Harry's, a bar overlooking the San Francisco Bay, James Cook poured a fresh glass of amber-colored Golden Gate Lager and dropped a bottle cap onto the beer's head. The cap floated like a lily pad on the foam. "That's what you get from using all malt, no rices or corn—a very firm head," he said. "It looks like whipped cream and acts like egg whites, as my father used to say." When Cook's glass was finished, the inside was coated with strips of foam, *Belgian lace* in brewer's jargon, and a sign of a beer's purity. "People usually think of a local beer as crummy, cheap beer. I plan to change the way they think," Cook said.

Cook is apt to talk this way, because (1) he is President of the fledgling Golden Gate Brewing Company, (2) he is the brewer of Golden Gate Lager, and (3) he is the sixth consecutive eldest son to become a brewer.

Cook, 36, is a former high-paid, high-powered management consultant with the Boston Consulting Group; he holds a Harvard B.A., M.B.A., and J.D. In 1984, Cook's idea of brewing and distributing a high-quality beer, capable of luring discerning beer drinkers away from European and Canadian imports, was just an idea. Golden Gate Lager was introduced in San Francisco on July 4, an appropriate day, but accidental timing according to Cook. The Golden Gate Brewing Company was incorporated in 1984.

Cook's goal is clear: "I intend to go head to head against imported beers. Nowhere in the world but America do they drink so much imported beer. Here, imported beer is popular because our domestic beer is so bad. My work is to give Americans an alternative to drinking foreign beers. I want to start a revolution in the way people think about American beer. There is nothing wrong with

This case was re-written by Brent Callinicos, Research Assistant, under the direction of Professor Richard I. Levin, University of North Carolina at Chapel Hill—Graduate School of Business, as a basis for class discussion and not to illustrate either effective or ineffective handling of an administrative situation. Copyright © 1988. Reprinted by permission.

EXHIBIT 8.1 **San Francisco Bay Area**

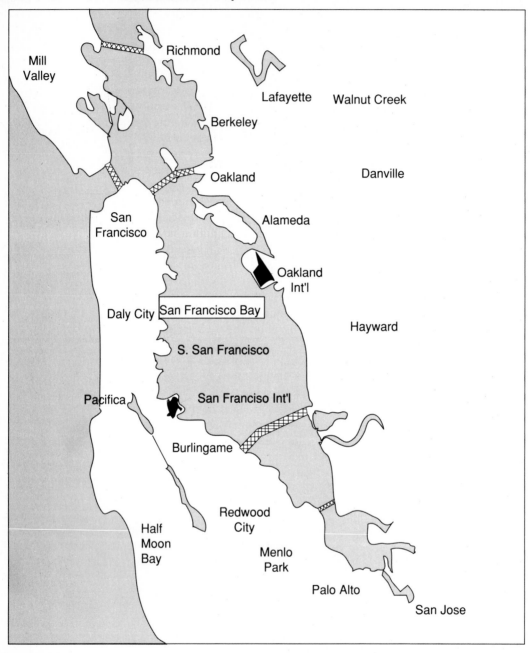

standard domestic beers, for what they are. They are clean, consistent and cheap. But they are also bland and mediocre. They are mass market products. People can recall, off the top of their heads, the advertising, the slogans and the music for most beers, but they can't remember the taste."

For years, small local breweries have been swallowed up by the giants like Anheuser-Busch. The advent of small boutique breweries, in California, Colorado, and New York, making limited quantities of quality beer, has opposed this trend. Analogous to David confronting Goliath, Cook acknowledges that the odds and the history are against small regional breweries. But Cook is betting on a combination of his family brewing background, his own management training, and a limited target market to create long-term Golden Gate Lager drinkers.

Golden Gate Lager is currently sold in two locations, San Francisco and Munich. As of November 1985, the current sales volume of 6,000 cases per month represents less than one minute of production for Anheuser-Busch. Cook reports that he has sold as much beer in the past six months as Anheuser-Busch makes in about six minutes: "They spill more beer every hour than I make in a month." In six months, the Golden Gate Brewing Company has sold 25,000 cases in California. His more than 200 accounts range from liquor stores to exclusive hotels to neighborhood bars, such as Harry's. Exhibits 8.1–8.3 provide information regarding the population demographics of the San Francisco SCSA (Standard Consolidated Statistical Area) and general demographics of U.S. beer drinkers.

"By my standards I have been very successful," said Cook. Demand had been strong, but he wondered if it would last. "People who drink imports will try it because it's new, but will Golden Gate Lager be just a flash?" Cook is hoping there are enough beer aficionados in San Francisco, but he is wondering if he should try to expand in Europe, or if he should concentrate on the west coast, the east coast, or selected cities throughout the country. How fast should he expand? Can Cook sustain his momentum as regionals, such as Coors, expand distribution nationwide? With several comparable local brews being sold in the area, will his marketing strategy have to change? Given the complex issues facing the beer industry, how should he proceed? What are the risks involved? Cook realized he needed to make some strategic decisions.

THE BEER INDUSTRY IN THE UNITED STATES

Dimensions of the Industry

The annual retail value of the brewing industry's products is near $3.7 billion. Total employment in the industry is close to 40,000 persons.

The average hourly earnings of a brewing industry employee was $18.27 in 1985, a 3.2% increase over 1984.

In a recent typical year, the industry's gross assets amounted to $6,639,979,000. Its net worth, computed from income tax returns, was $3,377,780,000.

EXHIBIT 8.2

Population Characteristics, San Francisco/Oakland SCSA-1980

During the decade 1970 to 1980, the population of San Francisco/Oakland SCSA (Standard Consolidated Statistical Area) increased by 142,000 people, or 4.57%.

Number of People

YEAR	SF/OAKLAND SCSA*	PERCENT CHANGE
1960	2,649,000	N/A
1970	3,109,000	17.37
1980	3,251,000	4.57

*SCSA = Standard Consolidated Statistical Area

Age Composition

AGE	# PEOPLE	PERCENT OF SCSA
Under 18	1,296,000	25.02
18–24	666,000	12.86
25–34	989,000	19.10
35–44	668,000	12.90
45–54	536,000	10.35
55–64	491,000	9.48
65–over	533,000	10.29
Under 21	1,571,000	30.33

Ethnic Data

RACE	PERCENT OF SF/OAKLAND SCSA
White	62.37
Black	10.71
Spanish	9.64
Indian	10.93
Eskimo	.47
Other**	5.88

Education, Persons 25 years old and over

YEARS OF EDUCATION	PERCENT OF SCSA
Less than 5	3
High School Only	71
Four year college or more	26
Median school years completed	13

**Includes Japanese, Chinese, Filipino, Korean, Asian Indian, Vietnamese, Hawaiian, Samoan, etc.

Of the persons 16 years old and over, 66.5% were in the labor force. (This includes those in armed forces) Of these 43.4% were females and 56.6% were males.

Occupation

GROUP	PERCENT OF SCSA
Managerial and Professional	28.28
Technical and Sales-related	35.43
Service Occupations	11.84
Farming/Forestry/Fishing	1.15
Craft/Repair Group	11.12
Operators/Laborers	12.18

Income Breakdown

INCOME	HOUSEHOLDS	PERCENT OF SCSA
Under $5,000	199,763	10.12
$5,000–$9,999	243,278	12.32
$10,000–$19,999	511,225	25.90
$20,000–$34,999	611,279	30.97
$35,000–$49,999	258,758	13.11
$50,000–Over	149,577	7.58
Total households	1,973,880	
Median income	$20,607	

EXHIBIT 8.3   **1983 U.S. Beer Drinker Demographics**

	PERCENTAGE OF THE POPULATION DRINKING					
	Domestic	Light	Imported	Malt	Ale	Draft
All Adults	39.6%	24.4%	15.8%	8.3%	8.6%	26.2%
Males	54.0	28.6	22.0	11.0	12.0	35.6
Females	26.6	20.6	10.3	5.9	5.5	17.7
Age:						
18–24	51.2	29.1	26.6	14.8	14.0	36.5
25–34	49.0	30.8	20.8	10.9	10.9	36.1
35–44	39.3	27.8	15.8	7.3	7.8	26.8
45–54	35.5	23.5	13.5	5.6	7.0	22.8
55–64	30.9	16.7	8.5	4.1	5.6	16.9
65 or older	23.4	13.0	4.6	4.3	3.8	9.8
Grad. college	47.5	32.2	28.0	6.0	12.4	36.3
Attended college	45.3	30.0	22.0	8.9	11.9	33.5
Grad. high school	38.4	23.9	13.6	8.4	7.8	25.8
Not grad. high school	23.6	17.4	8.5	9.2	5.6	16.7
Employed full time	46.2	30.2	20.4	9.0	10.5	33.2
Part time	36.7	24.9	17.7	8.0	9.0	26.5
Not employed	32.1	17.3	10.1	7.6	6.2	17.7
Professional	48.2	32.8	27.1	7.4	12.8	37.0
Clerical/Sales	38.6	29.8	17.6	7.3	9.2	29.2
Craftsman/Foreman	52.9	30.7	17.7	9.1	8.4	36.3
Other employed	44.3	25.5	16.2	11.5	9.6	28.9
Single	50.8	28.5	29.0	14.9	14.5	36.5
Married	38.3	24.1	12.9	6.1	7.1	24.6
Divorced	30.7	20.2	11.0	8.7	6.7	19.6
Parents	41.0	26.5	14.5	8.8	7.7	27.9
White	39.8	24.9	15.8	6.1	8.4	27.4
Black	36.8	19.3	14.4	25.4	9.8	16.4
Other	42.0	27.6	25.6	12.7	7.5	27.6
Geographic location:						
Northeast	42.9	22.0	22.3	7.2	13.5	27.7
East central	39.1	24.2	11.6	7.5	9.3	27.2
West central	42.3	29.0	13.1	7.4	5.6	30.3
South	32.7	22.8	11.1	9.6	6.4	21.0
Pacific	45.1	26.1	22.3	9.5	7.8	28.4

(Continued)

EXHIBIT 8.3   (Continued)

| | PERCENTAGE OF THE POPULATION DRINKING | | | | | |
	Domestic	Light	Imported	Malt	Ale	Draft
Household income:						
$40,000+	45.6	29.7	24.1	6.0	11.8	32.7
$30,000+	44.2	28.8	22.5	6.0	10.7	32.0
$25,000+	44.1	28.4	21.3	6.4	10.3	31.4
$20–24,999	38.1	26.0	14.0	6.8	7.7	27.5
$15–19,999	42.5	26.7	14.5	10.9	8.7	28.8
$10–14,999	36.0	20.9	11.2	9.1	7.1	21.7
under $10,000	32.3	16.5	9.5	11.3	6.5	16.6

What the Industry Buys

Agricultural commodities, the output of more than four million acres of farm land worth over $700 million, are used annually by the brewing industry. These include

- 4.9 billion pounds or 143.8 million bushels of choice malt—worth $380M;
- other select grains, chiefly corn and rice—worth $221 million; and
- hops—value to the grower of $80 million.

Some 86.9% of all beer sold is packaged in cans or bottles. In one year, the brewing industry uses more than

- 33.1 billion steel and aluminum cans;
- 19.2 billion bottles in returnable and non-returnable form; and
- $525 million for interest, rentals, repairs, maintenance, etc.

The industry's annual bill for containers—cans, bottles, kegs and related packaging materials purchased from other American industries—is close to $4.5 billion. Supplies and services of numerous kinds are also required in brewing and distributing malt beverages. Annual average outlays for these include

- fuel, power and water, $420 million;
- wholesale payroll, $1.8 billion; and
- brewery equipment and improvements, $550 million.

The Industry's Products and Terminology

Beers fall into two broad categories—those that are top-fermented and those that are bottom-fermented.

Bottom-fermented

Pilsner/Pilsener. The world's most famous beer style, it was named after the excellent beer brewed in Pilsen, Czechoslovakia, for the past 700 years. The term became generic, but the finest example remains Pilsner Urqueil from Pilsen. It is a pale, golden-colored, distinctly hoppy beer.

Lager. All bottom-fermented beers are lagers. This is a generic term, though it is sometimes applied to the most basic bottom-fermented brew produced by a brewery. In Britain and the United States, the majority of lagers are very loose, local interpretations of the Pilsner style.

Bock. Bock Beer is a special springtime brew, made like lager beer, but of a somewhat deeper color and more pronounced flavor.

Top-fermented

Ale. Generic term for English-style top-fermented beers. Usually copper-colored, but sometimes darker. It is usually paler in color and differs in flavor from lager beer.

Porter. Originally a local London beer made with roasted, unmalted barley, well hopped, and blended. Dark brown, it is as heavy as most ales.

Stout. Darker in color and sweeter or maltier than ale. The darkest, richest, maltiest of all regularly produced beers.

"Malt Liquor." This is a term conjured up to describe beers that exceed the legal alcohol levels—5% in the United States—of that nation. They are most often made as lagers, but the American version can be sweetish or more bitter than the traditional lagers.

Barrel. This refers to a full barrel, which has a volume of 31 gallons.

Industry Overview

Historically, the U.S. beer industry had many small regional producers, but now it is emerging as an oligopoly—a market structure dominated by only a few firms. In 1876, there were 2,685 breweries and in 1947 there were only 500. The number of operating breweries declined from more than 350 in 1952 to fewer than 80 in 1982 (see Exhibit 8.4). Acquisition, consolidation and standardization has characterized this industry. While this trend has been mirrored in each of the four census regions, it was least pronounced in the South and the West, where the overall demand for beer grew rapidly. Major national firms were more willing to purchase struggling regional producers or construct new facilities in the South and West. Today there are six major national brewers which control over 90% of the domestic sales. The companies are Anheuser-Busch, Miller, Stroh, Heileman, Coors, and Pabst (see Exhibit 8.5).

After several years of flat or nearly flat sales, beer consumption declined about 0.7% in 1984. This represents the first decline in twenty-seven years. The

EXHIBIT 8.4

Number of Operating Breweries by Census Region

REGION	1952	1960	1970	1982	PERCENT OF TOTAL 1952	PERCENT OF TOTAL 1982
Northeast	100	62	45	18	28.0	22.8
North central	164	99	61	25	45.9	31.6
South	42	33	26	20	11.8	25.3
West	51	35	22	16	14.3	20.3
Total U.S.	357	229	154	79	100.0	100.0

EXHIBIT 8.5

Leading U.S. Brewers' Domestic Beer Market Share
(In %)

Brewer	1970	1975	1980	1982	1983	1984
Anheuser-Busch	18.2	23.7	28.9	33.5	34.1	34.6
Miller	4.2	8.7	21.5	22.3	21.1	22.1
Stroh[1]	2.7	3.5	3.6	13.0	13.7	13.5
G. Heileman	2.5	3.1	7.7	8.2	9.9	9.3
Adolph Coors	6.0	8.0	8.0	6.8	7.7	7.2
Pabst	8.6	10.5	8.7	6.8	7.2	6.8
Genesee	1.2	1.5	2.1	1.9	1.8	1.9
C. Schmidt	2.5	2.2	2.1	1.8	1.8	1.7
Falstaff	5.4	5.0	2.3	1.8	1.5	1.8
Pittsburgh			.6	.6	.6	.5
Other	48.7	33.8	14.5	3.3	.6	.6
Total	100.0	100.0	100.0	100.0	100.0	100.0

[1] Stroh acquired F.M. Schaefer Brewing and Jos. Schlitz Brewing in 1981 and 1982, respectively.

year 1984 also closed with a decline in production of approximately 1.2%. Per capita consumption of beer has also declined, and for 1985, per capita consumption is estimated to remain at the 1984 level—24 gallons. The long-term outlook for the industry is less encouraging. Chris Lole of The Stroh Brewery Co. believes beer sales will remain flat for the next ten, possibly twenty, years (see Exhibits 8.6–8.9).

However, there is one segment of growth in this troubled industry—imports. Imported brands have grown from 0.7% of total consumption in 1970 to 3.4% in 1983 (aided somewhat over the years by a strong U.S. dollar). Imports occupy the highground in terms of quality in consumers' perception; and trading up continues to benefit imports. As import volume has grown, an increasing num-

EXHIBIT 8.6

U.S. Beer Sales—Domestic and Imported, 1984 and 1983
(Total Does Not Include Exports)

	31-GALLON BARRELS (IN MILLIONS)		% OF TOTAL		% GAIN/LOSS
	1984	1983	1984	1983	1984
Domestic beer	175.3	177.5	96.1	96.6	−1.2
Imported beer	7.2	6.3	3.9	3.4	14.3
Total sales	182.5	183.8	100.0	100.0	−0.7

EXHIBIT 8.7

Production of Malt Beverages in the United States, Selected Years
(In Thousands)

YEAR	BARRELS	YEAR	BARRELS
1904	48,265	1977	172,229
1914	66,189	1978	171,639
1924	4,891	1979	183,515
1934	37,679	1980	188,374
1944	81,726	1981	194,542
1954	92,561	1982	193,984
1964	103,018	1983	195,664
1974	153,053	1984	193,416

EXHIBIT 8.8

U.S. Per Capita Consumption of Malt Beverages, 1974–1984
(Years In Gallons)

1974	20.9	1978	23.1	1982	24.4
1975	21.3	1979	23.8	1983	24.2
1976	21.5	1980	24.3	1984	24.0
1977	22.4	1981	24.6		

ber of brands have appeared, and many more are now being advertised. The continued growth in this segment, coupled with the decline in domestic sales, meant an increase in imports' share to almost 4% in 1984.

For regional and smaller brewers, it is becoming increasingly difficult to move a product that is falling in demand and cannot be backed by the advertising

EXHIBIT 8.9

Barrelage of Top Ten Brewers, 1984 vs. 1983

(In 31-Gallon Barrels;
Total Includes Exports But No Imports)

	1984	1983	GAIN/LOSS (Barrels)	GAIN/LOSS (%)
Anheuser-Busch	64,000,000	60,500,000	3,500,000	5.8
Miller	37,520,000	37,470,000	50,000	0.1
Stroh	23,900,000	24,300,000	(400,000)	−1.6
G. Heileman	16,760,000	17,549,000	(789,000)	−4.5
Adolph Corrs	13,187,000	13,719,000	(532,000)	−3.9
Pabst	11,562,000	12,804,000	(1,242,000)	−9.7
Genesee	3,000,000	3,200,000	(200,000)	−6.3
C. Schmidt	2,500,000	2,800,000	(300,000)	−10.7
Falstaff	2,338,000	2,705,000	(367,000)	−13.6
Pittsburgh	950,000	1,000,000	(50,000)	−5.0
All others	2,134,000	3,597,000	(1,463,000)	−40.7
Total	177,851,000	179,644,000	(1,793,000)	−1.0

revenues of the large national breweries. Interestingly, the microbrewer/brew pub trend continues. More and more entrepreneurs are allured by the prospects of concocting their own distinctive beer and operating their own business.

Some explain the disappointing sales trends by pointing to the 7% price hike many brewers took at the beginning of 1983. This put beer prices well ahead of the inflation rate. However, there was no discernible improvement in sales when prices were discounted and income and employment levels improved.

External Factors: Threats to the Industry

The beer industry must operate in a changing environment, where the name of the game is survival for some domestic breweries. There are several external threats that affect the beer industry. First is that the U.S. population is increasingly interested in healthier lifestyles, which could reduce beer consumption. Consumption and purchase-pattern preference of 25–40-year-olds have changed dramatically in recent years. This group, because of interests in appearance, exercise, and career advancement, exhibits a preference for drinks with fewer calories and lower alcohol content. Over-40 drinkers are also increasingly health and diet conscious.

An important negative factor for future beer sales is demographics. Growth of the 18–34-year-old age group is winding down. Beer sales have closely tracked the baby boom age bulge in the population. Domestic industry sales grew at only a 0.6% compounded rate in the 1950's and 3.5% in the 1960's and 1970's.

EXHIBIT 8.10   **U.S. Population by Selected Age Groups, 1983–1990**

AGE GROUP	POPULATION			COMPOUND ANNUAL CHANGE 1983–90
	1983	1985	1990	
Young children Under 15 Years	22.0%	21.7%	21.9%	0.8%
Teens, 15–19	8.2	7.7	6.8	−1.7
Young adults, 20–29	18.3	18.1	16.0	−0.3
Middle years 30–39	15.1	15.9	16.8	2.5
40–49	10.4	10.8	12.7	3.9
Older adults, 50–64	14.3	13.8	13.1	−0.3
Senior citizens, 65 and older	11.7	12.0	12.7	2.2
Total population (millions)	243.3	238.6	249.8	0.9

Exhibit 8.10 shows that the teenage population (the source of most new drinkers) has been decreasing and is forecast to continue its decline. Brewers, therefore, confront a decline in potential new users. In addition, the young adult population (20–29 years) is also declining. The beer industry relies on this segment to replace sales lost due to attrition in the future drinking population. Finally, people between the ages of 30 and 49 will increase substantially and by 1990 will constitute 30% of the population. Historically, this group has been an important age group. However, industry analysts say this group is the one most concerned about alcohol abuse and drunk driving. This category has been nicknamed the neo-prohibitionists.

The beer industry faces another demographic change that will create problems. Blue collar workers have traditionally been the heaviest consumers of beer. Today, the economy is shifting toward the service sector and the blue collar work force is declining.

The emergence of wine coolers is also taking a toll on the beer industry. Wine coolers appeal to beer drinkers and to non-beer drinkers. Coolers are, to some extent, a beer substitute. Introduced five years ago, there are about 50 cooler brands now available, which contain 6% alcohol. Retail sales in 1984 were $360 million and in 1985 approached $700 million. However, cooler sales for 1986 are projected at 35 million cases, versus the 2.5 billion cases of the beer market. Some analysts believe that wine coolers are firmly established, while others contend that coolers are just a fad.

The market will shrink further due to the enforcement of drunk driving laws and the rise of the national drinking age to 21. The growing awareness of the need for responsible drinking habits has been fostered by groups such as Mothers Against Drunk Drivers (MADD). According to MADD, about 55% of all highway fatalities in 1983 were drinking related; 1984 figures indicated a small decline to 54%. The sobering truth has brought attention to the dangers of alcohol abuse and has resulted in stiffer penalties for drunk drivers and new laws to combat alcohol abuse.

In July 1984, President Reagan signed into law the National Minimum Drinking Age Act, which grants the federal government the authority to withhold federal highway funds from states that fail to raise their legal drinking age to 21 by 1987. When the law was enacted there were 27 states and the District of Columbia with a minimum age below 21, but many have introduced legislation to raise the age, or are expected to.

Some 360 new drunk driving laws have been passed nationwide since 1981, and many states and municipalities have banned "happy hour," which encourages increased alcohol consumption through discount prices. Also, there are 37 states with statutes holding the establishments and hosts liable for the subsequent behavior of intoxicated patrons or guests. These could also serve to reduce beer consumption.

The Industry's Reaction

Faced with these problems, many other industries would retrench, concentrate on keeping primary profit-making brands afloat and try to ride out the storm. The brewery industry's response has been almost the opposite. New brands and extensions have appeared on retailers' shelves at a record pace. Beers that had been available only regionally are being moved into broader distribution. New light beers, low-alcohol beers, low-priced beers, super-premium beers and malt liquors have emerged. Exhibit 8.11 lists the brands introduced in 1984 by both national and regional brewers.

The major U.S. brewers introduced twenty-one new products or line extensions in 1984. Two-thirds of these new product introductions were low-alcohol or low-calorie products. Anheuser-Busch (A-B) was the first major brewer to unveil its low-alcohol entry, LA; and regional brewers soon got into the act. To date, however, the low- and no-alcohol products have not worked out well. They are viewed as weak with no zing. They seem to appeal to the drinker who does not drink very much beer to begin with, in contrast to light beers, which appeal to the heavy beer drinker.

Although new product introductions slowed in 1985, the beer industry is doing everything possible to attract new customers. A shrinking market means brewers must steal share from competitors. Large brewers generally desire to have something for everyone. Today, brewers do not want to be underrepresented. The lower-price/lower-profit beer category has also seen introduction. Traditionally, in the low-price segment, price is supposed to move the

EXHIBIT 8.11   ## Domestic Beer Brands Introduced in 1984

BRAND	BREWER
Black Label 11-11 Malt Liquor	Heileman
Black Label LA[1]	Heileman
Blatz LA[1]	Heileman
Big Man Malt Liquor	Eastern Brewing
Choice[1]	F.X. Malt
Golden Hawk	Schmidt
Ice Man Malt Liquor	Pabst
I.C. Golden Lager	Pittsburgh
King Cobra Malt Liquor	Anheuser-Busch
LA[2]	Anheuser-Busch
Light-N-Lo[1]	Latrobe
Little Kings Premium	Schoenling
Lone Star LA[1]	Heileman
Low Alcohol Gold[1,2]	Pabst
Low Alcohol Pabst Extra Light[1,2]	Pabst
Meister Brau Light	Miller
Milwaukee's Best	Miller
Old Style LA[1]	Heileman
Oscar Wildes's	Pearl
Plank Road Original Draft	Miller
Rainier LA[1]	Heileman
Schaefer Low Alcohol[1]	Stroh
Schmidt LA[1]	Heileman
Select Special 50 Low Alcohol[1]	Pearl
Sharpe's LA[1]	Miller
Silver Thunder Malt Liquor	Stroh

[1] Low in alcohol.

[2] Repositioned brand.

product, and no advertising is performed due to the thin margins. National firms are now doing away with tradition by expanding marketing budgets.

Taxes

The brewing industry confronts another problem, the ever-present threat of a federal excise tax increase. In 1984, Congress enacted legislation to increase the excise tax on distilled spirits. This increase is most likely an indication of what is almost certain to follow. Increases in the rate have accompanied each national emergency since the first dollar-a-barrel tax was applied during the Civil War. Federal legislators look at the excise tax as part of the solution to the nation's huge deficit. The anti-alcohol movement seeks to link the excise tax to a Medicare/Medicaid bailout. The distillers are seeking tax equity with beer and wine. An increase in this tax, however, would squeeze profit margins even more.

Beer is one of the most highly taxed consumer products. Taxes constitute the largest individual item in the price of beer. The federal excise tax is $9 a barrel, and state taxes average approximately $5.41 a barrel. (Effective February 1977, a brewer who produces not more than 2 million barrels of beer in a year has a $7 a barrel federal tax rate on the first $60,000 sold or consumed.) In addition, there are federal and state occupational taxes on brewers, wholesalers and retailers, as well as local taxes in some states.

In 1983, the United States government received $1.6 billion in excise taxes on malt beverages. Combined annual federal, state and local taxes equal almost three billion dollars. The government earns over $14 for each barrel of beer or ale sold; the brewing industry's average profit rate per barrel after taxes is estimated between two and three dollars.

Internal: Industry Factors

The major causes of the national beer industry oligopoly appear to be economies of scale and product differentiation. Economies of scale, which occur when large plants produce at lower unit costs than smaller ones, appear to exist in the beer industry in which brewing and bottling processes have become increasingly mechanized. The increased capacity attained by many individual breweries over the past twenty years has forced the closing or sale of numerous regional producers. Industry experts contend that the wave of consolidation has not ended. Additional economies of scale in volume and production are necessary. Currently there is excess capacity and certain plants are inefficient (see Exhibit 8.12). Except for A-B, the industry is operating between 75% and 85% of capacity. If plants are consolidated, resulting in increased volumes, profitability can be increased.

Even though the U.S. beer industry is suffering from overcapacity, two brewers announced expansion plans during 1985. The Adolph Coors Company intends to build a $70 million beer packaging plant in Virginia, and, if sales justify it, the facility will be expanded to include full brewing facilities. The G. Heileman Brewing Company plans to construct a new brewery in Milwaukee. The facility will specialize in more costly imported-style beers. The industry's overcapacity was accentuated by Miller Brewing's decision to write-down $140 million of its $450 million new plant and Stroh Brewery Company's decision to close its older, underutilized Detroit plant.

Successful product differentiation occurs when a firm convinces customers that real or imagined differences in its beer render it preferable to that of the competitors. Larger brewers, with national sales and multi-plant operations, can

EXHIBIT 8.12

U.S. Brewing Industry Capacity and Usage, 1983
(Total Capacity and Shipments in Millions of Barrels)

BREWER	NUMBER OF PLANTS	TOTAL CAPACITY	SHIPMENTS	% OF CAPACITY
Anheuser-Busch	11	66.5	60.5	91.0
Miller	7	54.0	37.5	69.4
Stroh	7	32.6	24.3	74.5
G. Heileman	12	25.5	17.5	68.6
Adolph Coors	1	15.5	13.7	88.4
Pabst	4	15.0	12.8	85.3
Genesee	1	4.0	3.2	80.0
C. Schmidt	2	5.0	3.2	64.0
Falstaff	5	5.0	2.7	54.0
Pittsburgh	1	1.2	1.0	83.3
All others	34	7.4	3.7	50.0
Domestic total	85	231.7	180.1	77.7

often more easily attain this "high-quality" image than local or regional brewers. There also appear to be economies of scale in brand proliferation and product extensions. Large brewers can more easily (and cost-effectively) segment all price and product categories. The high fixed costs associated with advertising new brands can be spread over a large sales volume that smaller brewers do not have. Large firms can realize lower advertising costs on each barrel than can small firms. If the larger brewers can induce their smaller competitors to expend huge amounts on media advertising, the former are better able to withstand the resulting cost-price squeeze.

Advertising has grown considerably in importance and in expense. In 1984, brewers spent an estimated $780 million. Advertising expenditures in 1983 averaged $2.74 per barrel. The evidence that high advertising expenditures and high-profit levels are positively correlated is, however, somewhat mixed. At Schlitz, for example, advertising expenditures on each barrel rose dramatically at a time when sales and operating profit per barrel both fell. Similarly, Coors had higher profit figures when advertising expenditure levels were extremely low and lower profits when advertising outlays accelerated. However, A-B and Miller have increased both profit on each barrel and market share, at a time when advertising expenditures increased.

Imports

To the dismay of domestic brewers, imports are expected to perform well throughout the remainder of the 1980s. Between 1980–1984, the quantity of beer imported increased about 12% annually. Five countries, the Netherlands, Canada, West Germany, Mexico, and the United Kingdom, account for about 90% of all U.S. imports, but over forty other countries also ship beer to the United States. The imports' share of the U.S. beer market has grown from 1.1% in 1975 to 3.9% in 1984. A New York based research firm projects a 15% increase in import shipments for 1986. By 1990, it predicts the import market will almost double in worth. Of the 120 beer wholesalers that the firm interviewed, 68% felt imports would capture at least 10% of the total U.S. beer market by the end of the decade.

Ten years ago, imported beers were esoteric products consumed by a small elite, in a handful of markets. Since then the industry has exploded, with beer drinker's desire, taste and imagery fueling this growth. According to industry analyst Emanuel Goldman, "The imports have image. We live in a self-indulgent age that's getting more and more self-indulgent, and people want something different. They can get something different, upscale and feel good about it with imports. There is tremendous selection, too. The consumer seems to feel that imports are superior beers."

The top ten imported brands dominate about 87% of import sales. Heineken maintains the lead with an estimated 34% of the market, while Molson holds second place with 13.4%. Fortifying the Canadian segment is Moosehead in the number four spot and Labatt in the fifth place with 6% and 4.5% of the market, respectively. Beck's is in third place with 8.9% of the market and its closest German competitor, St. Pauli Girl, ranks seventh. Rounding out the top ten is Mexico's Dos Equis in sixth place; Australia's Foster's Lager, eighth; Amstel, the leading imported light beer, number nine; and Corona from Mexico in tenth place. (See Exhibit 8.13.)

EXHIBIT 8.13   **Imported Brands (by Sales)**

TOP TEN	SECOND TEN (ALPHABETICALLY)
1. Heineken (Netherlands)	Carta Blanca (Mexico)
2. Molson (Canada)	Dinkelacker (Germany)
3. Beck's (Germany)	Dortmunder (Germany)
4. Moosehead (Canada)	Grolsch (Netherlands)
5. Labatt (Canada)	Guinness (U.K.)
6. St. Pauli Girl (Germany)	Kirin (Japan)
7. Dos Equis (Mexico)	Kronenbourg (France)
8. Foster's Lager (Australia)	O'Keefe (Canada)
9. Amstel Light (Netherlands)	San Miquel (Philippines)
10. Corona (Mexico)	Tecate (Mexico)

Favorable demographics and an improving economy have aided this segment. The rise of the Hispanic population and the popularity of Mexican cuisine have fared well for Mexican beers, while the growing oriental population has given rise to a host of Chinese and Japanese brews. Most significant has been the appeal of imported beer to status-conscious consumers. A prime market eager for imported beers has been the young urban professionals, with a desire for unusual and different products, especially those of a foreign bent.

In addition, imports have seen only two price increases in the last five years, and as long as imported beer prices stay close to the superpremium domestic brews, they will remain a good buy for the consumer. With the domestic category remaining relatively flat, Americans looking for full-flavored beers are trading up to the imports.

The strong U.S. dollar has encouraged importation. An estimated ten new imported beers entered the U.S. every month in 1984. Exhibit 8.14 provides a partial list of the imported brands introduced in 1984. If the dollar becomes

EXHIBIT 8.14

Imported Beer Brands Introduced in 1984

BRAND	COUNTRY	BRAND	COUNTRY
ABC Stout	Singapore	Hombre	Mexico
Affligem	Belgium	John Peel Export	Britain
Alfa Beer	Holland	Jever Pilsner	West Germany
Anchor Pilsener	Singapore	Kaiser	Germany
Bamburger Hofbau	Germany	Koff Stout	Finland
Brador	Canada	Kronenhaler[1]	Austria
Broken Hill	Australia	Lindener	West Germany
Castillio Beer	Italy	Lorimer	Britain
Castle St.	Britain	Maes Pils	Belgium
China Beer	Taiwan	Oktober Beer	West Germany
China Clipper	China	Orangebloom	Holland
Danish Light	Denmark	Pacifico	Mexico
De Koninck	Belgium	Rolland Light	Germany
Dempseys	Ireland	Scandia Gold	Denmark
Elan[1]	Switzerland	Tientan	China
Feingold Pils	Austria	Vaux	Britain
Felinfoel	Britain	Vienna Lager	Austria
Festive Ale	Britain	Warteck[1]	Switzerland
Glacier	Sweden	Wolfbrau	Germany
Golden Ox	Germany	Yuchan Beer	China
Grizzly Beer	Canada	Zero[1]	Germany

[1] Denotes low or non-alcoholic brand.

weaker, many of these beers may disappear, because they will be unable to pay the price of admission.

There are two major obstacles in trying to capture American market share. The first is Van Munching & Company, which distributes Heineken. Heineken, with its commanding market share, essentially sets the benchmark pricing level for much of the import category. Many feel you cannot enter the U.S. market if you are above Heineken in price. The second major problem is a paradox created by the very success of the category, namely brand proliferation and the resulting market dilution.

Success hinges on the ability to come up with the "unique selling proposition" to cut through the multitude of brands competing for available market share. One technique used by imports is a unique packaging profile. The theory behind this is that the consumer knows none of the beers, but he will try the one that looks a little different. This is supported by the number of American beer drinkers who first bought Grolsch, if for no other reason than to see what sort of brew was in its distinctive bottle with the old-fashioned wire closure and ceramic stopper. More imports are also moving to a green bottle for their products. Consumer research shows that Americans feel green glass is more appealing for a light-colored beer.

Although beer tasting and tavern promotion nights are the most cost-effective ways to promote public awareness, reliance on heavy advertising is increasing. In 1985, Van Munching spent an estimated $22 million advertising and promoting Heineken. For Molson $15 million was spent. St. Pauli Girl had a $14 million budget, and Mexican Tecate plans regional advertising at $4 million in 1986. Although imports account for less than 4% of the beer market, the category held 10% of all beer advertising in 1984. About five imported beers represent 78.9% of all imported beer advertising. Heineken leads the list of import advertisers with 33.9%, Molson has 20.5%, Amstel Light follows with 15.8%, Moosehead and St. Pauli Girl trail with 4.5% and 4.2%, respectively. However, some importers are not marketing at all and some import companies have ten to twenty restaurants and delicatessens to whom they sell beer.

Exports

Confronted with a static-to-declining domestic market, beer producers are being forced to seek new markets abroad. A-B sees the international market, which is more than twice as large as the U.S. market, as critical to U.S. brewers' long-term success. Miller's Vice-President Alan Easton echoes this view, "Anybody who is really serious about being in the beer industry is going to have to consider participating in non-U.S. markets." Because substantial foreign opposition exists, brewers are seeking to expand government efforts to negotiate for trade barrier reductions. Exhibit 8.15 illustrates 1983 U.S. beer exports and imports by continent of destination and origin respectively.

During the first seven months of 1985, Canadian imports of U.S. beer increased more than 250%, to about $10 million. The major cause behind this

EXHIBIT 8.15

U.S. Beer Imports and Exports

1983 EXPORTS BY CONTINENT OF DESTINATION		1983 IMPORTS BY CONTINENT OF ORIGIN	
Continent	Percentage	Continent	Percentage
North America	28.9	North America	35.1
Europe	2.8	Europe	59.9
Asia	33.1	Asia	2.8
Caribbean	20.8	Caribbean, Central America, South America, Africa, Australia/Oceania	2.2
Central America	1.0		
South America	2.3		
Africa	1.7		
Australia/Oceania	9.4		

increased export activity occurred because some Canadian brewery workers went on strike, and Canadian retailers turned to the U.S. brewers for supplies. Immediately following settlement of the labor dispute, U.S. sales to Canada fell to the prestrike levels. Under normal conditions, Canadian provinces protect local producers by severely limiting beer imports.

Currently, the U.S. is Canada's major export customer for beer. In contrast, the U.S. is a residual supplier of beer to Canada. This may change, making Canada a promising market. Some provinces, particularly in Western Canada, are insisting that foreign beers be imported freely. The new Liberal government in Ontario (37% of Canada's beer drinkers reside in Ontario) is promising to break up the Ontario brewers' retail monopoly.

Anheuser-Busch provides an example of how domestic producers can develop overseas markets. Anheuser is relying on licensees to brew regular Budweiser for its overseas production, marketing, and distribution. To meet A-B standards, the licensees import ingredients from the U.S. and their production must be approved by Anheuser's four international brewmasters, as well as Chairman August A. Busch, III. Licensees are brewing Bud in Britain, Japan, and Israel. Negotiations are being conducted in Australia, Korea, and the Philippines. Anheuser is also considering the purchase of foreign breweries and exports to about ten other countries. Budweiser has failed, however, to crack the West Germany market, and France has been a disappointment.

National Brewers

Anheuser-Busch, Inc.

The St. Louis-based "King of Beers" has the most profitable product mix in the industry and is least in need of price increases. The key to its growth has been the world's best-selling beer, Budweiser. Bud has taken a big part of the youth market from Miller High Life and now commands a 24% market share (see Exhibits 8.16 and 8.17). A good product reputation and a powerful distribution network of virtually exclusive distributors contributes to A-B's success. A-B has marketing muscle and the average wholesaler does a 50% greater volume than his counterpart at Miller. A-B also has exposure; advertising expenditures in

EXHIBIT 8.16

Top Five National Brewers

1984 RANK	COMPANY NAME	PRINCIPAL BRANDS
1.	Anheuser-Busch, Inc. St. Louis, MO	Budweiser, Bud Light, Michelob, Michelob Light, Busch, Natural Light, LA, King Cobra Malt Liquor
2.	Miller Brewing Co. Milwaukee, WI	Miller High Life, Miller Lite, Plank Road, Milwaukee's Best, Meister Brau, Sharpe's LA, Lowenbrau, Genuine Draft
3.	The Stroh Brewery Co. Detroit, MI	Stroh's, Stroh's Light, Old Milwaukee, Piels, Schlitz, Signature, Schaefer, Goebel, Silver Thunder Malt Liquor
4.	G. Heileman Brewing Co. La Crosse, WI	Old Style, Old Style LA, Special Export, Blatz, Rainer, Black Label, Lone Star, 11-11 Malt Liquor
5.	Adolph Coors Company Golden, CO	Coors, Coors Light, Herman Josephs, George Killian's Irish Red

EXHIBIT 8.17

Top Ten Brands for 1984

RANK	BRAND	1984 MARKET SHARE	1984 BRAND GROWTH
1	Budweiser	24.0%	5.0%
2	Miller Lite	10.0%	2.0%
3	Miller High Life	7.8%	−18.0%
4	Coors	5.0%	−5.0%
5	Old Milwaukee	3.8%	1.5%
6	Michelob	3.8%	−3.5%
7	Pabst	3.4%	−20.0%
8	Stroh	3.2%	2.0%
9	Old Style	2.9%	−5.0%
10	Bud Light	2.3%	10.5%
Top 10 Total		66.2%	−30.5%

1985 were $440 million. A-B has created the ability to outspend its competitors, because its gross margin and gross profits are growing while others are not. Moreover, A-B is in the driver's seat as far as pricing goes.

Miller Brewing Company

Acquired in 1970 by Philip Morris, Inc., Miller surged during the 1970s and continues to be in the number two position. Unfortunately, the premium-priced High Life brand has been losing momentum and its luster as sales erode. However, the Lite brand is doing well, but faces more competition. The strategy of introducing two low-priced, low-profit beers, Meister Brau and Milwaukee's Best, is questioned by analysts. They believe this maneuver, coupled with a large advertising budget, cannot succeed. Miller is innovating at the higher segment with Plank Road and Miller High Life Genuine Draft. It is trying to reposition Lowenbrau as a brand with worldwide image. Because the beer is brewed in Milwaukee, not Munich, this campaign has failed in the past. Miller remains hopeful about its future.

The Stroh Brewery Company

Until 1981, this family-owned brewery, founded in 1849, was primarily a regional brewer. Since acquiring F&M Schaefer Brewing Co. in 1981 and Jos. Schlitz Brewing Co. in 1982, Stroh has carved a comfortable lead over its nearest competitor, G. Heileman. The acquisition of Schlitz gave Stroh a strong national wholesalers' network to distribute the rest of its products. Stroh's national rollout had some bad introductions in the Northeast, but it has a solid product line—Stroh's, Old Milwaukee, Schaefer and superpremium Signature. A company with good management, Stroh will be a difficult force to contend with: it has minimized unit costs and is operating at full capacity. Moreover, because it is a private company, it does not have to show good quarterly returns; it just has to generate enough cash flow to cover the family's needs.

G. Heileman Brewing Company

The G. Heileman Brewing Co. entered 1984 leading the industry in five-year profitability and growth. The return on equity averaged 31.7%. It has eleven breweries—five in the Midwest and two each in the South, Southwest and Northwest. Heileman's growth is a result of acquisition, and it has expanded its own distribution network by acquiring companies with well-established distribution systems. Despite excellent, street fighting management and good marketing, Heileman lacks a national image for its brands. This makes competing with A-B difficult. Heileman is, however, competing with the imports by building a new small plant exclusively for the production of a specialty beer. It does not want to mix the new beer with its domestic brands.

Adolph Coors Company

Famous for its mountain spring water, Coors is expanding from its regional mystique to become a national brewery. The rollout has worked very well, especially in New England, where it now advertises at the rate of one TV commercial per resident per second. Also, Coors seems to have stemmed the market share erosion in its core territories out west and hopes to regain the lost ground. Coors Light is doing very well, and in 1985 accounted for 40% of Coors' total barrelage. The success of Coors Light is helping to elevate the confidence that both the consumers and the wholesalers have in the Coors brand name. The imported superpremium George Killian's Irish Red is also making strong headway.

The Regional, Small Brewers

In an industry increasingly dominated by a few firms, several regional brewers have endured and continue to flourish. Some are large, nearly "Big-Six" status, while others are small-scale. Some have 150-year histories and others have only recently emerged. All stand as evidence that hometown loyalties and the strength of the regional market can be cornerstones of success.

This distinctive group must grapple with the issues confronting their specific markets while trying to find ways to survive. Some of the strategies being used include (1) the specialty brewer serving the moderate beer drinker and catering to the growing market of image-enhanced goods in select markets, (2) the dual-purpose brewer who wants to serve his loyal and home market while developing more prestigious and distinctive beers for select markets, and (3) the more traditional regional brewer whose markets are blue-collar and whose customers are more loyal than those in the more transient metropolitan areas.

The Genesee Brewing Company, Rochester, NY

Founded just after Prohibition's demise, Genesee is now the seventh largest brewery in America. Genesee's territory has been expanding and now includes all of the East Coast, Ohio, Indiana, Kentucky, West Virginia and the Province of Ontario. For a brewery considered to be a regional, Genesee has also implemented major advertising campaigns. Genesee had an impressive growth rate throughout the 1970s, with sales increasing at an average annual rate of 10.3%.

The F.X. Matt Brewing Company, Utica, NY

The F.X. Matt Brewing Co. reflects the tradition of family involvement that characterizes the industry. F.X. Matt, II understands both the romance and the realities of the industry. He realizes the necessity of an economical operation. Therefore, he constantly upgrades equipment not justified for a brewery this size. Besides the strategy of capital improvements, three other factors have been keys to success: consistent quality, loyal personnel and a "hands-on" management philosophy. The extensive product line includes Utica Club, Utica Club Light, Utica Club Cream Ale, Matt's Premium, Matt's Premium Light' Choice (a low-alcohol beer), Maximus Super Beer (with 6.5% alcohol content), and Saranac 1888, the newest product. Approximately 125 distributors carry Matt products throughout New York, Pennsylvania, parts of New England and north-central Colorado. Distributors must have a good game plan, ability to cover the market, competence and a particular way of doing business.

The newest product, Saranac 1888, an ultrapremium all-malt lager, was created in response to the phenomenal growth of imported beers. This is not a mass-produced/mass-promoted product. It is sold with a combination of point-of-purchase materials and placement in proper places.

Dixie Brewing Company, New Orleans, LA

Neal Kaye, Jr., President of Dixie, bought the company in June of 1983. The brewery was founded by the Merz family in 1907. It produces Dixie and Dixie Light, Coy International Private Reserve (a superpremium), and Rhinoceros (a malt liquor). The company also imports two French beers, Panache and 33. Dixie's advertising dollars go into national cable television spots and distribution is handled through their own subsidiary. Kaye points out that there is no other brewery like it in the Deep South, so unless one is built, he is confident Dixie will survive.

Anchor Brewing Company, San Francisco, CA

In 1965, Fritz Maytag, heir to part of the Maytag appliance fortune, bought this bankrupt brewery. Using his personal finances, he embarked on an extensive capital investment plan to renovate and replace equipment. Anchor, operating at a loss for ten years, went into the black in 1975. Anchor's initial annual capacity of 600 barrels has been expanded to 50,000 barrels. In 1984, Anchor produced over 37,000 barrels. The brewery's flagship, Anchor Steam Beer, accounts for 80% of sales, and Anchor Porter and Anchor Liberty constitute 7% of total sales. The remaining sales volume is made up by a barley ale, wheat beer, and its Christmas ale.

The brewery initially self-distributed its products, but it now uses two distributors on the West Coast. With over 100 total distributors, Anchor is available on the West Coast, in parts of Maryland, Delaware, Virginia, Washington, D.C., New Jersey, Connecticut and Massachusetts. The company has done almost no advertising, but relies instead on distinctive packaging.

A quasi-market research study provided the following buyer profile: The buyers are young adults, upscale, predominately college-educated and very knowledgeable about beer. Many drink a variety of beers and consider themselves aficionados. They drink primarily imported brands and enjoy a rich, distinctive taste in the beer they consume.

Maytag explains Anchor's success: "We start with a respect for the brewing tradition and a reputation for integrity. It's a concept that starts with the product. Our brew is low-key, high-quality and non-establishment. We actually try to make a beer that most people don't like—heavy, hoppy, and flavorful. It's traditional and distinctive, not designed for high volume, but for rapid growth, with relatively high margins, on a small scale."

Walter Brewing Company, Eau Claire, WI

Mike Healy, Jr. recently purchased this brewery for $1 million. He will transform it, with the help of Alan Dikty, a brewing consultant and managing editor of *New Brewer*, into a specialty brewery, to capture a part of the lucrative import market. "Selling a standard beer is the road to disaster," says Dikty. "You can't beat the big boys at their own game."

The Microbrewers

The American brewing industry has one small, dedicated group of mavericks. These are the microbrewers, with annual production under 15,000 barrels. Microbreweries are as individual as the personalities of their owners, yet all share an attitude of respect and enthusiasm for the brewer's art.

The majority of micro brews represent an historic genus of malt beverage that was common in pioneer America and until shortly after World War II in Great Britain. By the 1940s this had disappeared from the U.S., and by 1960 was difficult to find in Great Britain. During the 1970s, this traditional mode of brewing was renewed in England, primarily due to the country's "real ale" partisans. Brewed by top-fermentation, the generic term for this type of beer is *ale*.

Jack McAuliffe, an unemployed sailor who started the first microbrewery in 1976 in Sonoma, California, reintroduced this English-type brew in the U.S. His New Albion Brewery survived only a few years, but others have followed. Today there are about twenty-five micros and another thirty are set to begin production in 1986. Exhibit 8.18 provides a comprehensive list of American microbreweries.

The "real ale" is not the only style produced by microbreweries. A new American style—"nouveau lager"—has emerged on the market. This bottom-fermented beer is decidedly more hoppy and is brewed in the German Reinheitsgebot tradition. Reinheitsgebot dates from 1516, when the Bavarian ruler of that day, Wilhelm IV, limited the ingredients in beer to water, malted barley, hops, and yeast. This edict may be the oldest consumer protection law still on the books. In West Germany, Norway, and a few other countries, all beer produced for local consumption must be "Reinheitsgebot Pure," with only those four ingredients, no cereals, no additives and no enzymes. This new wave of American beers are nearly all made to these specifications.

EXHIBIT 8.18   ## American Microbreweries

NAME	LOCATION
Riley-Lyon Brewing Co.	Little Rock, AR
Palo Alto Brewing Co.	Mountain View, CA
Sierra Nevada Brewing Co.	Chico, CA
Stanislaus Brewing Co.	Modesto, CA
Thousand Oaks Brewing Co.	Berkeley, CA
Golden Gate Brewing Co.	Berkeley, CA
Boulder Brewing Co.	Boulder, CO
Snake River Brewing Co.	Caldwell, ID
Millstream Brewing Co.	Amana, IA
Boston Beer Co.	Boston, MA
Montana Beverage Co.	Helena, MT
The Manhattan Brewing Co.	NY, NY
Old New York Brewing Co.	NY, NY
Wm. S. Newman Brewing Co.	Albany, NY
Columbia River Brewing Co.	Portland, OR
Widmer Brewing Co.	Portland, OR
Reinheitsgebot Brewing Co.	Plano, TX
Chesapeake Bay Brewing Co.	Virginia Beach, VA
Hart Brewing Co.	Kalama, WA
Hales Ales Ltd.	Coleville, WA
Independent Ale Brewing Inc.	Seattle, WA
Kemper Brewing Co.	Rolling Bay, WA
Kuefner Brewing Co.	Monroe, WA
Yakima Brewing and Malt Co.	Yakima, WA
BREW PUBS:	
Buffalo Bill's Microbrewery & Pub	Hayward, CA
Mendocino Brewing Co.	Hopeland, CA
Hopeland Brewery	Hopeland, CA

The West Coast is a hotbed of microbrewery activity. The area is an ideal geographic market for these niche beers, because of the generally high personal incomes, coupled with a widespread awareness and appreciation of small wineries. The classic flavor and quality these breweries achieve, combined with their anti-establishment stance, has resulted in attractive alternatives for the price-inelastic, high-end beer drinker.

Microbrewing, however, is not ironclad. In 1982, in the San Francisco Bay area, there were five micros in business. Only two are still brewing. With a failure rate of more than 40%, this business is not for amateurs. Micro success is often unattainable, because of competition from imported labels and the inescapable economies of scale involved. Microbreweries are faced with the dilemma of needing to increase production in order to sell more aggressively and to exploit economies of scale. At the same time, they must contend with a mature and oversaturated market that simply does not justify scaling up.

Because of their low volume, it is also difficult for them to find a distributor. The few distributors that are receptive are normally attracted by label graphics and by superlative quality. Electric labels offset the generic identity of many of their primary products. Most distributors cannot, or will not, distribute a label that represents such small numbers. Therefore, most microbrewers must rely on personalized pre-selling of their brew to retailers. First-hand contact is essential for success. It is also invaluable for gauging a constantly changing marketplace. Furthermore, even if one can attract a regional distributor, personal calling regularly outsells the distributor.

Another marketing device used by micros is point-of-purchase materials. Microbreweries need to cut through the array of labels confronting the consumer in the import and specialty segment. The volume does not warrant a comprehensive advertising campaign, so point-of-purchase materials are the most cost-effective.

Micros are surviving for now, by charging a little more, by maintaining a rigorous quality-conscious image and by providing more and more beer drinkers with the joys of fresh, wholesome, handmade brews. *Premium* is again becoming an adjective that means something.

Profiles of Several Microbreweries

Sierra Nevada Brewing Company, Chico, CA

Located in a farming and college town near Sacramento, this ale brewery has a current production of 3,000 barrels. Started in 1979, the first brew was sold in 1981. Sierra Nevada produces pale ale, porter, and stout, which all retail for about $18 a case. The firm also sells full and half kegs of draft ale and a Christmas ale. Operating efficiency and a steadily growing reputation among serious beer lovers have proven to be keys for survival. But owner/brewer, Camusi, predicts a shakeout among microbrewers, a direct result of dilution in the specialty market. The critical areas of size and capacity may be the deciding factors in its long-term success. Sierra Nevada has added to its capacity every year and now approaches an annual capacity of 7,500 barrels. Its draft beer, accounting for a large percentage of its volume, enables the brewery to avoid the crowded single bottle market. Camusi believes growth is essential for survival. He must exploit economies of scale and achieve efficiency. According to Camusi, "The really small brewery is just not a viable business anymore."

Mendocino Brewing Company, Hopeland, CA

Situated 100 miles north of San Francisco, this brewery was formed from the equipment and staff of the defunct New Albion Brewery. This micro has overcome many of the economic viability issues of distribution and scale by operating a "brewpub." Approximately 660 barrels a year of ale, porter and stout are sold through the pub under the name of the Hopeland Brewery. Mendocino produces a wide variety of products, with Red Tail Ale its mainstay.

This amber, heavy bodied, English-style brew sells in a one-and-a-half-liter magnum bottle for $6. Its Black Hawk Stout, pale ale, and Christmas, summer, and spring ales sell on draft at the pub. The owners describe the Mendocino Brewing Co. as a "domestic alternative" which provides a small group of beer drinkers with a fresh, premium product. By selling exclusively to a local market, this micro has overcome the problem of finding distributors. Because of the vagaries of foreign exchange, and the cost of glass and brewing materials, the brew pub may be the solution to running a small brewery.

Boulder Brewing Company, Boulder, CO

Founded in 1979 by a small group of home brewers, this brewery sold its first beer on July 3, 1980. Boulder's products are unpasteurized, English-type brews. The two products, Boulder Extra Pale Ale and Boulder Stout, are sold in 12 ounce non-returnable bottles. No draft is produced. Accounts are served by those wholesale distributors who approached the company.

Distribution is confined to the state of Colorado, with a network of twelve outlets currently handling the brewery's products. Although the company enjoys considerable free publicity, word-of-mouth advertising serves as its primary source of demand. Marketing resources are focused on upgrading packaging graphics. These are products consumers drink for taste. A public stock offering in September 1983 financed the company's capitalization and construction of its recently completed $1.1 million brewery. Forty million common shares were issued at 5 cents a share, raising a total of $2 million. The new facility covers about 14,000 square feet and annual capacity now stands at 15,000 barrels.

The Old New York Beer Company, New York, NY

The first of the nouveau lagers came from New York in 1982, when Matthew Reich introduced New Amsterdam Amber, a rich, hoppy, full-bodied, all malt lager beer. Reich invested his life's savings, $10,000, and hired Dr. Joseph Owades, an international brewing consultant and director of the Center for Brewing Studies in San Francisco, to design a lager beer similar to Anchor Steam.

Reich had always dreamed of being a brewer. While working as the director of operations at Hearst Magazine, he often wished he was out creating his own beer. He believed there was room for a connoisseur's beer, the kind that poured from kegs, without rice or corn—a "pure" beer. For two years Reich and Owades slaved over the beer's body, color, and taste, during which time Reich still worked at Hearst.

Basing their decision on a fifteen-page business plan, twenty-two private investors invested $255,000 to form a limited partnership. In the summer of 1982, Reich left Hearst, and that August he began buying brewing time at F.X. Matt Brewing Company in Utica, NY. New Amsterdam Amber ferments for one week and ages for twenty-six days before being bottled or kegged and shipped to Manhattan.

In 1983, Old New York Beer Co. sold 44,000 cases for $600,000. Sales doubled to $1.2 million in 1984, with earnings of $50,000 (after taxes). Reich expects to reach a sales level of $1.8 million in 1985 on 100,000 cases. The average retail price for a six-pack is $6.

Like other micros, Reich personally sold his brew, first approaching trendy restaurants and bars in Manhattan. While he originally intended to target only NY, his beer is now available in 21 states, including the West Coast. Reich's initial success has enabled him to raise an additional $2.2 million from two venture capital firms. He is using the money to construct a new brewery in Manhattan that will also have a restaurant, a tap room and a visitors' center. Although this action dilutes Reich's holding in the company to 25%, it improved Old New York's image and increased its annual production capacity to 30,000 barrels. When the brewery is completed late in 1986, he will be able to triple 1985's expected production.

THE GOLDEN GATE BREWING COMPANY

Background

With a Cambridge home, an office overlooking the Boston Harbor from the thirty-first floor of a prestigious downtown address, and a quarter-million-dollar annual salary, James Cook was the picture of yuppie success. But something was missing.

James Cook, christened Charles James, attended Harvard College, where he majored in government and graduated with honors in 1971. For the next three years, he was a mountaineering instructor with Outward Bound. In 1974, he returned to Harvard to study law and business administration. In 1977, Cook climbed to the snow-covered peak of Alaska's 20,320 ft. Mount McKinley. "After traveling for weeks and seeing nothing but white," he recalls, "I wondered what magic sight awaited me at the summit. And when I got to the top, there it was, glowing in the light, an empty beer can, planted like somebody's flag. Ah," he exclaims, "the power of beer is transcendent!"

With a J.D. and an M.B.A. James joined the renown Boston Consulting Group (BCG). He never took the bar exam, as he had no desire to practice law. He spent seven years honing his management skills and advising industrial, primarily international, managers. After six years he got tired of telling other people how to run their company and decided to start his own. "I wanted to create something, I wanted to make something of my own," said Cook. As noted in BCG's annual report, 30% of those who leave go on to start new businesses. Another 46% join small companies in top executive positions. BCG's corporate structure encourages many consultants to start their own companies and it is a training ground for some of the brightest, most successful risk-takers in the country. James' choices boiled down to either brewing beer or building a chain of for-profit medical clinics in Seattle.

The consultant in Cook voted for the doc-in-the-box set-up. But as the eldest son of a fifth generation brewer, he figured he really did not have a choice.

Cook's family has the longest line of brewmasters in the U.S. The first Cook brewmaster immigrated in the 1840s from Bohemia, near what is now Pilsen, Czechoslovakia. Cook's great-great-grandfather, Louis, operated a tiny brewery (the Louis Cook Brewery) in St. Louis, not far from the original A-B brewery and used a lager recipe he inherited from his fathers. Louis brewed beer when Eberhard Anheuser was still selling soap and Budweiser was a European beer. James' father, Charles Joseph, Jr., worked as a brewmaster at several breweries in Cincinnati. However, this was the time when all the local breweries were going belly-up. After four breweries fell out from under him, his father abandoned the family trade, moved to California, and opened an industrial chemical distributorship.

James vividly remembers the smell of fermenting beer on days he visited his father at work. "I liked it. I never liked hard liquor and never understood wine. Even now I drink two–three beers a day, rarely less, rarely more. Breweries are neat places and the brewmaster has the best job. He walks around, tastes beer and makes changes. It's almost like playing God," notes Cook. Cook believes he was put on earth for one thing—"to make the greatest beer in the U.S."

James' father discouraged his idea. He was proud of the fact that, after generations of brewers, James was the first to go to college. He said, "James, it took us 150 years to get the smell of the brewery out of our clothes, and you want to go back there?" He thought James was out of his mind. But as James points out, "On the surface it was an insane thing to do, but I was convinced there was a small emerging market for what I wanted to do. It was the time for microbreweries and hand-crafted beers, and it seemed tragic that I was ending a line of five generations of brewers. I realized Americans had begun to appreciate premium beers in recent years, especially on the West Coast, but I felt they relied too heavily on imported beers, which are inherently inferior. I think that the American appreciation of beer is very much in its infancy. We're in the Blue Nun stage of beer drinking. There was a time when people thought that Blue Nun was a great wine, just as now there are people who think Heineken and Beck's are great beers. In fact, they're the Schlitz of Europe. They have a certain mystique, but it's a phony mystique. These beers aren't fresh. Beer has a shelf life that's not a whole lot longer than orange juice. And you'd never think of buying orange juice from Germany. In Germany, they don't drink Beck's. They drink the local beer. Americans have this notion that the farther away a beer is made, the better it is. But the imports we get in America not only have preservatives, which are illegal in Germany, but by the time they arrive here, they are almost always spoiled, stale and/or skunked. Beer must be fresh. It deteriorates the instant you put it in a bottle. The day it leaves the brewery, it goes downhill. The travel time in importing beer and use of green bottles that expose beer to damaging light can often mean the expensive imported beer is not what it claims to be."

The Start-up

Although Cook has no formal education in brewing, he studied notes and material his father had saved from the Siebel Institute of Brewing in Chicago where he learned to be a brewmaster. Although American tastes in mass marketed beers has drifted toward light, paler versions, Cook decided to buck the tide, go with family tradition, and brew a full-bodied lager. He wanted a connoisseur's beer, brewed in an "old world" tradition.

His father suggested he revive the old family formula. After searching his father's attic in Cincinnati, Cook found his great-great-grandfather's original recipe, first developed by his ancestor in the 1870s. With his family's formula, Cook hired biochemist and brewery consultant Joseph L. Owades to aid in devising the final formula. In the summer of 1984, Cook traveled to the fermentation lab at the University of California at Davis and worked with Owades on translating Louis Cook's Midwestern American lager into a 1980s West Coast superpremium beer.

The formula is water, malt, hops, and a special yeast strain developed by Owades. The hops are the best in the world, Tettnang and Hallertau Mittlelfreuh hops, imported from Bavaria at a cost of $4.50 per pound. A pound of ordinary hops costs $.55. The hops, according to Cook, are key, as they give the beer its flavor. Two-row summer malted barley and some caramel malt are used for color and body. Although many people think that water is the most important ingredient that goes into beer, it is, in fact, the least important. The quality of the yeast strain is much more important, but is seldom talked about as it lacks advertising appeal. Cook points out, "When you listen to what people advertise about their beers, it's things that have real macho appeal—fire brewing, beechwood aging, mountain spring water. What matters are things like hops, malt, and yeast. Unfortunately, they don't have the advertising appeal of cool mountain streams."

To make this beer formula a reality Cook needed to raise capital. He tossed in all his personal savings, $100,000, and raised an additional $300,000 from friends, business associates, clients, and even his father. "While you can start a small boutique brewery with $400,000, a good lager is difficult to produce in a microbrewery. A lager requires more sophisticated brewing equipment and more careful handling than the ale produced by most micros. I was forced to find an existing brewery, and luckily, I was able to find a brewery in Berkeley that was perfect for my purposes," relates Cook. The Berkeley Brewery, by contract and federal regulation, becomes the Golden Gate Brewing Company while James' beer is being produced there.

The Brewing Process

This 100-year-old recipe requires a craft brewing process not used by American brewers in this century. The sweetness is drawn from the malt through a decotion mash, a process traditional in Germany, but rarely used any more by American brewers. Fresh hops are added in six stages during the brewing process to give the beer its complex hop character. (The usual process is to add hops only during the cooking stage of production, when boiling extracts the greatest amount of bitterness; this process, therefore, is more economical.) Cook's beer is then *krausened* (a second fermentation that carbonates the beer and also removes some of its impurities) for a smoother taste and a natural carbonation. A final addition of fresh hops is made to the beer as it ages to impart the striking aroma. This is a labor-intensive technique.

Molded after Czechoslovakia's Pilsener Urqueil and the original Lowenbrau, this time-consuming brewing process requires a level of personal attention that would be difficult to maintain in a modern mass-production brewery. Golden Gate takes 40–45 days to make—one day to "cook," seven days to ferment, and about two weeks to krausen. The rest of the time is lagering, or aging. These efforts in the brewing process create the full-bodied flavor, rich with coppery color.

The beer is produced in batches, between 250–300 barrels per batch. Cook was not pleased with the first batch, some of which was used to pitch prospective accounts. The problem was over-filtration. "The technician tried to get it to look like Budweiser," said Cook. "I am more interested in flavor than clarity, and the over-filtration removed some of the subtle flavors and hops bouquet." Cook currently travels to Berkeley every one to two weeks to oversee the brewing of a new batch. He follows the process step by step to ensure that his recipe is followed precisely.

Packaging

All Golden Gate beer is currently bottled; no draft beer is produced. The classic American beer bottle, the 12-ounce longneck, or bar bottle, that requires an opener, is used. This shape and the cap offer the most protection from light and oxidation. The bottle is also a dark brown, because a dark bottle protects beer from light, a deadly enemy of beer. Beer left in light for more than ten minutes begins to spoil.

Because of U.S. consumers' perceptions of quality, many imported beers come in green bottles. All the research focus groups show that Americans believe they're getting a better product in a green bottle. According to Cook, "That's why Heineken, Beck's, and Molson come in green bottles—which is a shame.

Nobody in the world drinks beer out of green bottles except Americans. In Canada, Molson is sold in a brown bottle."

After being bottled in Berkeley, the beer arrives in San Francisco four hours later. Cook has hired two truck drivers and leases trucks. Each trip to San Francisco costs about $800 per truck. Initially, 500 cases per week were delivered, but this has grown to about 1,500 cases per week. (Each truck has a maximum capacity of 2,500 cases.) The beer is delivered to an old San Francisco brewery, where Cook rents office and warehouse space, prior to distribution.

Organization

The employment roster of the Golden Gate Brewing Co. numbers five people, including James Cook—the brewer and chief salesman. In addition to two truck drivers, there are a part-time bookkeeper and an accounts manager, Rhonda Kallman, who was James' secretary at BCG. Her numerous and varied duties include selling and even delivering when necessary. To keep overhead as low as possible, the business has no secretary, no typewriter, and no computer. Cook also took a 75% pay cut from his BCG salary.

Financial Information

According to Cook, the Golden Gate Brewing Co. stopped losing money around July or August. "It is still in the red, but we're getting back toward recovering our losses. The business after six months is doing remarkably well," reports Cook. Exhibit 8.19 shows the Golden Gate Brewing Company's income statement for the first six months of operations.

Golden Gate sells for about $0.25 more per bottle than Heineken, or $1.75–$3.50 per bottle retail. A six-pack retails for about $6.50 and a case varies from $20 to $24. Asked if he thought the high price might limit sales, Cook said, "I don't drink wine, but I understand a good bottle of wine costs about $30. Well, for the price of a mediocre bottle of wine, you can go out and buy a six-pack of the best beer in America." Golden Gate wholesales for about $16 a case.

This fresh, smooth brew, with strong overtones of fruit and honey, and a creamy head, costs two to three times what it costs to brew the popular imported beers. The delivered cost into San Francisco was initially listed at $12 a case, but, because of increased volume, it is now down to $10.50 a case. Other expenses include salaries, office and warehouse rent, truck leasing, marketing and promotion, public relations, general selling and administrative expenses and taxes.

Advertising and Marketing

Golden Gate Lager is an unadvertised beer in a business in which advertising dominates the consumer's purchase decision. It is primarily a locally marketed beer in a business in which the national brands have driven out many small

EXHIBIT 8.19   **1985 Income Statement, Golden Gate Brewing Company**

Sales	$408,000[1]
Cost of goods sold	273,000[2]
Gross margin	$135,000
Less:	
Shipping	840[3]
Salaries & wages	101,003[4]
Office/warehouse rent	4,800[5]
Truck leasing	20,800[6]
Marketing and promotion	55,000[7]
Repairs	1,000[8]
Depreciation	7,500[9]
Gen. sell/admin & other exp.	9,057[10]
Net income (loss) before taxes	($65,000)

[1] Includes 25,000 cases sold in California and 500 in Munich.

[2] The first 3,500 cases cost $12/case, the rest cost $10.50/case.

[3] Includes shipping costs of $.07/bottle for 500 cases shipped. (Larger shipments would decrease the per bottle cost)

[4] Includes Cook's salary of $25,000 for July–December and average hourly earnings of his four employees of $18.27/hr. (Another 4% increase is expected in 1986)

[5] Office and Warehouse rent totals $800/month.

[6] 26 truck trips were made into San Francisco in the first six months.

[7] Includes $35,000 for booklet and $10,000 for placards used in July and August.

[8] Cost of incidental repairs, including labor and supplies, which do not add materially to the value of the property.

[9] Depreciation is on the straight-line basis, assuming a 20 yr useful life, no salvage value, one-half year's depreciation taken in the first year and $300,000 of assets acquired.

[10] Included are salaries and wages not deducted elsewhere, amounts not otherwise reported, such as administrative, general and office expenses, bonuses and commissions, delivery charges, research expenses, sales discounts, travel expenses, etc.

breweries. And Golden Gate is a beer whose flavor Americans have rarely tasted in the popular domestic, or even imported, beers.

Even though his strategy has been to create a brand identity without advertising, one of the first things Cook did was to hire an advertising agency and a public relations firm. James stated, "I looked for companies that were enthusiastic about this venture. I needed people who could start at the beginning with me, help with name selection, product positioning, packaging, and promotional material. I needed an intelligent sounding board for what I was doing."

All the marketing and promotion has been done with a budget that would not begin to pay for one 30-second spot on Monday Night Football. The main marketing element is quality and freshness, and the main marketing tool is personal selling and word-of-mouth. Tabletop display cards are also placed in bars and restaurants in and around San Francisco. In addition, a little blue miniature booklet, each hand-applied, dangles from each long-stem bottle. The booklet is entitled "Why Is This Special Beer Different?" and describes the beer, brewing process, and flavor. The first order alone cost $35,000.

There is no advertising budget, but during the summer of 1985 Cook experimented with advertising. Placards were placed on the sides of San Francisco's tour buses. While it was relatively cheap advertising at $5,000 per month, Cook is not sure it was worth it. "I don't think we generated enough sales to pay for it." This experience confirmed his gut feeling that small, specialized companies do better relying on word-of-mouth advertising and publicity. "The first thing you must have in business is a solid, substantial advantage over the alternatives. Somehow you're got to have a reason for people to buy your product, and it's got to be more solid than anything advertising can create. There are very few products that have really lasted long-term on marketing alone," says Cook. "However, nothing is so good that it automatically sells itself. You have to go out and hustle."

He links the logistics of introducing this beer to those of a fine wine, with the best advertising being word-of-mouth, but Cook was fortunate to gain a credible third-party endorsement. Less than two months after the introduction of Golden Gate Lager, this superpremium, full-bodied, amber brew was crowned the Best Beer in America at the annual Great American Beer Festival in Denver. One beer is selected the best by the 4,000 attendees. This year's contest had over 102 entries. The resulting publicity played a major role in boosting sales. Cook, thrilled by the victory, said, "For a family that has been making beer for 150 years to suddenly get recognized as making the best beer in the country—that is the ultimate accolade."

James Cook also conducts his own market research and studies. Three nights per week he visits local pubs and restaurants. He questions patrons as to why they drink imports when they can have Golden Gate. He asks what they like about imported brands. He asks beer drinkers for their opinion of Golden Gate. If they have not tasted Golden Gate, he describes the flavor and suggests they try it. After a short conversation, he identifies himself as the brewer. Aside from polling patrons, Cook chats with bartenders and questions waitresses and waiters about sales. According to Cook, "The neatest thing is to come into a bar and see people drinking my beer. The second neatest thing is to take the empty cases out."

Distribution

"Getting the beer on the market boils down to a door-to-door campaign with restaurants, bar managers, and liquor store owners," says Cook. Cook converts his BCG briefcase into a cooler by adding cold packs, places four or five bottles of Golden Gate in it, and asks potential carriers to taste the beer. "The response is incredible," boasts Cook. "Bar managers and owners like the personal attention. It show them how much you believe in your product."

Beer is sold today through massive advertising. Beer salespeople today are primarily order takers. They do not sell the beer—the advertising does. The distribution system of large wholesalers often provides retailers with indifferent service on popular brands with marketing power. The outlet has no choice. Even if the delivery service is poor, there are brands an establishment has to carry. Because Golden Gate requires an amount of personal attention and credibility that the normal beer sales and distribution channels cannot give, Cook has set up his own distribution company. He even goes as far as making deliveries, pinstriped suit and all, out of his station wagon. Normally, his drivers will handle this.

Cook realizes all this costs money, probably twice what traditional distributors pay. Cook is currently negotiating with a major regional beer distributor. Affiliation with a large distributor provides access to numerous, established accounts that Cook would otherwise have to pursue one by one. He wonders if this is a sound strategy.

Target Market

The Golden Gate Company's Golden Gate Lager is trying to reach less than 4% of all beer drinkers. The target is the beer drinker who knows how to distinguish a well-made beer from an average to below-average one, and who cares more about quality and taste than advertising appeal. Cook believes the typical Golden Gate drinker could be anyone, from gourmets to yuppies to construction workers, who likes a good beer. The current diverse cross-section of drinkers cuts across traditional demographics.

Export Plunge

In October 1985, James Cook performed an unusual feat. He shipped 12,000 bottles (500 cases) of Golden Gate Lager to Munich, West Germany, a city with the most finicky beer drinkers in the world. Golden Gate is the first U.S. brewed beer to be sold in West Germany outside U.S. military bases. Good taste is not enough in Germany. The beer must pass the strict Reinheitsgebot, or German Beer Purity Law. It took four weeks before the Wiehenstathan, or beer institute, gave his beer their seal of approval. Obtaining an import license was the next task. The 500 cases were sent to George Thaler, a business consultant friend and now part-time beer distributor, who attempts to get Germans to try, and then order, Golden Gate. Thaler explains his sales techniques as follows, "I bring three cold bottles with me, then I tell them what has happened to beer in America and then discuss the brewing process. Then we taste." Thaler says Germans like the beer, which helps both sales of Golden Gate and the image American products have. "It's a quality image for a U.S. product."

The Munich market is not without problems. In Munich, six breweries own 90% of all pubs and they will only serve their brand of beer. Therefore, Golden Gate is locked out of all but a few of Munich's restaurants, delicatessens and hotels (the so-called "free bars"). In addition, although shipping costs add only $.07 to the price of a bottle of Golden Gate, the beer costs 30%–50% more than German draft beers, or about $5\frac{1}{2}$ marks more per beer. But Thaler explains that this is a consistent with the product positioning. "We don't want student beer drinkers to get drunk on Golden Gate. We want the beer connoisseur to drink Golden Gate." Thaler presently has five accounts taking seventy cases per week, which he delivers in the trunk of his Mercedes-Benz. The accounts range from a high-class delicatessen to a New York style bar.

Cook's plunge into West Germany is designed primarily to demonstate his product's quality; he is now considering expansion. Thaler hopes to soon expand to Dusseldorf and Austria. Cook wonders what other markets he should pursue, how fast he should expand and how much time he should devote to export possibilities. He is confident that his time-consuming brewing process and choice ingredients make Golden Gate competitive with the best of European brews.

Capital Expansion

Cook formed his company with two goals initially: (1) to brew the best lager in the U.S.—"an answer to the best Europe has to offer, a beer with absolutely no compromises" and (2) to brew the beer in San Francisco. Cook has achieved his first goal, but his second has yet to be realized. "The beer is as good as I thought," says Cook. "But I guess it will take longer than I wanted to get it brewed in San Francisco. Maybe next summer."

The Golden Gate Brewing Co. currently rents office and warehouse space at an old San Francisco brewery. This brewery, with three feet thick walls, was abandoned in 1965. It was cheaper to abandon than tear down. It is now owned by the nonprofit Neighborhood Development Corporation, but Cook has an option on about one-fourth of the building's 170,000 square feet. He hopes to be able to buy the building, renovate it, and brew Golden Gate in 40,000 square feet, after funding completion. Cook estimates his needs at $3.75 million, with $1.1 million going for renovations and $2.1 million for new tanks and bottling gear. His goal is an annual capacity of 30,000 barrels. The project is initially expected to create twelve to fifteen new jobs and has the potential to create fifty-five to sixty. Actual renovation and equipment installation is estimated to take four to ten months. Cook says it would be cheaper to build a brewery in the suburbs, but "romance" led him to the old SF brewery. "I could save $800,000 if I moved to a suburban industrial park, but I don't want to make California, or West Coast Lager Beer. I want to make Golden Gate Lager."

Cook has explored several financing possibilities—Industrial Revenue Financing, Urban Development Action Grants, and market rate financing. Are there other sources that he should consider? He needs to evaluate the pros and cons of each source and determine if proceeding with his second goal is viable at this time.

Industrial Revenue Financing

Industrial Revenue Bonds (IRB) are vehicles that developers and corporations use to raise low interest financing for construction projects. They are issued by a municipality only to achieve tax exempt status, and are not guaranteed by the full faith and credit of the government. IRB's are backed by the future revenue of the project. IRB's were originally designed to attract industry into communities for employment and economic benefits through the use of tax exempt financing. IRB loans in San Francisco generally carry interest rates of 70% of prime with a 15-year balloon and a 30-year amortization.

The San Francisco Industrial Development Financing Authority (SFIDFA) must give initial approval to an application by Cook's Golden Gate Brewing Company. The revenue bonds must then gain city council and mayoral approval. Cook is confident that the mayor will bestow enthusiastic support; he campaigned on revitalizing San Francisco neighborhoods. Once the IRB's are approved, a bank must agree to loan the funds. Most banks require the IRB loans to be secured by the personal guarantees of the principals.

Urban Development Action Grants

The UDAG is another possibility. By financing projects that otherwise would not be feasible, the UDAG program is designed to create jobs and expand the city's real estate tax base.

The UDAG is a flexible program which offers a source of cheap money. The maturity and interest rate are negotiated between the city and the borrower. The collateral is normally limited to the assets being financed (and personal guarantees). The UDAG can be used for fixed assets whose life expectancy exceeds seven years. The terms and conditions negotiated between the city and the borrower must be approved by the city council and the U.S. Department of Housing and Urban Development. The UDAG process averages three to four months. Another important advantage of this subsidy is that the UDAG can be mixed with IRB's and other federal programs. Exhibits 8.20, 8.21, and 8.22 highlight other criteria of this program.

The UDAG subsidy does have one drawback. To raise money for future projects, the local program shares in the profits of the subsidized projects. This can restrict profit potential. Cook was not excited about sharing profits and/or giving up control or ownership.

Market Rate Financing

Another option for capital, explored by Cook, is market rate financing from local commercial banks. San Francisco has five major banks, one of which, the

EXHIBIT 8.20

UDAG Criteria for Selection

The following criteria have been developed by the central office staff for the review, rating and ultimate selection of UDAG applications, for approval:

1. Relative distress of the applicant.

2. Private leverage: the ratio of private investment to UDAG funds. The national average is now 6.2 to 1, and the ratio should be at least 5 to 1 to insure competitiveness. A ratio below 5 to 1 must be strongly supported by other factors and less than 2.5 to 1 will not be considered.

3. Repayment of action grant recipient. At least a portion of the grant should be returned to the city for recycling. The repayment may be structured as a "soft" second mortgage or lease so the developer virtually has a grant if the project is not successful.

4. Permanent jobs. Weight is given to the total number of jobs created, the number of low/moderate income jobs created, and the ratio of UDAG funds to jobs created. Currently, a cost of $5,000 or less per job created is considered competitive. Retained jobs are also important.

5. New taxes. New taxes created and the ratio of new taxes to Action Grants dollars. A return of $.10 per dollar is competitive.

6. Commitment to minority participation. The creation of minority jobs and the inclusion of minority entrepreneurs is weighted heavily.

7. Commitment to hire and train hard-core unemployed is a plus factor.

8. Other public participation. Investment of funds by the state and/or city is a good measure of their support of the project.

9. Feasibility. The project must be feasible socially and economically, and the participants should be capable of starting within one year of preliminary approval and completing the project within four years of that date.

The program seeks to fund an equal number of commercial, industrial and neighborhood projects. To date, approvals have been 36% industrial, 34% commercial and 30% neighborhood.

Bank of San Francisco, has already solicited the Golden Gate Brewing Company. Cook has yet to supply necessary financial statements or projections, however. The loan would be a mortgage, used to cover all the expenses associated with the completed property. The interest rate would be based on the prime rate. Cook feels that the rate on a commercial mortgage would be prime + 1% for a 15-year balloon with a 30-year amortization.

Expansion/Growth Strategy

Winning America's Best Beer Award, and the resulting publicity, caused many distributors from other states to solicit the Golden Gate Brewing Co. and Golden Gate Lager. Cook has put several possible new accounts temporarily on

EXHIBIT 8.21   **Ten Questions Corporations Ask about UDAG**

1. Why does the federal government help businesses finance plant and equipment?
   Creating jobs in distressed cities is a national goal. UDAG will help companies finance fixed assets that create jobs.

2. Is it free money? What's the catch?
   - UDAG won't finance the whole project. At least 72% of the project's cost must come from private sources.
   - Businesses reimburse the city for use of Action Grant funds.
   - UDAG won't finance working capital/assets with useful lives under 5 years.

3. If the funds must be repaid, what's the rate?
   Terms are negotiable. Repayments are tailored to the project's economics and allow a fair return to the owner. UDAG may ask for a share of cash flow as an equity kicker.

4. Which cities are eligible?
   Almost half the cities and towns in the United States meet HUD's distress criteria, ranging from New York, NY (population—7,800,000) to Woodlawn, ID (population 321). Call Frank Ridenour, (202) 755-6784, to find out if a city is eligible.

5. Do successful companies qualify?
   UDAG has made awards for projects involving large and profitable companies. UDAG looks for a financing short-fall in a single project's economics.

6. How bad is the red tape?
   UDAG's requirements are similar to those of private lenders. The application is not short, but the city prepares most of it with information you provide. UDAG guarantees an answer in two months.

7. Is there a loan ceiling?
   There are no ceilings on Action Grants; awards have ranged from $35,000 to $30,000,000. UDAG can lend up to 28% of project costs when sufficient private capital cannot be raised.

8. Can action grants be combined with other government programs?
   UDAG encourages developers and cities to seek other public funds. Action Grants can facilitate tax-free bond financing on projects up to $20,000,000.

9. Do my competitors know about this program?
   Absolutely! UDAG has participated in over 900 industrial and commercial ventures in over 80 different industries.

10. What are my chances of getting a UDAG?
    UDAG's are awarded competitively. Chances are excellent, if you have
    - A project which creates jobs and increases city tax revenues.
    - Private funding for about 80% or more of the project cost.
    - Firm, private financing commitments.
    - Evidence the project needs the Grant.
    - A project ready to proceed.

EXHIBIT 8.22   How the Funds Flow in a UDAG Funding

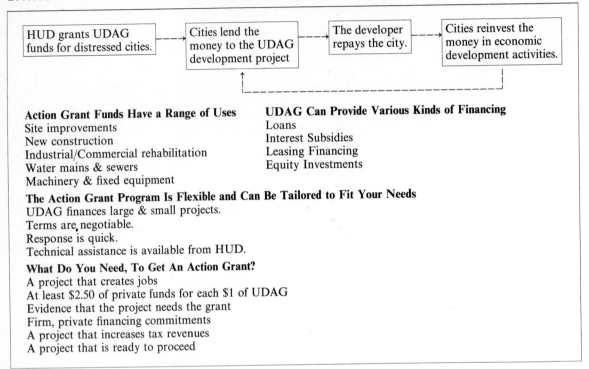

Action Grant Funds Have a Range of Uses
Site improvements
New construction
Industrial/Commercial rehabilitation
Water mains & sewers
Machinery & fixed equipment

UDAG Can Provide Various Kinds of Financing
Loans
Interest Subsidies
Leasing Financing
Equity Investments

The Action Grant Program Is Flexible and Can Be Tailored to Fit Your Needs
UDAG finances large & small projects.
Terms are negotiable.
Response is quick.
Technical assistance is available from HUD.

What Do You Need, To Get An Action Grant?
A project that creates jobs
At least $2.50 of private funds for each $1 of UDAG
Evidence that the project needs the grant
Firm, private financing commitments
A project that increases tax revenues
A project that is ready to proceed

hold and has turned down requests from distributors in Washington, Colorado, Kentucky, and Alaska. Cook's current agreement with the Berkeley Brewery limits production and Cook felt it was important to penetrate and service San Francisco first. Renovating the old San Francisco brewery, however, would provide a much higher production capacity level. Exhibits 8.23 and 8.24 illustrate beer-consumption trends in various states and regions. Cook also realized that beer is regulated in fifty different ways in the U.S. The bureaucratic red tape is complicated and time-consuming. Cook sometimes thinks it is easier to sell Golden Gate in Munich than in the U.S. Germany requires only that the beer be pure.

Regardless, Cook wonders, should I expand, how quickly should I expand and where? Cook concedes that he will never slay the major domestic giants. "I don't compete with them. I make a different product and sell it for a different price. I compete with foreign beers." But he is uncertain of the strategy he should use. Should he just pursue California, or should he select particular cities? (Los Angeles, for example, contains the third largest market for imported beer, after New York and Chicago.) Or should he go for West Coast states, the East Coast, the country? Should he pursue the foreign markets? Should he approach distributors and, if so, how should he screen them? Is his marketing strategy satisfac-

EXHIBIT 8.23   **Beer Consumption Statistics for Several U.S. States**
(Gallon and Dollar Amounts in Thousands)

	PACKAGED GALLONS	DRAFT GALLONS	TOTAL GALLONS	WHOLESALE DOLLARS	RETAIL DOLLARS
New England					
Maine	22,402	3,200	25,602	$102,409	$159,758
New Hampshire	28,903	5,920	34,822	144,513	226,885
Vermont	12,306	1,637	13,943	55,492	86,012
Massachusetts	117,321	24,030	141,351	572,471	858,707
Rhode Island	20,930	3,225	24,155	96,619	140,097
Connecticut	54,138	9,824	63,962	259,047	375,619
Middle Atlantic					
New York	305,532	62,579	368,111	1,472,444	2,282,289
New Jersey	138,460	23,482	161,942	644,528	999,018
Pennsylvania	221,903	74,871	296,774	1,142,579	1,770,998
E.N. Central					
Ohio	234,138	33,390	267,528	1,070,111	1,626,568
Indiana	107,096	14,068	121,164	502,829	769,328
Illinois	249,523	34,026	283,549	1,091,662	1,735,742
Michigan	176,066	34,408	210,473	837,684	1,315,164
Wisconsin	128,732	28,258	156,991	627,962	954,502
South Atlantic					
Delaware	4,247	2,051	6,298	65,517	87,792
Maryland	90,898	13,724	104,622	276,363	403,490
Wash, D.C.	16,366	1,819	18,185	73,102	97,226
Virginia	113,741	12,638	126,379	502,990	674,006
Florida	289,779	28,982	318,761	1,198,540	1,594,058
West S. Central					
Louisiana	95,670	10,630	106,300	430,515	576,891
Texas	442,226	33,797	476,023	1,785,086	2,374,164
Pacific					
Washington	75,910	18,884	94,794	364,956	481,742
Oregon	46,397	13,964	60,361	240,238	319,517
California	575,622	63,958	639,580	2,398,424	3,213,888

tory, or are changes necessary? Should the product line be extended? Should he proceed with plans to brew Golden Gate in San Francisco? If so, how should he finance that project? Are there other sources of financing available which he needs to evaluate? What volume would be necessary to break even? Are there other decisions he needs to make to insure a viable brewing company?

EXHIBIT 8.24   **U.S. Beer Consumption
1985 Gallons***

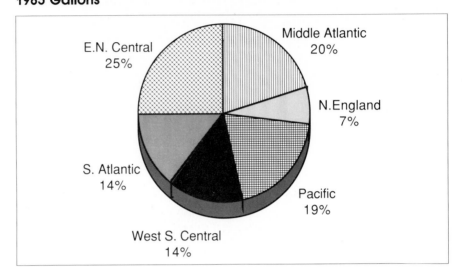

* (Includes both packaged and draft)

Cook understands that success hinges on moving Golden Gate out of the trial/novelty category and making it a regular, if not exclusive, choice for the customers. Cook realizes that brand loyalties change slowly in the beer market and, even with strong initial sales, a small brewer faces long odds. Cook, a divorced father of two, Megan, six and Charlie, five, is determined to produce a first-rate beer and have a brewery to pass on to his son or daughter. He hopes there will be a seventh generation of brewers.

Anheuser-Busch Companies, Inc. . . . August A. Busch, III

THOMAS L. WHEELEN • JANIECE L. GALLAGHER

Sitting in his office on March 15, 1986, Mr. August A. Busch, III was reviewing his staff's analysis of his first ten-year strategic plan. He was preparing himself for the next day's staff meeting, in which the company's next ten-year strategic plan would be developed. Many changes had been made in the company since its founding more than a century ago. He was proud. Anheuser-Busch had come a long way in its corporate development. Diversification strategies had proven successful and continued growth seemed evident. But, where would the company go within its fast-paced competitive environment? Its primary objective is well-planned and well-managed growth, and the company's long-term strategies of vertical integration, internal development of new business areas, and diversified acquisitions reflect this commitment. Busch stated that "Beer . . . will remain our top priority, as evidenced by substantial future capital commitments." The plan couldn't stop there.

COMPANY HISTORY—AN ENTREPRENEURIAL SPIRIT

In 1852, George Schneider founded the Bavarian Brewery in St. Louis, Missouri. On the brink of bankruptcy in 1857, the brewery was sold to a competitor, who renamed it Hammer and Urban. By 1860, the new company defaulted on a loan to Eberhard Anheuser. Anheuser, a successful soap manufacturer, assumed control of Hammer and Urban and four years later asked his son-in-law, Adolphus Busch, to join the brewery in the position of salesman. Busch, who became the driving force behind the new venture, became a partner (1873), and President (1880–1913) of the brewery. In 1879, the name of the brewery was changed to Anheuser-Busch Brewing Company.

Adolphus Busch was a pioneer in the development of a new pasteurization process for beer and became the first American brewer to pasteurize beer. In 1894, he and Carl Conrad developed a new beer that was lighter in color and body than the previous one. This new beer, Budweiser, gave Busch a national beer, for which he developed many marketing techniques (such as giveaways—tokens and pocketknives) to increase its sales. By 1901, the annual sales of Anheuser-Busch surpassed the million-barrel mark.

In 1913, August A. Busch succeeded his father as president of the company, and served as President through the Prohibition era (1920–1933) to 1934. He

This case was prepared by Professor Thomas L. Wheelen, and Ms. Janiece L. Gallagher, MBA student, of the University of South Florida. Research Assistance was performed by Kelli Anderson, Kim Hart, and Cathy Lee of the University of South Florida at Sarasota. It was presented at the North American Case Research Association Meeting, 1987. Distributed by the North American Case Research Association. All rights reserved to the authors and the North American Case Research Association. Reprinted by permission of the authors and the North American Case Research Association. Copyright © 1987 by Thomas L. Wheelen.

led the company into many new diversification endeavors, such as truck bodies, baker's yeast, ice cream, corn products, commercial refrigeration units, and non-alcoholic beverages. With the passage of the Twenty-first Amendment, Anheuser-Busch returned to the manufacture and distribution of beer on a national basis, and in 1934, the company went public.

August A. Busch, Jr., succeeded Adolphus Busch III as President and Chief Executive Officer in 1946. In 1949 Eberhard Anheuser was elected the first Chairman of the Board. August A. Busch, Jr. was elected Chairman in 1956. During his tenure, eight new breweries were constructed and sales increased eleven-fold, from 3 million barrels in 1946 to 34 million barrels in 1974. He also guided the company's pursuit of diversification strategies into real estate, family entertainment parks, transportation, the St. Louis Cardinals baseball team, and can manufacturing. Busch is currently serving as Honorary Chairman of the Board of Anheuser-Busch Companies, Inc., and Chairman and President of the St. Louis National Baseball Club, Inc.

August A. Busch III was elected President in 1974, and Chief Executive Officer in 1975 (see Exhibit 9.1). As of 1986 he is serving as Chairman and President. During his tenure, sales doubled, from 34 million barrels in 1974 to 68 million barrels in 1985. The company has eleven breweries with a total annual capacity of 75.27 million barrels, and under his direction Anheuser-Busch has continued its successful diversification efforts.

August A. Busch III, born on June 16, 1937, is the fifth generation of the Busch brewing dynasty. He started his career hauling beechwood chips out of 31,000-gallon aging tanks. In his youth "Little Augie" was a hell-raiser, but is now a conservative "workaholic" after attending the University of Arizona and the Siebel Institute of Technology, a Chicago school for brewers.

In his ten years of managing the company, Busch has transformed it from a large, loosely run company into a tightly run organization with an emphasis on the bottom line. Busch is known for his tough-mindedness and intensity, his highly competitive nature, and his attention to detail. As Mr. Dennis Long, President of the company's brewing subsidiary, said, "There is little that goes on that he doesn't know something about." Busch, a brewmaster, is known for making unscheduled visits to the breweries at all hours of the day and night. He daily compares beers from different plants and suggests remedies for any variations in look and taste. Mr. Long added, "Let there be no doubt. He's at the helm and he sets the tone."

Encouraging openness and participation from his executives, Busch provides them with plenty of responsibility and freedom, and promotes group decision-making. His Policy Committee is a nine-member forum in which each member must present an opinion on the current topic or issue and substantiate his position. Mr. Busch feels that "executives do not learn from success, they learn from their failures." What is his philosophy on success? As he states, "The more successful that we become . . . the more humble that we must be . . . because that breeds future success."

EXHIBIT 9.1   **Historical Organization Chart, Anheuser-Busch Companies, Inc.**

Steps in Ownership Development

YEAR	FIRM	TYPE
1852–1857	George Schneider	Proprietorship
1857–1858	P. and C. Hammer & Co.	Partnership
1858–1860	Hammer & Urban	Partnership
1860–1875	E. Anheuser & Co.	Partnership
1875–1879	E. Anheuser Co.'s Brewing Association	Corporation
1879–1919	Anheuser-Busch Brewing Association	Corporation
1919–1979	Anheuser-Busch, Inc.	Corporation
1979–(current)	Anheuser-Busch Companies, Inc.	Corporation

Presidents of Anheuser-Busch

NAME	TENURE
Eberhard Anheuser	President of E. Anheuser & Co. from 1860 to July 7, 1875
	President of Anheuser Co.'s Brewing Association from 1875 to April 29, 1879
	President of Anheuser-Busch Brewing Association from April 29, 1879, to May 2, 1880 (death)
Adolphus Busch	President of Anheuser-Busch Brewing Association from May 10, 1880, to October 13, 1913 (death)
August A. Busch, Sr.	President of Anheuser-Busch Brewing Association from December 8, 1913, to Novemeber 22, 1919
	President of Anheuser-Busch, Inc. from November 22, 1919, to February 13, 1934 (death)
Adolphus Busch III	President of Anheuser-Busch, Inc. from February 22, 1934, to August 29, 1946 (death)
August A. Busch, Jr.	President of Anheuser-Busch, Inc. from September 5, 1946, to April 27, 1971
Richard A. Meyer	President of Anheuser-Busch, Inc. from April 27, 1971, to February 27, 1974
August A. Busch III	President of Anheuser-Busch, Inc. from February 27, 1974, to October 1, 1979
	President of Anheuser-Busch Companies, Inc. from October 1, 1979, to present

During the summer of 1985, Mr. Busch's 21-year-old son, August A. Busch IV was employed in the Corporate Yeast Culture Center at the St. Louis headquarters. Commenting about the succession of his four children, Mr. Busch says, "If they have the competency to do so, they'll be given the opportunity.

You learn from the ground up. Those of us who are in this company started out scrubbing the tanks." So the younger August Busch begins his career with Anheuser-Busch.

THE ORGANIZATION

On October 1, 1979, Anheuser-Busch Companies, Inc. was formed as a new holding company (see Exhibit 9.2).

The new company's name and organizational structure more clearly reflect Anheuser-Busch's mission and diversification endeavors of the past decades. Because each subsidiary of Anheuser-Busch Companies, Inc. has its own Board of Directors and officers, management has gained operational and organizational flexibility. The Policy Committee for Anheuser-Busch Companies, Inc. establishes policies for all the subsidiaries, one of which is Anheuser-Busch, Inc.

For strategic planning purposes, the company is organized into three business segments: (1) beer and beer-related companies, (2) food products companies, and (3) diversified operations. The Board of Directors consists of fifteen members (see Exhibit 9.3). The executive officers of the company are described in Exhibit 9.4.

In 1985, the beer and beer-related business segment contributed 77.3% of the corporation's net sales and 95.8% of the operating revenue. Exhibit 9.5 sketches the eighteen companies that comprise the three business segments, and the financial information for each of the business segments is shown in Exhibit 9.6.

Because of the company's vertical integration strategy, the knowledge of the economics of those businesses has increased, the quantity and quality of supply is better assured, and both packaging and raw materials are more strongly controlled. In cultivating internally developed businesses such as Eagle Snacks, Anheuser-Busch continues its philosophy of maintaining premium quantity and quality of supply, and control of both packaging and raw materials through self-manufacture. In 1985 Eagle Snacks added plant capacity through the acquisition of Cape Cod Potato Chip Company and through plant expansion.

EXHIBIT 9.2   **Anheuser-Busch Companies' Subsidiaries**

Anheuser-Busch, Inc.
Metal Container Corporation
Busch Agricultural Resources
Container Recovery Corporation
Anheuser-Busch International, Inc.
Campbell Taggart, Inc.
Eagle Snacks, Inc.
Busch Industrial Products Corporation

Busch Entertainment Corporation
Busch Properties, Inc.
St. Louis National Baseball Club, Inc.
Civic Center Corporation
St. Louis Refrigerator Car Company
Manufacturers Railway Company

EXHIBIT 9.3

Board of Directors, Anheuser-Busch Companies, Inc., 1986

DIRECTORS

August A. Busch, Jr.
Honorary Chairman of the Board

August A. Busch III
Chairman of the Board and President

Richard T. Baker
Former Managing Partner and present Consultant—Ernst & Ernst (now Ernst & Whinney); certified public accountants

Margaret S. Busch
Vice-President—Corporate Promotions

Peter M. Flanigan
Managing Director—Dillon, Read & Co. Inc.; an investment banking firm

Roderick M. Hills
Distinguished Faculty Fellow and Lecturer, International Finance—Yale University School of Management

Edwin S. Jones
Former Chairman of the Board—First Union Bancorporation (now Centerre Bancorporation); a multibank holding company

Fred L. Kuhlmann
Vice-Chairman of the Board and Executive Vice-President of St. Louis National Baseball Club, Inc.

Vilma S. Martinez
Partner—Munger, Tolles & Olson; attorneys

Sybil C. Mobley
Dean of the School of Business and Industry—Florida A&M University

Bernard A. Edison
President and Director—Edison Brothers Stores, Inc.; retail specialty stores

James B. Orthwein
Chairman of the Board—Newhard, Cook & Co. Inc.; an investment brokerage firm

Walter C. Reisinger
Special Representative—Customer Relations—Anheuser-Busch Companies, Inc.

Armand C. Stalnaker
Professor of Management—Washington University School of Business

Fred W. Wenzel
Chairman of the Board—Kellwood Company; a manufacturer of apparel and home fashions

ADVISORY MEMBER

W. R. Persons
Former Chairman and Chief Executive Officer—Emerson Electric Company; a manufacturer of electrical and electronic equipment

DIRECTOR EMERITUS

M. R. Chambers
Former Chairman of the Executive Committee and Director—INTERCO, Inc.

EXHIBIT 9.4

Executive Officers of Anheuser-Busch Companies, Inc., 1986

August A. Busch III (age 48) is presently Chairman of the Board, President, Chief Executive Officer, and Director of the company and has served in such capacities since 1977, 1974, 1975, and 1963, respectively. He is also Chairman of the Board and Chief Executive Officer of the company's subsidiary, Anheuser-Busch, Inc. and has served in such capacity since 1979. He serves as a member of the Corporate Office.[1]

(Continued)

EXHIBIT 9.4   **(Continued)**

Dennis P. Long (age 50) has served as Vice-President and Group Executive of the company since 1979. Also since 1979, he has been President and Chief Operating Officer of the company's subsidiary, Anheuser-Busch, Inc. He serves as a member of the Corporate Office.[1]

Jerry E. Ritter (age 51) has served since 1984 as Vice-President and Group Executive of the company. During the past five years he has also served as Treasurer of the company (1981) and Vice-President, Finance (1981–1983). He serves as a member of the Corporate Office.[1]

Barry H. Beracha (age 44) has been Vice-President and Group Executive of the company since 1976. He is also presently (1986) Chairman of the Board and Chief Executive Officer of two of the company's subsidiaries, Metal Container Corporation and Container Recovery Corporation, and has served in such capacities since 1976 and 1978, respectively. Since 1984 he has served as President of another subsidiary, Metal Label Corporation.

Patrick T. Stokes (age 43) has been Vice-President and Group Executive of the company since 1981. He is also the Chairman and President of Campbell Taggart Inc. He has held these positions since 1985. He was previously Vice-President and Group Executive of the company and served in such capacity from 1981. During the past five years he also served as Vice-President, Materials Acquisition (1980–1981).

John H. Purnell (age 44) has served as Vice-President and Group Executive of the company since 1982. During the past five years he also served as Vice-President, Corporate Planning and Development (1981). He has also been Chairman of the Board and President of two of the company's subsidiaries, Anheuser-Busch International, Inc. and Eagle Snacks, Inc., since 1980 and 1982, respectively.

W. Randolph Baker (age 39) has been Vice-President and Group Executive of the company since 1982. He has also served as Chairman of the Board and President of two of the company's subsidiaries, Busch Entertainment Corporation (since 1979) and Busch Properties, Inc. (since 1978), and Chairman of the Board and Chief Executive Officer of another subsidiary, Busch Creative Services Corporation (since 1983).

Stephen K. Lambright (age 43) has been Vice-President and Group Executive of the company since 1984. During the past five years he has also served as Vice-President, National Affairs (since 1981) and as Vice-President, Industry and Government Affairs (1981–1983).

Stuart F. Meyer (age 52) has served since 1984 as Vice-President, Corporate Human Resources. During the past five years he also served as Vice-President, Employee Relations (1981–1983).

Raymond E. Goff (age 40) has been Vice-President and Group Executive of the company since January 1986. Since that time he has also been Chairman of the Board and Chief Executive Officer of two of the company's subsidiaries, Busch Agricultural Resources, Inc., and Busch Industrial Products Corporation. He has also served as Vice-President, Administration of a subsidiary, Anheuser-Busch, Inc. (1981–1985).

---

[1] The Corporate Office consists of Mr. Busch, Mr. Long, and Mr. Ritter.

EXHIBIT 9.5   **Anheuser-Busch Companies, Inc.: Segments**

COMPANY	YEAR FOUNDED	ACTIVITIES
Business Segment: Beer and Beer-Related		
1. Anheuser-Busch, Inc.	1852	The world's largest brewer in 1985, selling 68.0 million barrels; has been the industry leader since 1957. Distributes 11 naturally brewed products through 960 independent beer wholesalers and 10 company-owned wholesalers.
2. Busch Agricultural Resources	1962	Processes barley into malt. In 1985, supplied 32% of the company's malt requirements. Grows and processes rice, and can meet 20% of the company's rice need.
3. Container Recovery Corp.	1979	Largest aluminum recycler in U.S.A. in 1985.
4. Metal Container Division	1974	Expected to produce 5.8 billion lids and 5 billion cans in 1986: 35% of the company's requirements and 6.4% of all beverage cans and lids in the U.S.
5. Anheuser-Busch Beverage Group	1985	Responsible for the non-beer beverages. In 1985, acquired two mineral water companies—the Saratoga Spring Co. and à Santé Mineral Water Co. Offers three wine products—Master Cellars Wines, Baybry's champagne coolers, and Dewey Stevens premium light wine coolers.
6. Anheuser-Busch International, Inc.	1981	International licensing and marketing subsidiary. The world beer market is 3.5 times the domestic market.
7. Busch Media Group	1985	In-house agency to purchase national broadcast media time.
8. Promotional Products Group	N/A	Responsible for licensing, development, sales, and warehousing of the company's promotional merchandise.
Business Segment: Food Products		
1. Campbell Taggart, Inc.	1982	75 plants and approx. 19,000 employees. Consists of the following subsidiaries: (1) bakery operations, (2) refrigerated products, (3) frozen food products, and (4) international.
2. Eagle Snacks, Inc.	1978	Produces and distributes a premium line of snack foods and nuts. In 1984 began self-manufacturing virtually all of its snack products, and in 1985 purchased Cape Cod Potato Chip Company.
3. Busch Industrial Products Corp.	1927	Leading producer and marketer of compressed yeast in U.S.; also produces autolyzed yeast extract.
Business Segment: Diversified Operations		
1. Busch Entertainment Corp.	1959	Family entertainment subsidiary, with (1) The Dark Continent, (Fla.), (2) The Old Country (Va.), (3) Adventure Island (Fla.), (4) Sesame Place (Pa.), and (5) Exploration Cruise Line—6 ships. In 1985, more than 2.9 million people visited the Dark Continent, and 2.05 million visitors came to The Old Country.
2. Busch Properties, Inc.	1970	Real estate development subsidiary with commercial properties in Va., Ohio, and Calif. Developing a planned community in Williamsburg, Va.
3. St. Louis National Baseball Club, Inc.	1953	St. Louis Cardinals, St. Louis, Mo.

(Continued)

EXHIBIT 9.5 (Continued)

COMPANY	YEAR FOUNDED	ACTIVITIES
4. Civic Center Corp.	1981	Owns various properties in downtown St. Louis, Mo.
5. Busch Creative Services	1980	Full-service business and marketing communications company, selling its services to Anheuser-Busch and other Fortune 500 companies.
6. St. Louis Refrigerator Car Co.	1878	Transportation subsidiary with 3 facilities. Provides commercial repair, rebuilding, maintenance, and inspection of railroad cars.
7. Manufacturers Railway Co.	1878	The other transportation subsidiary, operates 42 miles of track in the St. Louis area, 525 insulated railroad cars used to ship beer, 48 hopper cars and 77 boxcars. Includes a fleet of 200 trailers.

Another internally developed diversification, Master Cellars Wines, has become part of the newly created Anheuser-Busch Beverage Group. Two other acquisitions were the Saratoga Springs Company and à Santé Mineral Waters bottled water companies.

In 1985, the company became an investor in its first venture capital fund, Innoven, an established fund that has been very successful over the years. With this company, Anheuser-Busch gains exposure to new business areas being developed by the small start-up companies in which Innoven invests capital.

Busch Entertainment in 1985 acquired Exploration Cruise Lines. This six-vessel fleet cruises such areas as Mexico, Tahiti, and Alaska.

The company extended its research and development program with Interferon Sciences, which has been developing and clinically testing both material and recombinant forms of interferon, an anti-viral agent found in the human body. The program has been extended. Planning for the future, Anheuser-Busch will continue its long-term plans for diversification. These efforts are to be maintained as long as they are consistent with the company's objectives.

ALCOHOL ABUSE AND CORPORATE CITIZENSHIP

Anheuser-Busch ". . . is deeply concerned about the abuse of alcohol and the problem of driving while intoxicated. It supports the proposition that anything less than responsible consumption of alcoholic beverages is detrimental to the individual, to society, and to the brewing industry." The company has been a leader in developing programs that support this position.

The TIPS program was developed in 1985 by Health Communications Corporation, Anheuser-Busch, and the Miller Brewing Company to train retail personnel to deal effectively with the patrons who overindulge. Approximately 1,500 Anheuser-Busch wholesaler employees are now certified trainers. Their goal is to train 10,000 servers nationwide.

Anheuser-Busch was the first major brewer to promote on network television the control of alcohol abuse. The company is an active sponsor of SADD (Students Against Drunk Driving), and it developed operation ALERT (Action,

EXHIBIT 9.6 — Financial Information for Business Segments, Anheuser-Busch Companies, Inc.

(Dollar Amounts in Millions)

	BEER AND BEER-RELATED	%	FOOD PRODUCTS	%	DIVERSIFIED OPERATIONS	%	ELIMINATIONS	%	CONSOLIDATED
1985									
Net sales	$5,412.6	77.3	$1,416.4	20.2	$189.6	2.7	$(18.3)	(0.2)	$7,000.3
Operating income	797.0	95.8	28.5	3.4	6.8	0.8			832.3
Depreciation and amortization expense	161.7	—	53.2	—	21.2	—			236.1
Capital expenditures	416.2	—	103.7	—	36.1	—			601.0
Identifiable assets	3,515.6	—	935.9	—	174.6	—			4,626.1
Corporate assets									495.3
Total assets									$5,121.4
1984									
Net sales	$5,001.7	76.9	$1,343.9	20.7	$169.5	2.6	$(13.9)	(0.2)	$6,501.2
Operating income	728.2	96.5	16.5	2.2	10.0	1.3			754.7
Depreciation and amortization expense	141.1	—	42.3	—	20.0	—			203.4
Capital expenditures	393.1	—	106.7	—	19.4	—			519.2
Identifiable assets	3,214.7	—	811.8	—	128.0	—			4,154.5
Corporate assets									370.2
Total assets									$4,524.7
1983									
Net sales	$4,586.0	76.0	$1,311.9	21.7	$149.3	2.5	$(13.0)	(0.2)	$6,034.2
Operating income	649.9	92.8	47.3	6.7	3.6	0.5			700.8
Depreciation and amortization expense	129.5	—	40.3	—	17.5	—			187.3
Capital expenditures	348.1	—	54.8	—	25.1	—			428.0
Identifiable assets	2,994.1	—	768.6	—	143.7	—			3,906.4
Corporate assets									423.8
Total assets									$4,330.2

Leadership, Education, Responsibility and Training), which serves as an umbrella covering a variety of educational and awareness programs.

In 1985, Anheuser-Busch contributed $11 million to charitable organizations such as the Muscular Dystrophy Association, Job Employment Programs, Urban League Scholarship programs, and the Economic Development Program. It also donated funds for disaster relief to victims of the 1985 Mexico earthquake and West Virginia flood.

LEGISLATION AND LITIGATION	In recent years, Anheuser-Busch has become more active in monitoring and taking positions on issues that could have a major impact on the company. The Industry and Government Affairs Division has expanded in order to identify and respond to such issues with specific programs.

The PUSH Campaign

In 1983, the Reverend Jesse Jackson's campaign PUSH against Anheuser-Busch Companies, Inc., accused the company of discrimination against blacks and encouraged minorities to boycott Anheuser-Busch's products. Using the battlecry "Bud is a Dud," Jackson claimed that the company (1) did not do business with enough minorities, (2) did not hire and promote black employees, (3) did not patronize black-oriented community organizations, and (4) did not have enough black wholesalers in the distribution system. Eventually, Mr. Wayman Smith, Vice-President of Corporate Affairs, was able to make the Reverend Jackson aware of the company's minority hiring and promotion practices, support to minorities throughout the country, and the role of minority suppliers. Anheuser-Busch also agreed to (1) spend $23 million in procurements from minority businesses, (2) spend $8 million on advertising in minority media, (3) spend $10 million in construction performed by minority-owned firms, (4) hold $2 million in certificates of deposit in forty-one minority-owned banks, and (5) establish lines of credit for $6 million and deposit $6 million in payroll accounts with twenty-five of these banks.

The Minimum Drinking Age

The National Minimum Drinking Age Act of 1984 grants the federal government the authority to withhold federal highway funds from states that fail to raise their legal drinking age to 21 by 1986. Currently, forty states have mandated or approved a 21-year-old minimum drinking age.

The Thayer Suit

An insider-trading lawsuit field by Anheuser-Busch against Paul Thayer, a former director, was resolved in 1985. The suit for $285 million claimed that, during the 1982 acquisition of Campbell-Taggart, Inc., Mr. Thayer leaked information that increased Campbell-Taggart's price before the take-over was complete. Thayer settled SEC civil charges and pleaded guilty to obstructing justice by lying to the SEC. When the suit was resolved, Mr. Thayer's sentence included four years in prison, a $5,000 fine, and the payment of $550,000 in profits earned by others through his tips.

Wholesale Distribution Rights

Anheuser-Busch is also active in the legal issue of allowing distributors to have exclusive wholesale-distribution rights. The state of Indiana is the only state to forbid exclusive-distribution contracts, and twenty-seven states require the contracts. In 1977, the Supreme Court ruled that exclusive contracts can be legal, if the contracts don't hamper competition, but that decisions would be made on a case by case basis. Distributors and brewers say that this court decision has created lawsuits—any wholesaler or retailer can challenge its competitor's exclusive-distribution contracts.

The Malt Beverage Interbrand Competition Act of 1985, which has been cleared by the Senate Judiciary Committee, would preserve the industry's right to sue for antitrust violations. The 140-member U.S. Brewers Association and the 2,000-member National Beer Wholesaler Association have lobbied for the bill, because they believe that it would clarify the existing antitrust law. The bill's opponents, including the Federal Trade Commission, Senator Strom Thurmond (Chairman of the Senate Judiciary Committee), Senator Howard Metzenbaum, and numerous consumer groups, believe that exempting the beer industry from the antitrust laws would increase prices and reduce competition. In fact, the New York Attorney General has filed a class-action lawsuit against Miller, Stroh, Heileman and Anheuser-Busch, and claims that their exclusive agreements with distributors have caused price increases and decreased competition.

Use of "LA" Name

A lawsuit has been filed by G. Heileman Brewing and joined by Miller Brewing Company against Anheuser-Busch's use of "LA" (low alcohol) as a brand name. As in a previous suit by the Stroh Brewery, these breweries claim that this is a generic term. Anheuser-Busch won the Stroh Brewery suit with their claim that LA is a trademark and not a generic term.

COMPETITION   In 1984, there were 92 domestic brewery plants with a total capacity of 232.7 million barrels of beer. Operating at an average 78.7% of capacity, shipments were 178.4 million barrels (see Exhibit 9.7). This is quite a contrast to the 430

EXHIBIT 9.7 | **U.S. Brewing Industry Capacity and Usage—1984**
(Total Capacity and Shipments in Millions of Barrels)

BREWER	NUMBER OF PLANTS	TOTAL CAPACITY	SHIPMENTS	% OF CAPACITY
Anheuser-Busch	11	66.5	64.0	96.2
Miller Brewing (Philip Morris)	7	54.0	37.5	69.4
The Stroh Brewery	7	32.6	23.9	73.3
G. Heileman Brewing	12	26.5	16.8	63.4
Adolph Coors	1	15.5	13.2	85.2
Pabst Brewing	4	15.0	11.6	77.3
Genesee Brewing	1	4.0	3.0	75.0
Christian Schmidt[1,2]	2	5.0	2.1	42.0
Falstaff Brewing[3]	5	5.0	2.3	46.0
Pittsburgh Brewing	1	1.2	1.0	83.3
All others	41	7.4	3.2	43.2
Domestic total	92	232.7	178.6	78.7

[1] Includes 2.8 million barrels which are tax-free exports and military shipments.

[2] Includes Ohio plant which closed Nov. 1984.

[3] Includes Pearl Brewing Co. and General Brewing Co.

SOURCES: Anheuser-Busch Companies, Inc. *Annual Reports*; *Modern Brewery Age Blue Book*; and *Impact* Databank.

brewers in 1850 who produced 750,000 barrels per year. By the end of the 1890s, the number of brewers had grown to 1,169, and over 1,000,000 barrels were produced per year. However, by mid-century the industry had begun to consolidate. In 1954 there were 310 plants and 263 brewers, and by 1963 these numbers had shrunk to 211 plants and 171 brewers. This concentration of the industry continued through the next decade, so that there were 88 plants and 41 brewers in 1980. The top five brewers in the nation accounted for 87.1% of total beer sales in 1985, a 2.6% increase over the previous year.

In 1985, Anheuser-Busch held a 37.1% market share, compared with 35.0% in the previous year, and 23.4% a decade ago. It has set a corporate objective of 40% market share by the late 1980s. As Mr. Long, President and CEO, said, "We have always seen yesterday's success not as our ending point or a conclusion, but as a springboard into tomorrow's challenges." The challenging objective for the 1990s will be a 50% market share. The sales and market-share figures of Anheuser-Busch's competitors are shown in Exhibit 9.8.

Since Philip Morris Company acquired it in 1970, Miller Brewing has been Anheuser-Busch's prime competitor. Miller's market share in 1970 was 4.2% (5.1 million barrels), and it ranked seventh in the industry. The company experienced rapid growth in the 1970s because of the successful introduction of Lite beer. Anheuser-Busch countered with two separate strategies. First, the company increased its advertising budgets and took on Miller in head-to-head competition. Then, Anheuser-Busch developed a strategy of flanking Miller's beers in each category with two Anheuser-Busch beers (e.g., Budweiser and Busch flanked Miller High Life in the premium beer category).

Over the past three years, Miller has introduced eight new brands of beer. Although the company had to mothball its Trenton, Ohio, brewery in 1984, its market share had grown to 20.3% (37.1 million barrels) by 1985, and the company now ranks second in the industry. Miller's sales volume did decline by 1.1 percent in 1985. This decline was attributed to continued weakness in Miller High Life's sales. Miller's other premium beer, Lowenbrau, was also competing poorly at this time. However, Miller's profits were up by approximately 17% in 1985 over the depressed profit on 1984.

In 1981, the Stroh Brewery purchased F&M Schaefer and closed their Detroit brewery (7.2 million barrel capacity). On April 27, 1982, the Joseph Schlitz Brewing Company was merged into the Stroh Brewery, and Stroh became the third largest brewer. The company's shipping of 13.1 million barrels in 1985 represents a 12.8% market share and a 2.1% decline in volume sales over the previous years.

G. Heileman Brewing, the United States' fourth largest brewer, has been very effective in competing against Anheuser-Busch in regional markets. It has successfully developed and implemented a strategy of acquiring struggling local brewers at a low cost. After acquiring the new brewery, Heileman reintroduces its brands with an aggressive marketing plan. Anheuser-Busch has countered with a strategy focused on heavy price competition from its Busch brands. Although G. Heileman halted its planned expansion into the Southwest market, the company's market share grew from 2.4% (3.0 million barrels) in 1970 to 8.8% (16.2 million barrels) in 1985. However, the company's earnings from its brewing industry declined by 11% in 1985, and it closed its small Phoenix plant (500,000 barrels).

The fifth largest brewer, Adolph Coors Company, had a 13% volume increase in sales in 1985. This increase was the result of an aggressive expansion into the New England and Illinois markets. Coors's profits from beer increased by 77% from its poor 1984 performance.

Pabst Brewing, the sixth largest brewer, experienced a decline in market share from 6.5% in 1984 to 5.0% in 1985, when the company's new owners aggressively increased prices.

DISTRIBUTION CHANNELS

The company distributes its beer in the United States and the Caribbean through a network of 10 company-owned wholesale operations, employing approximately 1,600 people, and about 960 independently owned wholesale companies (see Exhibit 9.9). The independent wholesalers employ approximately 30,000

EXHIBIT 9.8 Sales of Leading U.S. Brewers
(Volume in Thousands of Barrels)

COMPANY	1970		1980		1984		1985		% CHANGE IN VOLUME, 1984–1985
	Volume	Market Share (%)	Volume	Market Share (%)	Volume	Market Share (%)	Volume	Market Share (%)	
Anheuser-Busch	22,202	18.1	50,160	28.2	64,000	35.0	68,000	37.1	+6.3
Miller Brewing	5,150	4.2	37,300	21.0	37,520	20.5	37,100	20.3	−1.1
The Stroh Brewery	3,276	2.7	6,161	3.5	23,900	13.1	23,400	12.8	−2.1
G. Heileman Brewing	3,000	2.4	13,270	7.4	16,760	9.2	16,200	8.8	−3.3
Adolph Coors Co.	7,277	5.9	13,779	7.7	13,187	7.2	14,738	8.1	+11.8
Top 5, total	40,905	33.3	120,670	67.8	155,367	85.0	159,438	87.1	+2.8
Other domestic	80,995	68.0	52,830	29.6	20,133	11.1	15,662	8.6	−22.1
Total domestic	121,900	99.3	173,500	97.4	175,500	96.1	175,100	95.7	−0.2
Imports	900	0.7	4,600	2.8	7,200	3.9	7,900	4.3	+9.7
Total	122,800	100.0	177,900	100.0	182,700	100.0	183,000	100.0	+0.2

EXHIBIT 9.9   National Distribution Map, Anheuser-Busch Companies, Inc.

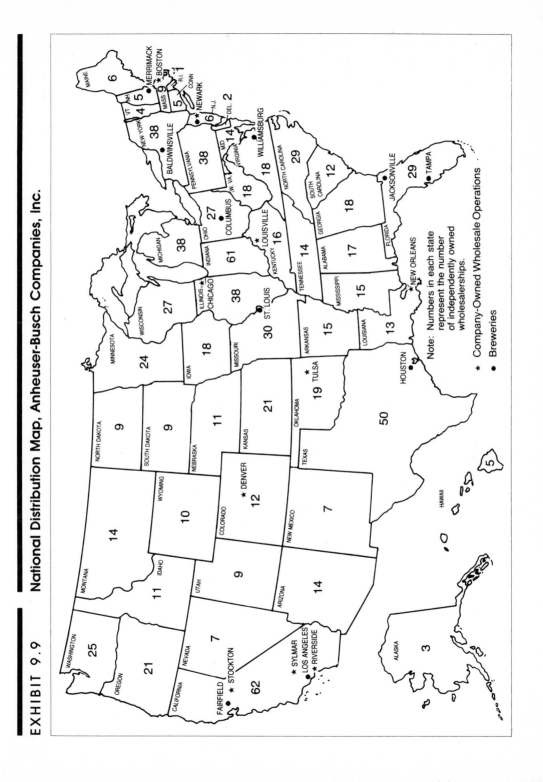

people. Canadian and European distribution is achieved through special arrangements with foreign brewing companies.

Sales volume at the wholesale level ranges from 870 barrels to 1.1 million barrels annually. However, the LA and Busch brands are presently available only in selected markets around the country.

MARKETING, ADVERTISING, AND PRODUCTS

Beer uniquely fits contemporary lifestyles. The five hallmarks of beer as a consumer beverage are convenience, moderation, health, value, and thirst-quenching properties. Each member of the Anheuser-Busch family of eleven beers is positioned to take advantage of this image. Exhibit 9.10 describes the targeted market for each of the company's beers.

There has been a major shift in consumption of beer by type or class (see Exhibit 9.11). It is expected that per capita beer consumption will decline about 1% or less in 1986, and remain flat throughout the balance of the 1980s. This decline is expected to be accompanied by a 2% rise in beer prices in 1986 and 1987. Also, the Census Bureau projects a drop in the 20–39-year-old age group, a major beer market (see Exhibit 9.12).

Anheuser-Busch has had its beers affiliated with sports for years (see Exhibit 9.13), and is probably the largest sponsor of sporting events, vehicles, and broadcasts. In fact, the company sponsored the 1984 Olympics, and in 1985 spent in excess of $100 million for advertising on television and radio sporting events. Out of a total $522,900,000 spent on advertising in 1985, Anheuser-Busch spent

EXHIBIT 9.10

Anheuser-Busch Beers

BEER	CLASS	TARGET MARKET
Budweiser	Premium	Any demographic or ethnic group and any region of the country
Bud Light	Light	Young to middle-aged males
Michelob	Super premium	Contemporary adults
Michelob Light	Light	Young, active upscale drinker with high-quality lifestyle
Michelob Classic Dark	Premium dark	Yuppies
Busch	Premium	Consumers who prefer lighter-tasting beer
Natural Light	Light	Beverage to go with good food
LA	Low alcohol	Health-conscious consumers
King Cobra	Malt liquor	Contemporary male, adults, aged 21–24
Carlsberg	Lager	Import market
Elephant Malt Liquor	Malt liquor	Consumers who enjoy imported beer

EXHIBIT 9.11

Apparent Beer Consumption by Type
(In Millions of Barrels)

TYPE	CONSUMPTION					% CHANGE, 1983–1984
	1975	1980	1982	1983	1984	
Popular	65.4	30.0	29.5	30.5	38.0	+18.0
Premium	71.6	102.3	95.7	94.6	87.0	−8.0
Super-premium	5.0	11.5	10.8	10.1	9.5	−5.9
Light	2.8	22.1	32.5	34.1	35.3	+3.5
Low alcohol	—	—	—	*	0.8	—
Imported	1.7	4.8	5.8	5.3	7.2	+14.3
Malt liquor	3.8	5.5	6.4	8.4	5.8	−9.4
Ale	N.A.	1.9	1.8	1.7	1.4	−17.6
Total	150.3	177.9	182.5	184.7	185.0	−0.5

N.A.—Not available.
* Less than 50,000 gallons.
SOURCE: *Impact* Databank.

EXHIBIT 9.12

U.S. Population Projections

AGE GROUP*	1985		1990		2000	
	Number (thous.)	% of Total	Number (thous.)	% of Total	Number (thous.)	% of Total
Under 5 yrs.	18,453	7.7	19,198	7.7	17,826	6.6
5–14 yrs.	33,408	14.0	35,384	14.2	38,277	14.3
15–19 yrs.	18,416	7.7	18,968	6.8	18,943	7.1
20–24 yrs.	21,301	8.9	18,580	7.4	17,145	6.4
25–29 yrs.	21,838	9.2	21,522	8.6	17,396	6.5
30–34 yrs.	19,950	8.4	22,007	8.8	19,019	7.1
35–39 yrs.	17,894	7.5	20,001	8.0	21,753	8.1
40–44 yrs.	14,110	5.9	17,848	7.2	21,990	8.2
45–49 yrs.	11,647	4.9	13,980	5.6	19,763	7.4
50–54 yrs.	10,817	4.5	11,422	4.6	17,356	6.5
55–64 yrs.	22,188	9.3	21,051	8.4	23,787	8.9
65 yrs. & over	28,609	12.0	31,697	12.7	34,921	13.0
All ages	238,631	100.0	249,658	100.0	267,955	100.0

* Includes Armed Forces abroad.
SOURCE: Department of Commerce, Population Series P-25, as of July 1, 1985.

EXHIBIT 9.13   **Anheuser-Busch's Sports Affiliations**

BUDWEISER	BUD LIGHT	MICHELOB	BUSCH	MICHELOB LIGHT
Horse racing	Triathlon	Lacrosse	NASCAR	Skiing
Soccer	Track	Rugby	Auto racing	Volleyball
Boxing	Boat racing	Golf	Billiards	Tennis
Boat racing		Sailing		

SOURCE: Anheuser-Busch 1986 Fact Sheet.

EXHIBIT 9.14   **1985 Anheuser-Busch Advertising Expenditures**
(Expenditures in Thousands of Dollars)

MEDIUM	EXPENDITURES
Magazines	$ 13,956
Newspapers	5,611
Newspaper suppliers	327
Business publications	724
Network television	154,503
Sports television	70,747
Network radio	8,929
Sports radio	39,713
Outdoor	5,105
Network cable	16,395
Total Measured Media	$316,011
Total Unmeasured	206,889
Total	$522,900

SOURCE: *Advertising Age*, September 4, 1986.

$225,250,000 in television advertising (see Exhibit 9.14). The top fifteen beer advertisers spent a total of $497,163,000 on television advertising in 1985 (see Exhibit 9.15).

Budweiser advertising and sales are very important to Anheuser-Busch, as Bud accounts for more than two-thirds of the company's beer production and one-quarter of the whole domestic market. To promote Bud, Anheuser-Busch began running advertisements exploiting patriotic fervor, the current resurgence in the pride of being an American.

Following this strategy, Anheuser-Busch has fine-tuned the campaign "For All You Do, This Bud's for You" into the very successful "You Make America

EXHIBIT 9.15   **Top Fifteen Beer Advertisers on Television, 1985**

	EXPENDITURES		
	Network	Spot	Total
Anheuser-Busch Cos.	$143,235,200	$ 55,820,000	$199,055,200
Philip Morris Cos. (Miller, et al)	112,641,600	27,337,300	139,978,900
Adolph Coors Co.	18,076,400	33,586,800	51,663,200
Stroh Brewery Co.	31,847,700	8,163,800	40,011,500
G. Heileman Brewing Co.	6,931,300	8,782,700	15,714,000
Brauen Beck & Co.	—	4,160,300	4,160,300
RJR Nabisco, Inc. (Fosters, Moosehead)	90,900	1,198,900	1,289,800
Genesee Brewing Co.	192,000	4,962,500	5,154,500
Van Munching & Co.	6,502,900	9,165,800	15,668,700
S&P Co. (Pabst, Pearl, Hamms)	—	1,847,300	1,847,300
Molson Cos.	99,200	1,800,400	1,899,600
Latrobe Brewing Co.	—	444,500	444,500
Pittsburgh Brewing Co.	—	853,700	853,700
John Labatt, Ltd.	—	567,400	567,400
Masters Brewing Co.	—	929,000	929,000
Total	$329,202,500	$167,961,100	$497,163,600

SOURCE: *Modern Brewery Age*, April 13, 1987, p. 1.

Work, and This Bud's for You." In 1985, measured media ads and promotions topped $80 million for Bud, the most heavily advertised beer in the United States. Miller also followed the same advertising strategy; however, as Budweiser sales increased, Miller sales decreased.

HUMAN RESOURCES MANAGEMENT

In 1983, Anheuser-Busch established its Office of Corporate Human Resources to focus on human resources activities and issues. Human resource planning has become an integral component of business planning at all levels of the organization.

The company's philosophy concerning its approximately 39,000 employees is that all employees are to be treated with courtesy and respect. The company tries to foster an atmosphere for open, two-way communications. Functioning on a national level, labor-management committees involve employees in issues and decisions that directly affect them and their working conditions. Additionally, in 1985 the beer division introduced "The New A-BI," a communication program to encourage the employees to suggest productivity improvements and cost reductions.

The Teamsters' Union represents approximately 15,600 employees in Anheuser-Busch Companies, Inc. A new labor contract with the International

EXHIBIT 9.16   **Production Facilities, Anheuser-Busch Companies, Inc.**
(Capacity in Millions of Barrels)

			TYPE OF BEER PRODUCED		
BREWERY	YEAR OPENED	1986 CAPACITY	Bud	Bud Light	Michelob Light
St. Louis	1880	12.70	X	X	X
Newark	1951	5.30	X	X	X
Los Angeles	1954	10.90	X	X	X
Tampa	1959	1.80	X	X	
Houston	1966	9.00	X	X	X
Columbus	1968	6.30	X	X	X
Jacksonville	1969	6.60	X	X	X
Merrimack	1970	2.97	X	X	X
Williamsburg	1972	8.70	X	X	X
Fairfield	1976	3.90	X	X	X
Baldwinsville	1982	7.10	X	X	X
Total capacity		75.27			

Brotherhood of Teamsters was ratified in 1985 and is effective through February, 1988.

PRODUCTION FACILITIES

Anheuser-Busch has eleven breweries located in nine states, and their annual capacity is 75.27 million barrels of beer (see Exhibit 9.16). A twelfth brewery at Fort Collins, Colorado, is scheduled to be operational in 1988, and its annual capacity will be 5 million barrels. Only the St. Louis plant brews all nine beers.

Productivity continues to be an integral part of Anheuser-Busch's growth strategy. In 1985, Anheuser-Busch, Inc., received the Excellence in Productivity Award from the Institute of Industrial Engineers because of the company's continued commitment to reducing waste and increasing efficiencies. Also, the Williamsburg Brewery received the U.S. Senate's Productivity Award. Capital investment in new and existing plants and equipment resulted in $1.8 billion of cost savings over the past six years. In 1985, Anheuser-Busch's Employee Suggestion Program resulted in $1 million of productivity savings. Nevertheless, productivity is not the sole goal. Anheuser-Busch has an equal commitment to quality because management believes that quality and productivity complement each other.

While many other brewers are shutting down or selling their existing facilities and running at lower capacity levels (see Exhibit 9.7), Anheuser-Busch must expand its capacity and operate with a high utilization of existing capacity, in

TYPE OF BEER PRODUCED				
Michelob	Busch	Natural Light	LA	Michelob Classic Dark
X	X	X	X	X
X				X
X		X	X	X
	X	X		
X		X		
X	X	X		
X	X	X		
X	X	X		
X	X	X	X	
X		X		X
X		X	X	

order to meet the increasing demand for its beer. Therefore Anheuser-Busch has developed an extensive expansion and modernization program. For example, the expansion of the Houston brewery, completed in 1985, added 5 million barrels of capacity, and the St. Louis, Newark, and Merrimack plants have been modernized.

The plants that manufacture and recycle cans continue to expand as well. Metal Container Corporation produced 4 billion cans and 2 billion lids in 1985. To meet the company's goals, the Gainesville plant was expanded in 1985; a new Oklahoma City plant, to manufacture ecology-type lids with stay-on tabs, will be completed in 1986; and the Jacksonville, Columbus, and Arnold plants are scheduled for modernization and expansion. In addition, Container Recovery Corporation now has three plants and is the largest recycler in the U.S. As Mr. Busch said, "We intend to adapt our proven management and production abilities to expand over horizons into areas previously uncharted by Anheuser-Busch."

FINANCE

Recently, Standard and Poor's raised the bond ratings on $800 million of Anheuser-Busch's senior debt from A+ to AA−, in recognition of its improved financial performance. The Busch family owns approximately 23% of the company's stock, and for the fifty-third consecutive year, Anheuser-Busch has paid dividends. Financial data for the company can be found in Exhibits 9.17–9.19.

For the next five years, the company has planned for extensive capital expenditure programs to take advantage of growth opportunities in its three business segments. The company is not opposed to long-term financing for some of its capital programs, but cash flow from operations will be the principal source of funds to support these programs. For short-term capital requirements, the company has access to a maximum of $500 million from a bank credit-line agreement.

EXHIBIT 9.17   Consolidated Balance Sheet, Anheuser-Busch Companies, Inc.
(Dollar Amounts in Millions)

	1985	1984
Assets		
Current Assets		
Cash and marketable securities (marketable securities of $119.9 in 1985 and $69.3 in 1984 at cost, which approximates market)	$ 169.6	$ 78.6
Accounts and notes receivable, less allowance for doubtful accounts of $3.1 in 1985 and $2.8 in 1984	301.7	275.6
Inventories		
Raw materials and supplies	225.4	212.7
Work in process	73.5	65.7
Finished goods	38.8	37.5
Total inventories	337.7	315.9
Other current assets	156.5	106.2
Total current assets	965.5	776.3
Investments and Other Assets		
Investments in and advances to unconsolidated subsidiaries	56.7	42.9
Investment properties	16.5	18.1
Deferred charges and other non-current assets	97.5	87.1
Excess of cost over net assets of acquired business, net	99.3	85.3
Total investments and other assets	270.0	233.4
Plant and Equipment		
Land	91.8	85.4
Buildings	1,578.7	1,399.3
Machinery and equipment	3,381.4	2,920.6
Construction in progress	288.9	395.3
Total	5,340.8	4,800.6
Less: Accumulated depreciation	1,454.9	1,285.6
Total plant and equipment	3,885.9	3,515.0
Total assets	$5,121.4	$4,524.7

EXHIBIT 9.17   **(Continued)**

	1985	1984
Liabilities and Shareholders' Equity		
Current Liabilities		
Accounts payable	$ 425.3	$ 338.2
Accrued salaries, wages, and benefits	177.1	150.3
Accrued interest payable	30.1	26.8
Due to customers for returnable containers	33.1	31.8
Accrued taxes, other than income taxes	56.9	43.6
Estimated income taxes	31.3	39.0
Other current liabilities	84.0	66.3
Total current liabilities	837.8	696.0
Long-Term Debt	861.3	835.8
Deferred Income Taxes	961.7	755.0
Convertible Redeemable Preferred Stock (Liquidation Value $300.0)	287.6	286.9
Common Stock And Other Shareholders' Equity		
Preferred stock, $1.00 par value, authorized 32,498,000 shares in 1985, 1984, and 1983; none issued	—	—
Common stock, $1.00 par value, authorized 200,000,000 shares in 1985, 1984, and 1983; issued 146,633,977, 48,641,869 and 48,514,214 shares, respectively	146.6	48.6
Capital in excess of par value	90.4	173.2
Retained earnings	2,142.3	1,829.3
Foreign currency translation adjustment	(4.4)	(6.6)
	2,374.9	2,044.5
Less: Cost of treasury stock (8,114,453, 4,692,456 and 358,656 shares in 1985, 1984, and 1983, respectively)	201.9	93.5
	2,173.0	1,951.0
Commitments and Contingencies	—	—
Total Liabilities and Shareholders' Equity	$5,121.4	$4,524.7

EXHIBIT 9.18 Financial Summary—Operations, Anheuser-Busch Companies, Inc.

(Dollar Amounts in Millions, except Per-Share Data)

Eleven Years

	1985	1984	1983	1982	1981	1980	1979	1978	1977	1976	1975
Consolidated Summary of Operations											
Barrels sold	68.0	64.0	60.5	59.1	54.5	50.2	46.2	41.6	36.6	29.1	35.2
Sales	$7,683.3	$7,158.2	$6,658.5	$5,185.7	$4,409.6	$3,822.4	$3,263.7	$2,701.6	$2,231.2	$1,753.0	$2,036.7
Federal and state beer taxes	683.0	657.0	624.3	609.1	562.4	527.0	487.8	442.0	393.2	311.9	391.7
Net sales	7,000.3	6,501.2	6,034.2	4,576.6	3,847.2	3,295.4	2,775.9	2,259.6	1,838.0	1,441.1	1,645.0
Cost of products sold	4,676.1	4,414.2	4,113.2	3,331.7	2,975.5	2,553.9	2,172.1	1,762.4	1,462.8	1,175.0	1,343.8
Gross profit	2,324.2	2,087.0	1,921.0	1,244.9	871.7	741.5	603.8	497.2	375.2	266.1	301.2
Marketing, administrative and research expenses	1,491.9	1,332.3	1,220.2	752.0	515.0	428.6	356.7	274.9	190.4	137.8	126.1
Operating income	832.3	754.7	700.8	492.9	356.7	312.9	247.1	222.3	184.8	128.3	175.1
Interest expense	(93.4)	(102.7)	(111.4)	(89.2)	(89.6)	(75.6)	(40.3)	(28.9)	(26.7)	(26.9)	(22.6)
Interest capitalized	37.2	46.8	32.9	41.2	64.1	41.7	—	—	—	—	—
Interest income	21.3	22.8	12.5	17.0	6.2	2.4	8.4	11.7	7.7	10.3	10.9
Other income (expense), net	(16.9)	(31.8)	(18.8)	(8.1)	(12.2)	(9.9)	5.4	0.7	4.1	1.7	1.9
Loss on partial closing of Los Angeles Busch Gardens	—	—	—	—	—	—	—	—	—	(10.0)	—
Gain on sale of Lafayette plant	—	—	—	20.4	—	—	—	—	—	—	—

Income before income taxes	780.5	689.8	616.0	474.2	325.2	271.5	220.6	205.8	169.9	103.4	165.3
Income taxes	336.8	298.3	268.0	186.9	107.8	99.7	76.3	94.8	78.0	48.0	80.6
Income before cumulative effect of an accounting change	443.7	391.5	348.0	287.3	217.4	171.8	144.3	111.0	91.9	55.4	84.7
Cumulative effect of change to the flow-through method of accounting for the investment tax credit	—	—	—	—	—	—	52.1	—	—	—	—
Net income	$ 443.7	$ 391.5	$ 348.0	$ 287.3	$ 217.4	$ 171.8	$ 196.4	$ 111.0	$ 91.9	$ 55.4	$ 84.7
Per share—Primary											
Income before cumulative effect of an accounting change	2.84	2.47	2.17	1.99	1.60	1.27	1.07	.82	.68	.41	.63
Cumulative effect of change to the flow-through method of accounting for the investment tax credit	—	—	—	—	—	—	.38	—	—	—	—
Net income	2.84	2.47	2.17	1.99	1.60	1.27	1.45	.82	.68	.41	.63
Per share—Fully diluted	2.84	2.47	2.17	1.96	1.54	1.27	1.45	.82	.68	.41	.63
Cash dividends paid											
Common stock	102.7	89.7	78.3	65.8	51.2	44.8	40.7	37.0	32.0	30.6	28.8
Per share	.73 1/3	.62 2/3	.54	.46	.37 2/3	.33	.30	.27 1/3	.23 2/3	.22 2/3	.21 1/3
Preferred stock	27.0	27.0	29.7	—	—	—	—	—	—	—	—
Per share	3.60	3.60	3.60	—	—	—	—	—	—	—	—
Average number of common shares	156.3	158.7	160.5	144.3	136.2	135.6	135.6	135.3	135.3	135.3	135.3

EXHIBIT 9.19

Financial Summary—Balance Sheet and Other Information
(Dollar Amounts in Millions, Except Per Share and Statistical Data)

	1985	1984	1983	1982	1981	1980	1979	1978	1977	1976	1975
Balance sheet information											
Working capital	127.7	80.3	175.1	45.8	45.9	26.3	88.1	223.7	175.4	182.1	255.4
Current ratio	1.2	1.1	1.2	1.1	1.1	1.1	1.3	1.8	1.8	2.0	2.5
Plant and equipment, net	3,885.9	3,515.0	3,204.2	2,988.9	2,257.6	1,947.4	1,461.8	1,109.2	952.0	857.1	724.9
Long-term debt	861.3	835.8	961.4	969.0	817.3	743.8	507.9	427.3	337.5	340.7	342.2
Total debt to total debt plus equity	25.9%	27.2%	31.9%	35.4%	42.4%	43.4%	36.0%	36.4%	33.4%	35.8%	36.8%
Deferred income taxes	961.7	755.0	573.2	455.1	357.7	261.6	193.8	146.9	119.1	93.0	74.6
Convertible redeemable preferred stock	287.6	286.9	286.0	285.0	—	—	—	—	—	—	—
Common stock and other shareholders equity	2,173.0	1,951.0	1,766.5	1,526.6	1,206.8	1,031.4	904.3	747.9	673.9	611.9	587.1
Return on shareholders equity	18.9%	18.2%	18.0%	19.9%	19.3%	17.8%	16.9%	15.6%	14.3%	9.2%	15.2%
Total assets	5,121.4	4,524.7	4,330.2	3,902.8	2,875.2	2,449.7	1,926.0	1,648.0	1,403.8	1,268.1	1,202.1
Other information											
Capital expenditures	601.0	519.2	428.0	355.8	421.3	590.0	432.3	228.7	156.7	198.7	155.4

Depreciation and amortization	236.1	203.4	187.3	133.6	108.7	99.4	75.4	66.0	61.2	53.1	51.1
Total payroll cost	1,547.7	1,427.5	1,350.8	853.3	686.7	594.1	529.1	421.8	338.9	271.4	268.3
Effective tax rate	43.2%	43.2%	43.5%	39.4%	33.1%	36.7%	34.6%	46.0%	45.9%	46.4%	48.7%
Price/earnings ratio	14.9	9.8	9.6	11.0	8.9	7.3	7.1	9.8	9.8	18.8	18.1
Percent of pre-tax profit on gross sales	10.2%	9.6%	9.3%	9.1%	7.4%	7.1%	6.8%	7.6%	7.6%	5.9%	8.1%
Market price range of common stock (high/low)	$45\frac{3}{4}-23\frac{5}{8}$	$24\frac{3}{4}-17\frac{7}{8}$	$25\frac{3}{8}-19\frac{1}{2}$	$23\frac{5}{8}-12\frac{7}{8}$	$14\frac{3}{4}-9\frac{1}{4}$	$10\frac{3}{8}-7$	$9-6\frac{1}{2}$	$9\frac{1}{4}-5\frac{7}{8}$	$8\frac{3}{8}-6\frac{1}{4}$	$12\frac{7}{8}-6\frac{7}{8}$	$13\frac{1}{4}-8\frac{1}{8}$

Pro Forma Information, assuming retroactive application of the flow-through method of accounting for the investment tax credit

Net income	443.7	391.5	348.0	287.3	217.4	171.8	144.3	121.9	98.3	75.5	89.1
Net income per share:											
Primary	2.84	2.47	2.17	1.99	1.60	1.27	1.07	.90	.73	.56	.66
Fully diluted	2.84	2.47	2.17	1.96	1.54	1.27	1.07	.90	.73	.56	.66
Common stock and other shareholders' equity	2,173.0	1,951.0	1,766.5	1,526.6	1,206.8	1,031.4	904.3	800.1	715.1	646.8	601.9
Return on shareholders' equity	18.9%	18.2%	18.0%	19.9%	19.3%	17.8%	16.9%	16.1%	14.4%	12.1%	15.6%
Book value per share	15.69	13.81	12.17	10.54	8.86	7.61	6.66	5.91	5.28	4.78	4.45
Effect tax rate	43.2%	43.2%	43.5%	39.4%	33.1%	36.7%	34.6%	40.8%	42.1%	27.0%	46.1%

CASE 10

Food Service Industry

LYNDA L. GOULET

For the last two decades one of the most important trends in the U.S. economy has been the steady growth of the service sector. Of all the segments in the service sector perhaps none is more representative of this trend than the food service industry. Every day 22 million people eat at McDonald's alone.[1] The rise in the popularity of eating out has resulted in a food service industry in the U.S. that generated $200 billion in sales in 1987 and is expected to grow at an annual average compound rate of 7.5% through 1992.[2] In spite of such predictions, however, the expenditure for food as a percentage of total personal consumption is declining and the price of food consumed away from home is increasing faster than the consumer price index (see Exhibit 10.1). Although people obviously have to eat, firms in the food service industry would like to know what people will choose to eat, where they would rather eat, and how much they are willing to pay.

FOOD SERVICE

The food service industry includes all establishments that prepare food to be consumed away from home or to be taken out for consumption without additional preparation. As shown in Exhibit 10.2 below, restaurants, one of four categories of eating places, comprised 61% of all food service sales in 1987.

In addition to restaurants (95% of 1987 eating place sales) there are three other types of eating places: public cafeterias (3%), social caterers (1%), and ice cream stands (1%). Although cafeterias are very popular with senior citizens who are value-conscious, sales from these establishments are expected to grow 7.0% annually through 1992, compared to the 7.7% growth projected for both

This industry note was prepared by Professor Lynda L. Goulet of the University of Northern Iowa. Presented at the Midwest Society for Case Research Workshop, 1989. All rights reserved to the author and the Midwest Society for Case Research. Copyright © 1989 by Lynda L. Goulet. Reprinted by permission.

EXHIBIT 10.1   **Income, Spending, Price, and Population Data**
(Dollar Amounts in Billions)

	1987	1986	1983	1980	1975	1970
Disposable personal income	$3,181.5	$3,022.1	$2,428.1	$1,918.0	$1,142.8	$715.6
Personal consumption expenditures		2,799.8	2,234.5	1,732.6	1,012.8	640.0
Expenditures for meals & beverages[1]		155.2	123.5	100.2	55.8	34.9
Expenditures for off-premise food[2]		333.3	290.4	242.3	158.5	104.4
Consumer price index (1967 = 100)		328.4	298.4	246.8	161.2	116.3
Price of food away from home (1967 = 100)	374.4	360.1	319.9	267.0	174.3	119.9
Price of food at home (1967 = 100)	318.5	305.3	282.2	251.5	175.8	113.7
U.S. population (mil.)		241.6	234.8	227.8	216.0	205.1
Households (mil.)		89.5	85.3	82.4	72.9	64.8
Median household income ($)		$24,897	$21,018	$17,710	$11,800	$8,734

SOURCE: U.S. Department of Commerce.

[1] Includes purchases and tips made in all categories of food service establishments for food consumed on the premises.

[2] Includes grocery purchases and food consumed off the premises purchased from food service and grocery establishments.

EXHIBIT 10.2   **Food Service Sales**
(Dollar Amounts in Billions)

	1992E	1988E	1987	1986
Total food service sales	286.6	213.5	199.6	187.1
All eating places	185.9	132.2	128.5	120.1
All restaurants	176.4	131.0	121.8	113.8

SOURCES: *Standard and Poor's Industry Surveys*, "Leisure Time: Restaurants," March 10, 1988, p. L36; and M. Knapp, "Twenty-First Annual Restaurant Growth Index: Industry Summary," *Restaurant Business*, September 20, 1988, pp. 71–73.

EXHIBIT 10.3   **Food Service Industry Structure**

CATEGORY	FOOD SERVICE PROVIDED BY OR IN	PERCENT OF FOOD SERVICE SALES	PROJECTED GROWTH
Hotel/Motel	Hotels or motels	6	7.6%/year
Transportation	Planes, trains, ship terminals, truck stops, turnpike plazas, etc.	2	10.9%
Leisure	Sports facilities, camps, bowling alleys, theaters, theme parks	3	6.2%
Retail	Food service by grocery, convenience stores, service stations, & other retail stores	4	13.3%
Business/Industry	Contract & internal food for employees, on-street catering, food vending machines	6	6.4%
Student	Contract & internal food for all students	5	5.6%
Health Care	Contract & internal food for patients & employees of all other institutions	6	5.0%
Drinking Places	Food sales at establishments where alcohol sales exceed food	5	5.5%
Eating Places	(See Exhibit 10.2)	64	7.7%

restaurants and caterers. The ice-cream-stand category, projected to grow at 7.2% annually through 1992, is comprised of establishments whose sales derive primarily from ice cream, yogurt, and similar frozen desserts. Two major chains in this category are Baskin-Robbins (3,400 stores with $650 million in total sales) and TCBY (820 stores with $120 million in total sales). Although International Dairy Queen ($2 billion in total sales) is ostensibly the largest firm in the ice cream category, it is not included because it now operates 3,000 of its 5,000 units as fast food restaurants. In addition, IDQ has recently purchased the Karmel Korn and Orange Julius chains and intends to combine all three concepts in shopping mall locations.

In addition to eating places, the food service industry includes eight other types of establishments. Each of these food service categories is described in Exhibit 10.3. Additionally, the percentage of 1987 total food service (FS) sales and the projected annual growth in sales through 1992 are shown by category.[3]

By the end of 1986, there were approximately 600,000 food service establishments operating in the U.S., with average unit sales of about $313,000. Over 250,000 of these units were restaurants. The rate of growth in food service unit formation has exceeded both population growth and household formation growth. Exhibit 10.4 summarizes the distribution of units, total sales, and average unit sales for each food service category.

EXHIBIT 10.4

Units, Total Sales, Average Unit Sales, Food Service Industry, 1986

	% TOTAL UNITS	% TOTAL SALES	AVG. UNIT SALES
Eating places:			
Restaurants	42.3	60.9	$ 450,400
Cafeterias	1.0	1.9	565,400
Caterers	0.6	0.7	385,700
Ice cream stands	1.4	0.8	177,700
Hotel/Motel	4.4	6.1	431,400
Transportation	0.1	1.6	6,951,400
Leisure	3.3	2.8	264,300
Retail	17.7	3.8	66,700
Business/Industry	1.9	5.7	938,500
Student	15.8	4.9	96,000
Health Care	6.0	6.2	320,600
Drinking Places	5.4	4.8	277,800
Total Food Service	100.0%	100.0%	$ 313,200
	(596,940 units)	($187.0 bil.)	

Individual Expenditures, 1986

	ALL FOOD SERVICE	RESTAURANTS
Dollar Sales/person	$ 775	$ 470
Dollar Sales/household	$2,090	$1,270
Persons/food unit	405	955
Households/food unit	150	355

SOURCE: "Twenty-first Annual Restaurant Growth Index," *Restaurant Business*, September 20, 1988, pp. 71–126.

TAKE-OUT FOOD[4]

The food purchased for consumption by individuals is supplied by the food service establishments as well as by supermarkets and other similar retail food stores. Further, the consumption of food may take place at the establishment where it is purchased or off the premises. Most of the sales of food service units are for food consumed at the unit, whereas most of the food purchased in supermarkets is for at-home preparation and consumption. However, as Exhibit 10.1 shows, the expenditures for meals and beverages are not as large as total food service sales shown in Exhibit 10.2. This discrepancy is explained by the fact that a significant portion of food service sales is now consumed off the premises (taken out) and is thereby reported as part of the expenditure for off-premise consumption in Exhibit 10.1. Moreover, take-out, home delivery, and drive-through sales of food service units are expected to grow at an annual rate of 10% through 1992.[5]

Almost any type of food service unit can provide take-out food. Such service typically benefits the owner of the unit by increasing volume and productivity without much additional labor or capital cost. However, take-out counters in restaurants can create problems with traffic flow, both inside and outside the unit. Home delivery, on the other hand, can add significant costs for packaging, vehicles, insurance, delivery labor, and food spoilage. For delivery service to be profitable, the food should have a high perceived price–value relationship. Fierce competition in pizza delivery, for example, has dramatically reduced profit margins. An increasing number of food service units are being designed to provide take-out or drive-through service exclusively. Such units typically have limited menus, non-prime locations, lower capital costs, and lower operating costs.

SUPERMARKETS[6]

Take-out services provide opportunities for food service units to increase their sales, and take-out services are not limited to food service firms. Increasingly, supermarkets and convenience stores are providing prepared foods to take out or eat on the premises. In 1987, total sales by food stores, including take-out prepared food, exceeded $300 billion, reflecting annual growth of 4.7% since 1980. During the 1980s, operating margins for supermarkets have steadily improved. Much of this improvement is associated with the increased size of stores and increased sales of high-margin goods and services. "Hypermarkets" are perhaps the ultimate supermarkets. Super Valu Stores, K Mart, Wal Mart, and several French firms are experimenting with these new formats. Super Valu's hypermarkets will contain 180,000 square feet; have 51 checkout lines; require 600 employees; stock 25,000 food items and 60,000 non-food items; and provide numerous services through optical, pharmaceutical, floral, and portrait photography departments. Wal Mart's version will include a bank and a gas station.

EXHIBIT 10.5   **Retail Grocery Industry, 1987**

	% TOTAL UNITS	% TOTAL $ SALES	AVG. UNIT $ SALES
Supermarkets	20.3	73.0	$7.516 million
Convenience Stores (excludes gasoline)	33.3	7.2	.448
Other grocery	46.4	19.8	.892
Total	100.0	100.0	$2.087 million
	(150,000 units)	($313 bil.)	

SOURCE: "Retailing: Supermarkets," *Standard and Poor's Industry Surveys*, April 21, 1988, pp. R90–96, and December 22, 1988, p. R64.

Super Valu expects the gross sales of its hypermarkets to exceed $1 million per week in each unit, with food sales accounting for half of the total.[7] Exhibit 10.5 describes the composition of the retail grocery industry for 1987.

TRENDS AFFECTING FOOD-RELATED INDUSTRIES	Both the food store and food service industries depend heavily on the availability of labor to provide their services. An increase in the minimum wage is likely to more strongly hurt the food service industry, however, because labor costs in most supermarkets are already above the minimum wage.[8] Both industries would be severely affected by mandated minimum health insurance coverage to all workers, including part-time labor. Scarcity of labor may also become a problem as the population of 15 to 30-year-olds will shrink in absolute size by 1992. Increased usage of computer technology in both industries will place additional skill and training requirements on food establishments.

In the shorter run, food costs are expected to rise as a result of the 1988 drought. This applies especially to wheat and corn products, beef, fruits, and vegetables.[9] Increased competition within and between the food service and food store industries will make it difficult to increase prices to absorb cost increases. Competitive pressure will also require more promotional efforts, a need for new products and services, and higher cost locations in both industries.

Demographic trends pose both threats and opportunities for these industries. The number of single-person households continues to rise (from 17% of all households in 1970 to 24% in 1986). Such people tend to eat out more frequently than members of larger households. The number of women in the workforce is expected to rise to 65% by the early 1990s. This, too, encourages the purchase of convenience foods of all types. The proportion of families with two wage earners exceeded 50% in 1986. This has helped to increase the disposable income required to support the cost of eating out and the cost of high margin convenience foods. It may be noted that single men tend to spend significantly more on food than single women, with men consuming about $2,300 each compared to $1,600 for women. Of this men spend over $1,100 annually away from home, while the typical woman spends only $500 away from home annually.[10]

The number of households with a microwave oven has increased from 10% in 1976 to over 70% by 1986, which favors increased purchases of upscale frozen convenience foods. However, as many baby-boomers have recently begun having children—creating a "mini-boom"—they may have to scale back their purchases of high-margin convenience items and food away from home. In spite of the fact that less than 5% of food service sales are for children's meals, it is estimated that in over 80% of all families children are the chief influence on where the family eats out. Furthermore, an offer of a toy or other such premium by a restaurant is often the deciding factor influencing the child.[11]

Both food stores and food service firms are making it easier for customers to pay for their purchases. Many supermarkets now provide electronic data terminals in their checkout lanes to permit the use of bank debit cards. American

Express and Visa are experimenting with credit card purchases in fast food restaurants. Early experience seems to indicate that the average food purchase made by credit card exceeds those made with cash.[12]

CHAIN RESTAURANTS AND FRANCHISING

Although the food service industry has historically been a fragmented industry, the franchise concept has allowed considerable consolidation through the development of chains. Operators of chain restaurant units can benefit from the power of prime-time television advertising, increased bargaining power with suppliers, the training and site selection expertise of the franchisor, and access to R&D involving new food products and processes.

In general, the franchisee in a restaurant chain must bear the cost of capital requirements which can range from $100,000 for a delivery-only unit to over $1,000,000 for a full-service, theme unit. In addition, the franchisee must remit approximately 3–5% of dollar sales as a royalty/service fee, plus an additional percentage for advertising done by the franchisor. The need for capital can be reduced if the franchisee is allowed to lease facilities or equipment through the franchisor or a third party. McDonald's, for example, usually owns the restaurant site and charges the franchisee a rental fee of 8.5% of sales, in addition to its 3.5% royalty and 4% advertising fee.[13]

One of the main advantages franchising provides for the franchisor is the ability to support faster growth in units, while limiting the firm's capital requirement. However, the franchisor's sales growth is limited to the fees collected from the unit franchisees rather than the total sales generated by the franchise units. Thus, if the total fees collected from a franchised unit were 5%, the franchisor would need twenty franchise units to generate the equivalent dollar sales of one company-owned unit. (Note that the "systemwide" sales often reported by chains refers to the total retail sales of all units, not the total sales of the franchisor, which are generally considerably less.) On the other hand, the level of profit margins and the return on investment provided by franchise units is generally higher than for company-owned units because the firm incurs only limited expenses for these units, many of which are fixed costs such as advertising which are spread over a large number of units. The proportion of franchised units in selected major restaurant chains is presented in Exhibit 10.6.

In 1986, 488 restaurant chains accounted for 31% of the total restaurant units and 46% of total restaurant sales. The average unit sales for these chains was $668,400, compared to $352,600 for the typical independent restaurant. Exhibit 10.7 presents the rate of growth in units and dollar sales for chain restaurants. It may be noted that there is presently one chain restaurant unit for every 3,000 people in the U.S. Thus, in a town of 30,000 population one may expect to see ten recognizable name restaurants, as well as more than twice this number of independent restaurants.

McDonald's is by far the largest single chain, with almost 10,000 units generating systemwide sales of over $14 billion in 1987. However, PepsiCo's three chains—Kentucky Fried Chicken, Pizza Hut, and Taco Bell—accounted for a

EXHIBIT 10.6   **Twenty-Five Restaurant Chains**

CHAIN	FOOD TYPE	NUMBER OF UNITS			SYSTEM-WIDE SALES ($ MILLIONS)	
		1988E	1987	% Franchised	1988E	1987
McDonald's	Burger	10,513	9,911	75.2	$16,064	$14,330
Burger King	Burger	5,473	5,179	84.7	5,400	5,000
Wendy's	Burger	3,816	3,727	64.2	2,869	2,747
Hardee's	Burger	3,110	2,912	66.9	3,299	3,064
Dairy Queen	Burger	5,122	5,005	99.9	2,067	1,878
Jack-in-the-Box	Burger	957	897	28.8	775	665
Arby's	R. Beef	2,049	1,851	89.4	1,160	988
Rax	R. Beef	521	520	70.0	366	358
Kentucky Fried Chicken	Chicken	7,761	7,522	74.7	4,896	4,100
Church's	Chicken	1,368	1,486	27.9	450	534
Pizza Hut	Pizza	6,597	6,257	56.9	3,200	2,900
Domino's	Pizza	4,893	4,279	74.1	2,307	1,980
Little Caesar's	Pizza	2,375	1,820	75.8	1,000	725
Taco Bell	Mexican	2,881	2,695	45.3	1,699	1,500
Red Lobster	Seafood	483	451	15.7	1,240	1,080
Long John Silver	Seafood	1,469	1,420	37.5	753	737
Captain D's	Seafood	636	574	42.2	364	343
Ponderosa	Steak	715	677	40.9	800	758
Bonanza	Steak	612	602	99.9	571	530
Sizzler	Steak	611	548	67.2	750	705
Shoney's	Full Menu	636	604	56.8	1,477	1,321
Denny's	Full Menu	1,299	1,221	14.4	1,323	1,244
IHOP	Pancake	458	454	84.4	316	297
Subway	Sandwich	2,898	1,810	99.4	603	360
Dunkin' Donuts	Donut	1,765	1,669	98.3	790	729

SOURCE: *Restaurant Business*, March 20, 1988, p. 194, and March 20, 1989, pp. 144–145.

combined total of 16,500 units and $8.5 billion in systemwide sales. The success of chains in contrast to independent restaurants is manifested by the fact that ten years after opening, 90% of chain units are still operating, compared to 18% of the independents.[14]

The international market provides a potential for restaurant chain growth. In 1985 there were fewer than 6,000 units of U.S. chains overseas, primarily in Canada, Japan, Australia, and the U.K. Though these international units are generally based on the parent chain's concept, they often have different menus tailored to local tastes. Regardless of the potential from population overseas, cultural differences, cost structures, foreign exchange rate volatility, and limited disposable income levels all constrain the overseas expansion opportunities of chains.[15]

SERVICE AND PRICE DISTINCTIONS AMONG RESTAURANTS

Restaurants can be classified in a number of ways. The government classifies them into two groups: full-menu and limited-menu. Full-menu units are those which offer table service and a relatively broad variety of food. In 1987 the average check per person for this type of restaurant was $10.55.[16] In contrast, the limited-menu category contains fast food establishments and those where service is through a line, excluding cafeterias. Although the total number of establishments in both categories is about the same—slightly over 126,000 each in 1986—average unit sales were higher in the full-menu group—$492,450 versus $408,200 in 1986. The projected annual growth rate through 1992, however, is higher for the limited-menu category—8.3% versus 7.2%.[17] Another form of classification utilizes three price groupings: upscale, midprice, and fast food.

Fast Food Restaurants

Because the number of fast food chains likely to be represented in a given population area has increased significantly in the last decade, competition has intensified. As a result, most fast food chains are attempting to encourage repeat business, broaden their customer base, simplify operations, and broaden their menu with convenient foods or unique products. Packaged salads, for example, provide convenience while broadening the appeal to more health-conscious customers. Food bars are another innovation. Wendy's SuperBar contains fifty items including Mexican food, pasta, salad ingredients, and baked potatoes with numerous toppings. Finger and bite-sized foods, such as chicken pieces and small hamburgers, are also successful and tend to increase sales of between meals snacks. This is important because present traffic patterns favor sales during lunch (36%) and dinner (40%) compared to morning (13%) and afternoon (11%).[18]

In addition to menu modifications, many chains are developing alternative store formats and organizational forms. Mini operations emphasizing delivery or take out service have been utilized to increase returns by lowering the investment required for unit expansion. Some chains are also experimenting with joint ventures involving convenience or grocery stores. For example, Godfather's is selling its pizza in frozen food sections of food stores. Other chains are testing the sales of their breakfast products at convenience stores because breakfast traffic at these stores has increased 20% in recent years.

The consumer's image of fast food service seems to have improved throughout the 1980s. Menu diversity, especially through the introduction of salads, is one major reason. In addition, many large chains have responded to health concerns by switching to the use of vegetable oil for cooking. However, consumer advocate groups continue to press for ingredients labeling on food wrappers. Environmentalists are concerned with the use of food containers that are not biodegradable or that contain chlorofluorocarbons.[19]

Upscale Restaurants[20]

This category contains full-menu establishments that are primarily independent units. The few chain restaurants in this group tend to be more regional in nature and consist of relatively few units. Most upscale restaurants reflect a theme, although this is no longer sufficient to attract patronage. Higher prices, attractive decor, and high service levels must also be accompanied by quality food. A shortage of skilled chefs is a major constraint restricting growth in this segment. The upscale group is the most trendy and fashionable. At present, Oriental and Southwestern cuisines are popular. To expand sales many units are incorporating an upscale breakfast meal and brunch on weekends.

Midpriced Restaurants

Many of the chains in the midprice group were originally coffee shops with a primary emphasis on breakfast—such as Denny's, International House of Pancakes, Country Kitchen, Bob Evans, Village Inn, and Waffle House. Most of these chains are now expanding their menus to appeal to the lunch and dinner markets. Other chains in the midprice group focus on the dinner meal and often on a specialized food emphasis—Bennigans, Chi-Chi's, El Torito, Chili's, and Red Lobster. Many of the traditional steak houses are expanding menus to include other types of meat and salads.[21] The prime customers for this segment tend to be senior citizens and families. Food trends in these units tend to lag the upscale segment by two to three years as midprice customers tend to be less adventurous.

The primary advantage of midprice restaurants over those in the fast food group is that they can increase sales by offering the customer higher quality food and more service in a nicer environment. However, there are limits to how much customers are willing to pay for these amenities. Ten dollars seems to be the practical limit of the per person charge in such restaurants. Charging too little also affects the value perceptions of midprice customers.[22] Because of price sensitivity and the relative labor intensity of this group compared to fast food, the segment is highly sensitive to labor availability and cost. As fast food units expand menus and service and raise prices, customers may actually receive more value at midscale restaurants.

In addition to price sensitivity, midprice restaurants also face potential for waste as food is cooked to order. Increased use of self-serve food bars, such as that employed by Bonanza, may be a partial solution to both these problems. Another problem faced by midscale units is the need to update decor in response to decor improvements by fast food chains. Furthermore, while advertising expenditures have traditionally been lower than those in the fast food group, this is beginning to change as the line between the two groups begins to blur. Finally, to combat increased costs some midscale chains are offering take-out service, although this may disrupt the atmosphere and operations.

MENU DISTINCTIONS AMONG RESTAURANTS	Units or chains may be classified not only by service or price, but also by the type of food served. The major categories are presented in Exhibit 10.7. Characteristics of and trends in the major menu categories are briefly described below. In recent years, some restaurants and chains have begun to face identity problems as their menu innovations take them further afield from their original concept. Exhibit 10.6 identifies a selected set of the larger restaurant chains in these primary menu categories.

Hamburger, Roast Beef, and Hot Dog Menus[23]

This menu group is clearly dominated by fast food chains. There have been some successful midscale chains in this group, but as the "gourmet burger" fad collapsed, many of these units had to convert to full menu to survive. In 1987, 5.2 billion hamburgers were sold in the U.S. McDonald's is the king of this segment with almost twice as many units and more than twice the dollar sales as the number two chain, Burger King (Pillsbury). Both Burger King and Wendy's struggled in the mid-1980s, with both sales and operating profits suffering. Hardee's has the fourth largest number of units in this group, but surpasses Wendy's in dollar sales. International Dairy Queen (IDQ) is actually fifth in this category, as 70% of its sales are derived from hamburgers, hot dogs, and chicken sandwiches. Finally, Arby's, Rax, and Jack in the Box are also large chains in this group. The latter two are currently repositioning themselves as upscale fast food chains, and are targeting older, more affluent customers.

In spite of the dominance of the large national chains, many regional and local chains continue to thrive. Finding prime sites is becoming more difficult and many of the larger chains are seeking non-traditional sites on military bases and in schools, hospitals, and airports. McDonald's even has a site on a Mississippi riverboat. As a percentage of sales, hamburgers continue to decline as these chains expand their menus.

Steak/Full Menu[24]

When per capita beef consumption declined in the early 1980s, most traditional steak houses expanded their menus. Some of these steak restaurants retained service through lines, while others are now providing full service. However, as beef consumption has stabilized, some units are now returning to their original focus on steak. The use of leaner cuts and higher grades of beef has led to price increases in this group. Increased consumer interest in meatloaf, stews, and pot roast may permit these chains to diversify their menus and lower their average

EXHIBIT 10.7

Chain Restaurant Data by Food Category

	NUMBER OF CHAIN UNITS			
	1988E	1987	1986	1983
Hamburgers, etc.	34,647	33,031	31,511	28,270
Pizza	19,761	17,739	16,221	11,852
Chicken	9,688	9,391	8,968	8,147
Steak/Full menu	10,716	10,044	9,628	9,849
Mexican	5,090	4,733	4,460	3,469
Seafood	2,917	2,684	2,518	2,309
Sandwich/Other	4,504	3,788	3,067	2,074
Pancake	2,056	1,921	1,830	1,558
Total	89,379	83,331	78,203	67,528
= Company owned	27,042	25,398	24,364	21,785
+ franchised	62,337	57,933	53,839	45,743

(Dollar Amounts in Billions)

	SALES OF CHAIN UNITS			
	1988E	1987	1986	1983
Hamburgers, etc.	$30.386	$27.257	$25.158	$18.948
Pizza	9.087	8.126	7.459	4.649
Chicken	5.345	4.822	4.375	3.418
Steak/Full menu	10.724	9.811	9.046	7.716
Mexican	3.317	3.079	2.889	1.682
Seafood	1.666	1.480	1.364	.938
Sandwich/Other	1.186	.956	.778	.503
Pancake	1.435	1.309	1.203	.838
Total	$63.145	$56.840	$52.274	$38.692
= Company owned	$22.061	$20.027	$18.804	$14.244
+ franchised	$41.084	$36.813	$33.470	$24.447

SOURCE: *Restaurant Business*, March 20, 1988, pp. 182–183, and **March** 20, 1989, pp. 132, 139.

prices, while maintaining their beef emphasis. One serious problem facing upscale and midprice steak establishments is that about two-thirds of all full-menu restaurants serve some kind of steak entree.

Chicken Menu[25]

The chicken category is troubled by three trends: the potential revival of beef consumption, health concerns over fried chicken, and the use of chicken in menu expansion by other types of restaurants. Many of the larger chicken chains are experimenting with roasted, broiled, or barbecued chicken as an alternative to frying. Kentucky Fried Chicken (KFC—PepsiCo) is the largest chain and is expanding at the rate of one new unit per day. KFC has added sandwiches to appeal to luncheon customers and is testing oven-roasted chicken and home delivery. Several chains in this group provide table service, expand their menus beyond chicken, and serve breakfast.

Pizza/Italian Menu[26]

The pizza/Italian category consists of delivery-only pizza, pizza restaurants (line or table service), and broader-menu Italian restaurants. Much of the recent sales growth in this category can be attributed to take-out and delivery service and lunch. Domino's Pizza, the second largest chain, provides only delivery service, while PepsiCo's leading chain, Pizza Hut, provides full service, take out, and experimental delivery service. One of the reasons for increased interest in Italian foods is the change in consumer attitudes towards the nutritional value of Italian cuisine, such as pasta. This trend is especially favorable for the upscale, full service restaurants, primarily consisting of independents.

Mexican Menus[27]

The Mexican-food category faces a number of potential difficulties. Many upscale and fast food Mexican units are facing increasing competition from other types of restaurants that have added Mexican entrees to their menus. The high concentration of Mexican units in the economically depressed oil-producing areas of the South has resulted in overcapacity and increased rivalry. In contrast, the Northeast provides an opportunity for expansion for this segment. However, regional taste differences may make it difficult to transplant an established chain operation without significant changes in food preparation and/or menus. Northeasterners prefer much less spicy food. Finally, many of the regional chains have patio decors with open-air seating that may limit the range of their geographical expansion. The upscale end of this category is dominated by independents. Chi Chi's is the largest midscale chain. PepsiCo's Taco Bell chain controls over 50% of the Mexican fast food market and is the only national Mexican chain.

Seafood Menus[28]

The consumption of seafood is increasing as consumers recognize its nutritional benefits. This provides an opportunity for growth, especially since two-thirds of all seafood is consumed in restaurants. However, this trend is not without threats. Seafood supplies and prices are unstable. Some popular species have been overfished as a result of fads and increased demand. The Cajun blackened cooking craze nearly eradicated the redfish population. Pollution problems also threaten supplies. Though aquaculture (fish farming) is expanding, not all species can be farmed, and capacity is still limited. Fish substitutes such as surimi (a fish paste formed to imitate crab, shrimp, or lobster at one-third the cost) have met with consumer resistance in the U.S., although they are popular in Japan, for example. Increased imports of fresh fish have increased supplies, although the cost is much higher than domestic fish.

Most seafood restaurants are independents, especially in the full-service category. Expansion by chains is slow for two main reasons. Fish is highly perishable and requires significant expertise in handling. Complex computerized purchasing systems are required for large chains. Red Lobster (General Mills) is the largest full-service chain and annually uses 50 million pounds of seafood, purchased from thirty-two countries. The use of air freight service and dry ice, coupled with a sophisticated computer ordering system linked to each unit in the chain, enables the chain to deliver its fish within twenty-four hours of its being caught. Almost all other chains are in the fast food category. The leader in this group is Long John Silvers (Jerrico). Most of the fast food chains face increased competition from other fast food chains that are adding fish sandwiches and finger foods to their menus. Seafood fast food chains are also experimenting with broiling techniques as an alternative to frying.

Pancake/Waffle Menus[29]

This menu category is no longer the specialty area it once was. Most chains have upscaled their units and expanded their menus to attract lunch and dinner customers. This was, to a large extent, the result of the incursion of the fast food chains into the breakfast meal area. International House of Pancakes is the leading chain of this type. In contrast, the Village Inn chain is trying to differentiate itself by serving breakfast twenty-four hours per day. All the large chains are full service, midpriced restaurants.

Sandwich and Other Menus

The sandwich segment faces a growth opportunity as consumers view these foods as healthier than hamburgers. The largest chain in this group is Subway Sandwiches and Salads. This firm is expanding aggressively. For sandwich establishments to add a salad bar involves very little additional inventory or food preparation cost.

Oriental food is increasingly popular for a number of reasons, including the relatively low check price, traditional emphasis on service, and increasing acceptance of the food's nutritional value. Most chains have been relatively unsuccessful. Both General Mills and Pillsbury abandoned their Oriental chains. This group has relatively low barriers to entry and is dominated by an abundance of existing, local, independent units, owned and operated by Orientals. Customers of this group have a strong preference for patronizing establishments run by Orientals. Because the emphasis in Oriental cuisine is on fresh ingredients, especially vegetables, it is difficult to design efficient systems for managing this type of unit in a chain. In spite of the presence of numerous oriental establishments, skilled chefs are scarce and many small chains have had to recruit chefs overseas.[30]

Another large subgroup in this category is the donut/cookie/bakery segment. This group is facing intensified competition from convenience stores with on-premise baked goods, supermarkets with in-store bakeries, and other restaurants that do their own baking. Although fast food mall shops with bakery items are becoming more prevalent, they face problems because malls don't open until after the traditional breakfast hour. Vie de France operates full service, soup/salad/sandwich restaurants, coupled with bakery takeout counters in mall locations. The parent company also operates a wholesale bakery that supplies frozen dough to its units and to other firms across the country. Donut shops—Dunkin' Donuts and Mister Donuts—are introducing more upscale baked goods, expanding menus to include sandwiches, and providing more fast food service.[31]

OPERATING CONSIDERATIONS

The suppliers to the restaurant industry include firms that provide the basic restaurant equipment and furnishings, paper products, food, and labor. Food costs vary widely, depending on the menu; labor costs are typically higher for full service restaurants. Franchise chains have a potential advantage over independents in the acquisition of these inputs because they can make large, centralized purchases. The major chains also have an advantage in providing standardized training for both employees and managers. Many chains such as McDonald's supply many items to their franchisees. However, they also recognize that if they force their units to buy from them at adverse prices, they threaten the long-run profitability of the chain. Thus individual unit operators are allowed to buy locally if they can show that their supplier will provide the specified quality at a lower cost. As a chain grows, the expense of distribution centers can offset savings on purchases and present difficulty in distributing perishable food inputs. Wendy's recognized that buying fresh meat locally could provide them with a source of strategic advantage over competitors using frozen meat.

Starting a new restaurant at this time is obviously more difficult than it was in an earlier stage in the industry life cycle. New concepts are more difficult to develop and good locations are becoming scarce. The cost of construction has risen steadily, raising the investment requirements for either the parent or the franchisee. Chains face increasing competition, not only from other chains, but from local independents and from other food stores. Entry at the local level remains relatively easy. Although the risk of failure in the restaurant business is historically high, there seems to be no shortage of entrepreneurs willing to enter the market.

NOTES

1. P. Moser, "The McDonald's Mystique," *Fortune*, July 4, 1988, pp. 112–116.

2. Data from Standard & Poor's *Industry Surveys*, "Leisure Time: Restaurants," March 10, 1988, p. L36; and M. Knapp, "21st Annual Restaurant Growth Index: Industry Summary," *Restaurant Business*, September 20, 1988, pp. 71–73.

3. Knapp, "21st Annual Restaurant Growth Index," pp. 71–126.

4. J. Scarpa, "Meeting the Demand of the Meal-at-Home Market," *Restaurant Business*, October 10, 1987, pp. 179–201; and M. Elder, "Upscale Take-out," *Restaurant Business*, November 1, 1987, pp. 169–184.

5. "Insights," *Restaurant Business*, September 20, 1988, p. 30.

6. "Retailing: Supermarkets," Standard and Poor's *Industry Surveys*, April 21, 1988, pp. R90–96 and December 22, 1988, p. R64.

7. R. Gibson, "Super Valu Plans Two 'Hypermarkets' for Cleveland Area," *Wall Street Journal*, July 1, 1988, p. 18.

8. "Retailing: Supermarkets," p. R96.

9. "Lateline," *Restaurant Business*, August 10, 1988, p. 212.

10. H. Riell, "Business Barometer," *Restaurant Business*, May 20, 1988, p. 2.

11. J. Applegate, "Fast-Food Eateries Woo Wee Diners with Tokens," *Waterloo Courier*, October 23, 1988.

12. B. Marsh, "American Express Chases After Fast-Food Market," *Wall Street Journal*, April 5, 1989.

13. "Leisure Time: Restaurants," p. L37.

14. Riell, "Business Barometer," p. 2.

15. *1988 U.S. Industrial Outlook*, U.S. Department of Commerce, pp. 61–63.

16. B. Main, "The Bottom Line: Industry Benchmarks," *Restaurant Business*, June 10, 1989, pp. 100–108.

17. Knapp, "21st Annual Restaurant Growth Index," pp. 75, 82.

18. J. Scarpa, "Breakfast," *Restaurant Business*, February 10, 1988, p. 210.

19. "Fast Food," *Consumer Reports*, June 1988, pp. 355–361.

20. K. MacNeil, "Upscale," *Restaurant Business*, January 20, 1988, pp. 126–128.

21. "Chain Restaurants," *Consumer Reports*, July 1988, pp. 444–450.

22. K. Farrell, "Midprice," *Restaurant Business*, January 20, 1988, pp. 117–123.

23. J. Scarpa, "Hamburgers," *Restaurant Business*, March 20, 1988, pp. 92–95; and J. Kochak, "Hamburgers," *Restaurant Business*, January 1, 1988, pp. 95–113.

24. J. Kochak, "Steak," *Restaurant Business*, May 20, 1988, pp. 173–198; and E. D'Ambrosio, "Steak," *Restaurant Business*, March 20, 1988, pp. 98–100.

25. M. Elder, "Chicken," *Restaurant Business*, March 20, 1988, pp. 104–114; and D. Jeffrey, "Upscale Chicken," *Restaurant Business*, July 20, 1988, pp. 104–108.

26. M. Elder, "Pizza," *Restaurant Business*, March 20, 1988, pp. 116–120; and P. Frumkin, "Italian," *Restaurant Business*, July 20, 1988, pp. 145–175.

27. J. Scarpa, "Mexican," *Restaurant Business*, March 20, 1988, pp. 122–126; and J. Kochak, "Mexican," *Restaurant Business*, July 1, 1988, pp. 133–149.

28. E. D'Ambrosio, "Seafood," *Restaurant Business*, March 20, 1988, pp. 130–132; and J. Kochak, "Seafood," *Restaurant Business*, September 1, 1988, pp. 135–150.

29. E. D'Ambrosio, "Pancake," *Restaurant Business*, March 20, 1988, pp. 146–148.

30. J. Kochak, "Oriental," *Restaurant Business*, March 1, 1988, pp. 177–192.

31. D. Long, "Donut," *Restaurant Business*, March 20, 1988, pp. 158–159; and J. Kochak, "Bakery/Bake-off," *Restaurant Business*, April 10, 1988, pp. 179–202.

General Mills Restructured

LYNDA L. GOULET

In January, 1988, following a disappointing Christmas season, General Mills announced that it was putting its Specialty Retailing segment on the market. This segment, comprised of the Talbots and Eddie Bauer clothing retail chains and catalog sales operations, was expected by some analysts to provide the firm with $350 to $400 million, though others estimated it would yield only $200 to $250 million. The lower estimate was based on the belief that the historically high growth of these firms would slow in the future. Further, this prospect for slower growth, coupled with the effects of the October, 1987, stock market crash, reduced price–earnings ratios for many firms in this industry by two-thirds, from about 35 times in August, 1987, to around 10–12 times in early 1988. The company announced that the proceeds from this sale would be used to finance "aggressive internal investment plans" and a significant repurchase of the company's stock.[1]

In September, 1987, at the firm's annual meeting, Chairman H. Brewster Atwater had announced that the retailing unit would be significantly expanded with the addition of fifteen to twenty new Talbots stores, the introduction of new product lines for the Eddie Bauer chain, and nearly $200 million in new capital spending. However, by the end of the 1987 holiday period, security analysts were estimating that in spite of moderate increases in sales, the Specialty Retailing unit would suffer significant earnings declines in the second half of the fiscal year ending in May, 1988. These forecasts followed announced operating earnings declines of 10% for the first half of the fiscal year, in spite of the addition of ten stores in each chain.

BACKGROUND AND RECENT HISTORY

General Mills began in 1928 as a combination of six large grain milling companies. In addition to their milling capacity, these mills provided the firm with the Betty Crocker brand (invented in 1921) and the Wheaties brand (1924). From 1928 to 1945 the firm relied heavily on its flour milling business. However, during that time it also expanded its breakfast cereal sales and began its entry into packaged baking mixes, acquiring Bisquick in 1931.

After World War II, in response to maturation in the flour milling business, General Mills began to concentrate its development on the production of commodity-type packaged foods such as baking mixes and cereals. During the

This case was prepared by Professor Lynda L. Goulet of The University of Northern Iowa. Presented at the Midwest Society for Case Research Workshop, 1988. All rights reserved to the author and the Midwest Society for Case Research. Copyright © 1988 by Lynda L. Goulet. Reprinted by permission.

third stage of its evolution, which lasted from 1960 to 1966, the firm shifted its emphasis away from a commodity product orientation to a greater emphasis on consumer packaged goods. The firm also closed half of its flour mills during this period. Following this initial period of consolidation General Mills began a decade (1966–1975) of aggressive diversification into a variety of consumer industries including various packaged and frozen foods, toys, clothing, philatelic supplies, and others. In the decade from 1976–1985 the firm attempted to rationalize these businesses and focus its attention on those with the greatest prospects for future growth and profitability.[2]

The most recent phase of the company's history began when the Board of Directors approved a corporate restructuring plan in Spring, 1985. This plan followed General Mills' fiscal 1984 earnings decrease of 4.8%—the first such decline in twenty-two years. As part of this restructuring plan the firm was to divest operations representing over one-quarter of total corporate sales and year-end assets. These divestitures were completed during 1985 and 1986 and involved twenty-six individual companies or divisions.

The most complex set of these divestitures involved the formation of two new companies whose stock was distributed to existing General Mills' shareholders in November, 1985. The firm's Izod-LaCoste (Alligator brand clothing) and Ship n' Shore (women's clothing) units were combined to form Crystal Brands, Inc. The Parker and Kenner toy units were combined with a number of other consumer units to form Kenner Parker Toys, Inc. (This new firm was subsequently acquired by Tonka for $633 million in 1987.) In the first few days after their spin-off the shares of both of these newly formed companies fell below their respective book values. In spite of this fact it was generally believed that these units would prosper more on their own than as units of General Mills because the firm's "culture was ill-suited to the volatility of the toy and fashion industries."[3]

Other divestitures involved units in the firm's Restaurant and Specialty Retailing segments. Three small restaurant chains—Casa Gallardo, Darryl's, and The Good Earth—were sold. These units had combined sales of $152 million and operating profits of $5.5 million in fiscal 1985. The last of the divestitures involved the sale of Wallpapers To Go, Leewards, and We Are Sportswear. Finally, in 1987 the Pennsylvania House/Kittinger furniture unit of the Specialty Retailing segment was sold. This unit constituted about 2% of the firm's total sales and net income in fiscal 1986.

Though the major motivation for the sale of these various units was ostensibly to permit the firm to focus its attention on its core businesses, it may have also involved a desire to protect the firm from a possible takeover. At least one security analyst estimated the total value of all the firm's various businesses, valued separately, to be $97 per share (breakup value) before the divestitures began.[4] This was in contrast to a stock price at the time of about $55 per share. In early 1988, after these divestitures were completed, the stock sold in a range between $40 and $60.

EXHIBIT 11.1 **Sales Contributions and Targeted Growth, General Mills**

	% 1985 CORP. SALES	TARGET REAL GROWTH/YEAR
Consumer foods	65%	4.0%
Restaurants	25	12.0
Specialty retailing	10	10.0
Total	100%	6.6%

THE RESTRUCTURED ORGANIZATION

The major restructuring of 1985 resulted in a more focused firm with three major business segments: Consumer Foods, Restaurants, and Specialty Retailing. The five-year (1985–1990) goals for real growth (above inflation) in these segments are detailed in Exhibit 11.1 along with their contribution to corporate sales.[5] These goals may be compared to expected real growth rates in packaged foods, restaurants, and apparel of 1%, 3%, and 2%, respectively. In announcing these goals Chairman Atwater said he believed that "the secret to getting good returns and good growth is to get yourself in the right [market] segments."[6] The firm hoped to achieve these objectives by installing a team of new, younger managers with more entrepreneurial attitudes.

Overall, General Mills' corporate objectives emphasize maintaining a balance between good growth and high returns to provide a superior total return for its shareholders. The firm's financial objectives require its return on equity and growth in earnings per share to fall in the highest quartile of major U.S. corporations. To achieve this performance top management feels the company needs to obtain an ROE of 19% and growth in EPS of 6% above inflation for the remainder of the 1980's. In addition, management wishes to maintain a strong balance sheet and a bond rating of at least "A".[7]

General Mills management also seeks to achieve leadership positions in highly profitable market segments within its chosen industries by entering selected new markets with innovative products and by keeping established products competitively attractive. Approximately 60% of the firm's total sales are from products that are ranked #1 in their market segments.

SPECIALTY RETAILING SEGMENT

By the end of fiscal 1987, with the sale of the Pennsylvania House/Kittinger furniture unit, the Specialty Retailing segment of General Mills consisted of only two units: the Talbots chain of classic women's apparel and accessories, and Eddie Bauer, a leader in outdoor apparel and related products. Both units compete in the $100-billion retail apparel industry. In 1987, these companies collectively operated 148 retail stores with 933,000 square feet of floor space and three catalog outlet facilities serving over 2.5 million customers; catalogs accounted for approximately one-third of the total sales of the segment.

Eddie Bauer

This company is a leading marketer of down-insulated apparel, sold through retail stores and a retail catalog. In fiscal 1985, Eddie Bauer reported sales growth of 19%, opened nine new stores (bringing the total to thirty-nine), but suffered an earnings loss resulting from an unsuccessful change in its merchandise mix. In 1985, the unit also mailed 25,000,000 catalogs in ten mailings which generated $57 million in catalog revenues, representing 55% of the total catalog sales of the Specialty Retailing segment in that year. Because of this poor earnings performance the unit narrowed its product lines and focused primarily on outdoor products, with a greater emphasis on leisure apparel. In 1986, the unit reported a 15% gain in both catalog and retail sales and a return to profitability. During 1987, total sales grew by another 20% to slightly above $190 million, though catalog sales growth was still only 15%. The catalog customer base grew by 15% in 1986 and 20% in 1987. The unit exceeded performance objectives for the first time since it was acquired in 1971. The ten stores added in fiscal 1988 were the first since the 1985 expansion and brought the total to forty-nine stores.

During 1986 and 1987, Eddie Bauer's catalog merchandise distribution center was relocated to Columbus, Ohio (from Seattle) to improve customer service, speed order fulfillment, reduce parcel shipment fees, and increase capacity. Concurrently, a new information system was completed to improve service and responsiveness. These advances were expected to improve performance by lowering costs 20% in fiscal 1988. A new retail distribution center was planned for Columbus to support future store expansion plans which would double the number of stores to about 100 by the end of fiscal 1990. The unit introduced a children's apparel line in several stores and was also aggressively seeking to increase the number of catalog customers.

Talbots

By the end of fiscal 1987, the Talbots line of classic women's apparel was sold through 109 retail stores in 24 states and the District of Columbia, and through the firm's catalog. Talbots was originally concentrated in the New England states and was known for outstanding customer service and quality. By 1987, the Talbots private brand of exclusive merchandise accounted for 60% of its sales. The firm believed that the maturing population, the increase in the number of working women, and the growth in disposable income were all factors that would promote continued growth in this highly successful company.

In 1985, Talbots reported a record sales level of $144 million, a 44% increase from the previous year. These sales were achieved by a combination of record catalog sales of $47 million at an average of $100 per order (an average sales increase of 10.5% in its thirty-nine established stores) and the opening of twenty new stores during the year. Average sales per square foot of selling area in the retail stores reached $550 (rising to $600 by the end of fiscal 1987). During the year the catalog and retail operations were placed under separate managements to improve the efficiency of each.

In 1986, sales at Talbots grew by 55% to almost $225 million, while operating earnings more than doubled. The unit's established stores posted 6% sales growth. Further, twenty-five new stores were opened and mail order sales rose over 50%, as catalog circulation increased over 40% to over $60 million, distributed through twenty mailings. A "Red Line" telephone system was installed in each retail store to connect customers directly with catalog sales for immediate access to information about the inventory of catalog merchandise.

By the end of fiscal 1987, sales of the Talbots unit had almost reached $300 million from the combined effects of an 8% rise in the sales in established stores, the opening of another twenty-five stores, and continued gains of 18% in catalog sales. Plans were made to double the number of retail outlets, to about 220, by the end of 1990. Catalog mailings were increased through the use of eight major catalogs and fourteen smaller, focused catalogs aimed at groups such as working women. The firm's active buyer list increased over 35%. Direct marketing order fulfillment had increased from 9,000 to 18,000 units per day since 1985. During 1987, Talbots had begun using national advertising to stimulate sales. A new distribution center was under construction, with an expected completion date in 1988.

RESTAURANT SEGMENT

By the end of fiscal 1987, this segment encompassed four restaurant chains with a total of 613 company-owned units and 19 Japanese joint venture units. Exhibit 11.2 illustrates the unit growth in this segment since 1984.

The restaurant segment competes in an industry that reached $112 billion in sales in 1985. During the 1980–1985 period this industry experienced 3.4% annual real sales growth and was expected to achieve 3% real growth per year

---

EXHIBIT 11.2 **Restaurant Units, General Mills**

| | UNITS AT END OF FISCAL YEARS | | | | |
	1984	1985	1986	1987	1988 (planned)
Red Lobster (USA)	367	370	389	392	412
RL (Canada)	1	2	9	40	40
RL (Japan)	3	3	9	19	31
Olive Garden	4	4	14	52	92
York's	129	129	114	113	113
Leeann Chin	—	—	8	16	16
Total co.-owned	501	505	534	613	673
Joint venture	3	3	9	19	31

SOURCE: General Mills, *Annual Report*, 1985–1987.

for the remainder of the decade. By 1987, restaurant industry sales had reached $153 billion. This market for away-from-home eating accounted for 31% of all consumer food purchases and had a faster rate of growth than the market for food eaten at home. In addition to an emphasis on unit expansion, the restaurant segment of General Mills consolidated its administrative staff and functions, resulting in a 45% decrease in the average number of employees per restaurant over the past five years.

Red Lobster

When General Mills acquired Red Lobster in 1970, the chain consisted of only three units. By the end of fiscal 1985, the chain had grown to 375 units in thirty-five states and two foreign countries (Canada and Japan). Total domestic sales exceeded $825 million. For the ten years prior to 1986, Red Lobster's annual compound sales growth and operating profit growth had averaged 26% and 20%, respectively. By 1985, the chain accounted for a 13% share of the away-from-home seafood market and was the only national seafood dinner chain. Pillsbury, a major General Mills rival, refers to Red Lobster as the Goliath of the industry and will target its own new seafood chain to serve a different, more upscale market segment.[8]

During fiscal 1986, Red Lobster USA sales grew to over $850 million, with total domestic sales exceeding $975 million in 1987. Average annual domestic unit sales for the chain were almost $2.5 million in 1987. During the mid-1980s Red Lobster began a remodeling program to create a more casual atmosphere, which included a more contemporary decor, mesquite grills, new outdoor signs, and a new menu. By October, 1987, all remodeling was completed.

The Canadian Red Lobster chain is expanding primarily through the conversion of Ponderosa restaurants acquired in 1985. In Japan, Red Lobster operates a joint venture with Jusco, a leading Japanese retailer. Television advertising in Tokyo was initiated in 1987 with good results. These international Red Lobster units are treated as foreign investments in the firm's financial statements. Thus, the sales and operating profits of these units have been excluded from the segment results in Exhibit 11.8.

Olive Garden

The Olive Garden Chain features a casual, cafe-style atmosphere with a wide selection of moderately priced Italian food. By 1986, the chain had achieved annual sales exceeding $2 million per unit. This grew to over $2.5 million per unit by 1987. This chain is in an expansion phase, with 120 new units planned for fiscal 1988–1990.

York's

York's is a budget, family steak-house chain that has been undergoing a change in format since 1985 to reposition the individual units as high-quality, self-service, mall restaurants. These new units are called York's Choices and offer an expanded menu, with lighter items such as deli sandwiches, fried vegetables, and broiled chicken. By the end of 1987, over half of the entrees sold in the York's Choices units were non-beef items.

Leeann Chin

This Minneapolis-based entry into Chinese cuisine was acquired in late 1985, and was being tested as either a buffet-style restaurant (four units) or a carry-out unit (twelve), or both. In 1987, the Leeann Chin concept was expanded to the Chicago market where it is not performing as well as expected.

CONSUMER FOODS SEGMENT

This unit serves a market that had total sales of over $260 billion in 1985, and volume (real) growth of 1% per year during the first half of the 1980s. In contrast, the Consumer Foods segment of General Mills experienced 3.2% annual volume growth for the same period. By 1987, the size of this market had increased to $290 billion. New products introduced by General Mills since 1980 accounted for almost 25% of its domestic packaged food volume. The average market share for companies or divisions within the Consumer Foods segment in established markets is over 27%.

Though sales from Consumer Foods increased during fiscal 1985, profits declined. Increased marketing expenditures, including a 20% increase in media expenses necessary to support both new and established products, was a major cause of the problem. However, programs underway to improve productivity are expected to provide savings of about $20 million for the remainder of the 1980s. General Mills' financial objectives for this segment include real profit growth of at least 4% annually. Its sales growth objectives are to be achieved by a combination of internal development and external acquisition. Another objective is to become the low-cost producer for consumer food products. The firm believes its success will depend on its ability to interpret demographic and lifestyle trends correctly so it may continue to develop successful new products. The firm anticipates continued consumer support for product quality, convenience, and nutrition.

Cereals

The breakfast cereal unit (Big G) is General Mills' largest single business. The ready-to-eat cereal industry experienced average annual growth of 12% in dollar sales and 1.5% in real volume during the 1980–1985 period. At the same time, General Mills' cereal sales grew 13% and 3%, respectively. From 1986 to 1987 domestic Big G cereal sales grew from approximately $900 million to $1,015 million. Kellogg, General Mills, General Foods (Post), Ralston Purina, and Quaker Oats jointly control 80% of the cereal market. Recent cereal market trends are summarized in Exhibit 11.3.

Hot cereals are experiencing revived demand, with children under five years

EXHIBIT 11.3

U.S. Cereal Consumption and Shipments

	1985	1986	1987
Per capita consumption (lbs. per person)	14.5 lbs	14.9 lbs	15.3 lbs
Ready to eat	11.0	11.3	11.7
Hot cereal	3.5	3.6	3.6
Total $ shipments	$4.38 bil	$4.82 bil	$5.34 bil
Ready to eat	3.91	4.32	4.79
Hot cereal	.47	.50	.55

SOURCE: Dept. of Commerce. *1988 U.S. Industrial Outlook.*

and adults over sixty-five being the chief consumers. Though the population under five is growing at only a 0.5% annual rate, the over–sixty-five group is growing at an annual rate of 2%. Innovations, such as convenient packaging in single servings, new flavors, and microwave cooking, have attracted more adults to hot cereals. The market for hot cereals continues to be dominated by the traditional leader, Quaker Oats, with a two-thirds share of the market. General Mills successfully entered this market in 1987.

The demand for presweetened cereal has been under pressure from regulatory attitudes towards advertising to children and from increasing consumer health consciousness. The five-to-fourteen age group, to which such cereals have their primary appeal, is growing at a 1.6% annual rate. However, the adult cereal market segment is the fastest growing market for ready-to-eat cereals. Convenience and nutrition are increasingly important to this age group, who have shown a preference for bran, fiber, multi-grain, and vitamin-enriched cereals. The introduction of new adult cereals is frequently accompanied by heavy advertising expenditures.

The strategy of the Big G cereal unit is to increase its penetration of the adult cereal market. Presently the unit has a below-average share of this market segment in which it rates at about 70% of the industry average. The unit intends to build on its existing strength in the children's segment, where its share is 140% of the average, and the all-family segment, where it holds an average position. To accomplish this the unit has increased its advertising, reformulated and repackaged its products to sustain older brands, and increased its efforts to develop new products. Seven of the unit's top fifteen brands are over twenty years old. However, as of 1987, the unit has four cereal brands that are among the top ten in dollar sales: Cheerios, Honey-Nut Cheerios, Lucky Charms, and Total.

Flour and Mix Products

This product category includes a variety of baking products and main-meal and side-dish mixes, such as Hamburger Helper. The total market for retail flour, baking products, and mixes was roughly $2 billion in 1987, having experienced volume declines of 5% and 10% in 1986 and 1985, respectively. Though the unit's markets are relatively mature overall, certain segments are experiencing growth arising from increasing demand for high-quality convenience foods. Several trends contribute to this demand growth. The primary stimulus for new product development is the microwave oven. Microwave oven penetration has increased from 10% of all households in 1976 to 60% in 1987 and is expected to reach 75% by the early 1990s. Further, microwave ovens are now found in about 50% of all workplaces. Another factor contributing to the demand for convenience foods is the increase in the number of one- and two-person households, which is expected to reach 60% of all households by the early 1990s. The number of working women also contributes to the rising demand for convenience foods, as two-thirds of all women are expected to be in the workforce by the early 1990s.

The retail flour market is shrinking in both dollar sales (from $420 million in 1985 to $405 million in 1986) and volume, as home baking declines. General Mills' Gold Medal flour—over 100 years old—has increased its share (34%) to almost twice that of its nearest rival. Similarly, Bisquick has increased its share of the related general purpose baking mix market. In contrast, the market for commercial bakery flour, representing about 70% of total flour milling volume, has experienced slight growth. In addition, prepared bakery goods shipments were up from $18.3 billion in 1985 to $19.4 billion in 1987. Although the per capita consumption of bread, related products, and crackers was stable, cookie consumption had increased from 17.9 pounds per person in 1985 to 18.8 pounds in 1987. General Mills' bakery flour business, the Sperry Division, has recently recorded continuing volume increases and record earnings levels, while lowering the production cost of flour 10%. Altogether, the U.S. milling industry had sales of $3.8 billion in 1987.

The dehydrated potato market is also experiencing dollar sales and real volume declines ($220 million in 1985 versus $205 million in 1986). However, the Betty Crocker specialty potato product line is the market leader in this category and has experienced volume gains in recent years. Main meal and side dish mixes experienced double-digit volume growth in both 1985 and 1986. Betty Crocker add-meat dinner mixes such as the Helper lines are leaders in this $230 million segment. Several product introductions have been made in recent years and the unit's Suddenly Salad line introduced in 1987 has rapidly become a consumer hit.

The dessert mix product market is one in which General Mills maintains a strong leadership position with its many Betty Crocker products. The unit has over a 50% share in the ready to spread frosting market and an overall 40% share in dessert mixes. This market has been relatively stable with sales of $1.1 billion overall in 1987. Betty Crocker has experienced 7% annual volume growth in the last two years, compared to market volume growth of 1%.

Snack Foods

Since 1985, General Mills has significantly increased its activity in snack foods. In the fruit snacks market ($225 million in 1985 versus $280 in 1987) General Mills' product lines have experienced volume growth of nearly 30% annually as a result of new product offerings. The company is the market leader in this segment. The $425 million granola snack market, which Quaker Oats leads with a 43% share, is in a decline, although General Mills has maintained its profitability in this market. In the microwave popcorn market ($190 million in 1986 versus $285 million in 1987) General Mills' Pop Secret was second in sales after only two years.

The frozen novelties market ($1.3 billion in 1986 versus $1.5 billion in 1987) has been characterized by high levels of promotional spending and new product introductions. In 1985 General Mills acquired Vroman foods, a major producer of ice cream specialties and frozen snacks, and has been expanding its distribution of these established products. Yoplait yogurt, acquired in 1977, achieved a 22.5% market share by 1985 in the $880 million domestic yogurt market. This market grew at an annual compound rate in excess of 30% per year in the 1980–1985 period, although volume growth is now slowing. By 1987, the market had expanded to $1.1 billion and General Mills was maintaining its Number Two position in the market.

Seafood and Other

General Mills has achieved the Number Two position in the frozen seafood market with its Gorton's product lines. The market ($810 million in 1985 versus $955 in 1986) experienced a decline in units sold for both 1985 and 1986, but rebounded in 1987. Gorton's experienced double-digit volume increases in this period. Recent introductions have been aimed at the microwave segment of this market.

In addition to its domestic retail consumer food and bakery flour businesses, General Mills' Consumer Foods segment includes two non-food businesses and international food operations. O-Cel-O's line of commercial and household sponges and Pioneer Products' line of cake decorations and party supplies are doing well. The segment's international businesses include a French sandwich cookie and granola bar business, a Spanish frozen precooked entree unit, a Dutch snack food unit, and other operations in Canada, Latin America, and the Far East.

STRATEGIC SEGMENTATION

Within each of its three operating segments General Mills' management has defined three types of product-market units: core units, established units, and major growth units. Overall these three types of units are considered strategically as distinct categories, regardless of the segment housing them. Real growth objectives and capital spending plans for each category appear in Exhibit 11.4.

EXHIBIT 11.4

Growth Objectives and Capital Spending Plans, General Mills

	1986 % TOTAL CORP. SALES	1985–1990 TARGET REAL GROWTH/YEAR	1988–1990 PLANNED INVESTMENT
Core units	44%	7%	$ 800 mil.
Established units	37	3	$ 200
Major growth units	19	15	$ 600
Total	100%	7%	$1,600 mil.[1]

SOURCE: General Mills, *1986, 1987 Annual Reports*.

[1] Includes $1.3 billion in new fixed assets.

Core Units

General Mills' Core Unit category is composed of one major company or division from each operating segment: Consumer Foods' Big G cereals, Restaurants' Red Lobster USA chain, and Specialty Retailing's Talbots chain. The objectives for the three core businesses are presented in Exhibit 11.5. Management describes the Core category and its past and planned performance:

> These businesses provide both high returns and good growth, with large reinvestment opportunities. They each have a consumer franchise that is stronger than industry standards. Their size and profit contribution are substantial relative to their industry segment within General Mills.

Established Units

General Mills' established businesses include Betty Crocker desserts, Bisquick baking mix, Gold Medal flour, Helper dinner mixes, international foods, York's restaurants, and other units. According to the *1986 Annual Report* the primary

EXHIBIT 11.5

Objectives for the Three Core Businesses, General Mills

	1986 % TOTAL CORP. SALES	1985–1990 TARGET REAL GROWTH/YEAR	COMPOUND SALES GROWTH/YEAR LAST TEN YEARS
Big G cereals	20%	6.0%	11%[1]
Red Lobster (USA)	19	7.0	18[2]
Talbots	5	15.0	33
Total	44%	7.5%	

[1] 1980–86 market growth = 11.8%/yr. vs. Big G, 13.7%/year.

[2] 1980–86 sales growth 50% above industry average.

objective for each of these units in the Established category is to increase market share by "... developing distinctive product line extensions and by finding opportunities for innovation, establishing effective cost reduction programs, and improving overall productivity." With their strong returns these businesses are expected to generate excess cash to support growth opportunities throughout the firm.

Major Growth Units

The Major Growth units in General Mills include businesses positioned to provide significant opportunities for future expansion. These include Yoplait yogurt, fruit snacks, Gorton's frozen seafood, Red Lobster International (as opposed to the domestic operation), the Olive Garden restaurants, Leeann Chin's restaurants, and other new food categories under development.

FINANCIAL INFORMATION

The financial statements for the company are shown in Exhibits 11.6, 11.7, 11.8 and 11.9.

EXHIBIT 11.6

General Mills, Inc.: Consolidated Statements of Earnings
(Dollar Amounts in Millions, except Per Share Data)

For Fiscal Years Ending	1987	1986	1985
Sales	$5,189.3	$4,495.9	$4,206.2
Costs and Expenses:			
Cost of sales, exclusive of items below	2,834.0	2,497.1	2,418.7
Selling, general and administrative expenses	1,756.4	1,531.4	1,370.1
Depreciation and amortization expenses	131.7	111.4	109.0
Interest expense, net	32.9	36.7	44.8
Loss from redeployments	1.1	2.6	71.1
Total Costs and Expenses	4,756.1	4,179.2	4,013.7
Earnings from Continuing Operations before Taxes	433.2	316.7	192.5
Income Taxes	211.2	137.5	78.8
Earnings from Continuing Operations	222.0	179.2	113.7
Earnings per Share—Continuing Operations	$ 2.50	$ 2.01	$ 1.27
Discontinued Operations after Taxes	—	4.3	(186.6)
Net Earnings (Loss)	$ 222.0	$ 183.5	$ (72.9)
Net Earnings (Loss) per Share	$ 2.50	$ 2.06	$ (.81)
Average Number of Common Shares	88.7	89.2	89.5

SOURCE: General Mills, Inc., *1987 Annual Report*, p. 25.

EXHIBIT 11.7   **General Mills, Inc., Consolidated Balance Sheets**
(Dollar Amount in Millions)

	MAY 31, 1987	MAY 25, 1986
Assets		
Current Assets:		
Cash	$ 48.7	$ 56.4
Short-term investments	131.0	133.9
Receivables, less allowance for doubtful accounts of $5.9 in 1987 and $6.3 in 1986	236.7	220.0
Inventories	388.6	350.9
Prepaid expenses and other current assets	60.9	50.7
Total Current Assets	865.9	811.0
Land, Buildings and Equipment, at cost:		
Land	115.8	100.9
Buildings	652.4	583.2
Equipment	1,028.2	894.7
Construction in progress	142.7	132.2
Total land, buildings and equipment	1,939.1	1,711.0
Less accumulated depreciation	(689.6)	(626.1)
Net land, buildings, and equipment	1,249.5	1,084.9
Other Assets:		
Intangible assets, principally goodwill	56.4	53.4
Investments and miscellaneous assets	108.6	136.0
Total other assets	165.0	189.4
Total Assets	$2,280.4	$2,086.2
Liabilities and Stockholders' Equity		
Current Liabilities:		
Accounts payable	$ 434.0	$ 382.4
Current portion of long-term debt	94.4	10.5
Notes payable	2.2	4.7
Accrued taxes	116.4	97.5
Accrued payroll	105.1	100.6
Other current liabilities	170.9	176.9
Total Current Liabilities	923.0	772.6
Long-Term Debt	285.5	458.3
Deferred Income Taxes	65.7	49.7
Deferred Income Taxes—tax leases	216.9	78.1
Other Liabilities and deferred credits	58.9	45.0
Total Liabilities	1,550.0	1,403.7
Stockholders' equity:		
Common stock	220.9	215.9

	MAY 31, 1987	MAY 25, 1986
Retained earnings	924.1	812.9
Less common stock in treasury, at cost	(379.4)	(314.1)
Cumulative foreign currency adjustment	(35.2)	(32.2)
Total Stockholders' equity	730.4	682.5
Total Liabilities and Stockholders' equity	$2,280.4	$2,086.2

SOURCE: General Mills, Inc., *1987 Annual Report,* p. 26.

EXHIBIT 11.8 **Financial Summary by Operating Segments, Continuing Business Segments Owned in 1987, General Mills**

(Amounts in Millions of Dollars for Fiscal Years)

	CONSUM. FOODS	RESTAURANTS[1]	SPECL. RETAIL[2]	CORP. ITEMS	TOTAL
Sales					
1987	$3,449.9	$1,249.1	$490.3	$ .0	$5,189.3
1986	3,061.3	1,051.0	383.6	.0	4,495.9
1985	2,771.3	1,140.1	294.8	.0	4,206.2
Operating profit before asset redeployments					
1987	$ 368.6	$ 94.3	$ 31.0	($ 59.6)	$ 434.3
1986	286.1	80.8	16.5	(64.1)	319.3
1985	249.4	85.2	(13.0)	(58.0)	263.6
Operating profit after asset redeployments					
1987	$ 369.5	$ 92.5	$ 30.7	($ 59.5)	$ 433.2
1986	284.2	84.8	11.6	(63.9)	316.7
1985	245.3	45.9	(40.7)	(58.0)	192.5
Identifiable assets					
1987	$1,211.7	$ 594.0	$177.8	$ 296.5	$2,280.4
1986	1,091.8	467.8	128.2	398.4	2,086.2
1985	1,008.7	424.6	204.9	1,024.4	2,662.6
Depreciation					
1987	$ 78.9	$ 39.4	$ 9.0	$ 1.4	$ 128.7
1986	69.2	32.7	7.2	0.7	109.8
1985	60.9	37.5	6.3	1.7	106.4

EXHIBIT 11.8

(Continued)

	CONSUM. FOODS	RESTAURANTS[1]	SPECL. RETAIL[2]	CORP. ITEMS	TOTAL
Capital spending					
1987	$ 151.5	$ 145.3	$ 30.1	$ 2.2	$ 329.1
1986	153.6	74.0	13.7	3.6	244.9
1985	103.9	40.5	27.0	39.0	209.7

SOURCE: General Mills, *1987 & 1985 Annual Reports.*

[1] Restaurant Segment data for 1985 includes $152 million in sales and $5.5 million in operating profits for the three restaurant chains subsequently sold.

[2] The Specialty Retailing segment data for 1985 includes $13 million in sales and an operating earnings loss for a unit subsequently sold.

EXHIBIT 11.9   Selected Financial Results, General Mills
(Amount in Millions of Dollars)

YEAR	SALES	C.O.S.	R&D	ADVERT.	DEPREC. & AMORT.	E.B.T.	NET INCOME
1987	$5,189.3	$2,834.0	$38.3	$330.0	$131.7	$433.2	$222.0
1986[1]	4,586.6	2,563.9	41.7	317.0	113.1	326.6	183.5
1985	4,285.2	2,474.8	38.7	274.3	110.4	195.9	(72.9)
1984[2]	5,600.8	3,165.9	63.5	349.6	133.1	398.7	233.4
1983	5,550.8	3,123.3	60.6	336.2	127.5	409.7	245.1
1982	5,312.1	3,081.6	53.8	284.9	113.2	406.7	225.5
1981	4,852.4	2,936.9	45.4	222.0	99.5	374.4	196.6
1980	4,170.3	2,578.5	44.4	213.1	81.1	316.6	170.0
1979	3,745.0	2,347.7	37.3	188.9	73.3	263.9	147.0
1978	3,243.0	2,026.1	30.5	170.5	58.6	245.2	135.8
1977[3]	2,909.4	1,797.5	29.9	145.6	48.1	229.2	117.0

YEAR	TOTAL ASSETS	L.T. DEBT	S.H. EQUITY	CAPITAL EXPEND.	DIV'DS	E.P.S.[4]	AVER. PRICE/ SHARE
1987	$2,280.4	$285.5	$ 730.4	$329.1	$110.8	$2.50	$46.50
1986[1]	2,086.2	458.3	682.5	244.9	100.9	2.06	33.00
1985	2,662.6	449.5	1,023.3	209.7	100.4	(.81)	27.00
1984[2]	2,858.1	362.6	1,224.6	282.4	96.0	2.49	24.62
1983	2,943.9	464.0	1,227.4	308.0	92.7	2.45	24.00

YEAR	TOTAL ASSETS	L.T. DEBT	S.H. EQUITY	CAPITAL EXPEND.	DIV'DS	E.P.S.[4]	AVER. PRICE/ SHARE
1982	2,701.7	331.9	1,232.2	287.3	82.3	2.23	18.62
1981	2,301.3	348.6	1,145.4	246.6	72.3	1.95	14.75
1980	2,012.4	377.5	1,020.7	196.5	64.4	1.68	11.75
1979	1,835.2	384.8	916.2	154.1	56.1	1.46	14.50
1978	1,612.7	259.9	815.1	140.5	48.2	1.36	14.50
1977[3]	1,447.3	276.1	724.9	117.1	39.1	1.18	15.37

SOURCE: General Mills, *1987 Annual Report.*

[1] Discontinued furniture operations.

[2] Discontinued toy and fashion and other operations.

[3] Discontinued chemical operations.

[4] Stock prices and earnings per share are in dollars and adjusted to reflect stock splits prior to 1987.

NOTES

1. F. Schwadel and R. Gibson, "General Mills Is Putting Up for Sale Talbots, Eddie Bauer Clothing Chains," *Wall Street Journal*, January 8, 1988, p. 4.

2. General Mills, *1985 Annual Report.*

3. P. Houston and M. Pitzer, "Can the General Mills Babies Make It on Their Own?" *Business Week*, November 18, 1985, pp. 46–47.

4. P. Houston and R. Aikman, "General Mills Still Needs Its Wheaties," *Business Week*, December 23, 1985, pp. 77–80.

5. General Mills, *1985 Annual Report.*

6. Houston and Aikman, "General Mills Still Needs Its Wheaties."

7. General Mills, *1985–1987 Annual Reports.*

8. Houston and Aikman, "General Mills Still Needs Its Wheaties."

In addition to these sources, industry forecasts were obtained from the *1988 U.S. Industrial Outlook*. Catalog retailing information was also obtained for 1985 from *Inside the Leading Mail-Order Houses*, 3d ed. (Colorado Springs: Maxwell Sroge, 1987).

Hershey Foods Corporation

JOYCE P. VINCELETTE • THOMAS L. WHEELEN • J. DAVID HUNGER

INTRODUCTION

Hershey Foods Corporation and its subsidiaries engaged in 1985 in the manufacture and distribution of food and food-related items. Since the early 1960s, Hershey Foods had grown from a firm with one plant, a few chocolate products, and sales of $185 million to a multiplant, multiproduct corporation with sales of $1.8 billion in 1984. In addition to becoming a major domestic producer of chocolate and confectionery products, the company operated a chain of restaurants, manufactured and distributed pasta products, operated a coffee service plan, and managed various types of international operations.

To lessen its dependence on chocolate, Hershey began to diversify in the 1960s, but it was not until William Dearden took over as chief executive officer in 1976 that diversification was emphasized as a distinct strategy. When Dearden took office, he made strategic planning his first priority. He charged a corporate planning committee to develop a strategic plan for the company covering the period from 1976 to 1985. The resulting plan for Hershey to become more of a major, diversified, international food and food-related company included the following four strategies:

1. To capitalize on the considerable growth potential in existing brands and products in current markets.
2. To introduce new products.
3. To expand the distribution of long-established, well-known brands into new domestic and foreign markets.
4. To make acquisitions and other types of alliances, both in the United States and elsewhere in the world.

Richard A. Zimmerman was selected by Hershey's board to succeed Dearden as Chief Executive Officer in 1984 and as Chairman of the Board in March 1985. Dearden continued to serve on Hershey's Board of Directors. One of Zimmerman's first priorities in his new position was to assess Hershey Food

This case was prepared by Professor Joyce P. Vincelette of Trenton State College and Professor Thomas L. Wheelen of the University of South Florida, and Professor J. David Hunger of Iowa State University. Initial research was performed by the following MBA students: Marie Anderson, Peggy Gallup, Patty Gibbs, Michael Hall, and Glenn Wilt of the University of South Florida. This case was presented at the North American Case Research Association meeting, 1986. Reprinted by permission of the authors and the North American Case Research Association. Copyright © 1986 by Joyce P. Vincelette, Thomas L. Wheelen, and J. David Hunger. It is also scheduled to appear in the *Journal of Management Case Studies*.

Corporation's performance from 1976 to 1985 in light of Dearden's strategic plan. New strategic plans for the next five years also needed to be developed for presentation to the Board of Directors.

HISTORY

Milton S. Hershey dreamed of making candy, but he had many setbacks before he achieved success. His formal education ended at the fourth grade. As a teenager, Hershey worked as an apprentice to a confectioner in Lancaster, Pennsylvania. When he was nineteen, he set out on his own to make penny candy. After business failures in Philadelphia, Chicago, and New York, Milton Hershey finally found success, at the age of forty, making caramels in Lancaster. He sold his caramel business for $1 million in 1900, at age forty-two.

Milton Hershey had traveled to the World's Exposition in Chicago in 1893 and had seen some chocolate-making equipment on exhibit. At that time, only the rich were able to afford chocolate. It was Hershey's conviction that the world was ready for an inexpensive chocolate confection. He purchased chocolate-manufacturing equipment from Germany and began manufacturing chocolate candies. In 1894 he turned out the first Hershey bar, which was made of solid chocolate and sold for a nickel. When the caramel business was sold, Mr. Hershey retained the right to manufacture chocolate, and rented space from his former company. The chocolate business grew, and by 1901, sales were $622,000. Additional manufacturing space was required. Several locations were considered, but Milton Hershey finally decided to build his chocolate factory in Derry Church, Pennsylvania, where he had been born. Derry Church was renamed *Hershey* in 1906 in his honor.

This location was chosen for the Hershey Chocolate Company to capitalize on the availability of fresh milk, which was essential to its two basic products—milk chocolate and almond chocolate bars. By streamlining production methods and gearing output to large standardized quantities sold at moderate prices, the company achieved immediate success. Production in the new factory began in 1905; by 1911, sales had reached $5 million. Hershey became the Henry Ford of the confectionery field, with one major difference: Hershey had no serious competition for over forty years.

Milton Hershey built not only a company, but also a storybook town with street lights shaped like Hershey Kisses. Mr. Hershey used to consider the company, the town, and its inhabitants as a large farm of which he was the owner. If the residents wanted or needed something, such as a bank, they asked him and he built it. Among other things, he built two hotels (Hotel Hershey and the Hershey Lodge), an airport, a sports arena, a half-dozen golf courses, an amusement park, a zoo, a public garden, a monorail, and a professional hockey team called the Hershey Bears.

Because Milton and Catherine Hershey were unable to have children, they founded in 1909 the Milton Hershey School for orphan boys. (Girls have been admitted since 1976.) The school, through the Hershey Trust, owned 100%

interest in the company until 1927, when approximately 20% of the stock was sold to the public. In the same year, Hershey was incorporated under the laws of the state of Delaware as the Hershey Chocolate Company. When Hershey went public in 1927, Mr. Hershey thought that investors might be concerned about a company that owned things like a zoo and a hockey team. Until 1927 the administration of the company, the town, and the school were intermingled. At this time, all was reorganized, and the Chocolate Corporation acquired all the chocolate properties; Hershey Estates, now the Hershey Entertainment and Resort Company (known as HERCO), owned the amusement park, the hotels, and the hockey team, among other properties; and the Hershey Trust Company continued to oversee the funds of the Milton Hershey School. In 1985, HERCO was owned entirely by the Hershey Trust but had no legal ties to Hershey Foods. The Milton Hershey School received 100% of the profits of HERCO. The orphanage, through the Hershey Trust, still owned 50.1% of the Chocolate Corporation. Dividends from Hershey stock were the orphan school's biggest source of income.

Many people have wondered about an orphanage having as much control as it did at Hershey. As a Hershey officer admitted, "That place is sitting there with the power to remove all the directors of this company if it wanted to. It could do whatever it wants."[1] The orphanage, nevertheless, never wanted to do much more than collect its quarterly checks and educate children. It never traded its stock. Thus, Hershey Foods people tended to look on the school as nonthreatening.

Though Milton Hershey died in 1945, the company maintained much of his conservative philosophy. This included treating all employees fairly and with dignity; providing employees with good working conditions, competitive wages, and rewards according to performance; maintaining quality standards for all ingredients; and tasteful advertising. See Exhibit 12.1 for Hershey's statement of Corporate Philosophy.

In 1968, Hershey Chocolate Company adopted a new name, Hershey Foods Corporation, to reflect its broadened product line, represented by the following acquisitions:

1963—H. B. Reese Company (peanut butter candies)

1967—San Giorgio Macaroni, Inc. (pasta)

1967—Delmonico Foods (pasta)

1967—Cory Food Services, Inc. (coffee service)

1977—Y&S Candies (licorice)

1978—Procino-Rossi (pasta)

1979—Skinner Macaroni Company (pasta)

1979—Friendly Ice Cream Corporation (informal restaurants)

1982—Petybon Industries Alimenticias Ltd. (Brazil) (pasta and biscuits)

1984—American Beauty Macaroni Company (pasta)

EXHIBIT 12.1   **Statement of Corporate Philosophy[1]**

Hershey is in business to make a reasonable profit and to enhance the value of its stockholders' investment, pursuing a policy of profitable growth by further diversifying into other food and food-related business and/or such businesses which offer significant opportunity for growth.

1. All employees should be treated fairly and with dignity, provided with good working conditions and competitive wages, rewarded according to performance. To the fullest extent possible, promotions should be made from within the corporation.
2. Sincere commitment to Hershey's Affirmative Action Program with an obligation to follow it in both the spirit and letter of the law.
3. Results oriented, with all employees given the opportunity to express individual initiative and judgment.
4. Each employee should strive to improve the communications relating to his or her area of responsibility in order to successfully conduct the business of the corporation.
5. Individual and company relationships conducted on the basis of the highest standards of conduct and ethics. Success of the business depends upon the character and integrity of people working in a spirit of constructive cooperation.
6. Provide customers and consumers with products of consistent excellent quality at competitive prices which insure an adequate return on investment.
7. Inherent responsibility to be a good neighbor and to support community projects. All employees encouraged to take an active part in improving the quality of community life.
8. Responsibility to conduct operations within the regulatory guidelines and in a manner that does not adversely affect our environment.

It is imperative to conduct operations throughout our entire organization which cause these philosophies to become a way of life.

[1] This was adopted in 1975 and reaffirmed in 1983.

STRATEGIC MANAGERS

As of March 1, 1985, there were eleven directors; seven of them from outside the corporation represented the fields of investment banking, public accounting, industrial manufacturing, and education.

The Chairman of the Board and Chief Executive Officer was Richard A. Zimmerman, age 53. A graduate of Pennsylvania State University in 1953, Zimmerman did graduate work at Florida A&M University. He joined Hershey Foods Corporation in 1958 as an Administrative Assistant. After that he held a number of positions at Hershey, including President of Cory Food Services, Inc. between 1971 and 1974. He was named President and Chief Operating Officer in 1976. He was a member of the Board of Directors of a number of organizations including the Hershey Trust Company. He was also a member of the Board of Managers of the Milton Hershey School.

EXHIBIT 12.2   **Hershey Foods Corporation: Organizational Chart**

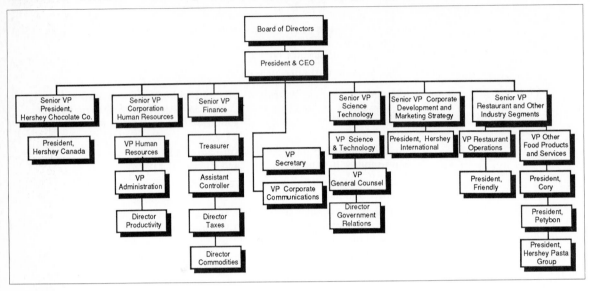

SOURCE: Hershey Foods Corporation, *1983 Annual Report.*

Also effective March 1, 1985, the Board selected Kenneth L. Wolfe, Senior Vice-President and Chief Financial Officer, to be President and Chief Operating Officer. Wolfe had joined Hershey in 1967 and had been promoted to a number of positions in the Finance Division. In 1984 he was named Senior Vice-President and Chief Financial Officer and was selected to the corporation's Board of Directors. Wolfe held a bachelor's degree from Yale University and a master of business administration in finance from the University of Pennsylvania. Exhibit 12.2 details the structure of Hershey Foods Corporation.

Each of Hershey's divisions operated as a strategic business unit. Joseph P. Viviano was President of Hershey Chocolate Company, replacing Earl J. Spangler, who retired in 1985; David Conn was President of Hershey Canada Inc.; Robert Gaudrault was Chairman and CEO of Friendly Ice Cream Corporation; and L. William Chiles was President and CEO of Cory Food Services. In 1984 the company's pasta operations were renamed the Hershey Pasta Group with C. Mickey Skinner as President and CEO.

HUMAN RESOURCES

As of December 31, 1984, Hershey Foods Corporation had a total of 15,200 full-time employees, many of whom were covered under collective bargaining agreements. In addition, Friendly Ice Cream Corporation employed approximately 18,000–23,000 restaurant personnel on a part-time basis. The company considered its employee relations to be good even though there had been a three-week strike at the main chocolate plant in Hershey in November 1980. Hershey Foods believed that its continued growth depended on its ability to manage effectively its human resources. Its stated goal was "to create a challenging, but satisfying, work environment and to provide employees with the opportunity to contribute and share in the future success of the corporation."[2]

To assist in meeting this goal, a number of human-resource-management programs have been established since 1977. Hershey initiated a formal, systematic human-resources-planning and organizational review process to improve the corporation's ability to project its future organizational needs and labor requirements. In addition, management launched a long-range planning program designed to identify the appropriate organizational structure, skills, and employee training and development needs for the next three years.

Critical to the overall planning and development program was the initiation of a new Corporate Management Succession Process. The major thrust of this activity was the identification and development of candidates for key management positions. A top management committee, chaired by the chief executive officer, was set up to provide the necessary guidance in this effort.

BUSINESS SEGMENTS

Hershey Foods Corporation operated in three business segments: *Chocolate and Confectionery Products; Restaurant Operations;* and *Other Food Products and Services.* Operations in the Chocolate and Confectionery segment involved the manufacture and sale of a broad line of chocolate and confectionery products. The principal product groups were bar goods, bagged items, baking ingredients, chocolate drink mixes, and dessert toppings. The Restaurant Operations segment operated restaurants and manufactured certain products sold in those restaurants. The Other Food Products and Services segment was involved in the manufacture and sale of pasta products in the United States and Brazil and in the operation of a coffee service plan for U.S. and Canadian businesses and institutions. In addition, Hershey was involved in a number of other ventures both within the United States and internationally. Exhibit 12.3 presents net sales, operating income, identifiable assets, and other information for the three business segments.

Chocolate and Confectionery Products

Hershey Chocolate Company

Despite an aggressive diversification program, the Hershey Chocolate unit still furnished 16% of the nation's chocolate and accounted for 80% of the operating profits and 68% of the sales of Hershey Foods Corporation in 1984. Hershey Foods' profits have dropped only twice in the past 10 years, in 1973 and 1977, two years when cocoa prices skyrocketed.

Hershey Chocolate Company's strategic plan was first developed in 1976 and remained essentially the same in 1985. Two of the company's principal strategic objectives were to achieve compounded annual real growth in operating income

EXHIBIT 12.3 Hershey Foods Corporation: Financial Statistics by Industry Segments
(Dollar Amounts in Thousands) For the Year Ended December 31

	1984	1983	1982	1981	1980	1979	1978	1977	1976
Net sales									
Chocolate and confectionery	$1,287,100	$1,159,065	$1,081,558	$1,015,106	$929,885	$822,813	$678,652	$586,882	$526,822
Restaurant operations	427,122	383,543	335,836	302,908	274,297	224,072	0	0	0
Other food products and services	178,284	163,497	148,342	133,137	131,107	114,410	89,228	84,345	75,138
Total net sales	$1,892,506	$1,706,105	$1,565,736	$1,451,151	$1,335,289	$1,161,295	$767,880	$671,227	$601,960
Operating income									
Chocolate and confectionery	$ 195,810	$ 179,253	$ 154,805	$ 142,648	$ 118,435	$ 99,880	$ 79,143	$ 69,834	$ 86,898
Restaurant operations	41,770	39,428	34,279	29,309	25,567	23,322	0	0	0
Other food products and services	4,804	4,692	4,947	7,250	51,482	6,397	5,061	4,528	5,005
Total operating income	$ 242,384	$ 223,373	$ 194,031	$ 179,207	$ 195,484	$ 129,599	$ 84,204	$ 74,362	$ 91,903
General corporate expenses	22,464	18,208	14,629	11,763	10,190	7,742	4,981	3,491	2,299
Interest expense (income)—net	10,349	15,814	7,859	12,512	14,100	17,764	(2,683)	(509)	357
Income before taxes	209,571	189,351	171,543	154,932	124,860	104,093	81,906	71,380	89,247
Less: Income taxes	100,889	89,185	77,375	74,580	62,805	50,589	40,450	35,349	45,562
Discontinued operations	0	0	0	0	0	0	0	(5,300)	(1,112)
Net income	$ 108,682	$ 100,166	$ 94,168	$ 80,352	$ 62,055	$ 53,504	$ 41,456	$ 41,331	$ 44,797

Identifiable assets

Chocolate and confectionery	$222,541	$221,928	$241,070	$297,296	$333,232	$445,815	$528,194	$552,422	$580,586
Restaurant operations	0	0	0	207,125	219,196	223,265	234,860	251,781	273,356
Other food products and services	44,325	47,023	50,450	63,886	62,553	63,446	83,345	84,964	152,747
Corporate	65,004	127,202	130,484	38,892	69,491	96,921	58,355	94,777	115,878
Total identifiable assets	$331,870	$396,153	$422,004	$607,199	$684,472	$829,447	$904,754	$983,944	$1,122,567

Depreciation

Chocolate and confectionery	$ 5,439	$ 5,702	$ 6,574	$ 7,389	$ 8,469	$ 9,554	$ 10,225	$ 14,393	$ 17,636
Restaurant operations	0	0	0	10,283	10,015	14,379	15,574	17,066	18,874
Other food products and services	1,755	1,789	1,720	2,185	2,671	2,675	3,670	4,597	5,524
Corporate	345	504	556	658	741	957	1,212	1,218	1,079
Total depreciation	$ 7,539	$ 7,995	$ 8,850	$ 20,515	$ 21,896	$ 27,565	$ 30,681	$ 37,274	$ 43,113

Capital additions

Chocolate and confectionery	$ 17,227	$ 22,381	$ 26,586	$ 29,472	$ 27,061	$ 57,504	$ 77,074	$ 51,779	$ 37,508
Restaurant operations	0	0	0	20,965	24,468	22,098	28,005	35,751	41,885
Other food products and services	1,754	3,014	4,420	2,233	6,141	5,525	7,022	7,462	5,574
Corporate	1,741	2,140	6,419	3,767	1,359	6,546	4,635	10,252	2,082
Total capital additions	$ 20,722	$ 27,535	$ 37,425	$ 56,437	$ 59,029	$ 91,673	$ 116,736	$ 105,244	$ 87,049

SOURCE: Hershey Foods Corporation, *Annual Reports 1984, 1983, 1980, 1978, and 1976.*

and to continue its market leadership position in chocolate and confectionery products. According to Earl J. Spangler, former President, the principal strategies to achieve these objectives were to (1) increase annual sales of existing products, (2) develop new products, (3) acquire new businesses, and (4) develop special markets.

MANAGEMENT   Earl J. Spangler retired as President of Hershey Chocolate Company on January 1, 1985, after thirty-four years of service to the company. Joseph P. Viviano was named as his successor. Viviano also served as a Senior Vice-President of Hershey Foods.

Viviano began his career in 1960 when he joined his family's pasta business, Delmonico Foods, Inc., in Louisville, Kentucky. Hershey acquired Delmonico in 1966. Viviano was named Vice-President of Operations in 1968 and promoted to president in 1972. After the merger of Delmonico with San Giorgio Macaroni, Inc. in 1975, he was appointed President of the combined companies. In 1979 the pasta division was again enlarged with the acquisition of Skinner Macaroni Company, and Viviano became President of the newly formed San Giorgio–Skinner Company.

PRODUCTS   Hershey Chocolate Company produced a broad line of chocolate and confectionery products. The principle product groups formed two major categories: *Confectionery Products*, including goods such as Hershey Chocolate Bars, Kisses, and Peanut Butter Cups; and *Grocery Products*, including cocoa syrup, chocolate chips, and chocolate milk, among other goods.

To increase the sales of existing products, Hershey Chocolate Company has restructured and expanded its consumer sales force to over 470 men and women. This restructured sales force created substantial incremental sales volume. Six of Hershey's traditional products—Hershey's Milk Chocolate Bars, Hershey's Almond Bars, Kisses, Syrup, Mr. Goodbar, and Reese's Peanut Butter Cups— had a compound annual growth rate of more than 11% in dollar sales between 1979 and 1983. Together these brands accounted for almost $600 million in sales in 1982.

The impetus behind Hershey Chocolate Company's strategies of developing new products and acquiring new businesses had been the need to lessen the impact of the cocoa bean prices on its overall business. In addition, Hershey's diversification efforts coincided with a shift in consumer tastes away from its traditional, predominantly chocolate candies. In 1963, predominantly chocolate products accounted for 80% of the candy division's sales; in 1983 the figure was down to 46%. America's candy eaters, once lovers of solid milk chocolate, seemed to prefer snacks that combined chocolate, nuts, and wafers. "People want a more complex, more interesting texture," said James F. Echeandia, a candy industry consultant in Orlando, Florida.[3] In 1985, more consumers appeared to be concerned about the nutritional value of the snacks they ate.

One way Hershey has been diversifying is through acquisition, as in the case of Y&S Licorice Products, which Hershey acquired in 1977. Hershey has also been broadening its product line through line extensions, such as Hershey's Big Block, which was introduced in 1980 at $0.50, and through internally developed new products, many of which contained significantly less chocolate, such as Reese's Pieces, and Whatchamacallit in the moderately priced area, and the Golden Almond Bar, Hershey Golden Almond Solitaires, and Skor in the luxury chocolate line. Skor was manufactured at the Hershey plant under license from Hershey's Swedish affiliate, AB Maribou. Skor was the most popular chocolate/toffee brand in the United States in 1984.

A number of new products have been introduced into regional markets as the foundation for future growth of new products. These included Reese's Pieces Peanut, the Golden Pecan Bar, and Take Five, a wafer bar layered with peanut butter creme and covered with milk chocolate, which was introduced and positioned as a light but satisfying adult snack. Hershey's management was now looking to Take Five to make important future contributions.

Responding to the $250 million granola industry, Hershey was courting health-conscious consumers with a product containing little or no chocolate—New Trail Granola Bars. Introduced nationally in late 1983 after almost two years in test markets, New Trail Bars had already captured by 1985 a sizable chunk of the rapidly expanding granola market. New Trail Bars came in six flavors (only two of which contained chocolate), and other varieties were planned. Hershey officials, who promoted New Trail as a snack, initially feared that a strong link with the Hershey name would make consumers think of the bars as candy. But the product has been so successful that Hershey has moved its name, previously in small print on the back of the package, to a prominent spot on the front.

New ground was broken in 1983 with Hershey's first franchised product, Hershey Chocolate Milk. The Company licensed the Hershey trademark for use on the milk carton and sold its own formulation of powdered chocolate-flavor mix to licensed dairies with market areas covering all fifty states. The dairies had full responsibility for producing the chocolate milk and selling it to retailers. Hershey promoted the product with consumer advertising and ensured that rigorous quality standards were met by the dairies. Hershey had become the largest selling national distributor of branded chocolate milk in the United States by 1985.

New product introductions have not always gone smoothly. Sales of Hershey's Whatchamacallit, a chocolate-covered crisped rice bar, have been slipping. Hershey's entry into the ready-to-spread frosting market, a four-product "Frostin" line, was not successful and was withdrawn in 1983 after two years. Hershey claimed that it was a victim of line and price promotion and could not compete with brands that had cake mixes to complement their frosting lines.

Internationally, Hershey was following the joint venture and licensing approach with already well-established food and confectionery companies. In 1983, Hershey was selling Kit Kat, Rolo, and After Eight under license from Roundtree Mackintosh of Great Britain and licorice products under license from Bassets of Great Britain. Hershey's rights under these agreements were extendable on a long-term basis at the company's option, subject to minimum sales limitations. As of 1985, these requirements have been substantially exceeded. In 1983, Kit Kat was one of the fastest growing major brands in the confectionery industry. In 1984 the Marabou Milk Chocolate Roll, which was imported from AB Marabou, Sweden, was successfully marketed on a nationwide basis.

Sales of new chocolate and confectionery products from 1980 to 1984 have increased from 5% to 22% of total unit sales. While lessening the company's dependence on chocolate, the new snacks have also added some variety to Hershey's line of products. Company officials believed that people rarely buy the same candy twice in a row. "All we can hope to do is get on your menu," said John H. Dowd, Vice-President for New Business Development in Hershey's Confectionery Division.[4]

To achieve their fourth growth strategy of developing special markets, a separate business unit, the Special Markets Department, was established in 1979 and assigned the responsibility for the sale of special confections, fund-raising projects (of the type in which scouting and school groups participate), food service, institutional products, and industrial products.

CONSUMERS Candy consumption in the United States hit a peak of 20 pounds per person per year in the late 1960s. Factors such as price rises, substitute products, and an increasing concern for health and nutrition combined to cause consumption to diminish to 16.7 pounds per person per year in 1984. This per capita consumption of chocolate was about half that in England and Western Europe.

MANUFACTURING AND DISTRIBUTION The success of Hershey's new products, coupled with the continued growth of its traditional products, caused Hershey Chocolate Company plants to run at full capacity. The Company took steps to remedy this situation with the construction of a new plant in Stuarts Draft, Virginia. This $90 million, 458,000-square-foot facility began production in October 1982. This plant increased Hershey's capacity for the production of recently introduced products as well as provided for the manufacturing needs of future products.

For many years the Hershey Chocolate Company's main plant in Hershey served as the primary distribution center in the East; it served volume customers as well as field warehouses strategically located throughout the continental United States, Hawaii, Puerto Rico, and Canada. New products and production facilities created a strain on the Hershey Plant to store finished product, mix inventories, and ship orders.

The need for a facility to perform these functions became obvious. After much study a 65-acre site in New Kingston, Pennsylvania, was selected. This location was 20 miles west of the main manufacturing facility in Hershey. Construction of an Eastern Distribution Center began in November 1982, and the 435,000-

square-foot, $16 million facility became fully operational in November 1983. The site for the distribution center was chosen for its centralized location in relation to the company's eastern manufacturing facilities and for its prime access to major interstate highways and railroad systems.

Hershey's products were distributed in the United States and abroad through a network of thirty-two field warehouses and by direct shipment to customers from the manufacturing plants. Location of customers and the quantity ordered determined the method of shipment and warehousing. Hershey's customers included convenience stores, grocery chains, independent grocery wholesalers, candy and tobacco distributors, syndicate stores, drug chains, and vending machine operators. These formed the link between Hershey and the consumer.

In 1985, finished goods moved from the manufacturing plants to the Eastern Distribution Center for storage and mixing. This center served as the stock replenishment point for twenty-four field warehouses, the Western Distribution Center, and volume customers located east of Colorado. The Oakdale, California, plant, serving as a distribution center in the West, replenished the western field warehouses and supported direct shipments to volume customers.

The field warehouses serviced most customers who placed orders for less than 25,000 pounds of product. They were commercial warehouses that provided temperature-controlled storage space in the major market areas. The field warehouses gave Hershey the ability to deliver in temperature-controlled trucks an order to any of their less-than-truckload customers within 48–72 hours of receipt. To improve customer service and information turnaround, as well as to enhance inventory control and reduce operating costs, Hershey computerized its field-order-processing and inventory-control system.

MARKETING AND SALES   Hershey's leadership in the chocolate and confectionery industry was based on three criteria: high quality of product, mass distribution, and optimum consumer value consistent with earning a profit in the competitive marketplace.

Hershey confectionery products were sold to some 65,000 wholesalers and retailers in 20,000 cities and towns by its sales and marketing forces. The field sales organization totaled over 470 full-time sales representatives and over 200 part-time sales merchandisers throughout the United States and Canada. This was a conventional selling organization in which sales representatives sold to the customer directly and then contacted retail outlets to draw the product out of customer warehouses.

The United States was divided into six sales divisions, twenty-four sales regions, and ninety-six districts, each with its own district manager. Canada was divided into six districts with independent wholesalers.

Hershey used the brand-manager concept of marketing management. The brands manager and the new-products manager were responsible for the development of the total marketing plan for the profitable growth of their assigned brands. They worked under the direction of the marketing manager, who along with the managers of marketing research and packing development, reported to the divisional vice-president for marketing. Exhibit 12.4 depicts a partial marketing and sales structure of Hershey Chocolate Company.

An innovative concept introduced by its Sales Department in 1983 was the retail merchandising force. This sales force of part-time people has enabled Hershey to economically expand its coverage of smaller retail outlets such as convenience stores. Before the formation of this retail merchandising force, Hershey's sales representatives did not have time to cover these outlets and concentrated on mass-merchandising outlets such as supermarkets. The additional

EXHIBIT 12.4 **Hershey Chocolate Company: Marketing and Sales Structure**

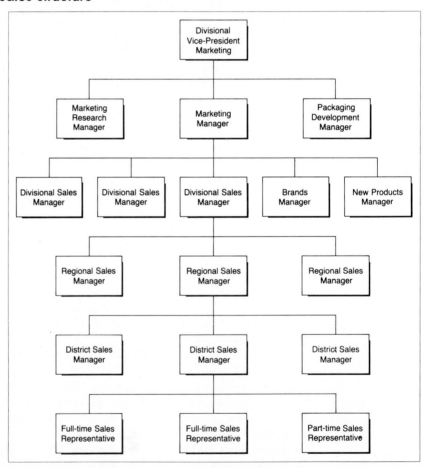

part-time sales coverage resulted in Hershey's capability to improve the position and salability of its products in previously uncontacted retail outlets.

For the purpose of developing special markets, the Special Markets Department was established in 1981 and assigned the responsibility for the sale of specialty confections, fund-raising projects, food service, and institutional and industrial products. To exploit the growth opportunities in these special market categories, Hershey developed an institutional broker network of over sixty brokers to sell to its special market customers. This selling organization has been very effective, as is shown by special-markets sales growth since 1976 of over 230%.

COMPETITORS In the $5 billion a year candy business, one percentage point of market share represents approximately $50 million in sales. In response to industry pressures, chocolate and confectionery-product manufacturers resorted to producing more chocolate-coated candies and reducing the sizes of bars while increasing prices to the retailer. Many retail stores sold similar sizes or types of candy at one price to avoid confusion, regardless of small wholesale price differences.

In November 1980, Mars, Inc. broke industry tradition: It increased candy bar size without increasing price. The 10% weight increase resulted in a 50% increase in sales. Mars' market share increased from 37% to 46%. Hershey's share decreased from 28% to 26% while Curtiss, Peter Paul Cadbury, D. L. Clark, and Nabisco suffered even more, because most of the market expansion went to Mars.

Confectionery companies change the prices and weights of their products from time to time to accommodate changes in the cost of manufacturing (including the cost of raw materials), the competitive environment, and profit objectives. In September 1981, Mars increased its bar prices to $0.30 retail. Hershey did not and advertised that it had not raised prices and was not responsible for the higher prices stores were charging. Most other candy makers followed Mars' lead, and most stores charged the same higher price to avoid confusion and pocketed the difference.

In March 1982, Hershey increased its price to $0.30 and increased the weight of its bars by 35%. In December 1983, Hershey increased its price to $0.35, a 17% wholesale price hike reflecting the increase in cocoa prices to about $1.20 per pound. Mars increased its bar prices to $0.35 in April 1984. Exhibit 12.5 details these price/weight changes.

By 1983, industry analysts estimated that Hershey and Mars were "locked in a head-to-head confrontation." Hershey's Marketing Department estimated the market share to be 33% for each firm. Six of the twelve top-selling bars were made by Mars. Hershey made four. The remainder of the top candy manufacturers included Standard Brands, Nestle, and Cadbury. Exhibit 12.6 lists the top-selling candy bars of 1983.

To battle Mars, Hershey had been regularly adding new confectionery products containing less chocolate. Mars made some aggressive moves of its own.

EXHIBIT 12.5   **Hershey and Mars Price and Weight Changes**

YEAR	MARS (SNICKERS)			HERSHEY (PLAIN)		
	Ounces	Price	Cost/oz.	Ounces	Price	Cost/oz.
1921				1.0	.05	5.0 cents
1930	2.5	.05	2.0 cents			
1968	1.16	.05	4.3	.75	.05	6.7
1969	2.3	.10	4.3	1.5	.10	6.7
1973	2.3	.15	6.5			
1976 (Jan.)	2.3	.20	8.7	1.2	.15	12.5
1976 (Dec.)				1.35	.20	14.8
1977				1.2	.20	16.7
1978	2.3	.25	10.9	1.2	.25	20.8
1980 (Apr.)				1.05	.25	23.8
1980 (Oct.)	1.69	.25	14.8			
1980 (Nov.)	1.8	.25	13.9			
1981 (Sept.)	1.8	.30	16.7			
1982	1.8	.30	16.7	1.45	.30	20.7
1983 (Dec.)				1.45	.35	24.1

SOURCES: 1921–1981: *Washington Post*, May 17, 1981; 1976–1982: *Washington Post*, July 11, 1982; and 1982–1983: Hershey Foods Corporation, *1983 Annual Report*.

To expand sales, it had started a campaign trying to convince customers that candy was an acceptable snack food rather than a cause of tooth decay, acne, or obesity. Mars paid about $5 million to sponsor the 1984 summer and winter Olympic games and promoted Snickers and M&M products as the "official snack foods" of the Olympics. In addition, Mars has been known in the industry for its aggressive sales force.

INDUSTRY FORECASTS   The confectionery industry anticipated changing demographics between 1985 and 1990. The under-18 age group, the dominant consumption group, will be shrinking; senior citizens will be growing in numbers; and the 35–54 age group, the main buyers of boxed chocolates, will be the dominant age group. Hershey's research revealed some important facts about the candy consumer. Consumers tended to make their purchases from a menu or roster of ten to twelve bars and never to buy the same bar twice in a row. In addition, the heavy users (six or more bars in thirty days), who made up 24.6% of the population, consumed 68.5% of all the candy sold. The light users represented 66.4% of the population and consumed 31.5% of the candy.

Research also indicated that traditional meal patterns have changed considerably with today's busy lifestyles. More and more people eat when they can

EXHIBIT 12.6 **National Candy Buyers' Survey of the Top Ten Candy Bars,[1] 1983**

RANK	BRAND	MANUFACTURER	1977 RANK
1	Snickers	Mars	1
2	M&M Peanut	Mars	3
3	M&M Plain	Mars	4
	Reese's Peanut Butter Cup	Hershey	2
4	3 Musketeers	Mars	5
5	Hershey Almond	Hershey	7
	Milky Way	Mars	6
6	Hershey Plain	Hershey	9
7	Kit Kat	Hershey	8
8	Almond Joy	Peter Paul Cadbury	
9	Mars Bar	Mars	
10	Mounds	Peter Paul Cadbury	

SOURCE: *Candy Industry*, May 1983, pp. 52–58.

[1] Because this survey was based on a regional basis (Northeast, Southeast, North Central, South Central, Mountain, and Pacific), national rankings were derived by summing regional rankings.

and when they choose. Snacking has become an acceptable way of eating for both children and adults. Because of the changing eating patterns, consumers' taste preferences have shifted away from the traditional, predominately chocolate bar to a combination bar that is a more nutritionally balanced snack.

In 1983, there were two noteworthy trends. First, per capita consumption of candy had been increasing since 1981, reversing an earlier trend, even though overall consumption declined at a compound annual rate of 0.9% between 1972 and 1983. Specifically, per capita consumption increased 2.5% in 1981, 3.7% in 1982, and 2% in 1983. In 1983, U.S. per capita consumption of all chocolate and nonchocolate candies, including imports, reached approximately 17.0 pounds. (In 1984, per capita consumption of chocolate was 16.7 pounds.) The most significant increase was in the consumption of imported candy, which reached 0.65 pound per capita in 1983, an increase of 8% over 1982. The second trend concerned the gain in popularity of ultra-expensive chocolate candies. In 1983, assortments of these ultra-expensive chocolate candies secured a larger share of the presentation-box candy market. These costly chocolates, which featured elaborate packaging and exotic ingredients, were usually available in a select group of retail outlets, such as department stores, and sold for about $18.00 per pound and up. In comparison, most domestic chocolate assortments, which were widely available, sold for $5.00–$7.00 per pound. To respond to this trend, Hershey had introduced the Golden Almond Bar and Skor and was researching and test marketing other products for inclusion in this product line.

Halloween has always been an important season for the sale of confectionery products, especially in the bar goods segment. In 1982, Halloween retail candy sales dropped between 10% and 25%, depending on area, because of the Tylenol scare and copycat product tampering. Halloween sales traditionally accounted for $1.5 billion of an annual industry total of $5.4 billion. In 1983 the industry mounted a consumer education program and made arrangements for a Halloween Hotline to the National Confectioners Association and the Chocolate Manufacturers Association in order to "nip in the bud" possible erroneous reporting. In addition, drug manufacturers introduced new, more secure, tamper-resistant packaging. Also in 1983, President Reagan signed into law a bill that defined willful adulteration of food products as a felony, with severe penalties attached. Because of these efforts, Halloween sales of candy in 1983 increased but had not regained 1981 levels.

Hershey Canada, Inc.

After thirty years of exporting its products through wholesale candy brokers in Canada, Hershey established its Canadian operation in 1963, with the opening of a 250,000-square-foot chocolate-making plant in Smith Falls, Ontario. This operation was augmented in late 1977 when Hershey acquired U.S.-based Y&S Candies, Inc., which included a 125,000-square-foot licorice plant in Montreal that became part of Hershey Canada, Inc. after the acquisition. By 1981 the Canadian operation was achieving record sales and substantial increases in tonnage in the chocolate, grocery, and licorice areas; new products accounted for over 25% of consumer sales. During 1981, Hershey's Canadian chocolate and confectionery operations were reorganized and transferred to a wholly owned subsidiary, Hershey Canada, Inc. In addition, a new company headquarters office was opened in Toronto to house the entire administrative and financial staffs.

In addition to introducing into the Canadian market several of the products for which Hershey was well known in the United States, Hershey Canada has also developed some unique products of its own, designed particularly for the Canadian market. These have included Brown Cow and Strawberry Cow, both cold milk modifiers, and Top Scotch, a butterscotch-flavored ice cream topping. In addition, Hershey Canada introduced in 1983 a completely new chocolate, which was designed, after extensive consumer testing, to satisfy the taste of the Canadian consumer. Hershey Canada implemented other significant changes in its business during 1983. The package graphics on the Hershey Bar line were completely redesigned; the weight of Reese's Peanut Butter Cups and Special Crisp were increased by 23% and 20%, respectively; bar prices were increased from $0.40 to $0.45 to match the competition; and part-time sales merchandisers were added to the company's sales organization.

In 1984, Hershey Canada, Inc. achieved record sales, and operating income improved substantially in comparison with 1983. The sales increase in 1984 came almost totally from volume increases on established products and the introduction of new products, as selling prices remained at the approximate levels of 1983. To take advantage of available plant capacity, a program to supply selected products to the United States was developed and implemented in the second half of 1984. This program was a major contributor to Hershey Canada's favorable operating results in 1984.

Restaurant Operations

Friendly Ice Cream Corporation

In 1979, Hershey Foods acquired the Friendly Ice Cream Corporation for $164 million ($75 million in debentures and $89 million in cash) and entered the restaurant industry. At that time, Friendly was a nonfranchised chain of 613 ice cream and sandwich shops located in the New England, Middle Atlantic, and Midwestern states. At the time of purchase it was vertically integrated, with two plants and products distributed in its own refrigerated trucks.

By the end of 1984, 707 family or mall restaurants, located in sixteen states, were in operation. The space in shopping centers was held under lease, while 68% of the freestanding sites were owned by Friendly. Essentially, all of Friendly's units were concentrated in suburban areas. Exhibit 12.7 lists the shops by state. A second O'goodies! ice cream dip shop was opened in 1984. At O'goodies! shops, customers could create their own sundaes and ice cream flavors, as well as obtain a variety of beverages and made-on-the-premises baked products. This concept was in a development and testing phase to determine its viability as a growth vehicle.

Friendly's plants at Wilbraham, Massachusetts, and Troy, Ohio, manufactured the ice cream and most of the syrups and toppings used in its units. Most of the meat used was processed in the Wilbraham plant and was shipped to the units in frozen form. Most of the other food and supplies were also furnished by these plants and distributed to each unit by a company-operated fleet of refrigerated trucks. A limited number of other items—mostly milk, baked goods, eggs, and produce—were purchased from local sources designated by Friendly's purchasing department. Friendly also maintained its own real estate, engineering, construction, carpentry, decorating, design, and maintenance departments. Approximately 10,400 square feet of additional production and office space was added to Friendly's Wilbraham, Massachusetts, headquarters in 1983, and new production equipment was installed, to enhance the company's capacity for the production of ice cream pies and extruded products such as Wattamelon Roll.

Between 1981 and 1984 a number of programs to improve productivity and customer service have been undertaken. Standardized and expanded menus were introduced for all restaurants, field sales supervision was realigned along geographic lines, sharp increases were made in promotional expenditures, and advances were made in prefabricated restaurant-building techniques. In addition, significant capital investment for future growth was being made through

EXHIBIT 12.7

Friendly Ice Cream Shops

State	1979	1980	1983	1984[1]
Connecticut	75	73	74	75
Delaware	3	3	3	3
Illinois	4	4	4	4
Indiana	4	3	2	2
Maine	5	5	5	6
Maryland	22	23	24	29
Massachusetts	182	187	179	179
Michigan	15	9	9	8
New Hampshire	11	11	12	13
New Jersey	48	49	60	64
New York	117	123	134	153
Ohio	76	78	82	89
Pennsylvania	37	42	46	53
Rhode Island	5	5	5	7
Vermont	3	4	4	5
Virginia	6	9	13	14
Total	613	628	656	707

SOURCE: Friendly Ice Cream Executive Office Pamphlet, June 1985.

[1]Number of stores as of June 1985, less those under construction.

the Restaurant Modification Program. By 1985, Friendly was in the process of modifying its restaurants from ice cream and sandwich shops to informal family restaurants serving high-quality, moderately priced menu items such as spaghetti.

"We have tried to strengthen the conviction of what we want Friendly to be," said Mr. Zimmerman. "Friendly has something special: the fourth meal. Everyone else has breakfast, lunch and dinner. We have a snack portion. We do a lot of business after eight o'clock at night, and it's not hamburgers, it's ice cream."[5]

Other Food Products and Services

Hershey Pasta Group

The history of Hershey's involvement in the pasta business began in 1967 with the acquisition of San Giorgio Macaroni Company of Lebanon, Pennsylvania, from the Guerrisi family. This brand was a familiar name in Central Pennsylvania, but distribution was limited mostly to the Pennsylvania, Washington, D.C., and New York areas. In the same year, Hershey acquired Delmonico Foods of Louisville, Kentucky, from the Viviano family. The Delmonico brand distribution was mostly in Kentucky, Ohio, and parts of West Virginia. The two pasta companies were consolidated into one in 1975 under the name San Giorgio Macaroni Company, Inc.

In 1978, San Giorgio acquired the Procino–Rossi Company of Albany, New York, a third family-owned business with a high-quality Italian-oriented brand. Sales of P&R were limited to upper New York state.

The pasta division acquired the Skinner Macaroni Company of Omaha, Nebraska, in 1979 for 398,680 shares of Hershey stock. Acquired from the Skinner family, this brand was sold predominantly in the southwestern and the southeastern parts of the United States and represented Hershey's first departure from an Italian-oriented brand name.

By 1981, San Giorgio was the fastest growing pasta brand in the United States, with a 10% market share (worth $800 million at retail) that was second only to Mueller, with a 16% market share. Record sales and operating income were achieved in both 1982 and 1983, as well as additions to operating capacity. The company marketed its products under several brand names, including San Giorgio, Skinner, Delmonico, P&R, and Light 'N Fluffy as well as certain private labels, to chain grocery stores, grocery wholesalers, convenience stores, and food distributors.

Hershey Foods Corporation announced on September 21, 1984, that it had reached an agreement with the Pillsbury Company for the purchase of American Beauty Macaroni Company, a division of Pillsbury. Under the agreement, Hershey purchased certain assets of the American Beauty business, including three plant facilities, fixed assets, inventories, and trademarks. American Beauty was a full-line, consumer-branded, dry pasta company, which conducted its business mostly in the central, southwestern, and western United States.

According to Richard A. Zimmerman, Hershey's President and Chief Executive Officer, "This acquisition is consistent with the company's stated objective of expanding its business into geographical areas where essentially it does not market its pasta products."[6]

This acquisition moved Hershey into the number one market-share position in branded pasta sales in the United States. To better reflect the character of the consolidation of Hershey's five strong regional brands, the company's pasta operations were renamed the Hershey Pasta Group in 1984.

Annual per capita consumption of pasta increased from 8.6 pounds in 1975 to almost 11 pounds in 1985 and was still growing. By comparison, Italians ate an average of 66 pounds of pasta per year in 1985. In the same period, pasta dollar sales in the United States grew by over 170%. Between 1980 and 1985, dry pasta sales grew at three times the growth rate of other dry groceries in supermarket sales and dry pasta continued to be one of the leading food categories in the grocery store. Much of this growth has gone to Italian imports. In waging an attack on the Italian imports and attempting to increase pasta consumption, U.S. pasta makers stressed quality, cut costs, and developed new products such as low-calorie, high-protein pasta.

Research also showed that pasta, relative to other carbohydrates, was inexpensive, and the long-term projections of high meat prices indicated a continued strong pasta market through 1990. The branded pasta industry as a whole was expected to reach a billion-dollar sales level at retail by the mid-1980s.

Cory Food Services, Inc.

Cory Food Services, Inc. was a Chicago-based provider of one of the largest coffee-service plans for businesses and institutions in the United States and Canada. The company provided and serviced its own brewing equipment in locations to which it sold and delivered coffee and other related products. In addition to coffee services, Cory provided allied product services such as hot tea, hot soup mixes, and hot cocoa and leased water-treatment units, microwave ovens, and compact refrigeration units. Cory was acquired in 1967 for $25 million and in that year became a wholly owned subsidiary of Hershey Foods.

The state of the economy affected Cory more than it did Hershey's other businesses. A depressed economy led to cutbacks in coffee use through layoffs and subsequent reduction in consumption. High inflation reduced expenditures for coffee. Hot summers have a depressing effect on coffee consumption. Because of weather and economic conditions in coffee-bean-growing countries, there were wide fluctuations in the prices of green coffee beans. In addition, customers' perceptions toward lowered caffeine consumption have changed dramatically since the coffee-service concept was introduced in the mid-1960s. Annual per capita consumption in the United States had declined from 39.2 gallons in 1964 to 32.8 gallons in 1972 and to 26.4 gallons in 1982.

In 1978, Cory withdrew from the consumer products market. In addition, Cory disposed of its manufacturing operations, because of reduced profitability in the manufacture of brewing equipment and other appliances. In 1979 a major market survey revealed that Cory had the largest market share and a lower account turnover than the industry average; but by 1980, Cory was experiencing a decrease in its consumer base. Cory President George E. Wilber, Jr. resigned in September 1980; Ogden C. Johnson, the corporation's Vice-President of Science and Technology, assumed the additional responsibility of acting President of Cory until a new president was selected.

L. William Chiles was appointed President and Chief Executive Officer of Cory in 1981. Sales in 1981 were hampered by inflation, unemployment, and decreased per capita consumption of coffee, although sales of allied products (tea, soup, canned juices, and leases of water treatment units, microwave ovens, and compact refrigeration units) showed growth. By 1982 the significant issues were considered to be the need for more effective sales and marketing programs, management training and compensation, restructured product pricing, and the addition and expansion of new lines of business such as a line extension to include gourmet coffees. By 1983, financial results were well below expectations because of competitive price pressures and hot summer months. At this time the field management structure was completely reorganized, and sales and customer service were separated, in an attempt to maximize productivity and focus management expertise in these areas.

To place greater emphasis on Cory's expertise with large accounts and its national service capability, a new sales team to focus on major account development and service was formed in 1984. These customers were particularly valuable to Cory because their high-volume purchases did not require a proportionate investment in brewers and related equipment. Another major change in 1984 was the revision of the sales force compensation plan, in an effort to improve the quality of the sales force.

Hershey International, Ltd.

The Hershey approach has been to form joint ventures with partners abroad who were willing to risk their own capital and who had strong, well-established businesses and a good knowledge of local market conditions. As with its domestic markets, Hershey's international investments and commercial activities concentrated primarily in the chocolate, confectionery, and pasta areas.

In 1977, Hershey staffed an International Department to actively pursue joint ventures, licensing, and export opportunities. In 1978, Hershey's investment and development activities in the international field expanded considerably. Special emphasis was placed on Brazil, which is larger than the United States in area and had half the population of South America. In 1981, all non-Canadian business interests were grouped into a new subsidiary company, Hershey International, Ltd., so that the monitoring, control, and reporting of international operations was strengthened. Despite a worldwide poor economy, exports were profitable in 1982, and joint ventures were profitable in local currencies, although Hershey experienced losses on foreign-exchange adjustments. By 1983, industry-wide profits were hurt by poor economic conditions worldwide, weak foreign currencies, and severe financial problems in South America and Latin America.

Hershey International, Ltd.'s sales and operating income in 1984 increased significantly over those of the previous year, in spite of the continuing high inflation levels and depressed economic conditions prevailing in two of the company's largest foreign markets, Brazil and Mexico. Export sales in 1984 surpassed the previous year's level despite the continued high value of the U.S. dollar. Marketing programs supporting these export sales activities were monitored closely and adapted as was necessary to meet local competition.

In the U.S. market, Hershey was working closely with three European manufacturers of chocolate and confectionery products: Roundtree Mackintosh of

York, England, for the sales and/or manufacture of Kit Kat, Rolo, and After Eight; P. Ferrero of Alba, Italy, for the test marketing of its Kinder line; and Bassets of Great Britain for the importation and distribution of high-quality licorice products.

PETYBON INDUSTRIAS ALIMENTICIAS LTDA. (BRAZIL) Petybon was originally a 40% joint venture between Hershey Foods Corporation and S. A. Industrias Reunidas F. Matarazzo of Sao Paulo, Brazil. This joint venture was formed in 1979 to manufacture and distribute pasta, biscuits, and margarine products, and to sell cooking oils, flour, candles, and soap manufactured by the Food Division of Matarazzo and other companies. Hershey purchased the remaining 60% for $13 million in 1982.

A. B. MARABOU (SUNDBYBERG, SWEDEN) Marabou was the leading chocolate and confectionery manufacturer in Sweden, and manufactured and distributed a complete line of chocolate and confectionery products. In 1977, Hershey acquired a 20% interest for direct investment and a joint research partnership for the exchange of production technology and know-how. In addition, Hershey began to import Marabou's fine-quality boxed chocolates into the United States. In 1979, Marabou completed the acquisition of Goteborgs Kex, Sweden's leading cookie and cracker producer. In 1983, Marabou expanded through the acquisition of Maarud, Norway's leading snack food producer. Marabou experienced significant growth in sales and earnings in 1984, supported by demand for its high-quality chocolate, confectionery, snack, and biscuit items and its continued export growth.

CHADLER INDUSTRIAL DA BAHIA S.A. (BRAZIL) In 1978, Hershey purchased 22.5% interest in this Brazilian processor of cocoa beans. Hershey agreed to provide technical assistance and quality-assurance inputs, to improve the quality and yield in the conversion of cocoa beans to semiprocessed products such as chocolate liquor, cocoa butter, and cocoa powder. By 1980, a plant expansion was completed. Chadler Industrial operations lost money in U.S. dollars between 1981 and 1983 but showed significant improvements in sales and earnings in 1984, because of more attractive conditions in world export markets for cocoa powder and cocoa butter.

NACIONAL DE DULCES (MEXICO) In 1978, Hershey initiated a 50% joint venture with Anderson Clayton & Co., S.A. High startup and financing costs associated with the opening of a new plant in Guadalajara burdened sales and profits through 1982, but 1983 saw improved results of operations despite the weakened Mexican economy and high interest rates. Two new products were introduced in 1983; and on the basis of improved operating performance and the long-range potential for chocolate and confectionery products in Mexico, both partners agreed to increase capital structure to provide additional funds for repair and replacement of production equipment and for working capital. In 1984, sales and operating income increased over the 1983 levels.

PHILIPPINE COCOA CORPORATION (PHILIPPINES) In 1978 a product-licensing agreement was signed that covered trademark, know-how, and technical assistance in the growth, production, and processing of cocoa beans, and the production and quality control of derived products. This agreement was approved by the Philippine government in 1980. In 1981 a 30% joint venture to provide technical assistance for the improvement of cocoa growing and processing was made. In 1982, sales and profits increased, with the completion of a new cocoa-processing plant and the first phase of an experimental farm for cocoa beans. Although 1983 brought slightly reduced sales and earnings, a new cocoa-processing operation, making possible the production of Hershey's Cocoa and other cocoa products, was completed. In addition, several new low-priced, bite-size chocolate items and hard candies were introduced. During 1984, locally produced Sweetened and Unsweetened Cocoa Powders were introduced, along with a new line of high-quality lollipops and the first locally produced, real milk-chocolate confectionery product. During this year the Philippine Cocoa Corporation showed growth in earnings, restructured its debt, and completed a major reorganization program.

FUJIYA CONFECTIONERY COMPANY (TOKYO) Fujiya was a leading manufacturer of chocolate and confectionery products, snack foods, beverages, ice cream, and bakery products. It also had a number of restaurant operations. Expecting a substantial increase in export sales of finished products and bulk to Japan, Hershey entered into trademark-license and technical-assistance agreements with Fujiya in 1979. These agreements gave the company the exclusive right to import, manufacture, and sell Hershey products in the Japanese market. Sales and earnings began expanding in 1980; and by 1983, Fujiya was manufacturing Hershey's Syrup in Japan and had introduced Hershey's Hellos (the international brand name for Reese's Pieces).

INDUSTRIAS DE CHOCOLATE LACTA, S.A. (BRAZIL) In 1980 the company entered into a joint venture partnership (no direct equity participation) with Lacta, Brazil's leading chocolate and confectionery company, to explore industrial and marketing projects in chocolate and confectionery.

RAW MATERIALS

The unique quality and flavor of Hershey's chocolate products were the result of the skillful blending of several basic ingredients, among which were cocoa beans, milk, sugar, almonds, and peanuts.

Cocoa beans were imported from West Africa, which accounted for approximately three-fifths of the world's crop, and from South American equatorial regions. Ghana was the largest supplier, followed by Nigeria and Brazil. Cocoa trees thrived only in tropical areas, within twenty degrees north or south of the equator, where the balance of temperature, rainfall, and soil conditions was precisely right. Cocoa beans were not uniform in quality and/or flavor, and the various grades and varieties were reflective of the different agricultural practices and environmental conditions found in the growing areas.

To meet its manufacturing objectives, Hershey bought a mix of cocoa beans. These beans were shipped to facilities in Hershey, Pennsylvania, Oakdale, California, and Canada for storage until needed. The main storage facility in Hershey had a capacity of more than 90 million pounds, enough for about five and one half billion Hershey bars.

The cocoa beans were the major raw material used in the production of Hershey's chocolate and confectionery products and as such, had the greatest impact on the cost of the candy bar. Cocoa beans had demonstrated wide price fluctuations that could be attributed to a variety of factors. These included weather and other conditions affecting crop size, the consuming countries' demand requirements, the producing countries' sales policies, speculative influences, international economics, and currency movements.

World output of cocoa exceeded demand between 1977 and 1981. Between 1982 and 1984, production fell below demand because drought, severe winds, and brush fires damaged the crop; world stocks were reduced. Speculation on the extent of damage to West African crops caused cocoa prices to jump from $1,900 per ton in 1983 to more than $2,700 per ton in 1984. The price of the cocoa bean jumped 184% between 1973 and 1984 and that increase forced some manufacturers to shift to more cocoa substitutes and extenders in their products. Exhibit 12.8 provides information on the prices of raw materials.

To minimize the effect of cocoa-bean price fluctuations, Hershey forward-purchased quantities of cocoa beans and cocoa products, principally chocolate liquor and cocoa butter, and bought and sold cocoa futures contracts. Hershey held memberships on the Coffee, Sugar and Cocoa Exchange, Inc. in New York and on the London Terminal Market Association. In addition, Hershey maintained West African and Brazilian crop-forecasting operations.

Fresh whole milk was vital to Hershey. Milk was purchased daily from more than 1,000 farms in the vicinity of Hershey's plants and was shipped directly to those plants in bulk tankers. The Hershey storage silos had a capacity of more than 300,000 gallons. Every day, Hershey used enough milk to supply all the people in a city the size of Salt Lake City. From 1973 to 1984 the price of milk rose 206%.

Sugar was another important raw material. In the East, most of the sugar was derived from cane and imported through eastern ports. The Oakdale plant used both beet and cane sugar processed in California. Because of the import quotas and duties imposed by the Agriculture and Food Act of 1981, which support the price of sugar, sugar prices paid by U.S. users were substantially higher than prices on the world sugar market.

Hershey was the largest user of almonds in the United States, all of which were grown in California. Peanuts, primarily from the southern and south-

EXHIBIT 12.8

Prices of Raw Materials

(In Dollars Per Pound)

YEAR	REFINED CANE SUGAR	COCOA	CORN SYRUP	PEANUTS
1984	.31	1.32	N.A.[1]	.241
1983	.32	1.08	N.A.	.256
1982	.30	0.92	.2670(E)[2]	.249
1981	.31	1.09	.1507	.162
1980	.41	1.35	.1441	.251
1979	.23	1.60	.1082	.206
1978	.21	1.74	.1044	.212

SOURCE: 1984: *Commodity Yearbook*, 1982–1983: Production, Consumption and Sales Values, *Current Industrial Reports—Confectionery* 1982; 1978–1981: Standard & Poor's *Industry*, January 1983.

[1] N.A. means that information was not available.

[2] E means that estimates were based on the 1984 *U.S. Industrial Outlook* and the 1984 *Commodity Yearbook*.

western states, were another important raw material. Market prices of peanuts and almonds were determined in the fourth quarter of the year, after the harvest of these crops. The prices per pound of peanuts between 1978 and 1984 can be found in Exhibit 12.8.

Pasta products were made from semolina flour milled from durum wheat. This wheat was a specialized, hard wheat grown almost exclusively in North Dakota. Recent crops had been excellent. Prices were reasonably stable.

General manufacturing costs have also escalated. Energy and wage costs increased by 495% and 112%, respectively, from 1975 to 1984.

RESEARCH AND DEVELOPMENT

Between 1978 and 1984 Hershey increased its spending from $2,786,000 to $9,942,000 on research activities, which involved the development of new products, improvements in the quality and safety of existing products, and improvement and modernization of production processes.

In November 1979, Hershey's 114,000-square-foot, $7.4 million Technical Center was completed. This center was considered to be the most complete and advanced research facility in the U.S. confectionery industry. This facility enabled Hershey to centralize many of its research and engineering operations, and contained offices, libraries, an auditorium, animal-testing facilities, and a pilot plant.

To facilitate the development and implementation of ideas, a reorganization of the company's technological and scientific functions into one unit took place in 1978. The resulting Department of Science and Technology consisted of four sections: *Research, Product and Process Development, Engineering,* and *Equipment Design and Development.*

The *Research Section* was responsible for developing new knowledge on issues that would keep the company competitive in its current businesses and provide for future growth. This section conducted nutritional research on Hershey products and developed one of the largest data banks in the world on the nutritional properties of chocolate and cocoa. In addition, research was conducted on tooth decay, chocolate allergies, and acne. This section was also responsible for ensuring that materials received from foreign countries met the company's quality specifications.

The *Product and Process Development Section* was responsible for investigating long-range product opportunities and consumer trends. The goal of this section was to provide Hershey's business segments with new products. Between 1978 and 1984 a number of new products and product modifications were introduced. Of these, eleven new products were for the Chocolate and Confectionery Division, four were for the Restaurant Division, and three were for the Other Food Products Division. New products introduced from 1980 to 1984 accounted for 22% of 1984 sales volume. Also being developed were new and improved chocolate-processing techniques to better control the products' quality and ingredient usage while conserving energy and maintaining the unique flavor and texture of Hershey's chocolate. In addition, a major thrust has been toward developing new products with a lower chocolate content.

The goal of the *Engineering Section* was to provide engineering support to assist in moving new products into production. The major responsibility of the *Equipment Design and Development Section* was to improve existing manufacturing systems. Newly designed equipment and manufacturing processes could be tested in an 8,500-square-foot pilot plant.

Hershey was continuously developing programs to improve the quality of its raw materials. Major programs involved efforts to improve the growing, harvesting, processing, and shipment of cocoa beans from farm to factory. The company's Agribusiness Department, a branch of the Science and Technology Department, was attempting to prove that modern organizational and production methods could be successfully applied to cocoa.

One project in this area involved Hershey's 1978 purchase of Hummingbird Hershey, Ltd., a cocoa farm located in the Central American nation of Belize. Another project involved a joint venture in Costa Rica. The purposes of these ventures were to demonstrate the feasibility of commercial cocoa production in the Western Hemisphere and to demonstrate the utilization of modern agricultural techniques in the growing of cocoa.

ADVERTISING AND PROMOTION

For sixty-eight years, Hershey did not advertise in mass consumer media. This attitude toward advertising had been based on the philosophy of the founder, Milton S. Hershey. He believed in point-of-purchase advertising and always said, "Give them quality. That's the best kind of advertising there is."[7] He believed that the best advertising was word-of-mouth endorsements from satisfied customers and good representation in retail outlets. By the middle 1960s, however, there was increased competition in the confectionery industry, coupled with the fact that young people were accepting advertising as an aid to discretionary purchasing. As new Hershey products were developed, it became necessary, to make profitable production feasible, to achieve mass distribution in a relatively short time. Without mass consumer advertising, Hershey was operating at a competitive disadvantage, and its new products' record was suffering as a consequence. These environmental changes brought a policy change in 1968, when Hershey announced its intention to initiate a consumer advertising program for its confectionery and grocery products.

Hershey learned a valuable lesson the hard way in 1974 when the price of cocoa beans soared and Hershey's advertising budgets were cut. Its chief competitor, Mars, continued full-scale advertising; and, for the first time in its history, Hershey was number two. Then Hershey became aggressive in both product advertising and product promotion. Hershey promoted to the trade (grocery chains, wholesalers, vendors, etc.) with promotions usually expressed in cents or dollars off the regular price of a box, case, etc. of its products. It also promoted to the consumer through point-of-sale promotions such as coupon and premium offers. In addition, it used television and radio forms of consumer advertising as well as advertising in newspapers, magazines, and other forms of printed media.

Promotional spending rose to $178 million in 1984 from $76 million in 1979. Hershey increased its advertising budget from $9.5 million in 1975 to $79.1 million in 1984. Sales during this period increased from $576 million to $1.9 billion.

According to then-President Dearden, in 1983 Hershey had recaptured the number one spot, but no official statistics were available, because Mars was secretive about its results. Under Dearden, Hershey Kisses were heavily promoted, and its sales tripled. The biggest success came through an accident of sorts. The Mars Company was approached by producers who offered to use M&M's in the movie *E.T.* When Mars refused the offer, the producers approached Hershey. After Hershey executive Jack Dowd, Vice-President for New Business Development, reviewed clips of the movie to ensure that it was not a monster movie, Hershey agreed to let them use Reese's Pieces in the film. Hershey also agreed to invest $1 million in a joint promotion with MCA, the film's distributor, over six weeks coinciding with the opening of the movie. Sales of the previously steady but unspectacularly selling candy increased 150% in the two weeks following *E.T.*'s release in June 1982; there followed an overall increase in sales of 80% over those of 1981. Furthermore, movie theaters started carrying the candy, whereas before they had refused. In 1982, Hershey negotiated a new agreement with Universal Studios to secure the rights to continue promotion of Reese's Pieces as *E.T.*'s favorite candy.

In 1984, Hershey Chocolate Co. became the first candy account for the Black Entertainment Network Cable System, Washington, D.C., with a multi-year, million-dollar advertising commitment. Hershey had been using other cable spots since 1980.

Hershey has always been concerned about the content of its advertising, as well as the type of program it supported. Its ads were constantly reviewed by child psychologists and public affairs specialists to make sure that they were not misleading and could not be misunderstood. Hershey did not indulge in advertisements that compared its products with those of a competitor, and advertising agencies were instructed not to position its ads on programs that featured sex or violence. Exhibit 12.9 outlines Hershey's advertising philosophy.

Hershey voluntarily began printing nutritional information on its labels in 1973 and for several years was the only manufacturer in the chocolate and confectionery industry to provide this customer service.

FINANCES

Hershey Foods Corporation's sales and earnings have improved yearly between 1978 and 1984. This period paralleled the existence of Hershey's strategic plan. During this time, sales grew at a compound annual rate of 16.0%, income from operations at 17.6%, and net income at 14.8%. Financial information is presented in Exhibits 12.3, 12.10, and 12.11.

EXHIBIT 12.9   Hershey's Advertising Philosophy

Simply stated, Hershey's advertising philosophy will observe the following guidelines:

1. *Honest*
   We will make no false or devious claims.
2. *Ethical*
   We will not degrade competition. We will not produce advertising whose tone or claims would offend or mislead. We will advertise in good taste.
3. *Respectful of Consumers' Intelligence*
   We can entertain and amuse, but never at the expense of truth. We will inform consumers of the merits of our products, but we will not take unfair advantage of our audience's lack of sophistication or technical background in presenting those merits.
4. *Effective*
   Hershey's advertising must be effective, while adhering to the above criteria.

Our intent is not just to be "legal" but to be as honest and ethical in our dealings with our unseen audience as we are with our direct customers—and as we would expect others to be with us.

SOURCE: Hershey Foods Corporation, College Packet, December 9, 1983.

EXHIBIT 12.10

Hershey Foods Corporation: Consolidated Balance Sheet
(Dollar Amounts In Thousands)

	1984	1983	1982	1981	1980	1979	1978	1977
Assets								
Cash and short-term investments	$ 87,917	$ 73,091	$ 34,503	$ 53,879	$ 48,906	$ 17,185	$111,756	$117,248
Accounts receivable—(net)	$ 80,977	56,456	65,129	56,241	45,964	37,423	31,787	27,008
Inventories	$ 185,953	194,666	178,585	151,890	113,701	106,078	65,611	61,950
Other current assets	$ 30,474	12,392	13,411	25,020	12,796	9,564	7,505	6,258
Total current assets	$ 385,321	336,605	291,628	287,030	221,367	170,250	216,659	221,202
Property/plant/equipment	$ 901,719	794,667	729,275	597,981	515,030	462,745	265,261	231,334
Less depreciation and amortization	259,110	219,546	189,361	157,797	135,589	113,480	94,481	88,164
Net property	$ 642,609	575,121	539,914	440,184	379,441	349,265	170,780	143,170
Goodwill	79,252	51,307	52,609	53,911	55,214	56,516	18,056	17,771
Investments and other assets	15,385	20,911	20,603	25,675	28,450	31,168	16,509	14,004
Total assets	1,122,567	983,944	904,754	806,800	684,472	607,199	422,004	396,153

(*Continued*)

EXHIBIT 12.10 (Continued)

	1984	1983	1982	1981	1980	1979	1978	1977
Liabilities								
Accounts payable	$ 96,378	67,107	61,971	48,085	52,498	51,636	43,696	55,650
Accrued liabilities	85,558	68,269	55,944	57,033	40,415	36,208	20,855	14,154
Accrued income taxes	14,247	10,287	11,399	10,006	17,107	7,546	9,864	13,345
Current portion of long-term debt	6,770	5,971	19,579	2,131	1,640	8,436	—	—
Total current liabilities	202,953	151,634	148,893	117,255	111,660	103,826	74,415	83,149
Long-term debt	150,316	127,990	140,250	158,182	158,758	143,700	35,540	29,440
Other long-term liabilities	—	22,367	9,350	—	—	—	—	—
Deferred income taxes	108,370	85,916	73,766	61,699	52,504	38,943	27,660	23,896
Common stock	31,337	31,337	15,669	15,669	14,160	14,159	13,745	13,730
Additional paid-in capital	54,006	54,006	54,006	54,006	2,259	2,255	2,169	2,083
Foreign currency adjustments[1]	(7,265)	(2,154)	—	—	—	—	—	—
Retained earnings	582,850	512,848	462,820	399,989	345,131	304,316	268,475	243,855
Total liabilities and stockholders' equity	$1,122,567	$983,944	$904,754	$806,800	$684,472	$607,199	$422,004	$396,153

SOURCE: Hershey Foods Corporation, *Annual Reports, 1984 and 1980.*

[1] 1983 restated to reflect the adoption of SFAS #52, "Foreign Currency Translations," January 1, 1983.

EXHIBIT 12.11

Hershey Foods Corporation: Eight-Year Consolidated Financial Summary

(All Dollar Amounts Are in Thousands Except Market Price and Per Share Statistics)

	1984	1983	1982	1981	1980	1979	1978	1977
Summary of Earnings								
Net sales	$1,892,506	1,706,105	1,565,736	1,451,151	1,335,289	1,161,295	767,880	671,227
Cost of sales	$1,293,446	1,168,109	1,084,748	1,015,767	971,714	855,252	560,137	489,802
Selling, general and administrative	$ 379,140	332,831	301,586	267,930	224,615	184,186	128,520	110,554
Interest expense	$ 15,291	16,766	11,441	15,291	16,197	19,424	2,620	2,422
Interest (income)	$ (4,942)	(952)	(3,582)	(2,779)	(2,097)	(1,660)	(5,303)	(2,931)
Income taxes	$ 100,889	89,185	77,375	74,580	62,805	50,589	40,450	35,349
Income from continuing operations	$ 108,862	100,166	94,168	80,362	62,055	53,504	41,456	36,031
Gain related to disposal of discontinued operations	—	—	—	—	—	—	—	5,300
Net income	$ 108,682	100,166	94,168	80,362	62,055	53,504	41,456	41,331
Net income per share	3.47	3.20	3.00	2.81	2.19	1.89	1.51	1.51
Dividends paid per share of common stock	$ 1.24	1.10	1.00	.875	.75	.675	.6125	.57
Dividends paid per share of Class B stock	$ .315	—	—	—	—	—	—	—
Average number of shares of common stock and Class B stock outstanding during the year.	31,337	31,337	31,337	28,643	28,320	28,306	27,484	27,444
Net income as a percentage of net sales	5.7%	5.9%	6.0%	5.5%	4.6%	4.6%	5.4%	5.4%

(Continued)

EXHIBIT 12.11 (Continued)

	1984	1983	1982	1981	1980	1979	1978	1977
Financial Statistics								
Capital additions	$ 87,049	105,244	116,736	91,673	59,029	56,437	37,425	27,535
Depreciation	$ 43,113	37,274	30,681	27,565	24,696	20,515	8,850	7,995
Advertising	$ 79,169	68,852	64,046	56,516	42,684	32,063	21,847	17,635
Current assets	$ 385,321	336,605	291,628	309,677	221,367	170,250	216,659	221,202
Current liabilities	$ 202,953	151,634	148,893	134,035	111,660	103,826	74,415	83,149
Working capital	$ 182,368	184,971	142,735	175,642	109,707	66,424	142,244	138,053
Long-term debt	$ 125,236	127,990	140,250	158,182	158,758	143,700	35,540	29,440
Stockholders' equity	$ 660,928	596,037	532,495	469,664	361,550	320,730	284,389	259,668
Total assets	$1,122,567	983,944	904,754	829,447	684,472	607,199	422,004	396,153
Return on average stockholders' equity	17.3%	17.8%	18.8%	19.3%	18.2%	17.7%	15.2%	16.8%
After-tax return on average invested capital	13.5%	13.8%	14.3%	13.9%	12.8%	14.3%	13.0%	14.2%
Stockholders' Data								
Outstanding shares of common stock and Class B stock at year-end	31,337	31,337	31,337	31,337	28,320	28,318	27,491	27,460
Market price of common stock								
At year-end	$ 38⅝	31⅝	28¼	18	11¾	12⅜	10⅜	9 15/16
Range during year	$41¼–28¼	35–24⅜	29¾–16¼	20½–11½	13–10	13¼–8⅝	11¾–9¼	11 3/16–8 5/16
Number of common stock and Class B stockholders at year-end	16,729	16,467	16,033	16,817	17,774	18,417	18,735	19,964
Employee Data								
Payrolls	$ 368,164	340,944	305,651	273,097	253,297	227,987	112,135	99,322
Number of full-time employees at year-end	15,200	14,310	13,600	12,450	12,430	11,700	8,100	7,660

SOURCE: Hershey Foods Corporation, *Annual Reports, 1984* and *1980.*

[1] All shares and per share amounts have been adjusted for the two-for-one stock split effective September 15, 1983.

[2] Financial statistics include certain reclassifications that have been made to the December 31, 1982 and 1981 consolidated financial statements.

In 1984, Hershey successfully completed its equity expansion program, to provide flexibility for growth as a major, diversified food company. Because of the company's unique ownership by the Milton Hershey School, it was necessary to devise a proposal that would allow the company to issue additional common stock while meeting the majority stockholders' desire to maintain voting control of the company. Stockholders approved and adopted amendments to the company's Certificate of Incorporation increasing the authorized shares of Common Stock from 50,000,000 to 150,000,000 and authorizing 75,000,000 shares of a new Class B Stock with greater voting power but lesser dividend rights. Under the amendments, holders of the Common Stock and the Class B Stock would generally vote together without regard to class on matters submitted to the stockholders, including the election of five-sixths of the Board of Directors; the Common Stockholders would have one vote per share and the Class B Stockholders, ten votes per share. The Common Stockholders, voting separately as a class, were entitled to elect one-sixth of the board of directors. With respect to dividend rights, holders of the Common Stock were entitled to cash dividends 10% higher than those declared and paid on the Class B Stock. To put this differential into effect during the fourth quarter of 1984, Hershey declared an increase in fourth quarter dividends to common shareholders to 35 cents per share. Dividends on Class B Stock remained at 31.5 cents per share.

To implement the amendments, Hershey offered shares of Class B Stock to all holders of Common Stock on a share-for-share basis in late 1984. At December 31, 1984, there were 26,235,110 shares of Common Stock and 5,102,002 shares of Class B Stock outstanding. Hershey Trust Company, as Trustee for the Milton Hershey School, owned 10,642,831 shares of the Common Stock and 5,051,001 shares of the Class B Stock as of December 31, 1984.

NOTES

1. *The New York Times*, July 22, 1984, p. 5.

2. Hershey Foods Corporation, *1979 Annual Report.*

3. Hershy Foods Corporation, *Second Quarter Report*, 1984.

4. *The Wall Street Journal*, July 11, 1984, p. 33.

5. *The New York Times*, July 22, 1984, p. 4F

6. Hershey Foods Corporation, *Third Quarter Report*, 1984, p. 4.

7. Hershey Foods Corporation, *1983 Annual Report*, p. 5.

CASE 13   Wendy's International, Inc.

SEXTON ADAMS • ADELAIDE GRIFFIN

Having emerged from obscure beginnings in 1969, Wendy's International has grown from a modest one-store operation to a multi-billion–dollar corporate giant. After sixteen years of successful operating results, Wendy's was beset by shrinking sales and profits and declining franchise confidence.[1]

John W. Weiss, an analyst with Montgomery Securities of San Francisco, stated it was "becoming increasingly uncertain whether the company will be able to successfully compete as a hamburger chain against McDonald's and Burger King."[2]

Wendy's had yet to convince Wall Street in early 1988 that it had turned the corner on its road to recovery. Michael J. Esposito of Oppenheimer and Company of New York stated, "We believe Wendy's still has several difficult quarters ahead before it gets back on track." Mr. Esposito had not recommended Wendy's stock, and Mr. Weiss was advising holders of Wendy's stock to sell off their shares.[3]

BACKGROUND/ HISTORY

Wendy's International, the third largest hamburger chain in the world, was started in the late 1960s. The founder, R. David Thomas, opened the first Wendy's Old Fashioned Hamburgers restaurant in downtown Columbus, Ohio, at 257 East Broad Street on November 15, 1969. Thomas named his first restaurant after his daughter Melinda Lou, who was nicknamed Wendy by her brother and sister.[4]

Thomas, Senior Chairman of the Board and Founder of Wendy's, dropped out of Central High School in Fort Wayne, Indiana, after the tenth grade. This

---

This case was prepared by Christina L. Alfertig, Naveen C. Bagh, Lulu Jasso, Van VanBebber and Bily M. Wilcox under the supervision of Professor Sexton Adams, North Texas State University, and Professor Adelaide Griffin, Texas Woman's University. Copyright c 1988 by Sexton Adams and Adelaide Griffin. Reprinted by permission.

self-made millionaire believes that more than a formal education is responsible for his success. Thomas states, "I believe what counts most in regard to work is whether you like to do it or not. Before I ever go into business for myself, I am going to know my business. I am going to start on a small scale and build my business and my experience together."[5]

Thomas began working at the age of eleven years. After being fired from his first two jobs, delivering groceries and working at Walgreen's Drug Store as a soda jerk, he landed a job working the lunch counter on weekends and during the summer at the Regas Restaurant in Knoxville.

Thomas worked at the Regas Restaurant for the next three years. When he turned fifteen, his family moved to Fort Wayne, Indiana. Thomas was able to get a job as a busboy at the Hobby House Restaurant. When his family left Fort Wayne a few months later, Thomas stayed behind, rented a room at the YMCA, and worked at the restaurant for the next fourteen years.[6]

In 1956, Thomas and his boss, Phil Clauss, opened their first restaurant in Fort Wayne. The restaurant served barbecue as its main meal and was named the Ranch House. During this time, Thomas met Kentucky Fried Chicken's founder Colonel Harland Sanders. Colonel Sanders eventually became one of the greatest influences on Thomas's life.

Initially, Thomas was not very impressed with Sanders. He opposed Clauss' idea of serving Sanders's chicken at the Ranch House. Clauss went against Thomas' beliefs and bought the franchise anyway and it soon prospered. Clauss bought three more Kentucky Fried Chicken franchises and in 1962, made a proposition to Thomas. Clauss said that if Thomas could turn the carryouts around, pay off a $200,000 deficit, and make a profit, Clauss would give Thomas 45% of the Columbus franchise for $65.[7]

Thomas jumped at the chance to go into business for himself. After reckoning that the stores were failing because they carried too many menu items, Thomas cut the menu to just a few items and focused primarily on chicken and salads. He advertised through radio to increase public awareness and paid for air time with buckets of chicken. The restaurants prospered and he was able to add four more Columbus locations. In 1968, he was able to sell his stores back to Kentucky Fried Chicken for $1.5 million and thus became a millionaire at thirty-five.[8]

Thomas was soon named Regional Operations Director for Kentucky Fried Chicken and was in charge of 300 restaurants. He continued to work closely with Colonel Sanders, who motivated and enhanced him. Thomas recalled, "He used to say: Be direct with people, tell 'em off when needed, but leave them feeling good."[9] The Colonel also introduced Thomas to Bob Barney, who not only began working for Thomas and Kentucky Fried Chicken in 1964, but ultimately became Chairman and Chief Executive Officer of Wendy's.

Thomas eventually left Kentucky Fried Chicken and opened an Arthur Treacher's Fish & Chips. While devoting a majority of his time in order to improve his restaurant, his desire to go into the hamburger business remained strong. This desire prompted the opening of the first Wendy's.

Thomas's competitors scoffed at his business methods. The first Wendy's menu consisted of fresh made-to-order hamburgers, chili, french fries, soft drinks, and the Frosty Dairy Dessert. Thomas wanted his restaurants to have a homey atmosphere and thus decorated them with carpeting, Tiffany-style lamps, and Bentwood chairs. Despite criticism, Wendy's prospered and expanded to four restaurants in Columbus.[10]

On July 16, 1971, Robert L. Barney joined Wendy's as President. A year later, after signing a franchise agreement for Indianapolis, Indiana, with L. S. Hartzog on August 17, 1972, Thomas began franchising Wendy's.[11] He borrowed $1 million from twenty investors who put up $50,000 each. Instead of franchising individual units, Thomas came up with the idea of selling franchises for entire cities and parts of states. Wendy's customers responded well to the Wendy's concept and the chain grew rapidly. After five years in operation, Wendy's net income exceeded $1 million and revenues topped $13 million. Total restaurant sales were nearly $25 million. On September 8, 1975, Wendy's stock was first traded on the over-the-counter market (WNDY). Later that same month, the first international restaurant was opened in Canada. Wendy's opened its five hundredth restaurant in Toronto, Canada and its thousandth restaurant in Springfield, Tennessee on December 15, 1976, and March 21, 1978, respectively. The opening of the thousandth restaurant was accomplished in 100 months—an industry record.[12] Wendy's also set a record for opening its two thousandth restaurant faster than any competitor.[13]

On November 15, 1979, Wendy's celebrated its tenth anniversary with 1,767 restaurants open in the United States, Puerto Rico, Canada, and Europe. Of these, Wendy's opened more than 750 restaurants in twenty-one months at a rate of 1.5% per day.[14] Also during November, 1979, Wendy's introduced its salad bar. This was the first new product added to the menu and was the beginning of Wendy's menu diversification program. Wendy's continued its diversification program with its acquisition of Sisters Chicken & Biscuits Restaurants on March 3, 1981. Sisters featured fried chicken and homemade biscuits served in a "classic country" atmosphere. On May 27, 1981, Wendy's was listed on the New York Stock Exchange with the symbol *WEN*.[15]

In September of 1982, the Board of Directors promoted R. David Thomas to the position of Senior Chairman of the Board. Robert L. Barney, President, was promoted to Chairman of the Board and Chief Executive Officer, and Ronald P. Fay was promoted to President and Continuing Chief Operating Officer.[16]

In January of 1984, Wendy's introduced the "Where's the Beef?" advertising campaign. The star of this campaign was Clara Peller, accompanied by Elizabeth Shaw and Mildred Lane. The campaign generated extensive media coverage and won three Clio Awards. It also resulted in the highest consumer-awareness levels in Wendy's history.[17]

Wendy's was the first national restaurant chain to offer salad bars. The Garden Spot Salad Bar offered more than twenty-five fresh vegetables, fruits, and other items, including six different dressings. Wendy's was also the first restaurant chain to offer baked potatoes nationwide. Wendy's Hot Stuffed Baked Potatoes offered five different toppings: sour cream & chives, cheese, chili & cheese, bacon and cheese, or broccoli and cheese. In September 1986, Wendy's introduced a new hamburger: The Big Classic. The Big Classic consisted of a quarter-pound hamburger loaded with fresh toppings and served on a corn-dusted kaiser-style bun. All of these new products were developed by Wendy's research and development department, which was established in 1979 to help Wendy's expand and stay competitive.[18]

As of December 1987, there were 3,816 Wendy's restaurants located in all fifty states and seventeen countries overseas. Systemwide sales had grown from less than $300,000 in 1970 to nearly $2.87 billion in 1987. Wendy's became the first chain to exceed $1 billion in sales in its first ten years of existence.[19]

Wendy's commitment to quality allowed it to expand its customer base to over 2 million served each day. Wendy's customers named Wendy's America's favorite hamburger chain for six years in a row, beginning in 1980, in the "Tastes of America" consumer survey conducted annually by *Restaurants and Institutions* magazine.

Wendy's creed, "Quality is Our Recipe," along with the company's philosophy of the customer being first priority, played important parts in helping the company maintain its third-position status among the hamburger chains. Wendy's also focused on new positioning and results orientation by developing new products, such as the SuperBar, which would allow for competitive expansion.[20]

Wendy's was primarily engaged in the business of operating, developing, and franchising a system of distinctive quick-service restaurants while maintaining quality and uniformity. By expanding the number of present restaurants, both company-owned and franchised, Wendy's management hoped to boost sales as well as stock prices. They also believed that they could increase Wendy's per-unit sales by $1 million.[21]

THE FAST FOOD RESTAURANT INDUSTRY

The restaurant industry during 1986 and 1987 was plagued by excess capacity, slower growth, and an increasingly price-sensitive market. It was a sluggish industry. So many new restaurants had been opened that there were only 685 people for every restaurant in the country, compared to 845 in 1972.[22] "Golden arches stretch from McSea to shining McSea, the Whopper has a home in every neighborhood, and the Colonel's visage peers down on his flock in every town," said industry expert Dan Cook.[23] Obviously, the boom years of the 1970s were over for the industry. The proliferation of fast food restaurants, coupled with the economic conditions of the time, resulted in average sales per unit declining for virtually all competitors. Thus, competition was fierce to maintain and improve market share in the environment.[24] Aggressive advertising, discounting, and couponing were the methods chosen by most to protect their share. Also, the "burger wars" of the 1970s were on again. Huge advertising budgets and humorous ads poking fun at burger rivals became the rage in a marketplace that remained stubbornly soft.[25]

Segments of the Fast Food Industry

The restaurant industry is highly fragmented and can be broken down into many different segments. In the entire fast-food segment, sharp declines were seen to be due to pressures to lower menu prices. A sub-segment of the fast-food segment is the burger chain. Once the fastest growing, this segment has since slowed dramatically.[26] Within this segment, the top contenders—McDonald's, Burger King, Wendy's and Hardee's—were fighting for a precious few percentage points to improve their market share.

Wendy's Major Competitors

The competition was intense within the burger segment. McDonald's was the market share leader. Burger King was a distant second. Wendy's and Hardee's were in close competition with each other, as can be seen by Exhibit 13.1.[27] Virtually everyone else within this segment was left in the dust behind these four big leaders. McDonald's continued to do very well, despite industry conditions. Its sales were up 11%.[28] It kept its title of the nation's most heavily

EXHIBIT 13.1 **Market Shares in the Burger Segment**

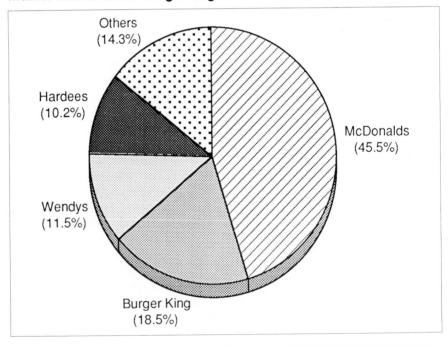

SOURCE: Nation's Restaurant News, August 11, 1986, p. 18.

marketed single brand name with an advertising budget of $311.6 million. This meant that it outspent Burger King three to one.[29] The familiar themes in McDonald's advertising continued to be convenience, speedy service, and consistency, which focused on brand awareness and customer loyalty. Burger King on the other hand touted a "Back to Basics" strategy. In its "burger war" ads, it differentiated itself with flame broiling and "Have It Your Way." Hardee's, meanwhile, used a head-on campaign to try to close the gap on Wendy's. Its full-scale marketing assault was aimed at showing consumers that its burgers were comparable to the "Big Three." Everyone else in the segment was trying to solidify their customer bases. For most, that meant using innovative marketing to foster a distinctive regional identity.[30]

Competition within the burger segment was extremely fierce. Competition also came from other areas. By selling hot foods in their mini-restaurants and delicatessens, grocery stores were vying for the same customers.[31] This put even more pressure on the restaurant industry, which was already facing tough times.

Trends Within the Fast Food Industry

Because of the intense competition, burger chains were trying many different ways to maintain their hard-earned market shares. Several trends emerged within the segment—breakfast items, chicken products, salads, non-traditional locations, and joint ventures. Even though Wendy's breakfast menu flopped, it proved successful for almost everyone else. To try to attract the increasingly health-conscious American public, many new restaurants were emphasizing quality, healthy, wholesome food. Chicken sandwiches and salads were a natural extension of America's health consciousness; most chains incorporated them into their menus. Not only were Americans more health-conscious, but they were also older. These older Americans wanted to be able to go to a restaurant and eat in a relaxed, unhurried atmosphere. They were also willing to spend more money for this kind of environment.

In addition, a major trend was opening restaurants in nontraditional sites, such as hospitals, hotels, discount stores, convenience stores, and even zoos.[32] Wendy's picked up on this idea, opening a unit in a Day's Inn hotel in Atlanta. Customers could order a Wendy's single through room service and have it charged to their room bill. Wendy's also experimented with units in K-Marts and in a zoo.[33]

A strategy that fast-food chains were beginning to utilize in order to substantiate profits was the "trend to combine" strategy, stated Don Jeffrey of *Nation's Restaurant News.* For instance, Churches and Hardee's joined forces with 7-Eleven to try to maximize profits. Winchell's Donuts had mini-stores within Arco gas stations and PepsiCo had acquired Pizza Hut, Kentucky Fried Chicken, and Taco Bell. Another trend was joint-ventures between different chains. For example, Wendy's installed a Baskin-Robbins ice cream concession in one of its stores.[34]

EXHIBIT 13.2

Advertising Expenditures

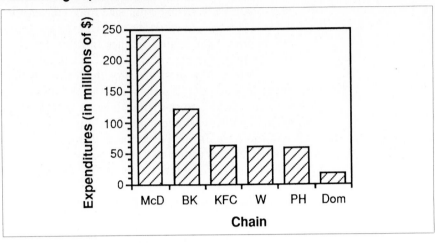

SOURCE: *Advertising Age,* March 2, 1987, p. 3.

Success Factors Within the Fast Food Industry

During these trying times, several success factors emerged. Marketing resources were obviously very important. Advertising was a major factor in determining and maintaining market share. It was up to the marketing departments to differentiate their products from those of their competitors. McDonald's spent overwhelmingly more than its competitors. It increased its expenditures by 5% over 1985. (See Exhibit 13.2.) Burger King and Kentucky Fried Chicken both increased their advertising expenditures by 14%, while Pizza Hut had a 15% increase. Dominos Pizza had an incredible 90% increase in advertising in 1986, yet they were still $222 million below McDonald's.[35]

Attention to customers' satisfaction was another success factor. Speed and quality of service were being improved, for example, by adding and expanding drive-through facilities. Cost cutting, another success theme, led many burger chains (including Wendy's) to cut overhead costs and even reduce staffs. Innovative products and distribution channels led to chains emerging in hospitals, military bases, and hotels.[36] The chains had to experiment in these ways to hold their market share while the industry continued to be sluggish.

Economic Factors

A minor recession and slow economic growth during this period made the consumers more price-conscious. Thus, the strategy of across-the-board increases in menu price was not feasible. Adding to this was an inflation rate that was moderate compared to the early 1980s. The Consumer Price Index rose only

2%.[37] Consumers, whose wages had not risen significantly, surely were not in a position to pay increased prices. In an effort to combat this, most chains tried using coupons and discounts, and introduced items with lower prices.[38]

Political/Legal and Technological Factors

Several legislative factors during this period affected not only Wendy's but the entire industry. Starting wages in fast-food outlets had gone up, and legislation was going through Congress to raise the minimum wage to $5.05 an hour (a $1.70 increase).[39] This increase obviously would greatly reduce profit margins to the stores. The Tax Reform Act of 1986, however, had a positive effect on Wendy's because of lower statutory rates, which more than compensated for loss of investment tax credits. It will continue to provide benefits in the future because of lower effective tax rates. Another benefit on the horizon was the new Financial Accounting Standards Board Statement on Income Taxes that enabled Wendy's to record their deferred tax liabilities at reduced rates.[40] A number of states had enacted legislation aimed at franchises. Basically, they required detailed disclosures and periodic registration to state agencies.

Legal Actions Affecting Wendy's

Wendy's was involved in various lawsuits in 1987. There were two proceedings in the Federal Districts Courts involving Pepsico, Inc. and Wendy's. In the first lawsuit, Wendy's was seeking a declaratory judgment concerning its obligations under a series of agreements with Pepsico. Wendy's sought damages on the basis of breaches of contract, tort, and antitrust violations on the part of Pepsico. Pepsico, in a counter lawsuit, alleged a breach of contract by Wendy's with respect to obligations to purchase products of Pepsico. However, even an adverse judgment wasn't seen as having a material impact on Wendy's.[41]

Wendy's was also involved in a sex discrimination suit by a former employee, Dorothy Kuenzi, who alleged discriminatory employment practices. The suit was settled out of court when Wendy's agreed to set up a $1.35 million fund for payments to certain female managers who believed they were denied promotions because of their sex, between 1983 and 1986. Breach of contract suits were also filed against several franchise owners. They, in turn, filed numerous counterclaims against Wendy's. Actual damages sought amounted to $9 million, while punitive damages sought were $48 million. The outcome of these suits was uncertain but Wendy's maintained its innocence and planned to vigorously defend itself.[42]

Technological Advances

Advances in technology were relatively few for the restaurant industry, but Wendy's became the first national chain to incorporate POS (point-of-sale) systems in their units. These were similar to automatic teller machines, except the machine issued $10 vouchers for food purchases. The customer then received his change in cash, while his bank account was automatically debited for the amount.[43]

Social and Cultural Factors

The fast-paced 1980s made greater convenience a growing demand of consumers. They wanted quick service and food that they could eat on the run—while doing other things (driving, working, etc.). "Everybody eats on the go, especially breakfast and lunch," according to Virginia Barnes of Midwestern Restaurant Corporation.[44] Wendy's responded with a smaller, 2 oz. burger that was convenient to hold and eat.[45] Consumers were also more conscious of price vs. value. Wendy's responded with less expensive burgers. Because the young family market was growing, Wendy's tried to carve out a niche there by upgrading its kids' menu, while offering promotional items, such as Tonka toys and GoBots aimed at getting children and their parents to visit Wendy's. Through much of the 1980s, Wendy's had targeted upscale adults. Thus they had "the smallest percentage of family trade," according to William Welter, then Wendy's top marketing official.[46]

MANAGEMENT

In 1987, Wendy's eliminated 160 positions, or 20% of its national administrative staff, to cut costs.[47] The employees ranged from vice-presidents to hourly headquarters staffers. Positions were eliminated from all administrative departments except operations. According to company spokesman Denny Lynch, the layoffs were not expected to save money in 1987 because of the cost of severance packages provided to the laid-off employees. The action taken at Wendy's was the latest in a growing number of retrenchments undertaken by chains looking to improve profits. The cuts followed the resignations of Richard Postle as President of Company Operations and William Welter as Executive Vice-President of Marketing. In addition, during 1986 Wendy's had reorganized company operations in order to put high-level executives in closer touch with store-level operations. An entire layer of management was eliminated in the process. The results were improved support of stores and better communication. Some levels of reporting in operations had been eliminated, so that more authority was given to those charged with actually running the store.[48] In addition to assisting the laid-off workers find new employment, the company also had a meeting for surviving staffers in order to boost morale. "We just talk about it so they can understand why we're doing it," Lynch said, "to get them involved."[49] The layoffs marked the first major reduction in Wendy's history according to a company spokesman.[50]

The organizational chart of Wendy's International can be seen in Exhibit 13.3. The executive officers of Wendy's included the following.

Mr. R. David Thomas, age 54, founded the company in 1969 and was its Chief Executive Officer until 1980. He served as Chairman of the Board from 1971 to 1982, when he became Senior Chairman of the Board.

EXHIBIT 13.3   **Organizational Chart, Wendy's International, Inc.**

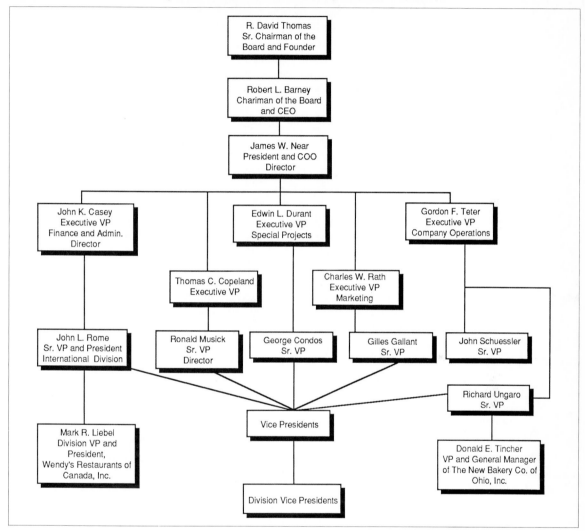

SOURCE: Wendy's International, Inc., *1987 Annual Report.*

Mr. Robert L. Barney, age 50, was President of the company from 1971 to 1982, and was appointed Chief Executive Officer in 1980. In 1982, he was named Chairman of the Board and retained his position as Chief Executive Officer. Mr. Barney began his food service career in 1962 as a franchise owner for Kentucky Fried Chicken in Athens, Ohio. There he met R. David Thomas and began a long business and personal relationship, which remained strong up through 1987 and beyond. Mr. Barney served as a Vice President for KFC from 1968 until joining Wendy's.

Mr. James W. Near, age 48, was appointed President and Chief Operating Officer in August of 1986. He served as President of Sisters International, Inc. from 1979 until August of 1986 and as Chief Operating Officer of Sisters from 1981 until August of 1986. He has been with the company since 1974. He was a franchisee of the company from 1974 until 1978, during which time he opened forty restaurants. He had thirty years of restaurant experience with a direct focus on operations and customer satisfaction.

Mr. John K. Casey, age 54, was appointed Executive Vice President of Finance and Administration in 1987. He joined the company in 1981 as Vice-President of Development, and was promoted in 1984 to Senior Vice-President of Corporate Development. Before joining Wendy's, he was a Group Vice-President at Bordens, Inc. Mr. Casey is a member of Wendy's Board of Directors.

Mr. Thomas C. Copeland, age 46, had served as Executive Vice-President since 1984, as Senior Vice-President of Franchise Operations from 1981 to 1984, and as Staff Vice-President from 1979 to 1981. He joined Wendy's in 1978 as Executive Assistant to the President. Prior to that, he served in various positions with Nationwide Corporation and its life insurance subsidiaries.

Mr. Edwin L. Durant, age 55, was promoted to Executive Vice-President in 1986 after joining Wendy's in 1986 as Senior Vice-President of Special Projects. He had extensive restaurant executive experience from 1967 until joining Wendy's.

Mr. Charles W. Rath, age 52, joined Wendy's in 1987 as Executive Vice-President of Marketing. From 1980 to 1987 he was employed by Dancer, Fitzgerald Sample, an advertising agency in which he served as Senior Vice-President.

Mr. Gordon F. Teter, age 44, joined Wendy's in 1987 as a Senior Vice-President and was promoted to Executive Vice-President of Company Operations in 1988. He had extensive restaurant executive experience with Ponderosa, Inc. and Red Robin International before joining Wendy's.

Mr. John L. Rome, age 33, joined Wendy's in 1974. Since that time, he has held various positions within the International Operations division before being named President of International Operations in 1986.[51]

As of January 3, 1988, Wendy's and its subsidiaries employed approximately 45,000 people, of whom approximately 44,000 were employed in company-operated units. Wendy's management believed that its employee relations were satisfactory, and except for certain employees of The New Bakery Company of Ohio, Inc., the company was not party to any collective bargaining agreements.[52]

Management believed that a renewed commitment to people-oriented programs that included significant improvements to the training for manager trainees and crew members would result in a better quality of life for employees and would improve operating performance. They also believed that recognizing the importance of employees was a major step in reducing turnover of employees, an industry problem.[53] A substantial financial commitment to training was made in 1986 and a vice president was appointed to manage that commitment. It was the belief of management that turnover could be reduced as pride and confidence was built in the training programs. For this reason, training was a high priority. All of the company's training programs were undergoing an updating process, which included the addition of strict specifications on orientation and skill building techniques. Both written and video systems were brought to state-of-the-art levels. New franchise owners and operators underwent fourteen weeks of training, of which eleven weeks were spent on the job at certified training stores, which consistently performed at the highest levels of operational excellence.[54]

A major rift took place between Wendy's management and franchise owners with the announcement in August of 1987 of the plans to expand the test marketing of the SuperBar. "They say we are focusing on burgers, then they do this (the SuperBar)," said Lonnie Stout, president of Winners Corporation, a fifty-nine–unit franchise. "There seems to be some confusion about where we're going." Many franchisees were experimenting with their own menu items and advertising. All this came at a time when 15–20% of Wendy's franchisees were so strapped for cash that they had stopped paying full royalties, according to informed sources.[55] Franchisees were "invited" to join the test of the SuperBar, as opposed to the breakfast program in 1985 in which they were required to participate. Robert Barney, Wendy's CEO, played down the departure that the SuperBar seemed to take from the emphasis on hamburgers. He said in 1987 that hamburgers would remain the focus of the company's advertising.[56]

Wendy's management style was a direct reflection of the personal philosophy of R. David Thomas, Wendy's founder. Mr. Thomas's dream of creating a better burger led to a multi-billion dollar business, but he didn't forget the years he had spent behind the grill and the counter. He believed that only by working behind the counter and at the grill could employees gain the valuable experience necessary for success. As a result, most of Wendy's executives and all franchisees were required to complete an extensive in-store training program. "Everyone was to wear the stripes," he said, referring to the traditional blue-and-white striped Wendy's uniforms.[57]

The New Bakery Company of Ohio, Inc., a wholly owned subsidiary of Wendy's, was a producer of buns for Wendy's restaurants. At the end of 1986 the bakery had supplied a total of 1,678 units with its buns. At that time the bakery did not manufacture or sell any other products.[58]

OPERATIONS

On March 2, 1987, Wendy's announced that it would sell its Sisters units in order to spend more time reviving its 3,727-unit hamburger chain. Sisters International, Inc. was Wendy's second restaurant concept. It was a wholly owned subsidiary of Wendy's. The transaction included thirty-five company operated units and the related trademark and franchise rights. Sisters was sold for $14.5 million in cash and notes. The proceeds of the sale would be used for Wendy's back-to-burgers retrenchment program in addition to bolstering its cash reserves.[59] "We're focusing our efforts on the hamburger business where we have been most successful," said Robert L. Barney, Chief Executive Officer and Chairman.[60] Refocusing on and protecting the hamburger business were main priorities for Wendy's executives at the end of 1986. Mandatory testing of a breakfast menu in 1985 resulted in dismal performance for Wendy's owners who welcomed the return to greater emphasis on hamburgers. After a $4.9 million loss in 1986, positioning Wendy's for a recovery in operating performance was a main objective for 1987.[61] Getting back to basics, the hamburger, was seen as the key to recovery.

Each Wendy's unit offers a relatively standard menu featuring hamburgers, chicken breast sandwiches, chili, chicken nuggets, a salad bar, baked and french fried potatoes, desserts, soft drinks and other nonalcoholic beverages, and a child's meal. The hamburgers and sandwiches were cooked to order with the customer's choice of condiments. A breakfast menu was served at certain units during morning hours. Effective March 10, 1986, the breakfast menu was made optional in each unit.[62] Although the breakfast program was not a success, management remained committed to the development of the breakfast menu. Alternatives were being explored in menu selection, operational efficiency, pricing, and all other facets of the breakfast program.[63] It was disclosed on October 13, 1987, that Wendy's would expand a test of its SuperBar to almost all of its 1,120 company-owned units.[64] The SuperBar was expected to increase store traffic and thus generate additional sales. Wendy's management felt that it was necessary to reevaluate the menu according to customer demand.[65] The SuperBar was a result of that thinking.

Engaged in ongoing research and development, Wendy's tested new products for possible introduction into the Wendy's system. Management believed that research and development should be stepped up in 1987 to help with the turnaround in operating performance.[66] While research and development was considered to be a major factor to good operating performance, the amounts expended on research and development in 1986 were not deemed to be material by management.[67]

Wendy's restaurants were built to the company's specifications as to interior decor and exterior style. Most units were constructed on sites of approximately 30,000 square feet. Parking space was provided for thirty-five to forty cars. The typical unit was a freestanding, one-story building containing 2,700 square feet. Each unit had a cooking area, a dining room for ninety-four persons, and a drive-through pick-up window. The units were usually located in urban or heavily populated suburban areas. The success of each unit depended heavily on serving a large number of customers.

In 1987 Wendy's opened 202 new stores, of which 52 were company-operated and 150 franchise. At the end of 1987, there were 3,816 total stores (see Exhibits 13.4, 13.5 and 13.6).[68] At the beginning of 1987, plans called for the opening of about 260 new units, with a long-term objective of lowering the overall percentage of company-owned units.[69] However, in 1987 it was reported that

EXHIBIT 13.4

Number and Ownership of Domestic Wendy's Units, by States

	COMPANY	FRANCHISE
Alabama	22	40
Alaska	—	9
Arizona	29	24
Arkansas	—	33
California	8	243
Colorado	33	39
Connecticut	—	34
Delaware	13	1
Florida	58	201
Georgia	94	62
Hawaii	—	13
Idaho	—	12
Illinois	108	61
Indiana	33	92
Iowa	—	31
Kansas	—	47
Kentucky	30	37
Louisiana	—	56
Maine	—	6
Maryland	—	73
Massachusetts	19	18
Michigan	57	119
Minnesota	—	34
Mississippi	14	29
Missouri	—	83
Montana	—	10
Nebraska	—	26
Nevada	—	23
New Hampshire	—	13
New Jersey	3	57
New Mexico	—	18
New York	25	114
North Carolina	45	74
North Dakota	—	9
Ohio	161	138
Oklahoma	29	17

(Continued)

EXHIBIT 13.4 **(Continued)**

	COMPANY	FRANCHISE
Oregon	—	39
Pennsylvania	66	92
Rhode Island	2	6
South Carolina	1	56
South Dakota	—	7
Tennessee	—	125
Texas	140	94
Utah	—	21
Vermont	—	5
Virginia	61	56
Washington	—	43
West Virgina	32	7
Wisconsin	31	8
Wyoming	—	9
Dist. of Columbia	—	4
Total	1,114	2,468

SOURCE: Wendy's International, Inc., *1987 Form 10-K*.

EXHIBIT 13.5 **International Wendy's Units**

	COMPANY	FRANCHISE
Bahamas	—	1
Canada	104	16
Guam	—	1
Ireland	—	2
Italy	—	6
Japan	—	30
Malaysia	—	3
New Zealand	—	2
Philippines	—	7
Puerto Rico	—	18
South Korea	—	9
Spain	11	5
Switzerland	—	4
Taiwan	—	11
United Kingdom	—	1
Virgin Islands	—	1
West Germany	—	2
Total	115	119

SOURCE: Wendy's International, Inc., *1987 Form 10-K*.

EXHIBIT 13.6   **Total Number of Wendy's Units**

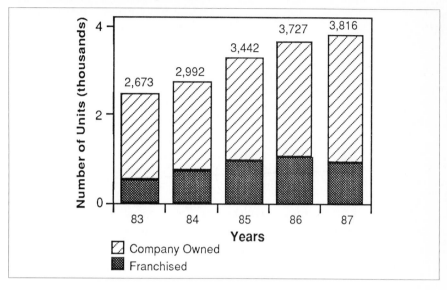

SOURCE: Wendy's International, Inc., *1987 Annual Report.*

Wendy's had scaled back its planned openings in 1987 to between 175 and 200 units.[70] It remained to be seen if the projected openings of 300 units in 1988 would actually materialize.[71]

A realignment program was implemented in 1986 in order to enhance royalty income and return on investment by franchising the vast majority of 120 under-performing domestic company-owned units. In addition, twenty-six international units were targeted for disposal under this program. Management believed that the realignment program would be instrumental in bringing Wendy's back to a strong competitive position.[72]

During 1986, Wendy's closed or sold twenty-two company-owned international units under the realignment plan that called for the elimination of units unlikely to provide a satisfactory return for an international unit, and to limit the company operated market to two countries, Spain and Canada. In addition, five franchise units were also sold. These international units were experiencing unfavorable profits, which prompted management to seek buyers; management sought to eliminate these unprofitable units and to increase royalty income through franchise agreements with the buyers.[73] At the end of 1987, the total number of international units stood at 234.[74] Because of the successful operating results of Far East licenses, especially those in Japan and Taiwan, and the strong Canadian market, management fully intended to continue international development through the use of company owned units and franchise licenses.[75] The

Canadian market could support 400 or more units.[76] In addition to the company operated markets that were being developed in Canada and Spain, franchise rights had been granted in Greece and Guam. The major emphasis for international development was through licensing, which allowed the company to conserve capital for domestic-development while maintaining an income stream from international operations.[77]

Wendy's began offering a financing program in 1981 to assist franchise owners. At the end of 1986 only twenty-one units had been opened in this program. The company received compensation from the operators of these units in the form of commitment fees and rent payments. Wendy's stood to receive all proceeds from the sale or liquidation of the ownership interest in the financed units' properties.[78]

At the end of 1987, franchise owners operated 2,587 units in all fifty states, the District of Columbia and seventeen other countries and territories. The Restaurant Franchise Agreement outlines the rights and franchises that were offered in the United States. This document gave the franchise owner the right to construct, own, and operate a Wendy's restaurant on a site approved by Wendy's.[79] In the past, units were franchised on a multi-unit basis; however, the company intended to franchise new units exclusively on a single-unit method, in which franchise rights were granted on a restaurant-by-restaurant basis. By franchising one store at a time, this program aided franchise growth; the company chose and developed the market location. Forty-six units were added under this method in 1986, and one hundred units were expected in 1987.[80] The Restaurant Franchise Agreement required the franchise owner to pay a royalty of 4% of gross receipts from the operation of the unit. In addition, a technical assistance fee of $25,000 was required for each unit, to defray the cost to Wendy's of providing site selection assistance, standard construction plans, specifications and layouts, and other business related matters.[81] Wendy's did not select or employ personnel on behalf of the franchise owners.[82] In addition to reducing the overall percentage of company operated units, Wendy's management also planned to franchise other company units, while taking advantage of opportunities to buy franchised units under the right circumstances. Management believed that the benefits of this action would be to increase administration efficiency and a more productive alignment of company units.[83]

Management believed that, because of lower operating performance in 1986, the development and strategy for operations was of utmost importance. Excellence in restaurant operations was perceived to be the key to success for Wendy's. Management began to reassess virtually every aspect of how the units were operated in 1987. A task force system was utilized. This task force was comprised of small groups of experts from several different fields, which reviewed the various aspects of in-store operations. The use of the task force allowed for concentration on specific problems, with direct resolutions.[84] Specifically, in operations, the issues that were addressed included menu simplification, new and increased levels of training, kitchen and equipment redesigns, and easier operational procedures.[85] To maintain quality and uniformity throughout all units, Wendy's provided detailed specifications for food products, preparation, and service. This was hoped to be achieved through the continual training of employees and from field visits from company supervisors and members of the task force.[86] In 1984 Wendy's began a program called Project BEST, which stood for Beat Every Sales Tactic. The major thrust of this program involved image enhancement of individual units, new menu items, new serving hours, separate marketing campaigns, redefinition of roles and responsibilities of store managers, and new state-of-the-art restaurant operating systems.[87]

MARKETING

Wendy's National Advertising Program (WNAP)

Wendy's restaurants were advertised through the use of television, radio, newspapers, and numerous promotional campaigns. In order to integrate company advertising with the various franchisees, Wendy's distributed to franchise owners a newsletter that informed them of current advertising techniques and promotions. To share the costs for such marketing between the company and the franchisees, the Restaurant Franchise Agreement provided that franchise owners spend 4% of their gross receipts for advertising and promotions: 2% for local and regional advertising and 2% as a required contribution to Wendy's National Advertising Program (WNAP). Wendy's had the right under the agreement to increase the required local expenditures to 3%, for a total of 5% per franchise, as long as Wendy's contributed 5% for all domestic company owned restaurants.[88]

WNAP is a non-profit corporation. It is headed by a committee of nine elected franchise owners and seven corporate representatives. During 1986, 1985, and 1984, the company contributed $17,843,000, $18,143,000 and $12,312,000 respectively to WNAP as is shown in Exhibit 13.7. In 1986, Wendy's International and its franchisees spent an estimated total of $140 million on advertising and promotion.[89]

There had been many changes occurring within the Marketing Division of Wendy's. During the past decade, these changes involved the use of advertising agencies and product mix.

Advertising Agencies

From the middle to the latter part of the 1970s, Wendy's retained Dick Rich, Inc. as its advertising agency. Rich was a one-man operation in New York. His primary objective was to focus on the Wendy's hamburger. Rich was retained as the ad agency for Wendy's for four years. During his tenure, Rich created the "Hot 'N Juicy" ad campaign, which catapulted Wendy's to become a national power. However, in 1980, three factors contributed to the end of the Wendy's–Rich relationship: the escalating price of beef, consumers supposedly getting tired of "just hamburgers," and Wendy's wanting to broaden its product mix. In 1980, Rich was fired.[90]

EXHIBIT 13.7   **Wendy's Contributions to WNAP**

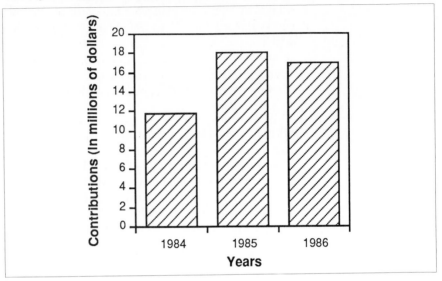

SOURCE: Wendy's International, Inc., *1986 Annual Report,* pp. 8 and 29.

The results of product diversification and the accompanying diverse advertising approaches were the slowing down of Wendy's system, customer confusion, and loss of the burger-oriented identity as a trade-off for developing new products and a wider scope.[91] Wendy's then hired DFS Dorland Worldwide to be its ad agency. DFS succeeded in aiding Wendy's to maintain its third position among the burger chains, behind McDonald's and Burger King. DFS created such classics as the "Where's the Beef?" campaign with Clara Peller and the "Big Classic" features. Although these ads established visibility for Wendy's from 1984 through most of 1986, Wendy's reported a third quarter loss in 1986. The reasons cited for this loss were the failure of a breakfast campaign, and Wendy's having the smallest percentage of family trade among the big three burger chains. To alleviate these problems, Wendy's fired DFS and decided to once again concentrate on burgers.[92]

To better emphasize product focus, Wendy's returned to the previously hired and fired ad man, Dick Rich, in November of 1986. Why was Rich chosen again? William Welter, Wendy's top marketing official, who later resigned, stated, "He is probably one of the most brilliant strategists. He knows the Wendy's business better than anyone else."[93] However, Rich's "Give a little nibble" ads flopped in the Spring of 1987, and Rich was once again on his way out.[94] *Advertising Age* commented that these ads were "irritating"; however, Wendy's competitors were pleased with the ads because they did not work.[95]

The most recent ad agency to take the Wendy's advertising account was Backer Spielvogel Bates (BSB). BSB had dropped the $10 million annual account of Arby's to take the Wendy's account. BSB also handled Campbell Soup Company, Miller Brewing Company, NCR Corporation, Fisher-Price, and Hyundai Motor of America, among others. The recently hired Executive Vice-President of Marketing for Wendy's, Charles W. Rath, said that Backer had the resources, discipline, and creative capabilities "to reach beyond where we have been in the past." The ad campaign most recently featured by BSB was the "Hamburger A" spots. These spots were based on a creation of the DFS agency, but the new tagline on the commercial stated, "Wendy's. The Best Burgers in the Business." These ads presented an interviewer located in a public area asking interviewees their choice between "Hamburger A" and "Hamburger B." "Hamburger A" is Wendy's burger and is obviously the best choice, but the weird and bizarre interviewees always picked "Hamburger B" for all the wrong reasons. These newest "Hamburger A" commercials were to be used during the interim period by BSB until it came out with its first major campaign for Wendy's during the winter of 1987–1988.[96] Randolf C. Lindel, Senior Vice-President of BSB and Account Director for Wendy's, said that Wendy's future plans included being "very aggressive in new products to expand its competitive position." Future products under consideration included a small burger called Hot 'N Junior, a double deluxe sandwich, a soft-serve ice cream dessert, a line of biscuit breakfast sandwiches, a prepackaged chef's salad, and a "super" bar.[97] Wendy's many changes in advertising firms and their related campaigns and expenditures are summarized in Exhibit 13.8.

EXHIBIT 13.8   **Wendy's Advertising Campaigns, 1977–1988**

YEAR(S)	NAME	AGENCY	SPENDING
1977–1980	Hot 'n Juicy	Dick Rich	$ 4 mil/yr
1981	Wendy's Has the Taste	Colarossi	$ 56 mil/yr
1981–1982	Ain't No Reason	DFS	$ 64 mil/yr
1982–1984	Wendy's Kind of People	DFS	$ 75 mil/yr
1984	Where's the Beef?	DFS	$ 90 mil/yr
1985	Choose Fresh. Choose Wendy's.	DFS	$100 mil/yr
1986	This is the Good Stuff	DFS/Dorland	$110 mil/yr
1987	Give a Little Nibble	Dick Rich	N/A
1987–1988	Hamburger "A"	BSB	N/A

SOURCE: Wendy's International, Inc., 1988.

SuperBar

Among the various products tested were the small hamburgers and SuperBar. The small hamburgers were a result of growing consumer demands for greater convenience. These burgers weighed 2 ounces and were priced at $.54. They had been tested at Milwaukee for several months.[98]

The other new product was the SuperBar. The SuperBar was a mini-smorgasbord with an array of fifty items. The 18-foot long spread included such items as fresh fruits, vegetables, desserts, a Mexican Fiesta station featuring tacos and nachos, a pasta selection that included fettuccine and rotini macaroni, and a top-your-own-baked-potato division. Wendy's had earmarked $35 million for the addition of SuperBars and had invited franchisees to install them at a cost of $30,000 to $40,000 per restaurant. Wendy's officers said they had asked the board of directors to establish a lending fund for franchisees needing financial aid for the changeover. At company test sites, the SuperBar had generated 15% incremental sales gains. Wendy's had considered lunch, dinner, and breakfast bars, and had explored ways of using the bar as a marketing tool to bolster customer traffic during slack periods.[99]

FINANCE

Despite recording a $4.5 million net profit in 1987 compared to a $4.9 million net loss in 1986, Wendy's suffered several financial setbacks. Retail sales declined 4.8% in 1987 over 1986. Similarly, total revenues from all sources declined from $1,139.9 million in 1986 to $1,058.6 million in 1987. The year 1987 had been the first year in the last ten years that Wendy's posted a decline in retail sales and total revenues from all sources. In 1978, the company had retail sales and total revenues of $198.5 million and $226.2 million respectively as compared to $987.1 million and $1,058.6 million respectively at the end of 1987.[100]

Wendy's stock price slumped to a low of $5.63 at the end of 1987 from a high of $18.00 during 1985.[101] Several Wall Street analysts and observers were advising "investors to hold the stock and sell on strength."[102] Po Folks, Inc., one of Wendy's larger franchisees (owning 141 units of Wendy's), had, like several others, been plagued with operating losses that stemmed, in part, from Wendy's inability to fully recover from increased competition, sales declines, and the disastrous breakfast program that had been scrapped in 1986.[103]

Average net sales for domestic company-operated restaurants increased 2.7% in 1987, following a decline of 10% in 1986; but there was a decline in franchise restaurants from $748,000 in 1986 to $721,000 in 1987. Exhibit 13.9 shows the average net sales per domestic restaurant in 1987, 1986 and 1985. Although the number of franchise restaurants in operation increased in both years, average net sales per domestic restaurant declined 3.6% and 11.6% in 1987 and 1986 respectively. This decline reflected that Wendy's franchisees were against the wall financially. It is yet to be seen how well the franchisees can recover from the slump despite Wendy's assistance in cost and financial management.[104]

EXHIBIT 13.9

Average Net Sales for Domestic Restaurants, Wendy's International, Inc.

	1987	1986	1985
Company	$786,000	$765,000	$850,000
Franchise	721,000	748,000	846,000
Total domestic	741,000	754,000	847,000

SOURCE: Wendy's International, *1987 Annual Report*, p. 10.

EXHIBIT 13.10

Consolidated Balance Sheet, Wendy's International, Inc.

(Dollar Amounts in Thousands)

	JAN. 3, 1988	DEC. 31, 1986
Assets		
Current assets		
Cash and short-term investments	$ 31,847	$ 31,911
Accounts and notes receivable (net)	20,334	15,213
Inventories	19,568	23,989
Income taxes receivable and deferred	20,962	—
Assets held for realignment	5,469	26,799
Total current assets	98,180	97,912
Property and equipment, at cost	822,976	820,484
Less accumulated depreciation	(219,322)	(184,261)
Other assets	71,939	67,023
Total assets	$773,773	$801,158
Liabilities and shareholders' equity		
Current liabilities		
Accounts and drafts payable	$ 55,982	$ 51,430
Accrued expenses	63,154	54,483
Realignment reserve	3,889	14,758
Current portion of long-term debt	8,136	4,378
Total current liabilities	131,161	125,049
Long-term obligations	187,456	215,903
Deferred income taxes	42,993	35,507
Shareholders' equity		
Common stock	9,667	9,622
Capital in excess of stated value	126,063	123,211
Retained earnings	281,775	300,235
Translation adjustments	3,204	1,509
Less treasury stock	(8,546)	(9,878)
Total shareholders' equity	412,163	424,699
Total liabilities and shareholders' equity	$773,773	$801,158

SOURCE: Wendy's International, Inc., *1987 Annual Report*.

The year 1987 was a year of transition for Wendy's from both operational and financial points of view. Wendy's almost concluded the realignment plan initiated in 1986 aimed at turning around the company's operating performance and its financial outlook.[105] "The steps we've taken to improve restaurant operations ... are beginning to pay off," said Chairman and Chief Executive Robert Barney. However, observers remained skeptical as to whether the chain's turnaround efforts would show up. "They have a batch of problems and they don't have a clear-cut strategy," said Neal Kaplan of Interstate Securities.[106]

The consolidated statement of income and consolidated balance sheet of Wendy's International, Inc. for the years ended 1987 and 1986 appear as Exhibits 13.10 and 13.11. Changes in revenues for 1987 and 1986 primarily reflect gains from dispositions of restaurant properties amounting to $11.7 million in 1987 and $27.9 million in 1986. Net income in 1987 includes a $1 million extraordinary gain on early extinguishment of debt. Other revenues in 1987 also

---

EXHIBIT 13.11 **Consolidated Statement of Income, Wendy's International, Inc.**

(Dollar Amounts in Thousands)

	JAN. 3, 1988	DEC. 31, 1986
Revenues		
Retail sales	$ 987,071	$1,036,528
Royalties and other	71,486	103,324
Total revenue	1,058,557	1,139,852
Costs and expenses		
Cost of sales	610,971	610,983
Operating and personnel expenses	308,810	299,013
General and administrative expenses	77,333	70,233
Depreciation and amortization	53,894	56,419
Interest (net)	19,565	18,455
Realignment expenses	—	73,421
Total costs and expenses	1,070,573	1,128,524
Income (loss) before taxes & extraordinary gain	(12,016)	11,328
Income taxes (benefits)	(15,488)	16,254
Income (loss) before extraordinary gain	3,472	(4,926)
Extraordinary gain	1,033	—
Net income (loss)	$ 4,505	$ (4,926)

SOURCE: Wendy's International, Inc., *1987 Annual Report.*

included $7.3 million in charges for asset write-offs in preparation for installation of the SuperBar concept in company operated restaurants.[107]

Shareholders' Equity declined from $425 million in 1986 to $412 million in 1987. Cash flow from operations was $61.9 million in 1987, substantially lower than the 1986 figure of $92.4 million. Earnings per share figures reflect the fluctuation in income during the last three years: from a high of $0.82 in 1985 to a negative $0.05 in 1986, and then to a positive $0.05 in 1987. This is shown in Exhibit 13.12. However, dividends distributed had consistently shown a moderate rise. The decrease in long-term obligations reflects the purchase of convertible debentures and the elimination of debt associated with the West German operations. The company's ratio of current assets to current liabilities was .75 versus .78 at the end of 1986. Net accounts receivable increased from year-end 1986, primarily reflecting royalties due from franchise owners.[108] Some selected financial data taken from Wendy's 1987 Annual Report are reproduced in Exhibit 13.13 for comparative analysis.[109]

EXHIBIT 13.12   **Earnings (Loss) per Share**

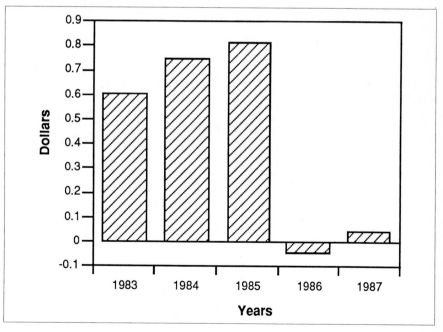

SOURCE: Wendy's International, Inc., *1987 Annual Report,* p. 12.

EXHIBIT 13.13

Selected Financial Data, Wendy's International, Inc.,

	1987	1986
Operations (in millions)		
Retail sales	$ 987.1	$1,036.5
Revenues	1,058.6	1,139.9
Operating profits	81.9	137.7
Net income (loss)	4.5	(4.9)
Financial position (in millions)		
Total assets	$ 773.8	$ 801.2
Property & equipment (net)	603.7	636.2
Long-term obligations	186.1	213.9
Shareholders' equity	412.2	424.7
Per share data		
Net income (loss)	$ 0.05	$ (0.05)
Dividends	0.24	0.21
Shareholders' equity	4.29	4.45
Market price, year-end	5.63	10.25
Other (year-end)		
Shareholders of record	52,000	48,000
Number of employees	45,000	50,000

SOURCE: Wendy's International, Inc., *1987 Annual Report,* p. 14.

CLOSING REMARKS

Commenting on the Wendy's of the 1990s, Robert L. Barney, Chairman and Chief Executive Officer, said, "I have a clear picture of what our image will be and what we will be known for: serving the highest quality, best-tasting hamburger in the quick-service industry; fast accurate service; a menu with a broader appeal to families and customers for all dayparts, weekdays and weekends; a competitive price–value perception; and a pleasant, contemporary eating environment."[110]

The CEO further commented, "We have a clear direction for 1988 and there is growing momentum throughout the Wendy's system. We will concentrate on our hamburger business and use SuperBar to attract new customers and encourage repeat business. And we have a consistent marketing message that will bring customers into our restaurants. These and other programs make me very optimistic about Wendy's future."[111]

Notwithstanding the above remarks by Barney, industry experts and analysts remained skeptical about Wendy's competitiveness, financial viability, and quick-service image. In addition to their own financial woes, takeover rumors have surfaced. Both Coca-Cola Company and Anheuser-Busch were named as potential buyers; however, neither would comment on the rumors.[112] Whether Wendy's can hold the dreams of its founder, therefore, is questionable.

NOTES

1. "Wendy's Road To Recovery Still Bumpy," *Nation's Restaurant News*, August 31, 1987, p. 44.

2. *Ibid*, p. 44.

3. *Ibid*, p. 44.

4. Wendy's International, Inc., "Backgrounder," p. 1.

5. Wendy's International, Inc., "How Wendy's Founder Worked His Way To Success," p. 1.

6. *Ibid*, p. 1.

7. *Ibid*, p. 2.

8. *Ibid*, p. 2.

9. *Ibid*, p. 2.

10. *Ibid*, p. 3.

11. Wendy's International, Inc., "Historical Highlights of Wendy's International, Inc.," p. 1.

12. *Ibid*, p. 1.

13. Wendy's International, Inc., "Backgrounder," p. 1.

14. Wendy's International, Inc., "Historical Highlights of Wendy's International, Inc.," p. 2.

15. *Ibid*, p. 2.

16. *Ibid*, p. 2.

17. *Ibid*, p. 2.

18. Wendy's International, Inc., "Backgrounder," pp. 1 & 2.

19. Wendy's International, Inc., *1987 Annual Report*, inside front cover page.

20. Wendy's International, Inc., *1986 Annual Report*, p. 1.

21. Wendy's International, Inc., *Form 10-K* (Washington, DC: Securities and Exchange Commission, December 31, 1986) p. 2.

22. Dan Cook, "The Fast Food Industry is Slowing Down," *Business Week*, May 18, 1987, p. 50.

23. *Ibid*, p. 50.

24. Wendy's International, Inc., *1986 Annual Report*, p. 2.

25. James Cox, "New Ads Aim to Whop McDonald's," *USA Today*, February 17, 1988, p. 1–2B.

26. "Restaurant Industry," *Value Line*, October 2, 1987, p. 312.

27. David Zuckerman, "Burger Biggies Caught In Copycat Quandary," *Nation's Restaurant News*, August 11, 1986, p. 18.

28. Scott Hume, "Wendy's Aims to Get Better With Its BEST," *Advertising Age*, April 30, 1984, pp. 4 & 64.

29. James Cox, "New Ads Aim to Whop McDonald's," *USA Today*, pp. 1 & 2B.

30. *Ibid*, p. 2B.

31. Dan Cook, "The Fast Food Industry is Slowing Down," *Business Week*, May 18, 1987, p. 50.

32. Don Jeffrey, "Wendy's Opens First Hotel Unit At Day's Inn, Sells 31 Outlets," *Nation's Restaurant News*, April 15, 1986, p. 3.

33. *Ibid*, p. 3.

34. Don Jeffrey, "Wendy's Joins Baskin-Robbins In Second Venture," *Nation's Restaurant News*, February 2, 1987, p. 3.

35. James Cox, "New Ads Aim to Whop McDonald's," *USA Today*, pp. 1 & 2B.

36. "Restaurant Industry," *Value Line*, October 2, 1987, p. 312.

37. Wendy's International, Inc., *1986 Annual Report*, p. 2.

38. "Restaurant Industry," *Value Line*, October 2, 1987, p. 312.

39. Ken Rankin, "House Mulls Minimum Wage Hike," *Nation's Restaurant News*, January 26, 1987, p. 1.

40. Wendy's International, Inc., *1986 Annual Report*, p. 17.

41. Wendy's International, Inc., *1986 Form 10-K*, (Securities and Exchange Commission), December 31, 1986, p. 10.

42. *Ibid*, p. 10.

43. "Wendy's Becomes First Food Chain to Join POS Funds Transfer System," *American Banker*, March 13, 1987, p. 16.

44. Don Jeffrey, "BK, Wendy's Test Small Hamburgers," *Nation's Restaurant News*, January 26, 1987, p. 83.

45. *Ibid*, pp. 1 & 83.

46. Marilyn Alva, "Wendy's Returns To A Single-Minded Focus On Hamburgers," *Nation's Restaurant News*, November 17, 1986, p. 15.

47. "Wendy's International Cuts 20% of Administrative Jobs," *Wall Street Journal*, May 21, 1987, p. 4.

48. Don Jeffrey, "Wendy's Opens First Hotel Unit At Day's Inn, Sells 31 Outlets," *Nation's Restaurant News*, April 15, 1986, p. 3.

49. Rick Van Warner, "Wendy's Slashes Support Staff," *Nation's Restaurant News*, June 1, 1987, pp. 1 & 166.

50. "Wendy's International Cuts 20% of Administrative Jobs," *Wall Street Journal*, May 21, 1987, p. 4.

51. Wendy's International, Inc., *1986 and 1987 Form 10-K*.

52. Wendy's International, Inc., *1987 Form 10-K*, p. 7.

53. Wendy's International, Inc., *1986 Annual Report*, p. 2.

54. *Ibid*, p. 6.

55. Peter J. Romeo, "Wendy's Franchisees Draft Own Turnaround Strategies," *Nation's Restaurant News*, August 17, 1987, p. 1.

56. Richard Koenig, "Wendy's to Expand Test of 'SuperBar' to Most of Its 1120 Owned Restaurants," *Wall Street Journal*, October 13, 1987, p. 38(E) col. 3.

57. Wendy's International, Inc., "How Wendy's Founder Worked His Way to Success," p. 2.

58. Wendy's International, Inc., *1986 Form 10-K*, p. 3.

59. *Ibid*, p. 7.

60. Peter Romeo, "Wendy's Okays Sale of its 70 Sisters Units," *Nation's Restaurant News*, March 2, 1987, pp. 1 & 16.

61. Wendy's International, Inc., *1986 Annual Report*, p. 2.

62. Wendy's International Inc., *Form 10-K* (Securities and Exchange Commission) December 31, 1986, p. 2.

63. Wendy's International, Inc., *1986 Annual Report*, p. 17.

64. Richard Koenig, "Wendy's to Expand Test of 'SuperBar' to Most of its 1120 Owned Restaurants," *Wall Street Journal*, October 13, 1987, p. 38(E) col. 3.

65. Wendy's International, Inc., *1986 Annual Report*, pp. 2 & 3.

66. *Ibid*, p. 17.

67. Wendy's International, Inc., *1986 Form 10-K*, p. 4.

68. Wendy's International, Inc., *1987 Annual Report*, p. 3.

69. *Ibid*, p. 4.

70. "Wendy's International Cuts 20% of Administrative Jobs," *Wall Street Journal*, May 21, 1987, p. 4.

71. Wendy's International, Inc., *1986 Annual Report*, p. 16.

72. *Ibid*, p. 2.

73. *Ibid*, p. 2.

74. Wendy's International, Inc., *1987 Form 10-K*, p. 8.

75. Wendy's International, Inc., *1986 Annual Report*, p. 13.

76. *Ibid*, p. 13.

77. *Ibid*, p. 17.

78. Wendy's International, Inc., *1986 Form 10-K*, p. 6.

79. Wendy's International, Inc., *1987 Form 10-K*, p. 8.

80. Wendy's International, Inc., *1986 Annual Report*, p. 4.

81. Wendy's International, Inc., *1986 Form 10-K*, p. 5.

82. *Ibid*, p. 6.

83. Wendy's International, Inc., *1986 Annual Report*, p. 17.

84. Ibid., p. 6.

85. *Ibid*, p. 17.

86. Wendy's International, Inc., *1986 Form 10-K*, p. 2.

87. Scott Hume, "Wendy's Aims to Get Better with its Best," *Advertising Age*, April 30, 1984, pp. 4 & 64.

88. Wendy's International, Inc., *Form 10-K* (Securities and Exchange Commission, December 31, 1986) page 6.

89. Wendy's International, Inc., *1986 Annual Report*, pp. 8 & 29.

90. Charles Bernstein, Editor's Corner, "Back to Burgers: Wendy's Resurrects Dick Rich," *Nation's Restaurant News*, December 1, 1986, page 9.

91. *Ibid*, p. 9.

92. Marilyn Alva, "Wendy's Returns to a 'Single-Minded' Focus on Hamburgers" *Nation's Restaurant News*, November 17, 1986, page 15.

93. *Ibid*, p. 15.

94. Marilyn Alva, "Wendy's New Agency Stages Second Coming of 'Hamburger A,'" *Nation's Restaurant News*, October 5, 1987, page 12.

95. Dan Cook, "Wendy's Tries Warming Up the Basic Burger," *Business Week*, May 1987, page 51.

96. Marilyn Alva, "Wendy's New Agency Stages Second Coming of 'Hamburger A,'" page 12.

97. Marilyn Alva, "B&S in Hand, Wendy's Aim:

Broad Ad Focus," *Nation's Restaurant News*, June 29, 1987, pp. 1 & 71.

98. Don Jeffrey, "BK, Wendy's Test Small Hamburgers," *Nation's Restaurant News*, January 26, 1987, pp. 1 & 83.

99. Peter J. Jones, "Wendy's Rolls Superbar in New Turnaround Bid," *Nation's Restaurant News*, October 26, 1987, pp. 1 & 52.

100. Wendy's International, Inc., *1987 Annual Report*, p. 14.

101. Rick Telberg, "Wendy's Retrenchment Surprises, Dismays Wall Street Analysts, "*Nation's Restaurant News*, November 17, 1986, p. 94.

102. "Wendy's Road to Recovery Still Bumpy," *Nation's Restaurant News*, August 31, 1987, p. 44.

103. Rick Van Warner, "Po Folks To Sell Wendy's Franchise For $1.75M Cash," *Nation's Restaurant News*, August 10, 1987, p. 3.

104. Wendy's International, Inc., *1987 Annual Report*, p. 11.

105. *Ibid*, p. 10.

106. "Wendy's International Profits Tumble 92 Percent," *Nation's Restaurant News*, August 10, 1987, p. 4.

107. Wendy's International, Inc., *1987 Annual Report*, p. 11.

108. *Ibid*, p. 12.

109. *Ibid*, p. 14.

110. Wendy's International. Inc., "1986 Annual Meeting Highlights—First Quarter Results," p. 2.

111. Wendy's International, Inc., "Press Release dated February 15, 1988," p. 2.

112. Gene G. Marcial, "Coke May Be Going Where The Beef Is," *Business Week*, March 30, 1987, p. 74.

The Hardee's Dilemma

WARD D. HARDER

On December 8, 1987, John Gibson, Vice-President and General Manager of the West Tennessee Restaurant Corporation (WTRC), was reviewing the latest financial statements of the company at November 30, 1987, which he and his wife had prepared. The results showed that revenues were declining and losses were mounting.

Gibson placed a conference call to the other three stockholders to inform them of the latest financial results. Jerry Soles, Fred Musselwhite, and Henry Lewis were extremely upset when Gibson told them the company had lost $223,000 in the last three months.

MUSSELWHITE: "How can we make $85,000 for fiscal year ended August 31 and turn around and lose $223,000 in September, October, and November? I just don't understand it."

SOLES: "John, you had better have a good explanation or else—I'm for hiring a new general manager."

LEWIS: "If I ran my CPA firm like we are running WTRC, I would be out of business . . . and that may be where we are."

Each of the four stockholders agreed to consider various alternatives which might be available to them.

HISTORY

In July 1986, John Gibson was employed as Executive Vice-President of Regency Investments, Inc. Regency was organized in 1980 to secure Hardee's franchises in North Carolina. Shortly after Gibson began to work with Regency, the company secured the franchise rights to six locations in North Georgia. Gibson supervised the construction and opening of these units.

While working in North Georgia, Gibson met Nelson Storrie of Boone, North Carolina. Storrie had secured the franchise rights to four locations in West Tennessee—Lexington, Milan, Savannah, and Waverly. (See Exhibit 14.1.) He was operating under the name of H & S Restaurants. Storrie was interested in selling these four units because it was over 600 miles from Boone, North Carolina, to the closest unit in Waverly. In addition, he was aware of the problems associated with absentee ownership.

Storrie opened his first unit in Lexington in May 1983. This unit had achieved the highest sales volume of any unit. In October 1983, a second unit was opened

This case was prepared by Professor Ward D. Harder of Motlow State Community College. It was presented at the Midwest Society for Case Research Workshop, 1988. All rights reserved to the author and the Midwest Society for Case Research. Copyright © 1988 by Ward D. Harder. Reprinted by permission.

EXHIBIT 14.1   **Map of West Tennessee**

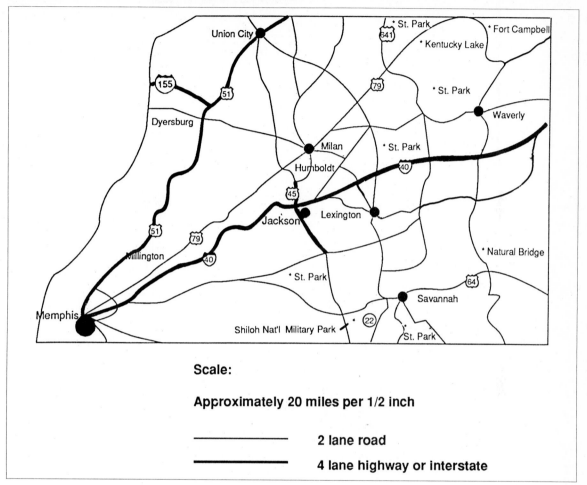

Scale:

Approximately 20 miles per 1/2 inch

————————   **2 lane road**

━━━━━━━━   **4 lane highway or interstate**

in Savannah. Sales at this unit had been unstable. Financing for both units was secured from Franchise Finance Corporation of America (FFC) in Phoenix, Arizona. In June 1985, units were opened in Milan and Waverly. Sales at the Waverly location had been consistently higher than at Milan. (See Exhibit 14.2.)

With his background at Regency, Gibson was very interested in forming a corporation to purchase the four units from Storrie. (See Exhibit 14.3.) Gibson contacted three of his business associates in Boone, North Carolina, about investing in this venture. Henry Lewis was a CPA who owned his own practice in

EXHIBIT 14.2

Unit Sales, January 1983–August 1986, West Tennessee Restaurant Corporation
(Dollar Amounts in Thousands)

MONTHLY SALES

FRAN. NAME	Jan 86	Feb 86	Mar 86	Apr 86	May 86	Jun 86	Jul 86	Aug 86
Lexington	71.905	67.412	84.272	82.960	92.457	87.956	86.271	74.723
Savannah	46.738	43.733	59.703	52.354	57.647	54.455	57.086	52.415
Waverly	56.670	50.702	61.036	58.045	64.278	70.032	62.878	56.770
Milan	39.655	39.542	47.027	41.811	51.142	52.072	50.336	46.270

	Jan 85	Feb 85	Mar 85	Apr 85	May 85	Jun 85	Jul 85	Aug 85	Sep 85	Oct 85	Nov 85	Dec 85
Lexington	48.129	49.308	68.598	68.448	75.343	78.453	80.387	77.209	70.632	80.866	76.923	77.392
Savannah	36.191	33.032	46.485	45.826	48.293	52.010	52.429	47.155	44.893	48.750	48.605	47.450
Waverly	0	0	0	0	0	114.921	87.058	87.412	72.040	78.324	71.745	66.066
Milan	0	0	0	0	0	24.382	68.778	53.329	46.816	46.515	44.809	43.610

	Jan 84	Feb 84	Mar 84	Apr 84	May 84	Jun 84	Jul 84	Aug 84	Sep 84	Oct 84	Nov 84	Dec 84
Lexington	50.588	53.151	63.468	65.139	67.515	75.172	67.794	66.245	62.382	61.794	60.010	66.888
Savannah	44.070	46.259	53.273	48.844	51.213	56.215	56.162	53.764	52.279	57.615	49.093	52.203
Waverly	0	0	0	0	0	0	0	0	0	0	0	0
Milan	0	0	0	0	0	0	0	0	0	0	0	0

	Jan 83	Feb 83	Mar 83	Apr 83	May 83	Jun 83	Jul 83	Aug 83	Sep 83	Oct 83	Nov 83	Dec 83
Lexington	0	0	0	0	4.451	96.296	75.163	63.460	53.866	50.845	53.659	57.443
Savannah	0	0	0	0	0	0	0	0	0	79.815	61.279	53.429
Waverly	NA	NA	NA	0	0	0	0	0	0	0	0	0
Milan	NA	NA	NA	0	0	0	0	0	0	0	0	0

EXHIBIT 14.3   ## Resumé of John A. Gibson

EXPERIENCE

September, 1986–February, 1988
Vice President and General Manager
West Tennessee Restaurants, Inc.
Milan TN.

Franchisee and chief operating officer for company operating four (4) Hardee's restaurants in the West Tennessee area (Lexington, Savannah, Waverly and Milan). Responsible for the entire operation of the company.

March, 1982–August, 1986
Executive Vice President
Regency Investments, Inc.
Boone N.C.

Chief executive officer for company reporting directly to the board of directors. Responsible for the entire operation of a Hardee's franchisee operating at one time as many as eleven (11) units. Duties include supervision of the administrative staff. During the first three years of employment with Regency the company opened six (6) Hardee's.

July, 1981–March, 1982
Manager
Peaches, Inc.
Greenville N.C.

Manager of Private club with mixed beverages featuring live entertainment as well as recorded music presented by in-house disc jockeys. Duties included: purchasing all inventory; employing and training all personnel; scheduling all entertainment; supervision of bookkeeping; payroll; filing all tax reports; coordinating advertising.

January, 1979–July, 1981
Partner and Manager
Quincy's Old Place
Lumberton, N.C.

Managed a 48-seat restaurant and 300 seat-club featuring live entertainment as well as recorded music presented by in-house disc jockeys. Duties included: purchasing all inventory; employing and training all personnel; scheduling all entertainment; supervision of bookkeeping; payroll; filing all tax reports; coordinating advertising.

June, 1978–January, 1979
Partner
Jerico Enterprises
Lumberton, N.C.

Operated a management firm for two convenience stores, two restaurants and one restaurant/discotheque. Duties included: supervision of management at each location, plus supervision of bookkeeping, payroll, tax reports, etc., of entire operation.

(Continued)

EXHIBIT 14.3 **(Continued)**

January, 1977–June, 1978
Owner and Manager
Fins, Furs & Feather Pet Shop
Lumberton, N.C.

October, 1975–January, 1977
Assistant Commissioner of Labor
North Carolina Department of Labor
Raleigh, N.C.

Administrative and managerial employment as immediate assistant to the Commissioner of Labor. Duties included: directing, managing, and coordinating the
day-to-day operational functions of the department working closely with the
Deputy Commissioner in evaluating existing programs, deciding questions of
policy, and in planning   for future services.

July, 1970–October, 1975
Executive Vice President
North Carolina Jaycees
Asheboro, N.C.

Served as chief administrator for the State Jaycee organization with overall
management responsibilities for the corporation. Duties included: supervision
of the office staff; preparing and administering yearly budget; securing corporate
sponsors for major state projects; coordinating all regional and state meetings;
i.e., programs, publicity, agendas, etc.; developed marketing program for Jaycee
sales items (plaques, jewelry, clothing items, etc.); coordinated travel schedule
of state Jaycee president (speaking engagements); served as liaison officer between state organization and national Jaycee organization. Also coordinated
public relations programs.

1964–1970
Agent and Staff Manager
State Capital Life Insurance Company
Lumberton and Newton, N.C.

Originally appointed as a sales representative and later promoted to a staff
manager's position supervising five agents.

1958–1964
Sales Representative
Gibson Sales Company
(Wholesale farm equipment dealer)
Lumberton, N.C.

Traveled eastern North and South Carolina calling on retail farm equipment
dealers.

EDUCATION

Littlefield High School
Lumberton, N.C.
Graduated, 1958

Attended Carolina School of Broadcasting
Charlotte, N.C.

Raleigh Institute of Realty, Inc.
Raleigh, N.C.
Graduated, 1977
(Holder of a current North Carolina Broker's License)

Hardee's Management Internship
Graduated June 30, 1982

Hardee's BASIC for Crew Selection
Presented Certificate of Achievement December 15, 1982

Hardee's Management BASIC
Behavior Assessment Selection Interview Course
June, 1985

State of North Carolina, Division of Health Services
Food Service Manager's Training Course in Food
Protection and Sanitation
November, 1985

Hardee's Performance Planning and Review
July, 1985

PERSONAL

Born:	August 16, 1941 (age 46)
Height:	5′ 11½″
Weight:	190 lbs.
Married:	5 children
Health:	Good–No physical limitations
Hobbies:	Camping, Fishing, Swimming
Affiliations:	Former president of Newton, North Carolina, Jaycees
	Life Member of the Newton, North Carolina, Jaycees
	Life Member of the North Carolina, Jaycees
	JCI Senator
	Former member of the Newton, North Carolina, Elks Lodge
	Member of Boone Area Chamber of Commerce
	Elected member of the Hardee's Area III Business Planning Council
	Elected member of the Hardee's Marketing Advisory Review Council (one of only 22 elected members representing the franchise community in the entire Hardee's system)
	Member Milan Lions Club

Lumberton, North Carolina. Fred Musselwhite was a prominent attorney in Boone who had an established law practice. Jerry Soles was the owner and operator of a very successful 300-seat restaurant in Boone. He had started the restaurant ten years before, and it was very profitable.

After an initial meeting with the three potential stockholders, Gibson scheduled a visit to each of the four units in West Tennessee. Lewis was a licensed pilot with his own airplane. On August 3, 1987, the group flew to Jackson, Tennessee, and drove to the Hardee's in Lexington, Milan, and Waverly. The weather forecast included thunderstorms, so the group returned to Boone without visiting the Savannah location. Additional information concerning each

EXHIBIT 14.4   Supplemental Information on Locations

	LEXINGTON	MILAN	SAVANNAH	WAVERLY
Population				
City	6,200	8,300	7,100	5,100
County	22,500	51,000	22,000	18,000
Date competitors opened				
Dairy Queen	1965	1966	1970	1972
McDonald's	—	—	1987	—
Burger King	—	1984	—	—
Wendy's	—	—	—	—
Sonic	1982	1980	—	1981
No. of major industries	7	18	10	7
Average per capita income	8,659	10,236	7,090	7,265

location was secured from the individual chambers of commerce. (See Exhibit 14.4.)

The group was excited about the potential of owning four Hardee's franchises. Each of the units was strategically located and possessed great potential for profits based on the sales figures provided by Hardee's. (See Exhibit 14.5.)

Musselwhite secured the corporate charter for the West Tennessee Restaurant Corporation. Each of the four stockholders contributed $70,000 to capitalize the new corporation. It was agreed that Gibson would resign from his current position and move to Milan to serve as Vice-President and General Manager of the corporation.

EXHIBIT 14.5   Actual Average Sales Volume, Hardee's

As of March 31, 1987, there were 1,793 domestic licensed Hardee's restaurants and 899 Hardee's restaurants owned by Hardee's and its affiliates ("company-owned") in operation. Of the company-owned restaurants, 601 were in operation for the entire 12-month period ending March 31, 1987, and had sales volumes of $600,000 or more. The Licensor does not receive regular reports providing detailed financial data from licensees and consequently, the table on the following page reflects the results of company-owned restaurants only.

The Licensor offers essentially the same services to company-owned restaurants as is offered to licensed restaurants of Hardee's. The Licensor provides greater supervisory services in connection with company-owned restaurants than it offers licensees; however, the Licensor believes that this difference is generally compensated for by closer control and supervision provided by individual licensees.

Company-owned restaurants offer substantially the same products and services to the public as those offered to the public by licensees of Hardee's. (Services offered to the public vary in some instances, e.g., providing varied breakfast service and providing 24-hour (or extended hour) service, but such variation exists among both company-owned and licensed restaurants and is reflected in the table.) Data from company-owned restaurants used in the Table represent free-standing as well as mall-located restaurants. Licensed restaurants include similar locations in approximately the same distribution. The data presented in the table was received from restaurants reporting on a uniform accounting method. Revenue is actual reported sales accumulated for a standard accounting period. Costs/operating expenses are actual expenses paid or accrued in order to match expenses with revenues. Reports are prepared consistent with generally accepted accounting principles.

The table does not include data from approximately 298 company-owned restaurants that have reported gross sales volumes of less than $600,000. The Licensor believes that data provided from company-owned restaurants reporting sales under $600,000 is not representative of sales and the associated costs in company-owned restaurants or sales which may be achieved by licensed restaurants because (a) these units have been in operation less than 12 months, or (b) these units are generally older restaurants with fixed costs generally lower than those shown in the table. Included in this older restaurant category are 234 restaurants. Of those, 105 reached the break-even point which the Licensor estimates as $500,000. 43 of these 234 restaurants are less than five years old, 85 restaurants are over five, but less than ten years old, and 106 restaurants are over 10 years old.

There were 2,442 domestic Hardee's restaurants (both company-owned and licensed) opened and reporting sales for 12 continuous months ending as of March 31, 1987. Of these,

- Approximately 82% (or 601 company-owned and 1,409 licensed restaurants) had annual sales volumes in excess of $600,000.
- Approximately 69% (or 473 company-owned and 1,208 licensed restaurants) had annual sales volumes in excess of $700,000.
- Approximately 52% (or 317 company-owned and 965 licensed restaurants) had annual sales volumes in excess of $800,000.
- Approximately 38% (or 218 company-owned and 711 licensed restaurants) had annual sales volumes in excess of $900,000.
- Approximately 25% (or 140 company-owned and 476 licensed restaurants) had annual sales volumes in excess of $1,000,000.

The highest annual sales volume for all domestic company-owned and licensed restaurants was $2,194,000; and the lowest annual sales volume of any restaurant was $141,000, at a restaurant located on a college campus. The average annual sales volume of domestic Hardee's company-owned and licensed restaurants was approximately $842,000. The break-even point for the company-owned restaurants noted on the table is approximately $650,000, when royalty expenses, depreciation and rent are implied or included per the table. (As noted above, older restaurants, for which reports are not included in the table, generally have a lower break-even point.) The median sales volume for the 2,442 restaurants was approximately $817,000.

EXHIBIT 14.5 (Continued)

Table of Hardee's Average Restaurant Performance: 12 Months Ending March 31, 1987

SUMMARY ACCOUNT	GREATER THAN $1 MILLION SALES	BETWEEN $900,000 & $999,999 SALES	BETWEEN $800,000 & $899,999 SALES	BETWEEN $700,000 & $799,999 SALES	BETWEEN $600,000 & $699,999 SALES
Net Sales	$1,156,170	$ 943,980	$ 845,406	$ 746,631	$ 653,830
Cost of food	−333,288	−276,448	−246,045	−218,971	−192,856
Cost of paper	−47,083	−38,926	−34,579	−30,999	−27,197
Labor hourly	−179,188	−153,708	−141,050	−126,923	−117,787
Labor manager	−85,857	−80,750	−73,279	−68,966	−65,923
Taxes payroll	−25,660	−22,249	−19,669	−18,136	−16,728
Benefits	−6,035	−6,080	−5,959	−5,905	−5,879
Labor other	−2,431	−2,404	−2,318	−2,368	−2,398
Utilities	−35,675	−33,275	−32,712	−29,695	−30,320
Supplies	−13,691	−11,801	−10,649	−9,674	−9,115
Other controllables	−13,619	−12,568	−11,199	−9,684	−9,589
Co-op adv. expenses	−35,883	−30,136	−26,481	−23,876	−21,416
Coupon food costs	−14,906	−13,051	−11,111	−11,278	−8,815
Local non-broadcast	−13,970	−14,074	−13,113	−11,506	−10,478
All other advertising	−3,270	−3,294	−3,256	−3,232	−3,216
Taxes property	−5,005	−5,800	−5,482	−5,740	−6,087
Repair & maintenance	−16,013	−14,826	−14,187	−13,159	−13,212

Workers comp	-6,851	-6,120	-5,886	-5,276	-5,191
Other occupancy	-3,215	-2,677	-3,295	-2,557	-2,219
Other expenses	-7,129	-6,237	-5,741	-5,216	-5,396
Other income—exp	4,861	3,323	3,613	2,819	2,566
	$312,262	$ 212,879	$ 183,008	$ 146,289	$ 102,574
Royalty expense	-46,247	-37,759	-33,816	-29,865	-26,153
Depreciation	-48,571	-48,571	-48,571	-48,571	-48,571
Rent	-28,000	-28,000	-28,000	-28,000	-28,000
Pre-tax profit (loss)	189,444	98,549	72,621	39,853	-150
Pre-tax margin	16.4%	10.4%	8.6%	5.3%	—%

SOURCE: Hardee's, Inc.

NOTES:

Royalty rate 4.0% of net sales.

Depreciation based on straight-line method with average equipment and building package of $600,000 (equipment $200,000, building $400,000 (inclusive of site preparation costs)), and as calculated using a seven year life for equipment and a twenty-year life for building and site work.

Rent based on 14% of average land cost of $200,000.

No provision in the Table has been made for supervisory costs or other administrative overhead above the store management level.

No provision in the Table has been made for financing costs, if any, associated with the purchase of equipment or construction of the restaurant(s).

Licensees are required to pay a minimum of 5% of net sales per month on advertising.

On August 31, 1986, Storrie sold the four units to WTRC for $650,000 with a $150,000 cash down payment and a note for $500,000 at 10% interest for twelve years. The inventory was valued at $40,000, which was purchased by WTRC for cash of $40,000 in addition to the $650,000 selling price. WTRC agreed to assume all liabilities of the lease with Franchise Finance Corporation of America (FFC). Storrie had financed his first two units with FFC. Under the provisions of the agreement, FFC owned the land, building, and equipment at the two locations. FFC negotiated a 13% fixed interest rate on the land and building for ten years, or $8\frac{1}{2}$% of the annual sales volume, whichever was greater. FFC set the interest rate at 8% on the equipment for seven years. The average amount financed by FFC at the two locations was $505,000 on the land and building and $119,000 on the equipment. At the end of the lease period, the land, building, and equipment could be acquired for the fair market value as determined by three independent MAI (Member of Appraisal Institute) appraisers. In addition, WTRC assumed the loans on the Milan and Waverly units, which were secured for $600,000 each at a fixed rate of $10\frac{1}{2}$% for fifteen years.

WTRC CORPORATION

The WTRC was formed when each of the four investors contributed $80,000 to form the initial capitalization of $320,000. Each stockholder owned 25% of the corporation's stock. The officers were Fred Musselwhite, President; John Gibson, Vice-President; and Henry Lewis, Secretary. The stockholders personally guaranteed the $500,000 note to Nelson Storrie, the lease to FFC, and two notes on the Milan and Waverly units.

The stockholders were anticipating profits based on the information secured from the Hardee's Corporation and the sales information provided by Storrie (Exhibit 14.2). Storrie did not provide any financial statements to the investors, but supplied only sales figures by each unit. With Gibson's background and experience, the other three stockholders were content in their role of absentee investors.

Financial Information

During its first year of operation, WTRC reported a consolidated net income of $84,985. The units in Lexington and Waverly reported net income of $115,237 and $45,432, respectively. In Milan and Savannah, net losses of $44,958 and $30,726 were shown, respectively. (See Exhibits 14.6—14.10.) During September, October, and November 1987, sales declined dramatically. At November 30, 1987, WTRC was showing a loss of $223,944. (See Exhibit 14.11.) The units at Lexington and Waverly reported net income of $93,659 and $33,489, respectively. But losses were reported at Milan of $38,978 and at Savannah of $39,919. (See Exhibits 14.11–14.16.) These amounts did not include any allocations of the expenses of the general office in Milan. Gibson prepared quarterly financial statements and distributed them to the stockholders.

EXHIBIT 14.6   **West Tennessee Restaurants, Inc.**
Consolidated Statement of Revenue and Expenses for the
Twelve Months Ended August 31, 1987

Sales	$2,580,753.33	Advertising	
Cost of sales		Advertising national program	$ 9,664.28
Purchases food	$ 746,879.15	Advertising coupons & promo.	5,288.42
Purchases nonfood	120,797.50	Advertising local	18,884.18
Raw waste	13,302.75	Promotion items	80,964.20
Finished waste	36,814.84	Advertising co-op	82,864.38
Purchase discounts	(10,892.03)	Advertising pop kits	8,461.64
Total cost of sales	$ 906,902.21	Billboard rent	3,350.20
Total income	$1,673,851.12	Total advertising	$ 209,477.50
Labor		Occupancy	
Salaries employees	$ 447,191.48	Rent	$ 379,129.72
Salaries managers	187,142.86	Repairs and maintenance	48,362.96
Payroll taxes	61,707.14	Insurance general	20,117.28
Insurance group	7,258.50	Property taxes	5,081.25
Insurance workmen's comp.	12,194.77	Total occupancy	$ 444,691.21
Employees benefits	1,230.10	Miscellaneous	
Total labor	$ 716,724.85	Dues & subscriptions	$ 1,700.76
Manager controllables		Contributions	1,304.31
Cash short & over	$ (301.00)	Travel & entertainment	2,502.23
Outside services	40.00	Taxes & licenses	10,501.85
Uniforms	6,420.08	Office supplies & expense	624.53
Laundry	3,807.73	Stationery & printing	536.87
Store supplies	26,261.04	Postage & freight	183.82
Birthday cake	778.61	Bank charges	206.34
Office supplies	443.35	Royalties	77,691.75
Cleaning supplies	4,520.26	Total miscellaneous operating expense	$ 95,252.48
Small equipment	5,693.26	Total expenses	$1,620,690.94
Electricity, water and gas	89,387.15	Net income operations	$ 53,160.18
Telephone	5,709.11	Other income	
Landscaping	32.33	Sale of by-product	$ 1,293.98
Waste removal	10,951.59	Commissions earned	3,180.85
Extermination	802.19	Promo item net profit	$ 27,349.96
Total manager controllables	$ 154,544.90	Total income	$ 84,984.97

EXHIBIT 14.7 | **West Tennessee Restaurants, Inc.: Hardee's of Lexington**
Unit Statement of Revenue and Expenses for the Twelve
Months Ended August 31, 1987

Sales	$834,041.38	Advertising	
Cost of sales		Advertising national program	$ 3,012.02
Purchases food	$235,957.41	Advertising coupons & promo.	1,387.85
Purchases nonfood	36,249.58	Advertising local	2,295.15
Raw waste	3,251.01	Promotion items	21,924.42
Finished waste	10,617.74	Advertising co-op	24,849.07
Purchase discounts	(4,254.73)	Advertising pop kits	1,820.23
Total cost of sales	$281,821.01	Billboard rent	813.80
Total income	$552,220.37	Total advertising	$ 56,102.54
Labor		Occupancy	
Salaries employees	$134,675.32	Rent	$ 90,146.32
Salaries managers	49,527.01	Repairs and maintenance	16,396.21
Payroll taxes	18,005.57	Insurance general	5,029.32
Insurance group	2,093.64	Property taxes	553.75
Insurance workmen's comp.	3,063.96	Total occupancy	$112,125.60
Employees benefits	355.03	Miscellaneous	
Total labor	$207,720.53	Dues & subscriptions	$ 270.66
Manager controllables		Contributions	706.49
Cash short & over	$ (1,987.83)	Travel & entertainment	768.98
Uniforms	1,799.03	Taxes & licenses	5,281.04
Laundry	817.08	Office supplies & expense	134.51
Store supplies	7,335.07	Stationery & printing	131.93
Birthday cake	79.22	Postage & freight	74.90
Office supplies	81.90	Bank charges	48.30
Cleaning supplies	1,388.49	Royalties	25,144.96
Small equipment	1,813.09	Total miscellaneous operating expense	$ 32,561.77
Electricity, water and gas	23,566.55	Total expenses	$446,713.51
Telephone	1,745.84	Net income operations	$105,506.86
Landscaping	32.33	Other income	
Waste removal	1,332.30	Sale of by-product	$ 726.56
Extermination	200.00	Commissions earned	1,041.54
Total manager controllable	$ 38,203.07	Promo item net profit	$ 7,962.04
		Net income	$115,237.00

EXHIBIT 14.8   **West Tennessee Restaurants, Inc.: Hardee's of Milan**
Unit Statement of Revenue and Expenses for the Twelve
Months Ended August 31, 1987

Sales	$511,886.44	Advertising	
Cost of sales		Advertising national program	$ 2,277.42
Purchases food	$149,153.67	Advertising coupons & promo.	1,596.25
Purchases nonfood	24,016.69	Advertising local	4,589.28
Raw waste	4,171.24	Promotion items	18,232.08
Finished waste	8,243.67	Advertising co-op	15,244.81
Purchase discounts	(1,484.99)	Advertising pop kits	1,863.12
Total cost of sales	$184,100.28	Billboard rent	1,153.80
Total income	$327,786.16	Total advertising	$ 44,956.76
Labor		Occupancy	
Salaries employees	$ 98,745.93	Rent	$102,318.27
Salaries managers	45,258.00	Repairs and maintenance	9,333.59
Payroll taxes	14,086.43	Insurance general	5,029.32
Insurance group	1,506.98	Property taxes	1,092.50
Insurance workmen's comp.	3,327.85	Total occupancy	$117,773.68
Employees benefits	295.02	Miscellaneous	
Total labor	$163,220.21	Dues & subscriptions	$ 392.81
Manager controllables		Contributions	223.33
Cash short & over	$ 680.07	Travel & entertainment	642.62
Outside services	40.00	Taxes & licenses	2,007.81
Uniforms	1,661.65	Office supplies & expense	135.69
Laundry	734.45	Stationery & printing	131.91
Store supplies	6,397.06	Postage & freight	30.92
Birthday cake	569.40	Bank charges	51.70
Office supplies	121.61	Royalties	14,116.01
Cleaning supplies	1,009.66	Total miscellaneous operating expense	$ 17,732.80
Small equipment	1,514.50	Total expenses	$379,463.27
Electricity, water and gas	19,228.07	Net income operations	$ (51,677.11)
Telephone	1,374.88	Other income	
Waste removal	2,148.47	Sale of by-product	$ 257.03
Extermination	300.00	Commissions earned	493.91
Total manager controllables	$ 35,779.82	Promo item net profit	$ 5,968.45
		Net income (Loss)	$ (44,957.72)

EXHIBIT 14.9

West Tennessee Restaurants, Inc.: Hardee's of Savannah

Unit Statement of Revenue and Expenses for the Twelve Months Ended August 31, 1987

Sales	$574,524.32	Advertising	
Cost of sales		Advertising national program	$ 2,097.42
Purchases food	$178,589.10	Advertising coupons & promo.	1,433.24
Purchases nonfood	29,741.67	Advertising local	7,046.85
Raw waste	4,377.31	Promotion items	21,948.82
Finished waste	6,597.32	Advertising co-op	17,061.22
Purchase discounts	(2,715.67)	Advertising pop kits	2,252.77
Total cost of sales	$216,589.73	Billboard rent	1,358.80
Total income	$357,934.59	Total advertising	$ 53,199.12
Labor		Occupancy	
Salaries employees	106,847.73	Rent	$ 90,665.13
Salaries managers	45,598.47	Repairs and maintenance	8,176.46
Payroll taxes	14,731.76	Insurance general	5,029.32
Insurance group	1,913.84	Property taxes	1,633.75
Insurance workmen's comp.	3,165.00	Total occupancy	$105,504.66
Employees benefits	250.03	Miscellaneous	
Total labor	$172,506.83	Dues & subscriptions	$ 308.34
Manager controllables		Contributions	278.30
Cash short & over	527.12	Travel & entertainment	675.59
Uniforms	754.48	Taxes & licenses	1,428.06
Laundry	1,086.78	Office supplies & expense	239.42
Store supplies	6,431.79	Stationery & printing	137.91
Birthday cake	148.98	Postage & freight	30.09
Office supplies	139.85	Bank charges	73.93
Cleaning supplies	1,160.85	Royalties	17,279.45
Small equipment	1,366.99	Miscellaneous operating expense	$ 20,451.09
Electricity, water and gas	26,276.56	Total expenses	$397,190.75
Telephone	1,634.19	Net income operations	$ (39,264.16)
Waste removal	5,829.46	Other income	
Extermination	$ 180.00	Sale of by-product	$ 160.04
Total manager controllables	$ 45,537.05	Commissions earned	764.60
		Promo item net profit	7,613.28
		Net income	$ (30,726.24)

EXHIBIT 14.10   **West Tennessee Restaurants, Inc.: Hardee's of Waverly**
Unit Statement of Revenue and Expenses for the Twelve
Months Ended August 31, 1987

Sales	$660,301.19	Advertising	
Cost of sales		Advertising national program	$ 2,277.42
Purchases food	$183,178.97	Advertising coupons & promo.	871.08
Purchases nonfood	30,789.56	Advertising local	4,952.90
Raw waste	1,503.19	Promotion items	18,858.88
Finished waste	11,356.11	Advertising co-op	25,709.28
Purchase discounts	(2,436.64)	Advertising pop kits	2,525.72
Total cost of sales	$224,391.19	Billboard rent	23.80
Total income	$435,910.00	Total advertising	$ 55,219.08
Labor		Occupancy	
Salaries employees	$106,922.50	Rent	$ 96,000.00
Salaries managers	46,759.38	Repairs and maintenance	6,456.70
Payroll taxes	14,883.38	Insurance general	5,029.32
Insurance group	1,744.04	Property taxes	1,801.25
Insurance workmen's comp.	2,637.96	Total occupancy	$109,287.27
Employees benefits	330.02	Miscellaneous	
Total labor	$173,277.28	Dues & subscriptions	$ 728.95
Manager controllables		Contributions	96.19
Cash short & over	$ 478.84	Travel & entertainment	415.04
Uniforms	2,204.92	Taxes & licenses	1,784.94
Laundry	1,169.42	Office supplies & expense	114.93
Store supplies	6,097.12	Stationery & printing	135.12
Birthday cake	(18.99)	Postage & freight	47.91
Office supplies	99.99	Bank charges	32.41
Cleaning supplies	961.26	Royalties	21,151.33
Small equipment	998.68	Total miscellaneous operating expense	$ 24,506.82
Electricity, water and gas	20,315.97	Total expenses	$397,315.41
Telephone	954.20	Net income operations	$ 38,594.59
Waste removal	1,641.36	Other income	
Extermination	122.19	Sale of by-product	$ 150.35
Total manager controllables	$ 35,024.96	Commissions earned	880.80
		Promo item net profit	$ 5,806.19
		Net income	$ 45,431.93

EXHIBIT 14.11

West Tennessee Restaurants, Inc.

Consolidated Statement of Revenue and Expenses
For the One Month and Eleven Months Ended
November 30, 1987 (Unaudited)

	CURRENT MONTH		YEAR TO DATE (11 MONTHS)	
	Amount	%	Amount	%
Sales				
Sales food	$199,834.60	100.0	$2,274,682.12	100.0
Gift certificates	0.00	0.0	19.50	0.0
Total sales	$199,834.60	100.0	$2,274,701.62	100.0
Cost of sales				
Purchases food	$ 57,386.01	28.7	$ 665,596.01	29.3
Purchases nonfood	10,000.67	5.0	107,029.64	4.7
Raw waste	1,169.33	0.6	15,881.64	0.7
Finished waste	608.60	0.3	13,090.53	0.6
Purchase discounts	(691.11)	(0.3)	(9,770.66)	(.4)
Total cost of sales	$ 68,474.38	34.3	$ 791,827.16	34.8
Total income	$131,360.30	65.7	$1,482,874.46	65.2
Labor				
Salaries employees	$ 38,096.48	19.1	$ 402,074.65	17.7
Salaries managers	13,488.05	6.7	157,180.41	6.9
Casual labor	60.72	0.0	413.78	0.0
Payroll taxes	4,716.98	2.4	55,318.61	2.4
Insurance group	1,320.16	0.7	7,286.61	0.3
Insurance workmen's comp.	800.49	0.4	10,898.62	0.5
Employee benefits	0.00	0.0	350.00	0.0
Total labor	$ 58,482.88	29.3	$ 633,522.68	27.9
Manager controllables				
Cash short & over	$ 384.43	0.2	$ 3,043.81	0.1
Uniforms	575.02	0.3	6,032.91	0.3
Laundry	138.10	0.1	3,016.94	0.1
Store supplies	2,406.42	1.2	21,353.97	0.9
Birthday cake	64.25	0.0	753.60	0.0
Office supplies	15.00	0.0	400.71	0.0
Cleaning supplies	834.93	0.4	3,532.68	0.2
Small equipment	139.05	0.1	4,800.63	0.2
Electricity, water and gas	6,752.60	3.4	87,681.31	3.9
Telephone	356.70	0.2	5,588.65	0.2
Landscaping	0.00	0.0	32.33	0.0
Snow removal	0.00	0.0	12.00	0.0
Waste removal	899.23	0.4	11,462.95	0.5

	CURRENT MONTH		YEAR TO DATE (11 MONTHS)	
	Amount	%	Amount	%
Extermination	89.00	0.0	890.77	0.0
Total manager controllable	$ 12,654.73	6.3	$ 148,611.26	6.5
Advertising				
Advertising national program	$ 800.00	0.4	$ 9,294.60	0.4
Advertising coupons & promo.	929.24	0.5	9,205.84	0.4
Advertising local	855.55	0.4	16,246.46	0.7
Promotion items	3,538.57	1.8	62,844.43	2.8
Advertising co-op	6,481.39	3.2	73,830.51	3.2
Advertising pop kits	1,062.35	0.5	10,611.57	0.5
Billboard	750.00	0.4	7,110.35	0.3
Total advertising	$ 14,417.10	7.2	$ 189,143.76	8.3
Occupancy				
Rent	$ 31,405.39	15.7	$ 345,459.29	15.2
Repairs and maintenance	3,015.88	1.5	39,509.83	1.7
Insurance general	2,600.59	1.3	20,264.14	0.9
Total occupancy	$ 37,021.86	18.5	$ 405,233.26	17.8
Misc. operating expenses				
Dues & subscriptions	$ 58.30	0.0	$ 1,484.25	0.1
Contributions	0.00	0.0	435.60	0.0
Travel & entertainment	246.60	0.1	2,094.66	0.1
Taxes & licenses	524.50	0.3	11,499.51	0.5
Office supplies & expense	0.00	0.0	88.42	0.0
Stationery & printing	0.00	0.0	227.45	0.0
Postage & freight	21.90	0.0	216.90	0.0
Bank charges	13.77	0.0	195.65	0.0
Royalties	6,070.11	3.0	68,657.88	3.0
Misc. operating expense	$ 6,935.18	3.5	$ 84,899.72	3.7
Total expenses	$129,511.75	64.8	$1,461,410.68	64.2
Other income				
Sale of by-product	$ 56.13	0.0	$ 916.56	0.0
Commissions earned	0.00	0.0	2,647.46	0.1
Promo item net profit	1,908.73	1.0	23,222.64	1.0
Total other income (loss)	$ 1,964.86	1.0	$ 26,786.66	1.2
Net income (loss) before General and Administrative	$ 3,813.41	1.9	$ 48,250.44	2.1
Labor				
Officers's salaries	$ 2,884.61	1.4	$ 32,115.30	1.4

(Continued)

EXHIBIT 14.11 **(Continued)**

	CURRENT MONTH		YEAR TO DATE (11 MONTHS)	
	Amount	%	Amount	%
District managers'	0.00	0.0	7,614.23	0.3
Training expense	0.00	0.0	4,884.31	0.2
Office salaries	898.30	0.4	10,806.85	0.5
Ins.—workers comp.	9.16	0.0	18.32	0.0
Payroll taxes	255.40	0.1	4,442.48	0.2
Labor total	$ 4,047.47	2.0	$ 59,881.49	2.6
Manager controllables				
Vehicle expense	$ 0.00	0.0	$ 1,846.70	0.1
Utilities	107.55	0.1	467.14	0.0
Telephone	653.13	0.3	8,540.65	0.4
Office rent	300.00	0.2	2,100.00	0.1
Total manager controllables	$ 1,060.68	0.5	$ 12,954.49	0.6
Occupancy				
Amortization expense	$ 9,044.48	4.5	$ 108,930.86	4.8
Depreciation	656.67	0.3	5,349.79	0.2
Insurance general	32.75	0.0	74.92	0.0
Insurance group	293.22	0.1	1,878.76	0.1
Total occupancy	$ 10,027.12	5.0	$ 116,234.33	5.1
Misc. operating expenses				
Miscellaneous	$ 85.00	0.0	$ 1,468.58	0.1
Dues & subscriptions	79.95	0.0	296.28	0.0
Contributions	0.00	0.0	50.00	0.0
Travel & entertainment	404.90	0.2	8,805.39	0.4
Taxes & license	0.00	0.0	911.98	0.0
Office supplies & expense	179.73	0.1	3,213.64	0.1
Printing	0.00	0.0	288.91	0.0
Postage	289.25	0.1	3,690.31	0.2
Bank charges	90.00	0.0	3,478.77	0.2
Interest expense	6,014.93	3.0	62,769.28	2.8
Professional fees	1,025.00	0.5	11,025.00	0.5
Life insurance	435.16	0.2	4,059.22	0.2
Total misc. operating expense	$ 8,603.92	4.3	$ 100,057.36	4.4
Total general & adm. expenses	$ 23,739.19	11.9	$ 289,127.67	12.7
Net operating income (loss)	$ (19,925.78)	(10.0)	$ (248,877.23)	(10.6)
Other income	—	—	—	—

EXHIBIT 14.12

West Tennessee Restaurants: Hardee's of Lexington

Unit Statement of Revenue and Expenses
for the One Month and Eleven Months Ended
November 30, 1987 (Unaudited)

	CURRENT MONTH		YEAR TO DATE (11 MONTHS)	
	Amount	%	Amount	%
Sales				
Sales food	$63,419.12	100.0	$734,742.21	100.0
Total sales	$63,419.12	100.0	$734,742.21	100.0
Cost of sales				
Purchases food	$18,177.51	28.7	$209,870.18	28.6
Purchases nonfood	3,269.83	5.2	32,125.44	4.4
Raw waste	213.27	0.3	3,627.39	0.5
Finished waste	156.15	0.2	3,160.01	0.4
Purchase discounts	(298.43)	(0.5)	(3,959.57)	(0.5)
Total cost of sales	$21,518.33	33.9	$244,823.45	33.3
Total income	$41,900.79	66.1	$489,918.76	66.7
Labor				
Salaries employees	$11,321.12	17.9	$120,527.17	16.4
Salaries managers	3,438.20	5.4	43,787.66	6.0
Casual labor	0.00	0.0	270.43	0.0
Payroll taxes	1,331.04	2.1	16,310.11	2.2
Insurance group	309.64	0.5	2,035.82	0.3
Insurance workmen's comp.	201.00	0.3	2,699.97	0.4
Employee benefits	0.00	0.0	100.00	0.0
Total labor	$16,601.00	26.2	$185,731.16	25.3
Manager controllables				
Cash short & over	$ 312.76	0.5	$ 1,054.88	0.1
Uniforms	289.16	0.5	2,237.89	0.3
Laundry	48.73	0.1	742.63	0.1
Store supplies	533.40	0.8	5,875.82	0.8
Birthday cake	6.50	0.0	106.51	0.0
Office supplies	6.73	0.0	169.41	0.0
Cleaning supplies	201.63	0.3	1,048.66	0.1
Small equipment	27.49	0.0	1,494.79	0.2
Electricity, water and gas	1,830.42	2.9	23,251.83	3.2
Telephone	94.85	0.1	1,571.87	0.2
Landscaping	0.00	0.0	32.33	0.0
Waste removal	222.52	0.4	2,082.80	0.3
Extermination	20.00	0.0	200.00	0.0
Total manager controllable	$ 3,594.19	5.7	$ 39,869.42	5.4

(Continued)

EXHIBIT 14.12   **(Continued) West Tennessee Restaurants: Hardee's of Lexington**

	CURRENT MONTH		YEAR TO DATE (11 MONTHS)	
	Amount	%	Amount	%
Advertising				
Advertising national program	$ 200.00	0.3	$ 2,874.60	0.4
Advertising coupons & promo.	247.45	0.4	2,433.18	0.3
Advertising local	201.54	0.3	1,993.21	0.3
Promotion items	963.01	1.5	16,025.80	2.2
Advertising co-op	1,924.92	3.0	22,219.68	3.0
Advertising pop kits	278.85	0.4	2,466.76	0.3
Billboard rent	160.00	0.3	1,238.80	0.2
Total advertising	$ 3,975.77	6.3	$ 49,252.03	6.7
Occupancy				
Rent	$ 7,407.08	11.7	$ 81,477.88	11.1
Repairs and maintenance	185.07	0.3	14,267.55	1.9
Insurance general	316.25	0.5	4,700.12	0.6
Total occupancy	$ 7,908.40	12.3	$100,445.55	13.7
Miscellaneous				
Dues & subscriptions	$ 0.00	0.0	$ 228.16	0.0
Contributions	0.00	0.0	400.00	0.1
Travel & entertainment	0.00	0.0	353.59	0.0
Taxes & licenses	179.75	0.3	5,579.50	0.8
Office supplies & expense	0.00	0.0	21.49	0.0
Stationery & printing	0.00	0.0	58.18	0.0
Postage & freight	9.80	0.0	96.20	0.0
Bank charges	0.90	0.0	1.44	0.0
Royalties	1,924.92	3.0	22,219.68	3.0
Misc. operating expense	$ 2,115.37	3.3	$ 28,958.24	3.9
Total expenses	$34,194.73	53.9	$404,256.40	55.0
Other income				
Sale of by-product	$ 23.63	0.0	$ 236.88	0.0
Commissions earned	0.00	0.0	810.66	0.1
Promo item net profit	507.28	0.0	6,949.17	0.9
Total other income (loss)	$ 530.91	.0	$ 7,996.71	1.1
Net income (loss) bef. G.&A.	$ 8,236.97	13.0	$ 93,659.07	12.7
Net operating income (loss)	$ 8,236.97	13.0	$ 93,659.07	12.7
Net income (loss) bef. taxes	$ 8,236.97	13.0	$ 93,659.07	12.7
Net income (loss)	$ 8,236.97	13.0	$ 93,659.07	12.7

EXHIBIT 14.13

West Tennessee Restaurants: Hardee's of Milan

Unit Statement of Revenue and Expenses
for the One Month and Eleven Months Ended
November 30, 1987 (Unaudited)

	CURRENT MONTH		YEAR TO DATE (11 MONTHS)	
	Amount	%	Amount	%
Sales				
Sales food	$42,238.01	100.0	$458,003.00	100.0
Total sales	$42,238.01	100.0	$458,003.00	100.0
Cost of sales				
Purchases food	$11,171.14	26.4	$133,440.45	29.1
Purchases nonfood	1,600.17	3.8	21,515.90	4.7
Raw waste	183.06	0.4	4,661.29	1.0
Finished waste	106.03	0.3	3,376.89	0.7
Purchase discounts	(89.45)	(0.2)	(1,304.68)	(0.3)
Total cost of sales	$12,970.95	30.7	$161,689.85	35.3
Total income	$29,267.06	69.3	$296,313.15	64.7
Labor				
Salaries employees	$ 8,445.31	20.0	$ 86,371.24	18.9
Salaries managers	3,458.45	8.2	37.470.51	8.2
Casual labor	0.00	0.0	50.20	0.0
Payroll taxes	1,106.74	2.6	12,158.80	2.7
Insurance group	335.96	0.8	1,653.27	0.4
Insurance workmen's comp.	199.83	0.5	3,047.11	0.7
Employee benefits	0.00	0.0	150.00	0.0
Total labor	$13,546.29	32.1	$149,901.13	30.8
Manager controllables				
Cash short & over	$ 52.11	0.1	$ 530.04	0.1
Uniforms	176.93	0.4	1,674.76	0.4
Laundry	0.00	0.0	489.37	0.1
Store supplies	581.81	1.4	5,163.09	1.1
Birthday cake	49.75	0.1	634.85	0.1
Office supplies	8.27	0.0	49.49	0.0
Cleaning supplies	121.53	0.3	739.59	0.2
Small equipment	69.32	0.2	1,471.39	0.3
Electricity, water and gas	1,611.10	3.8	20,760.17	4.5
Telephone	98.77	0.2	1,370.83	0.3
Snow removal	0.00	0.0	12.00	0.0
Waste removal	197.61	0.5	1,961.50	0.4
Extermination	25.00	0.1	330.00	0.1
Total manager controllable	$ 2,992.20	7.1	$ 35,187.08	7.7

(Continued)

EXHIBIT 14.13   **(Continued)**

	CURRENT MONTH		YEAR TO DATE (11 MONTHS)	
	Amount	%	Amount	%
Advertising				
Advertising national program	$ 200.00	0.5	$ 2,140.00	0.5
Advertising coupons & promo.	225.25	0.5	2,953.22	0.6
Advertising local	28.00	0.1	3,512.03	0.8
Promotion items	716.62	1.7	14,342.22	3.1
Advertising co-op	1,284.24	3.0	13,829.37	3.0
Advertising pop kits	252.99	0.6	2,356.46	0.5
Billboard rent	320.00	0.8	2,151.38	0.5
Total advertising	$ 3,027.10	7.2	$ 41,284.68	9.0
Occupancy				
Rent	$ 8,458.31	20.0	$ 93,041.41	20.3
Repairs and maintenance	1,314.75	3.1	9,404.31	2.1
Insurance general	1,662.52	3.9	6,185.14	1.4
Total occupancy	$11,435.58	27.1	$108,630.86	23.7
Miscellaneous				
Dues & subscriptions	$ 35.30	0.1	$ 343.00	0.1
Contributions	0.00	0.0	10.00	0.0
Travel & entertainment	0.00	0.0	487.66	0.1
Taxes & licenses	117.36	0.3	2,135.62	0.5
Stationery & printing	0.00	0.0	55.17	0.0
Postage & freight	0.00	0.0	34.24	0.0
Bank charges	12.87	0.0	130.47	0.0
Royalties	1,284.24	3.0	12,523.65	2.7
Misc. operating expense	$ 1,449.77	3.4	$ 15,719.81	3.4
Total expenses	$32,450.94	76.8	$341,723.56	74.6
Other income				
Sale of by-product	$ 8.00	0.0	$ 282.03	0.1
Commissions earned	0.00	0.0	653.16	0.1
Promo item net profit	645.31	1.5	5,496.74	1.2
Total other income (loss)	$ 653.31	1.5	$ 6,431.93	1.4
Net income (loss) bef. G.&A.	$ (2,530.57)	(6.0)	$ (38,978.48)	(8.5)
Net operating income (loss)	$ (2,530.57)	(6.0)	$ (38,978.48)	(8.5)
Net income (loss) bef. taxes	$ (2,530.57)	(6.0)	$ (38,978.48)	(8.5)
Net income (loss)	$ (2,530.57)	(6.0)	$ (38,978.48)	(8.5)

EXHIBIT 14.14

West Tennessee Restaurants: Hardee's of Savannah
Unit Statement of Revenue and Expenses
for the One Month and Eleven Months Ended
November 30, 1987 (Unaudited)

	CURRENT MONTH		YEAR TO DATE (11 MONTHS)	
	Amount	%	Amount	%
Sales				
Sales food	$40,070.62	100.0	$481,236.49	100.0
Total sales	$40,070.62	100.0	$481,236.49	100.0
Cost of sales				
Purchases food	$12,009.98	30.0	$148,219.75	30.8
Purchases nonfood	2,324.73	5.8	25,343.34	5.3
Raw waste	334.48	0.8	4,820.56	1.0
Finished waste	97.58	0.2	2,412.33	0.5
Purchase discounts	(153.65)	(0.4)	(2,311.38)	(0.5)
Total cost of sales	$14,613.12	36.5	$178,484.60	37.1
Total income	$25,457.50	63.5	$302,751.89	62.9
Labor				
Salaries employees	$ 7,952.04	19.8	$ 92,278.34	19.2
Salaries managers	3,199.11	8.0	36.991.77	7.7
Casual labor	0.00	0.0	18.43	0.0
Payroll taxes	989.70	2.5	12,887.99	2.7
Insurance group	309.63	0.8	1,766.11	0.4
Insurance workmen's comp.	199.82	0.5	2,773.41	0.6
Total labor	$12,650.31	31.6	$146,716.05	30.5
Manager controllables				
Cash short & over	$ (37.41)	(0.1)	$ 656.61	0.1
Uniforms	21.31	0.1	593.26	0.1
Laundry	62.62	0.2	924.30	0.2
Store supplies	481.91	1.2	5,047.62	1.0
Birthday cake	8.00	0.0	106.48	0.0
Office supplies	0.00	0.0	99.62	0.0
Cleaning supplies	203.30	0.5	815.01	0.2
Small equipment	42.24	0.1	757.68	0.2
Electricity, water and gas	1,630.82	4.1	25,364.18	5.3
Telephone	33.93	0.1	1,430.06	0.3
Waste removal	272.26	0.7	5,641.52	1.2
Extermination	20.00	0.0	200.00	0.0
Total manager controllable	$ 2,738.98	6.8	$ 41,636.34	8.7

(Continued)

EXHIBIT 14.14 **(Continued) West Tennessee Restaurants: Hardee's of Savannah**

	CURRENT MONTH		YEAR TO DATE (11 MONTHS)	
	Amount	%	Amount	%
Advertising				
Advertising national program	$ 200.00	0.5	$ 2,140.00	0.4
Advertising coupons & promo.	227.25	0.6	1,998.02	0.4
Advertising local	395.16	1.0	6,787.80	1.4
Promotion items	915.29	2.3	17,364.39	3.6
Advertising co-op	1,215.84	3.0	14,504.58	3.0
Advertising pop kits	251.66	0.6	2,718.99	0.6
Billboard rent	270.00	0.7	2,421.37	0.5
Total advertising	$ 3,475.20	8.7	$ 47,935.15	10.0
Occupancy				
Rent	$ 7,540.00	18.8	$ 82,940.00	17.2
Repairs and maintenance	814.72	2.0	6,737.20	1.4
Insurance general	310.91	0.8	4,639.44	1.0
Total occupancy	$ 8,665.63	21.6	$ 94,366.64	19.6
Miscellaneous				
Dues & subscriptions	$ 12.00	0.0	$ 269.59	0.1
Travel & entertainment	222.20	0.6	648.35	0.1
Taxes & licenses	80.22	0.2	1,494.02	0.3
Office supplies & expense	0.00	0.0	64.32	0.0
Stationery & printing	0.00	0.0	58.92	0.0
Postage & freight	0.00	0.0	28.46	0.0
Bank charges	0.00	0.0	37.00	0.0
Royalties	1,215.84	3.0	14,504.67	3.0
Misc. operating expense	$ 1,530.26	3.8	$ 17,097.33	3.6
Total expenses	$29,060.38	72.5	$347,751.51	72.3
Other income				
Sale of by-product	$ 10.00	0.0	$ 192.04	0.0
Commissions earned	0.00	0.0	$ 533.72	0.1
Promo item net profit	302.47	0.8	4,354.78	0.9
Total other income (loss)	$ 312.47	.8	$ 5,080.54	1.1
Net income (loss) bef. G.&A.	$ (3,290.41)	(8.2)	$ (39,919.08)	(8.3)
Net operating income (loss)	$ (3,290.41)	(8.2)	$ (39,919.08)	(8.3)
Net income (loss) bef. taxes	$ (3,290.41)	(8.2)	$ (39,919.08)	(8.3)
Net income (loss)	$ (3,290.41)	(8.2)	$ (39,919.08)	(8.3)

EXHIBIT 14.15

West Tennessee Restaurants: Hardee's of Waverly

Unit Statement of Revenue and Expenses
for the One Month and Eleven Months Ended
November 30, 1987 (Unaudited)

	CURRENT MONTH		YEAR TO DATE (11 MONTHS)	
	AMOUNT	%	AMOUNT	%
Sales				
Sales food	$54,106.85	100.0	$600,700.42	100.0
Gift certificates	0.00	0.0	19.50	0.0
Total sales	$54,106.85	100.0	$600,719.92	100.0
Cost of sales				
Purchases food	$16,028.18	29.6	$174,065.63	29.0
Purchases nonfood	2,805.94	5.2	28,044.96	4.7
Raw waste	438.52	0.8	2,772.40	0.5
Finished waste	246.84	0.5	4,141.30	0.7
Purchase discounts	(149.58)	(0.3)	(2,195.03)	(0.4)
Total cost of sales	$19,371.90	35.8	$206,829.26	34.4
Total income	$34,734.95	64.2	$393,890.66	65.6
Labor				
Salaries employees	$10,378.01	19.2	$102,897.30	17.1
Salaries managers	3,392.29	6.3	38,930.47	6.5
Casual labor	60.72	0.1	74.72	0.0
Payroll taxes	1,289.50	2.4	13,961.71	2.3
Insurance group	364.93	0.7	1,831.41	0.3
Insurance workmen's comp.	199.83	0.4	2,378.13	0.4
Employee benefits	0.00	0.0	100.00	0.0
Total labor	$15,685.28	29.0	$160,174.34	26.7
Manager controllables				
Cash short & over	$ 56.97	0.1	$ 802.28	0.1
Uniforms	87.62	0.2	1,527.00	0.3
Laundry	26.75	0.0	860.64	0.1
Store supplies	809.30	1.5	5,267.44	0.9
Birthday cake	0.00	0.0	(94.24)	(0.0)
Office supplies	0.00	0.0	82.19	0.0
Cleaning supplies	308.47	0.6	929.42	0.2
Small equipment	0.00	0.0	1,076.77	0.2
Electricity, water and gas	1,680.26	3.1	18,305.13	3.0
Telephone	129.15	0.2	1,215.89	0.2
Waste removal	206.84	0.4	1,777.13	0.3
Extermination	24.00	0.0	168.77	0.0
Total manager controllable	$ 2,329.26	6.2	$ 31,918.48	5.3

(Continued)

EXHIBIT 14.15 **(Continued) West Tennessee Restaurants: Hardee's of Waverly**

	CURRENT MONTH		YEAR TO DATE (11 MONTHS)	
	AMOUNT	%	AMOUNT	%
Advertising				
Advertising national program	$ 200.00	0.4	$ 2,140.00	0.4
Advertising coupons & promo.	229.29	0.4	1,821.42	0.3
Advertising local	230.85	0.4	3,953.42	0.7
Promotion items	943.65	1.7	15,112.02	2.5
Advertising co-op	2,056.39	3.8	23,276.88	3.8
Advertising pop kits	278.85	0.5	3,069.36	0.5
Billboard rent	0.00	0.0	1,298.80	0.2
Total advertising	$ 3,939.03	7.3	$ 50,671.90	8.4
Occupancy				
Rent	$ 8,000.00	14.8	$ 88,000.00	14.6
Repairs and maintenance	701.34	1.3	9,100.77	1.5
Insurance general	310.91	0.6	4,889.44	0.8
Total occupancy	$ 9,012.25	16.7	$101,790.21	16.9
Miscellaneous				
Dues & subscriptions	$ 11.00	0.0	$ 643.50	0.1
Contributions	0.00	0.0	25.00	0.0
Travel & entertainment	24.40	0.0	613.06	0.1
Taxes & licenses	147.17	0.3	2,290.37	0.4
Office supplies & expense	0.00	0.0	2.61	0.0
Stationery & printing	0.00	0.0	55.18	0.0
Postage & freight	12.10	0.0	58.00	0.0
Bank charges	0.00	0.0	26.74	0.0
Royalties	1,645.11	3.0	19,409.88	3.2
Misc. operating expense	$ 1,839.78	3.4	$ 23,124.34	3.8
Total expenses	$33,805.70	62.5	$367,679.21	61.2
Other income				
Sale of by-product	$ 14.50	0.0	$ 205.61	0.0
Commissions earned	0.00	0.0	649.92	0.1
Promo item net profit	453.67	0.8	6,421.95	1.1
Total other income (loss)	$ 468.17	0.9	$ 7,277.48	1.2
Net income (loss) before G. & A.	$ 1,397.42	2.6	$ 33,488.93	5.6
Net operating income (loss)	$ 1,397.42	2.6	$ 33,488.93	5.6
Net income (loss) bef. taxes	$ 1,397.42	2.6	$ 33,488.93	5.6
Net income (loss)	$ 1,397.42	2.6	$ 33,488.93	5.6

EXHIBIT 14.16

West Tennessee Restaurants, Inc.

Consolidated Balance sheet For the Month Ended
November 30, 1987 (Unaudited)

Assets

Current assets

Cash on hand	$ 2,200.00	
Cash in bank—Checking #1	34,206.32	
Cash in bank—Payroll	82.32	
Cash in bank—Savings	32,000.00	
Cash in bank—Checking #2	597.06	
Cash in bank—Checking #3	268.34	
Cash in bank—Checking #4	316.65	
Cash in bank—Checking #5	569.79	
Cash in bank—Checking #7	47.06	
Accounts receive.—Employees	288.07	
Inventory—Lexington	20,254.47	
Inventory—Savannah	14,541.68	
Inventory—Haverly	13,051.76	
Inventory—Milan	13,492.03	
Total current assets		131,915.55

Fixed assets

Machinery and equipment	$ 29,412.22	
Vehicles	7,174.49	
Accumulated depreciation	(8,991.38)	
Total fixed assets		27,595.33

Other assets

License agreement—Lexington	$ 37,000.00	
License agreement—Savannah	37,058.00	
License agreement—Waverly	37,285.00	
License agreement—Milan	37,285.00	
Goodwill	19,000.00	
Organization expense	562.50	
Covenant not to compete	749.95	
Utility deposits	6,900.00	
Development agreement—Hardees	37,499.95	
Lease agreement—Lexington	132,365.85	
Lease agreement—Savannah	104,275.80	
Lease agreement—Milan	61,999.95	
Total other assets		$511,982.80
Total assets		$671,493.68

EXHIBIT 14.16

(Continued) West Tenessee Restaurants:
Consolidated Balance Sheet

Liabilities and Equity
Current liabilities

Accounts payable	$154,700.76	
FICA tax payable	4.96	
Federal withholding payable	14.48	
Accrued state unemployment	1,944.84	
Accrued federal unemployment	576.55	
Accrued salaries	38,619.99	
Accrued interest	14,312.23	
Sales tax payable	15,800.00	
Accrued insurance	(2,895.03)	
Notes payable—H&S Rest.	24,267.21	
Notes payable—stockholders	59,059.16	
Total current liabilities		306,405.15
Long-term liabilities		
Notes payable—H&S Rest.	$446,405.26	
Notes payable—stockholders	208,058.96	
Total long-term liabilities		654,464.22
Total liabilities		$960,869.37
Stockholders' equity		
Capital stock outstanding	$ 4,000.00	
Retained earnings—beginning	(69,399.67)	
Current earnings	(223,976.02)	
Total stockholders' equity		(289,375.69)
Total liab. & stockholders' equity		$ 671,493.68

Organization

WTRC has 130 employees in four locations. Each unit has a manager, three assistant managers, and two breakfast supervisors. The managers' salaries range from $20,000 to $25,000 per year. All other employees are hired on a part-time basis. Their wages range from $3.35 to $5 an hour. Gibson and his wife are in charge of the daily operations. Gibson earns $36,000 and his wife earns $12,000 annually.

The manager of the Lexington unit has been employed since the unit opened. He takes a great deal of pride in his job and is very active in community activities.

The Savannah location has had three different managers since the unit opened. Several customer complaints have been received on the quality of the food and service. In addition, McDonald's opened a new store in September 1987, across the street from Hardee's.

The Waverly unit has had only one manager since it opened. Sales have been fairly stable at this location.

At Milan, eight different managers have been employed since the unit began operation. This has been a constant concern for Gibson: He intended to make the Milan store the showplace of his operation. Sales have been very disappointing at Milan.

Additional Information

In September 1986, Gibson secured the development rights to Madison County and Obion County. Jackson, the county seat of Madison County, has a population of 75,000. Union City in Obion County has a population of 10,500. In order to finalize the agreements for the development rights, Gibson had to send $25,000 to the Hardee's Corporation in Rocky Mount, North Carolina.

Gibson contacted FFC to secure information relative to building additional units in Jackson and Union City. The management of FFC was willing to provide financing for both units with no money down. In fact, financing in excess of the cost of constructing a unit could be secured. Joe Adams of FFC mentioned that funds in excess of $100,000 were provided to Nelson Storrie in order to start his businesses in Lexington and Savannah. Gibson attempted to convince the other stockholders to build units in the two other locations. It was a consensus of the other stockholders to make this decision after the business had been through a one-year operating cycle.

On December 15, 1987, Soles, Lewis, and Musselwhite met at Musselwhite's law office to discuss the financial condition of WTRC and to review the latest financial statements.

MUSSELWHITE: "I still for the life of me can't understand how we could make $84,000 in our first year of operation and lose $248,000 in the first three months of the second year. I can't understand these financial statements. Something is fishy about this whole thing."

SOLES: "Is John stealing us blind? Let's fire him and find us somebody else to run this operation."

LEWIS: "Let's look at our alternatives. Maybe we could sell to Boddie Noell who owns over ten Hardee's units in West Tennessee."

MUSSELWHITE: "What do we have to sell?"

LEWIS: "Let's try to sell all four units and not just the Lexington and Waverly units."

SOLES: "Does anybody want to go to West Tennessee and try to save our investment? Henry, you need to conduct an audit for us."

SOLES: "Is there anyway we can get out of the 13% fixed payment on the lease? The prime interest rate is now under 10% and we are still paying 13%."

MUSSELWHITE: "It's iron clad. They would be stupid to let us out of the lease. I don't think we can buy our way out."

Lewis suggested that each stockholder could contribute some additional funds to bail out the corporation.

SOLES: "How much do we need to contribute?"

Lewis had no idea how much would be required, but he knew they had to reduce the accounts payable.

SOLES: "I want to be sure that John puts in his fair share."

MUSSELWHITE: "Do you think we could borrow some money from some of the local banks in each town where we do business? I know that we would have to personally guarantee anything that we borrow."

LEWIS: "We don't have anything to use for collateral in Lexington or Savannah. I doubt that the bank in Milan would loan us anything based on our profit and loss there."

Musselwhite commented that Gibson had never paid the $25,000 to Hardee's for the development rights to Madison and Obion counties. Someone from Hardee's main office had told him that this was now open territory because the deposit had not been made.

LEWIS: "It looks like we made Storrie a rich man, and we are now paying for our ignorance. We need to find some short-term solutions and formulate some long-range plans if we plan to stay in business."

SOLES: "What shall we do to get out of this dilemma?"

Pioneer Hi-Bred International, Inc.

J. DAVID HUNGER ● DEBORAH READING ● DAVID SAVERAID
MARRETT VARGHESE ● LARRY MAXWELL

Perhaps Henry Agard Wallace will not be remembered as Vice-President of the United States under Franklin D. Roosevelt or as the Progressive Party's candidate for President in 1948, but the legacy he left to agriculture will never be forgotten. Chiefly responsible for the development of hybrid corn seed, Wallace provided the impetus for a doubling of American corn yields per acre in the last forty years. As an Iowa high school student, Wallace produced the famous Copper Cross variety of corn seed in 1924, and sold all fifteen bushels to finance his genetic experiments. In 1926, Wallace and a few friends founded the world's first hybrid seed company, the Hi-Bred Corn Company, to market the results of his research. Around 1936, Pioneer was added to the company name.

The native Americans who first domesticated corn had simply saved the best ears from the healthiest plants to plant the next spring. The typical American corn grower continued to use this same breeding method through the 1800s. This time-honored program cost little to implement and generally provided good results over the years. By around 1870, however, average U.S. corn yields had leveled off at twenty-six bushels per acre. Fifty years later, in the 1920s, corn growers harvested only about twenty-eight bushels of grain for every acre planted.[1]

Henry Wallace forged an agreement during the Great Depression of the 1930s with a Des Moines real estate agent, Roswell Garst, to distribute Pioneer's hybrid corn seed to the nation's skeptical farmers. The Garst–Pioneer relationship, cemented by a 1930 handshake, was to continue for more than half a century.

This case was prepared by Professor J. David Hunger, Deborah Reading, David Saveraid, Marrett Varghese, and Larry Maxwell of Iowa State University. This case was presented at the 1985 Workshop of the Midwest Society for Case Research. Copyright © 1985 by J. David Hunger. Reprinted by permission.

Garst returned to his native Coon Rapids, Iowa, taking with him Wallace's latest hybrid corn varieties. Unimpressed by tales of the hybrid's superiority over naturally produced seeds, farmers took Garst up on what they considered a sure bet. Any farmer planting Pioneer's hybrids alongside his own seed could harvest the results and pay Pioneer half the value of the difference between the two yields. To the farmer's surprise, Pioneer's hybrids out-produced generic seeds by twenty bushels to the acre.

As of January 1985, Wallace's corn company, known as Pioneer Hi-Bred International, Inc., provided more than a third of the nation's seed corn. More than half the farmers in the Corn Belt bought their hybrid corn seed from Pioneer.

THE HYBRID SEED INDUSTRY

A hybrid seed is the first-generation cross between two or more inbred or "parent" strains. A corn inbred is produced when the ear shoots of corn plants are covered with inverted paper bags so that no stray pollen from other corn plants can fall on the silks. Later, these bags are removed, and the female silks are pollinated by hand from the male tassels of the same strain. Bags are then replaced on the ear shoots to prevent further pollination from unwanted corn plants. The best ears are saved for the next year's seed. This self-pollination process is repeated until the unbred ears become uniform, although small, with the good traits of the inbred strain being firmly fixed in the seed. The crossing of two such inbred parent strains produces a hybrid seed that, when planted, grows into a large and vigorous plant.[2]

Interestingly, hybrids do not reproduce themselves with the same vigor. Although an estimated 90% of all corn and sorghum plus a small but growing proportion of other grains produced in the United States grow from hybrid seed, farmers cannot harvest their hybrid-grown crops, plant the resulting seeds, and expect the next generation to exhibit its parents' characteristics. Hybrids can be produced only from two or more inbred parent strains. These inbreds can be genetically engineered to increase yields, resist insects and diseases, withstand strong wind, and retain a desired moisture content in the kernels. Because of the necessity to use genetically engineered parent strains to produce hybrid seed, the modern farmer must look each year to companies like Pioneer to provide, at a price, the desired seed for planting.

By 1984 the only major field crops to be commercially successfully hybridized were corn and sorghum. Sunflower, still a minor crop, was also a hybrid. Corn, the United States' largest and most valuable crop, alone accounted for approximately $1.5 billion in sales out of an estimated $5 billion U.S. seed market. The hybrid corn seed market was felt by many, however, to be a mature business with low potential for growth. As a result, firms in the seed industry were trying to develop economically practical hybrids of wheat, soybeans, and cotton—each of which could become a billion-dollar seed market.

Unlike hybrid corn, the seeds of wheat, soybeans, and cotton could be saved from one year's crop and planted the following season. Therefore even though acreage devoted to corn and soybeans were roughly equal in size, the lack of a successful soybean hybrid resulted in much smaller annual sales of soybean seed than of corn. Nevertheless, in the early 1980s an estimated 65% of planted soybean seed came from the previous year's crop, compared to about 85% one decade earlier. Farmers were apparently willing to accept higher seed costs in exchange for better yields and stronger disease resistance.

Owing to its nature, wheat has been difficult to hybridize on a commercial scale. Believing that the potential of adding 20% or more to wheat yields has made wheat hybrids worth pursuing. Pioneer breeders have been developing several varieties for the U.S. market. James Windish, Director of Monsanto Corporation's plant-sciences business group, was very optimistic about wheat and soybean hybrid development. (Monsanto had bought DeKalb's wheat operation in 1982 and Hartz Seed Company's soybean seed business in 1983.) "We feel very strongly that in the 1990s, some combination of wheat and soybean breakthroughs will generate $300 million to $500 million in annual revenue for Monsanto."[3]

As a minor crop, hybrid sunflower seeds were a fairly recent commercial development, as 95% of the oil-type sunflower crop was grown from hybrids in 1977 compared to only 15% in 1974. Some people were optimistically comparing its stage of development in the 1980s to that of hybrid corn in the 1940s.[4] Pioneer's hybrid sunflower program, however, was not expected to result in Pioneer brand sunflower seed for several years.

MANAGEMENT PHILOSOPHY

Henry Wallace founded Pioneer on four principles:

- produce the best possible products,
- deal honestly and fairly with customers, vendors, and employees,
- sell vigorously, but without misrepresentation, and
- give service to customers.[5]

The current Chairman of the Board, Thomas N. Urban, described Pioneer's primary mission in a November 7, 1984, letter to the stockholders as "the same as it has been since the company's founding—making the production of food more efficient through the science of genetics."

Pioneer's traditional concern for its primary customer, the American farmer, was shown by its willingness during the 1930s depression to carry the debt of its customers on its books rather than demanding payment. Pioneer's top management believed that profits could be recovered, but customer loyalty could not. During the unusually poor growing year of 1978, Pioneer absorbed a 20% earnings drop rather than raise its prices above the 4.5% increase previously announced. "To raise prices further than we had originally set wouldn't have been justified," remarked then-Chairman, Dr. William L. Brown. "We're not in business for a year or two, but for the long-run."[6] In light of the 1984 depressed farm economy, Pioneer management elected not to raise seed prices for the 1985 growing season.

In comparison with business corporations in many other industries, Pioneer has a long-term time horizon. This orientation derived from its beginnings in the hybrid seed business. It typically takes ten years to develop new proven and accepted products from research. It takes fifteen to twenty years to develop new breeding techniques and to prove them in actual crops. This is generally slow, tedious work and rewards only those with persistence. Thomas Urban acknowledged this key part of the company in his remarks to the annual Pioneer stockholders' meeting of January 24, 1984. He was being promoted to the office of Chairman of the Board, replacing the retiring Chairman, Dr. William L. Brown.

We are not only preparing for 1985 but for the years beyond as well. We are continuing to emphasize our research programs. We have not lost sight of the fact that Pioneer is research driven.

EXHIBIT 15.1 **Board of Directors, Pioneer Hi-Bred International, Inc.**

C. Robert Brenton, President, Brenton Banks

Robert B. Wallace, National Co-Chairman, Population Crisis Committee/Draper World Population Fund
Stock ownership: 15.4%

Thomas N. Urban, President and Chairman
Stock ownership: 0.8%

Fred W. Weitz, President and CEO, The Weitz Corporation

Clifford L. Peterson, Retired Senior Vice-President—Finance, Deere and Company

Dr. Donald N. Duvick, Vice-President—Research, Director, Plant Breeding Division

John P. Wallace, President, Wallace Hatchery, Inc.

Raymond Baker, Retired Director of Corn Breeding
Stock ownership: 3.18%

Dr. Ray A. Goldberg, Moffet Professor of Agriculture and Business, Harvard University

Simon Casady, Retired Secretary, Chairman of the Executive Committee, United Central Bancshares
Stock ownership: 0.84%

Dr. Owen J. Newlin, Vice-President
Stock ownership: 9.5%

Robert J. Fleming, President, National By-Products, Inc.
Stock ownership: 0.37%

Charles S. Johnson, Vice-President—Finance and Treasurer

Raymond Lutjen, Retired Vice-President—Finance

SOURCE: Pionner Hi-Bred International, *1984 Annual Report.*

Pioneer continued in 1985 to be a successful, closely held corporation with its headquarters in Des Moines, Iowa. Although it became publicly held in 1973, "insiders" still controlled 70% of the 31,926,527 outstanding shares of common stock in 1984.[7] Wallace family and other heirs owned or controlled around 27% of the stock. Four members of the founding families served on Pioneer's Board of Directors: Robert B. Wallace, John P. Wallace, Owen Newlin, and Thomas N. Urban. In repeated statements in the 1982, 1983, and 1984 Annual Reports, the board announced its strong desire to keep Pioneer an independent company. This was apparently in response to the large numbers of mergers and acquisitions taking place in the seed industry. For a listing of board members, refer to Exhibit 15.1.

Top management was composed of Thomas N. Urban, Chairman and President, and seven other members of the Executive Committee. (See Exhibit 15.2.) Because of promotion from within, the average tenure at Pioneer of a member

---

EXHIBIT 15.2   **Officers and Executive Committee, Pioneer Hi-Bred International, Inc.**

NAME/EDUCATION	AGE	TITLE	YEARS WITH PIONEER
Thomas N. Urban[1] MBA, Harvard	50	Chairman and President	22
Owen J. Newlin[1] Ph.D., University of Minnesota Plant Breeding	56	Vice-President	29
Charles S. Johnson[1] B.S., Iowa State University Business	46	Vice-President—Finance and Treasurer	19
Carrol D. Bolen M.S., University of Illinois Agronomy	46	Vice-President	19
Donald N. Duvick[1] Ph.D., Washington University Plant Breeding	60	Vice-President—Research	33
Suri Sehgal Ph.D., Harvard Plant Breeding	50	Vice-President; President, Pioneer Overseas Corporation	21
Gordon McCleary B.S., University of Illinois Journalism	56	Director of Corporate Information	26
Dale L. Porter J.D., Drake University	59	Secretary and Corporate Counsel	32

SOURCE: Pioneer Hi-Bred International, *Leaders of Pioneer*, 1984.

[1] Member of the Board of Directors.

of the Executive Committee was twenty-five years. Firmly in charge of the corporate reins in 1985, Tom Urban had joined Pioneer in 1960 after earning an MBA from Harvard University. After serving a term from 1968 to 1971 as Mayor of Des Moines, he assumed the positions of President of the Illinois-Wisconsin Division in 1971, Corporate Vice-President in 1974, President in 1979, and Chief Executive Officer in 1984. Vice-Presidents Owen Newlin, Charles Johnson, and Carrol Bolen split responsibilities for overseeing thirteen of the sixteen corporate units. Newlin monitored the Eastern, Plains, and Southwestern Divisions, as well as Pioneer Hi-Bred Limited (Canada). Bolen handled the Illinois-Wisconsin, Cereal Seed, Soybean Seed, and Turf and Forage Divisions. As Vice-President of Finance and Treasurer, Johnson monitored the Central Division, Farm Information Management Systems, Green Meadows Limited, and Norand Corporation, plus the Administrative Services Group. Dr. Duvick was in charge of the research activities of the Plant Breeding and Microbial Genetics Divisions. Dr. Sehgal managed the Pioneer Overseas Corporation. Mr. Cleary served as Director of Corporate Information, and Mr. Porter as Secretary and Corporate Counsel.

With many successful years in the hybrid seed business, Pioneer's top management saw little need to diversify the company's product line beyond related offerings. Nonseed products contributed only about 9% to Pioneer's sales in 1984, sharply contrasting with the 66% provided by the diversified operations of the company's chief competitor, DeKalb Ag Research. Even before its 1982 merger with Pfizer, DeKalb had been involved in the breeding of swine and larger chickens, livestock marketing, commodity futures brokerage, oil and gas exploration, mining, oil well servicing, and irrigation systems, in addition to seeds.

According to former Chairman Dr. William L. Brown, in an interview in 1980, Pioneer's long-term growth will come from its diversification within the seed business. "If we were diversified, management time would be taken away from our major business and I can't help but think that would adversely affect our seed operations."[8] President Urban echoed these thoughts when he agreed that the company may not reduce its dependence on corn for a decade or more. "We would rather live or die on our ability to research new seed products than hedge that with an acquisition to provide earnings to offset any failure in research."[9]

In addition to a conservative attitude toward diversification, management philosophy encouraged decentralized decision-making, promotion from within, and the placement of maximum responsibility on each employee for performance of individual tasks. Some analysts felt that this decentralized management style allowed Pioneer's researchers free rein, and accounted for the firm's renowned creativity. The company has been proud of this laissez-faire relationship with its employees, which encourages initiative, creativity, and productivity. A member of Pioneer's Board of Directors remarked: "Employee attitudes are particularly important since many employees are in direct contact with the end users of our products."[10]

HUMAN RESOURCES

Pioneer directly employed 2,947 nonunionized employees in 1984, an increase of 10% over 1983. Scientists, engineers, and research support staff comprised 6% of the total work force.

The Department of Human Resources, according to Chairman Urban, was created at Pioneer in 1981 to "increase job satisfaction and further increase the productivity of our already productive people."[11] This new department was put in charge of two-year training and employee development programs, meetings to improve communication between levels of the company, management seminars, individualized job performance audits, and workshops on enhancing teamwork within Pioneer.

ORGANIZATION

Pioneer organized itself primarily around its product lines and geographic areas.[12] Key staff responsibilities were handled by the *Administrative Services Group* headed by Vice-President Charles Johnson with the assistance of the Corporate Controller, the Human Resources Director, and the President of Pioneer Data Systems. Pioneer Data Systems, in particular, provided data/information processing services for all units of the corporation. In addition to the Administrative Services Group were seven geographic units and eight product units. Except for the Plant Breeding Division, each unit was managed by a person with the title of President.

The seven geographic units were as follows:

- *Central Division:* produced Pioneer seed corn and marketed it along with Pioneer-developed wheat, alfalfa, soybeans, and other forages, plus sorghum and silage inoculants in Iowa, Minnesota, Missouri, the Dakotas, and eight western states. It operated seed corn production plants, soybean seed conditioning plants, and hard red spring wheat plants.
- *Eastern Division:* produced and marketed Pioneer corn, wheat, and soybean seed in much of the eastern and southern United States. Besides operating seed corn plants, it marketed silage inoculant and alfalfa and sorghum seed.
- *Illinois-Wisconsin Division:* produced and marketed Pioneer corn, soybean, and wheat seed. It also marketed sorghum, alfalfa, and forage seed, as well as silage inoculants produced by other Pioneer divisions.
- *Plains Division:* marketed pioneer seed and silage inoculant in Kansas, Nebraska, and Colorado. It also had some production facilities.
- *Southwestern Division:* marketed Pioneer corn, sorghum, soybean, wheat, and alfalfa seed in Texas, Oklahoma, and New Mexico. In addition to producing Pioneer soybean and wheat seed, it produced the total supply of sorghum seed marketed worldwide by Pioneer.
- *Pioneer Hi-Bred Limited:* a wholly owned subsidiary of Pioneer Hi-Bred International, it produced and marketed Pioneer corn and soybean seed in Canada. It also sold alfalfa, sorghum seed, and silage inoculants produced by other Pioneer divisions.

- *Pioneer Overseas Corporation:* marketed Pioneer corn, sorghum, and alfalfa seed plus silage inoculants outside North America. It also conducted its own research program for the development of corn hybrids for overseas markets. The division's President, Dr. Suri Sehgal, also served as Vice-President on Pioneer's Executive Committee.

The eight product units were as follows:

- *Cereal Seed Division:* produced parent seed for Pioneer wheat varieties, for production and marketing by the geographic units.
- *Soybean Seed Division:* produced parent seed for Pioneer soybean varieties, for production and marketing by the geographic units.
- *Turf and Forage Seed Division:* produced and procured forage seeds, such as alfalfa, for distribution by the geographic units and other channels.
- *Plant Breeding Division:* engaged in genetic research in corn, sorghum, soybeans, wheat, alfalfa, and sunflowers. Within the division, each crop had its own breeding department. The division's director, Dr. Donald Duvick, also served as Vice-President of Research on Pioneer's Executive Committee.
- *Microbial Genetics Division:* developed and produced bacterial inoculants to hasten the fermentation process that turned forage into a storage form for year-round animal feed. It was also researching bacterial intestinal-tract treatments for livestock. Its products were marketed by the geographic units.
- *Norand Corporation:* a wholly owned subsidiary of Pioneer, it developed, manufactured, and marketed microprocessor-based data handling systems for a variety of businesses, including wholesale and retail distributors, route truck operators, and field salespeople.
- *Farm Information Management Services Division:* marketed on-farm computer systems, educational packages, and specially developed computer software to farmers.
- *Green Meadows, Ltd.:* developed Pioneer-owned real estate for residential and commercial usage.

SEED PRODUCTION

To produce marketable hybrid corn seed, Pioneer planted a record 270,000 acres of parent inbreds in 1984; two parent strains alternated in rows of four. Because corn plants contained both male and female characteristics, the female parent was detasseled (Pioneer employed 80,000 temporary workers for this task in 1984), and the male plant left intact. Pollination crossed the two inbred parents to form the desired hybrid offspring. Seed produced in this manner generated fully half the fourfold increase in American corn yields over the last four decades. Without special characteristics bred into the plants, some parts of the country currently under production could not grow crops at all.

Some of Pioneer's seeds were grown in Florida, Texas, and Chile, where climatic conditions allowed the production of several generations in a single season. Even so, Pioneer experienced shortages of some popular new varieties of soybeans and forages because of uncooperative weather conditions in 1983.

Pioneer typically contracted with 2,000 farmers to produce its hybrid seeds, and paid them the market price for grain on the date of delivery. Some of these relationships dated back over a quarter of a century. However, this producton method required that Pioneer release its proprietary plant materials to the very farmers who bought its products. By planting Pioneer's parent varieties without crossing them, the astute agriculturalists could easily create their own breeding stock. This necessary release of trade secrets has been compared to Kentucky Fried Chicken's turning its recipe and ingredients over to every fry cook in the chain.[13] Because of a Pioneer lawsuit, however, hybrid seed corn producers were made liable for any proprietary inbreds planted to produce parent seed rather than hybrid crosses.[14]

Pioneer offered 115 varieties of hybrid seed corn, bred for different maturities and weather conditions, at three of the company's North American divisions. Ten of these 115 strains provided two-thirds of total corn seed sales in 1984. Two new varieties of wheat seed were developed by the Cereal Seed Division for the 1984 season. The Soybean Seed Division produced twenty-one varieties of soybeans, five of them new in 1984. The Turf and Forage Division developed two new alfalfa strains for 1985, which increased the plant's ability to return nitrogen to soil previously planted with nutrient-grabbing corn plants. In addition, the Southwestern Division introduced three new lines of sorghum seed in 1984.

PRODUCTION FACILITIES

Pioneer's production facilities were extensive and far-flung in 1985, and overall plant age was estimated at four years.[15] Twenty-four plants in North America conditioned commercial seed, a process requiring harvesting and drying before the first frost destroyed germination potential. Corn seeds underwent husking, sorting, and a six-month drying period before storage in one of Pioneer's facilities. Nine million bushels of bulk seed and 17.8 million 50-pound bags of corn could be warehoused in Pioneer's massive storage buildings. Corn dryers with a combined capacity of 1.9 million bushels were filled an average of eight times per season. Parent seed corn was conditioned at four plants in Iowa, Texas, Indiana, and Ontario, Canada. Separate production facilities were located in Spain, Brazil, Italy, India, and Austria.

Three unused seed-conditioning plants had been leased from competitors to handle 1984's bumper crop. Mr. James Ansorge, Financial Relations Manager at Pioneer, did not anticipate a recurrence of undercapacity problems in the next few years because of completion in fiscal 1984 of the new facilities at Mt. Pleasant, Iowa, and the remodeling of facilities at Marengo, Iowa, and Donipan, Nebraska.

Sorghum seed was conditioned at Pioneer's Plainview, Texas plant. Forage seeds were prepared in Idaho, California, and Minnesota. As part of Pioneer's move toward the sale of multiple seed products, plants in Iowa, Illinois, Ohio, North Dakota, North Carolina, Nebraska, Indiana, Michigan, and Ontario,

Canada, have been redesigned to condition a mix of corn, wheat, and soybean seeds.

Microbial culture research took place at Pioneer's Oregon and Iowa facilities, while plant breeding and biotechnology research were undertaken at the Johnston, Iowa, headquarters. Field research on plant breeding was conducted at forty-five stations in the United States and Canada and at an additional twenty locations throughout the world. Finally, Cedar Rapids, Iowa, was the site of Pioneer's production and distribution of data-handling systems through its Norand subsidiary.

NORAND CORPORATION

Pioneer acquired the Norand Corporation in October 1976 to develop, manufacture, and market electronic-information systems. Pioneer purchased Norand from George Chadima and his associates for $2.2 million. Mr. Chadima remained at Norand as Director of Research and Development, Executive Vice-President, and Chairman of Norand's board. The subsidiary was then managed by Arnold Sunde, who left what then became Pioneer Data Systems to become Norand's President.

Initially, Norand hoped to quickly boost its sales and earnings with the aid of Pioneer's abundant cash reserves. Pioneer's top management realized almost immediately, however, that drastic changes were needed. "We closed it after 30 days, shut it down, and started all over again," said Pioneer's Chairman, Thomas Urban. "They were at the low end of the market with their small inventory machine and we could see that the trend was for lower and lower prices in that market. So we decided to go for the high end of the market."[16] Norand's field sales and systems engineering staff have similarly been reorganized and expanded.

Norand's portable Route Commander computer, used by beer, soft drink, dairy and snack food delivery people, was the industry's standout in 1984 despite its premium price. The company's A-line buttonless cash registers have been installed in 823 Winchell Donut Shops and 814 Long John Silver's restaurants. Norand's big breakthrough came when Pepsico's Pizza Hut Inc. signed a contract for $40 million of A-line equipment for its nearly 2,000 restaurants. Norand was also in the running for a contract with Southland Corporation, owner of 7,400 7-Eleven convenience stores. The A-line equipment being tested in 1984 at 7-Elevens listed at $17,000 per store according to David Karney, Southland's Manager of Management Information Services in Dallas. A final decision on installation throughout Southland's chain was to be made during 1985.

Despite Pioneer's initial investment of $18 million in expansion funds and Norand's steadily increasing revenues, the subsidiary has accumulated more than $42 million in operating losses over the last seven years. Yet Pioneer has been patient with its subsidiary. "They are used to eight to ten year cycles in their seed corn hybrid development. But at the same time, it's true that they would have liked to have seen a little less investment cost," remarked one analyst.[17] Norand recently completed a $2.6 million expansion to its head-quarters and has hired 150 new employees, bringing its total employment in Cedar Rapids to 550. Half of the unit's products are made at the Cedar Rapids plant. The rest is subcontracted to other manufacturers in the United States and Mexico. Norand contributed positively to Pioneer's profits in 1984 with $875,000 in net income. According to Charles Johnson, Vice-President of Finance and Treasurer, Norand in 1985 had well over 90% of the installed route distribution base.

IBM, NCR, and a growing number of other companies were developing and selling systems to battle Norand's A-line. Service has been one of the strong points of the computer giants and one of the primary factors clients considered in choosing between competing systems.

Thomas Urban assessed the strategic importance of Norand:

> There is a lot of synergy in microbiology, biotechnology, genetic engineering, and computers. Our association with Norand has put us five to ten years ahead of our competition on the market side. By the end of 1985, we'll have 4,000 Norand portable computers with our seed salesmen. That product wouldn't even exist probably until 1990 if we hadn't made it, and it gives us the most efficient sales representative system in the seed business. What we want to do is put new products together to fit markets that we understand better than anyone.[18]

GREEN MEADOWS, LTD

Pioneer's Green Meadows, Ltd. subsidiary has been developing 529.5 acres of company-owned land in Johnston, Iowa, a suburb of Des Moines. No longer required for agricultural research, the land has sprouted homes, townhouses, apartments, shops, recreational facilities, a retirement home, and a convalescent home for children. Although development has lagged along with the depressed Des Moines real estate market, 1982 marked the opening of Village Square shopping center in Green Meadows. The Pioneer Overseas Corporation, Microbial Products Division, Employee Relations Department, and a Hy-Vee grocery store leased space in the new development.

FARM INFORMATION MANAGEMENT SERVICES

Developed in 1983, the Farm Information Management Services (FIMS) Division strove to bridge the gap between farmer and computer terminal. Pioneer's "Information Cultivation" program offered seminars, farm-friendly software, and a support system designed to help farmers make timely and accurate decisions regarding their operations. The package included an IBM personal computer, monitor, printer, and software to help a farmer examine the available alternatives as well as potential results of various actions. Also available were swine-production, corn-production, farm-accounting, and education-support packages developed by Pioneer. Newsletters, classroom instruction, local meetings, and a toll-free hotline were part of the FIMS support package. Pioneer hoped that its experience with its internal data processing division, Pioneer

Data Systems, would help it introduce FIMS to Iowa, Minnesota, and North Dakota in early 1985. Pioneer planned to expand quickly into other markets as soon as it had the necessary support staff in place.[19]

The consulting firm of Frost and Sullivan estimated that microcomputer and computer service sales to the farming industry will reach $104,232,000 per year by 1987. Spending on farm-related computer services, fueled by decision support systems, was expected to grow 24% per year through 1987. Total hardware unit sales for the period were projected at 94,000 units and dollar sales were projected to increase 15% per year.[20] To set the company apart from competitors, Pioneer's computer marketing strategists planned to offer a complete record-keeping and analysis system plus after-purchase service and support.

FINANCE

Although 1983 was a poor year for Pioneer, the company rebounded strongly in 1984. Pioneer rang up $554.9 million in seed corn sales, $12.5 million in sorghum seed, $45.4 million in soybean seed, and $12.1 million in cereal seeds, as well as forage, microbial products, and information products sales, totaling over $700 million. (See Exhibit 15.3.) Forages, the discontinued cotton seed operations, and the fledgling Farm Information Management Services suffered losses. However, corn's 27% contribution margin served to finance the development of the new and/or less successful lines. Overall, profits increased nearly 60% from 1983 to 1984. (See Exhibits 15.4 and 15.5 for financial statements.)

Seed sales and profits were typically high in the second and third quarters (December through May), and activity in the first and fourth quarters (June through November) was slow. In 1984, net income for the second and third quarters totaled $91,716,402, while a combined loss of $22,565,719 occurred in quarters one and four. Pioneer established a company borrowing record in 1984 by arranging $243 million in short-term credit to cover unusually high inventory levels.

Pioneer financed its growth primarily through internal sources, although $242 million in credit lines was available for seasonal and long-term borrowing in 1985. The company had increased its dividend every year since beginning dividends as a publicly held corporation in 1974. On August 31, 1984, 3,125 individuals and organizations held the 31,926,527 outstanding shares of common stock. Although 10,000,000 shares of preferred, cumulative stock have been authorized, none had been issued through 1984. Pioneer stock ranged in price from $23.25 in the third quarter of 1984 to a high of $32.25 in the second, having split two for one on March 19, 1982.

MARKETING

Pioneer's marketing system, developed in the 1930s by Roswell Garst, had evolved into the finest farmer-as-salesman network in the seed industry. Pioneer distributed seed primarily to farmers who sold it to other farmers on a part-time, commission basis. Over 5,000 such entrepreneurs were employed during

EXHIBIT 15.3 Net Sales and Contribution by Product: Pioneer Hi-Bred International, Inc.
(Dollar Amounts in Thousands)

Year Ended August 31	1984 Total	%	1983 Total	%	1982 Total	%	1981 Total	%	1980 Total	%
Net Sales										
Agricultural seeds										
Corn	$554,991	77.5	$376,142	74.4	$454,458	81.5	$382,883	80.1	$329,796	81.3
Sorghum	12,453	1.7	10,332	2.0	8,687	1.6	8,226	1.7	6,295	1.6
Soybeans	45,399	6.3	31,225	6.2	22,447	4.0	22,307	4.7	15,899	3.9
Forage	27,770	3.9	37,037	7.3	29,363	5.3	29,893	6.3	29,104	7.1
Cereal	12,107	1.7	8,624	1.7	9,386	1.7	6,100	1.3	3,116	.8
Cotton	684	.1	1,373	.3	2,073	.4	1,650	.3	3,233	.8
	$653,404	91.2	$464,733	91.9	$526,414	94.5	$451,059	94.4	$387,443	95.5
Electronic information systems										
Norand	$ 54,800	7.7	$ 31,698	6.3	$ 22,103	3.9	$ 15,871	3.3	$ 11,381	2.8
Pioneer Data Systems	—	—	—	—	—	—	2,899	.6	2,691	.7
Farm Information Management Services	28	—	—	—	—	—	—	—	—	—
	$ 54,828	7.7	$ 31,698	6.3	$ 22,103	3.9	$ 18,770	3.9	$ 14,072	3.5
Other	7,829	1.1	9,003	1.8	8,881	1.6	8,166	1.7	4,369	1.0
Total net sales	$716,061	100.0	$505,434	100.0	$557,398	100.0	$477,995	100.0	$405,884	100.0

(Continued)

EXHIBIT 15.3   (Continued)

Year Ended August 31	1984		1983		1982		1981		1980	
	Total	%	Total	%	Total	%	Total	%	Total	%
Contributions (loss)										
Agricultural seeds										
Corn	$151,899	123.4	$103,632	133.9	$150,972	107.9	$125,825	103.7	$129,547	114.5
Sorghum	2,257	1.8	1,917	2.5	2,501	1.8	2,150	1.7	899	.8
Soybeans	1,792	1.5	2,477	3.2	3,055	2.2	2,948	2.4	2,182	1.9
Forage	(617)	(.5)	1,728	2.2	1,344	1.0	2,221	1.8	1,023	.9
Cereal	52	—	(37)	—	1,316	.9	837	.8	(179)	(.2)
Cotton	(437)	(.4)	1,312	(1.7)	(299)	(.2)	(623)	(.5)	10	—
	$154,946	125.8	$108,405	140.1	$158,889	113.6	$133,358	109.9	$133,482	117.9
Electronic information systems										
Norand	$ 875	.7	$ (5,506)	(7.1)	$ (5,845)	(4.2)	$ (7,426)	(6.1)	$ (9,644)	(8.5)
Pioneer Data Systems	—	—	—	—	—	—	144	.1	348	.3
Farm Information Management Services	(1,463)	(1.2)	—	—	—	—	—	—	—	—
	$ (588)	(5.1)	$ (5,506)	(7.1)	$ (5,845)	(4.2)	$ (7,282)	(6.0)	$ (9,296)	(8.2)
Other	(6,277)	(5.1)	(1,851)	(2.4)	(421)	(.3)	295	.3	(1,260)	(1.1)
Total contributions	$148,081	120.2	101,048	130.6	152,623	109.1	126,371	104.2	122,926	108.6
Indirect expense	(24,943)	(20.2)	(23,702)	(30.6)	(12,766)	(9.1)	(5,052)	(4.2)	(9,753)	(8.6)
Pretax earnings from continuing operations	$123,138	100.0	$ 77,346	100.0	$139,857	100.0	$121,319	100.0	$113,173	100.0

SOURCE: Pioneer Hi-Bred International.

EXHIBIT 15.4   Consolidated Income Statements, Pioneer Hi-Bred International, Inc.

Year Ended August 31	1984	1983	1982	1981	1980
Net Sales	$716,061,483	$505,433,624	$557,397,642	$477,995,165	$405,884,401
Cost of Goods Sold	401,834,761	281,264,434	291,280,906	257,654,570	198,667,674
Gross Profit	$314,226,722	$224,169,190	$266,116,736	$220,340,595	$207,216,727
Operating Expenses					
Selling	$140,693,527	$104,765,746	$100,563,089	$ 85,087,756	$ 76,375,321
General and Administrative	37,280,265	31,099,363	24,563,042	17,665,478	15,853,029
	$177,973,792	$135,865,109	$125,126,131	$102,753,054	$ 92,228,350
Operating Income	$136,252,930	$ 88,304,081	$140,990,605	$117,587,541	$114,988,377
Financial Expense (Income)	13,115,366	10,957,884	1,133,253	(3,731,582)	1,815,021
Income before provision for income taxes and equity in net income (loss) of unconsolidated subsidiaries	$123,137,564	$ 77,346,197	$139,857,352	$121,319,123	$113,173,356
Provision for Income Taxes	56,656,161	32,527,680	67,808,796	59,651,214	56,026,114
Income before equity in net income (loss) of unconsolidated subsidiaries	$ 66,481,403	$ 44,818,517	$ 72,048,556	$ 61,667,909	$ 57,147,242
Equity in net income (loss) of unconsolidated subsidiaries	2,659,280	(1,094,119)	(444,438)	1,783,775	97,648
Net Income	$ 69,140,683	$ 43,724,398	$ 71,604,118	$ 63,451,684	$ 57,244,890
Earnings per Common Share	$ 2.17	$ 1.37	$ 2.24	$ 1.99	$ 1.80

SOURCE: Pioneer Hi-Bred International, Inc.

EXHIBIT 15.5   Consolidated Balance Sheets, Pioneer Hi-Bred International, Inc.

Year Ended August 31	1984	1983	1982	1981	1980
Current Assets					
Cash	$ 5,754,402	$ 1,724,827	$ 14,107,044	$ 18,116,420	$ 11,417,319
Marketable securities	18,684,951	6,489,833	3,393,253	16,440,833	60,182,539
Receivables					
Trade	44,701,282	40,525,360	29,661,624	18,506,807	14,378,185
Other	2,000,090	4,390,434	29,206,450	20,769,078	2,144,227
Inventories	213,685,893	271,543,088	199,920,862	121,947,657	130,095,924
Prepaid expenses	8,499,573	9,146,510	7,625,968	9,004,211	6,835,214
Deferred income tax charges	16,280,133	—	—	—	—
Total current assets	$309,606,324	$333,820,052	$283,915,201	$204,785,006	$225,053,408
Investments and Other Assets					
Equity in and advances to unconsolidated subsidiaries	31,667,274	22,789,754	21,804,413	14,015,118	8,516,233
Other	5,832,895	6,450,676	5,605,657	5,163,961	3,779,253
	$ 37,500,169	$ 29,240,430	$ 27,410,070	$ 19,179,079	$ 12,295,486
Property and Equipment					
Land and land improvements	$ 27,488,426	$ 25,161,381	$ 18,334,359	$ 14,993,901	$ 11,972,255
Buildings	125,679,659	117,626,822	77,874,232	66,040,455	58,541,329
Machinery and equipment	139,383,892	118,025,252	85,083,977	69,809,689	58,200,752
Construction in progress	28,094,209	20,502,555	65,598,619	34,844,771	12,113,618
	$320,646,186	$281,316,010	$246,891,187	$185,688,816	$140,827,954
Less accumulated depreciation	83,075,018	69,232,322	56,502,596	47,697,358	41,401,814
	$237,571,168	$212,083,688	$190,388,591	$137,991,458	$ 99,426,140
Intangibles					
Goodwill	$ 2,589,086	$ 3,805,794	$ 4,657,706	$ 5,538,601	$ 6,379,367
Other	1,197,741	3,810,994	6,424,247	—	—
	$ 3,786,827	$ 7,616,788	$ 11,081,953	$ 5,538,601	$ 6,379,367
Total assets	$588,464,488	$582,760,958	$512,795,815	$367,494,144	$343,154,401

Current Liabilities					
Commercial paper and line of credit borrowings	$ 62,082,640	$133,979,669	$ 66,676,069	$ —	$ —
Current maturities of long term debt	2,911,072	3,436,750	2,873,801	2,266,569	31,390,043
Accounts payable, trade	26,635,647	23,702,736	18,969,514	17,429,221	13,122,256
Accrued liabilities					
Salaries and wages	10,326,595	6,933,584	8,919,097	4,340,350	2,032,517
Dividends	6,385,305	5,746,987	5,745,943	4,149,380	3,827,359
Property and withholding taxes	5,698,588	4,252,003	3,834,914	2,571,758	2,741,605
Other	4,157,218	2,877,222	1,963,531	3,102,372	1,540,765
Income taxes payable	36,750,532	14,702,909	42,087,310	30,297,891	34,763,206
Deferred income tax credits, net	—	921,156	3,968,948	2,725,714	514,189
Total current liabilities	$154,947,597	$196,553,016	$155,039,127	$ 66,883,255	$ 89,931,940
Long-term debt	$ 17,826,328	$ 19,389,350	$ 14,747,879	$ 7,937,308	$ 9,881,940
Deferred income tax credit	$ 22,120,150	$ 14,552,070	$ 10,070,936	$ 7,184,975	$ 5,890,000
Stockholders' equity					
Common, $1 par value; authorized, 70,000,000; issued 32,084,606 shares[1]	$ 32,084,606	$ 32,084,606	$ 32,078,806[1]	$ 16,116,053	$ 16,104,228
Additional paid-in capital	9,870,357	9,861,065	9,806,746	9,769,377	9,556,809
Retained earnings	360,375,271	315,498,753	294,761,762	259,867,536	212,053,993
Cumulative translation adjustment	(7,144,579)	(4,189,636)	(3,445,081)	—	—
	$353,254,788 (*)				
	$395,185,655	$353,254,788	$333,202,233	$285,752,966	$237,715,030
Less:					
Cost of treasury stock	(303,644)	(264,360)	(264,360)	(264,360)	(264,360)
Unearned compensation[2]	(1,311,598)	(723,906)	—	—	—
	$393,570,413	$352,266,522	$332,937,873	$285,488,606	$237,450,670
Total liabilities and stockholders' equity	$588,464,488	$582,760,958	$512,795,815	$367,494,144	$343,154,401

SOURCE: Pioneer Hi-Bred International, Inc.

[1] Stock split two for one on March 19, 1982.

[2] Forfeitures by employees of stock tendered under compensation plan.

1984, some earning as much as $30,000 in a single year. A 1982 survey of Iowa farmers by *Wallace's Farmer* magazine concluded that 93.5% of all seed corn sold in Iowa was purchased from farmer-dealers. (See Exhibit 15.6.) To accommodate local buying habits in the southern states, Pioneer distributed through seed dealers.

The 1982 survey also indicated that 10.6% of Iowa farmers canceled or returned part of their 1982 seed corn order, up from 5.7% in 1979. Pioneer typically recorded sales as income when the customer took physical possession of the goods, not when the order was placed. Unopened bags of seed could be returned to Pioneer at any time for a full refund. Financing was provided independently by the farmer-dealer at his own risk.

During 1984 the average fifty-pound bag of Pioneer seed corn sold for approximately $70. Because seed typically represented less than 5% of a farmer's total costs, growers were willing to pay higher prices for genetically engineered hybrids that achieve increased yields. U.S. farmers spent $3,993 million on seed during 1982, while fertilizer costs totaled $9,024 million.[21]

According to Dr. Donald Duvick, Pioneer's Vice-President—Research, seed corn varieties remained in use an average of seven years (nine years for soybeans) before gradual replacement by "seeds believed to be better for several reasons, including enhanced yields and resistance to disease."[22]

Results of the 1982 *Wallace's Farmer* magazine survey indicated that 89.9% of Iowa farmers selected seed primarily for its yield performance. (See Exhibit 15.7.) The introduction of a new, higher-yielding hybrid can therefore have a dramatic, long-term effect on sales. Analysts believed that the emphasis on disease resistance over increased yields by DeKalb–Pfizer Genetics, Pioneer's main competitor in hybrid corn, had cost DeKalb–Pfizer dearly in the marketplace. Yields consistently 5% higher than those provided by DeKalb allowed Pioneer to pull ahead by twenty market share points in the 1970s. Company-sponsored field tests in 1983 indicated that Pioneer seed outproduced the competition by 6.9 bushels per acre. However, independent tests performed by Iowa

---

EXHIBIT 15.6 **Sources of Hybrid Seed Corn in Iowa 1976–1982**

	% 1976	% 1979	% 1982
Farmer-dealer	97.1	96.8	93.5
Seed store	6.2	6.7	8.8
Direct from seed company	6.9	5.2	9.4
Elevator	6.5	4.9	6.8
Farm center	1.2	2.2	2.1
Co-op store	0.5	0.9	NA
Buying group	0.9	0.2	0.8

SOURCE: "1982 Seed Corn, Soybean and Field Seed Survey Report," *Wallace's Farmer* magazine.

EXHIBIT 15.7   **Factors Considered in the Purchase of Seed Corn in Iowa, 1976–1982**

	% 1986	% 1979	% 1982
Corn performance	86.1	86.3	89.9
Company well known	23.1	20.7	21.9
Service is good	17.0	17.3	22.1
Dealer is friend	15.5	15.2	11.6
Price	13.4	12.5	17.2
University corn test	8.3	8.6	13.2
Private company research	NA	NA	9.3
Dealer widely known	6.0	6.3	5.4
Company sales incentive	NA	2.6	1.5

SOURCE: "1982 Seed Corn, Soybean and Field Seed Survey Report," *Wallace's Farmer* magazine.

State University placed Pioneer seed corn first in only two of Iowa's seven agricultural districts. The highest yields in the other five districts were generated by Stauffer Seeds, Renze Hybrids, Wilson Hybrids, Crows Hybrids, and Lynnville Seeds. None of these, however, had the highest yield in more than one district.[23] Despite the university's findings, Pioneer brand corn and alfalfa seeds continued in 1982 to be Iowa's front runners in terms of market share at 62.9% and 17.0%, respectively. Pioneer's soybean seed ranked second in its share of the Iowa market at 17.7% compared to Northrup King's 25.4%. (Information is provided only on Iowa because it typically ranks first among the fifty states in terms of acres planted in corn, and provided approximately one-sixth of the total U.S. corn acreage in 1984.)

Seed sales have tended to be highly seasonal. In past years, farmers placed their orders between July and December. During the 1980s, however, they have tended to delay their purchase decisions until August and sometimes were not fully committed until January.[24] During "Pioneer Days" each February, Pioneer dealers invited their customers for informal visits to settle their seed orders over a cup of coffee. At this time, early payment discounts encouraged customers to purchase and pick up seed for the following planting season.

Although the number of U.S. farms has been decreasing, the United States Statistical Reporting Service discovered an upward trend in average farm size from 420 acres in 1975 to 433 acres in 1982.[25] Larger farming operations tended to demand larger order volumes, special financing, and appointments for sales calls. Many analysts believed the days of informal, low-key marketing to be coming to an end.[26]

Until 1983 the agreement between Wallace and Garst had meant that the Garst Seed Company was Pioneer's exclusive distributor in western Iowa, Missouri, Colorado, Kansas, and Nebraska. With the termination of that agreement, Pioneer assumed complete control of the distribution of Pioneer brand products in the United States. In July 1982, Pioneer formed its Plains division with Kansas, Nebraska, and Colorado. The remaining ex-Garst territories of Missouri and western Iowa became the responsibility of the Central Division.

David Grieve, President of Pioneer's Plains Division, indicated in an interview that the total area formerly served by Garst represented 20.2% of the total U.S. corn acres in 1982. Pioneer's new Plains Division contained 12.2% of the U.S. corn acres in 1984. Nevertheless, recent water shortages, combined with the rising cost of energy needed to pump available irrigation water, are likely, according to Mr. Grieve, to result over the next decade in a gradual decline in acres devoted to corn in the Plains area. "Those acres will likely shift to more water-efficient crops such as sorghum and wheat," predicted Grieve.

In terms of overall market share, Pioneer's share of the U.S. market for its seed corn was approximately 35% in 1984. The next five companies' total share was slightly over 24%. The market shares of other Pioneer seeds were, however, far below that of corn. The company estimated its share of the hybrid sorghum seed market in 1984 at half that of the leader. The branded wheat and soybean seed concept was new and ill-defined. Pioneer claimed a growing although not significant share of these growing markets.[27] Analysts estimated Pioneer's soybean market share at 3% compared to 10% by the leader, Asgrow Seeds. Overall, Pioneer captured a 12% share of the $5 billion seed market in 1984, compared to DeKalb-Pfizer Genetics' 4%.

Similarly, market shares of Pioneer's fledgling bacterial products and cotton seeds were not dramatic. Pioneer bowed out of hybrid cotton seed production in 1983, stating that "it appeared unlikely that (the market for premium cotton planting seed) would grow large enough to support the kind of commitments to research and production we make in our other seed products."[28] Cotton research expenditures for 1980–1983 had totaled $1,260,000.

The company's cattle-breeding operations had been sold in 1976. Management felt poor bull performance reflected negatively on Pioneer's seed corn business. Pioneer divested its thirty-year-old Hy-Line and Indian River poultry concerns for book value (about $13 million) in 1978.[29] Although poultry had been a major Wallace family concern, created by Henry Wallace and run by his son, the division had consistently lost money.

Pioneer's print-media advertising budget of $2,132,121 ranked it thirteenth among agricultural advertisers for 1983. The typical agricultural concern spent 42.1% of its advertising budget on print media. Pioneer employed radio and television spots, trade shows, point-of-purchase devices, cooperative advertising schemes, newspaper and business publication advertisements (see Exhibit 15.8 for an example), outdoor displays, direct mail, premiums, catalogs, and directories to advertise its products. Each August, Pioneer hosted "Expo Days," during which neighboring farmers gathered to examine first-hand the various hybrids planted in a local Pioneer test plot. This two- to three-day event enabled farmers to discuss the performance of various hybrids with their neighbors as

Numbers you know... Numbers you know you should try.

It happens almost every year. Just when you think Pioneer can't come out with new and better hybrids than the ones you planted last spring, they do. Next year is no exception. The best Pioneer® brand hybrids you can plant on your farm include some "old and familiar" numbers ... and some "brand new". Hybrids like these:

3978

A hybrid that northern corn growers have come to know and trust, because it offers yield and drydown advantages that few competitive corns in this maturity can beat. **3978** performs very well on your better soils, and on "slower" peat ground, too.

3881 NEW

This exciting, new hybrid is about the same maturity as 3978, but with even higher yield potential. Better stalks and roots, and very good head smut tolerance are other reasons why you'll want to make **3881** part of your "new generation" team of Pioneer® brand hybrids.

3803 NEW

A hybrid that's a lot like 3906 for strong, dependable agronomic traits, but with even faster field drydown. You'll especially like the extended kernel "fill" period that enables **3803** to make the most of the season. Push your populations to boost yields even more.

3906

A full-season hybrid with the defensive agronomic traits it takes to maintain top plant health, and the yield punch it takes to be the "backbone" of your corn program. **3906** has strong stalks and roots, and the ability to turn higher populations into extra yield.

® **PIONEER**.
BRAND·SEED CORN ®

The Limitation of Warranty and remedy appearing on the label
is part of the terms of sale.
Pioneer is a brand name; numbers identify varieties. ®Registered
trademark of Pioneer Hi-Bred International, Inc., Des Moines, Iowa, U.S.A.

SOURCE: Farm Journal, January 1985. Reprinted courtesy of Pioneer Hi-Bred International, Inc., Des Moines, Iowa.

well as with Pioneer personnel. It was not unusual for farmers to receive a hat or jacket with the familiar green Pioneer logo, either at this event or when seed was purchased from the local farmer-dealer.

Word-of-mouth notoriety has been extremely important in seed marketing, because seed stocks are largely bought on faith. Their real merit could not be judged until the crop was "in the bin." Pioneer management believed that "there is no better advertising and no better selling aid than good performance by the product. We spend much more on research to improve our products than we spend to advertise them in the conventional ways."[30]

RESEARCH AND DEVELOPMENT

In-house research and development efforts were given most of the credit for Pioneer's dominance in the seed corn industry. Over the last five years, Pioneer budgeted an average of 3.7% of sales for research. (See Exhibit 15.9.) The Plant Breeding Division had been established to conduct independent research in corn, sorghum, soybean, wheat, alfalfa, and sunflower breeding. Within the division, each crop had its own breeding department.

Improved stress tolerance has been a major contribution of Pioneer plant breeders. By reducing the effects of stress on plants, researchers have been able to develop hybrids and strains that are capable of increased yields under a variety of conditions. Specific resistance to plant diseases, parasites, and adverse weather have been bred into Pioneer's hybrids.

Modern biotechnology was expected to allow Pioneer's researchers to make rapid progress in stress tolerance. One of the Department of Biotechnology's major goals was to allow plant breeders to transfer desired genes directly into

EXHIBIT 15.9

Pioneer's Research and Development Expenditures, 1980–1984

(Dollar Amounts in Thousands)

PRODUCT	1980	1981	1982	1983	1984
Corn	$ 8,255	$ 9,635	$13,309	$15,859	$19,015
Sorghum	763	843	912	1,428	1,395
Wheat	832	956	1,160	1,754	2,110
Soybeans	641	843	1,041	1,780	2,109
Alfalfa	405	632	773	1,239	1,123
Cotton	245	280	314	421	0
Sunflowers	51	141	182	219	258
Computer Systems	645	547	529	733	843
Microbial Cultures	632	780	825	1,297	1,331
Total	$12,469	$14,657	$19,045	$24,730	$28,184

SOURCE: Pioneer Hi-Bred International, *1984 Annual Report* and *1982 Annual Report*.

breeding material. This accomplishment could dramatically increase the rate of genetic selection.

In the Biotechnology Research Department, the Plant Breeding Division's newest unit, bioengineers worked to develop techniques for manipulating genes at the molecular level. Pioneer's scientists hoped to eventually move nitrogen-fixing genes from legume bacteria to corn, thus substantially reducing fertilizer requirements. However, this gene-splicing technique was considered by Pioneer to be a distant possibility.

The Corn Breeding Department, the largest subsection of the Plant Breeding Division, worked from twenty-five strategically located research stations. Each research station conducted location-specific yield tests at approximately fifteen outlying sites. Pioneer corn breeders continuously strove to develop hybrids that produced more harvestable bushels per acre than strains currently available.

A three-year study conducted by Pioneer researchers compared hybrids developed over the past fifty years with those in use in the 1980s. The study found annual yield improvements to average 1.4 bushels per acre. Modern hybrids were found to produce superior yields in both high- and low-fertility environments, yielding fifty more bushels per acre than the seed corn farmers planted fifty years ago.[31]

The goal of the Microbial Genetics Division in 1985 was to develop three new marketable products by 1987. This would bring to six the number of products in Pioneer's microbial genetics line. Silage and alfalfa inoculants and a bacterial digestive-tract treatment for livestock were already in Pioneer's product arsenal.

Gene splitting and microbial genetic research were becoming the targets of increasing controversy. Some public interest groups felt that mutant strains of potentially harmful organisms could result from attempts to develop organic herbicides and insecticides. While Pioneer lauded microbial genetic research as the newest tool whose application might result in advances even more exciting than those related to computer technology, some environmentalists feared that human-made genes could migrate and "create havoc."[32] Public opposition was successful in halting a major corn genetic research project at Stanford University. The University of Pennsylvania was in court in 1984 defending its right to perform genetically related experiments.

INTERNATIONAL ACTIVITIES

Through a network of subsidiaries, joint ventures, and independent distributors, Pioneer Overseas Corporation (POC) marketed Pioneer products in more than sixty countries outside North America. The majority of POC business in 1984 involved hybrid corn and sorghum seeds. In 1983, international sales contributed $18.7 million (24%) of total pre-tax income, a significant increase from a 10% contribution in 1982. In 1984, POC enjoyed an 8% increase in dollar sales and a 17% increase in unit sales over those of 1983. Nevertheless, the 1984 pre-tax contribution declined because of the relative strength of the dollar in international trade and abnormally high production costs due to the 1983 drought. Total unit sales of corn seed outside North America rose by 3% in 1984 over 1983; most of the increase came from Latin America. Nearly two-thirds of Pioneer's international sales were made in Europe. Although Asia's sales accounted for less than 5% of Pioneer's overseas sales, future growth in Asian corn seed demand was expected to grow as Oriental diets began to include more grain-fed meats.

Dr. William L. Brown, past Chairman of Pioneer, summarized Pioneer's situation in international activities in a 1984 speech to stockholders:

> Over the years the principal foreign markets for our products have been identified, effective and dedicated organizations are now in place in most of those marketing areas and breeding programs in areas where U.S. hybrids are not adapted are beginning to generate superior products.[33]

Nevertheless, in 1985, Pioneer was not as strong internationally as it was in North America.

COMPETITION

Traditionally, other than two to three major corporations the U.S. seed corn market has been the province of small, family-controlled companies. Nearly all of the 600-member companies of the American Seed Trade Association had sales in the range of $3 million to $10 million annually.[34] The lifeblood of these small firms was the propagation and sale of seeds developed by university and government experiment stations. These small, private seed companies conducted little to no research on their own. The industry's complexion, nevertheless, was changing.

In the last decade, more than 100 of these smaller companies have been acquired by large chemical and drug conglomerates with enormous research budgets. Developments in biotechnology have meant that instead of planting seeds and selecting those with desirable characteristics, scientists can now identify those traits in test tubes. "It takes 12 years to develop a classically bred variety; we think we can do the same thing (with biotechnology) in six years," predicted James E. Windish, director of Monsanto's plant-sciences business group.[35]

In place of the independent, family-owned seed companies, the industry has been consolidating behind giants like Monsanto, Sandoz, Celanese, and Ciba-Geigy. (See Exhibit 15.10.) Ownership of plant materials vital to the development of new strains has been attracting these bioresearch giants to private seed companies. Perhaps more important, the established hybrid companies occupied the front lines of the seed business. Without the channels provided by such experienced firms, the production, field testing, and marketing of new hybrids would be difficult for an acquiring company to perform.

L. William Teweles, seed company broker, predicted in 1984 that the major food companies would also begin snapping up smaller seed companies as a means to produce and test improved hybrids of grains used in common food products. Most new entrants were enchanted by Pioneer's profit margins ap-

EXHIBIT 15.10   **Seed Companies and Their Parents**

SEED COMPANY	PARENT ORGANIZATION
Asgrow	Upjohn
O's Gold	
Burpee	ITT
Harris	Celanese
Trojan	Pfizer
Dekalb	
Blaney Farms	Stauffer
Prairie Valley	
Ferry Morse	Purex
ACCO	Cargill
Jacques	Agrigenetics
Keystone	
Funk Seeds International	Ciba-Geigy (Switzerland)
Louisiana	
Ring Around Products	
Northrup King	Sandoz (Switzerland)
Wilson Hybrids	LaFarge Coppee (France)
DeKalb Wheat	Monsanto
Jacob Hart Soybeans	
Lynnville Seeds	Lubrizol

proaching 30% in corn. They recognized it as the industry leader in marketing and research. Teweles estimated that varieties produced by new genetic techniques would add $6.8 billion in sales to the industry by the end of the century.[36]

Commenting on the influx of multinational chemical companies into the seed industry, Pat R. Mooney, author of *Seeds of the Earth*, remarked, "Certainly the distribution mechanism for seeds and crop chemicals are the same and companies might be tempted to advertise the two products in package deals for farmers."[37] Pioneer's Dr. Duvick, Vice-President—Research, countered, "I doubt if such packages will ever be practical. Farmers are too individualistic to accept a complete package as long as they are free to choose."[38] Nevertheless, marketing efforts by seed-selling multinationals were becoming intense. Of 1983's top five seed advertisers, four were global conglomerates: Monsanto, Upjohn, Ciba-Geigy, and Stauffer. The fifth was Pioneer.[39]

Occidental Petroleum had planned to introduce the first hybrid cotton seed (and a hybrid rice seed it had received from the Chinese government during oil drilling negotiations) through its Ring Around Products subsidiary.[40] However, Ciba-Geigy's Funk Seeds International purchased the Dallas-based Ring Around Products in December 1984 to complement its new $7 million plant science and technology research facility in North Carolina.

Upjohn's operations combined agricultural chemicals with hybrid seed marketing in 105 countries of the world. Upjohn recently purchased O's Gold Seeds of Parkersburg, Iowa, to augment the pea, bean, sweet corn, field corn, sorghum, and soybean seed operations of its Asgrow Seed Company.

Stauffer Chemical's agricultural operations accounted for 16% of its $1,505.7 million in total sales for 1984. Stauffer continued to streamline its seed business through the consolidation of manufacturing and sales operations.

Mr. James Ansorge, Financial Relations Manager for Pioneer, denied in an interview feeling any widespread competitive pressure from these major corporations. He believed their entry into the industry was too recent and that they had too narrow a range of products to pose any immediate nationwide threat. Pioneer executives were aware, however, that the major attack, if and when it came, would be launched in the lucrative Midwestern Corn Belt market.

THE PIONEER–GARST "DIVORCE"

On May 18, 1983, Garst Seed Company and Pioneer Hi-Bred International issued a joint public statement. It read:

> Following the settlement, both companies will compete with one another. Pioneer will begin serving all of the area heretofore served by Garst; Garst intends to expand the area in which it operates. In the future Garst will be offering for sale its own brands of product produced from other than Pioneer breeding material.[41]

Thus ended the cooperative relationship forged by a Henry Wallace–Roswell Garst handshake fifty-three years before.

When Pioneer became publicly held in 1973, the company's outlook on profit and control changed. Henry Wallace had died in 1963. The Board felt that Garst's market share in the lucrative Western Corn Belt of Western Iowa, Missouri, Colorado, Kansas, and Nebraska was not increasing as rapidly as was Pioneer's in the rest of the nation. Upon Roswell Garst's death in 1977, Pioneer's management voted to terminate the unwritten distributor agreement with Garst at Pioneer's June 17, 1977, meeting. (The Wallace-Garst handshake had been made into a written contract in 1932. A new agreement was signed in 1940; when it lapsed in 1955, the two companies continued the relationship with no written contract in force.)

The Garst & Thomas Seed Company (Roswell Garst and Charles Thomas teamed up in the mid-1930s) was Pioneer's only distributor. Garst & Thomas regularly sold about 20% of all Pioneer's corn and grew 1.5% of Pioneer's seed. Alone, it was the third largest corn dealer in the country. The decades-old arrangement called for Garst to pay Pioneer a 7% royalty on all Pioneer seed produced, sold, and delivered by Garst (not to exceed half of Garst's net profits) and to reimburse Pioneer for the cost of parent seed production. In 1981, Pioneer netted $1.94 on each bag of hybrid corn seed sold by Garst, while Pioneer salesmen brought in profits of $7.88 per bag.[42] Pioneer's Board, citing smaller profit margins on the 20% of Pioneer's market held by Garst and diverging management styles of the two firms, signed a letter of intent with

Garst & Thomas Seed Company on October 13, 1980, outlining Pioneer's offer to buy Garst & Thomas for $18 million.

The situation changed in 1982 when the Garst family bought out the Thomases for $24.5 million. Disturbed by the loss of the Thomas family's stabilizing influence and by a lack of progress in the sales talks, Pioneer's CEO, Thomas Urban, served the new Garst Seed Company with an ultimatum on August 31, 1981: "You are hereby notified that the relationship which has existed between us is terminated as of August 31, 1983. Please take notice and govern yourselves accordingly."[43] Despite the prior sales agreement, Pioneer would not deliver products to the new Garst Seed Co. after August 31, 1983. The Garsts responded with an April 9, 1982 request for an injunction to forbid Pioneer from terminating the relationship, claiming that (1) Garst could not survive without Pioneer seed stock, (2) no good reason existed for termination, and (3) ten years, not two, was a reasonable period to allow Garst to develop its own parent seed stock. If the injunction were to be denied, Garst sought $140 million in damages. Pioneer soon responded with an injunction of its own.

Pioneer management discovered that 125 bags of proprietary parent seed had been removed from the Garst Seed Co. warehouses and stored in the basement of David Garst's residence. During the course of courtroom testimony, it became clear that the Garsts planted the 125 bags, not to produce more hybrid seed as agreed, but to create more parent stock. Pioneer filed suit on July 25, 1982, for the return of any parent inbreds in Garst's possession. Because corn reproduced itself 200 times each season, the 125 bags of seed could produce 25,000 bags of parent corn. With 25,000 bags of parent seed, Garst could harvest as much hybrid seed as Pioneer could, and have parents left in reserve.

In fighting the injunction, Garst claimed partnership with Pioneer, and cited their long history together, plus Garst's participation in Pioneer's research and testing, aid to Pioneer's sorghum program, and investment of $250 million earned from the sale of its Oklahoma sales group to Pioneer, allegedly in return for the right to sell the resulting wheat seed.

In a marathon hearing, Judge Thomas Smith of Carroll County, Iowa District Court, denied the Garst injunction request after sixty-four days and 10,000 pages of testimony. Judge Smith ruled that "Pioneer should not be forced to deal with a company that has said it wants to become a major competitor. An injunction continuing the relationship would be impossible to enforce because of the level of ill feelings between the Garsts and Pioneer." The judge further ordered the return of any and all "kidnapped" Pioneer genetic plant material in the Garsts' possession, claiming they had "acted with unclean hands" in retaining the parent seed.[44]

Before the suits and countersuits could be brought to trial, however, Garst and Pioneer issued their joint statement resolving the issue. The resolution outlined the following points: (1) Garst was terminated as Pioneer's distributor; (2) Garst agreed to return all plant-breeding material to Pioneer; (3) after the Spring 1983 season, Garst could no longer produce Pioneer seed but might sell any leftover Pioneer seed corn, sorghum, and wheat under the Garst name until

July 1, 1985; and (4) Garst must pay service charges to Pioneer for any retained inventory.[45]

The battle moved out of the courts and into the marketplace. Chairman Urban commented that "the full impact of the change in distribution won't be felt until fiscal 1985."[46] Garst lost eighteen out of thirty-two sales managers to Pioneer soon after the breakup. Garst, vowing to position itself as the number two seed corn producer, increased its print advertising budget by 97%, to $349,681 and began recruiting sales representatives in earnest.[47] Garst established six research centers, including one on Oahu, Hawaii, where it was growing three generations of breeding material per year. Research headquarters were under construction in 1985 in Slater, Iowa. Garst signed a breeding material sharing agreement with Coop de Pau, Europe's third largest seed corn company, and it purchased Clyde Black and Son Seeds to obtain its proprietary lines. Garst described its research program as "one of the largest and most productive in the industry."[48]

BREEDERS' RIGHTS

According to former-Chairman Brown, less developed nations have accused the major seed companies of collecting the world's plant genetic resources mainly from third world countries, storing these resources in the form of seeds in gene banks in the developed countries, and refusing to make them available to the developing nations from which they originally came. It has further been alleged that the seed companies took unfair advantage of the third world through their use of plant patents, plant breeders' rights, and the private exploitation of improved varieties of plants.[49] Those making the accusations demanded the free exchange of plant genetic material, regardless of breeders' rights, a development that could quickly bankrupt the seed companies. Although this movement was not a large one in 1984, support appeared to be growing throughout the less developed countries of the world.

This disregard for breeders' rights was bemoaned by Dr. Brown: "There was a time when the proprietary nature of lines and hybrids was respected by the competitor. This seems no longer to be true."[50] Chairman Urban echoed this concern as he pointed out a "rather peculiar turn in the competition in the seed corn business. We are selling against corn hybrids that look amazingly like those we have developed. The 'lookalike' problem has been building over the past five years or so."[51] The 1970 Plant Variety Protection Law provided some recourse against lookalike seeds, but techniques for identifying germ plasm had yet to be legally recognized.

OTHER FACTORS AFFECTING THE HYBRID SEED INDUSTRY

The hybrid seed corn market was relatively mature in 1985. Growth came only from increases in the number of corn acres planted. The government's policy has had a profound effect on crop acreage in recent years. One such effect stemmed from the 1983 Payment in Kind (PIK) program. In return for idling a portion of their cropland, farmers were paid with government surplus corn and wheat. Part of a broad acreage-reduction strategy, PIK sought to reduce agricultural surplus while increasing farm income. So successful was this strategy that corn acreage planted fell 27% in 1983. (See Exhibit 15.11.) Pioneer strongly supported the acreage reduction policy as being beneficial to the American farmer, although the resulting drop in corn plantings reduced Pioneer's profits 39%.

In addition to government policy, commodity prices, energy and fertilizer supplies, plant diseases, and, of course, the weather all influence the hybrid seed industry's profitability. In 1983, drought nearly doubled Pioneer's seed production costs and reduced seed production to 47% of normal. September 1984 freezes damaged a portion of that year's crop.

A doubling of per capita high-fructose corn sweetener consumption (see Exhibit 15.12), spurred by the recent switch from sugar to 100% corn sweetener in major soft drink formulations, and expanding production of ethanol for fuel use, provided incentives for corn growers. The federal tax credit for refiners who mixed alcohol with their gasoline increased from $.50 to $.60 per gallon of alcohol on January 1, 1985.[52] In addition, tariffs on imported fuel alcohol increased to $.63 per gallon.

Although farm prices were depressed and farm exports suffered from the strong dollar, Pioneer's Urban predicted permanent surpluses in U.S. grain bins. He estimated that research will provide average yields of 145 bushels per acre by the year 2000, an increase of 26% over yields achieved in 1982.[53]

U.S. agricultural policy in the 1980s focused on the use of price supports and acreage reductions to offset excess supply. However, economists and consumers feared that decreased yields would mean higher food costs and increased inflation. As attempts were being made in 1985 to deal seriously with the increasing U.S. federal deficit, city-dwelling congressmen were becoming

---

EXHIBIT 15.11   **Planted Acreage of Selected U.S. Crops**
(In Millions of Acres)

YEAR	CORN	WHEAT	SOYBEANS	SORGHUM
1975	78.7	74.9	54.6	18.1
1976	84.6	80.4	50.3	18.1
1977	84.3	75.4	59.0	16.6
1978	81.7	66.0	64.7	16.2
1979	81.4	71.4	71.6	15.3
1980	84.0	80.6	70.0	15.6
1981	84.2	88.9	67.8	16.0
1982	81.9	87.3	71.5	16.1
1983	60.1	76.8	63.5	11.8
1984	81.8	82.6	65.2	14.8

SOURCE: United States Department of Agriculture, Crop Reporting Board.

EXHIBIT 15.12   **U.S. Per Capita Consumption of Corn Sweeteners**
(In Pounds)

YEAR	HIGH-FRUCTOSE	GLUCOSE	DEXTROSE	TOTAL
1974	3.0	17.2	4.9	25.1
1975	5.0	17.5	5.0	27.5
1976	7.2	17.5	5.0	29.7
1977	9.5	17.6	4.1	31.2
1978	12.1	17.8	3.8	33.7
1979	14.9	17.9	3.6	36.4
1980	19.2	17.6	3.5	40.3
1981	23.3	17.8	3.5	44.6
1982	26.7	18.0	3.5	48.2

SOURCE: U.S. Department of Agriculture.

increasingly opposed to farm subsidies. Debate had already begun on a new farm bill to replace the 1981 law expiring on October 1, 1985. Critics of current farm policy estimated that in-place subsidy programs could cost up to $19 billion annually. Furthermore, they pointed out the worsening plight of mid-size, family-run operations in spite of current policy. Farm income and exports continued to contract as land values tumbled and farm debt increased.

The National Corn Growers Association and the Fertilizer Institute have begun lobbying for a nonsubsidy proposal, while wheat growers favored improving current price supports. The Reagan administration was expected to propose a free-market policy emphasizing soil conservation, fewer price supports, reduced farm loans, and less idle land. The administration's goal, to make U.S. farm prices more internationally competitive, would induce a survival-of-the-fittest farmer scenario, in order to lower commodity prices and reduce the federal deficit. Whatever the outcome of the current debate, Pioneer management believed that the state of the farm economy was the most crucial issue facing their company in the decade of the 1980s.

NOTES

1. *Pioneer in Applied Genetics* (Des Moines, Iowa: Pioneer Hi-Bred International, Inc., 1983), p. 3.

2. *Grains: Production, Processing, Marketing* (Chicago, Ill: Board of Trade, 1977), pp. 14–15.

3. "The Biotech Big Shots Snapping up Small Seed Companies," *Business Week*, June 11, 1984, pp. 69, 72.

4. C. H. Davenport, "Sowing the Seeds," *Barron's*, March 2, 1981, pp. 9–19, 33.

5. *The Long Look* (Des Moines, Iowa: Pioneer Hi-Bred International, Inc., 1981), p. 3.

6. "A Sustained Harvest," *Forbes*, October 15, 1979, pp. 120, 122.

7. *The Value Line Investment Survey*, August 31, 1984, p. 1493.

8. "Seed Corn's Long, Hot, Bruising Summer," *Business Week*, August 25, 1980, pp. 52–56.

9. *Ibid.*

10. Pioneer Hi-Bred International, Inc., *1984 Annual Report*, p. 6.

11. "Remarks of Thomas N. Urban and Dr. William L. Brown," Annual Shareholders Meeting (Pioneer Hi-Bred International, Inc., January 24, 1984), p. 8.

12. The information on Pioneer's organization structure was taken from *Leaders of Pioneer* (Des Moines, Iowa: Pioneer Hi-Bred International, Inc., 1984).

13. W. Cochran, "The Battle over a Little Bit of Seed Corn," *Des Moines Register*, November 28, 1982, pp. 1F, 3F.

14. L. Soth, "High Stakes in High-Tech Ag in Pioneer-Garst Legal Battle," *Des Moines Register*, May 2, 1983, p. 14A.

15. *The Value Line Investment Survey.*

16. C. Hawkins, "Patience with Norand Pays for Pioneer," *Des Moines Register* August 12, 1984, pp. 1F, 3F.

17. *Ibid.*

18. *Ibid.*

19. "Pioneer Announces Introduction of New Information Management System," Press Release (Des Moines, Iowa: Pioneer Hi-Bred International, Inc., Novemeber 9, 1984).

20. "Farm Computer Market to Be $428 Million in Five Years," *Agri Marketing*, October 1983, p. 23.

21. *Agriculture Yearbook* (Washington, D.C.: United States Department of Agriculture, 1984), p. 425.

22. G. Anthan, "Multinational Corporations Are Moving into Seed Business," *Des Moines Register*, June 24, 1982, p. 4A.

23. *The 1983 Corn Yield Test Report* (Ames, Iowa: Iowa State University Cooperative Extension Service).

24. "DeKalb-Pfizer Genetics Works to Keep Seed Sold," *Agri Marketing*, January 1983, p. 39.

25. *Agriculture Yearbook* (Washington, D.C.: U.S. Department of Agriculture), p. 381.

26. "DeKalb-Pfizer Genetics Works to Keep Seed Sold," *Agri Marketing*, January 1983.

27. Pioneer Hi-Bred International, Inc., *1983 Annual Report*, p. 24.

28. *Ibid.*, p. 4.

29. "A Sustained Harvest," *Forbes*, October 15, 1979, p. 122.

30. *The Long Look* (Des Moines, Iowa: Pioneer Hi-Bred International, Inc., 1981), pp. 3–4.

31. *Pioneer in Applied Genetics* (Des Moines, Iowa: Pioneer Hi-Bred International, Inc., 1983), p. 11.

32. P. A. Bellew, "Agricultural Research, Once Little Noticed, Grows Controversial," *Wall Street Journal*, November 21, 1984, pp. 1, 17.

33. "Remarks of Thomas N. Urban and Dr. William L. Brown," Annual Shareholders Meeting (Pioneer Hi-Bred International, Inc., January 24, 1984), p. 16.

34. "The Biotech Big Shots Snapping up Small Seed Companies," *Business Week*, June 11, 1984, p. 69.

35. *Ibid.*

36. *Ibid.*

37. G. Anthan, "Multinational Corporations are Moving into Seed Business," *Des Moines Register*, June 24, 1982.

38. *Ibid.*

39. "Top 150 Print Advertisers over Past Five Years," *Agri Marketing*, December 1983, p. 40.

40. "The Biotech Big Shots Snapping up Small Seed Companies," *Business Week*, June 11, 1984.

41. W. Cochran, "Garst-Pioneer Settlement Marks End of Era," *Des Moines Register*, May 18, 1983, p. 5S.

42. M. L. Cumins, "Seeds of Discontent," *Agri Marketing*, August 1982, pp. 20–24.

43. *Ibid*, p. 20.

44. W. Cochran, "Garst Told to Return 'Kidnapped' Seed Corn," *Des Moines Register*, April 20, 1983, pp. 1, 12.

45. "Pioneer Hi-Bred, Garst Settle Their Litigation," *Wall Street Journal*, May 19, 1983, p. 7.

46. "Remarks of Thomas N. Urban and Dr. William L. Brown," Annual Shareholders Meeting (Pioneer Hi-Bred International, Inc., January 24, 1984), p. 2.

47. "Divorce Creates New Competition," *Agri Marketing*, August 1983, pp. 22–26.

48. *The 1985 Garst Seed Catalog* (Coon Rapids, Iowa: Garst Seed Company), p. 1.

49. "Remarks of Thomas N. Urban and Dr. William L. Brown," Annual Shareholders Meeting (Pioneer Hi-Bred International, Inc., January 24, 1984), p. 13.

50. *Ibid.*

51. *Ibid.* p. 6.

52. N. Rask, "Brazilian Alcohol Could Fuel U.S Farm Export," *Wall Street Journal, December* 4, 1984, *p.* 28.

53. D. Muhm, "Urban Sees Permanent Surpluses in Farm Future," *Des Moines Register, December* 16, 1983, p. 10S.

CASE 16

The Maquiladora Operations Industry/Technical Note on U.S. Production Facilities in Mexico

WALTER E. GREENE

During World War II Mexico was neutral; however, many of its citizens were admitted into the U.S. under the Bracero Program to meet U.S. needs for workers. This program remained in effect until 1964, when the program was terminated and many Mexicans lost their "legal" status in the U.S. To alleviate the Mexican unemployment problems this caused, Mexico established the Border Industrialization Program or Maquiladora Program in May 1965. (*Maquiladora* is derived from an old Spanish word meaning "the amount of grain paid to the miller to grind the grain.") By 1967, 57 maquilas (plural for maquiladora) were operating in the border area and by 1976 the number had increased to 448 plants. By 1985 there were a total of 772 plants in Mexico on its Northern border, and Mexico had eased the requirements forcing all maquilas to be "on the Northern border".[1]

Until 1972 the maquiladora program was limited to roughly 19 kilometers from the U.S. border. In 1972, Mexico expanded maquiladora operations into the interior of Mexico, including such industrial areas as Mexico City and Monterey. This was done to encourage the inclusion of Mexican components in the assembly process.[2] Since 1972 the number of maquiladora plants operating in the interior had risen from 10 in 1973 to 76 in 1983. Plants in the interior have never accounted for more than 12% of the total number of plants.[3] Exhibit 16.1 shows the number of maquiladora plants operating in Mexico for the years 1975 through 1985. It is estimated that an additional 93 maquiladora

This case was prepared by Professor Walter E. Greene of Pan American University. Presented at the Midwest Society for Case Research Workshop, 1988. All rights reserved to the author and the Midwest Society for Case Research. Copyright © 1988 by Walter E. Greene, APS, Ph.D. Reprinted by permission. It also appears in *Annual Advances, 1988*, pp. 378–385, edited by Susan L. Wiley.

EXHIBIT 16.1   **Operating In-Bond Plants in Mexico**

	TOTAL	BORDER CITIES	INTERIOR CITIES
1975	454	405	49
1976	448	395	53
1977	443	388	55
1978	457	411	46
1979	540	480	60
1980	620	551	69
1981	605	533	72
1982	588	516	72
1983	629	562	67
1984	722	641	81
1985	772	683	89

SOURCE: *Business Mexico.*

plants were opened during 1986 bringing the total to 865.[4] Mexican officials believed the development of the maquiladora program, patterned after a model observed in the Far East on a tour by the Mexican Secretary of Industry and Commerce, could help solve Mexico's high unemployment problems.[5]

The basic concept of the maquiladora program was one of co-production. Under the program, a U.S. firm establishes two plants under one management, one on each side of the border. The U.S. plant provides components duty-free to its sister plant in Mexico for assembly, semi-processing and/or repair, and subsequently to be reexported to the U.S. for further processing or as completed goods. U.S. duty is levied on the returning products only to the extent of the value that was added in Mexico.[6] In designing the maquiladora program, the Mexican government sought to take maximum advantage of the U.S. Tariff Code, specifically Items 806.30 and 807, which allow the duty-free re-entry of U.S. goods assembled from materials and components of origin. The U.S. only levies duty on the non-U.S. components used and the value added by Mexican labor. Products that best fit the above parameters within the maquiladora concept involve operations that require manual dexterity. Products in which maquiladora plants have a comparative advantage include electronics, electrical equipment, ceramics, automotive parts, and toys[7,8]

There are generally three types of operating plants in the maquiladora program in terms of ownership and legal responsibility. Plants may be captured, sheltered, or subcontracted. The captured operation is majority U.S. owned, but located in Mexico. The sheltered plant is 100% Mexican owned but does not participate in management of the Mexican facility.[9,10] The subcontractor is 100% Mexican owned and does not allow foreign participation in its management. The subcontractor can therefore honor contracts with more than one

EXHIBIT 16.2

Direct Foreign Corporate Investments in Mexico, December 1987

COUNTRY	U.S. DOLLAR AMOUNT	PERCENTAGE OF PARTICIPATION
U.S.A.-based firms	$10,650,000	59.8%
Switzerland-based firms	1,762,000	9.9
West Germany-based firms	1,650,000	9.3
Japan-based firms	943,000	5.3
Canada-based firms	498,000	2.8
All other foreign-based firms	2,296,000	12.9
Total	$17,799,000	100.0%

SOURCE: *Lloyd's Mexican Economic Report*, Guadalajara, Jalisco, Mexico: Allen W. Lloyd y Asociados, S.A. de C.V., Investment Brokers, December 1987, p. 2.

NOTE: Figures released by the Mexican Government's Ministry of Commerce and Industrial Development indicate a 40% increase in direct investment in Mexico by firms of foreign countries over the past five years (1983–1987) over the previous five years (1977–1982). These figures include direct foreign investments in both maquiladora and border assembly plant operations and other multinational operations, excluding loans made by foreign lending institutions to the Mexican government.

foreign firm at the same time. U.S. firms normally start operations under sheltered or subcontractor arrangements. Once the U.S. firms are familiar with operating in Mexico, they change over to captured operations. In 1984, 60% of all maquiladora operations were either wholly or majority owned by non-Mexican interests.[11]

The direct foreign corporate investment in Mexico as of December 1987 is shown in Exhibit 16.2.

OPERATIONS AND OPPORTUNITIES IN MEXICO

Why this flight of U.S.-owned production capacity to another country? Many U.S. manufacturers have concluded that a major increase in "off-shore" (foreign) operations is the only viable choice remaining to them and is essential to their survival.[12] Several executives explained that their firm's decision to become more global was because their international competitors, with their excess capacity and lower costs, were attracting markets that the U.S. firms had served previously. Many of these firms are faced with price differences of 30%–50% and are being forced out of markets that they had developed over the last 40 years.[13] Most U.S. CEO's see their choice either to compete in the international and domestic market or retreat to the U.S. and beg for governmental protection. Most have chosen to compete by establishing production plants abroad, or what is most commonly known as "off-shore" production. (The terms *twin-plant operations* or *in-bond plants* are also used; one of each twin plant is located on each side of the border, and in-bond plant means that the goods are held in-bond and taxed on "value-added" when the goods are shipped out of the plant.)

In order to be more competitive in the U.S. market, corporations must reduce costs. The corporation can build a plant, hire and train a work force and put a management team in place. By establishing its own plant in Mexico, the U.S. manufacturer can save $12,000–$15,000 per worker each year.[14] (Note: Mexico does, however, have a history of seizing "foreign-owned" companies.)

Mexico's maquiladora industry ranks as the country's most rapidly expanding industrial sector and is now Mexico's second largest net foreign-exchange earner after petroleum. The real growth rate is expected to continue to be at least 10% per year[15] and to be particularly good in the automotive sector, and in television sets and other electrical goods. Since the inception of the program, employment within this geographic area has grown at an average annual rate of 24%. Maquiladora plants were estimated to employ some 255,000 persons at the end of 1986.[16]

ADVANTAGES

Operations in Mexico offer significant advantages over other foreign and domestic production sites for U.S. manufacturers. The maquiladora operations can offer significant wage-cost savings over locations in the U.S. or Asia. Minimum wages for unskilled labor are set by the Mexican federal government and are adjusted periodically to reflect different living costs in various economic zones throughout Mexico.[17]

The Mexican minimum labor wage in April 1987 was P$3,660 (US$2.80) per day for most of Mexico (lower in a few cities such as Monterey and Guadalajara), while the Hong Kong minimum wage per day as of September 1986 was HK$108 (US$13.85) per day.[18] The wage advantage of Mexico over both Hong Kong and the U.S.A. is obvious.

Geographic location at the U.S. border offers fewer communication and transportation problems than a location in Asia. By locating on the border, a plant can reduce shipping time, when compared to overseas manufacturing, from weeks (or months) to days.[19] In addition, the Mexican government provides sincere assistance and cooperation. It imposes few governmental regulatory restrictions when compared to the U.S. institutions such as Occupational Safety and Health Administration, Equal Employment Opportunity Commission, Environmental Protection Agency, etc. Mexico has a shortage of technically qualified personnel and low- to mid-level managers.[20,21]

DISADVANTAGES

Products from maquiladora operations may be sold in Mexico, but only up to 20%, and under certain conditions. The percentage is calculated item by item, not on total value of production, and second, there can be no similar Mexican production currently satisfying local market demand. Third, if local Mexican production is insufficient, sales must be authorized by Mexican authorities and must be requested annually.

Additionally, Mexico's infrastructure is not fully developed. Public roads, transportation, communications and electrical service is generally poor. Also, border crossing can be impeded by customs inspectors. Still, distribution time is significantly less than offshore production in Asia and other foreign sites.

CONCLUSION

The maquiladora program's benefits greatly outweigh the disadvantages. The maquiladora industry is the second most important source of revenue for Mexico as of 1988 and it is doubtful that either side of the border could adjust to economic conditions without the maquiladora operations. The unemployment rate in the four southernmost counties in Texas ranges between 15%–20%. Starr county, one of the four, is ranked as one of the poorest in the U.S.A. with an average annual income of just over $3,300.00.

Mexico's maquiladora industry offers considerable advantages to any company that wants to cut its production costs. One of the main savings that is offered is duty free import of raw materials to Mexico for use in production. There are many ways a firm can save costs; for example, set up a maquiladora plant, or subcontract, or use a shelter plant. Tariff rates under the U.S. Generalized System of Preferences are most advantageous, ranging from 0% to 10%–12% for electronic components, and textile tariff rates range from 8% to 35%. Finally the maquiladora industry has the advantage of total governmental support.

NOTES

1. Walter E. Greene, "Maquiladora, In-Bond, Twin-Plants, or Off-Shore Production, It's Still a Golden Opportunity," *Southwestern Small Business Institute Association Proceedings*, March 12–13, 1987, p. 134.

2. U.S. International Trade Commission, "Imports under Items 806.30 and 807.00 of the Tariff Schedules of the United States, 1981–1984," June 1986, p. 21.

3. Joseph Grunwald and Kenneth Flamm, *The Global Factory* (Washington, D.C.: The Brookings Institution), 1985, p. 140.

4. Mitchell Seligson and Edward J. Williams, *Maquiladora and Migration Workers in the Mexico–U.S. B.I.P.* (Austin, Texas), 1981, pp. 19–20.

5. Central Light & Power Co., Area Development Division, "The South Texas-Mexico Twin Plant Program" (Corpus Christi, Texas), 1987.

6. Greene, "Maquiladora, In-Bond, Twin-Plants, or Off-Shore Production," p. 136.

7. U.S. International Trade Commission, "Imports under Items 806.30 and 807.00," p. 23.

8. Grunwald and Flamm, *The Global Factory*, p. 166.

9. Greene, "Maquiladora, In-Bond, Twin-Plants, or Off-Shore Production," p. 135.

10. Grunwald and Flamm, *The Global Factory*, p. 166.

11. U.S. International Trade Commission, "Imports under Items 806.30 and 807.00," pp. 21–22.

12. Roger Turner, "Mexico Desk Officer, International Trade Administration," *Business America*, November 1984, p. 28.

13. *Ibid.*

14. William A. Orme, "Maquiladoras Thrive on Mexican Border," *Journal of Commerce*, November 1985, p. 7.

15. Steven Rosenberg, "Manufacturing in Mexico," *Mexico*, September 1985, p. 60.

16. Grunwald and Flamm, *The Global Factory*, p. 141.

17. Central Light & Power Co., "The South Texas-Mexico Twin Plant Program," p. 6.

18. Business International Corp., "Investing, Licensing, and Trading Conditions Abroad," 1987, pp. 15–30.

19. Central Light & Power Co., Area Development Division, "The South Texas-Mexico Twin Plant Program" (Corpus Christi, Texas), 1987.

20. U.S. International Trade Commission, "Imports under Items 806.30 and 807.00," p. 23.

21. Grunwald and Flamm, *The Global Factory*, p. 171.

ADDITIONAL REFERENCES

Juvenal Angel, *Marketing Your Skills in Mexico* (New York: World Trade Academy Press, 1977), pp. 10–18.

Jose L. Barraza, *Parques Industriales*, Mexico, September 1985, pp. 18–21.

Sue Birley and David Norburn. "Small U.S. Large Companies," *Journal of Business Strategy*, August 6, 1985, pp. 81–83.

Joseph M. Callahan, "Mexico's Hidden Treasure: The Magical Maquiladora," *Automotive Industries*, June 1986, pp. 87–88.

Gilbert Cardenas and Charles Ellard, *The Economics of the U.S.–Mexico Border* (Edinburgh, 1982), pp. 20–2.

Seamus Connolly, "Joint Ventures with Third World Multi-nationals," *Columbia Journal of World Business*, August 1984, p. 28.

Doing Business in Hong Kong, Price Waterhouse, 1983.

Doing Business in Mexico, Price Waterhouse, 1984.

Kenneth Drefyack, "Even American Know-How Is Headed Abroad," *Business Week*, March 1986, pp. 60–63.

Henry Eason, "Going South to Cut Costs," *Nations Business*, February 1987, p. 24.

Economic Report of the President (Washington, D.C.: Government Printing Office, 1987).

Martin Feldstein, "Correcting the Trade Deficit," *Foreign Affairs*, Spring 1987, pp. 795–805.

Kent Gilbreath, "A Businessman's Guide to the Mexican Economy," *Columbia Journal of World Business*, Summer 1986, pp. 3–14.

Thomas D. Gorman, "Hong Kong/China '86: Opportunities for Growing American Business." *Inc.*, May 1986, pp. 135–153.

Tien-tung Hsueh, and Tun-oy-woo. "U.S. Direct Investment in Hong Kong: The Present Situation and Prospects," *Columbia Journal of World Business* Spring 1986, pp. 75–85.

McCaughan and Peter Baird. *Las Maquiladora en Mexico* (ACLA, 1975), p. 21.

Carl A. Nelson, "Manufacturing in Mexico Using a Maquiladora," *American Import Export Management*, April 1985, pp. 66–67.

Brain O'Reilly, "Business Makes a Run for the Border," *Fortune*, August 18, 1986, pp. 70–76.

"PRI-Labour Pains," *The Economist*, May 1987, p. 46.

Francisco Rivera-Batiz, "Can Border Industry Be a Substitute for Immigration?" *American Economic Review*, May 1986, pp. 263–268.

Peter R. Scanton, "Collaborative Ventures," *The Journal of Business Strategy*, August 6, 1985, pp. 81–83.

J. Trevino, Import/Export Specialist, Customs-International Bridge, Hidalgo, Texas, Telephone Interview, April 18, 1986.

Carlos Uriarte, "There's a Cheaper Way," *American Import-Export Management*, July 1984, p. 30.

Richard Wygand, "Opportunities in the Maquiladora Industry," *Mexico*, November 1985, pp. 54–55.

The Plastic Suppliers, Inc.

WALTER E. GREENE

Plastic Suppliers, Inc. (PSI) commenced operations in April, two years ago. The company was an offshoot of its founder's lifelong dream of owning his own business that would provide services that he enjoyed and that he was considered highly qualified to do. At the onset he was named as the Chief Executive Officer (CEO) and the two other people who joined him were part owners and heads of the various functions within the organization. All three were friends who had worked in the plastics business as technicians for many years and shared the founder's personal objective of being their own bosses.

Mr. Edmunds, the founder of PSI, had sixteen years experience at IBM, where he started from the bottom and worked his way up until he became Head—New Products Division. Edmunds quit IBM and he and two of his friends with the same technical background invested their lifetime savings in a small company, Plastic Suppliers, Inc., and started operations in McAllen, Texas.

There were several advantages of the location in South Texas. First, the founder, Mr. Edmunds, was a native of south Texas. Second, most of the existing plastics-injection-molding outfits were located in the northeast or midwest USA and the nearest (a very small facility) was in Dallas, Texas, some 550 miles to the north of McAllen. Third, maquiladora operators were located just across the border in Mexico, some twelve miles away. Maquiladora plants are usually one half of twin plant operations: parts and technical operations are performed on the U.S. side, and manual operations are performed on the Mexican side. (See Case 16.) Mr. Edmunds realized that the maquiladora industry was a rapidly growing industry, and that some of its many manufacturing operations required parts made out of plastic.

Having a supplier that was close to the maquiladora operations could cut delivery time enormously. Inventory levels could be kept low (thus resulting in lower investments in inventory and all the pluses and minuses of JIT—Just-in-Time—inventory methods). The distance alone was an advantage for PSI as a supplier. If for any reason, problems occurred about the supplied parts, a customer (maquiladora) had the convenience of easily crossing the border into the U.S.A. and correcting the problem(s).

Maquiladora operators choose suppliers from the U.S. rather than Mexico primarily because of the higher quality and service available from the U.S. In

This case was prepared by Professor Walter E. Greene of Pan American University. Research assistance was provided by Mark E. George and Carminia D. Oris, graduate assistants, Pan American University. Presented at the Midwest Society for Case Research Workshop, 1988. All rights reserved to the authors and the Midwest Society for Case Research. This is a disguised case. Copyright © 1988 by Walter E. Greene, APS, Ph.D. Reprinted by permission. It also appears in *Annual Advances, 1988*, pp. 364–373, edited by Susan L. Wiley.

the Rio Grande Valley region of Mexico alone, there had been a 43% increase in maquiladora operations in the period 1978–1986 from 49 to 70 plants. Mr. Edmunds had projected, barring any drastic changes, a 10% annual growth rate for PSI, with 95% derived from the Mexican maquilas.

During the first two years of operations, growth of PSI had been tremendous. At first the plant was equipped with four 150-ton plastic-injection-molding machines (similar to the plastic-injection-molding machines that make toy soldiers, etc., only much larger). Twenty months later, four additional machines were installed; three 150-ton and one 500-ton machines. The plant had been expanded to accommodate the new equipment and the work force had grown from the original three to eighty-six employees.

COMPANY OBJECTIVES

Aside from Mr. Edmunds's personal desire to run his own business, the company had one major objective. All three partners agreed that the company was to become a full service supplier of plastic-injection-molding parts to local manufacturing firms on both sides of the border, i.e., in U.S. plants and in the Mexican maquiladora operations.

An organization chart is shown in Exhibit 17.1. PSI was Mr. Edmunds's dream of a lifetime: He had worked hard and put his lifetime savings into founding PSI. As a technician he had two major concerns: meeting clients' specifications and providing quality services and products. His cohorts were also technicians who wanted to be their own bosses. PSI found a niche in the market and grew at a tremendously fast pace during its first two years. As was common with entrepreneurs, they outgrew their original investments, and venture capitalists from both the U.S. and Mexico stepped in and provided much-needed capital.

PRODUCTS AND SERVICES PROVIDED

PSI had three profit generating departments: Engineering, Tooling, and Production. The Engineering Department created mold designs, the Tooling department made the actual molds and mold repairs, and the Production Department ran the mold to produce the various plastic parts.

Although each department's function could be considered a continuous flow from mold design to parts production, clients came in needing one or two or all of the services that PSI offered. Some clients had their own molds (which they brought down from northern U.S. locations so that delivery would be faster) so all that PSI had to do was produce the plastic parts and maintain the molds. Other customers came with specifications for the part that they wanted to produce, so PSI had to design and make the mold, then produce the parts. Added to all these functions, PSI was also capable of rendering local delivery services after it purchased a small delivery van.

The Engineering Department was responsible for designing the molds that would be used to make the parts. Its head was one of the original three that started the business. Two assistants prepared drawings showing all details of the

EXHIBIT 17.1   **Organization Chart, Plastic Suppliers, Inc.**

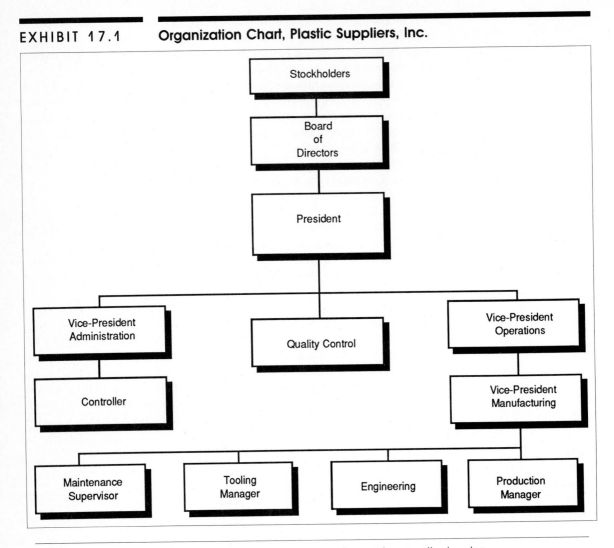

SOURCE: A report issued by PSI to third parties, customers, suppliers, and prospective investors.

mold. The drawings were made through a computer (CAD/CAM—Computer Assisted Design/Manufacturing) thus making the task easier. Designing the molds required highly skilled people, unavailable in the local job site.

The Tooling Department, supervised by one of the three founders, made the molds based on the drawing specifications prepared by the Engineering Department. Making a mold took anywhere from a couple of weeks at the very least to three months or more. Skilled personnel were a must for this department because of the complexity of the tasks involved. However, as was the case with the Engineering Department, skilled personnel were unavailable in the local area. After the molds were built, they were moved to the production floor for preliminary testing. If any flaws were discovered, the molds were sent back to Tooling for adjustments.

Adjusted and tested molds were turned over to the Production Department, manned mostly with semi-skilled operators. The only skills required for this department were in setting up the machine specifications to turn out the right number of plastic parts. Knowledge of cycle times, water levels, etc., was an important factor. Apart from this the machines did most of the work. Each machine was manned by a worker who saw to it that the parts were produced according to the quantity on the specification sheet and that the machine did not run out of water. This task did not require any special skills. Normally the only way big production schedules could be met was by second shift operations in the Production Department, and on rare occasions by using a third shift (24-hour operations).

QUALITY CONTROLS AND PROBLEMS

Mr. Edmunds realized that Quality Control was of the highest priority with maquiladora operators. Because PSI produced plastic parts that form part of larger components, all parts had to fit perfectly. (e.g., one of PSI's customers, which used a large portion of PSI's capacity, was a maquiladora plant which required the plastic parts for automobile seat belts. This maquiladora plant produced all seat belts required by one of the big three U.S. automobile manufacturers.) This required strict measurement and material quality controls. Therefore a Quality Control (QC) department was added.

Frequently, problems arose concerning a work order. Schedules were usually set up to insure that the parts got to the customer on time and to maximize the utilization of personnel and machines. However, delays could and did occur often, as caused by any of the following factors:

1. Too much time spent on designing the molds (Engineering), or in making the molds (Tooling), or in producing the parts (Production).
2. Sometimes parts did not conform to QC standards, and then each of the departments blamed the other departments for the failure.
3. Sometimes the molds broke or did not work correctly even if they passed QC checks.
4. Finally, machine breakdowns were a much too frequent problem.

ECONOMIC ENVIRONMENT

PSI's economic environment was greatly influenced by its being situated in the Rio Grande Valley of South Texas. While the U.S. national unemployment rate was about 7% (as it was throughout the state of Texas) unemployment in the valley area was between 15% and 18% during this period. Starr county (one of the four counties in the valley) had the dubious honor of being one of the four poorest counties in the U.S.A., with an average annual income of $3,300. Poor health, low educational achievement, and limited job opportunities characterized this region. The local economy was highly influenced by what happened to the oil industry and the Mexican economy. Mexico's rate of inflation during the first years PSI was in operation was 160% and had averaged over 100% for each of the past three years.

Most Mexicans residing near the border brought business to the area by purchasing goods on the U.S. side of the border. Because of the Mexican peso's being devalued a few years earlier, the high rate of Mexican inflation, the bottom dropping out of the oil market, and the killing freeze that had destroyed the valley's citrus crop three years before, business on the U.S. side of the border was basically at a standstill.

Unfortunately, local banks were geared to agriculture, oil, and small retail establishments. The failure rate of Texas banks during this period had been one of the highest of any state in the U.S.A. Bankers were scared, and in addition, none had any experience with manufacturing establishments like PSI.

Public officials in the region exhorted the development of a manufacturing sector. Because of the high unemployment rate, firms of any kind were encouraged to relocate to the valley from the industrial north. Aware that the economy had to become multi-faceted to lessen the impact of drastic changes in the local economy, a strong desire developed to encourage the manufacturing sector to grow in the valley region.

FAST EXPANSION

Rapid expansion was triggered by the increased demand from maquiladora operators. At the onset, PSI was doing small jobs and one big project (manufacturing bag handles). One machine was devoted entirely to the plastic handles. The other three machines were almost always idle because of small production runs. When the word spread that PSI was located in the valley, jobs came pouring in. Two maquiladora plants, Zenith Television and TRW (seat belts) alone took practically all of the original capacity. Expansion was inevitable, and four additional machines were acquired.

The Production Department's capacity in terms of machine hours had more than doubled over its first two years. The personnel complement had increased from three to eighty-six employees. The number of machines had grown from four to seven 150-ton, plus one 500-ton plastic-injection-molding machines. Raw materials were stacked in boxes beside the machines because of a lack of storage space. A small nearby warehouse had been leased for extra storage space. A small office for the Engineering Department had to be added because of overcrowding in the administrative office.

FINANCIAL PROBLEMS

During the first twenty months no accurate financial reports were maintained. The new stockholders were concerned about the lack of accounting information to support decision making. The original bookkeeper was just that, a bookkeeper. Mr. Earl, a CPA with consulting and work experience in one of the major accounting firms, was hired almost seven months ago.

Mr. Earl set up the accounting system from scratch and produced financial statements for the year. (See Exhibits 17.2 and 17.3.) As the controller, he per-

EXHIBIT 17.2

Balance Sheet, Plastic Suppliers, Inc.

Assets

Current Assets

Cash	($8,689)
Accounts receivable	146,547
Inventory	266,449
Prepaid expenses	3,765
Deposits	579
Total current assets	$408,651

Fixed assets

Autos & trucks	$75,880
Furniture & fixtures	14,191
Equipment	2,084,960
Building	283,246
Less accumulated depr.	(98,470)
Land	81,383
Leasehold improvements	49,525
Less accumulated amort.	(3,186)
Total fixed assets	$2,487,529
Total assets	$2,896,180

Liabilities

Current

Notes payable	$152,049
Accrued payable	22,590
Taxes payable	91,519
Other payable	52,421
Current portion long-term debt	343,487
Deferred income	67,771
Total current liabilities	$ 729,837

Long-term

Mortgage payable	$361,154
Notes payable	1,694,265
Total long-term liabilities	$2,055,419
Total liabilities	$2,785,256

Stockholders' equity

Common stock	$466,575
Paid-in capital	579,236
Treasury stock	(180,432)
Retained earnings	(754,455)
Total stockholders' equity	$110,924
Total liabilities & equities	$2,896,180

SOURCE: A report issued to third parties, i.e., suppliers, bankers and prospective investors.

EXHIBIT 17.3   Income Statement, Plastic Suppliers, Inc.

For this Year ended December 31	Production	Mold Build	Repairs	Total
Sales	$120,000	$140,000	$34,000	$294,000
Cost of sales				
Materials used	68,345	20,496		88,841
Direct labor	32,492	123,932	566	156,990
Overhead	31,434	26,058	3,515	61,007
Total cost of sales	132,271	170,486	4,081	306,838
Gross profit	(12,271)	(30,486)	29,919	(12,838)
General & administrative expenses				
Payroll				108,232
Maintenance				24,289
Depreciation				36,114
Amortization				1,213
Rent and leases				311
Insurance—assets				7,887
Travel and entertainment				11,546
Shipping				507
Taxes				741
Consulting fees				30,428
Office supplies				7,324
Telephone & telegraph				5,622
Mail/postage/courier				2,596
Electricity and water				19,835
Fuel and oil				122
Contributions and donations				51
Licenses and permits				491
Memberships, dues & subscriptions				1,418
Total general and administrative expenses				258,727
Operating income				(271,565)
Less other expenses (revenues)				
Financial expenses				42,083
Other expenses				3,824
Net income				($317,471)

formed functions like financial sourcing, financial information analysis and general accounting. He managed to secure several short-term and long-term loans. Cash flow problems had beset PSI from the start. Collections had been very late. To meet current expenses (such as payroll and regular monthly payments), short-term loans had been obtained. However, as loans matured, interest and principal payments became too high for PSI to handle. Eventually the debt grew so large that the debt–equity ratio and the debt–asset ratio precluded conventual debt financing. Long-term loans were hard to get because of the banking system's reservations about lending to manufacturing organizations.

When job costs were derived and compared against the revenues by Mr. Earl, it was discovered that PSI was barely making a profit on most of its contracts. In the absence of cost standards and a cost accounting system, the price quotations given to clients were not enough to cover costs of manufacturing the parts. A consulting team was hired to determine the standard costs for labor, raw materials, and overhead, and to set up a system to monitor expenses on a per job basis. The study was finished three months ago. However, the resulting cost accounting system was not implemented because Mr. Edmunds, the CEO, was too busy searching for more sales and financing.

With the existing plant already filled to capacity, management had plans for a bigger facility that could accommodate twenty plastic-injection-molding machines in the Production Department and officers for each of the departments. The number of jobs had increased, the company was producing at maximum capacity; therefore management believed that the proposed new facility was a must. Nevertheless financing was not available.

CHANGE OF MANAGEMENT

Mr. Edmunds relinquished his position to Mr. Earl just one month ago. Mr. Edmunds felt that the administrative duties were too much for him to handle and all sorts of paper work were piling up in the office. Besides, Mr. Edmunds was a technician and not fond of paper work. Mr. Earl had done an outstanding job of compiling PSI's financial statements.

Almost immediately, conflicts between Mr. Earl and the partners arose concerning company strategy and policies.

At the board meeting this morning, Mr. Earl tendered his thirty-day notice of resignation. Mr. Edmunds stated in the meeting that he would not resume duties as CEO, as he had more than he could handle generating sales (technical marketing).

TAKEOVER PROBLEMS

Aware of the financial problems of PSI and of their prospects as a maquiladora supplier, one of PSI's newest clients had become interested in acquiring PSI. This client was one of the larger maquiladora operators and it was its intention to integrate vertically and thus ensure an adequate supply of plastic parts at cheaper prices. This potential acquirer saw a definite advantage of a supplier located as close as PSI. In an attempt to prevent the takeover, the existing stockholders infused additional equity of approximately twice their original investments. Despite this, PSI still needed additional financing to build a larger facility.

The Caishikou Barbershop (Beijing, China)

STEVEN M. DAWSON

Inside the Caishikou Barbershop, Li Xing Yin sat in his third-floor office pondering several important decisions he needed to make soon about workers' salaries, benefits, and the acquisition of new equipment. On the first two floors below workers were busy giving haircuts, shampoos, and permanents. Outside on busy Guanganmennei Dajie bicycle bells could be heard from a steady stream of riders headed home from work in the late afternoon sun. Some paused to buy copies of *Renmin Rebao* (*People's Daily*), vegetables, and summer fruit from the small market stands that lined the street. Another warm evening was ahead for the Xuanwu District located southwest of Beijing's Tiananmen Square.

Several weeks earlier, in August, 1986, Li Xing Yin (pronounced "Lee Shing Yin") and his fellow workers took advantage of a major change in the way business is done in China. Since 1983 the authorities in Beijing had allowed private citizens, collectives, and families to lease certain small enterprises in the service trade in return for monthly lease payments. Officially the new policy on leasing was known as *separating ownership and management*. Leasing was intended to stimulate business activity while not changing the economy's socialist nature, as ultimate ownership remained with the state. By the summer of 1986 about one-third of the 3,300 barber, catering, repair, and non-staple food shops in Beijing's eight suburban districts were leased from the state.

The state had previously controlled virtually all enterprises, but leasing was said to make it possible for individuals to have management control and to retain profits. In leased enterprises the managers enjoy independence in business and labor decisions, and in the use of funds. Formerly their decisions were subject to many restrictions on matters of manpower, finances, materials acquisition, production, and marketing. A lease makes the enterprise, not the state, responsible for both profits and losses. This works both ways: If business is good profits can be kept by the enterprise instead of going to the state as before, but if losses are incurred the state does not simply provide the funds to make them up. How far the new economic reforms would be allowed to go, and how fast, was by no means certain, and Li Xing Yin felt a sense of relief and accomplishment that he had the two-year contract signed.

After sixteen years of working under government ownership and management at the Caishikou Barbershop, Li, as the signer of the lease, felt considerable motivation to be a good manager both for himself and for the seventy other employees. "Before we were the masters, but we did not have a sense of responsibility. Now we really feel we are the masters of the enterprise," said Li,

This case was prepared by Professor Steven M. Dawson of the University of Hawaii. This case has been accepted for publication in the *Case Research Journal*. Reprinted by permission of the author and North American Case Research Association. © 1988 by Steven Dawson.

"because the performance of each worker is directly linked to the honor and future of the shop."

One of Li's first actions after signing the lease was to ask his fellow workers for suggestions on how to improve the barbershop's operations. His objective was twofold: to learn from their experience and to build a sense of identification with the enterprise. The response to the request was overwhelming and encouraging: 210 suggestions were received in the first week. Li felt that the workers were really excited by the opportunity to have a say in management. Another 20 suggestions came in later. This was quite a change. Before the lease was signed the workers including Li felt little responsibility for the success of the enterprise. There was little incentive to do well since salaries were fixed, they often did not reflect a worker's contribution, workers couldn't be fired, and bankruptcy did not exist in China for state managed enterprises. Absenteeism was high among the barbershop workers and there were many complaints from customers about the bad quality of service provided.

After reviewing his fellow workers' suggestions, Li selected for early consideration three areas with a direct and significant financial impact. First, were proposals to change the payment of wages from the former fixed salaries to a basic wage plus a bonus which would recognize the workers' contribution to the enterprise's success. Second, was to initiate or continue several worker related benefit programs including a nursery, personal and health insurance, lunches, and housing for some single workers. Third, was a proposal to buy new equipment not included with the leased premises and to expand the services provided by the barbershop.

THE BUSINESS ENVIRONMENT

In China's socialist economy in the mid-1980s, virtually all medium- and large-sized enterprises were owned by the state as the representative of the people. Each enterprise reported to a specific state supervisory unit that was their "department in charge." The Caishikou Barbershop came under the Beijing Xuanwu District Service Corporation. An enterprise's fixed assets and regular "circulation fund" (net working capital) was provided free of charge by the state. In return the enterprise turned all its profit over to the state, its products were purchased at a fixed price by state commercial departments, and its labor force was provided by state labor departments. Each year the enterprise needed to apply to the department in charge for funds for working capital, equipment replacements, and any new ventures. Acceptance, revision, or rejection was more likely to be based on how the request related to the state's five-year plan than to its financial feasibility. With little power or responsibility, enterprises often did not emphasize profitability or efficiency and merely tried to meet state output plans. It was to the enterprises' advantage to keep their output target as low as possible so that it could be met or exceeded, and to increase financial and material allocation from the state. There were penalties for not meeting production targets, but not for having excess funds and materials.

In service enterprises prices were set by the state and the services were provided to the public on a more or less take it or leave it basis. Whether customers patronized the enterprise or not did not effect the interests of the staff one way or the other. This led to the inertia and inefficiency associated with the "iron rice bowl" of guaranteed employment and the "big pot" of state enterprise employment in which wages were not determined by the results of an individual's enterprise.

The difficulties encountered with state management and ownership of enterprises did not escape notice. The problems were particularly noticeable and disturbing in service industries. A consensus gradually evolved that these enterprises should be responsible for the efficient use of state funds and that service to customers might improve if enterprises were given the right to retain part of their profit. Part of the extra profit earned through improved management could be used for the workers' collective welfare or distributed as bonuses among those workers who made greater contributions. As the economist Xue Muqiao noted, "The superiority of the socialist system cannot be brought into full play unless the interests of the state, the workers, and staff, including the factory leaders, are integrated and all are interested in increasing production and practicing economy."

The first enterprise lease agreement was made in January, 1982, when Wu Jilong signed a contract with an electroplating copper factory in Taiyuan, Shanxi Provence, to manage its industrial silicon production workshop which had lost almost 2 million yuan the previous year. Under the contract all the workshop's equipment was still owned by the factory and the lessee bought the raw material, produced the product, and sold it to the factory. Following five years of losses before the lease, a profit was made and by the end of 1985 the cumulative profit was 4.18 million yuan. Reports about the workshop lease reached Hu Yaobang, General Secretary of the Communist Party of China's Central Committee, who suggested that what Wu Jilang had done should be tried in other smaller state enterprises. In Beijing experimental leases were made in small service related enterprises like green groceries, restaurants, bicycle repair shops, and barbershops. The authorities were especially interested in leasing enterprises that were operating at a loss and thus draining available state financial resources.

Leasing of state owned enterprises to individuals marked a major reversal of official policy, especially after the ten years of the Cultural Revolution from 1966 to 1976, when an often fierce campaign was waged against all capitalistic tendencies. It was firmly believed that having all businesses owned and managed by the state was the best choice for China's socialistic economy. The need to justify the new economic policy was noted in the 1984 *Decision of the Central Committee of the Communist Party of China on Reform of the Economic Structure* which pointed out that "As market theory and the practice of socialism have shown, ownership can be duly separated from the power of operation by the state institution." Commenting on this policy statement, the *Beijing Review* said:

> When the state leases the enterprises to the lessee, the ownership remains in the hands of the state. Feudal society was based on landlords leasing land to the peasants; in capitalist society, what is leased is companies or factories from one capitalist to another. In socialist China, the nature of leasing is different. The

lessor is the state, the lessees are laborers identified as masters of the state and the enterprise. Ownership remains with the state, the enterprise is still publicly owned. The only thing that has changed is the method of operation. The form of ownership of the means of production and of distribution is an important criterion for judging the nature of a social system. Therefore, the leasing business of China remains socialistic in nature.

THE LEASE

A two-year lease was signed by Li Xing Yin, representing his fellow workers, and the Xuanwu District Service Corporation. The monthly lease payment to the state was set at 6,000 yuan plus an additional 1.5% of sales revenues, to be paid to the state's worker education fund. Because this was a collective lease in which Li signed for all the barbershop workers, rather than a lease to individuals, no deposit was needed. One of the other six barbershops in the district was leased to an individual and he had to put 10% of the profit target down as the deposit. The Caishikou lease set targets of 450,000 yuan per year (37,500 per month) for sales and 82,000 yuan (6,833 per month) for profits before bonus and tax. If sales were below 450,000, the percentage of pretax income available for bonuses could be lowered by the service corporation, but the amount of reduction was not known then and would depend upon the results of the other six barbershops in the district. Alternatively, the bonus percentage would be raised if the sales target was exceeded. If the agreed profit target was not met, no bonuses would be paid and the base salaries would be cut by an amount equivalent to the profit target deficit. If the financial shortcomings were serious enough, the lease could be terminated by the state. All the workers would retain their jobs, but the barbershop would again be under state management. If profits were made after tax and other required payments, the lease provided that they could be retained by the barbershop. Initially it was agreed with the District Service Corporation that 50% would go to the enterprise development fund and 50% to the worker benefit fund. The development fund could be used for working capital, to buy new assets, and to repay loans used to finance assets. The workers benefit fund was for bonuses above those that are tax deductible and for other outlays that would benefit the workers.

Two years is a fairly short term: Many of the decisions to be made have long-term implications and Li already anticipated applying for renewal. Also under discussion with the District Service Corporation was an extension of the existing lease. Because it is a collective lease and all the workers were part of the leasing unit, when it came time to renew the lease they could vote for Li Xing Yin to represent them again, or if they wanted someone else they could change managers. Li Xing Yin could also be replaced before the lease's expiration if the workers wanted to do so. The District Service Corporation was on record as saying they did not care who signed the lease or represented the workers as long as they were confident the person had the ability to run the barbershop.

As its part of the lease the state provided the existing equipment and premises occupied by the barbershop. Also included was the circulation fund, the equivalent of net working capital, owned by the state but available for use by the barbershop. The circulation fund remained at 93,600 yuan, the same as before the lease was signed. The building, and the equipment provided by the state should be maintained and returned in the same condition, given reasonable wear and tear, at the conclusion of the lease. Offsetting credit or a refund could be provided by improvements or new assets paid for by the barbershop. The Xuanwu District Service Corporation also made available the services of Liu Yong Ming, Secretary of the Party Branch for all seven barbershops in the District. His main responsibility was to see that the barbershop was operated according to the lease contract. He could also "give ideas on management," but the barbershop can still make its own decisions, do ideological work, get market information, and help locate needed materials.

FOLLOWING THE LEASE

Initial results were very encouraging. Not only did the workers respond positively to the request for ideas on how to improve management by preparing 210 suggestions, but also the first month's financial results showed a big jump in revenues, a smaller jump in expenses, a healthy reported profit, and a balance sheet that was in good shape. Sales revenues rose to 44,731 yuan from 36,000 a year earlier and profit after tax as shown in the income statement in Exhibit 18.1 was 2,924 yuan. In theory the profit could have been even larger but Li had found that although some expenses were fixed and remained constant with the rise in revenues, other expenses, specifically fuel, water and electricity, materials, repairs, incidental expenses, the lease payment to the worker education fund, and the turnover tax, went up about in line with the revenue increase.

The distribution of profit before tax in the income statement was fairly structured. Profits before tax were distributed in these allotments:

1. 48% goes to income tax.
2. 10% is paid to the District Service Corporation as a location tax. The amount is based upon the enterprise's location; those in the city center pay more than 10% percent and those in the outer districts less.
3. 15% goes to the Ministry of Commerce.
4. 15% of profit after income tax and after the payment to the Ministry of Commerce goes to the State Energy Fund.

Li suspected that the large revenue increase in September might have occurred because many customers wanted to see whether better service was now being provided after the publicity the barbershop received when it was leased. Expenses were also lower than they would probably be in the future if the additional financial incentives he was now considering were implemented.

Regarding the revenues, Li recognized that there were enough barbershops in south Beijing; there were also individual barbers who set up shop in the outdoor markets. So the shop's revenues would probably fluctuate widely. In the past the state-run barbershop did not provide high quality and satisfactory service. Li realized that if he could gain a reputation for providing quality service at a fair price with a well trained and courteous staff, he would have a decided

EXHIBIT 18.1

Income Statement, Month of September 1986, Caishikou Barbershop

(Amounts in Chinese Yuan)

Income		44,731
Less expenses		
Fuel	268	
Water and electricity	626	
Materials used up	2,102	
Base salaries	5,254	
Welfare	956	
Repairs	403	
Depreciation[1]	849	
Incidental expenses	492	
Lease: State	6,000	
Lease: worker education fund	671	
Pension for retired workers	2,545	
Other expenses	369	
Turnover tax	1,476	
Total expenses		22,011
Operating profit before bonus		22,720
Bonus	9,088	
Profit before tax		13,632
Income tax	6,543	
Location tax	1,363	
Ministry of Commerce	2,045	
Energy fund	757	
Total taxes	10,708	
Net profit after tax		2,924
Distribution of profits		
Enterprise development fund		1,462
Worker benefit fund		1,462

[1] Paid to state for state-owned assets.

market advantage. Given the population in the area and the existence of other barbershops, 60,000 yuan per month was Li's best estimate of the high end of the possible revenue scale while the worst outcome short of an outright reputation disaster was 25,000.

The balance sheet as of September 30, 1986, is presented in Exhibit 18.2. Because it is against state policy in China for the actual balance sheet of an enterprise to be made public, the balance sheet in Exhibit 18.2 shows reasonable

EXHIBIT 18.2

Representative Balance Sheet, Caishikou Barbershop, September 30, 1986[1]

(Amounts in Chinese Yuan)

Sources of Funds (Liabilities and Net Worth)

State-owned circulating fund[2]	10,000
Enterprise development fund	5,000
Accounts payable	500
Pre-deductions[4]	1,000
Total	16,500
Renewal (equipment)[2]	1,000
Worker benefit fund[3]	1,000
Bonus payable	1,000
Pension	500
Welfare fund[5]	1,000
Total	4,500
State-owned net fixed assets	10,000
Depreciation	3,000
Total	13,000
Total sources of funds	34,000

Uses of Funds (Assets)

Materials	5,000
Furniture and utensils	10,000
Cash	1,000
Accounts receivable	500
Total	16,500
Specialized deposits	4,500
Fixed assets	13,000
Total uses of funds	34,000

[1] Yuan figures do not equal actual figures, but the relationships between accounts are believed to represent relationships between the real figures.

[2] Provided by the state.

[3] From profit after tax.

[4] Expensed in advance: included items like provisions for repairs.

[5] From income statement.

relationships among the individual entries for an enterprise like the Caishikou Barbershop but the figures for each outlay are not accurate.

VISITS WITH WORKERS

As a first step toward building a new attitude among his fellow workers, Li Xing Yin asked to visit each of the seventy employees in their home to learn about their problems and to identify ways in which the enterprise could assist them. The visits to the workers' homes went well and a number of people commented to him that this was the first time anyone from the barbershop had indicated an interest with their problems of daily living. In thinking back over his visits, Li put together a list of problems which were frequently raised. These included the following:

1. Inadequate access to a place to bathe.
2. No lunches provided at work, nor a place to eat.
3. No kindergarten at work for small children.
4. Problems getting to work by public transportation, especially in bad weather when bicycles could not be ridden.
5. No health insurance.
6. No personal insurance.
7. No place for a midday rest.

Although Li sensed that creating a new and more positive attitude among the workers toward the barbershop was important, he could not just seek to improve their welfare without regard to their attitude and ability. Those workers who wanted to work hard could have morale problems if workers were kept who were not suitable and thus Li fired one of the workers in the first month because he did not do the work well. This was the first worker fired in many years. Finding new workers was not a problem, because they could be hired by the barbershop directly. As long as the present policy toward leased service enterprises continued, it would not be necessary to work with the state labor office.

The visits to the workers' homes, the 210 suggestions he received, and his review of the initial income statement led Li Xing Yin to consider three principal modifications in the way the shop was managed that would have an early and potentially significant impact on the financial results.

THE CHOICES

One reason for the poor quality of service was clear: Salaries were too low. There also was little relationship between the workers' salaries, the amount of work done, and the profit made by the barbershop. This should be changed if there was to be hope of improving worker attitudes, the quality of service provided, and the reputation of the barbershop.

The existing base salary range was from 60 to a little over 100 yuan per month and the average was just 74 yuan for the 71 workers. No bonuses of any significance were paid before the lease was signed: Each worker merely received his or her base salary. Now that the barbershop was leased, bonuses could be paid either as tax deductible salary expenses or out of the worker benefit fund after taxes were paid. The Xuanwu District Service Corporation required that the deductible bonuses should be equal to a minimum of 36% to a maximum of 50% of the reported profit before taxes and bonuses. The actual percentage for each month was set by the Service Corporation using a method which was not clear to the barbershop. In September profits before tax and bonus were 22,719 yuan of which 40% or 9,088 was paid out to workers as a bonus. As the elected manager, Li's salary was equal to 65 yuan plus 15 yuan as manager. His bonus each month would be equal to the average bonus paid to each of the barbershop's other workers who received bonuses.

The September bonus reflected the substantial improvement in the barbershop's profitability during the first month and it was clear that the system of base salary plus bonus could be a powerful factor in improving worker attitudes. There were two primary alternatives proposed for consideration. First, the September experiment with the existing base salary averaging 74 yuan plus bonus could be retained. Second, some workers thought that all employees could receive an increase in their base salary, perhaps to around 150 yuan on average, with accordingly smaller bonuses available. A base salary of just 74 yuan, these workers said, did not recognize the skills, dedication, and experience of the workers in a leased enterprise rather than a state enterprise. The higher base would also take into consideration the workers' risk of a wage cut if the sales and profit targets were not met.

The method for determining the size of each worker's bonus was to award one point for every 30 yuan of revenues the worker generated above the base task. At the end of each quarter the total bonus available was divided among the workers based upon the points they accumulated. Workers who did not generate revenue directly received a bonus equal to the average bonus paid to all the barbershop workers. The only exception was the accountant whose bonus was 2.3% of total bonuses. So as to avoid too much emphasis on the quantity rather than the quality of work, workers whose work quality was not good or who quarreled with customers only received one half point for each 30 yuan of revenue generated. When there were serious problems, no point would be given. If each worker merely met his or her basic task, Li estimated that monthly revenues would be about 25,000 yuan.

The second issue involved expenditures for worker welfare. After making the home visits and identifying a number of problems that his fellow workers faced in their daily life, especially as it involved the barbershop, Li continued some worker welfare programs made available by the barbershop when it was a state enterprise and identified others that might be added. None of the costs identified below were included in the September revenue and expense statement in Exhibit 18.1 because existing benefits like the kindergarten were paid for by the workers.

The costs per month at current employment levels would be as follows:

1. Shower room: 135 yuan per month for supplies.
2. Provide lunch and a lunchroom: 250 yuan.
3. A kindergarten for workers' children: 180 yuan.
4. Rent rooms: 100 yuan.
5. Provide personal insurance: 71 yuan.
6. Provide health insurance: 350 yuan.
7. Place for a midday rest: no charge, use an existing room.
8. Recuperation trips: 167 yuan.

A tough problem to be solved involved transportation. Although there were six million bicycles in Beijing, not all workers had one and bicycles were a problem in bad weather. The Beijing bus service was often crowded and difficult to use. Some workers thought that a van should be purchased; but that would create too many problems, Li thought. An alternative to the van was to rent rooms from individuals near the barbershop in which eight to ten workers could stay when going home was inconvenient; perhaps these rooms could also be used as housing for single workers who had problems getting access to an apartment because of the priority given to married couples. Another partial solution to the transportation problem was flexibility in the starting or finishing times for workers with difficult commutes.

Although there was some feeling that the barbershop should start its own kindergarten for the preschool children of workers, this seemed to be much more expensive and difficult than sending the children to the kindergarten run by the District Service Corporation. The total cost was only 180 yuan per month and this is what was done before the lease.

The workers also identified concerns about insurance. Li investigated and found that personal insurance, which would make a payment of 1,000 yuan to the worker's family in case the worker died, could be purchased for just 1 yuan per worker per month. Health insurance could be purchased for 4 yuan per worker per month. In addition the barbershop paid 95% of health costs not covered by the insurance if the worker had worked at the barbershop for twenty years, and 90 percent if they had worked there for less than twenty years. All hospital costs were paid by the barbershop. The total cost of the health insurance and other health benefits was about 350 yuan per month.

The last worker benefit under consideration was intended to make the barbershop a prestige place to work. Each year ten workers can go to a nice place, such at the beach resort at Beidaihe or another scenic spot, for rest and relaxation with all expenses paid by the barbershop. Workers' selection would be based upon their contributions to the success of the barbershop.

The expenditures for worker benefits, both the existing outlays of 956 yuan for welfare in September and the added expenses identified here, required a substantial outlay and Li viewed them as desirable in theory but they would mean less profit would be available. Two alternatives to the fixed monthly payments were suggested. The first suggestion was to allocate a portion of revenues to these purposes. That way if the barbershop did well the funds would be available. If revenues were larger than needed, extra services could be added. Of course, if revenues dropped some services would need to be curtailed. If this was the choice, Li tentatively decided to set the percentage of revenue allocated to employee benefits equal to the amount needed to finance these outlays using September's revenue level. Existing benefits would thus be allocated 2.14% of revenues and the new benefits, assuming all were funded, would be covered by 2.8% of revenues. The second alternative was to eliminate all worker benefits from tax deductible expenses and to pay for them from the worker benefit fund consisting of 50% of after-tax profits.

The third issue involved the purchase of new equipment for the barbershop. Although the total demand in the Xuanwu District for haircuts and related personal services remained reasonably constant over time, individual shops were vulnerable to considerable competition and instability of revenues. This was especially true in the lower end of the market, the simple haircut. To upgrade the appearance of the barbershop and to provide services that would be relatively free from competition with other barbershops and the individual barber with scissors and a chair who set up shop in an outdoor market, Li decided to substantially improve his equipment to provide diversified and upgraded services. Included were the following outlays:

1. Ironing Machine (6,000 yuan): The barbershop already had a washing machine. The ironing machine would be used for workers' uniforms. The appearance of the staff was an important part of the new image of the barbershop.

2. Air Conditioner (35,150 yuan): This could be a real competitive advantage during the summer months.

3. New Barber Chairs (35,400 yuan): The present ones have been in the shop for a long time and new chairs would improve the barbershop's appearance and provide better service.

4. Work Tables (8,800 yuan): These would be in front of each chair and would hold the workers' equipment.

5. Equipment (6,000 yuan) for use by the workers.

6. New Boiler (4,635 yuan): The present one does not supply enought hot water.

7. Face Lift for Barbershop (13,400 yuan): Many years had passed since the walls had been repainted. The entrance way and waiting room also needed attention and many new pictures showing the latest styles could be placed on the walls. New working rooms were also needed for new services.

8. Laser Medical Machines (13,000 yuan): This would be a major expansion of services. Many customers had facial skin problems, especially acne, and these machines could be used to treat them.

Monthly depreciation for the eight expenditures would be approximately as follows:

1. 24 yuan
2. 141 yuan
3. 142 yuan
4. 35 yuan
5. no depreciation
6. no depreciation
7. 54 yuan
8. 52 yuan

Items that individually cost less than 5,000 yuan are not subject to the regular depreciable. Instead, 50% of the purchase price goes into the income statement as an expense when the assets are purchased using accelerated depreciation and another 50% is expensed when the asset is disposed of. Normally state enterprises in China pay the state an amount in cash equal to depreciation, but as a leased enterprise the barbershop would not need to do this if it purchased the equipment with its own funds.

Payment for these purchases should not be a problem. Although the enterprise development fund did not have nearly enough in it to pay for everything, the Beijing Service Corporation, the Government of Xuanwu District, and the Xuanwu District Service Corporation were prepared to provide funds. No interest would be charged and repayment would be in two equal payments at the end of 1988 and 1989. If the lease was terminated, the loan would be payable at that time. The first payment was still twenty-eight months away. There was the possibility that the Beijing Service Corporation would provide up to 100,000 yuan of the full loan with no need to repay, but that had not yet been fully decided upon and Li decided to assume the full purchase price would be borrowed and repayment would be made for the entire loan. If the non-repayment part of the total loan was used, the barbershop would have the use of those funds and assets, but not the ownership, and would need to pay the related depreciation expense to the state each month. The new assets would also not count toward the "maintenance of the value of leased assets as of the time the lease ends" clause in the lease. Manager Li needed to decide whether to take the repayable loan and thus get ownership of the assets, decide not to go ahead with these expenditures (a course of action with negative implications for the success of the barbershop), or to hold out for the no-repayment loan.

The operating procedures of the Caishikou Barbershop specified that Li's financial plans must be presented to the workers council for approval before he could proceed. This was a group of twenty-four workers who were selected by their fellow workers and it had a voice in management, policies, and workers' benefits. Now that the information had been obtained, it was time to begin making decisions about the way workers' salaries would be paid, what benefits would be financed, how they would be paid for, and the acquisition of new assets. Adding to Li's desire to do a good job managing the barbershop was an item in today's paper. After some delay for revisions, China's new Law on Bankruptcy has been submitted for approval to the Standing Committee of the Sixth National People's Congress. In the past the state held that "bankruptcy is a capitalist concept and incompatible with socialism." According to the new draft law state enterprises with serious deficits due to poor management will be declared bankrupt upon application by creditors. The draft law stipulates that those responsible for the failure will be disciplined.

Ying May Garment Factory, Limited (Hong Kong)

CHRISTINE SPECTER • XENIA WONG

The Ying May Garment Factory, Limited (Ying May) was founded in Hong Kong in 1978 by Mrs. Wong May Yuk, who at that time was a worker on an assembly line in a large garment factory, and a fellow worker, Mr. Shau Yin Hui, who was an experienced pattern maker. Their initial goal was to subcontract with the garment factory, sewing cut pieces into garments for export. As Hong Kong grew to be the largest exporter of apparel in the world, opportunities for Ying May continued to expand.

In late 1986 Mrs. Wong was reviewing her company's recent performance in preparation for a planning session with Mr. Shau. Over the past three years, Ying May had experienced tremendous growth surpassing the co-founders' expectations. The factory, recognized as a mid-sized manufacturer in Hong Kong, was producing ladies' pants, skirts, blouses, jackets, as well as children's wear. Garments were being exported to the U.S., West Germany, Italy, Austria, and Switzerland. (Export sales for 1986 are summarized in Exhibit 19.1.)

A REVIEW OF YING MAY'S PERFORMANCE

Production increases had required investments in machinery and equipment. The total number of machines had grown from forty to eighty over the past three years. Types of machines included those for button attaching, buttonhole sew-

EXHIBIT 19.1

1986 Sales by Country, Ying May Garment Factory, Limited
(Amounts In U.S. Dollars)

MARKETS (BY COUNTRY)	SALES VOLUME	% OF TOTAL SALES
U.S.A	$2,945,500	91.0
West Germany	156,170	5.0
Italy and Austria	104,241	3.2
Switzerland	13,896	.4
Hong Kong (local)	15,550	.4
Total	$3,235,357	100.0

This case was prepared by Professor Christine Specter of Florida International University and Ms. Xenia Wong of Townson State University. Research assistance was provided by Ms. Andrea Shaw. This case was presented at the North American Case Research Association Meeting, 1987. Reprinted by permission of the authors and the North American Case Research Association. Copyright © 1987 by Dr. Christine Specter and Ms. Xenia Wong.

ing, and attaching electric snaps, as well as twin-needle feed lockstitch machines, and overlock sewing machines. Renovated single-needle lockstitch machines were Ying May's most recent purchase. (These partly computerized machines cut thread endings automatically and were instrumental in increasing productivity at the factory.) A telex communications system had been installed to foster better information exchange with Ying May's customers.

Growth in the number of employees was equally impressive. The number of workers had doubled, from forty-five to ninety, over the same three-year period. The hiring process involved interviews with prospective workers. New employees were given verbal job descriptions and objectives were communicated in a similar fashion. Most of the workforce were engaged in sewing cut pieces of fabric into finished garments. The standard practice in Hong Kong was to pay workers by the piece rate system. (The more they produced, the more money they earned.) Ying May followed this standard practice; Mrs. Wong believed that working class people in Hong Kong were motivated by monetary rewards. While the industry's average labor turnover rate was quite high, Ying May had maintained a relatively low rate of turnover during the past year. Mrs. Wong thought this was due to the company policy of paying its employees more than the average industrial wage. She believed that the lower turnover rate had been instrumental in lowering costs of production, increasing productivity, and improving product quality.

Another motivating technique used at the factory had grown out of the co-presidents' recognition of the importance of informal groups and the effect they have on performance of individual workers. They had divided the workers into two production lines. One consisted of employees who spoke Mandarin, and the other consisted of those who spoke Cantonese. These two groups held slightly different values and attitudes. The result was that they tended to compete against each other on the basis of the amount of money they earned, which was based on the productivity of the two production lines. Mrs. Wong thought this technique had proven successful as well. She realized that one of Ying May's greatest assets was its management group, comprised of ten dedicated individuals. The organization chart shown in Exhibit 19.2 provides a summary of the managers' responsibilities, as well as notes written by Mrs. Wong concerning the strengths of the individuals holding the positions. (Ms. Au Yuen Shuk Ling had just taken the position as foreman of production line A; Mrs. Wong was not yet prepared to evaluate her performance.) One middle-level manager was responsible for purchasing, quality control, and packaging. Five of the managers reported directly to the two presidents. At times Mrs. Wong and Mr. Shau were overburdened by this reporting system.

To provide some relief, they had discussed giving more authority and responsibility to the production line foremen. However, they both believed that the production processes were so complicated and involved so many details, that nobody else would put in the time and effort required to maintain a smoothly operating organization. Part of the problem related to their dual responsibilities. Mrs. Wong and Mr. Shau served not only as co-presidents, but also as heads

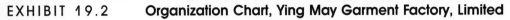

EXHIBIT 19.2   **Organization Chart, Ying May Garment Factory, Limited**

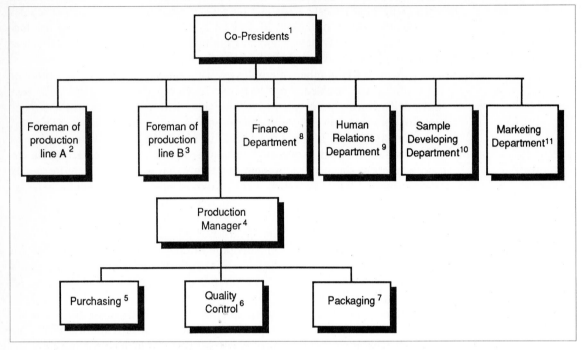

NOTES: The two co-presidents, Mrs. Wong May Yuk and Mr. Shau Yin Hui, serve as department heads also.

[1] Mrs. Wong May Yuk and Mr. Shau Yin Hui
Responsibilities: Overall planning, organizing, coordinating and controlling of the organization's activities.
Traits: Hardworking, dependable, organized, good communication skills and good interpersonal relations.

[2] Ms. Au Yuen Shuk Ling.
Responsibilities   Subdivide garments into component parts which would be assigned among specialized workers; keep cost of production low but enough to keep workers motivated; give technical assistance to workers.
Traits: Relatively new to position, traits not yet known.

[3] Ms. So.
Responsibilities: (Same as above).
Traits: Careful, good interpersonal relations, organized and responsible.

[4] Mr. Chan Wei Kueng.
Responsibilities: Make sure that specified kind of accessories like zippers, buttons, labels and linings are purchased and delivered on time for production; set up standard for quality control according to clients' specifications, and make sure that standards are met and defects are sorted out; supervise the button sewing, ironing and packaging crew to meet shipment deadlines.
Traits: Very careful with all the details requested by different clients. Good communication and interpersonal skills.

EXHIBIT 19.2   (Continued)

[5] Annie Ho.
Responsibilities: Place orders for raw materials.
Traits: Careful and conscientious about production schedule.

[6] Amy Ng.
Responsibilities: Make sure that standards are met and defects are sorted out.
Traits: Understands the importance of quality control.

[7] Chan Man Shung.
Responsibilities: Prepare garments ready for shipment.
Traits: Responsible and hardworking.

[8] Lee Fung Sheung.
Responsibilities: Record keeping, calculate workers' wages, prepare pay checks and manage petty cash.
Traits: Good in mathematics, and careful.

[9] Wong May Yuk.
Responsibilities: Make sure different groups are working in harmony to achieve the organization goals.
Traits: Understanding, good reasoning power, and sensitivity to people's needs.

[10] Fund Wei Sheun.
Responsibilities: Make sure samples are in accordance with client's specifications.
Traits: Responsible and reliable.

[11] Shau Yin Hui.
Responsibilities: Contact clients, give quotations and negotiate the price and quantity for contracts.
Traits: People-oriented.

of the human relations and marketing departments respectively. Mr. Shau frequently disagreed with Mrs. Wong concerning personnel management issues. However, since she was head of the human relations department, she frequently made the final decision in these matters.

Mrs. Wong picked up a recent set of financial statements from her desk. (See Exhibits 19.3–19.5.) These statements provided ample evidence of Ying May's strong performance. Profits from operations were over 185,000 Hong Kong dollars for the six-month period ending March 31, 1985. The net book value of Ying May equaled 617,208 Hong Kong dollars on the same date. Yet there were certain operational problems that would need to be addressed. Mrs. Wong was concerned that the increased production capacity had not been matched with an equivalent increase in sales. The problem was related to seasonal fluctuations in demand from Ying May's major markets in the U.S. and West Germany. This led to an uneven production schedule at the factory. At the beginning of the year, production capacity was not fully utilized and some resources lay idle. Mrs. Wong and Mr. Shau thought they might compensate for this situation by exporting to China during slow periods. However, this plan had not yet reached fruition. On the other hand, at the end of the year, there was more demand than the factory could handle comfortably. This situation created a different set of problems: delays in shipment of finished goods, lowering of the quality of the output, and increased costs of production due to the lengthened work hours of employees on the production lines.

EXHIBIT 19.3

Trading and Profit and Loss Account Statement, Ying May Garment Factory, Limited

For the Six-month Period, October 1, 1984, to March 31, 1985[1]
(Amounts in Hong Kong Dollars[2])

Sales	$11,532,200.45
Less cost of production	10,410,626.29
Gross profit	1,121,574.16
Less	
Trading expenses	
Certificates and declaration	24,525.30
Packing expenses	157,624.23
Quota charges	45,655.43
Transportation	75,213.16
Total trading expenses	303,018.12
Gross profit less trading expenses	818,556.04
Add	
Sundry income	17,871.90
Total	836,427.94
Less operation expenses	
Selling	123,332.26
Administrative	513,297.39
Financial	14,149.07
Total operating expenses	650,778.72
Net profit from operation before extraordinary items	185,649.22
Less extraordinary items	6,470.00
Unappropriated profit carried forward	$ 179,179.22

NOTES:

[1] Since this is the first set of audited accounts of the Company, no comparative figures from other periods are available.

[2] In Hong Kong dollars, USD:HKD = 1:7.78

Another production concern was that of quality control. Each finished garment was carefully inspected before export. Mrs. Wong believed that too many garments failed to pass this inspection process. Her initial analysis revealed that quite often defective merchandise was related to raw materials, such as fabric, thread, buttons and zippers. She and Mr. Shau had numerous discussions about quality control. It was not clear from these talks whether or not the two owners could reach agreement about the best way to improve quality. This situation would require a thorough investigation.

EXHIBIT 19.4

Statement of Operating Expenses, Ying May Garment Factory, Limited

For the Six-Month Period October 1, 1984 to March 31, 1985[1]
(Amounts in Hong Kong "Dollars"[2])

Selling expenses	
Advertising	$ 1,351.00
Commission paid	98,091.56
Entertainment	4,146.00
Motor vehicle expenses	434.00
Sample charges	19,309.70
Total selling expenses	$123,332.26
Administrative expenses	
Audit fee	$ 4,000.00
Building management fee	19,410.00
Business registration fee	350.00
Cleaning expenses	3,840.00
Cable and telex	3,173.35
Depreciation on furniture & fixtures	51,528.00
Depreciation on motor vehicle	3,400.00
Insurance	17,157.40
Loss on exchange	5,723.04
Messing	27,020.80
Printing & stationery	12,730.10
Professional charges	2,500.00
Salaries	285,835.50
Stamp & postage	4,210.80
Sundry expenses	24,169.40
Telephone charges	5,605.00
Travelling—Local	19,046.00
—Overseas	23,598.00
Total administrative expenses	$513,297.39
Financial expenses	
Bank charges	$ 7,638.81
Interest paid	6,510.26
Total financial expenses	$ 14,149.07

NOTES:

[1] Since this is the first set of audited accounts of the Company, no comparative figures from other periods are available.

[2] In Hong Kong dollars, USD:HKD = 1:7.78

EXHIBIT 19.5

Fixed Assets Statement, Ying May Garment Factory, Limited

For the Period Ended March 31, 1985[1]
(Amounts in Hong Kong Dollars[2])

	PLANT & MACHINERY	FURNITURE & FIXTURES	MOTOR VEHICLE	TOTAL
Assets, at cost				
Additions during the period	$511,870.00	$257,640.00	$17,000.00	$786,510.00
Disposals during the period	15,000.00	—	—	15,000.00
Balances as of March 31, 1985	$496,870.00	$257,640.00	$17,000.00	$771,510.00
Accumulated depreciation charges for the period	$ 99,374.00	$ 51,528.00	$ 3,400.00	$154,302.00
Disposals during the period	—	—	—	—
Balances as of March 31, 1985	$ 99,374.00	$ 51,528.00	$ 3,400.00	$154,302.00
Net book value as of March 31, 1985	$397,496.00	$206,112.00	$13,600.00	$617,208.00

NOTES:

[1] Since this is the first set of audited accounts of the Company, no comparative figures from other periods are available.

[2] In Hong Kong dollars, USD:HKD = 1:7.78

Other operational problems were linked to a need for better communications. Neither of the presidents nor the production manager was fluent in English and this caused numerous breakdowns in communications with their clients overseas. Misunderstanding and misinterpretation of terms had led occasionally to serious production mistakes. Mrs. Wong recalled one such example. A foreign client sent Ying May a sample with production specifications written in English; Mr. Chan had proceeded with production in accordance with the sample, neglecting the changes made on the specification sheet that he could not understand.

Internal communications needed to be improved as well. Mrs. Wong remembered a situation in which one of the production managers had been notified that a certain task was to be completed by the end of the week. The task was not finished on time because a problem encountered by the production manager was not communicated to either of the presidents. Only when the deadline arrived and the task was not finished did Mrs. Wong learn of the unattended problem.

Production mistakes frequently were caused by lack of sufficient information supplied to production line workers. When employees did not receive adequate instructions for production, they tended to make a "best guess." They did not realize that this process could lead to disasterous results for the organization.

THE HONG KONG TEXTILE/GARMENT INDUSTRY AND THE FUTURE OF YING MAY

As Mrs. Wong turned her attention to the future, there were certain environmental concerns that needed to be addressed. The overall business climate in Hong Kong was excellent and business was booming. The colony's gross domestic product was predicted to grow by 12% in 1986, making it one of only three Asian countries to reach double-digit growth. (South Korea and Taiwan were booming as well, but certain analysts were predicting that their growth rates could slow in the near future.) Much of the heat from the booming economy was being absorbed by the export sector. The government had recently raised its 1987 forecast for export growth to 27% above 1986.

The clothing industry had been the mainstay of the economy since World War II. The growth of the industry was due to the influx of emigrants from Shanghai with a tradition of working in textiles and apparel, and especially the large influx of immigrants during the 1970s who provided the human capital required. Of course, success was tied to the pro-business, laissez-faire policies of the Hong Kong government as well.

At the present time the textile and apparel industry was Hong Kong's largest industry, employing close to a third of the industrial workforce and supplying approximately 40% of the colony's export revenue. Ying May was one of over 9,000 companies in Hong Kong responsible for these achievements. Hong Kong was the major exporter of apparel in the world and its major customer was the U.S.

Mrs. Wong considered Hong Kong's performance impressive, especially when she considered the importance of the industry worldwide. The textile and apparel industry is the world's largest source of manufacturing employment, providing jobs for approximately 25 million people in both developed and developing countries. Significantly lower labor cost gave developing countries the competitive edge, threatening the loss of jobs in developed countries, including the U.S.

The sensitivity of this issue had led to the formation of numerous multilateral and bilateral agreements concerning trade in textiles and apparel, with some of the most stringent originating in the U.S. One long-standing agreement which specifically affects the industry is the Multifibre Arrangement (MFA). Instituted in 1974, it places numerous restrictions on the import of textiles into the U.S. The original MFA provided for certain import restrictions for fabrics made of wool, cotton, or man-made fibers. In 1986 the agreement was renewed for five more years and now includes ramies, silks, and linens. However, the United States textile industry is not pleased with the language of the agreement. Although these new fabrics are covered, domestic injury must be proven before quotas are imposed and these can be challenged by a Geneva-based Textile Surveillance Body.

Through numerous bilateral agreements between the U.S. and major textile exporting nations, yearly quotas limit the amount of goods that can be exported to the U.S. The traditional system in Hong Kong works as follows: The Hong Kong government receives a year's quota supply from the U.S. government which it, in turn, distributes to quota holders in the garment industry. The system is efficient—those purchasing quota allocations have to "use it or lose it." The purchaser has to use at least 50% of the allocation himself, but can sell the rest of the allocation to secondary purchasers. In this way, Hong Kong's quota is never wasted, and producers can gear their production to a set demand figure equal to the amount of their quota allocations. Each time a quota allocation is transferred, a quota broker collects a commission.

In an attempt to beat the quota system and to avoid paying quota prices, many Hong Kong companies were developing alternative sourcing possibilities, and setting up production facilities elsewhere to safeguard their options. In exchange for investments in Sri Lanka, Indonesia, and Mauritius, companies were guaranteed a large share of these countries' quotas. Another alternative was to move production to non-quota countries like Dubai or to countries with free trade agreements with the U.S.—such as Israel. Another strategy has been to move to Europe. This may seen odd because of the higher labor costs; however, this move allowed the companies to have freer access to the U.S. markets because the quota restrictions placed on Asia are not placed on Europe. One problem that the Hong Kong producers were experiencing in Europe was lower productivity rates than those in their own country. Another possibility was to move production to the Caribbean. Under the Caribbean Basin Initiative and the new Super 807 program, liberal access to the U.S. was provided for Caribbean-made garments stitched from fabric woven and cut in the U.S. Evidence suggested that Far Eastern manufacturers were beginning to shift production to this area. Mrs. Wong and Mr. Shau would have to consider these alternatives to continued expansion of their Hong Kong operations.

Now, due to growing concern in the U.S. over the trade deficit, imports of textiles and apparel were under the increasing scrutiny of U.S. policy-makers. Herein lay the most immediate problem facing the Hong Kong clothing industry: increasing protectionism aimed at the global clothing industry. One indication of this was an interest among certain members of the U.S. Congress to change the system of quota allocation. The new process would have the U.S. government auction off quota allocations directly to factories in Hong Kong and elsewhere. The rationale was that in this way the U.S. government would reap the quota allocations fees. Estimates of the total that could be collected ran as high as $2 billion. (Proceeds from the auction would be used to help industries adjust to foreign competition and improve skills of U.S. workers.) The downside of this plan meant that only the largest, most efficient factories could afford to purchase quotas, and mid-sized factories like Ying May would not be able to compete.

Another proposition before Congress was that of a global quota system. Under this plan, there would be global quotas for each category of textiles, thus eliminating the system of bilateral agreements between the U.S. and its trading partners and also eliminating the quota system in Hong Kong that had been functioning so well. Even if the traditional quota system remained in place, other forms of protectionism could lead to a weakening of U.S. demand for apparel from Hong Kong.

Competitors had arisen in Taiwan, South Korea, the Philippines, Indonesia, and China. Competition from these countries was based primarily on their ability to produce textiles at lower costs per unit. With the Hong Kong dollar tied to the U.S. dollar since 1983, the devaluation of the U.S. dollar was initially considered a positive consequence because it lowered the cost of Hong Kong products in parts of Europe. However, the garment industry soon learned this was not the case. The cost of raw materials and piece goods from countries whose currencies were strengthening against the dollar led those in the Hong Kong apparel industry to pass on these increased costs to U.S. purchasers through higher prices. This made other countries' offerings look even more attractive to U.S. customers. In reaction to this, some Hong Kong-based factories had moved into the production of higher priced, higher quality clothing.

A long-term issue facing Ying May related to the political future of Hong Kong. The Colony will revert to the People's Republic of China (PRC) in 1997, so a cloud of uncertainty hung over the economic landscape. Some experts were saying that the system could not survive the transformation to PRC control. Others were insisting that China's leadership would be intent on maintaining the capitalistic, free-market activities for which Hong Kong had been famous. During the past year investors seemed to be regaining confidence and businesses were benefiting from the Chinese Open Door policy that was providing ample trading opportunities with the PRC.

Mrs. Wong leaned back in her chair. She had concluded her review of Ying May's recent performance and those factors that needed to be considered if the Factory were to continue to prosper. She was prepared for tomorrow's planning meeting with Mr. Shau. The meeting would be an important one.

CASE 20

Applied CAD Knowledge, Inc. (A)

JOHN A. SEEGER ● RAYMOND M. KINNUNEN

> Something is seriously wrong with this planet. Look at us. I'm working a hundred and twenty hours a week or more, and not catching up. I've got these two friends—both recently divorced, like me—who aren't working at all: they're living off their girl friends, and loving it. One of them is basking in Hawaii. But here I am, busting my ass and giving my customers problems anyhow.
>
> Some guys go on television and say, "Send money now," and people *do*. I ask my best customer to send money, and he goes bankrupt instead. What's wrong with this picture?

Jeff Stevens, President and 90% owner of Applied CAD Knowledge, Inc., was reporting on current sales and production levels to the two business school professors who comprised his Board of Directors. It was late August, and the three men sat in a booth at Bogie's restaurant. The waitress, Patty, was accustomed to these monthly meetings; she offered another round of Lite beer. "Make mine cyanide," said Stevens. "On the rocks, please."

Applied CAD, a small service bureau that designed electronic circuit boards, was experiencing the highest sales levels in its three-year history. June sales had reached $50,000—leaving a backlog of $90,000; July shipments had set a record at $58,000; August would be nearly as high. The problem facing Stevens through the summer of 1987 was a shortage of good designers to work as part-time freelancers. The surge in business saw Stevens sitting at the computer consoles him-

---

This case has **accompanying video tape** of Jeff Stevens in a question-and-answer session in front of an Executive M.B.A. class that can be purchased from Office of the Dean, Northeastern University, College of Business Administration, Hayden Hall, Boston, MA 02115.

This case was prepared by Professor John A. Seeger, Bentley College, and Professor Raymond M. Kinnunen, Northeastern University. Presented at the North American Case Research Meeting, 1988. All rights reserved to the authors and the North American Case Research Association. Copyright © 1988 by John A. Seeger and Raymond M. Kinnunen. Reprinted by permission of the authors and the North American Case Research Association.

self, doing design work on second and third shifts, six or seven days a week. After eight weeks of this schedule, the strain was showing. One director asked about the longer-range sales picture, and Stevens summed it up:

> Can I borrow a .45 automatic? I'd like a good game of Russian Roulette.
>
> There's nothing on the books at all for late fall, and not much likely. Every major customer we have is in "busy phase" right now. When these designs are finished, it will be another four to six months before their next generation of product revisions. In the meantime, everybody is burned out. All I'm hoping for right now is a front porch, a rocking chair, a lobotomy and a drool cup.

THE ELECTRONICS INDUSTRY AND CIRCUIT BOARD DESIGN

The United States electronics industry in 1987 was a sprawling giant, some of whose sectors were growing while others remained in a protracted slump. In 1986, total industry size was estimated by *Electronic Business* magazine (December 10, 1985) as $100.5 billion to $182 billion. The same article projected industry revenues for 1995 to be $295.4 billion to $512 billion. The magazine concluded that its industry represented a major driving force for the American economy. The Value Line investment service reports separately on four segments of the electronics industry (see Exhibit 20.1).

Printed Circuit Boards

A basic part of nearly every electronic product—whichever segment of the industry produced or used it—was the printed circuit board to which a variety of electronic components were attached. These components ranged from old-fashioned resistors, capacitors, and vacuum tubes, to transistors and the most modern integrated circuit chips. All components needed some sort of platform to sit on, and some way to make connection with the other components of the circuit.

In the 1930s and 1940s, circuit boards were made from thin, non-conducting fiberboard with metal pins and sockets attached. Assembly operators wound the wire leads of the circuit's resistors, capacitors, etc. around the proper pins

EXHIBIT 20.1

Electronics Industry Revenues
(Dollars in Amounts in Billions)

INDUSTRY SECTOR	NUMBER OF COMPANIES	1982	1983	1984	1985	1986	1987 (Est')
Electronics	35	$16.4	$17.7	$ 21.6	$ 21.2	$ 22.0	$ 24.0
U.S. semiconductors	14	11.4	13.0	17.2	15.6	16.0	17.8
Computers/peripherals	34	78.6	88.4	104.4	110.5	115.0	127.5
Electrical equipment	25	50.9	51.2	54.9	56.5	64.7	72.0

SOURCE: *Value Line*, May 8, 1987.

I

and soldered them in place. By the 1960s, the technology of wiring boards and assembling components had advanced to a highly automated stage. Numerically controlled machines positioned components and connected pins to one another with wires. During this decade, electronic components became increasingly miniaturized and more reliable, complex and powerful. With these technological developments, the printed circuit board (PCB) was developed; its use and technical sophistication accelerated rapidly.

In a printed circuit, the wires leading from one pin to another are replaced by electrically conductive lines "printed" or plated onto (or under) the surface of the board itself. The pins themselves are gone; wire leads from electrical components are inserted through small holes in the board and soldered on the underside. By the 1980s, components could be mounted directly on the board's surface, in contact with the printed "wires."

The increasing complexity of electronic circuits presents a problem for PCB technology. When connections were made with wires, assemblers simply attached one end, routed the wire over the top of everything between the two pins involved, and attached the other end where it belonged. With printed circuits, however, designers are constrained to two dimensions on a flat board; they must route the line between two pins without touching any other lines, and they cannot go "over the top" without leaving the surface of the board. Furthermore, efficient design calls for the components to be tightly packed together, grouped by function. Designers frequently find that they cannot lay out a trace from one point to another without interfering with other traces.

"Multilayer" PCBs ease this problem by providing "upstairs" layers on the board, allowing the designer to go over the top. Multilayer boards contain at least three layers of traces, and sometimes more than twenty layers. Skilled designers seek to minimize the number of layers required for a given circuit, in order to reduce manufacturing costs of the board: Multilayer PCBs are far more expensive to manufacture. In 1983, multilayer boards had sales of $900 million, or 26% of the PCB market. By 1993, they are forecast to reach sales of $5.6 billion, or 41% market share. Exhibit 20.2 shows PCB sales and projections by type of board.

Board design was made more complicated by increasing density of components, by sensitivity of components to heat (some threw off large amounts of heat, while others would go haywire if their operating temperature was disturbed), and by radio-frequency interference (some components generated static, while others might "hear" the noise and try to process it). The layout of components on the board had tremendous impact on how well the finished product worked, as well as on its manufacturing cost.

Printed circuit boards offered many technical advantages over the previous method for fashioning circuits:

1. *Greater miniaturization:* PCBs can be highly miniaturized, allowing progressively more powerful and complex electronic circuits for smaller, lighter products.

EXHIBIT 20.2   **Sales and Projections for PCBs by Type of Board**

PCB TYPE	1983 Sales in $ Millions	1983 Market Share (%)	ANNUAL GROWTH RATE	1993 Sales in $ Millions	1993 Market Share (%)
Multilevel	900	25.3	20%	$5,600	41.0
Double-sided	2,000	56.1	13%	6,700	49.0
Flexible	353	10.0	10%	916	6.7
Single-sided	307	8.6	4%	454	3.3
Total	$3,560	100%		$13,670	100%

SOURCE: *Electronic Business* February 1, 1985, p. 87.

2. *Improved performance:* product reliability is much greater than in pin-to-pin circuitry, so that applications can be made in extreme environmental conditions.
3. *Manufacturing advantages:* for high volume products, manufacturing costs are greatly reduced. PCB applications range from simple consumer products to the most powerful mainframe computers.
4. *Maintenance advantages:* PCBs allowed designers to "package" electronic systems into discrete modules which, if not functioning properly, could be replaced without the immediate need of determining where the problem was within the board.

Frost and Sullivan, Inc., a New York market research firm, estimated (in "The Printed Circuit Board Market in the U.S.," July, 1986, quoted by permission) that the total U.S. PCB market reached $3.7 billion in sales in 1985, a decrease of 12% from 1984's production. PCBs were projected to grow to a likely $6.5 billion by 1990 and to $10.8 billion in 1995. Multi-layer PCBs were expected to be the fastest-growing type, averaging 15.7% annual growth. A little over half the market was served in 1985 by independent PCB makers, as opposed to captive suppliers, Frost & Sullivan said.

Trends in Equipment Used in Circuit Board Design

Originally (and still, for simple circuits), an engineer or technician worked from a "schematic" drawing of the circuit, which showed how the various components were connected. On a large layout table, the PCB designer manually drew in the components and linked them with black tape (or ink), to produce a "photo master" film which was in turn used to project the design photographically onto the base material of the circuit board. As circuits became more complex, the manual process bogged down.

As boards became more complex, specialized computer hardware and software began to help designers and engineers solve complex design problems. By the mid 1970s, system vendors began to offer CAD (Computer-Aided Design) systems specifically developed for PCB designing. Racal–Redac, Inc., a British firm, was the first to offer a powerful special-purpose PCB-oriented system. Based on Digital Equipment Corp.'s PDP-11 computer, the Redac product was the first to permit PCB designers to interact with the computer; designers could try various routings of traces and see how they looked on the graphic display. This approach competed well against established systems such as Computervision, whose general-purpose equipment was priced in the $500,000 class and still lacked the interactive design capability.

By 1982, prices for PCB design systems had fallen below $100,000. New CAD equipment makers entered the field, with automated routing or documentation features that carried substantial advantages over the established Redac software. Calay and Cadnetix, as examples, introduced strong entries— neither being compatible with the Redac or Sci-Cards equipment already in the field. Racal–Redac Ltd., however, had perhaps taken the greatest strides to tailor its software to run on a variety of hardware platforms. Said Ian Orrock, Chief Executive of Redac's electronics CAD division in England, "We're all going to end up being software houses."

Another important feature of the new CAD equipment was ease of use; the older CAD/CAM systems might require months of learning time before a designer became proficient. In the late 1970s, with high equipment costs and low availability of trained designers, only the largest electronic firms designed and produced their own PCBs. Service bureaus took advantage of the market opportunity, acting as the primary design resource for smaller clients and as peak load designers for firms with in-house capacity. As electronics firms purchased and began to use the newer systems, however, they wanted service bureaus to be equipped with similar or compatible machines. Service bureaus felt the pressure to acquire the most up-to-date hardware and software available, in order to qualify as bidders on that work.

Service Bureau Operations

When a service bureau invested in CAD equipment, the sheer size of the investment created pressure to use the equipment intensively. Multi-shift operations were common, but the supply of designers to man them was severely limited. Typically, a service bureau did not hire permanent staff for all three shifts: the work load was too unpredictable. Service bureaus generally hired moonlighting designers from established electronics firms to staff their second and third shifts.

The design of printed circuit boards requires a peculiar combination of skills, primarily in spatial geometry, circuit insight, memory, and persistence. A talented designer—perhaps capable of completing a complex design in three weeks of console time—might be several times more productive than a "journeyman." In the early 1980s, talented designers willing to work odd shifts were earning over $100,000 per year; few of them had college educations.

Most customers requested separate quotations for each board; often, customers asked for bids from several service bureaus. Design clients always ran on tight schedules, Jeff Stevens observed, wanting their work to be delivered "yesterday":

> Circuit board design is usually one of the last steps before a new product goes into production. Our design time is the customer's time-to-market. It's natural for them to be in a hurry.

For the design of a large, complex, 4-layered PCB a client might pay between $10,000 to $15,000. Such a project might require five to six man-weeks of labor input (two thirds of which might be designer's time); it might involve extensive communication between Applied CAD personnel and a wide variety of the client's technical personnel, and it would often require Applied CAD personnel to work through the night at various project stages to make deadlines. In such a typical project, much of Applied CAD's time would be spent sorting out and coordinating conflicting information and directions from different technical people in the client company. Stevens noted,

> Even our clients themselves won't always know completely what they want. When we take their directions to their logical conclusions, problems often occur. Then we have to show them what developed. You spend a lot of time on the phone with clients, sometimes at 3 A.M. Often, I wind up making decisions for the client, so the work can go ahead; later, I have to convince the client the decision was right.

Design reliability remained a key attribute of a service bureau's reputation, since whole product lines (or engineers' jobs) might depend on the PCB design's working properly, and on its prompt delivery:

> We had one job, in the old days, where a satellite was literally sitting on the launch pad, waiting for a corrected module design. The engineers had discovered a design flaw. They flew into town with the specs, and then took turns sitting behind the designer at the scope, or sitting beside their hotel room telephone, waiting to answer any questions that might come up. In this business, you have to deliver.

When the design phase of a job was finished, the computer tape or disk would be carried to a second service bureau for creation of the film photoplots needed for manufacturing. The equipment for photoplotting was far more complex and expensive than the computer systems needed for design. Only a few design shops in New England had their own photoplotting capability; they performed this work for other service bureaus and in-house design departments as well as for their own design clients.

The actual production of PCBs might be done by the client company itself or by a fabrication shop which specialized in the work. New England was home to some 80 to 100 fab shops, many of which offered design as well as manufacturing services. A few large firms (Hadco at $125 million in sales) were equipped to service very large orders—100,000 or more boards of a design—but most

EXHIBIT 20.3 **Low-Cost PC Board Design Software Available, Spring, 1987**

COMPANY	PRODUCT	BASE PRICE	REQUIRED HARDWARE	OPERATING SYSTEM	AUTO-ROUTER	AUTO-ROUTER PRICE
Abacus Software	PC Board Designer	$195	Atari 520ST or 1040ST	GEM	●	
Accel Technologies	Tango-PCB	$495	IBM PC/XT or PC/AT	MS-DOS	●	
Aptos Systems	Criterion II	$4,000	ARTIST 1 CARD and IBM PC/XT or PC/AT	MS-DOS	●	$5000
Automated Images	Personal 870	$8,000	IBM PC/XT or PC/AT	MS-DOS		
B&C Microsystems	PCB/DE	$395	IBM PC/XT or PC/AT	MS-DOS (and the Autocad Drafting package)		
CAD Software	Pads-PCB	$975	IBM PC/XT or PC/AT	MS-DOS	●	$750
Case Technology	Vanguard PCB	$4,250	IBM PC/AT, SUN-3. or DEC Microvax	MS-DOS, UNIX, or VMS	●	$5500
Daisy Systems	Personal Boardmaster	$8,000	IBM PC/AT or Daisy PL386	DNIX		
Dasoft Design	Project: PCB	$950	IBM PC/XT or PC/AT	MS-DOS	●	
Design Computation	Draftsman-EE	$1,147	IBM PC/XT or PC/AT	MS-DOS	●	$2450
Douglas	Douglas	$395	Apple Macintosh	Macintosh		
Electronics	CAD/CAM					
Electronic Design Tools	PROCAD	$2,495	IBM PC/XT or PC/AT and 68000 Coprocessor	MS-DOS	●	$2495
Electronic Industrial Equipment	Executive CAD	$11,000	IBM PC/XT or PC/AT	MS-DOS	●	
Futurenet	Dash-PCB	$13,000	IBM PC/AT and 32032 Coprocessor	UNIX	●	
Hewlett-Packard	EGS	$7,000	HP 9000	HP-UX		
Kontron	KAD-286	$10,400	IBM PC/AT	MS-DOS		
Personal CAD Systems	PC8-1	$6,000	IBM PC/XT or PC/AT	MS-DOS	●	$6000
Racal-Redac	Redboard	$12,000	IBM PC/XT or PC/AT	MS-DOS	●	
Seetrax (in U.S., Circuits and Systems)	Ranger	$5,000	IBM PC/AT	MS-DOS	●	$2000
Softcircuits	Pcloplus	$1,024	Commodore Amiga 1000	Amigados	●	
Vamp	McCAD	$395	Apple Macintosh	Macintosh	●	$995
Visionics	EE Designer II	$1,875	IBM PC/XT or PC/AT	MS-DOS	●	$1475
Wintek	Smartwork	$895	IBM PC/XT or PC/AT	MS-DOS	●	
Ziegler Instruments (in U.S., Caddy)	Caddy Electronic Systems	$2,495	IBM PC/XT or PC/AT	MS-DOS	●	$2500

SOURCE: *EDN*, March 18, 1987, pp 140–141. Used by permission.

AUTO-PLACEMENT	COMPATIBLE NET LISTS	MAXIMUM NUMBER OF COLORS	MAXIMUM NUMBER OF TRACES	MAXIMUM NUMBER OF COMPONENTS	MAXIMUM NUMBER OF LAYERS	PACKAGING TECHNOLOGIES
		2	1100 Lines	250	2	
	Accel, Omation, Orcad	16	26,000 Lines	1000	9	SMD
•	Aptos, Futurenet, P-CAD	16	2000 nets	1000	50	SMD, ECL, Analog
	Applicon, Futurenet, Orcad	16			16	SMD, Hybrid
	B&C	16				
•	Futurenet	16	4511 nets	764	30	SMD, Fine-Line
•	Case	16	2000 nets	1000	256	SMD
	Daisy	7	14,000 Lines	14,000	255	SMD
	Dasoft	6			4	SMD
•		16	4000 nets	300	20	Fine-Line
		2				SMD, Analog
•	Electronic Design Tools	16	10,000 nets	3000	56	SMD, Constant-Impedance
•	Electronic Industrial Equipment	16			4	SMD, ECL
	Futurenet	4			10	Fine-Line
	HP	15			255	Hybrid
	Kontron	64	5300 Lines	3200	255	ECL, SMD, Hybrid
•	P-CAD, Futurenet	16	1000 nets	300	50	SMD
•	Racal-Redac	16	1900 nets	511	16	SMD
•	Seetrax	16	10,000 Lines	1400	16	SMD
		16				
•	Vamp	2	32,000 Lines	32,000	6	SMD, Metric
•		16		999	26	SMD
	Wintek	3			6	
	Ziegler	16			128	Analog

fab shops fell in the $1–$2 million size range, with an average order size of 25–30 relatively small boards. One shop estimated its average PCB was priced at $22 each, with a setup charge of $150.

Trends in PCB Design

By the end of 1986, a number of vendors had developed PCB design packages to run on personal computers—mostly the IBM XT or AT machines. These software systems, some including automatic routing, were priced as low as a few hundred dollars or as high as $13,000, and varied widely in their features and capabilities. In-house design capability became practical for most electronics firms, although many lacked the PCB expertise that still marked the better service bureaus. Freelance designers, too, could acquire their own equipment. Exhibit 20.3 compares the features and prices of twenty-four such software packages.

Clients were inclined to stay with their existing service bureaus, unless they were severely burned. Good relationships between service staff and engineering personnel helped minimize communication errors, and availability of the data base from the original job allowed for revisions or modifications at much lower cost.

In the 1980s, as the cost of entering the service bureau business dropped, many new firms appeared. Jeff Stevens observed, "When I started at Redac in 1978, there were three service bureaus in New England. By 1993 there were maybe a dozen. Now there might be seventy-five, and it could reach 100 in another year." In 1987, several competing service bureaus in the area were owned by former employees of Racal–Redac, where Jeff himself had learned the business. Exhibit 20.4 lists the major competitors in the northeastern United States in 1986.

For the longer, run, some industry analysts speculated that constant advances in miniaturizing electronic circuits might permit semiconductor technology to reduce certain whole PCBs (such as those developed for computer memory) into a single IC chip.

APPLIED CAD KNOWLEDGE, INC.: HISTORY	Jeff Stevens had learned the rudiments of circuit board design in his first job after high school graduation, as a technician in a five-person product development laboratory. Here, in 1975, one of his duties was to prepare enlarged prints of circuits, using black tape on white mylar. In another, concurrent job as a technician in an electronics manufacturing firm, he learned how the circuits themselves worked.

In 1977, Stevens left his two technician jobs for an entry-level design position with Racal–Redac in Littleton, Massachusetts. Redac operated a service bureau to complement its sales of DEC hardware and British software. As a pioneer in the field, Redac at the time boasted a near-monopoly in powerful systems

EXHIBIT 20.4	**PC Design Service Bureaus in New England**

Design Houses (Grouped by Sales Volume in Millions of Dollars)

0–$1 Million per Year	*$1–$2 Million per Year*
Abington labs.	Automated Images, Inc.
Berkshire Design	Automated Design, Inc.
CAD Tec	CAD Services, Inc.
Cadtronix, Ltd.	Antal Associates
Computer Aided Circuits, Inc.	Multiwire of New England
Dataline PCB Corp.	Teccon
Design Services	Tech Systems & Design
Energraphics	Kenex, Inc.
Graphics Technology Corp.	Alternate Circuit Design Technology
Herbertons, Inc.	Photofabrication Technology Inc.
Het Printed Circuit Design	
High Tech CAD Service Co.	*$2–$5 Million per Year*
Jette Fabrication	Tek-Art Associates
LSI Engineering	Strato Reprographix
PC Design Company	Altek, Co.
PAC-Lab, Inc.	Eastern Electronics Mfg. Corp.
Packaging for Electronics	Datacube, Inc.
PC Design Services	Owl Electronic Laboratories, Inc.
Point Design, Inc.	*$5–$10 Million per Year*
Power Processing, Inc.	Triad Engineering Co.
Product Development Co.	Photronic Labs, Inc.
Qualitron Corp.	*$10+ Million per Year*
Quality Circuit Design, Inc.	Algorex Corp.
Research Labs, Inc.	ASI Automated Systems, Inc.
Scientific Calculations, Inc.	Augat Interconnection Systems Group
Tracor Electro-Assembly Inc.	Racal–Redac Service Bureau
Winter Design	Synermation, Inc.

SOURCE: Beacon Technology, "New England Printed Circuit Directory." Copyright © 1985. Reprinted by permission.

dedicated to PCB design. Jeff Stevens, in a training rotation, joined Redac's service bureau as a data-entry technician.

> We had three computer systems—about twenty people altogether. A system then cost about $200,000 and a lot of companies didn't have enough design work to justify buying one.
>
> In data entry, you prepare code to represent all the terminals and components on the board. I refused to code the first job they gave me, and nearly got fired. Finally I convinced them that the job *shouldn't* be coded: the turkey who engineered it had the diodes in backward, and the circuit wasn't going to work. About a week later, they put me in charge of data entry, supervising the guy who had wanted to fire me.

Stevens became a designer, then a lead designer, then operations manager of the service bureau. Under his leadership, the operation dramatically im-

---

EXHIBIT 20.5   **Balance Sheet, Applied CAD Knowledge, Inc.**

Balance Sheet	1985	1986	1987
Assets			
Current assets			
Cash	$128,568	$ 14,148	$ 33,074
Accounts receivable, trade	18,865	15,375	14,250
Prepaid taxes and other current assets	4,853	1,200	5,074
Total current assets	152,286	30,723	52,398
Property and equipment	174,079	190,079	203,079
Less accumulated depreciation	48,697	86,357	124,062
Total property and equipment	125,382	103,722	79,017
Total assets	$277,668	$134,445	$131,415
Liabilities and stockholders' equity			
Current liabilities			
Accounts payable, trade	$127,685	$ 9,025	$ 21,823
Current maturities of long-term debt	13,300		
Income taxes payable	4,008		2,303
Other current liabilities	5,000	5,373	70
Total current liabilities	149,993	14,398	24,196
Long-term debt, less current maturities	41,121	83,247	53,663
Stockholders' equity			
Common stock, no par value; authorized 15,000 shares, issued and outstanding 1,000 shares	25,000	25,000	25,000
Retained earnings	61,554	11,800	28,556
Total stockholders' equity	86,554	36,800	53,556
Total liabilities and stockholders' equity	$277,668	$134,445	$131,415

proved its reputation for quality and on-time delivery, as well as its financial performance:

> When I took over in October of 1981, monthly sales were $50,000 and monthly expenses were $110,000. In six months we turned it around: monthly sales were $110,000 and expenses were $50,000. There had been a tremendous amount of dead wood. We had a big bonfire with it, and went from twenty-six people to sixteen. In some ways, it was a brutal campaign, I guess.

In June 1983, Stevens left Racal–Redac to work as a consulting designer, helping electronics firms with their CAD decisions as well as doing freelance design work. He had developed design and management expertise and established a reputation in industry circles which he could now broker directly to clients who were familiar with his previous work.

In December 1983, Jeff established Applied CAD while still working from his home in Pepperell, Massachusetts. By purchasing used computer equipment and installing it himself in his living room, Stevens was able to hold his initial investment to $35,000; the largest cost element was $28,000 for the software purchased from his former employer. (Financial data on Applied CAD's last three years of operation are shown in Exhibits 20.5 and 20.6.)

> The equipment pretty well filled up the living room, and through the summer I couldn't run it during the daytime: we didn't have enough electricity to cool it down. Winter solved that problem, though; I heated the house with a PDP-11.

EXHIBIT 20.6   Income Statement, Applied CAD Knowledge, Inc.

	1985	1986	1987
Net revenues	$328,262	$232,540	$346,267
Cost of revenue			
Salaries, wages and outside services	134,686	116,835	209,998
Research and development	14,154	7,551	13,731
Software costs	65,131	18,864	
Total cost of revenue	$213,971	$143,250	$223,729
Gross profit	114,291	89,290	122,898
Selling, general and administrative expenses	72,320	143,051	77,732
Operating profit	41,971	(53,761)	45,166
Bad debt expense			(28,660)
Interest income (expense), net	2,331	3,576	(10,103)
Income before income taxes	44,302	(50,185)	6,403
Income taxes	4,508	0	0
Net income	39,794	(50,185)	6,403
Retained earnings, beginning of year	21,760	62,385	22,154
Retained earnings, end of year	$ 61,554	$ 11,800	$ 28,557

In late 1984, Applied CAD leased a 1,000-square-foot office suite on the ground floor of a new building near the Merrimack River in Tyngsboro, Mass. Jeff Stevens designed the interior space to hold a central computer room (with special air conditioning), a darkened "console room" for the actual design work, and a large front office. By January 1985, the computing equipment was installed and operating. The console room was furnished with two Recaro ergonometric chairs (at $1,100 each) for the designers' use; the front office held a large receptionist's desk and a sparse collection of work tables, file cabinets, and spare hardware.

Applied CAD's Organization

Jeff oversaw all operations in his company, did all the high level marketing and sales contact work with clients, and did much of the technical design work as well. Another full-time designer was hired in May 1985 but had to be terminated in September 1986 because of persistent personal problems. Steve Jones, Jeff's data manager and former assistant at Redac, became a full-time employee in January, 1986. Among other duties, Steve covered the telephone, coordinated technical work done by freelance contractors in Jeff's absence, and performed various administrative duties. Steve had a B.S. in Engineering and, before Redac, had worked for other PCB electronics companies. In April 1987 Jeff hired John MacNamara, a former subcontract designer, on a full-time salaried basis.

In May 1987 Jeff also hired a part-time person to keep the books, write checks, and handle other office related matters. For her first three months she focused on straightening out the books and tax related items. She was also trying to find time to set up an accounting package on the personal computer. The package had been purchased in August 1986 (at the request of Board members), for the purpose of generating accurate monthly statements. Since the company's founding, the Board had been asking for accurate end-of-month data on sales, accounts receivable, cash balance, backlog and accounts payable. It also wanted monthly financial statements, although Stevens himself saw little point in them: Cash flow projections served his immediate needs. The accounting package was chosen by one of the Board members, based partly on its broad capabilities. For example, it could assist in invoicing and aging receivables.

Jeff had other capable designers "on call"—available for freelance project work when the company needed them. Depending upon the market, there were time periods when Jeff could obtain the services of several contractors to meet peak work loads. In general, design contractors worked on a negotiated fixed-fee basis for completing a specific portion of a design project. In July 1987, however (after sales in June reached approximately $50 thousand and the backlog reached $90 thousand), Jeff found it difficult to attract contract designers who had free time. The backlog consisted of about fifteen boards ranging in price from $800 to $15,000. Sales in the electronics industry had turned upward and in busy times everyone was busy. Consequently, free-lance designers were committed to their own customers or employers who were also busy.

Jeff's Board of Directors consisted of Jeff and two college professors from well-known institutions in the Boston area. Since the fall of 1985 the Board had met monthly for three to four hours, usually during the first week of the month. At most meetings the Board first discussed the previous month's sales and current levels of cash, accounts receivable, backlog and payables. Other typical agenda items ranged from the purchase of new equipment and/or software, to marketing and personnel problems.

At most meetings, the Board spent considerable time discussing the current business climate and the future sales outlook. This usually led to a discussion of hiring someone to take over the marketing and sales function. It was generally agreed that such a person could not only contribute to the company's growth in sales but also free up a considerable amount of Jeff's time that could be devoted to design and operational matters. When Applied CAD was busy, however, Jeff had very little to devote to finding, hiring, and working with such a person. When the firm was not busy, Jeff's concern over the reliability of future cash flows made him hesitant to make the major salary commitment that a marketing professional would require. He was aware of the contrary pressures: "I can't get out of the 'boom–splat' syndrome," he said.

To Jeff, the "splat" came when backlogs and cash balances fell. The winter of 1987, for example, had felt to him like hitting a wall. (Exhibit 20.7 shows monthly totals of sales, accounts receivable, backlogs and cash balances, as estimated by Jeff at monthly Board meetings.)

Hardware and Software

After moving into his new quarters, Jeff Stevens located another PDP-11/34 computer—this one for sale at $7,000. Adding it to his shop required purchase of another Redac software package, but the added capacity was needed. Other, competing CAD systems were now available, but the decision to stick with Redac seemed straightforward to Jeff:

> Racal–Redac systems had several advantages. They were specifically dedicated to PCB design work and they had software that was brutally efficient. They were familiar to most of the freelance designers in the area. Wide acceptance of Redac's software makes it easier to get overflow work from companies that demanded compatibility with their own equipment. Not to mention that I know this gear backward and forward, and could keep several machines busy at once.

The Redac software was originally developed in 1972, which made it very old by industry standards. Jeff pointed out, however, that because machines were slower in 1972 and had much less memory, the software *had* to be extremely efficient. Having used this software for a long time, he said, "I've been able to

EXHIBIT 20.7

Monthly Sales and Month-End Receivables, Backlogs, Cash Levels, Applied CAD Knowledge, Inc.

(Dollar Amounts in Thousands)

	ACCOUNTS RECEIVABLE	SALES	BACKLOG	CASH
January 1986	**$18**	**$20**	**$20**	**$98**
February	—	10	—	N/A
March	18	10	12	62
April	18	10	20	28
May	24	20	26	26
June	—	10	—	N/A
July	14	25	—	18
August	70	50	30	15
September	90	40	—	8
October	50	30	—	26
November	19	5	10	17
December	24	10	18	14
January 1987	**13**	**3**	—	**7**
February	40	21	—	8
March	35	28	22	6
April	32	22	37	11
May	25	22	50	5
June	50	50	90	10
July	90	58	30	10

make process modifications to improve its efficiency, and I know all its intricacies." Jeff had developed some proprietary software for PCB design work which he believed kept him at the cutting edge of the competition. At times, he wondered about the possibilities of licensing his proprietary software to other PCB design firms. He concluded, however, that the small market for this type of software product would probably not justify the necessary marketing and additional product development costs.

In addition to the original equipment purchased by Jeff in 1983 the company purchased a VAX Model 11/751 and a Calay Version 03 in December 1985 at a cost of approximately $170,000. (See Exhibit 20.8 for the cash flow statements prepared for the bank to obtain a loan.) The VAX was intended to be used as a communications and networking device and as a platform for developing new software. The Calay was a dedicated hardware system that included an automatic router which could completely design certain less complex boards

EXHIBIT 20.8   Cash Flow Projections as of December 16, 1985, Applied CAD Knowledge, Inc.

(Dollars Amounts in Thousands)

	DEC 1985	JAN 1986	FEB 1986	MAR 1986	APR 1986	MAY 1986	JUN 1986	JUL 1986	AUG 1986	SEP 1986	OCT 1986	NOV 1986	DEC 1986	TOTAL
Sales	25	30	30	30	30	30	30	30	30	30	30	30	30	360
Expenses[1]	20	24	29.5	29.5	29.5	29.5	29.5	29.5	29.5	29.5	29.5	29.5	29.5	348.5
Profit	5	6	0.5	0.5	0.5	0.5	0.5	0.5	0.5	0.5	0.5	0.5	0.5	11.5
Opening cash	141	148	102	102.5	88	88.5	89	89.5	90	90.5	91	91	91.5	
Receivables	37	17	30	30	30	30	30	30	30	30	30	30	30	
Disbursements[2]	30	24[3]	29.5[4]	29.5	29.5	29.5	29.5	29.5	29.5	29.5	29.5	29.5	29.5	
Taxes[5]		39[6]		15										
Closing cash	148	102	102.5	88	89	89.5	90	90.5	91	91	91.5	92		

[1] Expenses include rent, heat, light, power, salaries, contract work, telephone, etc. This level of expenses will support sales double those projected.

[2] Figures do not include depreciation which would only influence total profit.

[3] Includes loan payment of 4K/mth.

[4] Includes new employees at 66K/yr.

[5] Taxes based on the following assumptions: 1985 profit of 150K; 50K software expense on new equipment; 20K depreciation on new equipment; 10K misc. expenses; investment tax credit of 15K.

[6] 25% of equipment costing 156K.

without an operator. On more complex boards it could complete a major percentage of the board, leaving a designer to do the remainder. In September 1986, a software upgrade to Calay Version 04 was purchased at a cost of approximately $28,000. Although bank financing was available, Jeff decided to pay cash for this equipment, to avoid raising his monthly fixed expenses. The new purchases gave Applied CAD enough machine capacity to support some $2 million in annual sales.

When the Calay machine was purchased, Jeff and the Board felt that its automatic routing capability might open a new market for the company for less complex boards. Because the Calay was virtually automatic on certain applications the final price of these boards could be much less than if they were done by hand. Because of the lower price to the customer the Calay was also appropriate for designing boards that would be produced in smaller quantities. Finally, Jeff and the Board felt that the manufacturer of the Calay as well as the Calay user group would supply new customer leads. Some of these expectations had been met.

The VAX, however, was not being fully used as originally intended—to allow hands-off automation of the firm's varied pieces of computing equipment, as well as providing batch data processing capacity. In its ultimate form, the VAX might actually operate the older, more cumbersome systems. It would be able to juggle dozens of design tasks between work stations and autorouters, queueing and evaluating each job, and calling for human intervention when needed. One director, visualizing robots sitting in Applied CAD's Recaro chairs, called this the "Robo-Router plan." To carry it out would require an additional investment of approximately $15,000 in hardware and another $10,000–$20,000 in programming, along with a significant amount off Jeff's time. The investment would result in very substantial cost reductions and reduced dependence on freelance designers, but it would only pay for itself under high volume conditions.

CURRENT BUSINESS OPTIONS

In August 1987, Jeff was contemplating the current business climate, his accomplishments with Applied CAD over the past three years, and the direction in which the company was headed. His major objective, and the Board's, was growth. Jeff had discussed many times with his Board the need for a marketing person and a promotional brochure for the company. On occasion, he had talked with marketing people about Applied CAD's needs, but most of these prospective employees lacked the level of skills and PCB experience Jeff hoped to acquire. He had also talked with commercial artists about design of a brochure. Jeff and his Board felt that a "first class" brochure would cost $5,000–$10,000.

Marketing in the PCB business, especially among companies with sales of under $1 million, was characterized as informal. Very few companies had full-time people devoted to the marketing task; in most cases it was the owner-president who handled marketing and sales. Most small companies had their own list of faithful customers and new customers tended to come by word of mouth. In the under $1 million segment it was not uncommon for a company when extremely overloaded with work to farm out a board to a competitor. Also, certain other services, such as photoplotting, were done by shops that also did design work. Consequently, there was considerable communication among the competitors; the players seemed to know who got what jobs.

The marketing job at a company like Applied CAD consisted mainly of coordinating the advertising and a sales brochure, calling on present customers, and attempting to find new customers. Such a person needed a working knowledge of PCB design, which required experience in the industry. People with the qualifications necessary normally made a $40,000–$50,000 base salary plus commissions; frequently their total compensation exceeded $100,000 per year. Of major concern to Jeff was Applied CAD's erratic history of sales and cash balances, and the difficulty of predicting sales volume any further than two months in advance (see Exhibit 20.7). He balked at taking on responsibility for an executive-level salary, lacking confidence in the future. "This would probably be somebody with kids to feed or send to college," Jeff said. "How could I pay them, in slow times?"

Still, marketing appeared to be the function most critical to achieving the growth rates Jeff Stevens and his Board hoped for. It was key, also, in meeting the major potential threat posed by the recent availability of inexpensive software that could enable personal computers to design printed circuit boards (see Exhibit 20.3). Jeff had heard that some of that software could perform almost as well as the more expensive equipment that was being used by Applied CAD. He wondered how the advent of PC-based design might be viewed as an opportunity, not a threat.

Four possible responses had occurred to Jeff and his people: Applied CAD could ignore the PC software, adopt it, distribute it, or sell its own software to the PC users. Ignoring the new technology might work in the short run, since the complex boards designed by Applied CAD would not be the first affected; in the long run, however, failure to keep up with technology would leave more and more jobs subject to low-cost competition.

By adopting the new software for his next equipment expansion, Applied CAD could take a proactive stance. Jeff could buy a system or two to see how good they were, and hire people to work on the new systems on a freelance basis. Of course, he would need a flow of jobs to experiment with. A variation of this alternative was to sit back and wait while ready to move quickly if he saw something developing.

A third alternative, acting as a distributor for the PC software, would give Applied CAD a product to sell to prospects who insisted on doing their own design. This could establish relationships with people who might later need overload capacity.

Fourth, Applied CAD could proceed with development of its proprietary software, creating a product to sell to PC users. Jeff estimated that his Automated Design Review System could save both time and grief for other designers. In some tasks, it could cut the required design time in half. In all jobs, the capability to check the finished design against the original input automatically and completely could improve quality. ADRS already existed in rough form; it was one of the elements which would make up the "Robo-Router" system, if that were implemented.

Many of these options seemed to require significant marketing skills— areas where the company was presently weak. The technical questions could be answered, if Jeff had the time to work on them. But the marketing questions called for a person with extensive industry experience, broad contacts, a creative imagination, and the ability to make things happen.

Amid all the other problems facing the owner of a small business, Jeff was trying to figure out how to shape his business for the long-range future, and how to attract the kind of person he could work with to assure growth—and survival.

Applied CAD Knowledge, Inc. (B)

RAYMOND M. KINNUNEN ● JOHN A. SEEGER

In September 1987, as the summer rush slowed, Jeff Stevens began to talk seriously with Jerry King, Regional Sales Manager of Calay Systems, Inc., about the marketing problems of Applied CAD Knowledge, Inc. Stevens wanted someone to become in effect a co-owner and officer of the small firm. King had been a principal in his own service bureau in the very early days of automated PCB design, and retained friendships and contacts with high level personnel in many electronics firms. (Exhibit 21.1 shows King's résumé.)

After a month of conversations and negotiations, including a meeting with the Board of Directors, the two men reached tentative agreement on employment terms which would give King a 3% commission on all company sales, a car allowance, and a base salary of $40,000 per year. Because the marketing person would be influential in pricing many jobs, it was important to preserve his regard for profitability; King was offered a stock interest in Applied CAD, contingent on the bottom line at the end of 1988. With a handshake of agreement, Stevens set out to reduce the terms to an employment contract letter.

The following night, Jerry King called Stevens to express his regret that he would be unable to accept the Marketing VP position, after all: he had just received an offer from AT&T, to set up Australian operations for a new venture. It was simply too good an offer to refuse, King said. A dejected Jeff Stevens reported the development at the next Board meeting; "We're back to square one," he said. "And the next 'splat' is just about to arrive."

Applied CAD's monthly sales dropped to half their mid-1987 level, and the backlog dropped to near zero. On December 8, however, Jerry King called Jeff to say he had just decided against Australia, and would like to apply again for the Marketing Vice President position, if it was still open. Jeff agreed, and the next day Jerry presented to Jeff and the Board a plan for reaching $1 million in sales in 1988, and for growing by $1 million per year in the following two years. (This plan is partially reproduced in Exhibit 21.2.) Concerned with the timing of cash flows, one of the directors asked how long it would take to generate enough new sales to cover their added marketing expenses. King responded, "If I couldn't provide more than enough sales to cover my pay, I wouldn't take the job."

This case has an **accompanying video tape** of Jeff Stevens in a question-and-answer session in front of an Executive M.B.A. class that can be purchased from Office of the Dean, Northeastern University, College of Business Administration, Hayden Hall, Boston, MA 02115.

This case was prepared by Professor Raymond M. Kinnunen, Northeastern University and Professor John A. Seeger, Bentley College. Presented at the North American Case Research Meeting, 1988. All rights reserved to the authors and the North American Case Research Association. Copyright © 1988 by Professor Raymond M. Kinnunen and John A. Seeger. Reprinted by permission of the authors and the North American Case Research Association.

EXHIBIT 21.1   **Resumé**

Jerry King

Married
Four Children
Excellent Health

EDUCATION

Fairleigh Dickenson University, Madison, New Jersey
Major: Business Administration

U.S. Navy, Electronics "A" School, Pearl Harbor, Hawaii

Continuing Education, including numerous seminars and workshops in Corporate Finance, Power Base Selling, Territory Time Management, The Art of Negotiating, Computer Graphics in Electronics, Sales Management and Marketing Techniques.

EXPERIENCE

General Business Management: Establishing policies and procedures for high volume cost efficient business operations, planning promotions for new business development, hiring, training and supervising personnel, including management level, designing and conducting management, sales, marketing and CAD/CAM training seminars internationally.

Technical Background: Twenty-one years of direct Printed Circuit Design, Fabrication and Electronics CAD/CAM marketing experience. Helped to create detailed business plans for three start-up companies including a high volume printed circuit design service bureau and raised five million dollars in venture capital used to purchase state-of-the-art CAD/CAM systems and other related equipment. Managed the development and marketing of a PCB Design Automation turn-key system which was sold exclusively to Calma/GE in 1977 and integrated with their GDS1 TRI-DESIGN system. Very strong market knowledge in Computer Aided Engineering (CAE), Computer Aided Design (CAD), Computer Aided Test (CAT), and Computer Aided Manufacturing (CAM).

ACCOMPLISHMENTS

Particularly effective in areas of personnel management, motivation and training, thereby increasing sales volume, production flow, productivity and employee morale. Significant career accomplishments in customer relations, marketing and sales leadership and management.

EMPLOYMENT HISTORY

1986–Present   Calay Systems Incorporated, Waltham, Massachusetts
                Senior Account Manager.
Responsible for a direct territory consisting of Northern Massachusetts, Vermont, New Hampshire, Maine and Quebec.

1985–1986   Automated Systems Incorporated, Nashua, N.H.
                Eastern Regional Sales Manager.

Responsible for regional design and fabrication service sales with a regional quota in excess of $5 million.

1981–1985   Engineering Automation Systems, Inc., San Jose, CA.
              Western Regional Sales Manager.
Responsible for new Printed Circuit Design CAD/CAM system. Set up regional office, hired and trained sales and support staff of twelve people. Western regional sales were in excess of fifty percent of the company's business.
              September 1984 Promoted to **National Sales Manager**.

1978–1981   Computervision Corporation, Bedford, Massachusetts
              National Product Sales Manager.
Responsible for all electronic CAD/CAM system sales and related products. Provided direct sales management and training to the national field sales team, conducted sales training internationally, assisted in developing competitive strategy, technical support and new product development. Reported to the Vice President of North American Division.
              March 1980 Promoted to **Manager, Corporate Demonstration
              and Benchmark Center**.
Managed team of 38 people who performed all corporate level demonstrations and benchmarks. Supported field offices with technical information and people worldwide. Reported to the Vice President of Marketing Operations.

1966–1978   King Systems, Inc., San Diego, California (A
              Printed Circuit Design CAD/CAM and NC Drilling
              Service Bureau.)
              Founder, President, Chairman and Major Stockholder.
Served as Chief Executive Officer in charge of all aspects of the operation. Primary activities in sales management, direct field sales and customer relations. Responsible for financial administration, production operations and personnel administration. Assessed future needs and created business planning for increasing market share, facilities capability and penetrating new market opportunity. Developed a new concept in contract services for blanket sales to large government and commercial prime contractors.

Although not officially joining Applied CAD until January 4, Jerry spent the rest of December in joint calling, with Jeff, on customers where Calay and Applied CAD shared some interests. In these first weeks, the "chemistry" Jeff Stevens had hoped for became readily apparent. The two men's skills complemented each other well: this would be a highly effective team, Stevens believed.

As 1988 began, King and Stevens continued to work closely together. Because Applied CAD's office layout did not provide the privacy needed for telephone prospecting, Jerry worked out of his home, joining Jeff several times per week on joint sales calls. At the January 8 meeting of the Board of Directors, the two men presented detailed sales projections for the first quarter and broader

EXHIBIT 21.2　　**Excerpts from Jerry King's December 9, 1987 Presentation to the Board**

INTRODUCTION

The plan is a detailed road map for taking Applied CAD Knowledge, Incorporated (ACK) from the current sales volume to more than three million annual sales volume over the next three years. It identifies target markets, competitive environment, and sales tactics which will be used for achieving the sales projections during the plan period from January 1st 1988 through December 31st 1990. The projections show a monthly breakdown for 1988 and a yearly number for 1989 and 1990. The monthly projections were created on Lotus and provide for projected, forecasted and actual sales bookings for each month. As each month passes the actual numbers are entered and a goal status report is generated as part of the end of month reporting. At the end of each quarter a new quarter will be added so that there will always be four consecutive quarters of monthly projections.

The aggressive growth which is outlined will require significant expansion of facilities, personnel and equipment in order to maintain consistent QUALITY and ON TIME deliveries and insure REPEAT BUSINESS from established customers. It is required that the management and the Board of Directors of ACK provide the necessary production controls and capital/operating budgets to support expansion commensurate with sales volume increases over the term of the plan.

The PCB design service market can be divided into three major segments. Each of these segments will include companies that design and manufacture electronic equipment for Commercial, Industrial, Aerospace and Military vertical market areas.

Major Accounts and Government Sub-contractors (MA)

Major Accounts and Fortune 1000 companies. They present a significant opportunity for multiple board contracts and blanket purchase agreements. Any one company could fill ACK's capacity.

Primary Accounts (PA)

Primary accounts are companies that have been doing business for more that three years (not a start-up) and typically do between 5-500 million dollars in annual sales. These companies represent the most consistent level of business. The type of contracts available from this market segment are usually on the level of one to four board designs per month. Typically, each board or project has to be sold separately at the project engineering level.

Venture Start-up Accounts (VA)

Venture start-up companies usually are operating on stringent budgets. They typically have no internal CAD capability and therefore must rely on outside service. The business potential for this market segment is very significant. This market represents a high risk and therefore is avoided by the major competitors leaving more opportunity for the smaller operation. It is not unusual to obtain sole source product level contracts from companies in this market.

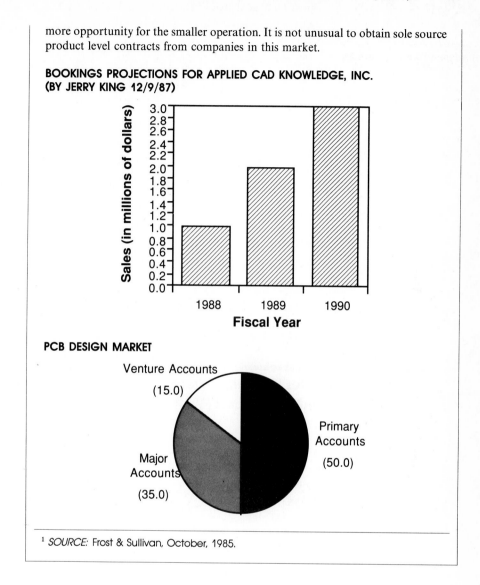

BOOKINGS PROJECTIONS FOR APPLIED CAD KNOWLEDGE, INC. (BY JERRY KING 12/9/87)

PCB DESIGN MARKET

Venture Accounts
(15.0)

Major Accounts
(35.0)

Primary Accounts
(50.0)

[1] *SOURCE:* Frost & Sullivan, October, 1985.

estimates for the entire year (see Exhibit 21.3). One account alone—California PrinCo—held the promise of some $250,000 in sales over the next four months. An old and steady customer of Applied CAD, PrinCo was nearing a decision on a major expansion in their use of circuit boards.

January sales totalled only $6,000 but many prospects seemed close to signing for large orders. At the February 19 Board meeting, Jeff and Jerry predicted sales of $100,000 per month for February and March; it appeared a 1988 sales goal of $1,000,000 might still be reachable. (Exhibit 21.4 shows monthly sales and backlogs through January, 1988.)

EXHIBIT 21.3

Sales Projections Presented to the Board, January 8, 1988
PART A: Forecast First Quarter 1988: Sales by Customer

ACCOUNT NAME	JAN 50%	90%	FEB 50%	90%	MAR 50%	90%	TOT 50%	TOT 90%	GRAND TOTAL
Customer A	.0	20.0	.0	8.0	20.0	.0	20.0	28.0	48.0
Prospect I	.0	7.0	.0	.0	.0	.0	.0	7.0	7.0
Prospect II	5.0	.0	2.0	.0	2.0	.0	9.0	.0	9.0
Customer B	.0	.0	12.0	.0	.0	.0	12.0	.0	12.0
Customer C	12.0	.0	.0	.0	.0	.0	12.0	.0	12.0
Customer D	.0	.0	12.0	.0	.0	.0	12.0	.0	12.0
Customer E	.0	30.0	.0	.0	20.0	.0	20.0	30.0	50.0
Prospect III	.0	.0	15.0	.0	20.0	.0	35.0	.0	35.0
Prospect IV	.0	.0	15.0	.0	20.0	.0	35.0	.0	35.0
Prospect V	.0	6.5	.0	.8	.0	3.8	.0	11.1	11.1
Customer F	.0	.0	.0	7.0	.0	.0	.0	7.0	7.0
Total	17.0	63.5	56.0	15.8	82.0	3.8	155.0	83.1	238.1

NOTE: The above percentages (50% and 90%) are the estimated likelihood of receiving an order from a particular customer.

EXHIBIT 21.3

Sales Projections Presented to the Board, January 8, 1988
PART B: Forecast Fiscal Year 1988: Bookings by Product Type

	SERVICE	SOFTWARE	TOTAL	ACCUMULATIVE TOTAL
January	33	15	48	48
February	48	5	53	101
March	53	15	68	169
Quarter 1	134	35	169	
April	60	5	65	234
May	68	15	83	317
June	75	5	80	397
Quarter 2	203	25	228	
July	80	15	95	492
August	85	0	85	577
September	88	15	103	680
Quarter 3	253	30	283	
October	90	8	98	778
November	95	15	110	888
December	98	15	113	1001
Quarter 4	283	38	321	

EXHIBIT 21.3   Sales Projections Presented to the Board, January 8, 1988
PART C: Total Forecasted First Quarter 1988 Sales
by Customer

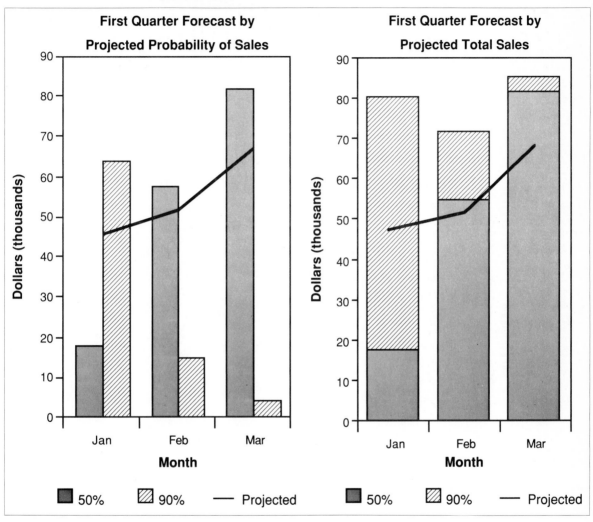

EXHIBIT 21.4

Monthly Sales and Month-End Receivables, Backlogs, Cash Levels, Applied CAD Knowledge, Inc.

(Dollar Amounts in Thousands)

	ACCOUNTS RECEIVABLE	SALES	BACKLOG	CASH
January 1986	**$18**	**$20**	**$20**	**$98**
February	—	10	—	N/A
March	18	10	12	62
April	18	10	20	28
May	24	20	26	26
June	—	10	—	N/A
July	14	25	—	18
August	70	50	30	15
September	90	40	—	8
October	50	30	—	26
November	19	5	10	17
December	24	10	18	14
January 1987	**13**	**3**	**—**	**7**
February	40	21	—	8
March	35	28	22	6
April	32	22	37	11
May	25	22	50	5
June	50	50	90	10
July	90	58	30	10
August	—	25	—	10
September	34	25	50	21
October	62	48	9	8
November	50	24	—	—
December	14	34	9	33
January 1988	**8**	**6**	**—**	**19**

Fared Robot Systems, Inc.

JAMES W. CLINTON

Fared Robot Systems, Inc., was incorporated in the State of Colorado on May 20, 1981, to provide consulting services to industrial customers who wished to adapt robotics technology to their manufacturing processes. (The name of the company is an acronym for Flexible Automation, Robotic Engineering, and Distribution.)

Fared quickly learned that customers were less interested in learning from Fared's salesmen about equipment specifications than they were in obtaining the equipment hardware. Fared's customers, therefore, wanted both consulting services and automated equipment provided by the same vendor. Fared responded by changing both product and service mix to accommodate these customer preferences.

By the summer of 1987, Fared provided custom design of precision assembly automated equipment focused on four major industries: (1) automotive manufacturers and their suppliers, (2) home appliances, (3) electronics, and (4) ordnance (munitions and weapons systems). Fared currently was creating assembly systems for General Motors for use in the manufacture of automobile instrument gauges. The company also was developing a system to manufacture ice cube makers for the Whirlpool Corporation, as well as a $5 million system (the third of its kind) to produce washing machines.

Fared can provide customers with a "one-stop" or turnkey automation capability of robotic equipment that the company manufactures itself, assembles from parts and components manufactured by others, or obtains from other manufacturers and distributors as complete systems. Fared has the capability to custom design and manufacture assembly systems to the specifications of customers who wish to automate assembly of precision parts and components used in applications such as computer keyboard products, home appliances, and automobile assembly. All of Fared's systems involve computerized controls.

In addition to providing robotics and automated hardware equipment to customers, Fared offers software and communications systems that create a completely integrated macro-system of hardware, software, control, and communications. Fared's 1986 annual report states that

> A typical FARED system assembles a product by using programmable conveyors which direct product flow to as many as one hundred functional tasking elements. These elements include custom-designed automation, standard machinery, and robotic cells that have the ability to self-correct many assembly problems. The systems also use elements of FARED's generic automation equipment, such as

This case was prepared by James W. Clinton of the University of Northern Colorado. Presented at the Midwest Society for Case Research Workshop, 1987. All rights reserved to the author and to the Midwest Society for Case Research. Copyrighted © 1987 by James W. Clinton. Reprinted by permission.

robot hands, pallet identification systems and precision-part tray handlers, which allow us to increase system reliability while reducing costs. Pertinent information generated at these cells can be stored, retrieved or passed to other operating elements within the system, to diagnostic centers, or to a plant host computer.

We know of no other assembly-systems integrator in the world, within the areas in which we compete, that has achieved the degree of hardware/software integration and in-process control typically found in FARED-developed products.

Fared Robot Systems has undergone a transformation during its history through acquisition and the formation of subsidiaries. (See Exhibit 22.1.) In February, 1982, Fared incorporated a separate and wholly-owned subsidiary, Fared Automation, Inc., in the State of Michigan. Fared Automation was created primarily to acquire Intec Corporation, an automation design engineering company. Fared Automation acquired Intec on March 1, 1982 through the issue of Fared common stock and promissory notes.

In November, 1982 Fared formed a subsidiary, Fared Drilling Technologies, Inc. to research the feasibility of an automated pipe-handling system. In 1984, however, Fared Robot Systems reduced the company's ownership to approximately 13% of Fared Drilling's outstanding stock. A decline in oil prices and cutbacks in both onshore and offshore oil and gas drilling during 1985 and 1986 further reduced the potential demand for an automated pipe handling system. In addition, development of this pipe-handling system required several millions of dollars—money that Fared believed could be better applied to its core businesses.

Fared Robot Systems acquired Automated Robotic Systems (ARS) on September 15, 1983 in exchange for 2.2 million shares of Fared's common stock. ARS, a holding company, consisted of two wholly-owned subsidiaries (Equus Automated Systems, Inc. and Equus Robotic Systems). ARS acquired both of these subsidiaries on January 1, 1983, for a combined purchase price of $4,984,400. This purchase price included $3.7 million in goodwill—the difference between the fair market value of assets acquired and their purchase price.

EXHIBIT 22.1   **Major Transactions, Fared Robot Systems, 1981–84**

DATE	TRANSACTION
May 20, 1981	Incorporated in Colorado.
February, 1982	Created Michigan subsidiary, Fared Automation.
March, 1982	Acquired Intec.
November, 1982	Formed subsidiary, Fared Drilling Technologies, Inc.
1983	Disposed of Fared Automation assets.
September, 1983	Acquired Automated Robotic Systems.
1984	Reduced ownership in Fared Drilling.

According to current Fared President Harold Spidle:

> I wasn't here at the time, but I question that Fared could have survived without this merger. A steep price was paid in additional debt; but, in exchange, Equus, which wanted to go public, saved the expense that would have been involved with a public offering of stock through an investment banker.

As a result of the merger, according to President Spidle, "instead of two companies with major problems, there resulted one larger company—with even larger problems."

During fiscal 1984, Fared Robot Systems relocated corporate offices to Arlington, Texas, and consolidated most of its operations among facilities located in the Dallas/Fort Worth area. The move was made because the Texas market appeared to offer more growth potential than that found in the Rocky Mountain region around Denver.

In 1985, Fared constructed a new plant in Fort Worth, Texas, which consolidated the company's offices and manufacturing facilities under one roof. The plant and offices were built to the company's specifications as part of a ten-year lease obligation. Fared was offered attractive terms that President Spidle considers "a gift." The developers of the property are committed to the economic development of the Fort Worth area and in their wish to emphasize high technology enterprise, viewed Fared as a desirable tenant. In an adjoining part of the industrial park, the University of Texas is building a Robotics Research Center. Fared believes that there is the potential for synergy between the company and the University's research center.

MARKETING

Fared Robot Systems (FRS) markets its products and services within the continental United States through a company sales force. FRS' marketing is focused on the central and western states.

Target customers of primary interest to Fared are manufacturers that (1) assemble small precision devices, (2) produce machine components or parts, (3) move or reposition mechanical assemblies, or (4) make electronic circuit boards. These production processes, for robotics to be economically feasible, require a volume or frequency of 50,000 operations per week.

Fared advertises its products and services in trade journals, participates in robotics trade shows, and is a member of several trade associations committed to the promotion of robotics and automation applications.

Several major customers account for a substantial portion of Fared's consolidated sales. In fiscal 1986, Whirlpool Corporation and IBM Corporation accounted for 69% and 18%, respectively, of Fared's sales. In the previous year, Apple Computer, IBM Corporation, Whirlpool Corporation, and Xebec accounted for 11%, 42%, 14%, and 13%, respectively, of the company's total sales. Equipment built by Fared for Apple is shown in Exhibit 22.2.

EXHIBIT 22.2

An Example of a Fared Designed and Built Product, As Shown in a Fared Marketing Brochure

For APPLE COMPUTER, FARED provides assembly cells for an automated assembly line designed to build the APPLE IIc product. This robotic system assembles a complete computer at the rate of one every 16 seconds.

Fared's marginal financial condition (see Exhibits 22.3 and 22.4) adversely affects the company's marketing efforts, according to President Spidle.

Some potential customers won't consider entering into a contract unless they clearly believe that Fared has the resources to complete, e.g., a $150,000 or $1 million contract. Customers' progress payments sometimes are awfully slow. We've lost contracts because we just didn't have a good enough balance sheet.

EXHIBIT 22.3

Consolidated Income Statements, 1983–1986, Fared Robot Systems

(Dollar Amounts in Thousands Except Per Share Data)

Year ended September 30	FISCAL 1986	FISCAL 1985	FISCAL 1984	11 MOS. 9/30/83
Sales	$12,677	$16,771	$16,151	$9,942
Cost of goods sold	11,264	15,497	15,495	8,582
Gross margin	1,413	1,274	656	1,360
Sales, administrative, and general expenses	2,618	2,397	3,431	3,628
Research & dev. expense	—	—	909	1,746
Operating loss	(1,205)	(1,123)	(3,684)	(4,014)
Interest expense	(666)	(741)	(1,007)	(585)
Other income (expense)	(162)	(130)	(1,248)	162
Gain from sale of subsidiary stock	—	—	—	1,255
Acquisition costs	—	—	—	(192)
Net loss before minority interest	(2,033)	(1,994)	(3,443)	(3,374)
Minority interest in net loss of consolidated subsidiary	—	—	241	395
Net loss	(2,033)	$(1,994)	$(3,202)	$(2,979)
Net loss per common share	$(0.12)	$(0.12)	$(0.30)	$(0.33)
Weighted average common shares outstanding (000)	17,379	16,179	10,770	8,925

EXHIBIT 22.4

Consolidated Balance Sheet, 1983–1986, Fared Robot Systems

(Dollar Amounts in Thousands)

Year ended September 30	1986	1985	1984	1983
Cash	$ 232	$ 470	$ 253	$ 746
Accounts receivable	756	2,618	2,403	1,924
Costs/earnings in excess of billings on uncompleted contracts	305	1,733	2,121	1,687
Inventories	209	326	368	549
Other	41	41	28	176
Total current assets	1,543	5,188	5,173	5,082
Net property/equipment	1,755	1,639	2,223	3,096
Net intangible assets	3,375	3,498	3,622	3,804
Other	233	288	220	238
Total long-term assets	5,363	5,425	6,065	7,138
Total assets	6,906	10,613	11,238	12,220
Notes payable	17	—	—	3,140
Accounts payable	335	1,031	2,218	2,051
Billings in excess of costs and earnings on uncompleted contracts	182	513	1,065	319
Current portion of L-T debt	828	847	712	614
Accrued interest payable	209	339	245	53
Other	496	692	509	459
Total current liabilities	2,067	3,422	4,749	6,636
Notes payable to bank	785	1,134	4,683	1,200
Subordinated notes payable	3,150	2,928	465	3,178
Capital lease obligations	82	281	459	614
Minority interest in consolidated subsidiaries	—	—	—	277
Other	—	142	29	41
Total long-term liabilities	4,017	4,485	5,636	5,310
Total liabilities	6,084	7,907	10,385	11,946
Stockholders' equity				
Common stock	87	86	67	47
Addit'l paid-in capital	12,480	12,331	8,504	4,742
Retained earnings (deficit)	(11,745)	(9,711)	(7,718)	(4,515)
Stockholders' equity	822	2,706	853	274
Total liabilities and stockholders' equity	6,906	10,613	11,238	12,220

The *1985 Annual Report* contains the following information concerning Fared's Notes Payable to Bank: "The $4,770,309 Notes payable to bank at September 30, 1984 consisted of $2,396,992 borrowed under a $3,000,000 revolving line of credit, $873,317 borrowed under a $1,500,000 bridge loan, and a $1,500,000 term loan. These loans had been in default and were restructured concurrent with the issuance of $2,800,000 of 14½% Convertible Subordinated Debentures. The bank converted $1,700,000 of debt into 1,700,000 shares of FARED common stock, received $1,500,000 in cash from the proceeds of the debenture, and structured the $1,570,309 balance of the debt as a long-term note requiring quarterly principal payments of $87,239 commencing September 30, 1985."

OPERATIONS

Fared uses a "mixed technology assembly," consisting of robotics, machine tools, and manual operations, which are electronically monitored. Concurrent with all assembly processes are integral inspection systems that monitor production efficiency and product quality and also create a data base for reference, control, and assessment. Fared has produced an electronic console that displays a complete manufacturing system as presently functioning in Fared's plant facility and as it is intended to be installed in the customer's plant. The console display shows reject frequencies and sources of problems and significantly reduces adding value to defective assemblies, thus reducing cost of goods sold and improving production efficiency.

Fared's manufacturing operations include materials arrival; materials processing, including machining, welding, and painting; product assembly; and finished goods packaging and shipment.

Fared is attempting to develop generic robotic applications for use in common industrial manufacture and assembly operations. Such recycled applications will permit Fared to spread research and development costs over more units and enable Fared to price systems and products more competitively.

Several of Fared's major contracts experienced cost overruns in 1985. These contracts, for which Fared either will experience a loss or achieve minimal profit, continue to place a strain on Fared's working capital. Fared, however, hopes to develop standard hardware and software applications so that the company can apply the learning curve to comparable systems, parts of systems, or processes, and thus spread developmental costs over a greater number of applications and minimize the likelihood of future cost overruns.

Fared designed and built one of the world's largest robotic assembly systems for International Business Machines (IBM) to manufacture typewriters and letter quality printers. The total system included more than eighty automated work stations, and cost $13 million to produce.

Fared provides assembly cells for an automated assembly line designed to build the Apple IIc computer. This robotic system assembles a computer every 16 seconds.

Fared built a system for General Electric to drill multiple holes simultaneously through steel discs. The system drills the discs at a rate of 108 discs per minute. Fared also designed and built a machine for the Whirlpool Corporation that assembles washing machine parts, and detects and rejects improperly assembled parts, at a rate of 150 assemblies per minute. Fared also designed and built a machine that automatically cuts, seals, and ties a rope on the starter used in McCulloch chain saws.

Frank Romeo, Executive Vice-President, offered the following comments:

> Recently we completed a robotic application that can replace eight people working 16 hours a day. The rapid ROI is there—just as a university would replace an instructor if it could develop a robot that could perform all of the instructor's teaching functions and have it pay off within a year.
>
> We're doing what we can to advance the technology and make it cost effective for our customers. The first unit of a robotic cell we recently constructed cost

$180,000; the second $120,000; and the third, $90,000. We developed a circuit board to replace a complicated set of wires and connections. The improved grasping and control element is significantly lighter and reduced costs by 75%.

The computer industry has yet to capitalize upon the potential of automated assembly of its products. We built an entire assembly operation for Apple Computer at their Dallas plant. Apple, however, in an economy move, closed the plant before it became operational. As a result, Fared lost the opportunity to point to a local operating facility that used Fared technology. The plant was state of the art in automation and robotics. We have, nevertheless, a videotape of the operation which we use as a marketing tool.

MANAGEMENT

None of the original founding officers and directors of the company presently are associated with the company. All have been replaced by present management.

Fared's present President, CEO, and Chairman, Harold D. Spidle, was appointed in June, 1984, as noted in the 1984 Annual Report, "to address various operational problems within the company and gain the confidence of customers, creditors, and prospective investors." President Spidle said that he was particularly attracted by the caliber of the company's employees and was very impressed by the quality of equipment being produced for IBM, using FARED-developed systems. Prior to coming to Fared, President Spidle had been president of a California company that manufactured equipment for the transport of liquid nitrogen and oxygen. That company, however, sold out to the Richmond Tank Car Company of Houston, Texas, and Spidle was transferred to Houston as an executive for Richmond, but he was not comfortable with this new parent company and was anxious to run his own company. In his search for acquisition opportunities, he attracted the attention of several venture capitalists, including the venture department of Texas Commerce Bank which had invested $1 million in Fared. Through their efforts, he was offered the presidency of Fared, which he accepted. Spidle has an undergraduate degree in engineering and a graduate degree in fluid mechanics. According to the President,

> Investors come to this plant, are enthusiastic about what they see, and want to invest in the company. For example, Caterpillar Tractor invested $2 million in the company in December, 1985. They are interested for the long-term in the things that we are doing.
>
> We're disappointed in the market performance of the company's common stock. We believe that the company and the industry are experiencing a temporary malaise which will turn in the future. Manufacturers know that robotics and automation must be considered; it's just a matter of when.
>
> Competition is fierce. All competitors have underbid to obtain contracts. Furthermore, it's difficult to accurately estimate engineering time to develop a customized manufacturing application. Regardless, however, we've got to make money. After all, that is what enables us to operate and attract investors. In regard to planning, we would like to look down the road two to three years, as is typically done in strategic management, but under our present situation we can take only one year at a time.

Frank Romeo, Executive Vice-President, came to Fared from Mooney Engineering, where he had been an engineer and designer. Scott Musselman, Chief Financial Officer, joined Fared in 1982. He previously worked for a Big Eight accounting firm. Don Jackson, Manager, Support Services, previously worked for Mooney Engineering.

The directors of the company are

Harold D. Spidle, President, CEO, and Chairman;

Nolan Lehmann, President, Equus Corporation International;

Fred R. Lummis, II, Vice-President, Texas Commerce Investment Company;

Robert L. Powers, President, Caterpillar Venture Capital, Inc.; and

Thomas W. Wright, President, Sunwestern Venture Group.

ORGANIZATION

Fared uses what Frank Romeo terms a modified matrix organizational design. Technical management consists of (1) mechanical engineers, (2) software engineers, (3) controls engineers, and (4) CAD/CAM systems specialists (see Exhibit 22.5). Technical specialists and engineers are assigned to project managers as needed. Fared, as of August 14, 1986, employed 130 employees—about 45% of whom were engineers, 40% tradesmen and technicians assigned to manufacture and assembly, and 15% management.

EXHIBIT 22.5   Organization Chart, Fared Robot Systems

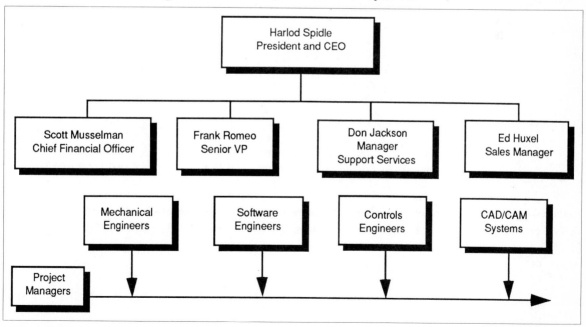

FINANCE

Fared Robot Systems has yet to earn a profit in five years of operations (see Exhibits 22.3). Fared went public in 1982, issuing 16 million shares of common stock at $0.25 per share. On October 18, 1983, the company declared a reverse stock split, exchanging one share of the newly issued stock for five shares of previously issued stock. The highest bid prices for the company's stock during 1984–86 is shown in Exhibit 22.6. On May 26, 1987, the stock sold at $.06 bid and $.09 asked.

Throughout 1986, President Spidle attempted to obtain an additional $6 million in venture capital to add to the company's working capital so that

> we can do those things that we haven't been able to do because of the company's constrained financial condition. The funds would be used for increased marketing and additional research and development, as well as for possible acquisitions of vertically integrated companies.

In early June, 1987, President Spidle indicated that he expected to secure an additional $1.3 million financing from four venture capitalists and the owner of the plant which Fared presently is leasing. Of this amount, $950 thousand is scheduled to be subordinated debt; the remainder, $350 thousand, will be in stock.

Under terms of a debt agreement with a bank creditor, Fared cannot pay a dividend without prior consent of the bank. Fared also is required to maintain a minimum working capital of $1 million, a minimum stockholders' equity of $2 million, and a current ratio of at least 1.2 to 1.

Standard and Poor's *Stock Reports* noted on February 28, 1986, that Fared Robot Systems

> reported to the Securities and Exchange Commission that . . . [Fared's] operations reflected low gross margins resulting from cost overruns; also, its level of backlog had declined. Should possible resulting demands placed upon Company's liquidity cause delayed payments to creditors (Company not having access to working capital credit facilities), Company might have delays in shipments from suppliers, causing additional project delays and cost overruns which could have a material adverse effect on future operations.

Fared presently is leasing various computer equipment, software, and related peripheral equipment as part of a computer-aided design system. Fared was obligated to make lease payments of $213,927 for 1986 and 1987 and $92,059

EXHIBIT 22.6   **High Bid Prices for Fared's Common Stock, 1984–1986**

YEAR	HIGH BID PRICE
1984	$12^{13}/_{16}$
1985	$2^{15}/_{16}$
1986	$5/_8$

in 1988. Fared also has non-cancellable leases for additional facilities and equipment. Under these operating leases, Fared is obligated to pay $781,054 in 1986, $735,763 in 1987, $498,089 in 1988, and $478,885 in 1989 and 1990.

According to President Spidle, leases shown on the balance sheet for Computer Assisted Design (CAD) can presently be duplicated for one half of Fared's original outlay for these leases. Fared committed itself to these lease agreements to obtain equipment necessary for research. Unfortunately, the technology changes so rapidly in this field that management continually is confronted with the dilemma of either waiting for the price of the technology to drop or taking current technology and initiating developmental effort.

Fared has leased 95,000 square feet of office and manufacturing space in Fort Worth, Texas, for a ten-year period. Lease payments are $390,000 the first year, increasing to $520,000 in the tenth year. The lessor has agreed to finance leasehold improvements of $590,000. Fared issued a note of $100,000 for a one year period, a $340,000 promissory note payable over ten years, and issued the lessor 200,000 shares of Fared's common stock to pay the remaining $150,000.

LEGAL

In September, 1985, a customer terminated a contract with Fared, alleging that Fared had defaulted on the contract by failing to deliver equipment that operated as specified in the contract. The customer indicated that he planned to correct deficiencies in the equipment and bill Fared for the expense. Fared has initiated legal action to recover the amount billed to the customer that was unpaid—$251,430. Fared, according to a note in the company's *1986 Annual Report*, "does not anticipate any losses with respect to this lawsuit." No other major legal issues are pending or anticipated.

COMPETITION

Fared's competitors are varied and possess substantial resources. They consist of (1) domestic assembly automation manufacturers, (2) foreign robot manufacturers, (3) distributors of assembly equipment components, including those manufactured overseas, (4) robot consulting and service companies, and (5) major American manufacturers who produce robots as an incidental part of their operations.

Domestic Manufacturers

Important manufacturers of automation equipment (and considered by Fared executives to be the company's major domestic competitors) are Cincinnati Milacron, Unimation (a division of the Westinghouse Corporation), and Adept Technology, Inc. (which according to Dun & Bradstreet's 1987 *Million Dollar Directory*, had sales of $7 million in 1986 and 170 employees). Cincinnati Milacron's sales in 1985 were $732.2 million. Milacron spent $36.6 million in 1985 on research and development.

Foreign Manufacturers

Fujitsu of Japan, ASEA of Sweden (the largest robot manufacturer in the world, has only a small share of robots used in the United States and makes robots for the spray painting of automobiles and larger operations), Sankyo/Seiki of Japan, which manufactures robots for IBM (Japanese manufacturers of robots are concentrated in the field of small parts assembly), KUKA and Volkswagen of Germany, and Automatic Tooling Systems of Canada, are major international manufacturers and distributors or robots.

Domestic Distributors

Esab/Heath distributes the Swedish-made ASEA robot in the United States.

Robot Consulting and Service Companies

There are numerous companies that offer robot and automation consulting and service. These include

> *Productivity Systems, Inc.,* Detroit MI: Develops robot applications, conducts training seminars on robots, and evaluates vendor robot proposals.
>
> *LTI, Inc.,* California: Develops robot applications, conducts training seminars in robotic systems, and evaluates candidate robotic products for users.
>
> *Robotics Systems, Inc.,* Atlanta GA: A subsidiary of Brown and Sharpe Manufacturing (also a manufacturer of robots), offers services similar to those provided by Fared; Robotics has operated a robot demonstration facility since 1981.
>
> *Kohol,* Dayton OH.
>
> *Finch Robotics Company,* Philadelphia PA.
>
> *D. Appleton Company,* Manhattan Beach CA: Specializes in integrating computer systems such as those used in factory automation.
>
> *Automatix,* Burlington MA.
>
> *Electronic Data Systems (EDS) Corporation,* a subsidiary of General Motors Corporation, acquired by GM in 1984 for $2.5 billion.

American Manufacturers That Also Manufacture Robots

The following companies manufacture robots for use in company-related manufacturing operations and also for sale to other companies. These manufacturers are

> *General Motors,* which with the Japanese manufacturer, Fanuc, formed the joint venture, GMF. GMF was the world's largest robot supplier in 1985, with sales that were almost three times those of Cincinnati Milacron.

General Electric, which joined with Fanuc of Japan in a $200 million joint venture in June, 1986, called GE Fanuc Automation Corporation.

Westinghouse (Westinghouse acquired Unimation, Inc. for $107 million in 1983.).

IBM.

THE INDUSTRIAL ENVIRONMENT

Major United States manufacturers are increasing their use of factory automation systems, more than doubling such systems from $7.4 billion in 1980 to $18.1 billion in 1985, and expected to double 1985 levels by 1990 (see Exhibit 22.7). Several major manufacturers plan to spend billions of dollars on factory automation that include substantial use of robotic systems. Investment in computer aided manufacturing is more than doubling every five years (see Exhibit 22.8). IBM expects to invest more than $15 billion in automation between 1985 and 1990. General Electric will spend $1 billion on automation during this same five-year period. American manufacturers' investment in factory automation,

EXHIBIT 22.7

U.S. Domestic Investment in Automation, 1980, 1985, and 1990 (Estimated)

(Dollar Amounts in Millions)

	1990 (est.)	1985	1980
Computer-Aided Design (CAD)	$ 6,500	$ 2,456	$ 389
Computer-Aided Mfg. (CAM)	32,300	15,375	6,853
Communication links, misc.	800	264	113
Totals	$39,600	$18,095	$7,355

EXHIBIT 22.8

U.S. Domestic Investment in Computer Aided Manufacturing, 1980, 1985, and 1990 (Estimated)

(Dollars Amounts in Millions)

	1990 (est.)	1985	1980
Factory computers and software	$ 6,500	$ 2,861	$ 935
Materials handling systems	9,000	4,500	2,000
Machine tools and controls	7,000	4,800	3,000
Programmable computers	3,000	550	50
Robots and sensors	2,800	664	68
Automated test equipment	4,000	2,000	800
Totals	$32,300	$15,375	$6,853

nevertheless, is only about one-half the amount spent by Japanese companies for similar automation systems.

Robotics and automation are expected to be of increasing importance to American manufacturers as they attempt to raise worker productivity, lower costs, and compete with both foreign manufacturers and other American firms that have relocated manufacturing facilities overseas. According to *Value Line Investment Survey*, August 22, 1986:

> The industry's mix of incoming orders already appears to be gradually shifting from relatively standard stand-alone machine tools (like lathes) to highly sophisticated manufacturing systems made up of several machine tools linked by material handling devices, the entire system controlled by computers. And the high-tech content of even stand-alone machines seems to be rising. More incorporate robots, lasers, and the like than they did several years ago.
>
> The machine tool companies (rather than their potential customers) bear the cost of designing these manufacturing systems, and even after proposals to build such systems are drafted, there are no assurances that all of the work that went into developing the proposal will result in a firm order.

Advantages of Factory Automation

Factory automation offers the following benefits:

- Faster turnaround on product design and manufacture. Integrated computer systems are used to design, engineer, manufacture, package, and ship products tailored to the customer's specifications.
- Improved information exchange, access, and storage.
- Improved accuracy of manufacturing and operations data.
- Lower labor costs to process manufacturing information, including materials requirements planning information.
- Reduced inventory costs where automation is related to just-in-time inventory planning and control.
- Improved reliability of manufacture that can improve product quality.
- Improved manufacturing flexibility that allows smaller batches of product to be manufactured more quickly and economically. Lower break-even points in production are possible. Computer-integrated manufacturing (CIM), which is also known as flexible automation or manufacturing, allows machines to make different products without time-consuming retooling or setups. Manufacturers will be able to respond more quickly to changing consumer tastes as well as concurrently responding to multiple customer segments. Factory automation will cause learning curve theory to be reevaluated because economies are realized without the need for large volume production.
- Manufacturers are encouraged to adopt a more integrative approach to their total operation and identify, e.g., marketing benefits associated with improved responsiveness of factory automation, and long-term production

economies obtained at the expense of major short-term capital investment. Automation affects every functional area of the firm, and thus requires extensive coordination if potential benefits are to be realized.

· Factory automation will reduce labor costs to the degree that companies will find it just as economical to manufacture in the United States as they would in a lower cost overseas location. Consequently, according to Patrick A. Toole, a Vice-President for Manufacturing, as reported in *Business Week*, "The ideal location for the factory of the future is in the market where its products are consumed."

Current Industry Situation

According to *Value Line Investment Survey*, February 20, 1987, prospects for the machine tool industry

> ... for 1987 remain highly uncertain. Continued weakness in domestic industrial growth and the existence of inventories of Japanese machine tools suggest that orders won't pick up much.... Earnings prospects for just about all of the companies in this group are dismal.
>
> By the late Eighties, interest in factory automation systems ought to be considerably stronger, supporting a partial earnings recovery for those companies able to survive until then.
>
> ... There's a lot of interest in sophisticated, unmanned factory automation systems ... we expect the move to full factory automation to get underway by the 1990s.

General Electric announced in January, 1987 that it was closing its robotics plant in Florida. The company said that, "the robotics industry is taking longer than expected to develop and that the segment in which it [GE Fanuc Automation Corporation] concentrated, automated welding, is much smaller than originally anticipated." According to *Business Week*, robotics accounts for less than 2% of GE's total revenues from factory automation.

In August, 1986, GMF Robotics, a joint venture of General Motors and Fanuc of Japan, reduced its workforce from 700 to 200 and cancelled plans to build an automated factory designed to build robots that build robots. General Motors also has experienced difficulty in introducing automated systems within a major automobile assembly plant that is considered to be state of the art. General Motors' difficulty has affected the entire field of robotics since most of the capital expenditures in robotics have been in the automotive industry. *Business Week* reported that the auto industry accounted for "nearly two-thirds of 1985 investments in automation, and GM spent more than half of that."

The 1986 Tax Reform Act eliminated the investment tax credit and extended depreciation periods, discouraging investment in new plant and equipment. Decline in demand for factory automation systems caused the Eaton Corporation, for example, to withdraw from this segment of the machine tool industry.

The *Value Line Investment Survey*, August 22, 1986, reported that "there still are large inventories of low-priced Japanese machine tools in the United

States . . . waiting to be sold." Similarly, *Business Week*, January 12, 1987, noted that "A big U.S. inventory of low-cost, foreign-made machines must be worked off before orders of domestic manufacturers pick up."

Business Week, in a special report of September 29, 1986, reported that

> The great wave of automation that has swept through offices and factories since 1980 is losing momentum, largely because not enough companies are adopting the innovative work practices that get the most out of automation. Many managers are reluctant to run the kind of social revolution at work that is needed to make technology pay for itself . . .

According to an article that appeared in *The Wall Street Journal* on May 14, 1987:

> Factory automation lags expectations as firms take a piecemeal approach. . . . The University of Michigan Business School . . . puts the 1985 market at $24 billion . . . Most automation is done on a machine-by-machine basis rather than through companywide planning. Moreover . . . the yen's rising value may make manufacturers slower to automate because they believe they're getting a "breather" from Japanese competition.

CASE 23

The Limited, Inc.

SEXTON ADAMS • ADELAIDE GRIFFIN

Where are hottest names in women's apparel today? Some would argue that they are not on Seventh Avenue, or in Paris, or in Milan. They are in Columbus, Ohio, where Leslie H. Wexner has built The Limited, Inc. into one of the nation's fastest-growing and most admired retailers. It offers apparel tailored to the tastes and lifestyles of fashion-conscious, contemporary women and provides fashion, quality, and value through multiple retail formats. The Limited, Inc. has positioned itself to penetrate the women's fashion apparel market through specialty stores and mail order catalogues. Its portfolio in 1986 consisted of six retail divisions with nearly 2,400 stores and seven nationally distributed mail order catalogues. In 1985 The Limited sold more than 200 million garments, three for every women in the country between the ages of 15 and 55. Profits were $140 million on $2.4 billion in sales.[1] The Limited may be the most misnamed company in America.

BACKGROUND AND HISTORY

Leslie Wexner left his parents' general apparel store in 1963, borrowed $10,000 from his aunt, and opened his first Limited store in the Kingsdale Shopping Center near Columbus, Ohio.[2] The store covered strictly sportswear for women in the 16- to 25-year-old range—hence the "Limited" name. Industry analysts reflected that this approach was distinctly ahead of its time considering that most women's apparel was marketed in department stores.[3] In 1969, The Limited went public with a six-store chain.

In 1977, everything seemed to be going well for The Limited. Growth had been steadily remarkable; there were 188 stores with annual sales of $175 million and a respectable new income of $13.2 million. Suddenly in 1978, major problems seemed to be crawling out of the woodwork. The causes of these problems, however, had been brewing for some time.

This case was prepared by Jeff Friant and Elsie Fletcher under the supervision of Professor Sexton Adams, North Texas State University and Professor Adelaide Griffin, Texas Woman's University. Copyright © 1988 by Sexton Adams and Adelaide Griffin. Reprinted by permission.

In 1978, sales rose to a record $218 million; however, most of the gain was attributed to the opening of 70 new stores. Despite this record earnings, net income actually fell to $5.9 million. Sean O'Leary, contributing editor for *Visual Merchandising & Store Design*, stated that this scenario was common when companies tried to grow too fast. The year 1978 was also marked by several major events for The Limited. The Limited moved into a new $20 million distribution warehouse/headquarters, a facility that was ten times beyond the current needs of the company according to industry analysts, in the thick of a recession in one of the hardest hit areas of the country. A new computer system that would serve to computerize inventory and distribution was installed and inevitably was not working right. At the same time, management was devoting their attention to acquiring Mast Industries, Inc., an apparel supplier with worldwide manufacturing connections.[4] This acquisition would give The Limited major supply side advantages over its competitors.

The Limited did survive these adversities of the late 1970s. The way in which Wexner and his management responded to these problems played an integral part in the creation of The Limited legend. Mast Industries was purchased. This acquisition gave The Limited large worldwide advantages and options on the supply side. The distribution center, with its excess capacity, proved invaluable when The Limited began its series of acquisitions. Last, but not least, the computer was reprogrammed. Company operations were tightened. Industry analysts noted that one significant event of this period was that Wexner backed off from the financial end of the company and allowed Vice-Chairman Robert Morosky, a CPA, to fully assume responsibility.[5]

In 1981, The Limited decided to try to recapture the 1980s model of the young woman they had begun in the 1960s. Limited Express was launched, specializing in popular-priced sportswear for the 15 to 25-year-olds.[6] By the end of 1982, thirty stores were open nationwide.

The corporate name was changed to The Limited, Inc. in 1982 and the company was listed on the New York Stock Exchange. This was also the year of acquisitions—The Limited, Inc. acquired Lane Bryant, a $419 million volume large-size apparel specialist; Brylane, the nation's largest catalogue retailer of women's special size apparel and shoes; Victoria's Secrets, a five-unit $5 million better lingerie chain plus catalogue; Sizes Unlimited, which offers off-price, special size apparel for women; and Roamans, a $100 million chain of women's special size apparel store and mail order operation that was merged into Sizes Unlimited. In the years to come, The Limited, Inc. would acquire three more women's apparel chains. In 1984, Pic-A-Dilly, which specialized in budget women's apparel, was acquired and merged into Sizes Unlimited. The year 1985 brought the final two acquisitions—Lerner Stores, a $400 million chain that specialized in budget-priced women's apparel, and Henri Bendel, the $2.4 million prestigious New York specialty store.[7] These acquisitions, financed largely by large debt issues, have given The Limited a niche in almost every segment of the women's clothing market. Exhibit 23.1 illustrates the growth and acquisi-

EXHIBIT 23.1   **History of Growth, The Limited, Inc.**

Retail Division	DATE STARTED	DATE ACQUIRED	NO. OF STORES, FISCAL YEAR END				FIRST QUARTER 1986	SECOND QUARTER 1986
			1982	1983	1984	1985		
Limited	1963		489	521	562	597	610	619
Limited Express	1980		30	70	133	218	233	244
Lane Bryant		1982	222	245	322	401	416	438
Victoria's Secrets		1982	6	16	46	93	104	120
Sizes Unlimited (consolidated with Pic-A-Dilly)		1982	78	85	349	293	287	239
Roamans (merged into Sizes Unlimited)		1982						
Pic-A-Dilly (merged into Sizes Unlimited)		1984						
Lerner		1985				750	737	736
Henri Bendel		1985				1	1	1
Totals			825	937	1,412	2,353	2,388	2,397

Mail Order Divisions	DATE ACQUIRED

Brylane
  Lane Bryant
  Roaman's
  Lerner Woman
  Sue Brett
  Lerner Sport
  Tall Collection
	1982

Victoria's Secret	1982

SOURCE: The Limited, Inc.

tion pattern of The Limited. Exhibit 23.2 illustrates the sales volumes for 1984 and 1985 of The Limited.

Art Carpenter of Goldman, Sachs & Co. stated, "It doesn't take a shrewd analyst to figure out that The Limited has specialized in specializing and that the sum total of the empire covers just about every segment of the women's apparel market—working contemporary women, trendy juniors, large sizes, fashion lingerie, and catalogs." In its 1984 Annual Report on American Industry, *Forbes* called The Limited the fastest growing, most profitable specialty apparel retailer.[8] Net sales have grown from $70,303,000 in 1975 to $2,387,110,000 in

EXHIBIT 23.2

1985 Sales Rank, The Limited, Inc.
(Dollar Amounts in Thousands)

COMPANY	1984 SALES	1985 SALES	% SALES CHANGE
Limited	$552,289	$637,825	+15.5
Lane Bryant	356,076	431,736	+21.2
Lerner Stores	—	521,988	—
Limited Express	46,963	69,406	+47.8
Victoria's Secrets	30,814	51,677	+67.7
Sizes Unlimited	281,000	254,784	−9.0
Henri Bendel	—	8,500	—
Others	—	411,194	—

SOURCE: *Apparel Merchandising*, June 1986.

1985 (Exhibit 23.3). According to these simple facts, The Limited, Inc. could well be the world's largest specialty retailer of women's clothing.

THE STORE BASE

The Limited, Inc. had nearly 2,400 retail outlets throughout the United States. In 1985, The Limited, Inc. opened its flagship store on Manhattan's miracle mile amid designer boutiques like Yves Saint Laurent.[9] Included in this complex were three stores: The Limited, Limited Express, and Victoria's Secrets. The way Wexner saw it was "if you can make it everywhere, you can make it in New York." Exhibit 23.4 shows the store base in July of 1986.

Its distribution facility and corporate headquarters were in Columbus, Ohio. A secondary corporate headquarters was planned to open in New York City so that The Limited, Inc.'s executives would be closer to the heart of the fashion industry.[10]

THE INDUSTRY

The specialty apparel retail industry was one of the largest industries in the world. Over $60 billion were spent in 1985 for the purchase of specialty clothing in the United States.[11] A wide variety of companies competed in the industry and were classified into three basic categories.

The first category was *department stores*, which was further segmented into three groups: (1) those that targeted upscale customers, (2) companies that targeted the middle-income market; and (3) the companies such as Mervyn's that competed in the popular-priced market. There were two groups in the *specialty retailing* category. The first was the narrowly focused chains such as The Limited and the Gap. The second group was the specialty department stores

EXHIBIT 23.3 **The Limited's Growth**

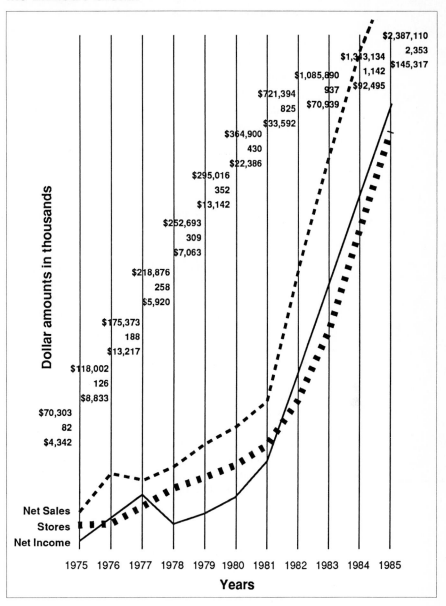

SOURCE: The Limited, Inc., *1985 Annual Report.*

EXHIBIT 23.4

The Store Base, The Limited, Inc.

(Number and Type of Stores)

STORE	TYPE	NUMBER
The Limited	Medium-priced women's sportswear	619
Limited Express	Popular-priced teen sportswear	244
Victoria's Secrets	Lingerie	120
Lane Bryant	Women's large sizes	438
Sizes Unlimited	Large women's budget	239
Lerner	Women's budget sportswear	736
Henri Bendel	Upscale women's sportswear	1
Total Stores		2,397

SOURCE: The Ohio Company, *Investment Research*, August 14, 1986.

like Neiman-Marcus which competed for the upscale market. *Discount stores,* such as K mart and Target, were in the third category and were subgrouped by the type, price, and quality of merchandise.[12]

According to Aimee Stern, a retailing industry analyst for *Dun's Business Month,* a vast restructuring was changing the shape of retailing, creating new opportunities for the quick and resourceful, leaving the less prepared companies behind. The winners were identified as the creative specialty chains that developed unusual merchandising and operational techniques, the innovative department stores that repositioned themselves with new consumer-driven marketing strategies, and the savvy discounters that have overturned the pricing structure of the industry by turning the country into a nation of bargain hunters.[13] Industry analysts agreed that the key to success in the highly competitive specialty apparel business was a well-defined merchandising strategy or focus.[14] According to *Barnard's Retail Marketing Report,* two factors were essential to the successful merchandising strategy of a specialty retailer. The factors were the ability to identify and fill high-growth niches and to provide superior customer service.[15]

In order to develop a successful focus, retailers had to consider continually changing fashions as well as transitional and divergent consumer shopping habits and values. "The trick is to identify a life-style and demographic segment and create a store for them [the customers]," observed Joseph Ellis, Vice President with Goldman, Sachs & Co. Through merchandise selection, price level, and ambiance, a focused store developed a distinctive and consistent identity that allowed shoppers to decide if it fit their preferences and budget.[16]

To further develop a focus, retailers had to understand the consumers. This was no small task considering that the basic demographics of the United States were changing. In the 1960s, most people were in the 15- to 25-year-old age group. The population grew older in the 1970s and this trend was expected to continue throughout the rest of the century.[17] Another demographic factor was the changing role of women. Many more women were working which increased their income; however, because of work they had less time to shop. According to the Greater Washington Research Center, many nine-to-five retailers were considering expanding business hours to snare the female labor force.[18]

At the same time, retailers had to recognize the changing makeup and shopping patterns of their customers. For example, the previous success of many retailers was directly related to their dependence on the growth and evolution of the shopping mall. The shopping mall was becoming more of an entertainment center where people went to spend much of their time and money. However, shopping mall growth had flattened considerably since 1982, limiting one of the main avenues of growth.

Another limit to growth was that the United States was "overstored," especially with apparel retailers. According to *Dun's Business Month*, an industry survey showed that the country had ample retail space for that time as well as for the next four or five years. Apparel sales were expected to increase only 1% or 2% a year at least until 1990.[19]

Because of these limits, retailers could no longer just add stores in order to grow. "If you're going to grow, you have to do it by taking someone else's market share and by literally killing off a competitor," said Cyrus Wilson, president of the retail consulting firm, Management Horizons.

Economic factors had also changed consumer shopping patterns. A larger share of wealth was being distributed among fewer people, increasing the significance of the upscale market. After two recessions, consumers were debt-ridden and more willing to shop around at a number of stores because they wanted both quality and value.[20] This pattern held true even though there was a lower inflation rate and a relatively attractive employment picture.[21] This new attitude forced many stores to cut prices while their operating costs had been increasing.

The industry was also subject to fluctuations from changes in customer preferences, which were dictated by both fashion and season. These fluctuations affected the inventory selection of apparel retailers, because merchandise usually was ordered a significant time in advance of the specific season and in some instances before the fashion trends were evidenced by customer purchases. It was the general practice to build up inventory levels prior to peak selling seasons. Companies usually had to enter into contracts for purchase of materials and manufacturing well in advance of the season. Therefore retailers were vulnerable to demand and pricing shifts.[22]

Identifying the right merchandise selection was perhaps the most elusive part of developing a store's focus. "It is difficult to impossible for a store's product managers to design a fashion line; so what usually has ended up happening is that they study the season's fashions, find the things they like, and then have them knocked off," said Stan Schwartz, President and Chief Executive Officer of Guy Laroche North America.[23] "Knock off" meant to copy the popular styles of an established designer and was common among apparel retailers.

Schwartz added, "On the other hand, working with a designer on an exclusive licensing basis gives the store access to a true design house. Then the store is free to concentrate on details of coordination and marketing those designs."[24]

Licensing was also used for knock-off lines that were endorsed by celebrities. Cheryl Tiegs had such an agreement with Sears, as did Jaclyn Smith with K mart. Commenting on the agreement with Smith, Joseph Antonini, Senior Vice-President of K mart, said, "What our customers are asking for is a little better styling, and we think this line will fill that need."[25] Such licenses are not limited to celebrities. Coca-Cola, Disney, and the American Ballet Theatre have all signed licensing agreements.[26]

Each store had a need to set itself apart from the crowd.[27] That was certainly what stimulated the growth of many department stores' private-label programs in the 1950s. However, the private-label programs in fashion are changing, Schwartz reported. Private labels were becoming associated with a designer name rather than a store name. Exclusive licensing agreements with designers were providing many stores with new private-label merchandise. Consumers were causing this change because of their desire for a unique identity at an affordable price.

Licensing agreements were not without risk, however. "There is a certain aura to a designer name, but much depends on how it is packaged and marketed," said Richard Carty, Fashion Marketing Manager for Bloomingdale's.[28]

PROFILES OF COMPETITORS

Clothestime Inc.

According to *Business Week*, this California-based company was one of the fastest growing companies in the United States. Started in 1974 by brothers Michael and Ray DeAngelo, Clothestime had over 235 stores in the Sun Belt in August 1986. It tripled its 1985 sales to $10 million based on $127 million in sales.[29]

The DeAngelos' ability to bargain had made Clothestime one of the few success stories in the popular-priced teen apparel business. Clothestime typically located its stores in strip malls where rent was lower rather than in large shopping centers. Also, much of its merchandise was purchased from manufacturers' closeouts or canceled orders. Both of these tactics were part of the overall strategy to keep the cost of overhead and goods low. Chairman Michael DeAngelo adamantly stated, "We don't pay full price for nuthin'."[30]

Because the strip malls did not get much traffic, heavy emphasis had been placed on advertising through direct mail and radio ads on rock and roll stations. Clothestime spent roughly 3% of sales on advertising, more than most other retailers.[31]

The DeAngelos, who started in business together by selling odds and ends out of their van at flea markets, recognized the riskiness of their business. "Junior apparel is like dynamite. It can explode in your hand," remarked Ray DeAngelo. "Styles change so quickly that some chains have trouble keeping up."[32]

Critics had questioned Clothestime's ability to become a national chain. Most of its growth came from opening new stores rather than increasing sales at current locations. Sales growth at existing locations dropped from 24% in 1983 to 7.2% in 1984, although sales growth had averaged 40.5% in 1982, 1983, and 1984. In response to their critics, Michael DeAngelo stated that they were "fine tuning" the Clothestime concept.[33]

Petrie Stores Corporation

In 1986 Petrie Stores, a $1.2 billion women's specialty retailer, was headed by 83-year-old Milton Petrie, Chairman and CEO. Petrie Stores was comprised of 14 chains with 1,400 stores in the United States, Puerto Rico, and the Virgin Islands. Petrie also owned 27% interest in Toys 'R' Us and 26% of Paul Harris stores, an Indiana-based specialty retailer.[34] In addition to the Petrie name, the Secausus, New Jersey, retailer operated under different trade names like Marianne, Stuarts, Rave, Jean Nicole, and Three Sisters.[35]

The company had recently completed an electronic point-of-sale systems development program. This program included new merchandising and markdown systems through which the company was able to minimize its costs by enhancing communication between merchandising, stores, and distribution centers. Additionally, the company spent $74 million in 1984 and 1985 to renovate over 520 stores.[36]

Milton Petrie and Leslie Wexner had long been acquainted. In 1965, Petrie offered Wexner a $75,000 per year job as his understudy. "Those numbers were like the GNP to me," Wexner recalled. "But I still said no. I wanted to run my own business." Wexner also turned down Petrie's offer to by a 49.5% interest in The Limited, Inc. for $500,000 when total sales were only $400,000.[37]

A few years ago Wexner almost took over Petrie Stores, but Milton Petrie backed out at the last minute. After The Limited, Inc. bought Lerner in 1985, Wexner and Petrie became direct competitors. About The Limited, Inc.'s entry into the low-cost apparel business, Petrie said, "He [Wexner] won't find it as easy in our field."[38]

Petrie Stores continued to be a target for takeovers. Petrie's strong financial performance, its interest in the profitable Toys 'R' Us and Paul Harris Stores, Milton Petrie's age, and no heir apparent to head the company were all contributing factors to its attractiveness as a takeover target.[39]

The Gap, Inc.

Until 1985, the 600 nationwide Gap stores focused on the jean and teenager clothing markets. With the growth of the traditional business slowing, Gap management, headed by president Donald F. Fisher, changed the Gap's merchandising mix and renovated "The Gap" stores and added the "Super Gap" stores.[40] Although still the largest vendor of Levi Strauss jeans (27% of sales), the new emphasis was on fashion-oriented, medium-priced sportswear. The Gap, established in 1969, began to target 20- to 45-year-olds with a quality look and up-to-date styling.[41] Sixty percent of its merchandise was under its own private label.[42]

The San Bueno, California-based company had also expanded into one of the newest areas of specialty retailing: travel and safari wear. The Banana Republic, which was expected to have 30 stores by the end of 1986, had about twice the average sales volume per store ($2 million) as the average Gap store.[43]

The new merchandising strategy seemed to pay off. In the first nine months of fiscal 1985, the Gap's total sales increased 23% over the same period in the previous year, to $423.8 million. Earnings jumped 143% to $1.46 a share.[44]

Carter Hawley Hale Stores, Inc.

Carter Hawley Hale (CHH) was a Los Angeles-based holding company of five department store and three specialty retailing chains. The stores, which had a wide selection of fashionable and competitively priced merchandise, targeted middle- and upper-income segments. The department store chains included The Broadway—Southern California, The Broadway—Southwest, Emporium Capwell, Thalhimers, and Weinstock's. Bergdoff–Goodman, Neiman-Marcus, and Contempo Casual were the specialty units.[45]

In the 1980s, the CHH divisions were producing marginal results. Between 1980 and 1985, CHH's return on equity was 10.3% as opposed to 20% and 14.5%, respectively, for competitors R. H. Macy and Federated. In the same time period, net income as a percentage of sales was 1.9% for CHH while it was 4.5% for Macy's and 3.5% for Federated.[46] Although 1985 saw a 77% increase in sales over 1984 to nearly $4 billion, CHH Chairman Philip Hawley said a greater customer service orientation was required for continued improvement.[47]

Hawley, who started with The Broadway in 1958 as a buyer, became president of CHH in 1972. Since 1980, Hawley has overseen the development and installation of new computer system. This system aided in better management of inventories and buying and greater customer service by decreasing credit approval time and speeding sales transactions in the stores. Hawley also introduced more employee training programs to improve product and fashion knowledge and to enhance communication and selling skills.[48]

In 1984, CHH faced one of its greatest challenges when it became a takeover target of The Limited, Inc. CHH fiercely resisted the takeover by selling 37% of its equity to the General Cinema Corporation in exchange for an agreement that restricted General Cinema's rights to sell its stock until 1991. Additionally, CHH sold its profitable Waldenbooks division to K mart and changed its corporate bylaws to make a takeover more difficult.[49] Later that year Limited chairman Leslie Wexner, who had been interested in CHH since 1980, halted the takeover attempt. Commenting on the failed takeover, Wexner said, "The war isn't over yet."[50] Wexner was not kidding. In 1986, The Limited, Inc., in a joint venture with shopping center mogul Edward J. DeBartolo, began a second takeover attempt by offering $1.7 billion for CHH.[51] (See Exhibit 23.5.)

EXHIBIT 23.5   **The Takeover Fight for Carter Hawley Hale**

1. Mr. Richard Smith, CEO, of General Cinema Corporation could have accepted the takeover offer of Wexner and DeBartolo and realized a $432 gain of the of Carter Hawley Hale stock holdings.

2. Mr. Smith countered the offer of Wexner and DeBartolo by purchasing an additional 3.6 million shares of stock for $178 million. This boosted General Cinema Corporation's equity position to 49.1% of the stock.

3. Under the terms of an agreement between the management of Carter Hawley Hale and General Cinema, General Cinema cannot seek majority ownership of the company until 1991.

4. In December 1986, the board of Carter Hawley Hale approved a restructuring plan to split the company into two separate companies—Neiman–Marcus Group and Carter Hawley Hale Group.

    Neiman–Marcus, a separate company, consisted of the speciality department store business of
    Neiman Marcus,
    Bergdorf Goodman,
    Contempo Casuals,
    Holt, Renfrew and Co. of Canada.

    The Carter Hawley Hale Group consisted of five divisions:
    Broadway—Southern California,
    Broadway—South West,
    Emporium Capwell,
    Thalhimers and
    Weinstock.

    General Cinema Corporation received 60% of the stock of the new Neiman–Marcus Company and 12% of the new Carter Hawley Hale Company.

5. Selected financial information for Carter Hawley Hale

    Stock Price

Range	1986	1985	1984	1983	1982
High	$57\frac{1}{2}$	$31\frac{1}{4}$	$32\frac{1}{4}$	$24\frac{3}{4}$	$17\frac{1}{4}$
Low	$26\frac{1}{2}$	$22\frac{5}{8}$	$18\frac{1}{4}$	$15\frac{1}{8}$	$10\frac{1}{2}$

Voting rights: One vote per share with cumulative voting rights for directors.

Number of stockholders: January 28, 1986–12,205

Number of Employees: January 28, 1986–56,000

Property: The company operated 128 full line department stores with 22,103,000 square feet of gross store space principally in California and 156 specialty stores with 4,026,000 square feet.

Financial data

	1986	1985	1984	1983
Sales ($ millions)	3,977.9	3,724.2	3,632.6	3,054.7
Net income	48.0	89.7	67.5	49.0
Operating income	278.8	232.2	262.0	74.6
Long-term debt	697.6	548.7	521.5	504.9
Net worth	659.4	648.1	783.5	693.0
Net profit margin(%)	50.6	27.1	56.6	38.5

SOURCES: *Moody's Industrial Manual; Standard and Poor's* April 1989; Lynn Fleary "The New Show at Neiman-Marcus," *Fortune,* April 27, 1987; and *Value Line.*

MANAGEMENT

More than two decades after its founding in Columbus, Ohio, The Limited was something of a legend among retailers and so was Leslie Wexner, the man who originated it and who kept it going. "The Limited's billionaire founder was regarded as a merchandising genius as well as one of retailing's most tough-minded managers," stated Richard Stevenson in *The New York Times.*[52] Milton Petrie, President of Petrie Stores, called Wexner "the greatest merchandising talent in America."[53]

Wexner served as Chairman of the Board of The Limited, Inc. His associates credited him with keeping an entrepreneurial spirit alive in the company, despite its mushroom-like growth. He and his family control 35.1% of company stock. Leslie Wexner studied business administration at The Ohio State University. He enrolled in law school but dropped out to work at his father's store. His Limited creation has made him a billionaire and helped him acquire the tangible items that accompany this status—five residences, corporate jets, and rare automobiles. In addition to his passion for fashion, he is on the board of Sotheby's and the Whitney. His major philanthropies are The Ohio State University and the city of Columbus, Ohio. "Les Wexner belongs in with Watson of IBM, Ray Kroc of McDonald's," said Tom Peters who included The Limited in his book *A Passion for Excellence.*[54]

The most well-known members of the Board of Directors in addition to Wexner, were Robert Morosky as Vice-Chairman, and Bella Wexner, Leslie's mother, as Secretary. Robert Morosky, who had been with The Limited since 1972, believed in Wexner so much that he sold his house to buy Limited stock. A CPA by trade, Morosky handled financial affairs. Through his association with The Limited, he became a millionaire.[55]

The presidents of each of the nine divisions reported directly to Wexner and Morosky. According to Michael Weiss, head of Limited Express, each president was given a totally free hand in running his/her divisions.[56] The country was divided geographically into regions. Regional managers reported directly to their respective president. Below regional managers were district managers and then individual store managers. An overview of management is represented in Exhibit 23.6.

LABOR RELATIONS AND EMPLOYEES

The company has acknowledged that the number one incentive was not money, but self-realization and recognition. "We start with the fundamental premise that work is an uplifting experience that can be just as fun as the golf course," said Thomas Hopkins, Vice-President of Organizational Development.[57] The Limited exemplified this philosophy in its employee relations. The philosophy contended that employees are part of the company and when they feel that way, they will be their most productive.

The corporate culture at The Limited was intense. Employees at The Limited, Inc. were called "associates." These 33,000 full time associates, about 50 of them

EXHIBIT 23.6   Table of Organization, The Limited, Inc.

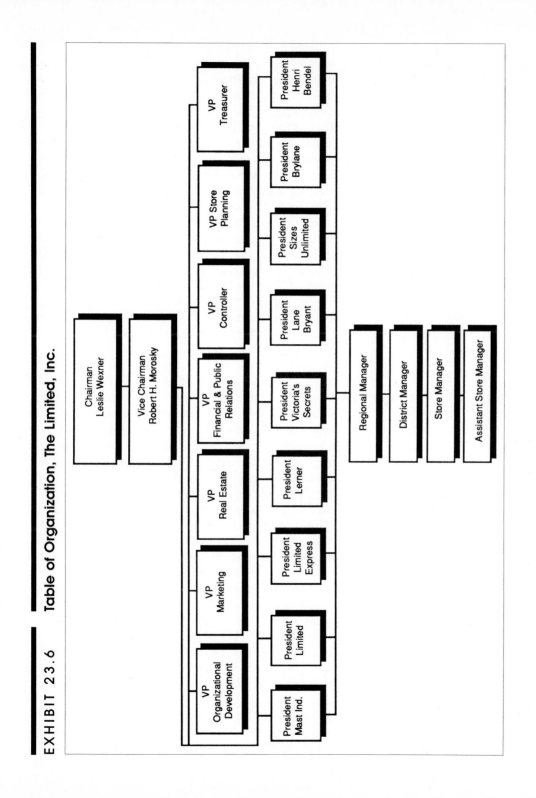

millionaires, controlled roughly half the company's stock. Top managers were flown once a year to Vail to celebrate. Wexner held yearly dinners for the staff and gave awards for outstanding contributions. He freely admitted that he copied these employee awards programs from IBM.[58] On the staff of The Limited, Inc. was a full time manager of nonmonetary compensation and incentives, Lynn Beckmaster-Irwin. One of her projects was to develop the company magazine, *Applause, Applause*, to recognize employee and company achievement.[59] Associates are warned not to talk to competitors or the press. Some critics said The Limited is more a corporate cult than a culture, that conformity was as important as creativity. Industry analysts noted that this conformity tended to induce some management turnover.

A policy of The Limited was to promote from within. Store managers became vice-presidents of distribution and merchandise clericals became executive vice-presidents of merchandise. For example, Verna Gibson, who was President of the Limited store's flagship division, started in 1971 as a trainee. Robert Grayson, the President of the Lerner stores division, started as a store manager. This was The Limited family. Wexner stated that "his executives are good people—they don't get divorced and are good to their parents."[60] Most of them have worked for him from the beginning and were fiercely protective around him.

MERCHANDISING STRATEGY

When studying the success of The Limited, analysts first point to its merchandising ability. These analysts believed that The Limited's success has been due to its ability to identify what fashions American women were going to buy, just before American women knew it and just before their competitors knew it. It also has an uncanny knack for bailing out of a style before demand for it collapsed.[61] The Limited's fashion strategy was to design a look. When asked what women want, Wexner answered "Anything they don't have. Every woman already has enough clothes to last 100 years. You have to sell excitement."[62]

Many of The Limited's most successful fashions were private-labeled "knock-offs" of more expensive designer labels. Buyers and executives reported from their continuous shopping tours of markets at home and abroad. In 1983, on a trip through Italy, Verna Gibson noticed teenagers in Florence wearing bulky yachting sweaters. The sweater was copied under the division's private label, Forenza, and sold by the millions. "It was probably the most successful sweater to hit the American retailing market," said Gibson.[63] Many stores attempted to clone the sweater but The Limited managed to sell more than three million at about $29 apiece. Wexner himself dreamed up the Italian sounding name "Forenza." *The Wall Street Journal* stated that Forenza was the number three best seller in sportswear in the world in 1986.[64] The marketing approach created by The Limited led buyers to believe that the tuxedo-clad man on the Forenza ads was the designer Forenza himself. There was even an Italian address on the garment tags. But alas, a small amount of research would have shown that the fictitious Forenza was invented in 1984 by the marketing staff of The Limited.[65]

These private-label goods carried large margins because they were produced at low cost and sold for whatever price the market would bear. This technique of selling private brands served to enhance The Limited's marketing strength.

In addition to its private label merchandising, The Limited also entered into agreements with several European designers to design lines of apparel and accessories to be sold in its stores. The first designer label chosen by The Limited in 1985 was Kenzo, a Japanese designer well known in Europe but not in the United States. The Limited's "Album by Kenzo" line was distinctly different from his Paris collection.[66] The designer chosen for 1986 was Krizia, an Italian designer.

Analysts questioned why a "knock-off" store such as The Limited would hire designers to create lines exclusively for them—the answer is simple—it sells. A spokesperson from The Limited's public relations department said, "American women are more sophisticated in their fashion taste than they are given credit for. The only thing stopping them is the price tag."[67]

In late 1985, another new and vastly successful private label brand was introduced. Outback Red was a new line of stylish safari clothing—basically a "knock-off" on the popular Banana Republic clothing store. Unlike most other retailers, The Limited routinely test-marketed its new clothing lines. This prevented bloated inventories which could ultimately lead to drastically marked down prices. The line was an instant success.[68]

MARKETING

One thing that The Limited did extremely well was turn around the ailing companies it acquired. Marketing in the other Limited retail-divisions was very similar to the flagship stores. After acquisitions, major changes usually occurred. For example, when The Limited acquired Victoria's Secrets the lingerie was priced to accommodate only about 12% to 15% of the market. The Limited kept the tasteful look of the lingerie but reduced the prices to attract a larger market. After the Lerner acquisition, The Limited shocked the business community by canceling an estimated $100 million worth of merchandise orders with various manufacturers and reestablishing its on-order inventory.[69] A similar process occurred in other Limited acquisitions, that is, replacing a large amount of inventory with lower cost, and in most cases private label, clothing.

The Limited, Inc. managed its marketing, production, and distribution from one central location in Columbus, Ohio. All retail stores were tightly controlled. The whole system was monitored by the POS (Point Of Sale) computer. This computer tracked what items, sizes, and styles of merchandise were being sold so that replacements could be ordered and slow-moving items could be dropped. The computer system allowed a new item to be in the stores within six weeks after the original design approval. The industry average was ten weeks.

The fact that all stores looked alike was no accident. Every other Tuesday the displays were torn apart and rearranged. Pictures were taken in the model stores and sent to the other stores. By the next Monday, they were all identical.

No deviations were allowed. The stores were decorated in high-tech chrome and glass with plants and wicker furniture. Lifelike mannequins were dressed and accessorized in the latest fashions. Each week managers received a plan, developed by the marketing department at Limited headquarters in Columbus, that dictated changes in pricing, presentation, and merchandise mix.[70]

MANUFACTURING AND DISTRIBUTION

Mast Industries, acquired in 1978, was The Limited's manufacturing and buying arm. Mast had interest in twelve factories in Asia and long-standing relationships with 190 others around the world. According to Milton Petrie, "Mast is The Limited's trump card."[71] Most retailers depended on middlemen such as wholesalers, importers, and independent buying offices and waited considerably longer periods of time for their orders. According to Wexner, "You can't patent anything in the clothing business, so you've got to be the first to get your stuff to the consumer if you want to be successful."[72] Mast had helped bail The Limited out of serious difficulties. For example, in 1984, The Limited stocked cotton career clothing that was not selling. It placed new orders with Mast and within months had new lines to offer.[73]

In addition to Mast Industries, The Limited was vertically integrated. Most retailers relied on New York middleman suppliers. Mast owned the steamers used to bring cotton fabric from China to factories in Hong Kong. It owned the planes that rush the goods to the United States. After clearing customs, a fleet of tractor-trailers owned by The Limited and operated by Walsh Trucking, a New Jersey-based company, rushed the goods to the distribution center in Columbus, Ohio.[74] There each style was sorted by size and color and assigned to containers destined for particular stores. They computer read the bar codes on the containers and directed them to the proper shipping location and again the company-owned truck fleet delivered the merchandise to the stores. It took an average of 48 hours for a garment to pass through the distribution center, whereas other less automated warehouses took weeks to process a garment. The Limited fed fresh merchandise into its stores at the rate of two shipments per week.[75]

One problem revealed by Bettye Benton, the manager of The Limited Prestonwood–Dallas store, was the delays associated with processing goods through customs. Ms. Benton sighted a recent example of a popular blouse, known as a "Ten Buttons" that buyers were demanding daily but she was unable to provide because the blouses were tied up in the red tape associated with customs. The Limited was addressing this problem by trying to obtain zoning approval for an airstrip near their distribution center so that goods could be flown directly to Columbus.

The Limited turns over its inventory ten times per year compared to an industry average of three times a year. Mr. Morosky, Vice Chairman of The Limited, Inc. boasted that its chains had the highest sales per square foot of any stores in its market segments. Management relied on high traffic locations to draw customers and was willing to pay in mall rent what others spend on advertising. The flagship Limited stores had sales of almost $300 a square foot, triple the industry average.[76]

It was not The Limited's strategy to advertise. Their first advertising began in 1985. Advertisements appeared in youthful magazines such as *Glamour* and *Elle*. In the past, The Limited had depended on store display and choice, higher cost mall locations to secure business. The new advertisements promoted the designer lines.

FINANCE AND ACQUISITIONS	The Limited, Inc. had made spectacular use of leverage, the strategy whereby companies use borrowed money to finance acquisitions. The risk associated with this strategy was that the company must produce enough cash flow to cover interest charges and pay off the debt or face a financial crunch.

Leslie Wexner faced this crunch in 1978 when The Limited issued $30.9 million debt to acquire Mast Industries, to install the computer network, and to build the distribution center. Cash flows slowed dramatically when sales started to slump and inventories piled up. At this point, Wexner halted the expansion program and tightened operations. By January 1981, long-term debt was down to $16.6 million.

In July 1982, Wexner took on $97.2 million of debt, in the form of bank loans and debt issues, and went on an acquisition binge that doubled the size of the company. In 1982 The Limited, Inc. acquired Lane Bryant, Brylane, Victoria's Secrets, Roamans, and Sizes Unlimited. Sales soared 100% and earnings rose 50% from 1981 figures. The entire loan was repaid in eighteen months.

In April 1984, The Limited borrowed $515.4 million to finance a hostile takeover of the Carter Hawley Hale department store chain. The specialty line department store would have completed The Limited, Inc.'s coverage of the women's clothing market. Wexner lost the battle and the debt was eventually trimmed to $92 million.

In April 1985, Wexner purchased Lerner Stores, leaving The Limited with a debt of $353.9 million. In addition, The Limited opened hundreds of new stores across the country.[77] This debt was in the form of convertible debt issues. Many of these issues were called in so as to force conversion in mid-1986. This action brought The Limited's debt-to-total capital ratio under 20% from nearly 50%.

On October 21, 1986, The Limited, Inc. increased its available bank credit lines to $1.4 billion from $700 million. Robert Morosky, Vice-Chairman, said, "This move sends a signal to the investment community that we are a potential buyer of retail operations; however, there is nothing specific in way of a pending acquisition."[78]

Net sales have increased 37.5% in the first six months of 1986 and net income has increased 52%. There are 119,946,441 shares of outstanding stock with a market value of $3,078,000.00. (See Exhibits 23.7–23.10.)

EXHIBIT 23.7   **Consolidated Balance Sheets, The Limited, Inc.**
(Dollar Amounts in Thousands)

	FEBRUARY 1, 1986	FEBRUARY 2, 1985
Assets		
Current assets		
Cash and equivalents	$ 12,948	$ 7,494
Accounts receivable	62,077	45,912
Inventories	320,305	190,014
Prepayments and other	20,994	13,056
Total current assets	416,324	256,476
Property and equipment	648,314	267,528
Investment in and advances to finance subsidiaries	74,795	23,672
Other assets	72,077	19,476
Total assets	$1,211,510	$567,152
Liabilities and shareholders' equity		
Current liabilities		
Accounts payable	$ 184,368	$103,010
Accrued expenses	103,381	47,719
Income taxes payable	9,253	9,378
Deferred income taxes	56,416	29,109
Total current liabilities	353,418	189,216
Senior long-term debt	213,744	60,139
Subordinated convertible debt	175,000	—
Deferred income taxes	44,506	42,394
Other long-term liabilities	20,767	—
Shareholders' equity		
Common stock	59,917	29,807
Paid-in capital	24,695	22,466
Retained earnings	319,463	223,130
Total shareholders' equity	404,075	275,403
Total liabilities and shareholders' equity	$1,211,510	$567,152

SOURCE: The Limited, Inc., *1985 Annual Report.*

THE FUTURE   The Limited's management believed the company's existing businesses had the potential to grow from about 2,400 stores to 5,000 and produce revenues of $5 billion in the next few years. Wexner wanted nothing less than to dominate the $50 billion-a-year women's clothing business. Industry experts reported that the future of retailing could be summed up in two key words: specialization and

EXHIBIT 23.8 Consolidated Statements of Shareholders' Equity, The Limited, Inc.

(Dollar Amounts in Thousands)

	COMMON STOCK		Paid-in Capital	Retained Earnings
	Shares Outstanding	Par Value		
Balance, January 29, 1983	29,216	$14,608	$12,267	$ 95,703
Net income	—	—	—	70,939
Cash dividends	—	—	—	(7,056)
Exercise of stock options and other	588	294	5,821	—
Two-for-one stock split	29,376	14,688	—	(14,688)
Balance, January 28, 1984	59,180	29,590	18,088	144,898
Net income	—	—	—	92,495
Cash dividends	—	—	—	(14,263)
Exercise of stock options and other	434	217	4,378	—
Balance, February 2, 1985	59,614	29,807	22,466	223,130
Net income	—	—	—	145,317
Cash dividends	—	—	—	(19,118)
Exercise of stock options and other	488	244	2,229	—
Two-for-one stock split	59,732	29,866	—	(29,866)
Balance, February 1, 1986	119,834	$59,917	$24,695	$319,463

SOURCE: The Limited, Inc., *1985 Annual Report.*

EXHIBIT 23.9 Consolidated Statements of Income, The Limited, Inc.

(Dollar Amounts in Thousands except per Share Amounts)

	1985	1984	1983
Net Sales	$2,387,110	$1,343,134	$1,085,890
Costs of goods sold, occupancy and buying costs	1,668,267	938,813	758,274
Gross Income	718,843	404,321	327,616
General, administrative and store operating expenses	442,631	231,219	192,239
Operating Income	276,212	173,102	135,377
Interest Expense	(41,230)	(16,662)	(10,248)
Other income, net	4,335	1,055	9,810
Income before income taxes	239,317	157,495	134,939
Provision for income taxes	94,000	65,000	64,000
Net Income	$ 145,317	$ 92,495	$ 70,939
Net income per share	$1.20	$.77	$.59

SOURCE: The Limited, Inc., *1985 Annual Report.*

EXHIBIT 23.10 **Consolidated Statements of Changes in Financial Position, The Limited, Inc.**

(Dollar Amounts in Thousands)

	1985	1984	1983
Cash was provided from:			
Operations			
Net income	$145,317	$ 92,495	$ 70,939
Add expenses not requiring working capital			
Depreciation and amortization	80,128	34,526	28,427
Deferred income taxes and other	(3,030)	7,587	12,511
Working capital from operations	222,415	134,608	111,877
Cash flow additions (requirements) resulting from			
Inventories	(51,342)	(67,157)	(20,698)
Payables	62,567	36,240	2,147
Income taxes	11,082	16,326	8,779
Other current assets and liabilities	4,528	288	4,490
Cash provided from operations	249,250	120,305	106,595
Other sources of cash			
Subordinated convertible debt	175,000	—	—
Other long-term debt	346,590	38,290	—
Disposal of assets	8,323	2,716	25,252
Total cash provided	779,163	161,311	131,847
Cash was used for:			
Net cash to acquire subsidiaries and retire debt	331,462	14,142	24,493
Reduction of long-term debt	196,398	—	52,648
Investment in property and equipment	180,269	117,684	52,016
Investment in and advances to finance subsidiaries	47,456	8,000	—
Cash dividends	19,118	14,263	7,056
Other, net	(994)	1,010	(159)
Total cash used	773,709	155,099	136,054
Increase (decrease) in cash and equivalents	5,454	6,212	(4,207)
Cash and Equivalents, beginning of year	7,494	1,282	5,489
Cash and Equivalents, end of year	$ 12,948	$ 7,494	$ 1,282

SOURCE: The Limited, Inc., *1985 Annual Report.*

consolidation.[79] Recognizing that the future of retailing was a battle over a largely stagnant market, the industry knew that future growth would be at the expense of competitors. The Limited, Inc. planned to continue to use its expertise to carve out unexploited niches in the women's clothing market. Wexner believed that a weakened major retailer or department store chain could become available as a merger partner.[80] Although it appeared the company still had plenty or segments to expand into now, a saturation level would eventually occur. Where will the new growth come from then?

NOTES

1. Susan Dentzer, "Parlaying Rags into Vast Riches," *Newsweek*, December 30, 1985, p. 30.

2. Julie Baumgold, "The Bachelor Billionaire: On Pins and Needles with Leslie Wexner," *New York*, August 5, 1985, p. 35.

3. Sean O'Leary, "Les's Successes," *Visual Merchandising & Store Design*, June 1986, p. 107.

4. *Ibid.*, p. 107.

5. *Ibid.*, p. 109.

6. *Ibid.*

7. Delinda Karle, "Limited's Growth Knows No Bounds," *The Plain Dealer*, September 20, 1985, p. 3.

8. *Ibid.*, p. 1.

9. Dentzer, "Parlaying Rags into Riches," p. 30.

10. The Ohio Company, "Second Quarter Results," *Investment Research*, August 14, 1986, p. 3.

11. Paula Lashinsky, "The Big Get Bigger," *Apparel Merchandising*, June 1986, p. 28.

12. Aimee Stern, "Retailers Restructure," *Dun's Business Month*, February 1986, p. 30.

13. *Ibid.*, p. 28; Lashinsky, "The Big Get Bigger," p. 29.

14. Stern, "Retailers Restructure," p. 28.

15. Faye Foster Hughes, "Retail Winners Find a Niche," *USA Today*, March 4, 1986, p. 4B.

16. Stern, "Retailers Restructure," p. 28.

17. *Ibid.*

18. "Where Woman's Place Isn't the Home," *The Wall Street Journal*, November 11, 1986, p. 30.

19. Stern, "Retailers Restructure," p. 28.

20. *Ibid.*; Foster Hughes, "Retail Winners Find a Niche," p. 4B.

21. Foster Hughes, "Retail Winners Find a Niche," p. 4B.

22. The Gap Stores, Inc., *Form 10-K*, January 28, 1985.

23. "Retailers Press Direct Licensing," *Stores*, February 1985, p. 12.

24. *Ibid.*

25. *Ibid.*, p. 14.

26. "Mouseketeer Wear," *Newsweek*, July 22, 1985, p. 65; "Retailers Press Direct Licensing," p. 14.

27. *Ibid.*, p. 12.

28. *Ibid.*, p. 14.

29. Julie Flynn, "This Business Is Anything But Threadbare," *Business Week*, August 18, 1986, p. 98.

30. *Ibid.*, p. 98.

31. *Ibid.*, p. 99.

32. *Ibid.*, p. 98.

33. *Ibid.*, p. 99.

34. Jean G. Marcial, "A Triple Play at Petrie?" *Business Week*, August 11, 1986, p. 54.

35. "Petrie Stores Corp.," *The Insider's Chronicle*, June 30, 1986, p. 3.

36. Petrie Stores Corporation, *1985 Annual Report*.

37. William H. Meyers, "Rag-Trade Revolutionary," *The New York Times Magazine*, June 8, 1986, p. 4.

38. *Ibid.*, p. 4.

39. Marcial, "A Triple Play at Petrie?" p. 54.

40. The Gap Stores, Inc., *Form 10-K*, January 28, 1985; Stern, "Retailers Restructure," p. 32.

41. "The Gap, Inc.," *The Insider's Chronicle*, September 23, 1986, p. 3.

42. Stern, "Retailers Restructure," p. 32.

43. The Gap Stores, Inc., *Form 10-K*, January 28, 1985.

44. Stern, "Retailers Restructure," p. 32.

45. Carter Hawley Hale Stores, Inc., *1985 Annual Report*.

46. Roger Neal, "Phil Hawley's Last Chance," *Forbes*, January 28, 1985, p. 44.

47. Carter Hawley Hale Stores, Inc., *1985 Annual Report*.

48. Neal, "Phil Hawley's Last Chance," p. 44.

49. "CHH's Year Of Living Dangerously," *Chain Store Age*, General Merchandise Edition, June 1985, p. 46; "Carter Hawley Hale Takes Steps Seen Aimed At Buying Time," *The Wall Street Journal*, April 13, 1984, p. 14.

50. "CHH's Year Of Living Dangerously," p. 46.

51. "Limited, DeBartolo Plan to Launch Offer for Carter Hawley Hale," *The Wall Street Journal*, November 26, 1986, p. 3.

52. Richard W. Stevenson, "The Limited Is Aiming Higher," *The New York Times*, November 2, 1985.

53. Brian O'Reilly, "Leslie Wexner Knows What Women Want," *Fortune*, August 19, 1985, p. 155.

54. Baumgold, "The Bachelor Billionaire," p. 32.

55. *Ibid.*, p. 30.

56. Karle, "Limited's Growth Knows No Bounds," p. 2.

57. *Ibid.*, p. 2.

58. Dentzer, "Parlaying Rags into Vast Riches," p. 31.

59. Nancy Austin and Tom Peters, *A Passion for Excellence* (New York: Random House, 1985), p. 253.

60. Baumgold, "The Bachelor Billionaire," p. 32.

61. Stevenson, "The Limited Is Aiming Higher," p. 2.

62. O'Reilly, "Leslie Wexner Knows What Women Want," p. 156.

63. Meyers, "Rag-Trade Revolutionary," p. 41.

64. Julie Solomon, "Bartles & Jaymes Aren't Real Guys, But You Knew That—Forenza Is a Phoney Too," *The Wall Street Journal*, July 8, 1986, p. 1.

65. *Ibid.*, p. 2.

66. Richard Shellwood, "Retailers Press Direct Designer Licensing," *Stores*, February 1985, p. 12.

67. O'Leary, "Les's Successes," p. 109.

68. Meyers, "Rag-Trade Revolutionary," p. 2.

69. Karle, "Limited's Growth Knows No Bounds," p. 5.

70. Baumgold, "The Bachelor Billionaire," p. 34.

71. Meyers, "Rag-Trade Revolutionary," p. 2.

72. *Ibid.*

73. Dentzer, "Parlaying Rags into Vast Riches," p. 31.

74. Molly Brant, "Yesterday's Vision Becomes Today's Reality at The Limited," *Chain Store Age Executive*, September 1986, p. 22.

75. Meyers, "Rag-Trade Revolutionary," p. 3.

76. Stevenson, "The Limited Is Aiming Higher," p. 2.

77. Baumgold, "The Bachelor Billionaire," p. 32.

78. Julie Soloman, "Limited's Wexner Rebuts Acquisition Rumor," *The Wall Street Journal*, October 21, 1986, p. 33.

79. Foster Hughes, "Retail Winners Find a Niche," p. 4B.

80. Dentzer, "Parlaying Rags into Vast Riches," p. 32.

Federated Department Stores, Inc.: Major Diversification Strategies Revisited

SEXTON ADAMS ● ADELAIDE GRIFFIN

Federated Department Stores, headquartered in Cincinnati, Ohio, was a diversified retail firm serving customers across the nation through its department stores, mass merchandising stores, specialty stores, and supermarkets. Federated was the largest department store chain with 1986 sales of $10.5 billion. This level of performance has gained it the image among its peers as the "Grande Dame" of retailing.[1]

However, the "Grande Dame" of retailing in 1986 posted two consecutive quarters of declines in earnings; a third was on its way in 1987. "Long considered the granddaddy of the industry, Federated this year played the part of a stepchild on Wall Street: a stock you want to avoid at this time," stated one retail industry analyst in late 1986.[2] The company concluded 1986 with 15 operating divisions and 631 stores in the major retail markets of 36 states.[3,4] (See Exhibits 24.1 and 24.2.)

Incorporated in Delaware in 1929, Federated was established as a holding company that consisted of William Filene's and Company, Abraham and Straus, and F & R Lazarus. Subsequent years brought other retailing establishments under the corporate umbrella. These stores included such retail giants as Bloomingdales, I. Magnin, and Burdines.[5]

FEDERATED BUSINESS SEGMENTS

Each of the business segments operated on a decentralized basis and emphasized the needs of the people it served in the merchandise it sold, the store atmosphere, and the personal service. In addition, Federated's stores were highly marketing oriented with each positioned to offer a specific range of merchandise and services to specific consumer groups.

Federated had historically pursued a strategy of department store acquisition and expansion. However, in the mid-1960s, Federated redefined its expansion strategy when a consent decree was handed down by the Federal Trade Commission after Federated's acquisition of California's Bullock's and I. Magnin stores. Under its terms, Federated was prohibited from acquiring any more

This case was prepared by H. Bell, L. Brooks, J. Capron, and C. Gibson under the supervision of Professor Sexton Adams, North Texas State University, and Professor Adelaide Griffin, Texas Woman's University. Copyright © 1988 by Sexton Adams and Adelaide Griffin. Reprinted by permission.

department stores for the next five years. At that point, Federated chose to expand into other non-department store areas.[6]

In 1967 Federated acquired Ralph's, a supermarket chain in California, and ventured into discounting by creating the Gold Circle chain of stores. Federated focused its efforts on the growth and expansion of these businesses throughout the 1970s and early 1980s. During this decade, Federated's department and specialty stores contributed over 70% of sales and about 90% of operating profits.[7] (See Exhibit 24.3.) However, annual growth in sales from the department store segment had declined from 10.8% in 1984 to 4.2% in 1986. The specialty store segment had also experienced a decline in sales growth from 31.4% in 1984 to 19.4% in 1986. (See Exhibit 24.4.)

EXHIBIT 24.1   **Federated Department Stores by Business Segment**

(Dollar Amounts in Millions)

DIVISIONS	DATA ESTABLISHED	1986 NUMBER OF STORES	1986 SALES
I. **Department Stores**			
Abraham & Straus	1865	15	$ 778.6
Bloomingdale's	1872	16	1,050.0
Bullock's	1906	22	751.8
Burdines	1898	29	809.7
Filene's	1852	16	390.8
Foley's/Sanger–Harris	1900/1857	37	1,107.0
Goldsmith's	1870	6	174.0
Lazarus	1830	32	904.7
Rich's	1867	20	690.6
I. Magnin	1876	26	317.1
II. **Mass Merchandising (Discount)**			
Gold Circle-Richway	1967	76	969.2
MainStreet	1983	15	109.3
III. **Specialty (High Fashion)**			
Bullocks-Wilshire	1929	6	N/A
The Children's Place	1969	166	161.8
Filene's Basement	1909	22	252.1
IV. **Supermarkets**			
Ralph's	1873	127	2,045.7
Total Stores		631	

SOURCE: Federated Department Stores, Inc., *1986 Annual Report*, pp. 16–20.

EXHIBIT 24.2   **Geographic Locations, Federated Department Stores, Inc.**

Abraham and Straus
15 department stores in the New York City and Philadelphia metropolitan areas, on Long Island and in northern New Jersey

Bloomingdale's
15 department stores in the New York City, Philadelphia, Washington D.C., Boston, Stamford, Dallas and Miami metropolitan areas, on Long Island and in northern New Jersey

Bullock's/Bullocks–Wilshire
21 department stores and six specialized fashion stores in the Los Angeles, San Diego and Palm Springs, California; Las Vegas, Nevada; and Scottsdale, Arizona, metropolitan areas

Burdines
29 department stores throughout Florida, including the Miami, Fort Lauderdale, West Palm Beach, Gainesville, Daytona Beach, Orlando, Melbourne, Tampa-St. Petersburg, Fort Myers and Sarasota metropolitan areas

The Children's Place
158 children's apparel stores in California, Colorado, Connecticut, Delaware, Florida, Georgia, Illinois, Indiana, Kansas, Kentucky, Louisiana, Maine, Maryland, Massachusetts, Michigan, Missouri, New Jersey, New York, North Carolina, Ohio, Oklahoma, Pennsylvania, South Carolina, Tennessee, Texas, Virginia and Wisconsin

Filene's
16 department stores throughout the northeastern United States, including the Boston, Massachusetts; Warwick, Rhode Island; Manchester, New Hampshire; Portland, Maine; Waterford, Connecticut; and Albany, New York, metropolitan areas

Filene's Basement
17 stores throughout the northeastern United States, including the Boston, Massachusetts; Warwick, Rhode Island; Manchester, New Hampshire; New York, New York; and Hartford, Connecticut, metropolitan areas, and on Long Island

Foley's
17 department stores in southern Texas, including the Houston, Austin, San Antonio and Bryan/College Station metropolitan areas

Gold Circle/Richway
76 mass merchandising stores in Ohio, New York, Kentucky, Georgia, Florida, Tennessee and North and South Carolina

Goldsmith's
Six department stores in Memphis and Jackson, Tennessee

Lazarus
(includes Shillito-Rikes)
31 department stores in the Columbus, Cincinnati, Dayton, Springfield, Mansfield and Lima, Ohio; Indianapolis and Evansville, Indiana; Louisville and Lexington, Kentucky; and Huntington, West Virginia, metropolitan areas

I. Magnin
26 stores in the San Francisco, Oakland, Los Angeles, Sacramento, Palo Alto and Palm Springs, California; Seattle, Washington; Portland, Oregon; Phoenix, Arizona; Chicago, Illinois; and Washington D.C. metropolitan areas

MainStreet
Nine stores in the Chicago metropolitan area

Ralph's
127 supermarkets in southern California, including Los Angeles, Orange, San Bernadino, Riverside, San Diego, Ventura and Kern counties

Rich's
17 department stores in the Atlanta and Augusta, Georgia; Columbia and Greenville, South Carolina; and Birmingham, Alabama, metropolitan areas

Sanger–Harris
18 department stores in the Dallas, Fort Worth and Tyler, Texas; Tulsa, Oklahoma; Tucson, Arizona; and Albuquerque, New Mexico, metropolitan areas

(Continued)

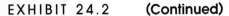

EXHIBIT 24.2   (Continued)

SOURCE: Federated Department Stores, Inc., *1985 Annual Report.*

The Traditional Department Store: Premiere in a Premier Market

Federated was uniquely positioned with leading department stores in the premiere markets of the nation. Many of Federated's department stores pioneered retail development in some of today's major urban areas. Beginning in the early 1980s, the company expanded its department store franchises within their geographic markets to take advantage of suburban and regional growth.

Federated viewed its strength in the department store segment as the ability to recognize and consistently meet the expectations of its target customers. "This ability is an important factor in our strategic objective of building market share within existing markets for each of the department store divisions," stated one senior executive.[8]

Federated's traditional department stores included Abraham and Straus, Burdine's, Filene's, Foley's/Sanger–Harris, Goldsmith's, Lazarus–Shillito–Rikes, and Rich's. Based on market research of customer expectations for its traditional department stores, Federated exercised a unified strategy for the segment, upon which all strategic decisions were made. Strategic actions taken from 1982 to 1986 focused on reducing inefficiencies in Federated's operations. Federated restructured and consolidated its Ohio-based Lazarus and Shillito–Rikes department stores in 1986, and in January 1987, Federated merged Texas-based Sanger–Harris and Foley's.

EXHIBIT 24.3   **Sales by Business Segment and Percentage of Total, Federated Department Stores, Inc.**

(Dollar Amounts in Millions)

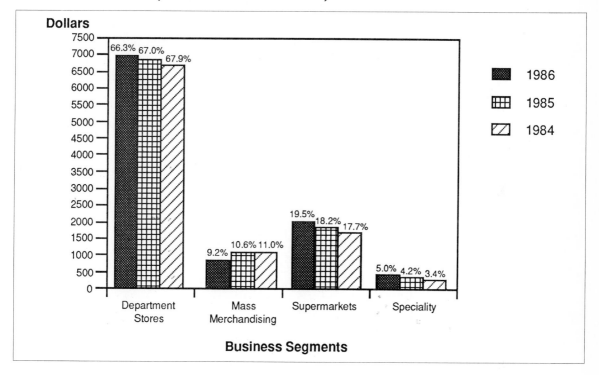

SOURCE: Federated Department Stores, Inc., *1986 Annual Report,* p. 32.

To further reduce inefficiencies, Federated established a centralized regional data processing center, headquartered in Atlanta, to serve three of the company's southern department store divisions. These divisions included Rich's, Burdine's, and Sanger–Harris, with plans to incorporate Foley's in 1987. In addition, a department store remodeling and expansion program costing nearly $300 million was implemented in 1986 with the intent of increasing market share.[9]

Programs were implemented to enhance the department store's merchandise in the moderate and upper-end categories. Federated management planned for its future stores to carry a full line of goods, a concept that many other department stores had abandoned because of cost pressures from discounters and specialty hard-goods stores. Chief Executive Officer Howard Goldfeder recognized the difference in emphasis; however, he believed that by adding more

EXHIBIT 24.4   **Sales by Business Segment and Percentage Growth or Decline, Federated Department Stores, Inc.**

(Dollar Amounts in Millions)

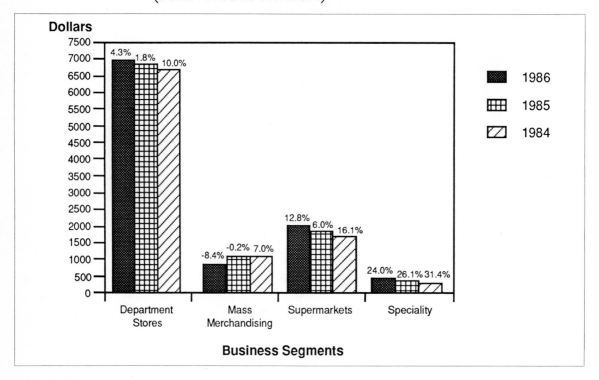

SOURCE: Federated Department Stores, Inc., *1986 Annual Report,* p. 32.

classifications, Federated would gain higher sales volumes, thereby holding down overall costs and boosting profitability.

The Upscale Department Store: Marketing Its Best

Refined customer expectations for fashion and quality gave impetus to the growth of Federated's upscale department store segment. Bloomingdale's, Bullock's and Bullocks-Wilshire, and I. Magnin were designed to appeal to a more selective, higher-income customer than Federated's traditional department stores.

Bloomingdale's was the largest of the upscale department store divisions.[10] It developed a nationwide reputation for trendy merchandise and slick promotions. Based on this reputation and its strong marketing niche, Bloomingdale's national expansion into new high-potential markets was an important part of

Federated's overall growth strategies. Bloomingdale's operated in seven major markets—New York, Washington, Philadelphia, Boston, Dallas, Miami and Boca Raton, Florida—and planned to enter its eighth major market in Chicago in 1987.[11]

Since 1980, Bullock's concentrated on merchandising and marketing strategies that were designed to capture an increasing share of the large upscale apparel and home furnishings market in the affluent southern California region.[12] Bullocks-Wilshire, Bullock's separate and unique retail operation, followed a similar marketing strategy for its smaller apparel- and accessory-oriented stores. It focused merchandising efforts on its traditional position in the upper market segment.

I. Magnin, another of Federated's upscale department store divisions, was recognized as a high-fashion, quality-conscious store with outstanding sales, service, and merchandise presentation. The division operated twenty-six stores in California, Oregon, Washington, Arizona, Illinois, and Maryland. Despite the strong profile of the Magnin name, the specialty store floundered in 1984 in the intensely competitive California market. Industry observers stated that I. Magnin, like other retailers in saturated markets, would have to establish a more strongly defined store identity in terms of desired target markets.[13]

Federated's upscale units expanded their business through an aggressive mail-order catalog program. Bloomingdale's successfully developed a national sales program through their catalog operations. In 1984, Bullocks-Wilshire embarked on a similar national catalog sales program. Howard Goldfeder expected solid earnings growth in this portion of Federated's business throughout the 1980s.[14]

The Mass Merchandiser/Supermarket: Marketing Opportunities

One reason for Federated's size was the diversity of its retail portfolio—one that took advantage of a broad range of marketing opportunities in most consumer market segments. For example, mass merchandising divisions and supermarkets added diversity and marketing opportunities to Federated's retail portfolio.

Federated's mass merchandising division, Gold Circle/Richway, consolidated in January 1986, targeted the middle market customer who placed more emphasis on price when equating value than many department store shoppers and more accent on fashion than many traditional discount store shoppers. This division represented over a billion dollar per year retail business, but its performance fell below Federated's expectations in 1986 with sales of $969.2 million compared to 1985 sales of $1,057.9 million. As of February 1987, the division operated forty-five Gold Circle stores in the Midwest and thirty-one Richway stores in the Southeast.[15]

The division strengthened its competitive position by focusing specifically on enhanced fashion assortments, low everyday pricing in consumables, and intensified customer service programs. Furthermore, Federated planned to increase the per-square-foot sales of this division by at least one-third over the 1984–1989 time period by intensifying underdeveloped merchandise areas, updating and improving in-store merchandise placement, increasing turnover, and providing enhanced visual presentations.[16]

Federated's supermarket division, Ralph's, was another example of the company's diversified portfolio. Ralph's stores, which operated in southern California, achieved a leading position in the market by targeting upscale and middle-market customers with quality products and an aggressive pricing strategy. In January 1986, Federated opened a new 70,000-square-foot Ralph's prototype store. This spacious shopping format combined low prices, warehouse-style displays of packaged goods, fresh produce, bakery, and seafood items that generated enthusiastic consumer support. Fourteen additional Ralph's giant stores and four 40,000-square-foot superstores were opened in southern California in 1986.[17]

The Specialty Store: Meeting Customers' Special Needs

Federated's retail portfolio included specialty stores designed to meet the changing needs of a dynamic marketplace. Federated had two specialty divisions—Filene's Basement and The Children's Place—both positioned to meet a unique market segment.

Filene's Basement began operating in 1909 when merchandise that was not selling from Filene's department stores was placed into the basement and offered to value-conscious shoppers at bargain prices. Filene's Basement was the original "bargain basement" department.[18] In 1984, Filene's Basement was established as a separate division of Federated in order to develop and manage its growth more effectively. As part of the growth plan, an upscale prototype branch of Filene's Basement was developed to target professional and working women who placed emphasis on both fashion and value. An accelerated expansion program which included entry into the New Jersey and Philadelphia markets was scheduled for completion by 1988.[19]

The Children's Place was uniquely positioned to respond to specific consumers. With the children of the "baby boom" generation starting families of their own, a significant market existed for retailers. This division, which was acquired by Federated in 1982, was an established retail entity with a growing and well-defined target customer base—a key ingredient of success in specialty retailing, according to one industry analyst.[20]

Federated's management viewed The Children's Place as a vehicle in which to build future growth in specialty retailing. The division, which operated 158 outlets and superstores nationally, continued to expand through product development and private labeling programs. The Children's Place manufactured nearly half of all its merchandise offered. By the end of the 1980s, Federated management expected the division to be operating 300 stores.[21]

MainStreet Strategies for Future Growth

Federated pursued an aggressive expansion strategy with its newest retail chain, MainStreet. The store was established in 1983 with the opening of three stores in the Chicago area. In 1985, six new Chicago area locations were added and plans were announced for the opening of ten new stores in 1986 and 1987.[22] Seven of the ten stores would be in metropolitan Detroit, the chain's first expansion market. Federated management planned to expand the chain nationally, and future markets were being evaluated. Federated management expected this chain to be an important source of earnings growth for the company in the late 1980s and throughout the 1990s.

The chain's target customers ranged in age between twenty-five and forty-five years, which was younger than the typical department store customer.[23] The combination of quality and value was designed to make MainStreet attractive to households in the $20,000 to $40,000 income bracket.[24] The creation of MainStreet stores signaled a new approach for Federated. In the past management preferred to buy successful regional concerns or spin off departments of existing stores rather than build retail chains from scratch. Targeted at middle-income consumers, MainStreet stores were intended to fill a gap between discounters and department stores and to directly compete with the highly successful Mervyn's, a division of Dayton–Hudson. MainStreet served price-conscious shoppers exclusively. Approximately 80% of the merchandise consisted of moderately priced apparel, with the remainder primarily housewares.

Through its affiliation with Federated, MainStreet was able to take advantage of increased buying clout coupled with substantial cost-cutting opportunities. For example, Gold Circle did all of MainStreet's data processing requirements, which resulted in savings due to the elimination of duplicate functions.

THE FOLEY'S/ SANGER–HARRIS MERGER

Federated continued to use consolidation as a means of enhancing efficiency and positioning for future growth, by merging its two Texas-based operations, Foley's and Sanger–Harris, in January 1987. The newly consolidated division operated out of Houston under the Foley's name. Prior to the merger, Foley's and Sanger–Harris's annual sales in 1985 were $680.3 million and $450.7 million, respectively. With combined sales of approximately $1.1 billion, the new Foley's was Federated's largest sales volume department store division and was ranked the nation's sixth largest retailer according to *Stores* magazine.[25]

Foley's was established in Houston in 1900 and by 1922 was Houston's largest department store. In 1945, Federated acquired all seventeen Foley's stores located in southern and eastern Texas. Sanger–Harris was founded in Dallas in 1857 and expanded quickly into other areas of Texas. Sanger's joined Federated in 1951. In 1961, the division acquired A. Harris & Co., another Dallas-based retailer. Expansion of the division continued into other southern states. Sanger–Harris contributed eighteen department stores located in Texas, Oklahoma, New Mexico, and Arizona to the merger with Foley's.

Federated's primary motivation for the merger, as presented by Lasker M. Meyer, Foley's new Chief Executive Officer, was to "improve and expand in the levels of service and merchandise selections we are able to offer our customers in all store locations, in all cities and in every state in which we operate. By eliminating costly duplications and operating redundancies, we can concentrate more of our resources in the areas of the business that matter most to our customers."[26]

Although Federated Department Stores' management claimed the merger was a "match made in heaven," some industry analysts believed that there were potential problems. Sanger–Harris and Foley's operated under two very different business strategies. Foley's pursued a strategy of "big is better." Large stores were established at significant distances apart. In addition, Foley's always catered to a moderate-priced market.[27] In contrast, Sanger–Harris placed increasing emphasis in the 1980s on targeting an upscale fashion conscious consumer. Stores were established in close proximity within designated market areas. Industry concern was that the two diverse strategies would be unable to successfully merge.

Early reaction to the merger was confusion and frustration from the public, vendors, and employees. Loyal Sanger–Harris customers were concerned that they would lose the quality fashion items they had come to expect. Many shopped Foley's stores and were not pleased with the merchandise assortment.

The stage of transition caused confusion for Sanger–Harris/Foley's vendors. Functions such as distribution and accounts payable operated out of both Dallas and Houston. According to one Sanger Harris buyer, who transferred to the headquarters in Houston, "we are experiencing difficulty adjusting to Foley's systems and procedures."[28] Before Sanger–Harris's data was integrated into the Atlanta data processing system, buyers were forced to operate under Foley's archiac manual record-keeping system as opposed to the on-line computer system they had enjoyed at Sanger–Harris. According to one executive, an attitude of Sanger–Harris superiority developed among Sanger's former employees. "The merger is developing into a sort of Civil War between the North (Sanger's) and South (Foley's)."[29]

Furthermore, there was talk of a potential power struggle at the top-management level. Insiders were concerned that Lasker Meyer would try to redefine the already successful upscale stores in Dallas, because of his emphasis on "value" merchandise. Michael Stenberg, current President of the new Foley's organization, was instrumental in moving Sanger–Harris into its dominant market position by developing its upscale image and emphasis on fashion.

MERCHANDISING   In order to keep pace with an eclectic, dynamic marketplace, Federated emphasized its efforts to meet customer expectations for the right fashion at the right time at the right place. Management accomplished this through intensified merchandise selections and enhanced assortments in the moderate and upper ends of its department store business in order to satisfy the expectations of its target customers for department store merchandise. In its mass merchandising and other retail segments, Federated developed and implemented strategies that concentrated on merchandise selections in customer-preferred areas for those shopping formats.

Federated developed its Federated Merchandising Services (FMS) function to work closely with its buying staff to anticipate and identify emerging fashion trends throughout the world and to select merchandise in accordance with local market tastes.[30] The FMS function assisted Federated divisions in making decisions in a broad range of merchandising considerations and assisted buyers in their efforts to bring distinctive fashion quality and value to product offerings. In addition, FMS developed and managed more than thirty-five private designer labels, including the popular Allen Solly line for men and Lauren Alexander line for women.

TOP MANAGEMENT

Federated's corporate management team and support staff were regarded by many as the most effective innovative decision makers in the retail business.[31] Included among these advocates were competitors who continuously praised the intellect and expertise inherent in Federated's management. "It is the type of respect one gives to elders—based more on historical existence rather than current performance," stated an industry analyst.[32]

During the mid-1980s, Federated's management formulated a new set of strategies geared to increase market share and to rethink its position as an innovator. The objective of these new strategies was to regain the competitive edge Federated once enjoyed in the retail industry by concentrating its efforts and resources on efficiency in each decentralized division. These seven strategies were to:

• Capture greater market share through more aggressive promotions and stocking deeper inventories,
• Renovate key units in major markets,
• Expand department stores into high-growth areas in the Sunbelt,
• Develop and nurture new divisions,
• Develop management stability,
• Reposition and expand Ralph's supermarkets, and
• Dispose of or merge unprofitable operations for greater efficiencies.[33]

The long-term result (three to five years), said analysts, would be growth outpacing that of the retail industry. Short-term expectations were less optimistic; "I think retail sales in the near-term will see a little bit of improvement against a depressed basis," stated Jeffrey Edelman, First Vice-President at Dean Witter.[34]

Howard Goldfeder attained the position of Chairman of the Board and Chief Executive Officer in 1981 by working his way up through the Federated ranks.

Goldfeder spent all but four years of his 34-year career with Federated and he strongly adhered to a system of autonomy among management's decision-making processes and means of implementation. In addition, he incorporated several new performance assessment techniques for identifying strengths and weaknesses within each division. The most significant technique was the five-year strategic plan required annually by each divisional manager submitted to the corporate officer in Cincinnati for review. These plans ascertained the division's current position, listed desired goals and objectives, stated strategies or means for achieving these objectives, and provided alternative options pursuant to deviations in the assumptions underlying the plan.[35]

A five-year plan was implemented in 1983 with each division submitting its plan to the corporate office, but, according to one employee, to what extent senior management utilized these plans was questionable. For example, variances to particular divisions' earnings projections occurred for two consecutive years but specific corrective actions were not identified.[36]

Under the direction of Goldfeder, Federated continued to support all of its business segments in expansion despite Allied Stores' decision to move up-market, thereby concentrating on fewer target markets. Goldfeder stated, "The premium will be on the quality of the implementation as opposed to a revision in strategies. Seven strategies are better for the shareholders than one simple strategy."[37]

EMPLOYEE RELATIONS

Federated's primary focus for employees was on providing professional training programs and challenging career opportunities. The Priority on People program was designed to assure that individuals at all levels were treated fairly, encouraged to succeed, and promoted accordingly. Goldfeder stated that "there is no better formula for success than making their associates (employees) a priority in everything they do."[38]

Federated's employee incentive plan was twofold: a pension plan and a contribution plan through profit sharing. In addition, certain retired employees qualified for health care and life insurance benefits.[39] The requirements for retirement benefits were generally based on age and number of years of service.

Employee-emphasis policies were recently put to the test. As previously mentioned, in January 1987, Federated announced the merger of Foley's and Sanger–Harris department stores. The union of these two Texas divisions caused approximately 500 employees to lose their jobs. In an attempt to ease this transition, severance packages and placement and counseling services were immediately offered to displaced employees. Jim Sluzenski, Federated's Director of Public Relations, stated in an interview, "we are actively seeking opportunities in all our divisions for people who are displaced by the merger."[40]

ECONOMIC FACTORS

The retail industry was a major beneficiary of the 1986 Internal Revenue Code. For example, the reduced personal income tax rates and increased personal exemptions led to higher after-tax income for most consumers, which in turn left a higher disposable income for retail purchases.[41]

However, a retail industry analyst stated that after-tax profits for retailers did not increase. This was due to the fact that the reduction in the corporate tax rate was passed on to the consumers in the form of lower prices. These lower prices were in turn a result of competitive pressures in the marketplace.

Consumer debt also affected available discretionary income. In 1987 this debt was at an historically high level as a percent of disposable income. The principal reasons for this increase were the bargain financing rates offered by U.S. automakers and lower mortgage rates.[42]

U.S. RETAILING INDUSTRY

Confronted by intense competition and unpredictable consumers, U.S. retailing underwent an extensive restructuring in the 1980s. Those that were maintaining a strong position in the market were the specialty stores that developed a unique image, the department stores that repositioned themselves with innovative marketing strategies, and the discount chains that catered to a value-conscious consumer.[43] The retailers that lost ground were those that failed to adapt to the changing marketplace and consumers' buying habits.

At the beginning of 1987, the U.S. was saturated with retail stores, and a 1986 industry study showed that the country had sufficient retail space for the current population and for any reasonable future population growth.[44] With market growth stable, retailers could no longer achieve long-term profit growth just by adding stores. In addition, retailers' operating costs increased while consumers were more unwilling to pay higher prices. This resulted in an increase in markdowns from 9% of department store sales in 1975 to 16% in 1985, as reported by the National Retail Merchants Association.[45] Retailers experienced a classic profit squeeze.

The 1980s demographic and economic developments changed consumers' shopping patterns. First, the population was aging and a greater share of the wealth was distributed among fewer people, thus increasing the importance of the upscale market. Second, women in the workforce had more disposable income, but less time to shop. Finally, consumers who had experienced two recessions sought both quality and value in their purchases.

Consumers' preferences and shopping patterns were no longer predictable. Retailers were forced to address their customers according to lifestyles and demographics. "The retailer has begun to look at consumer needs both economically and socially and how they translate into shopping behavior," said Harry Barnard, Executive Vice-President of the New York apparel consulting firm Colton Bernard, Inc.[46]

The challenge for retailers was to identify a lifestyle and demographic segment and to create a store that projected a distinct and consistent image that allowed shoppers to quickly decide whether the store addressed their fashion and price requirements. "The consistency of some retailers compared to others pays off," noted Walter Lorb of Morgan Stanley Company, another leading industry analyst. "You see it at a Lord & Taylor, a Bloomingdale's or a Nordstrom. They have developed a focus and then marketed the hell out of it."[47]

Developing a focus however involved more than merely choosing a merchandise category and making a store attractive. The direction started with top management and permeated through buying, distribution, and inventory management, down to the selling floor. According to Daniel Dorsey, Vice-President of the retail consulting firms Nexus America, Inc., all these attributes must contribute to creating the store's personality. "You have to create a total mix of product, service and delivery that work together."[48] This increased emphasis on focus caused by the complexity of consumer shopping patterns created many new kinds of stores within the general department store, specialty, and discount categories.

Department Store Characteristics

Department stores were segmented into three subgroups: those that catered to upscale customers, those that focused on the middle of the market, and those that were upscale mass merchandisers such as Dayton-Hudson Corporation's Mervyn's and Federated Department Stores' MainStreet.

A study by Donaldson, Nafhin & Jennette showed how the nation's retailing categories performed in the period 1981–1985 and ranked department stores at the very bottom. Their average sales per square foot, the study noted, was $134, well below apparel stores' $222, jewelry stores' $541, and the top achiever, consumer electronic outlets' $1,098.[49]

Department stores throughout the country redefined their businesses. In the future, shoppers would find fewer high-expense, low-profit departments as the large department stores sought ways to improve their profitability. Stores removed items such as appliances, furniture, sporting goods, and toys—categories in which specialty stores had gained dominance. Department stores emphasized womenswear, sportswear for both men and women, cosmetics, and jewelry, which offered higher returns on investments.

To improve their competitive position, the department stores tried a number of cost-cutting measures. Some developed centralized buying systems and consolidated management. Others adopted sophisticated inventory control systems to help keep them on top of the market. Dillard's, one of the most innovative, systematized inventory control so that it could buy merchandise regionally that was tailored to the needs of its individual stores.

Private-label merchandising allowed retailers to cut costs and offset consumer reliance on brand names. The ratio of private-label to branded merchandise was as high as 40% in some department stores. Cyrus Wilson, President of Management Horizons, a retail consulting firm, cited two department stores that made major commitments to private labels: Dayton–Hudson with its Boundary Waters label, and Federated Department Stores with its Allen Solly line of men's clothing.[50]

Specialty Store Characteristics

The specialty store segment was divided into two groups. There were the narrowly focused chains, such as The Limited, Inc. and Bennetton, and specialty department stores, such as Neiman Marcus and Saks Fifth Avenue, which sold a broader assortment of soft goods.

Specialty stores that sold one kind of merchandise—records, women's clothing, or shoes—experienced increased success by using eye-catching displays, better service, and lower prices to attract customers. In addition, they developed very sophisticated marketing strategies. The specialty chains carefully defined their customers and employed the target marketing techniques of direct marketers. Practitioners included Fedco, Federated's MainStreet Stores, and Tandy/Radio Shack. A specialty retailer relied on target marketing to help it make better inventory decisions for specific stores, depending on the psychographic makeup of consumers who lived in the stores' market areas. Others used target marketing to track their best customers and their lifestyles as they aged.

Discount Store Characteristics

Discounters were separated into three groups. At the lower end were the chains such as Zayre Discount Department Stores and Wal-Mart Stores that aimed merchandise primarily at a lower-income audience; in the middle were those such as K-mart Corporation and Dayton–Hudson's Target that carried medium-priced branded merchandise; and at the top were discounters such as Caldor, Inc., and Bradlees that targeted the department store customer in some product lines. Another type of merchandiser in the discount category that recently increased in popularity was the off-price apparel stores that sold branded and designer labels at 20% to 40% below retail price.[51]

Although the discount segment of the retail industry experienced strong growth and success through the 1970s, new challenges developed from a variety of sources. These included the deep discount drug chains such as Drug Emporium, membership warehouses such as Sams, and the drug/grocery combination stores. Many of the large discounters formerly maintained a large sales volume in toys, hardware, and electronics. Superstores such as Toys 'R' Us, Home Depot, and Highland dominated the market in sales and volume by offering greater assortments, lower prices, and better service.[52] In fashion softlines, the discount stores lost markets to merchants such as The Limited and The Gap, off-price retailers, and Mervyn's or MainStreet-type stores.[53]

Mergers/Acquisitions: A Growing Trend

Mergers, acquisitions, and divestitures among the nation's retail stores were expected to continue, according to Wall Street predictions.[54] Although the new tax code took away some of the reasons for retail consolidations, this trend was not likely to stop in 1987. "The only way to get high growth is to buy out the people you're competing with," said Carl Studtmann, Chief Economist for Management Horizons.[55] "There will be a great deal of shuffling of properties," said Walter F. Lock, industry analyst for Morgan Stanley Co. Newly merged retailers shedded unwanted assets, while companies looking to diversify tried to buy out some of the hot specialty retailers. Realization that parts of a company were more valuable than the whole inspired acquisition-minded retailers.[56]

Many retailers in the mid-1980s adopted anti-takeover defenses. "Everyone is vulnerable; the best defense is a high stock price," said Daniel Good, managing director and head of principal investments at Shearson Lehman Brothers.[57] Size was not a limitation given the huge amounts of capital raised by corporate raiders and buyout-pools. Even Federated, the nation's largest department store chain with $10 billion in revenue, became the subject of takeover talk by the Dart Group Corporation.[58] Like any other takeover target, a vulnerable retailer had low growth, low returns, and a stock price that was below the market price/earnings ratio and probably close to the company's book value.

The rush to acquire retailers was due to their "high and predictable cash flow that will support high leverage in an acquisition," said Edward Weller, E. F. Hutton's retail analyst. "That makes lenders willing to lend, especially with declining interest rates."[59] "Retailers had abundant hidden assets that never showed on the balanced sheet," added Fred Wintzer, an analyst at Alexander Brown & Sons in Baltimore.[60] As he saw it, the buried treasure in a retail company was real estate—especially long-term leases carried on the balance sheet at values substantially less than current market value.

There was a trend among real estate developers to acquire retailers, because of the saturation of stores in the U.S. One way for developers to expand was to buy into existing shopping centers. This helped explain why companies like Federated, with anchor stores in regional malls, were attractive acquisition candidates.

Raiders and real estate developers were not the only purchasers of retail chains. Other retailers found that the best way to expand business was to buy an existing chain of stores. One of the reasons stores went after each other was to gain space; it was simply less expensive to buy existing stores than to build from the ground up.[61]

Technological Advances

Traditionally, retail information systems were utilized for sales analysis, merchandise planning, and "open-to-buy." In 1986, retail information systems were used to help management consider customers' purchase factors for making many decisions as affected by in-store sales promotions, consumer expendable income, seasonal influences, in-store personal selling, advertising, number of brands, number of shoppers, and brand positioning.[62] This information assisted retailers in positioning and marketing their businesses. According to Randy

Allen, retail industry analyst for Touche Ross, "major new retail systems in the next three-to-five years would be concentrated in five major areas: customer service, planning, decision-making, productivity, control, and security."[63]

Customer service was a big issue facing retailers. Technology was used to improve service while controlling cost. Expected advances included customer self check-out, computer based merchandise selection systems, and systems that customize assortments of wardrobe or furniture.[64] Also, planning systems were developed to assist top management in effective target market selection and in corporate strategy development. Competitive analysis systems became more sophisticated to enhance management's decisions on store openings, site selections, and new ventures. In addition, more complete customer profiles were generated as part of the planning systems.

Control and security systems were developed to deal with a number of costly areas in the stores such as security, loss prevention, and energy conservation. Emphasis was placed on payment systems debit cards, on line authorization via autodial, and other devices that could read and authorize check payments to reduce stores' receivable problems.[65]

COMPETITORS' PROFILES

The Dayton–Hudson Corporation

The Dayton–Hudson Corporation was a growth-oriented company that focused exclusively on retailing. Retail operations were conducted by five companies which were organized into four business segments. The firm ran over 1,300 operations in 48 states in 1986, which included Target, a discount store, Mervyn's, a value-oriented department store, and two specialty merchandisers, B. Dalton Booksellers and Lerhmere, a New England hardlines retailers.

Since 1977, Dayton–Hudson's revenues increased annually at a minimum rate of 17%; 1986 sales levels were $9.2 billion.[66] The total number of stores grew from 350 to over 1,300 over this same time period. In addition, the strategic direction of the company changed from department stores to the Target and Mervyn's business segments. The percentage of revenues generated by Target and Mervyn's grew from 58% in 1980 to 73% in 1986. Operating profit increased from 59% in 1980 to 77% in 1986.

Dayton–Hudson planned a capital budget of approximately $4 billion over the period 1986–1990. The majority was directed to Target and Mervyn's in order to strengthen and expand existing markets and develop new markets in new geographic areas.[67]

Another plan of Dayton–Hudson was the expansion of its department store operation into additional markets with specialty oriented units. According to Raj Joneja, President of the Department Store Division, "the company plans to expand stores into new markets that resemble a specialty store format with focused content in addition to quick adaptation to trends and an increased concentration on service."[68] The stores were larger than the typical specialty store, enabling them to offer a department store's wider range of merchandise.

Allied Stores Corporation

Allied Stores Corporation was one of America's largest retailing organizations, operating 665 stores in 46 states, the District of Columbia and Japan, with total 1986 revenues of $4.3 billion.[69] Its operations included seventeen department store divisions, seven specialty store divisions, six regional shopping centers, and four subsidiary companies, which provided support to the Allied retail operations in the areas of marketing and merchandising research, and consumer credit, insurance, and real estate.

The Allied Stores direction for its department stores was to emphasize fashion and a "One-Step-Up" merchandising philosophy. The "One-Step-Up" program, established in 1977, was designed to provide customers with higher quality, more fashionable merchandise, and contributed significantly to the overall company profits.[70]

The Allied Stores Corporation entered the specialty stores market in 1979 with such prestigious names as Brooks Brothers, Bonwit Teller, Garfinckle's and Ann Taylor, which contributed 19% of total sales in 1985. In addition, Allied Stores Corporation was acquired during the third quarter of 1986 by a Canadian development company, Campeau Corporation.

R. H. Macy Corporation

R. H. Macy Corporation's business was in the operation of major department stores in regional shopping malls and central city areas. The company operated 99 stores in 14 states that occupied 24.4 million square feet of total store space.[71] During 1986, Macy's opened four additional stores, one each in Houston, New Orleans, Maryland and Atlanta, In 1986 sales were $4.6 billion.[72]

Macy's concentrated its efforts on its successful department stores. The company initiated some of the major innovations in department store merchandising such as the elimination of budget basements and turned the space into fashionable boutiques and also moved large inventories through aggressive merchandising. In the early 1980s, the company was the most successful department store in terms of gaining market share by emphasizing store promotions and inventory management.[73]

May Department Stores Company

In November 1986, the May Department Stores Company acquired Associated Dry Goods Corporation. Prior to the acquisition, the May Department Stores Company, one of the nation's largest retailing companies, had three principal retail businesses: department stores across the United States, a regional quality discount store chain, and a national self-service family shoe store chain. Through subsidiaries, the company was one of the largest national developers and operators of shopping centers. After the acquisition of Associated Dry Goods Corporation, combined 1986 sales were $10.4 billion.[74]

FEDERATED'S FINANCIAL POSITION

Over the past five years, Federated's consolidated financial results provided a cash-rich posture (see Exhibit 24.5), a position management enjoyed when analyzing diversification strategies. The ability to utilize internal funds for expansion or working capital reduced the amount of funds required from external sources, hence, a reduction in the cost associated with financing requirements—a cost that can be substantial during inflationary periods.

The downside to the cash-rich posture was the attraction of corporate raiders to companies that possessed a surplus of liquid assets and a low debt level in relation to its shareholders' equity. At the end of the fiscal year 1986, Federated had $791 million of long-term debt, compared with $2.7 billion of stockholders' equity (see Exhibits 24.6 and 24.7). One corporate analyst strongly believed the equity was greatly undervalued because "it failed to reflect the market value of the company's real estate assets or the true value of its well-placed department store franchises. In late 1986 Federated's land, buildings and equipment were on the books at $2.2 billion, but the company's approximate market value was more like $3.2 billion."[75]

With lots of cash and undervalued assets on hand, Federated drew a lot of attention from corporate raiders interested in the retail business. Leslie Wexner of The Limited, Inc., felt that Federated was in the shape corporate raiders liked best, "not strong enough to be unaffordable, not wretched enough to be

---

EXHIBIT 24.5

Cash Generated from Operations, Federated Department Stores, Inc.

(Dollar Amounts in Millions)

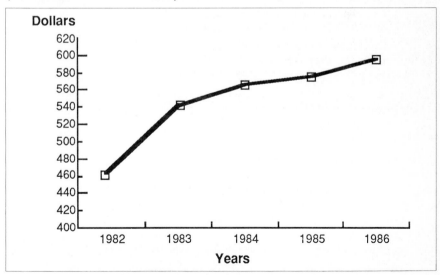

SOURCE: Federated Department Stores, Inc., *1986 Annual Report.*

EXHIBIT 24.6   **Consolidated Balance Sheet, Federated Department Stores, Inc.**

(Dollar Amounts in Thousands)

	JANUARY 31, 1987	FEBRUARY 1, 1986
Assets		
Current assets:		
Cash	$ 101,097	54,270
Accounts receivable	1,554,402	1,607,012
Merchandise inventories	1,405,992	1,320,097
Supplies and prepaid expenses	42,508	43,448
Total current assets	3,103,999	3,024,827
Property and equipment—net	2,451,629	2,249,624
Other assets	132,110	79,192
Total assets	$5,687,738	$5,353,643
Liabilities and shareholders' equity		
Current liabilities		
Notes payable and long-term debt due within one year	$ 240,053	$ 42,749
Accounts payable and accrued liabilities	1,249,149	1,125,626
Income taxes	119,149	320,748
Total current liabilities	1,608,351	1,489,123
Deferred income taxes	420,042	186,091
Deferred compensation and supplementary retirement	204,890	189,648
Long-term debt	791,901	781,513
Shareholders' equity[1]	—	—
Preferred stock	—	—
Common stock	118,876	62,196
Capital in excess of par value of common stock	25,597	98,506
Retained earnings	2,538,612	2,569,404
Less treasury stock at cost	20,531	22,838
Total shareholders' equity	2,662,554	2,707,268
Total liabilities and shareholders' equity	$5,687,738	$5,353,643

SOURCE: Federated Department Stores, Inc., *1986 Annual Report*, p. 23.

NOTE: [1] Shareholders' Equity reflects, as of January 31, 1987, the 2-for-1 common stock split.

beyond effort, but rather in between—floundering but still valuable, worth more in pieces than as a whole."[76]

To the extent that external funds were utilized, primarily through the issuance of debt or notes payable, Federated's policy was to finance fixed capital/

EXHIBIT 24.7   **Consolidated Statement of Income, Federated Department Stores, Inc.**

(Dollar Amounts in Thousands, Except Per Share Data)

	52 WEEKS ENDED JANUARY 31, 1987	52 WEEKS ENDED FEBRUARY 1, 1986	52 WEEKS ENDED FEBRUARY 2, 1985
Net sales, including leased department sales of $324,200, $294,300 and $264,000	$10,512,425	$9,978,927	$9,672,336
Cost of sales, including occupancy and buying costs	7,698,628	7,314,725	7,097,683
Selling, publicity, delivery and administrative expenses	2,103,315	1,962,537	1,893,649
Provision for doubtful accounts	50,558	45,599	33,924
Interest expense—net	79,801	86,386	116,259
Unusual items—net	13,082	35,054	(42,609)
Total costs and expenses	9,945,384	9,444,301	9,098,906
Income before income taxes and extra-ordinary item	567,041	533,726	573,430
Federal, state and local income taxes	265,100	247,100	244,100
Income before extraordinary item	301,941	286,626	329,330
Extraordinary item—loss on early extin-guishment of debt, net of tax effect of $14,527	(14,341)	—	—
Net income	$ 287,600	$ 286,626	$ 329,330
Earnings per share of common stock[1]			
Income before extraordinary item	$3.12	$2.94	$3.38
Extraordinary item	(.15)	—	—
Net income per share	$2.97	$2.94	$3.38
Fully diluted earnings per share			
Income before extraordinary item	$3.05	$2.87	$3.30
Extraordinary item	(.14)	—	—
Net income per share	$2.91	$2.87	$3.30

SOURCE: Federated Department Stores, Inc., *1986 Annual Report*, p. 22.
NOTE: [1] All per share data reflect the 2-for-1 common stock split on April 13, 1987.

expansion and base level working capital with long-term debt and to reserve short-term debt for seasonal working capital needs.[77] In 1985, the company issued $100 million, 11% Euronotes due in 1990 and $100 million, $10\frac{1}{8}$% Euronotes due in 1995. According to an economic analyst, Euronotes provided a cheaper source of financing than U.S. notes because of the strength of the dollar during this period and future expectations on interest rate levels.[78]

In February 1986, Federated issued $100 million $9\frac{1}{2}$% Sinking Fund Debentures due 2016, as part of a shelf registration statement filed with the Securities and Exchange Commission in 1982 for up to $300 million of debt securities. On March 21, 1986, the company filed a new shelf registration statement, which incorporated the $100 million of debt securities remaining available for issuance under the 1982 shelf registration and added an additional $100 million of debt securities.[79]

By filing additional debt securities with the SEC through shelf registration, Federated provided a financial mechanism for carrying out management's strategies of reaching out to additional target markets within all its business segments—department stores, mass merchandising, specialty stores, and supermarkets.

The retail industry faced intense competition that caused the quest for additional market share to be bought primarily with lower margins. With one third of Federated's capital budget tied up in other businesses (Exhibit 24.8), Goldfeder

EXHIBIT 24.8

Capital Expenditures by Segment and Percentage of Total, Federated Department Stores, Inc.

(Dollar Amounts in Millions)

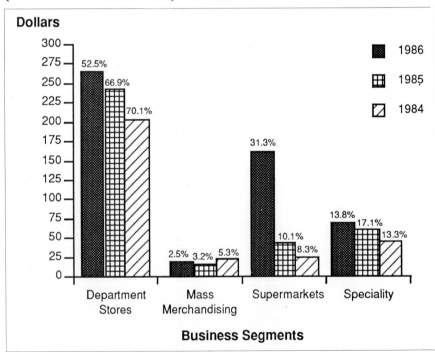

SOURCE: Federated Department Stores, Inc., *1986 Annual Report,* pp. 38–39.

pushed the department stores to expand market share by aggressive pricing rather than by a pursuit of additional store locations. Most of Federated's divisional heads said they met their sales targets in 1986 at the expense of their earnings targets.[80] (See Exhibit 24.9.)

Several points of interest should be noted: (1) In March 1987, the Board of Directors increased the quarterly dividend by 10.4% and declared a 2-for-1 stock split of its common stock in the form of a 100 percent stock dividend. The new quarterly dividend increased from $0.67 to $0.74 per share of common stock on a pre-split basis—the 226th consecutive dividend paid since October 1931. (See Exhibit 24.10.) (2) The Board, in declaring the split, also adjusted to 20 million shares on a post-split basis its previously approved authorization for the company to repurchase from time to time 10 million shares of its pre-split common stock at price levels deemed desirable. Under that authorization, Federated repurchased about 2.2 million shares on a pre-split basis during the

EXHIBIT 24.9   **Operating Income by Business Segment and Percentage of Total, Federated Department Stores, Inc.**

(Dollar Amounts in Millions)

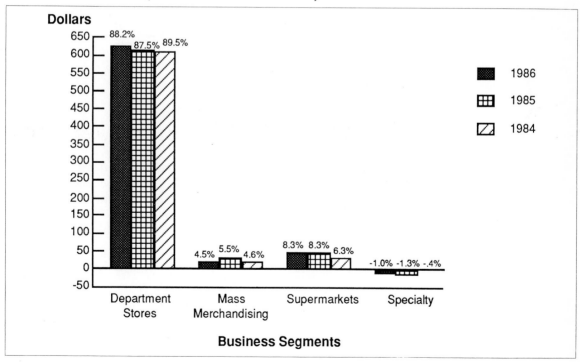

SOURCE: Federated Department Stores, Inc., *1986 Annual Report*, p. 32.

EXHIBIT 24.10 **Annual Cash Dividend per Share, Federated Department Stores, Inc.**

(Adjusted to Reflect 2-for-1 Split)

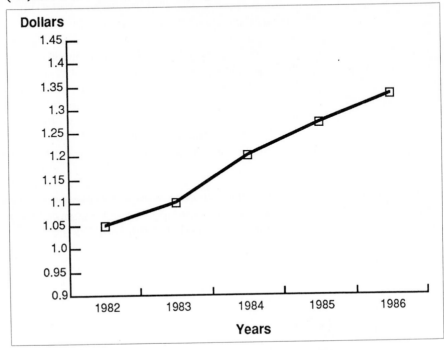

SOURCE: Federated Department Stores, Inc., *1986 Annual Report.*

fourth quarter 1986. (3) The merger of Foley's and Sanger–Harris resulted in a $17.1 million asset writedown recorded on the 1986 balance sheet. (4) In the third quarter of 1986, the company took advantage of favorable interest rates by repurchasing approximately $297 million of Sinking Fund Debentures. These repurchases resulted in an extraordinary loss of $14.3 million, net income tax benefit of $14.5 million.[81]

THE FUTURE

In 1986, Federated management remained committed to improving and developing their department store segment as the cornerstone of their retail portfolio. However, they continued to bring other business segments into their portfolio. This allowed them to continue to pursue additional markets.

Federated also began to take advantage of its enhanced operating strength due to consolidations. Its emerging growth vehicles—MainStreet, Ralph's, and

Filene's Basement in particular—benefitted from new store locations that have opened since 1984. These stores were positioned to offer significant growth and earnings potential to Federated in the upcoming year.

NOTES

1. Subrata N. Chakravarty, "Federated Chooses Not to Choose," *Forbes*, April 8, 1985, pp. 82–84.

2. *Ibid.*, p. 82.

3. Federated Department Stores, Inc., *Annual Report 1986*, p. 1.

4. "Retail Store Industry," *Value Line*, December 8, 1986, p. 1633.

5. *Moody's Industrial Manual—1986*, p. 2847.

6. Chakravarty, "Federated Chooses," p. 83.

7. *Ibid.*, p. 83.

8. Federated Department Stores, Inc., *Annual Report 1984*, p. 4.

9. Federated Department Stores, Inc., *Annual Report 1985*, p. 5.

10. Chakravarty, "Federated Chooses," p. 83.

11. Federated Department Stores, Inc., *Annual Report 1986*, p. 17.

12. *Ibid.*, p. 17.

13. *Ibid.*, p. 20.

14. Federated Department Stores, Inc., *Annual Report 1985*, p. 5.

15. Federated Department Stores, Inc., *Annual Report 1986*, p. 19.

16. Federated Department Stores, Inc., *Annual Report 1985*, p. 8.

17. *Ibid.*, p. 22.

18. Federated Department Stores, Inc., *Annual Report 1983*, p. 19.

19. *Ibid.*, p. 22.

20. Aimee Stern, "Retailers Restructure," *Dun's Business Monthly*, February 1986, p. 29.

21. Federated Department Stores, Inc., *Annual Report 1983*, p. 5.

22. "Going Middle Class: Federated Fashions a New Chain," *Business Week*, November 5, 1984, p. 129.

23. *Ibid.*, p. 129.

24. *Ibid.*, p. 129.

25. "Value Strategies," *Stores*, September 1986, p. 88.

26. Federated Department Stores, News Release, January 16, 1987, p. 1.

27. Interview with a Dallas-based Federated executive, March 21, 1987.

28. Interview with a former Sanger–Harris buyer, March 21, 1987.

29. Interview with a Dallas-based Federated executive, March 21, 1987.

30. Federated Department Stores, Inc., *Annual Report 1985*, p. 11.

31. Holly Klokis, "Retailing's Grande Dame: Cloaked in New Strategies," *Chain Store Age–Executive*, March 1985, p. 18.

32. *Ibid.*, p. 18.

33. *Ibid.*, p. 18.

34. Chakravarty, "Federated Chooses," p. 86.

35. *Ibid.*, p. 87.

36. Interview with a Dallas-based Federated executive, March 21, 1987.

37. Chakravarty, "Federated Chooses," p. 87.

38. Federated Department Stores, Inc., *Annual Report 1987*, p. 17.

39. *Ibid.*, p. 31.

40. Interview with Jim Sluzenski, March 19, 1987.

41. Ellen Benolt, "The Double Play in Retailing," *Financial World*, November 25, 1986, p. 24.

42. *Ibid.*, p. 24.

43. Stern, "Retailers Restructure," p. 28.

44. *Ibid.*, p. 28.

45. *Ibid.*, p. 28.

46. *Ibid.*, p. 28.

47. *Ibid.*, p. 29.

48. *Ibid.*, p. 29.

49. *Ibid.*, p. 30.

50. *Ibid.*, p. 32.

51. "The Discount Lines Are Stalking the Future," *Chain Store Age–General*, May 1986, p. 17.

52. *Ibid.*, p. 14.

53. *Ibid.*, p. 15.

54. Isadore Barmash, "Retail Environment Seen as Ripe for More Deals," *New York Times*, December 29, 1986, p. 26.

55. *Ibid.*, p. 26.

56. *Ibid.*, p. 26.

57. Chakravarty, "Federated Chooses," p. 86.

58. Benolt, "The Double Play," p. 20.

59. *Ibid.*, pp. 20–21.

60. *Ibid.*, p. 24.

61. *Ibid.*, p. 24.

62. "New Focus on Marketing," *Stores*, September 1986, p. 44.

63. *Ibid.*, p. 44.

64. *Ibid.*, p. 44.

65. *Ibid.*, p. 45.

66. "Ranking the Forbes 500," *Forbes*, April 27, 1987, pp. 199–231.

67. *Ibid.*, p. 8.

68. "Dayton–Hudson to Expand Department Store Operations," *Daily News Record*, July 22, 1986, p. 37.

69. "Ranking the Forbes 500," pp. 199–231.

70. Allied Stores Corporation, *Annual Report 1985*, p. 7.

71. R. H. Macy Corporation, *Annual Report 1985*, p. 2.

72. "Ranking the Forbes 500," pp. 199–231.

73. "Federated Chooses," p. 86.

74. "Ranking the Forbes 500," pp. 199–231.

75. "Federated Chooses," p. 86.

76. *Ibid.*, p. 77.

77. Federated Department Stores, Inc., *Annual Report 1986*, p. 36.

78. Amy Dunkin, "Some Growing Pains—But Nothing Serious," *Business Week*, January 12, 1987, p. 107.

79. Federated Department Stores, Inc., *Annual Report 1986*, p. 36.

80. "Federated Chooses," p. 87.

81. Federated Department Stores, Inc., *Annual Report 1986*, pp. 42–43.

JJ's—Women's Clothing Store

JOANN K. L. SCHWINGHAMMER ● CHARLES R. WAGNER

"I must admit owning JJ's has been fun, Beth, in spite of some of the uncertainties. We've had to work hard, but I think it's been worth it."

"Oh, I agree, Ann," replied Beth Sommers, co-owner of JJ's. "There were times I didn't think we'd make it to our second anniversary. I know we're not out of the woods yet, but I think we could already write a book!"

Ann Winters and Beth reflected on their two years of owning the women's fashion shop, and the ups and downs of retail business in a small, relatively rural Minnesota community. At present, they were considering how well they had done and were making future plans for their store.

"I just know we can increase traffic and sales here in the store, Beth. I suppose we could advertise more, but we never seem to know if it's working very well. We want to be sure that whatever we do is cost effective. This isn't exactly the best time to be wasting money on ideas that are chancey."

The women felt that it was their good "business sense" that had helped their store survive these past two years in a community basically dependent on agriculture; other businesses had not been so fortunate. Their concern for the coming summer of 1987 was how they could improve sales, how much money they would have available to spend on advertising and promotions, and what those programs should be.

BACKGROUND

JJ's was a women's clothing store located in St. Peter, Minnesota, and owned by Ann and Beth since April 1985. Ann, a resident of St. Peter for all of her 20-some years, and Beth, in her mid-40s, had learned the retail clothing business while working together at another St. Peter women's clothing store. Their dream had been to one day own a store of their own, and when they learned that JJ's was being sold, they decided to take advantage of the opportunity. JJ's had been in existence for three years when Beth and Ann purchased it, although it had had another name for part of that time. The previous owner, Jane Johnson, had done most of the work of running the store herself, and was tired of the demands it placed on her. The sale was "sealed with a hug" on April 1, and Beth and Ann energetically set about operating their own store.

This case was prepared by Professors JoAnn K. L. Schwinghammer and Charles R. Wagner of Mankato State University. The names of the store and the owners have been disguised. Presented at the North American Case Research Meeting, 1988. All rights reserved to the authors and the North American Case Research Association. Copyright © 1987 by JoAnn K. L. Schwinghammer. Reprinted by permission of the authors and the North American Case Research Association to be published in the *Case Research Journal*, 1989.

EXHIBIT 25.1 **A Map of The St. Peter Area**

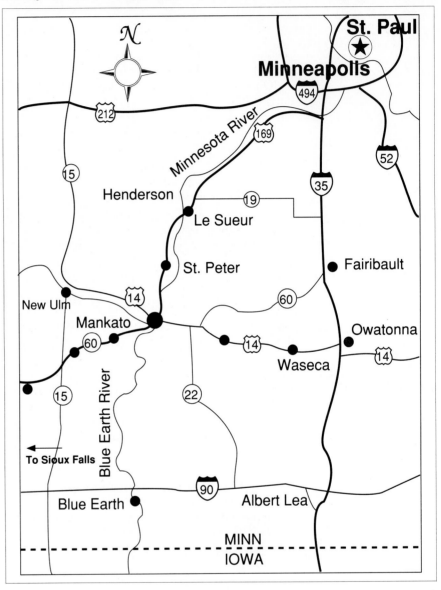

THE CITY AND SURROUNDING AREA

St. Peter, Minnesota, a city of approximately 9,000 residents, was located on the Minnesota River 65 miles southwest of Minneapolis–St. Paul, and twelve miles northeast of Mankato. (See Exhibit 25.1 for a map of the region.) The city enjoyed some recognition in the state, because it was one of the oldest cities in Minnesota, founded in 1853, and had thirteen sites on the National Registry. St. Peter had produced five governors, and might itself have become the state capital, had the bill designating it not been stolen while awaiting the Governor's signature.

Minnesota Avenue (U.S. Highway 169), running the length of the city, was lined with most of St. Peter's retail trade. The central business district could be defined as an area approximately one and one-half blocks on either side of Minnesota Avenue from Walnut Street to midway between Broadway Avenue and Chestnut Street (see Exhibit 25.2). Industries in St. Peter were varied; they ranged from a regional treatment center with extensive mental health facilities, educational facilities and electronics businesses, each employing several hundred persons, to a woolen mill, to a small organ factory, employing eight persons. St. Peter was also the home of Gustavus Adolphus College, a private, four-year, liberal arts school with a sound reputation. Because tuition at Gustavus Adolphus was higher than Minnesota state schools and several other regional private schools, students were likely to be from relatively wealthy familes or to work to partially support their college educations. Exhibit 25.3 provides information about St. Peter's population trends, retail sales, industry composition, transportation, community services, and education.

The extent of market potential among college women was estimated at approximately 1,250 women at Gustavus Adolphus College in St. Peter, and 7,200 college women in Mankato, resulting in about 8,450 prospective customers. The work force in Nicollet County and Blue Earth County summed to approximately 36,000 positions, which were largely non-manufacturing (mostly farming). Assuming that the female population was approximately half, then 26,450 (18,000 plus 8,450) represented the absolute market potential for women's clothing in the area. Per capita incomes were not especially high.

In the recent past, discussions had been held regarding potential downtown renovation. Options ranged from "streetscaping" in the core of downtown, to building a one-block small mall, to building a four-block larger mall. The current sentiment favored building a mall, although plans were not yet sufficiently developed to detail the size and location. At city meetings, residents and community leaders expressed overwhelming support for keeping retail and entertainment downtown, rather than on some outlying acreage yet to be determined. Of the factors considered in developing a retail area, those most important to the residents included retaining downtown retailing, stopping shopping center competition, and improving the retail mix. Discussions on financial feasibility were expected to narrow the choices, with a decision for action expected near the end of the year.

EXHIBIT 25.2 **A Map of Downtown St. Peter, Minnesota**

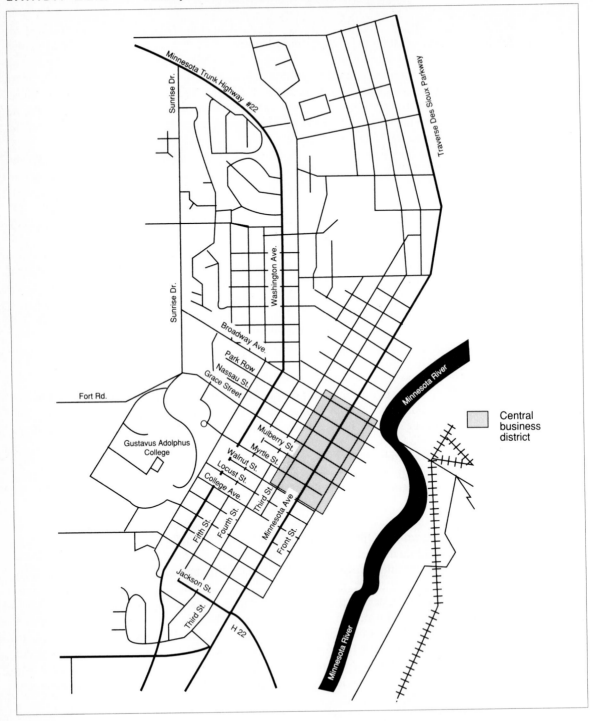

Central business district

EXHIBIT 25.3   ## St. Peter's Community Profile

Population

	1960	1970	1980	1985 (est)
St. Peter	8,484	8,339	9,056	9,082
Nicollet County	23,196	24,518	26,920	28,190

Industry

Number of Employees

Health care	1,025
Education	630
Electronics	245
Total manufacturing	2,900
Total non-manufacturing	4,960 (mostly farming)
Total labor force	13,601 (county)

Unemployment: 4.2% annual average

Transportation

Rail: 2 lines daily, no passenger service
Truck lines: 4
Bus: 1 intercity line
Air: 1 airport; nearest commercial airport: Mankato
Highways: 35 miles to I–35; 69 miles to I–90
   Federal: #169 through city; State: #99, 22, 295, 333

Community Services

Motels: 3; units: 50
Hospital beds: 46; Nursing home beds: 150
Doctors: 10; Dentists: 8
Churches: 12
Banks: 2; Deposits: $120 million
Sports: college
News Media: Newspaper: 1 weekly; Radio stations: 2 AM, 2 FM
   Television: 0
Retail sales: County $70.9 million (1985)
            St. Peter $41.9 million (1985)
Per capita income: County $11,123 (1984)

Education

	Number	Enrollment	Grades
Elementary schools	2	860	K–6
Senior high schools	1	805	7–12
Parochial schools	1	141	K–6
Colleges	1	2,230[1]	Gustavus Adolphus

SOURCE: Minnesota Department of Energy and Economic Development, 1987, St. Paul, MN.

[1] 1252 women, 978 men

EXHIBIT 25.4

Mankato–North Mankato Community Profile

Population

	1960	1970	1980	1985 (special census)
Mankato	23,797	30,895	28,637	28,692
Blue Earth County	44,385	52,322	52,314	52,964 (1985 est)
North Mankato	5,927	7,347	9,145	9,844
Nicollet County	23,196	24,518	26,920	28,190 (1985 est)

Industry

	Number of Employees
Total manufacturing	4,455
Total non-manufacturing	18,563 (mostly farming)
Total labor force	23,018 (county)

Unemployment: 5.3% annual average

Transportation

Rail: 7 lines daily, no passenger service
Truck lines: 6
Bus: 2 intercity lines
Air: 2 commercial airlines; charter and jet service
Highways: 40 miles to I–35; 51 miles to I–90
    Federal: #14, 169; State: #68, 65, 22

Community Services

Motels: 12; units: 679
Hospital beds: 272; Nursing home beds; 384
Doctors: 90; Dentists: 34
Churches: 47
Banks: 10; Deposits: $638 million
Sports: college; Professional: fall practice site for MN Vikings
News Media: Newspaper: 1 daily; Radio stations: 2 AM, 4 FM
    Television: 1 station
Retail sales: both counties $434.1 million (1984)
           both cities $326.6 million (1984)
Per capita income: Blue Earth County $10,945 (1983)
           Nicollet County $ 9,902 (1983)

Education

	Number	Enrollment	Grades
Elementary schools	8	3,414	K–6
Senior high schools	2	2,838	7–12
Parochial schools	12	1,493	K–12
Colleges	4		
Mankato State University		13,105[1]	
Bethany Lutheran College		N/A[2]	
Rasmussen Business College		N/A[2]	
Mankato Technical Institute		930[3]	

SOURCE: Minnesota Department of Energy and Economic Development, 1986, St. Paul, MN.

[1] 6,815 women, 6,290 men
[2] proprietary data, not available
[3] 375 women, 555 men

Beth and Ann themselves felt that there was a "new fresh attitude" among St. Peter retailers. The Retail Council, a committee of the St. Peter Chamber of Commerce, had undertaken numerous planned activities to encourage and support St. Peter's retail establishments. Retailers believed that the consumers in this region were quite typical of consumers throughout the country, though sometimes they seemed more prone to bargain hunting.

Much of the concern retailers and residents had for downtown improvement stemmed from growing recognition of the impact of competing market areas. A St. Peter resident could drive to Minneapolis in just over an hour. Large new malls in the south and west suburbs of Minneapolis, with their unlimited variety of nationally recognized brands and stores, enticed shoppers from outlying areas. St. Peter shoppers were also attracted to Mankato, which, together with North Mankato, offered many nationally known chain stores, services, and recreational opportunities. (See Exhibit 25.4.) The population of Mankato-North Mankato numbered around 40,000 people, and several educational institutions added to this population base: Mankato State University, Bethany Lutheran College, Mankato Technical Institute, and Rasmussen Business College. Many of these students, particularly those attending Mankato State University, lived in the twin cities of Minneapolis–St. Paul and their suburbs, and commuted there to work on the weekends.

THE STORE

JJ's was located on Third Street, one block west of Minnesota Avenue, between Grace and Mulberry Streets, in the Konsbruck Hotel building. Built in 1901, the hotel occupied about two-thirds of the length of Third Street on that block and was now divided into five business places on the first floor, with residences for low-income persons on the second floor. The business place closest to Mulberry Street was currently unoccupied. Other businesses in the hotel building included a bar, an art and framing gallery, a second-hand clothing store, and one unoccupied space. The bar was actually a private club established in the early 1900s as a men's fraternal organization. Although it is no longer restricted to men, its membership was made up of long-time residents of St. Peter; the bar tended to be patronized by older people. An empty lot lay between the hotel building and a restaurant on the corner of Third and Grace. Across the street from JJ's stretched a parking lot for a relatively large low-cost food store, and a fire station.

The store had characteristics of buildings of its age: high ceilings, narrow doorways, wooden floors. JJ's occupied approximately 1,500 square feet on the first floor and basement, although the basement was virtually unusable due to lack of upkeep through the years. In fact, the dirt basement floor had never been improved with floor covering. The sales area was divided from the work and storage area in the rear by a wall with a doorway on the right. (See Exhibit 25.5.) Clothing racks lined the walls; a central counter at the back wall and

EXHIBIT 25.5   **Store Layout, JJ's—Women's Clothing Store**

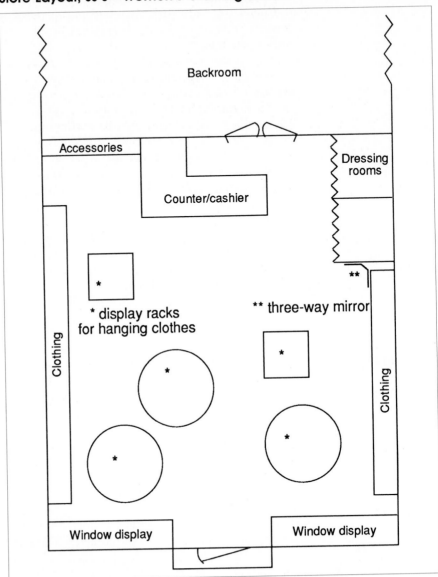

clothing racks left just enough room for shoppers to maneuver between the displays. The back room contained a desk for record keeping, a chaise and a few chairs, and several additional clothing racks for lay-a-ways and new inventory. The basement was accessible only through a trap door in the floor of this work area.

When Beth and Ann bought the store, they made few changes. Improvements they believed to be necessary, however, included window film to prevent clothes from fading, shades, carpet in the window display areas, and some decorative border around the doorway. Planned improvements included wall papering and air conditioning.

JJ's was open on Mondays through Thursdays from 9:00 to 5:30, even though typical closing time for retail businesses in St. Peter was 5:00. In addition, JJ's was open until 9:00 on Fridays, and 5:00 on Saturdays. No retail clothing stores were open on Sundays in St. Peter.

The owners believed Fridays and Saturdays to be their busiest days, although sometimes Mondays could be busy. A typical Saturday's sales would range from $500 to $600, while a typical weekday might might bring in between $250 and $500, although there was greater fluctuation by season. The owners also believed that about 50% of the people who entered the store were "just looking." These people were important, however, because they were likely to be good future business. The owners believed that if people once came into the store, they were likely to come back. One of Ann's and Beth's problems at this time was the low level of recognition and patronage of the store, even among residents of St. Peter. This was a small enough town that people were accustomed to leaving the area to look for and purchase unique goods.

Weather had an effect on sales. A blizzard or particularly frigid cold spell during the winter would reduce minimum daily sales to almost nothing. The past winter had been extremely mild, so little fluctuation in daily or overall sales was apparent.

Although the owners did not know exactly what their trade area was, they believed it to include St. Peter, towns to the north such as Le Sueur, where store selection was extremely limited, Henderson, and perhaps even Belle Plaine, 25 miles away. They were quite sure they drew from other small towns in the near vicinity. JJ's also drew some people from Mankato, on their way to Minneapolis. The owners even had some business from people who lived in towns such as Madelia, 20 miles south of Mankato. Occasionally, they would be visited by Minneapolis shoppers who desired smaller retail shopping areas for the services offered.

People were apparently willing to travel from areas in the near vicinity, although distances had not been measured to determine the trade area. Opportunities existed to draw on college women as they commuted to and from Minneapolis on weekends. The owners had a feeling about who were good customers, but didn't know approximately how many visits per year the average buyer made, the dollars spent on the average visit, or the proportion of dollars spent on clothing vs. accessories on a typical visit.

Of the other women's clothing stores in St. Peter, none carried clothing especially appropriate for the "young career" woman. One well-established store appealed to older people who were willing to pay higher prices, and another catered to women with children: their mix of merchandise combined women's and children's clothing. An additional children's clothing store was believed

EXHIBIT 25.6   **Retail Competition—Women's Clothing**

STORE	MERCHANDISE[1]			CUSTOMERS' AGES	QUALITY[2]	PRICES[2]
	Types	Styles	Sizes			
St. Peter						
Bonnie's	Casual business	Trad	6–20 half sizes	30+	M	M
Bunde's	Casual dressy	Trad	6–16 petites	25+	M–H	M
JJ's	Casual	Cont trad	6–18 petites	18–30	M	M
Mankato						
Mankato Mall—downtown:						
Brett's		Department store		Various	M–H	M–H
J. C. Penney		Department store		Various	M	M
Benetton	Casual	Trendy	3–13	13–40	H	M–H
County Seat	Casual jeans/tops	Trendy	1–16	13–24	M	M
Creeger Coat Company	Casual coats/dresses	Cont/tren	4–20	25+	M	L–M
Dahl House[3]	Casual business	Trad	Petite to 16	13+	M–H	M–H
Ehler's	Casual business	Trad/tren	3–24+	14–80	M–H	M
Just Girls	Sports dresses	Trad/tren	Infant to 14	Moms grandmas	H	M
Kristine	Cas/bus formal	Trad	4–14	15+	H	H
Lancers[3]	Casual business	Trad	6–18	20–60	M	M
Lorraine Shop	Casual bridal	Trad/ trad	6–20 4–42	40–70 18–35	M–H M–H	M–H M–H
Lundberg's	Casual sports	Trad	8–20	30+	M–H	M
Maurices[3]	Casual formal[4]	Trad/tren	3–14	13–60	M	M
Nina B	Casual	Trendy	3–13	17–30	M	M
Stevenson's[3]	Casual formal	Cont	3–28	13+	M	M
Vanity	Casual	Cont/tren	3–13	12–40	M	M
Madison East Mall—on east side of Mankato						
Sears		Department store		Various	M	M
F. W. Woolworth		Discount store		Various	L–M	L
Braun's	Casual	Trad	3–16	20–30	M	M

| STORE | MERCHANDISE[1] | | | CUSTOMERS' AGES | QUALITY[2] | PRICES[2] |
	Types	Styles	Sizes			
The Closet	Casual formal[4]	Trad/tren	3–14	13–25	M	M
Jean Nicole	Casual	Trendy	3–13	13–25	M	M
La Petite	Cas/bus formal	Trad	4–16 petites	16–40	M	M
M. E. Robinson	Cas/bus formal[4]	Trad/cont	4–18	30+	H	H
Peck & Peck	Casual business	Trad	4–16	30+	M–H	M–H
Free-standing stores:						
Kmart		Discount store		Various	L–M	L
Lewis Eastgate		Discount store		Various	L–M	L
ShopKo		Discount store		Various	L–M	L

NOTES

[1] Merchandise is described by the types of lines carried, from casual to business to formal; unless specified, refers to a mix of dresses, skirts, slacks, tops, coats, and accessories. Styles refers to how fashionable, from traditional styles to contemporary to trendy (faddish). Women's sizes usually are given in even numbers if misses sizes; junior sizes are given in odd numbers and are usually cut for a younger figure.

[2] Codes: H = high, M = medium, L = low.

[3] Also has store at Madison East Mall.

[4] Formal wear is seasonal only.

to be going out of business soon. (See Exhibit 25.6 for a brief summary of competition.) A clothing store that had been located on the river side of Minnesota Avenue and catered to the college and career woman had recently closed its doors. The owners of that store spent about $25,000 in redecorating, perhaps more than could have been recovered in a reasonable amount of time. Another reason given for the store's failure was "This is a small town and people didn't know the owners." With most of St. Peter lying to the west of Minnesota Avenue, businesses located on the east side of the busy street seemed to have a harder time. JJ's clothes were usually priced somewhat below other stores for the same brands, to maintain competitiveness. Retailers in the area recognized the prevalence of comparative shopping and the importance of price to customers.

THE RETAIL MIX

Merchandise

When Ann and Beth purchased JJ's in 1985, the lines of clothing carried by the store were appropriate for young women aged twelve to eighteen. Because it was Ann and Beth's belief that market potential for that age range was not likely to increase in the long run, they chose to keep only three vendor lines and added others that were suitable for college and young career women. In the two years since they purchased the store, they changed some lines for other reasons: Some were not the quality the owners were seeking, and some sales reps were difficult to deal with.

The owners characterized their lines as "young missy" and "young career." In the early phase of their business, they carried lines for which a mother would probably shop with or for her daughter; with their line changes, however, items were usually selected by the intended wearer. This change in focus was appropriate, the owners believed, because the young college women, and particularly the young career women (women who would be working in or near St. Peter), had the need and the ability to buy.

While JJ's did not carry "Guess?" or "Esprit" brands of clothing, which required a minimum order of $5,000, they did carry other popular brands: D. D. Sloane, Zena, White Stag, and Catalina, for example. The types of merchandise included slacks, skirts, blouses and tops, and casual and a few semi-dressy dresses. They carried several lines of accessories as well.

Of the Zena brand, JJ's carried jeans and denim clothing, some dyed and some twills, priced at retail about $43–45, considered to be a moderate price by Ann and Beth. These were available in missy (8–18) and junior (5–13) sizes, and could only be ordered in even dozens. Even so, Ann and Beth had no choice regarding the sizes or sometimes even the colors that were included in each dozen they would receive from Zena. This sometimes created a problem, because the larger sizes were often the first to sell, with little demand for the very small sizes. In addition, Zena used a "factor," a representative (often a bank), through which to handle payments from store owners and managers. Dealing with this channel facilitator sometimes added complexity to their communications with Zena, even to the point of holding up orders if there were misunderstandings on payments.

Under the D. D. Sloane label, JJ's stocked sweaters, knit dresses, sportwear, jackets, pants and shorts, usually priced at $40–$60 (retail), somewhat higher than most of JJ's other merchandise. Of this better line, the owners were able to buy pieces in lots of four. Garland was also considered by Beth and Ann to be a good-quality line. Well known for many years as a sweater manufacturer, Garland also produced print skirts. These items were priced moderately, $30–$40; JJ's purchased them in minimum quantities of six items.

White Stag was a widely distributed brand of good quality knit separates, with tops cut a little fuller, and pants, skirts, and shorts with elastic waist bands. These were available in missy sizes and were usually purchased by women over age 25. This moderately priced line had been a popular brand for JJ's. Catalina knitwear was also sized for the missy figure and included swim and sportswear, moderately priced. JJ's could order any amount and size from the manufacturer.

Either Ann or Beth would go to market five to six times a year, usually to Minneapolis, where several vendors could be called upon in one day. Some vendors' offices and showrooms were located in hotels; others sold out of their homes. Occasionally, sales reps would come to St. Peter. The owners had made an effort to find new lines through visiting with reps in each of these situations.

Merchandise was ordered at least four months early. Fall merchandise for July delivery was ordered in the first week in April. On occasion, Beth and Ann would be able to special order merchandise if they needed a special size or color, although most vendors did not make this service available to small retailers.

Because the two owners did not employ any other help, they were responsible for all the duties necessary to keep the store operating, including ordering, selling, planning and preparing displays and advertisements, pressing and marking clothing, making payments to vendors, handling customer service, and doing any other tasks that needed to be done. They shared responsibilities flexibly, adapting to each other's personal schedules as the need arose, though it did so infrequently. While they did not have a formal partnership agreement, they had recently discussed the benefits of having one.

Service

For their customers, Ann and Beth offered many services that would not be found in larger stores. Perhaps their most important service was the personal attention they were able to offer. For many women shopping for clothing, having assistance in selecting correct sizes and colors was desirable. In addition to accepting Visa and Mastercard, Beth and Ann offered a store charge, with monthly payments and no interest on the unpaid balance. Lay-away was available, with a 30% initial payment and future payments according to the customer's ability. After a length of time one of the owners would call the customers to check on their desire, then either keep the product on lay-way or put it back on the floor for sale. Customers could take home an item of clothing for trial, with next-day payment or return. The owners stressed that because this was a small town, they knew people and had a good idea of who could and who could not be trusted. To date, they had only had one bad account, a woman who charged merchandise worth $250 and didn't make payments.

JJ's also offered to take back any unacceptable merchandise. In fact, they sometimes felt that this service was too good, because occasionally customers would take advantage of it. They described one woman who purchased an oversized "balloon" style sweatshirt, with black animals printed on white fabric. Instructions printed on a garment tag, and reiterated verbally to the woman by Ann, cautioned against washing the garment in anything other than cold water. Several weeks later the woman returned the garment, quite worn and faded. It was taken back and replaced with a new, identical garment. The woman returned with the second garment equally worn sometime later. Ann took the garment back and gave the woman credit, even though she suspected that the sweatshirt had been washed in hot water or otherwise treated harshly. No other purchasers of the garment had similar problems.

Other services included free gift wrapping and simple alterations such as hemming, which Beth would do if the work was not too involved. For more difficult alterations, they preferred to recommend a local seamstress or tailor, although one was rarely available.

Pricing

The owners set their markups generally at 40% of their cost, then reduced them by a dollar or two, to maintain competitive prices. Some items, such as White Stag, came preticketed. For accessories, they generally used the standard 100% markup.

Their fee for handling Visa and Mastercard was 4%. They had more cash sales than credit. Other than that one bad debt, they had little or no difficulty with offering store charge. When a payment was received from their layaway customers, that amount was rung up as a sale for that day. Terms for payments to their vendors were typically $2/10$, net 30.

Promotions

Ann and Beth made their own advertising decisions, and understood the value of advertising in generating customer traffic and sales. They developed the message but usually had an artist-friend do the layout and design. Although they appreciated their friend's help, she was sometimes hard to motivate, so there was sometimes insufficient lead time to prepare good ads. Even though they were doing more advertising than the previous owner, they were uncertain whether they were doing enough, or whether what they were doing was effective. In addition, they wondered if there might be other forms of promotion that they hadn't yet tried that might work for their store.

There were several activities that the Retail Council organized for St. Peter retailers. These events were chosen by a subcommittee of the Council, and voted upon by the full membership. Ann and Beth had participated actively in many of these events. For 1987, the Retail Council's list of suggested events consisted of those activities in Exhibit 25.7.

In addition to those events, JJ's participated in a Hospital Auxiliary style show at the beginning of April, held at a local restaurant overlooking the Minnesota River. Attendance was in excess of 350 people. A fall style show was held in November with several other businesses for students of Gustavus Adolphus College. At this event, gift certificates and coupons for the following week were distributed. According to the number of coupons redeemed at the store, this event was quite successful in attracting new business.

The fall style show also contributed toward raising funds for another project sponsored by the Retail Council. On the evening after Thanksgiving, the community turned out for "The Big Turn On," lighting the elaborate Christmas lights and decorations on Minnesota Avenue. Fund raising events intending to raise $13,000 for this project brought in $20,000. Plans were underway to extend the lights and decorations to the retail areas along Third Street, but another $2,500 was needed, for which the Council had been soliciting $100 donations from businesses in St. Peter. In coordination with these activities, Ann organized cooperative advertising Christmas flyers to be placed in shopping bags, follow-

EXHIBIT 25.7   **Retail Council's–Retail Promotions for 1987**

February 27	Library Reserves
April 4	Style Show
May 15–16	Clean-Up Sale 8 A.M.–9 P.M. Friday
	8 A.M.–5 P.M. Saturday
June 10	Sunrise Sale 6 A.M.
July 28	Moonlight Madness 7–10 P.M.
August 22	Neighborfest
August	Back to School
August 6, 7, 8, 9	Nicollet County Fair
September 11, 12	Sidewalk Sale 8 A.M.–9 P.M. Friday
	8 A.M.–5 P.M. Saturday
October 30	Halloween Dress-up
November 27	Big Second Annual Turn On
December	Christmas Hours
13	Hospitality Sunday 1–5 P.M.
20	Sunday opening
7–23	Open every weekday night
24	Close at 4 P.M.
31	Close at 4 P.M.

ing the motif of the street designs and promoting the downtown merchants and local seasonal events.

In the fall of 1985 (their first fall), JJ's participated in the Welcome Wagon service, for which they paid $90 to have coupons printed and distributed. The service welcomed approximately 850 new and transfer students to Gustavus Adolphus. The number of coupons redeemed from this promotion was so negligible that Ann and Beth did not participate in subsequent years.

At Christmas, JJ's sponsored a Men's Night, during which on one special evening cheese, wine, and soda pop were served to men shopping for Christmas gifts. JJ's helped these men shop by maintaining lists prepared previously by women shoppers and kept on file at JJ's for their husbands or friends.

JJ's had an anniversary sale each year at the beginning of April. For several of their events, they utilized joint ads with a local men's clothing store.

For their numerous special events and regular awareness builders, Beth and Ann used newspaper and radio advertisements: the *St. Peter Herald* and *Valley*, the *Mankato Free Press*, KRBI, and KEEZ. The *Herald* was used for specials, perhaps twice a month; ads were placed in the *Valley* and *Free Press* about once a month. KRBI, the only local St. Peter radio station, was used for ads with the Retail Council (sometimes free ads were available with the Council)

EXHIBIT 25.8   **Media**

MEDIUM	REACH	COSTS
Newspapers		
Mankato *Free Press*	27,000 daily except Sunday	All rates on monthly basis; ads appear 6 days/week, 24 times/month Column inch: 1–19 = $8.01/in. 20–49 = 7.17 50–99 = 6.89 ¼ page (3 × 10) = $215.10 ½ page = 413.40 full page = 851.41
St. Peter *Herald* *Valley*	3,500 weekly 12,000 *weekly*	If a home gets the *Herald*, it does not get the *Valley*; rates are all on a per ad basis. Ad appears in both *Herald* and *Valley*. Basic rate: $5.70/col in. Yearly: 100 in/yr = $5.28/col in. 300 = 5.06 900 = 4.85 3000 = 4.64 ¼ page (31 × $5.70) = $176.70 ½ page = 353.40 full page = 706.80
Reporter on campus Mankato St. U., distributed T/Th only during year, W only in summer		$3.50/col. in. 3.25/col. in. if over 75″ 2.50/col. in. in summer ¼ page = $58.50 ½ page = $122 full page = $243
Gustavian Weekly Gustavus Adolphus College		On-campus distribution; Fridays only. Rates not available; not printed summers.
Television		
KEYC-TV Mankato	35 miles NE and 100 miles SW Minn.	TAP (Total Audience Participation), spots spread through viewing time. 44 spots/wk = $596 Prime time (7 pm–10 pm) 104 spots/yr = $99/spot 10 pm news $89/spot 6 pm news 79/spot Many other packages available.
Cable TV MTV USA 97% penetration rate Plays in many pizza and rest/bars in area, wired to all dorms.	48,000 families greater Mankato area	TAP, 30 sec., 3:30-midnight 100 spots = $600 (2–3 per night) $7/ad if less than 100 50% higher for 60 sec. ads production = $150 for 30 sec. 175 for 60 sec. To develop jingle, starts at $100 for background music, more for lyrics.
Radio		
KRBI St. Peter	30-miles radius	30 seconds ads = TAP Per year cost: 1–52 spots = $9.05/ad 53–156 = 7.70

MEDIUM	REACH	COSTS
		157–312 = 7.00
		313–624 = 5.75
		625–1248 = 5.40
		Weekly cost: 10–20/wk = 7.50/ad
		21–30 = 7.25
		31–60 = 7.00
		61–80 = 6.60
		81–100 = 6.30
		101+ = 5.95
		Noon hour rate: $12.10/ad/30 sec.
		19.50/ad/60 sec.
		Copy writing help available.
KDOG Mankato top 40, rock, some jazz	45-mile radius	TAP 6 am to midnight, 30 sec. ads. 300/yr = $6.50/ad 20/wk = 9.25 21–30/wk = 8.50 Prime time morning or afternoon = $9.00/ad.
KEEZ Mankato top 40, light rock, "classics"	200-mile radius	TAP 6 am to midnight, 30 sec. ads. 14 spots/wk = $147 35 spots/wk = 332.50 Morning drive: 25% increase. 13 week commitment: 10% decrease. Annual contracts, 10 sec. spots, and copy writing help available.
KTOE Mankato older songs, easy listening, MN Twins games	75-mile radius	TAP 6 am to midnight, 30 sec. ads. 14/wk = $10/spot 35/wk = 8.50 49+ = 7.50 150/yr = 7.00 600/yr = 6.25 Prime time: 25% increase; packages available. Special for ads during MN Twins games, including tickets.
KYSM North Mankato country	FM: 55-mile AM: n/a	TAP, 30 sec., special promotion: 30/month for 3 months = $6.00 50 = 5.50 75 = 5.25 (393.73/mo.) 15 sec. = $4; 60 sec. = $8
XL-93 Mankato light rock, mellow	80-mile radius	$8.50 prime time, 30 sec. spot 8.00 for equal number of ads/wk Special: 60 sec. for 30 sec. price = $8.50

about once a month, while KEEZ, from Mankato, was occasionally used on a "saturation" basis, when ads were aired at regular intervals over a week's time. A description of these media and other media available in the area is provided in Exhibit 25.8. In addition to these media, residents also watched or listened to several Minneapolis–St. Paul television and radio stations.

FINANCIAL RECORDS AND STATEMENTS

Limited financial records were maintained by the store owners. Essentially these consisted of cash register tapes, a check book, vendor files for unpaid and paid invoices, and a spreadsheet journal form on which daily entries were made for the operations. The spreadsheet journal was given periodically to a licensed public accountant's firm.

The accounting firm used the spreadsheet journal as a source medium for updating the store's computerized general ledger. Then, a balance sheet and an income statement were prepared. During 1985, monthly statements were issued for seven of the nine months after the new owners took over. Only three statements were issued for 1986: May, Preliminary End-of-Year, and Final End-of-Year (see Exhibits 25.9–25.10). In 1987, only the balance sheet for March and the income statements for January, February, March, and the first quarter had been furnished the store owners (see Exhibits 25.11–25.12).

One reason for the infrequent issue of statements was that the store's owners agreed to pay the accounting firm by letting the accountant's wife charge purchases, offset against the accounting fees. Although this arrangement worked well in the beginning, the lack of specific agreement about the regular issuance of statements caused problems for JJ's owners. They never knew exactly how much credit they had with the accountant, and were reluctant to press the issue with him.

The store's owners were concerned about maintaining the vendor files so as not to miss taking a discount. With approximately two dozen vendors used as their sources of merchandise inventory, the method used to pay vendors relied upon a combination of memory and calendar entries. One of the owners had primary responsibility for handling vendor invoices.

When an invoice was received it was reviewed for accuracy, the payment date (giving cognizance to any discount period) was entered on the calendar, and then the invoice was filed in the unpaid vendor file (actually, a stack of bills on the desk). On a daily basis, or nearly so, the calendar was reviewed to determine what bills needed to be paid. Such entries on the calendar resulted in the unpaid vendor's file being searched for the appropriate invoice. Then, a check was issued.

The owners admitted that this was not a foolproof system. Occasionally a vendor invoice did not get paid on time; even worse, they feared missing a discount. Both partners understood that missed discounts translated into a high effective interest cost.

The owners paid rent on a monthly basis, based on a flat fee; there was no per-square-foot charge or percent-of-sales charge. They were committed to a one-year lease. They had also borrowed $5,000 in March 1987 for inventory, and consequently had a lien against the inventory. In order to ease the burden of payments, they paid Jane Johnson on the 15th and Ann on the 15th, while Beth took her payment on the 30th of each month. However, in some months when sales were particularly low, the owners did not take a salary at all. They

EXHIBIT 25.9   ## Income Statement, JJ's—Women's Clothing Store

December 31	1986 12 MONTHS	1985 9 MONTHS
Income		
Sales—clothing	$83,746	$47,055
Sales—taxable	5,058	2,290
Less: returns and allowances	864	665
Total gross sales	87,940	48,680
Direct cost of sales		
Purchases	57,593	32,054
Freight	178	415
Store supplies	1,407	1,044
Laundry and alteration	31	0
Total direct cost of sales	59,209	33,513
Total gross profit from sales	$28,731	$15,167
General operating expenses		
Advertising and promotion	$ 3,452	$ 1,601
Accounting and legal	0	89
Bank and credit card charges	333	217
Contributions	316	0
Dues and subscriptions	112	90
Insurance	270	273
Interest	902	445
Rent expense	4,740	3,555
Utilities and telephone	1,214	980
Office supplies and postage	421	183
Travel and market	429	169
Repairs and maintenance	645	306
Miscellaneous expense	105	283
Depreciation expense	922	677
Amortization expense	400	297
Total general expenses	14,261	9,165
Net profit before partners' salary	$14,470	$ 6,002
Less: partner salary—Beth	3,300	4,169
Less: partner salary—Ann	3,300	3,100
Profit or (Loss)	$ 7,870	($ 1,267)

EXHIBIT 25.10   **Balance Sheet JJ's—Women's Clothing Store**

December 31	1986	1985
Assets		
Current assets		
Cash on hand	$ 626.89	$ 133.87
Change fund and petty cash	120.00	.00
Checking account	6,308.56	2,748.36
Accounts receivable	.00	.00
Inventory	14,290.15	12,718.83
Total current assets	21,345.60	15,601.06
Fixed assets		
Store equipment	4,511.07	4,511.07
Less: Accumulated depreciation	1,599.00	677.00
Covenant not to compete	2,000.00	2,000.00
Less: Accumulated Amortization	697.00	297.00
Goodwill	2,000.00	2,000.00
Total net fixed assets	6,215.07	7,537.07
Total assets	$27,560.67	$23,138.13
Liabilities and partner equity		
Current liabilities		
Accounts payable	$ 81.14	$ 302.17
Sales tax unremitted	95.14	53.82
Total current liabilities	176.28	355.99
Long-term debt		
Note payable—Jane Johnson	5,041.52	6,261.39
Note payable—bank	700.00	.00
Total long-term debt	5,741.52	6,261.39
Total liabilities	5,917.80	6,617.38
Owners' equity		
Owner equity—Beth	6,812.39	8,876.75
Owner equity—Ann	6,959.88	7,644.00
Current profit or (loss)	7,870.60	.00
Total owners' equity	21,642.87	16,520.75
Total liabilities and owners' equity	$27,560.67	$23,138.13

EXHIBIT 25.11

Income Statement for Three Months, JJ's—Women's Clothing Store

1987	JANUARY	FEBRUARY	MARCH
Income			
Sales	$6,943.43	$7,977.31	$8,259.66
Taxable sales	447.83	541.83	533.00
Sales returns and allowances	150.00	194.22	211.82
Total sales	7,241.26	8,324.92	8,580.84
Cost of goods sold			
Purchases	4,544.32	5,537.44	5,715.23
Freight	29.91	23.46	35.73
Store supplies	406.48	198.05	145.61
Laundry and alterations	4.55	0.00	0.00
Total cost of goods sold	4,985.26	5,758.95	5,896.57
Total gross profit from sales	$2,256.00	$2,565.97	$2,684.27
General operating expenses			
Advertising	$ 634.18	156.66	353.19
Bank and credit card charges	38.97	1.37	19.66
Contributions	5.00	12.00	90.00
Interest—Jane Johnson	42.01	41.12	40.23
Interest—bank	5.59	0.00	0.00
Rent	395.00	395.00	395.00
Utilities and telephone	81.14	120.65	126.25
Office supplies and postage	2.00	32.64	47.00
Travel and market	69.68	26.00	130.05
Repairs and maintenance	0.00	0.00	23.89
Miscellaneous	12.78	0.00	0.00
Total operating expenses	1,286.35	785.44	1,225.27
Less: Partners Salaries			
Partner salary—Beth	500.00	350.00	350.00
Partner salary—Ann[1]	500.00	1,259.00	350.00
Current profit or (loss)	($ 30.35)	$ 171.53	$ 759.00

[1] Ann drew a larger salary than usual in February (with Beth's approval) in order to pay taxes due on the farm her husband operated.

were considering making double payments to Jane, in order to retire that responsibility as soon as possible. For all of their debt payments, they kept careful records.

EXHIBIT 25.12 **Balance Sheet JJ's—Women's Clothing Store**
(March 31, 1987)

Assets

Current assets	
Cash	$ 87
Cash on deposit	282
Inventory	$25,514
Total current assets	25,882
Fixed and other assets	
Goodwill	2,000
Store furniture and fixtures	4,848
Covenant not to compete	2,000
Total other assets	8,848
Less: accumulated depr./amort.	2,296
Net fixed assets	6,552
Total assets	$32,434

Liabilities and Partnership Equity Liabilities

Liabilities	
Accounts payable	$ 81
Unremitted sales tax	91
Note payable—Jane Johnson	4,719
Note payable—Bank	5,000
Total liabilities	9,891
Partnership equity	
Partner equity—Beth	10,748
Partner equity—Ann	10,895
Profit or (Loss)	900
Total partnership equity	22,543
Total liabilities and partnership equity	$32,434

GOALS FOR THE FUTURE

Although the owners had no explicitly stated goals for their business, they had thought about a best case scenario. Both owners were anxious to earn a more rewarding level of compensation for the hours they devoted to the business. They wanted, eventually, to buy the building in which the store was operating, and perhaps to expand the store, or at least to move the wall backward to expand the sales floor area of their store. Comparable buildings in similar locations in St. Peter carried selling prices between $80,000 and $100,000.

For Ann, whose husband farmed, a dream was to be able to earn enough from the store to renovate their fifth-generation family farm home. Renovation of the kitchen and bath, and perhaps an added bedroom, would not cost less than $50,000. With the farming economy as restricted as it had been in this rural area, these were not easy times. This was all the more reason for them to have well-planned and well-implemented strategies and programs to stimulate demand for their store.

University Pharmacy

KATHRYN E. WHEELEN • THOMAS L. WHEELEN

By Spring of 1989, the 85.4% sales growth (over the past five years) of the University Pharmacy began to present difficulties for the 33 year-old owner-manager-pharmacist, Steffi Marshall. A policy of superior service and an aggressive pursuit of new business had provided the type of success Marshall sought. Various managerial problems had occurred over the past seven years since she had opened the pharmacy, but all seemed to be resolved.

However, the current and future growth rate of the business appeared sufficiently high that Marshall began to worry about potential problems. Specifically, the private hospital across the street from the pharmacy was planning to expand from 300 to 450 beds. As a result, five more doctors were moving their offices into the immediate neighborhood. This meant that a total of thirty-five doctors would soon be located within four blocks of the pharmacy.[1] The next closest pharmacy, Pettit Pharmacy, was about one mile away.

The physical premises of the University Pharmacy had been recently expanded to the 2,000-square-foot-limit allowed by the zoning codes for that location. Installation of display space and a fitting room for surgical appliances had been added during this remodeling. The sales and rentals of surgical appliances in particular were increasing rapidly and could soon present a space problem.

During the past four years, the assets of the corporation had increased by $266,000 for leasehold improvements and working capital. The equity position of the firm had increased by only $61,250. Accounts payable and a bank loan of $105,000 had been used to finance the asset increases. Ms. Marshall believed that her personal credit was good and that the success of the pharmacy had been sufficiently impressive that additional bank loans were possible. Nevertheless, she was uncertain about the amount and timing of additional financing that might be required in the next few years. She had a meeting scheduled with her banker, Dave Croll, to discuss her financial needs. Her accountant, Bill May, had brought to the pharmacy on Friday the company's past five years of financial information (see Exhibits 26.1–26.3) that Steffi had requested. Unfortunately, May came while Marshall was out to lunch. They met in the store's parking lot as May was leaving. "Hi Steffi! I dropped off the financial statements that you requested," greeted May. "As I already told you, I will gladly

---

[1] The number of doctors for the past four years were 1987—25 doctors; 1986—23 doctors; 1985—20 doctors; and 1984—20 doctors.

EXHIBIT 26.1   **Monthly Income, University Pharmacy**
(Amounts in Dollars)

MONTH	MERCHANDISE	PRESCRIPTIONS	DOCTORS	RENTALS	TOTAL SALES PER YEAR
January 1, 1984 to December 31, 1984					
January	23,345	38,668	6,482	1,071	69,566
February	20,545	38,665	4,575	154	63,939
March	18,204	38,780	5,170	1,246	63,400
April	25,242	43,677	4,176	1,628	74,723
May	19,642	41,867	3,248	270	65,027
June	18,053	39,792	4,855	140	62,840
July	20,969	47,009	5,369	319	73,666
August	20,227	46,662	3,794	151	70,834
September	20,237	41,017	4,757	522	66,533
October	21,816	41,731	4,886	2,772	71,205
November	21,480	38,637	3,724	410	64,251
December	21,494	40,681	5,019	490	67,684
Totals	251,254	497,186	56,055	9,173	813,668
January 1, 1985 to December 31, 1985					
January	28,861	45,140	5,975	1,841	81,817
February	23,884	40,891	5,124	287	70,186
March	21,609	40,912	3,812	221	66,554
April	30,597	43,712	4,043	557	78,909
May	26,275	42,679	5,117	221	74,292
June	23,650	40,999	5,180	18	69,847
July	26,201	46,571	4,988	35	77,795
August	25,883	44,272	6,759	2,170	79,084
September	24,283	47,180	6,913	0	78,376
October	24,346	42,060	4,988	0	71,394
November	21,707	38,962	4,120	2,468	67,257
December	26,320	42,256	5,387	0	73,963
Totals	303,616	515,634	62,406	7,818	889,474
January 1, 1986 to December 31, 1986					
January	30,216	55,255	6,248	2,401	94,120
February	28,403	46,561	5,758	0	80,721
March	28,907	49,700	4,522	35	83,164
April	32,851	52,010	5,142	1,302	91,305
May	30,289	60,505	5,957	1,792	98,543
June	26,142	48,734	6,388	0	81,264
July	28,070	51,919	5,366	2,538	87,898

(Continued)

EXHIBIT 26.1 (Continued)

MONTH	MERCHANDISE	PRESCRIPTIONS	DOCTORS[1]	RENTALS	TOTAL SALES PER YEAR
August	26,058	52,308	6,752	0	85,118
September	28,546	53,382	6,440	3,392	91,760
October	26,422	46,330	5,726	18	78,496
November	29,064	48,930	6,496	1,484	85,974
December	32,508	51,279	7,231	0	91,018
Totals	347,476	616,913	72,026	12,962	1,049,377
January 1, 1987 to December 31, 1987					
January	39,610	58,216	0	2,291	100,117
February	37,345	54,541	0	966	92,852
March	36,481	56,234	0	851	93,566
April	49,361	70,413	0	833	120,607
May	40,838	68,072	0	4,130	113,040
June	36,064	58,958	0	850	95,872
July	34,871	62,250	0	886	98,407
August	37,321	59,080	0	861	97,262
September	43,117	60,208	0	868	104,193
October	34,542	54,474	0	893	89,909
November	39,067	57,932	0	851	97,850
December	39,613	56,872	0	1,015	97,500
Totals	468,230	717,650	0	15,295	1,201,175
January 1, 1988 to December 31, 1988					
January	49,797	74,236	0	2,210	126,243
February	46,543	65,370	0	1,519	113,432
March	44,769	67,470	0	1,950	114,189
April	58,905	70,753	0	1,551	131,209
May	42,238	69,510	0	1,505	113,253
June	53,491	80,126	0	2,146	135,763
July	50,824	78,460	0	1,631	130,915
August	48,591	79,195	0	1,456	129,242
September	48,370	68,940	0	3,084	120,394
October	51,454	76,447	0	1,505	129,406
November	54,457	84,021	0	1,859	140,337
December	49,801	72,546	0	1,959	124,306
Totals	599,240	887,074	0	22,375	1,508,689

[1] Prescription sales to doctors were included in prescription sales beginning in 1987.

EXHIBIT 26.2   Income Statements, University Pharmacy

Year Ended December 31	1984	1985	1986	1987	1988
Sales	$813,668.50	$889,474.00	$1,049,377.50	$1,201,175.00	$1,508,689.00
Less: Returns	17,832.06	5,793.50	5,467.71	14,897.53	21,281.38
Net Sales	795,836.44	883,680.50	1,043,909.79	1,186,277.47	1,487,407.62
Cost of goods sold	503,571.39	562,673.66	683,032.65	766,467.86	935,985.07
Gross profit on sales	292,265.05	321,006.84	360,877.14	419,809.61	551,412.55
Operating Expenses					
Advertising	7,160.17	11,118.27	10,808.46	8,288.08	11,164.23
Bad accounts	2,766.43	3,557.85	4,827.09	4,924.81	4,073.43
Bookkeeping services	0.00	0.00	0.00	7,687.50	16,746.34
Contributions	813.66	1,067.35	1,574.05	1,801.76	1,695.48
Depreciation	6,916.07	7,916.21	8,604.81	9,369.14	15,237.66
Dues and subscriptions	1,627.31	1,423.14	1,783.92	2,522.46	2,715.62
Insurance	3,091.89	11,474.06	13,012.14	15,014.65	19,612.84
Miscellaneous	10,089.33	14,942.96	13,641.76	18,498.05	17,198.31
Professional services	7,322.90	12,452.47	11,647.97	5,765.63	8,901.21
Rent	35,719.48	39,670.01	38,092.00	38,197.27	49,786.44
Repairs & maintenance	1,871.41	1,601.03	4,827.09	2,522.46	3,620.83
Salaries	127,906.64	172,822.47	203,891.91	248,282.25	324,517.06
Supplies	7,404.27	5,158.88	6,296.20	7,327.15	14,307.24
Taxes & licenses	9,845.23	8,894.62	10,493.67	12,372.07	16,595.48
Telephone	3,335.99	3,291.01	3,882.66	5,044.92	8,599.47
Truck expenses	6,916.07	6,404.13	6,611.01	8,648.44	6,638.19
Utilities	4,881.93	4,803.09	5,141.90	5,285.16	6,638.19
Cash shortage	0.00	0.00	0.00	0.00	452.60
Total operating expenses	237,668.78	306,597.55	345,136.64	401,551.80	528,500.62
Income from operations	54,596.27	14,409.28	15,740.50	18,257.81	22,911.93
Other income[1]	7,485.63	8,005.16	16,684.93	15,375.00	24,440.62
Other expenses[2]	5,858.32	4,980.99	4,407.34	4,924.80	9,806.42
Income before taxes	56,223.58	17,433.46	28,018.09	28,708.01	37,546.13
Provision for taxes					
Federal	—	2,846.28	7,030.76	7,327.15	9,504.68
State	—	711.57	1,678.99	1,681.64	2,112.15
Total income taxes	11,635.27	3,557.85	8,709.75	9,008.79	11,616.83
Net income	$ 44,588.31	$ 13,875.61	$ 19,308.34	$ 19,699.22	$ 25,929.30

[1] Income from the hospital for sale of equipment and the filling of prescriptions as well as pharmacists' time when loaned to the hospital pharmacy.

[2] Expenses are materials and labor connected with sales to the hospital.

EXHIBIT 26.3

Balance Sheets, University Pharmacy 1985–1988

Year Ended December 31	1985	1986	1987	1988
Current Assets				
Cash	$ 7,885	$ 12,348	$ 1,813	$ 0
Accounts Receivable	93,166	109,728	118,258	133,388
Inventories	180,544	211,974	251,086	312,953
Prepared Expenses	1,729	0	0	4,952
Total Current Assets	283,324	334,050	371,157	451,293
Equipment				
Fixtures and equipment	57,186	65,523	71,340	90,482
Leasehold equipment	0	0	0	38,811
Trucks	16,327	16,327	16,716	16,152
Total	73,513	81,850	88,056	145,445
Less: accumulated depreciation	20,961	29,372	33,579	41,321
Net Equipment	52,552	52,478	54,477	104,124
Other Assets				
Miscellaneous	493	0	0	0
Land	0	0	0	23,303
Building	0	0	0	26,771
Total	493	0	0	50,074
Less: accumulated depreciation	0	0	0	668
Total other assets	493	0	0	49,406
Total assets	$336,369	$386,528	$425,634	$604,823
Current liabilities				
Bank overdraft	0	0	0	1,659
Notes payable	80,951	61,250	88,515	25,798
Mortgage payable	0	0	0	4,924
Accounts payable	77,451	115,790	107,926	154,056
Accrued taxes	3,076	5,187	4,532	4,424
Sales tax payable	945	1,281	1,512	7,564
Accrued income taxes	3,566	8,672	9,093	9,863
Accrued salaries	9,226	14,000	14,000	28,987
Total current liab.	175,215	206,180	225,578	231,275

Year Ended December 31	1985	1986	1987	1988
Long-term liabilities				
Notes payable	0	0	0	116,466
Mortgage payable	0	0	0	34,874
Total	0	0	0	151,340
Total long-term liab.	175,215	206,180	225,578	382,615
Stockholders' equity				
Capital stock	105,000	105,000	105,000	105,000
Retained earnings	56,154	75,348	95,056	117,208
Total stockh. equity	161,154	180,348	200,056	222,208
Total liab. and stockh. eq.	$336,369	$386,528	$425,634	$604,823

prepare the proformas for your meeting with Dave Croll, but I can't get them to you until late on Tuesday." Steffi responded, "Thanks Bill for the kind offer, but I have to deal personally with my cash flow problems. I feel if I prepare the proformas personally, I will have a better feel for the financial aspects of my company. I've set aside the entire weekend to work on these financial statements. Again, thanks for offering. I may call you Tuesday, if I have any problems. Have a great weekend Bill, and say hi to Sarah, Cary and Patrick for me."

As Steffi walked into the pharmacy, she decided to call Dave Croll, Senior Vice President of Terrace Bank, to confirm their appointment of 10:00 a.m. next Wednesday. In response Croll said, "Steffi—we need to focus Wednesday on your cash flow needs for the next five years. We don't want any major crisis to arise. Have a nice weekend." Steffi hung up the phone and decided to go home early to work on the financial statements. "I hope I'm not going to find any nasty surprises in this stuff Bill gave me," thought Steffi Marshall as she put the financial papers in her attaché case and proceeded to walk to her car.

CASE 27

Harley-Davidson, Inc.: The Eagle Soars Alone

STUART C. HINRICHS ● CHARLES B. SHRADER ● ALAN N. HOFFMAN

In May of 1987, Vaughn Beals, Chief Executive of Harley-Davidson, Inc., and Thomas Gelb, Vice-President of Operations, made a difficult decision. They had turned Harley-Davidson around on a dime and were now poised for continued success with a fine-tuned production process and an exciting new product line. However, in a continued effort to maintain low costs, Beals and Gelb were forced to give a contract for eight electronically controlled machining centers worth $1.5 million to Japanese-owned Toyoda Machine Works. Even though the Toyoda production site for the machining centers was in Illinois, Beals would have preferred to buy from an American company. But he was constrained because of the Japanese company's ability to deliver both high quality and low price.

Beals was well aware of the implications of the decision. He had previously toured several Japanese motorcycle plants during Harley's turnaround and had been impressed with their efficiency and quality. Beals understood the pressure that foreign competition had put on his company, and on other manufacturing-intensive companies in the U.S. as well.

Nonetheless, the decision reflected Harley's commitment to quality and reliability, and also indicated the company's willingness to change with the competitive environment.

Beals and his small management team turned around a company that really symbolized America. Harley-Davidson motorcycles represented freedom and rugged individualism. Beals had put Harley back as the market leader in the super-heavyweight (more than 851cc) motorcycle market. Harley owned 33.3%

This case was prepared by Lieutenant Commander Stuart Hinrichs and Professor Charles B. Shrader of Iowa State University, and Professor Alan Hoffman of Bentley College. The authors would like to thank Linda Zorzi, assistant to V.L. Beals, Kathryn Molling, Public Relations Director, Harley-Davidson Inc., and Don Wright, Holiday Rambler Corp., for information they provided in preparing this case. The authors would also like to thank Lieutenant Michael Melvin and Blaine Ballentine of Iowa State University for providing helpful information. © 1988 by Charles B. Shrader. Reprinted by permission.

of that market in 1986 compared to Honda's 30.1%. As of August 1987, Harley had 38% of the large-cycle market and total company sales were expected to rise from under $300 million in 1986 to over $600 million in 1987[1] (see Exhibit 27.1).

Yet Beals knew that to stabilize that performance, his company needed to diversify. The Milwaukee-based company manufactured motorcycles and

EXHIBIT 27.1

Harley-Davidson's U.S. Market Share, Super Heavyweight Motorcycles (850cc+)

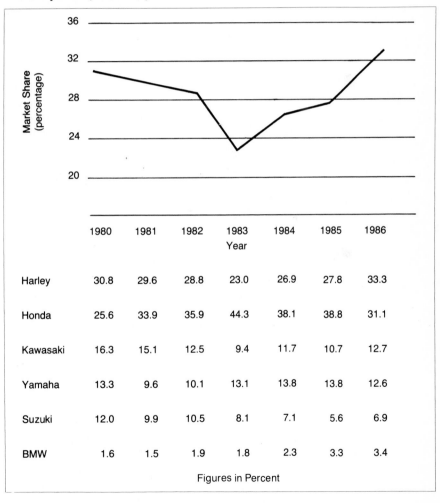

	1980	1981	1982	1983 Year	1984	1985	1986
Harley	30.8	29.6	28.8	23.0	26.9	27.8	33.3
Honda	25.6	33.9	35.9	44.3	38.1	38.8	31.1
Kawasaki	16.3	15.1	12.5	9.4	11.7	10.7	12.7
Yamaha	13.3	9.6	10.1	13.1	13.8	13.8	12.6
Suzuki	12.0	9.9	10.5	8.1	7.1	5.6	6.9
BMW	1.6	1.5	1.9	1.8	2.3	3.3	3.4

Figures in Percent

SOURCE: Harley-Davidson, Inc., *1986 Annual Report.*

motorcycle accessories, as well as bomb casings and other products for the military. In 1986, Harley acquired Holiday Rambler Corporation, a recreational vehicle company. Beals believed that it would fit perfectly with the other businesses, and it was in one industry that was free from Japanese competitors.

Beals knew that Harley had to continue to improve both its production and its human resource management techniques if it was to remain strong competitively. And he also realized that his company's basic product, super-heavyweight ("hog") motorcycles, had the loyal customers and brand image upon which successful competitive and diversification strategies could be built. The company's nonmotorcycle businesses were performing well and the Holiday Rambler acquisition looked promising. Now the challenge Beals faced was how to keep the company moving down the road at high speed.

HISTORY[2]

The Harley-Davidson story began in 1903 when William Harley, aged 21, a draftsman at a Milwaukee manufacturing firm, designed and built a motorcycle with the help of three Davidson brothers: Arthur, a pattern maker employed by the same company as Harley; Walter, a railroad mechanic; and William, a tool maker. At first, they tinkered with ideas, motors, and old bicycle frames. Legend has it that their first carburetor was fashioned from a tin can. Still, they were able to make a three-horsepower, twenty-five-cubic-inch engine and successfully road test their first motorcycle.

Operating out of a shed in the Davidson family's backyard, the men built and sold three motorcycles. Production was expanded to eight in 1904 and in 1906 the company's first building was erected on the current Juneau Avenue site of the main Milwaukee offices. On September 17, 1907, Harley-Davidson Motor Company was incorporated.

Arthur Davidson set off to recruit dealers in New England and in the South. William Harley completed a degree in engineering, specializing in internal combustion engines, and quickly applied his expertise in the company: He developed the first V-twin engine in 1909. He followed this with a major breakthrough in 1912—the first commercially successful motorcycle clutch. This made possible the use of a roller chain to power the motorcycle. The first three-speed transmission was offered in 1915.

During the early 1900s the U.S. experienced rapid growth in the motorcycle industry, with firms such as Excelsior, Indian, Merkel, Thor, and Yale growing and competing. Most of the early U.S. motorcycle companies turned out shoddy, unreliable products. But this was not considered to be true for Harley-Davidson and Indian cycles. Early continued success in racing and endurance made Harleys favorites among motorcyclists. The company's V-twin engines became known for power and reliability.

During World War I, Harley-Davidson supplied the military with many motorcycles. By virtue of very strong military and domestic sales, Harley-Davidson became the largest motorcycle company in the world in 1918.[3] The company built a 300,000 square foot plant in Milwaukee, Wisconsin in 1922, making it one of the largest motorcycle factories in the world.[4]

In the late 1930s, Harley-Davidson dealt a strong competitive blow to the Indian motorcycle company: it introduced the first overhead-valve engine. The large, 61-cubic-inch engine became very popular and was thereafter referred to as the Knucklehead. Indian could not make a motorcycle to compete with these Harleys.

Harley introduced major innovations in the suspensions of its cycles in the 1940s. However, in 1949 Harley first met with international competition, from Great Britain. The British motorcycles, such as Nortons and Triumphs, were cheaper, lighter, better handling, and just as fast, even though they had smaller engines.

To counter the British threat, Harley-Davidson further improved the design of the engines, and thereby increased the horsepower of their heavier cycles. The result, in 1957, was what some consider to be the first of the modern super-bikes: the Harley Sportster. It was also during the 1950s that Harley developed the styling that made it famous.

As the 1950s drew to a close, new contenders from Japan entered the light-weight (250cc and below) motorcycle market. Harley welcomed the little bikes because it believed that small-bike customers would quickly move to larger bikes as the riders became more experienced. The Japanese cycles proved to have some staying power, however, and Japanese products began to successfully penetrate the off-road and street cycle markets. In the 1960s Japan entered the middleweight (250–500cc) market.

As Harley entered the 1960s, it made an attempt to build smaller, light-weight bikes in the U.S. But the company found it difficult to build small machines and still be profitable. As a result, Harley acquired 50% of Aermacchi, an Italian cycle producer, and built small motorcycles for both street and off-road use. The first Aermacchi Harleys were sold in 1961.[5] The Italian venture endured until 1978, but was never highly successful. Few took Harley's small cycles seriously; some Harley dealers refused to handle them. In the meantime, Japanese cycles dominated the small and middleweight markets. Harley seemed trapped in the heavyweight segment.

In an attempt to expand its production capacity and raise capital, Harley went public in 1965. The company merged with the conglomerate AMF, Inc. in 1969. AMF, a company known for its leisure and industrial products, expanded Harley's production capacity from 15,000 units in 1969 to 40,000 units in 1974.[6] With the expanded capacity, AMF pursued a milking strategy, favoring short-term profits rather than investment in research and development, and retooling. The Japanese continued to improve while Harley began to turn out heavy, noisy, vibrating, laboriously handling, poorly finished machines.

In 1975, AMF failed to react to a serious Japanese threat. Honda Motor Company introduced the Gold Wing, which quickly became the standard for large touring motorcycles, a segment that Harley had owned. At the time,

Harley's top-of-the-line touring bike sold for almost $9,000 while the comparable Honda Gold Wing was approximately $7,000.[7] Not only were Japanese cycles priced lower than similar Harleys, but Japanese manufacturing techniques yielded operating costs that were 30% lower than Harley-Davidson's.

Motorcycle enthusiasts more than ever began to go with Japanese products because of their price and performance advantages. Even some loyal Harley owners and police department contracts were lost. The company was rapidly losing ground both in technological advances and in the market.

Starting in 1975 and continuing through the middle 1980s, the Japanese companies penetrated the big-bore, custom motorcycle market with Harley look-alikes with V-twin engines.[8] The Honda Magna and Shadow, the Suzuki Intruder, and the Yamaha Virago were representative of the Japanese imitations. In a short time the Japanese captured a significant share of the large cycle segment and controlled nearly 90% of the total motorcycle market.[9]

During AMF's ownership of Harley, its motorcycles were strong on sales but relatively weak on profits. AMF did put a great deal of money into Harley and production went as high as 75,000 units in 1975.[10] But motorcycles never seemed to be AMF's priority. For example, in 1978, motorcycles accounted for 17% of its revenues but for only 1% of profits. AMF was more inclined to emphasize its industrial products and services.

THE TURNAROUND[11]	Vaughn Beals served as Harley's top manager during its last six years under AMF control. Beals was uncomfortable with AMF's short-term orientation and unwillingness to confront the problems caused by imports. Consequently, in June 1981, a subgroup of Harley management, including Beals, completed a leveraged buyout of Harley-Davidson from AMF. To celebrate, Beals and the management team made a Pennsylvania–Wisconsin motorcycle ride, proclaiming, "The Eagle Soars Alone."

Beals knew that reversing the company's momentum would not be easy, especially without the help of the former parent. Indeed, things first began to get worse. Harley suffered its first operating loss in 1981. In 1982, many motorcycles were coming off the assembly line with defects, registrations for heavyweight motorcycles were falling, and the Japanese were continuing to penetrate Harley's market segments. Company losses for the year totalled over $25 million.[12] Several Japanese companies built up inventories in the face of a declining market and engaged in aggressive price discounting.

Beals petitioned the International Trade Commission (ITC) for temporary protection from Japanese "dumping" practices in 1982. He accused the Japanese of dumping large quantities of bikes in the U.S. and selling them for prices much below what they were in Japan. The U.S. Treasury had previously found the Japanese guilty of excess-inventory practices, but the nonpartisan ITC ruled that the practices had not adversely affected the sales of Harley-Davidson motorcycles. Therefore, no sanctions were placed on the Japanese companies.

The Japanese continued price competition and many thought that Harley would soon buckle from the pressure.

However, in 1983, with the help of many public officials including Senator John Heinz of Pennsylvania, Harley was able to obtain protection from the excess-inventory practices of the Japanese. In April of 1983, President Reagan, on the recommendation of the ITC, imposed a declining five-year tariff on the wholesale prices of Japanese heavyweight (over 700cc) motorcycles. The tariff schedule was as follows:

1983	45%
1984	35%
1985	20%
1986	15%
1987	10%

The effects of the tariff were mixed. Much of the Japanese inventory was already in the U.S. when the tariff went into effect, and prices of those units were not affected. Also, dealers selling Japanese cycles sharply reduced prices on older models, and thus hurt the sale of new bikes.

On the other hand, the tariff signaled that Japanese over-production would not be tolerated, so that Harley would have some breathing room and management would have a chance to reposition the company. Beals and others inside the company felt that the dumping case and the tariff protection helped focus the company on developing its competitive strengths and on improving the production process. They also believed that the tariffs were the result of the government's recognition of Harley's overall revitalization effort. The process of whipping the once proud American company back into shape had begun several years before the tariff went into effect.

IMPROVING PRODUCTION[13]

In the early years Harley had been successfully run by engineers. Beals' background was in engineering as well, and he began to focus on the beleaguered production process. Until 1982, the company used a batch production system that produced only one model at a time. The final line work force would vary from 90–140 people depending on which model was being produced on a given day.

To make the production system more efficient, Beals, Thomas Gelb, and others on the management team implemented what they called their productivity triad that included the following:

1. An inventory system that supplied materials as needed.
2. An employee involvement and development program.
3. A computer-aided design and manufacturing program.

The Materials As Needed (MAN) system stabilized the production schedule, and helped reduce excess inventory. Under this system, production worked with marketing to make more accurate demand forecasts for each model. Based on these forecasts, precise production schedules were established for a given month and were not allowed to vary by more than 10% in subsequent months. A production method was adopted whereby a different mix of models was produced every day. This was referred to as the "jelly bean" method.

Under the MAN system, Harley also required its suppliers to become more compliant to its quality requirements. Harley offered long-term contracts to suppliers who conformed to the quality requirements and who delivered only the exact quantity needed for a given period of time. Harley also integrated backward into transporting materials from suppliers: when the Harley-Davidson transportation company made scheduled pickups from suppliers, Harley had greater control over the shipments, and was thereby able to cut costs.

Before the 1983 tariff was imposed, Beals, Gelb, and others visited several Japanese motorcycle plants and learned the importance of employee development and employee involvement. As a result, rigorous training programs were developed. By 1986, over one-third of the employees were trained in statistical process control, or the ability to sample and analyze data while performing a job. Set-up times were reduced with the use of ideas gleaned from quality circles—problem-solving sessions between workers, managers, and engineers.

Further improvements in the production process were made by Walter Anderson, senior production engineer, with the help of Harley employees and management. Whereas components had formerly run down straight lines, Anderson organized workers into a series of "work cells." A work cell consisted of a few workers in a small area with all the machines and tools they needed to complete a job. The work cells were often arranged in U-shaped configurations that allowed for intensive work within a cell and reduced the total movement of components through the process. The use of cells also improved employee efficiency, because workers stayed at the same work station all day yet enjoyed variety in their tasks.

Harley also invested heavily in research and development. One payoff of this investment was a computer-aided design (CAD) system developed by the research and development group, that allowed management to make changes in the entire product line while maintaining elements of the traditional styling. The company's R&D group developed a more efficient engine in 1983 and a new suspension in 1984. Harley was soon recognized to be an industry leader in many aspects of production, including belt-drive technology, vibration isolation, and steering geometry. Since 1981, the company had allocated a major portion of its revenues to R&D each year.

Beals' emphasis on production brought big payoffs for the company. Harley's defect rate was reduced to nearly perfect, 1% in 1986. The company also lowered its breakeven point from 53,000 units in 1982, to 35,000 units in 1986.[14] Many companies visited Harley for seminars and advice on how to improve efficiency.

EXHIBIT 27.2   **Facilities, Harley-Davidson, Inc.**

Type of Facility	LOCATION	AREA (sq. feet)	STATUS
Executive offices, engineering and warehouse	Milwaukee, Wisconsin	502,720	Owned
Manufacturing	Wauwatosa, Wisconsin	342,430	Owned
Manufacturing	Tomahawk, Wisconsin	50,600	Owned
Manufacturing	York, Pennsylvania	869,580	Owned
Engineering test laboratory	Milwaukee, Wisconsin	6,500	Lease expiring 1991
Motorcycle testing	Talladega, Alabama	9,326	Lease expiring 1988
International offices	Danbury, Connecticut	2,850	Lease expiring 1988
Office and workshop	Raunheim, West Germany	4,300	Lease expiring 1989

SOURCE: Dean Witter Reynolds, *1986 Prospectus.*

Perhaps one of the greatest indicators of Harley's production turnaround was evidenced through one of their oldest pieces of equipment—a huge, sheet-metal forming machine known simply as the "Tool." The Tool, originally built in Milwaukee but later moved to the York plant in Pennsylvania, was used to forge the "Fat Bob" gas tanks for all the FX and FXR series bikes. There was no operating manual nor maintenance book for the Tool, yet the company still used this old legendary machine to crank out modern, high-quality products (see Exhibit 27.2).

In March, 1987, Vaughn Beals appeared before a Washington, D.C. news conference and offered to give up the tariff protection, which was intended to last until the middle of 1988. Congress praised the announcement and commended the company for its success. President Reagan even visited the York plant in celebration of the event.

CORPORATE STRUCTURE[15]

According to Beals, one of the most important contributions to the company's turnaround was the savings obtained by a drastic reduction in salaried staff, a result of Beals' exposure to the Japanese management systems. The number of managers at each plant was reduced, and each manager was given responsibility for everything at the plant: hiring, operations, productivity, etc.

The number of line employees was also reduced. Line employees were given individual responsibility to inspect products for defects, apply quality-control measures, determine quotas and goals, and make production decisions.

A majority of the company's employees participated actively in quality-circle programs. The quality circles were used not only to improve efficiency but also to address other issues. One such issue was job security. Both the reduction in staff and the increased productivity caused workers to worry about their jobs. However, the quality circles came up with the idea to move some sourcing and fabricating of parts in-house. In-house sourcing made it possible for many employees, who may have otherwise been laid off, to retain their jobs.

Harley's corporate staff was made very lean and the structure was simplified. Top executive officers were put in charge of functional areas. Under top management, the company was basically organized into two divisions—motorcycles and defense. Holiday Rambler Corporation became a wholly owned subsidiary in 1986.

TOP MANAGEMENT[16]

Vaughn L. Beals, Jr. was appointed as the Chief Executive Officer and Chairman of the Board of Directors of Harley-Davidson motor company following the buyout from AMF in 1981. He had originally earned an engineering degree from the Massachusetts Institute of Technology. He worked as a logging-machine manufacturer and as a diesel engine maker before joining AMF in 1975. In 1981, along with one of the grandsons of the founder and twelve other persons, he led the leveraged buyout of the Harley-Davidson Motor Company.

EXHIBIT 27.3

Board of Directors, Harley-Davidson, Inc.

Vaugh L. Beals, Jr.
Chairman, President and Chief Executive Officer—Harley-Davidson, Inc., Milwaukee, Wisconsin

Frederick L. Brengel
Chairman and Chief Executive Officer—Johnson Controls, Inc., Milwaukee, Wisconsin

F. Trevor Deeley
Chairman and Chief Executive Officer—Fred Deeley Imports, Richmond, British Columbia, Canada

Dr. Michael J. Kami
President—Corporate Planning, Inc., Lighthouse Point, Florida

Richard Hermon-Taylor
Management Consultant, South Hamilton, Massachusetts

Richard F. Teerlink
Vice President, Treasurer and Chief Financial Officer—Harley-Davidson, Inc., Milwaukee, Wisconsin

SOURCE: Harley-Davidson Inc., *1986 Annual Report.*

He was known throughout the company for his devotion and enthusiasm for motorcycles. He owned a Harley deluxe Electra-Glide and rode it on business trips whenever possible.

Harley's top management always demonstrated their willingness to take a "hog" on the road for a worthy cause. On one occasion, in 1985, Beals and a product designer, William G. Davidson (known as "Willie G"), led a caravan of Harleys from California to New York in an effort to raise money for the Statue of Liberty renovation. At the conclusion of the ride, Beals presented a check for $250,000 to the Statue Foundation.

Beals claimed that his major responsibility was for product-quality improvements. On one occasion, during a business trip, Beals noticed a defect in a 1986 model's seat. He stopped long enough to call the factory about the problem. The workers and test riders, however, had already found and corrected the flaw.

Beals made an all-out effort to keep managerial levels in the company to a minimum. The Board of Directors was composed of six officers, four of whom were from outside the company. The CEO often communicated with everyone in the company through memos known as "Beals'-grams" (see Exhibits 27.3 and 27.4).

Because of the company's success, and in an effort to provide additional capital for growth, Harley went public with an offering of approximately 6

EXHIBIT 27.4 | **Harley-Davidson Executive Officers**

	AGE	POSITION	YEARS WITH COMPANY[1]	ANNUAL COMPENSATION
Vaughn L. Beals	58	Chairman and CEO	10	$207,217
Richard F. Teerlink	49	Vice-President, Chief Finance Officer	5	$143,375
Jeffrey L. Bleustein	46	Vice-President, Parts and Accessories	15	$118,387
Thomas A. Gelb	50	Vice-President, Operations	21	$132,666
James H. Paterson	38	Vice-President, Marketing	15	$ 95,728
Peter L. Profumo	39	Vice-President, Program Management	17	$129,521

SOURCE: Dean Witter Reynolds., *1986 Prospectus.*
NOTE: [1] Years with Harley-Davidson or AMF, Inc.

million shares in the summer of 1986. Beals owned nearly 16% of the Harley-Davidson stock, which was then increasing in value.

HUMAN RESOURCE MANAGEMENT[17]

Harley-Davidson employed approximately 2,336 people in 1986. This number was down from that of 3,840 in 1981. Under Chief Executive Beals, the company made great strides in developing a participative, cooperative, less hierarchical work climate. Employees wrote their own job descriptions and actively participated in on-the-job training. Employees learned that they were responsible for not only their own jobs, but for helping others learn as well. Performance was evaluated through a peer review program.

The company developed many career and placement opportunity programs as a response to employees' concern over job security. Harley also entered into a cooperative placement agreement with other Wisconsin unions. The company even developed a voluntary layoff program, in which senior workers voluntarily took themselves off in down times to protect the jobs of newer workers. Harley offered sophisticated health and retirement benefits, and has also developed employee wellness and college tuition funding programs.

FINANCIAL PERFORMANCE

Harley was purchased from AMF through a leveraged buyout in 1981, for approximately $65 million.[18] The buyout was financed with a $30 million term loan and $35 million in revolving credit from institutional lenders. AMF also received $9 million of securities in the form of preferred stock. In 1984, the two companies reached an agreement whereby the preferred stock held by AMF was cancelled and subsequent payments were to be made directly to AMF from future Harley-Davidson profits.

In 1985, Harley negotiated an exchange of common stock for forgiveness of a portion of the loans. The company offered $70 million in subordinated notes and $20 million in stock for public sale in 1986. The proceeds from this sale were used to repay a portion of the debt to AMF, to refinance unfavorable loans, to provide financing for the Holiday acquisition, and to provide working capital.

Holiday Rambler Corporation was a privately held company until its acquisition by Harley in 1986. Holiday Rambler performed very well in its first year as part of Harley-Davidson. It.had total sales of approximately $257 million through September of 1987, compared to $208 million for the same period in 1986; this was nearly a 24% increase.

Harley-Davidson's net sales and profitability improved during the years 1982 to 1986. Net income and earnings per share fluctuated in that period. The motorcycle division's sales as a percentage of total sales decreased, because of the rapid increase in the defense division. In the years following the 1981 buyout, the company relied greatly on credit for working capital (see Exhibits 27.5, 27.6, and 27.7).

EXHIBIT 27.5   **Consolidated Balance Sheet, Harley-Davidson, Inc.**

(Dollar Amounts in Thousands)

Year Ended December 31	1984	1985	1986
Assets			
Current assets			
Cash	$ 2,056	$ 9,070	$ 7,345
Temporary investments	—	4,400	20,500
Accounts receivable net of allowance for doubtful accounts	27,767	27,313	36,462
Inventories	32,736	28,868	78,630
Prepaid expenses	2,613	3,241	5,812
Total current assets	65,172	72,892	148,758
Property, plant and equipment, at cost, less accumulated depreciation and amortization	33,512	38,727	90,932
Deferred financing costs	—	2,392	3,340
Intangible assets	—	—	82,114
Other assets	523	81	2,052
Total assets	$99,207	$114,092	$327,196
Liabilities and Stockholders' Equity			
Current liabilities:			
Notes payable	$ —	$ —	$ 14,067
Current maturities of long-term debt	2,305	2,875	4,023
Accounts payable	21,880	27,521	29,587
Accrued expenses and other liabilities	24,231	26,251	61,144
Total current liabilities	48,416	56,647	108,821
Long-term debt, less current maturities	56,258	51,504	191,594
Long-term pension liability	856	1,319	622
Stockholders' equity			
Common stock 6,200,000 issued in 1986 and 4,200,000 in 1985	42	42	62
Class B common stock, no shares issued	—	—	—
Additional paid-in capital	9,308	10,258	26,657
Deficit	(15,543)	(5,588)	(717)
Cumulative foreign currency translation adjustment	—	40	287
	(6,193)	4,752	26,289
Less treasury stock (520,000 shares) at cost	(130)	(130)	(130)
Total stockholders' equity	(6,323)	4,622	26,159
Total liabilities and stockholders' equity	$99,207	$114,092	$327,196

SOURCES: Harley-Davidson Inc., *1986 Annual Report*; Dean Witter Reynolds, *1986 Prospectus*.

EXHIBIT 27.6 Consolidated Statements of Income, Harley-Davidson, Inc.
(Dollar Amounts in Thousands Except Per-Share Data)

Year Ended December 31	1982	1983	1984	1985	1986
Income statement data:					
Net sales	$ 210,055	$ 253,505	$ 293,825	$ 287,476	$ 295,322
Cost of goods sold	174,967	194,271	220,040	217,222	219,167
Gross profit	35,088	59,234	73,785	70,254	76,153
Operating expenses:					
Selling and administrative	37,510	36,441	47,662	47,162	51,060
Engineering, research and development	13,072	9,320	10,591	10,179	8,999
Total operating expenses	50,582	45,761	58,253	57,341	60,059
Income (loss) from operations	(15,494)	13,473	15,532	12,913	16,096
Other income (expenses):					
Interest expense	(15,778)	(11,782)	(11,256)	(9,412)	(8,373)
Other	(1,272)	188	(311)	(388)	(388)
	(17,050)	(11,594)	(11,567)	(9,750)	(8,761)
Income (loss) before provision (credit) for income taxes, extraordinary items, and cumulative effect of change in accounting principle	(32,544)	1,879	3,965	3,163	7,335
Provision (credit) for income taxes	(7,467)	906	1,077	526	3,028
Income (loss) before extraordinary items and cumulative effect of change in accounting principle	(25,077)	973	2,888	2,637	4,307
Extraordinary items and cumulative effect of change in accounting principle	—	7,795	3,578	7,318	564
Net income (loss)	$ (25,077)	$ 8,768	$ 6,466	$ 9,955	$ 4,871
Average number of common shares outstanding	4,016,664	3,720,000	3,680,000	3,680,000	5,235,230
Per common share					
Income (loss) before extraordinary items and cumulative effect of change in accounting principle	$ (6.61)	$ 0.26	$ 0.79	$ 0.72	$ 0.82
Extraordinary items and cumulative effect of change in accounting principle	—	2.10	0.97	1.99	0.11
Net income (loss)	$ (6.61)	$ 2.36	$ 1.76	$ 2.71	$ .93

SOURCE: Harley-Davidson, Inc., *1986 Annual Report.*

EXHIBIT 27.7

Sales and Income by Business Segment, Harley-Davidson, Inc.

(Dollar Amounts in Thousands)

	1983	1984	1985
Net sales			
Motorcycles and related products	$229,412	$260,745	$240,631
Defense and other businesses	24,093	33,080	46,845
	$253,505	$293,825	$287,476
Income from operations:			
Motorcycles and related products	$ 16,513	$ 15,489	$ 9,980
Defense and other businesses	3,566	7,012	9,390
General corporate expenses	(6,606)	(6,969)	(6,457)
	13,473	15,532	12,913
Interest expense	(11,782)	(11,256)	(9,412)
Other	188	(311)	(338)
Income before income taxes, extraordinary items and cumulative effect of change in accounting principle	$ 1,879	$ 3,965	$ 3,163

SOURCE: Dean Witter Reynolds, *1986 Prospectus.*

MARKETING STRATEGY

Harley-Davidson's marketing efforts centered around the use of the Harley name. The company emphasized that its name was synonymous with quality, reliability, and styling. Company research indicated a 90% repurchase rate, or loyalty factor, by Harley owners.

Harley's marketing concentrated on dealer promotions, magazine advertising, direct mail advertising, sponsorship of racing activities, and the organization of the Harley Owners Group (HOG). The HOG club had enrolled 77,000 members by 1987, and permitted the company to have close contact with customers. Another major form of advertising was accomplished through the licensing of the Harley name, which was very profitable and served to promote the company's image.

In addition, Harley sponsored or co-sponsored organizations such as the Ellis Island Statue of Liberty Foundation and the Muscular Dystrophy Association.

The company was also the first motorcycle manufacturer to offer a national program of demonstration rides. Some dealers felt the program, introduced in 1984, resulted in a large number of Harley motorcycle purchases.

The company also directed a portion of its marketing expenditures toward expanding the field sales force, in an effort to assist the domestic dealer network. In some areas the sales force developed local marketing programs to train dealers.

THE HARLEY IMAGE

Few companies could elicit the name recognition and brand loyalty of Harley-Davidson. Harley's appeal was based on the thrill and prestige of owning and riding the king of the big bikes. Harleys were known as sturdy, powerful, macho bikes; not for wimps and kids, they were true bikes for the open road, bikes for driving through brick walls!

A worrisome problem with the Harley image, however, was the perceptual connection of Harleys exclusively with "outlaw" groups. The negative "Road Warrior" image affected sales in some areas to such a degree that the company initiated a public relations campaign. They gently attacked the biker image by directing much of their advertising toward young professionals. The message was that Harley-Davidson represented fun, recreation, and reliability. The company heralded the fact that famous professionals such as Malcolm Forbes and Reggie Jackson rode Harleys, and advertisements picturing these celebrities atop their "hogs" further helped the company's image. The campaign seemed to work. More doctors, lawyers, and dentists began to purchase Harleys.

Harley also put tighter controls on licensing its name, ensuring that it was not used in obscene ways. Harley was careful not to alienate their loyal "biker" customers, however. And the company continued to promulgate, even enhance, its tough image, through advertising in motorcycle magazines. For example, one ad pictured a group of rather tough looking bikers and had a caption which read: "Would you sell an unreliable bike to these guys? We Don't!" Another ad showed a junkyard filled with scrapped Japanese bikes. The caption was: "Can you find a Harley in here?"

A related problem with its image was that Harley could not attract very many women customers. This was due to the image and to the size of the bikes. Harleys were very big and heavy. The Harley low-rider series was attracting some women customers because the bikes were lower and easier to get on. Notwithstanding this partial success, some Japanese companies introduced smaller, lighter, low-riding, inexpensive, Harley look-alikes in a straightforward attempt to attract women buyers. Honda's Rebel (250cc) was one such bike that became fairly successful with women.

Perhaps the most objective indicator of the strength of the image came from an unlikely source—Japan itself! The Japanese made numerous attempts to copy Milwaukee designs.[19] For example, Suzuki's 1987 Intruder (1400cc) went to great lengths to hide the radiator—because Harleys were air cooled. Yamaha's Virago (1100cc) and Kawasaki's Vulcan (1500cc) were V-twin street bikes conspicuously styled in the Harley tradition. Nevertheless, some analysts felt that Japanese imitations only served to strengthen the mystique of the original. The more the Japanese tried to make look-alike bikes, the more the real thing increased in value. Beals agreed. He maintained that Harleys were built to last longer and have a higher resale than other bikes.

DIVERSIFICATION STRATEGY

Harley-Davidson competed in the heavyweight motorcycle market segment since the early years of the company. Heavyweight bikes were divided into three categories: touring/custom, standard street, and performance motorcycles. Harley was never totally successful in building smaller bikes, and at one time Beals was even quoted as saying that Harley would not attempt to build small bikes in the future.

Harley-Davidson had made attempts to diversify throughout its history. However, its current motorcycle product line was very narrow compared to those of its competitors. The company's management thought about breaking out of its narrow niche by expanding into international markets. The largest export markets for Harley were Canada, Australia, and West Germany.

In 1971, Harley attempted to diversify by manufacturing its own line of snowmobiles. The seasonal nature of the business and intense Japanese competition caused the company to abandon the product in 1975.

Another attempt at diversification was the company's purchase of a small three-wheeler firm named Trihawk in 1984. Shortly thereafter the company realized it could not make a go of it in this market because of high start-up costs, and the project was terminated.

Under Beals the company moved into the manufacturing of casings for artillery shells and rocket engines for military target drones. Beals set corporate goals to increase the level of defense-related business in an attempt to diversify the company. Thus, the company became very active in making bids for the design and development of defense products. The defense business was very profitable for Harley.

Accessories, bike parts, clothing, "leathers," even furniture associated with the Harley name were big business for the company. Brand-name licensing and related accessories generated about as much income as did the motorcycles.

But Beals wanted to move the company into other businesses not related to the rather narrow motorcycle line and not located in an industry with Japanese competitors. He felt Harley needed to diversify in order to be a truly stable performer. That is why Harley acquired the Holiday Rambler Company in December of 1986. Beals saw the fit as a good one because Holiday was a recreational vehicle producer and was what he called "manufacturing intensive" just as Harley was.

Holiday Rambler manufactured premium motorhomes, specialized commercial vehicles, and travel trailers. Holiday employed 2,300 people and was headquartered in Wakarusa, Indiana. Holiday was the largest privately owned maker of recreational vehicles at the time of the acquisition. The company was recognized as one of the leaders in the premium-class motorhome and towable-trailer markets. It ranked fourth, in 1986, in market share in the motorhome market and fifth in towable recreational vehicles. Its products were gaining share in the industry as a whole.

A Holiday subsidiary, Utilimaster, built truck trailers and bodies for commercial uses. The company had contracts with companies such as Purolator Courier and Ryder Truck Rentals. Other Holiday subsidiaries produced office furniture, custom wood products, custom tools, van conversions, and park trailers.

Even with the Holiday acquisition and with the success in defense, Harley looked for other means of diversifying. In September of 1986, a tobacco company purchased a license to test market Harley-Davidson brand cigarettes.

THE FUTURE

The Harley turnaround, in the face of stiff competition, caused the company to be viewed as an example of what can be accomplished by use of modern production and personnel-management techniques. Top management was committed to keeping the company lean and viable. Yet they knew they needed to diversify and change. Beals knew that this company needed to become as tough as its image.

Beals focused his turnaround effort on the internal operating efficiency of the company. Now he needed to provide leadership for a newly acquired subsidiary and plan for growth in the defense division.

He also faced the challenge of breaking the company out of its narrow market segment in its bread-and-butter division: motorcycles. Could he plan for growth and market penetration in the motorcycle industry? Or should he be content with maintaining Harley as a big bike company only?

Since 1903, 150 American motorcycle companies had come and gone. Harley-Davidson Motor Company, with Vaughn Beals at the helm, was the only one that survived. The eagle continued to soar alone.

NOTES

1. Harley-Davidson, Inc., *1986 Annual Report*.

2. David K. Wright, *The Harley-Davidson Motor Company: An Official Eighty-Year History*, second edition (Osceola, Wisconsin: Motorbooks International), 1987.

3. *Ibid.*, p. 17.

4. *Ibid.*, p. 17.

5. *Ibid.*, p. 35.

6. *Ibid.*, pp. 282–283.

7. "Uneasy Rider: Harley Pleads for Relief," *Time*, December 13, 1982, p. 61.

8. Wright, *The Harley-Davidson Motor Company*, pp. 244–262.

9. "Trade Protection: Mind My (Motor) Bike," *The Economist*, July 2, 1977, p. 82.

10. Wright, *The Harley-Davidson Motor Company*, p. 281.

11. *Ibid.*, pp. 244–262.

12. Dean Witter Reynolds, *Prospectus*, Harley-Davidson, Inc., July 8, 1986, p. 8.

13. Rod Willis, "Harley-Davidson Comes Roaring Back," *Management Review*, October 1986, pp. 20–27.

14. *Ibid.*

15. *Ibid.*

16. Jeff Baily, "Beals Takes Harley-Davidson on New Road," *Wall Street Journal*, March 20, 1987, p. 39.

17. Willis, "Harley-Davidson Comes Roaring Back," pp. 20–27.

18. Dean Witter Reynolds, *Prospectus*, Harley-Davidson, Inc., p. 10.

19. "Why Milwaukee Won't Die," *Cycle*, June 1987, pp. 35–41.

Bombardier

JOSEPH LAMPEL • JAMAL SHAMSIE

I want a company with a continuous flow, that is not subject to the drastic fluctuations of being in just one business.[1]

These were the words of Laurent Beaudoin, Chairman of Bombardier, as he
contemplated his company's dramatic rise to prominence during the 1960s and
1970s. The Canadian company's name had been at one point synonymous with
snowmobiles. Its pioneering efforts in the development and the launching of
the Ski-Doo had been handsomely rewarded. By the late 1960s, Bombardier
controlled close to 50% of the snowmobile market—about three times as much
as its closest competitor (see Exhibit 28.1).

Notwithstanding this success, Laurent Beaudoin had long believed that the
fortunes of his company were too closely tied to a single product. Thus, even
before the demand for snowmobiles began to slow down, Bombardier took
steps to insulate itself from the uncertainties of the recreational market.
Throughout the 1970s, Beaudoin led the company on an aggressive strategy of
diversification into other areas of leisure and transportation.

As the company moved into the 1980s, its revenues had grown considerably
beyond the $165 million that it had generated from snowmobiles at the start
of the previous decade. But while Bombardier's revenues grew dramatically, it
continued to experience wide swings in profits (see Exhibit 28.2). In fact,
Beaudoin had only recently managed to move Bombardier away from two consecutive years of losses, including the single largest loss that it had ever incurred.

GROWING WITH SNOWMOBILES

Birth of the Snowmobile

Work on the snowmobile was first started in the mid-1920s by Joseph-Armand
Bombardier in his father's garage at Valcourt, Quebec. But it took until 1935
before Joseph-Armand had built the first snowmobile. It consisted of a large
plywood body set on caterpillar tracks and driven by a heavy, conventional
internal combustion engine.

These early snowmobiles were hand-assembled in versions intended to accommodate from 5 to 25 passengers. In each case, the machine was individually
adapted for a specific use according to the wishes of different customers. By
1942, Joseph-Armand had incorporated his garage to form Bombardier Snowmobile, Limited, and was producing snowmobiles to serve doctors, missionaries,
woodmen, foresters, trappers, and farmers in outlying districts of Quebec.

This case was prepared by Professor Joseph Lampel of New York University and Professor Jamal
Shamsie of McGill University. Copyright © 1988 by Joseph Lampel and Jamal Shamsie. Reprinted
by permission.

EXHIBIT 28.1	**Snowmobile Sales in Units**		
	SEASON	INDUSTRY	BOMBARDIER
	1963–1964	17,000	8,000
	1964–1965	30,000	14,000
	1965–1966	60,000	26,000
	1966–1967	120,000	48,000
	1967–1968	170,000	78,000
	1968–1969	250,000	120,000
	1969–1970	415,000	170,000
	1970–1971	540,000	195,000
	1971–1972	530,000	190,000
	1972–1973	515,000	150,000
	1973–1974	400,000	110,000
	1974–1975	330,000	84,000
	1975–1976	245,000	67,000
	1976–1977	195,000	62,000
	1977–1978	225,000	68,000
	1978–1979	270,000	72,000
	1979–1980	200,000	55,000
	1980–1981	180,000	60,000
	1981–1982	145,000	55,000
	1982–1983	105,000	37,000
	1983–1984	115,000	38,000
	1984–1985	100,000	34,000
	1985–1986	110,000	39,000

SOURCE: Bombardier Annual Reports.

With the advent of World War II, the basic snowmobile design was adapted to produce an amphitrack armoured carrier called the "Penguin" for use by Canadian troops. Subsequently, the demonstrated durability and ruggedness of the snowmobile also led to the development and production of various forms of specialized industrial equipment. These consisted of machines that were especially suited for use in forestry, logging, oil exploration, and snow removal.

Eventually, Joseph-Armand and his son Germain tackled the challenge of developing and producing a smaller and lighter version of the basic snowmobile design intended to carry one or two persons. The key to the new design was the coupling of a recently introduced two-cycle motor-scooter engine with an all-rubber track that had internal steel rods built in for added strength. By 1959, the first snowmobile directed at the individual user was introduced into the

EXHIBIT 28.2

Income Statements, Bombardier, Inc.

(Canadian Dollar Amounts in Millions; Year Ended January 31)

	1981	1982	1983	1984	1985	1986
Net Sales	$394.4	$448.8	$551.1	$491.0	$515.5	$656.6
Cost of sales	310.8	368.1	452.6	418.9	428.8	557.5
Selling & administrative	72.2	85.4	62.1	50.0	58.7	56.2
Depreciation & amortization	8.1	9.9	11.3	10.8	15.6	21.5
Other income	(1.0)	(0.5)	(2.7)	(7.5)	(11.2)	(12.2)
Interest on long-term debt	3.1	8.3	7.5	5.6	6.7	5.2
Other interest	9.4	11.5	10.1	2.8	0.1	1.6
Income taxes	(2.4)	(15.4)	4.1	4.1	6.7	10.7
Net income (Net loss)	($5.8)	($18.5)	$6.1	$6.3	$10.1	$16.1

SOURCE: Bombardier Annual Reports.

market. Initially, Joseph-Armand thought of calling his invention the Ski-Dog, but he decided in favour of a more bilingual name, the Ski-Doo.

Development of the Snowmobile

When he died in 1964, Joseph-Armand Bombardier left behind a company that had 700 employees and a product that was enjoying increasing popularity: 16,500 Ski-Doos had been sold, and demand was clearly on the rise. Joseph-Armand's son, Germain, took over as President, but shortly thereafter relinquished his post for reasons of health. The company passed into the hands of son-in-law Laurent Beaudoin, a chartered accountant and one of the first management graduates of the University of Sherbrooke. Beaudoin realized that certain factors were standing in the way of the development of the full potential of the snowmobile:

> There were two fundamental problems arising from the nature of the company's beginnings. First, there was no research and development department because it had all taken place in the mind of Joseph-Armand Bombardier. Second, the company which he created was, very naturally, a production-oriented company. It produced machines to fill a market need, which was mainly for large machines to do practical jobs, rather than creating and seeking out new markets.[2]

Beaudoin introduced an R&D section, set up an integrated marketing system, and geared up facilities for efficient mass production. Extensive research confirmed that an untapped snowmobile market existed not only for transport, but also for recreation and sport. Bombardier invested heavily in the development of this potential market. Over the next several years, massive advertising, combined with the establishment of a dealership network, culminated in the setting up of eighteen regional sales groups covering Canada, the U.S., and Europe. These efforts resulted in making Bombardier a leader in the snowmobile market, and turned the Ski-Doo trademark into a generic term for snowmobiles.

But the success of Bombardier also brought about the entry of new producers of snowmobiles. Most of the new competition came from U.S. companies that had been closely watching the development of the snowmobile business. Beaudoin, however, was not fazed at the prospect of more competition. He was confident about the capabilities of his company to maintain its leadership:

> It's an industry that looks very simple. Everybody looks and says: "Gee, we can get in tomorrow morning and grab everything." But it's not that simple. The advantage we have over all those companies is that we eat snow, we know snow, and are snowmobilers ourselves.[3]

In order to ensure that he could meet this growing competition, Beaudoin also decided to start acquiring almost all of his suppliers, most of which were situated within the Province of Quebec. These acquisitions led to the development of a series of subsidiaries and affiliates that manufactured parts or accessories related to snowmobile production (see Exhibit 28.3). This push for acquisitions eventually climaxed in the $30-million purchase of Rotax-Werk A.G. Located in Austria, Rotax-Werk manufactured the two-stroke engines used in the Ski-Doos. By 1970, Bombardier's own production facilities or those of its subsidiaries and affiliates were supplying over 90% of the 1,400 parts that went into the manufacturing of the Ski-Doo. Beaudoin saw these moves as a necessary precaution against an eventual intensification of competition—in particular, the likely outbreak of price wars: "If there is any price war, we will be in a position to face it. This has been our first idea."[4]

Shortly thereafter, Bombardier moved to buy out its largest competitor. In 1971, it finalized the acquisition of Moto-Ski from its U.S. parent, Giffin Industries. This acquisition consolidated Bombardier's domination of the snowmobile market. By this time, the achievements and stature of Bombardier were acclaimed as a product of Canadian imagination and entrepreneurial vigour. An article, published at the beginning of 1972, bestowed praise upon the company:

> Not many companies can claim to have started an entirely new industry—fewer still to have done so and stayed ahead of the pack. Bombardier Ltd. has done just that ... It is a company owned and managed by Canadians, which several foreign companies would dearly love to own. It is the largest Quebec-owned company operating in the province, and is one of the 200 most profitable public companies in Canada.[5]

EXHIBIT 28.3   ## Acquired Manufacturing Companies, Bombardier Inc.

YEAR OF ACQUISITION	NAME AND LOCATION OF COMPANY	TYPE OF BUSINESS
1957	Rockland Industries Kingsbury, Quebec[5]	Rubber parts
1968	La Salle Plastic Richmond, Quebec[5]	Plastic parts
1969	Roski Roxton Falls, Quebec[5]	Fiberglass products
1970	Lohnerwerke Vienna, Austria Rotax-Werk Gunskirchen, Austria	Streetcars Engines
1970	Walker Manufacturing Company Montreal, Quebec[5]	Sportswear
1970	Drummond Automatic Plating Drummondville, Quebec[3]	Chrome plating
1970	Jarry Precision Montreal, Quebec[1]	Transmissions
1971	Moto-Ski La Pocatiere, Quebec[2]	Snowmobiles
1972	Ville Marie Upholstering Beauport, Quebec[4]	Foam seats
1976	Montreal Locomotive Works Montreal, Quebec	Locomotives Diesel engines
1980	Heroux Longueuil, Quebec[6]	Aeronautical parts
1984	Alco Power Auburn, N.Y.	Locomotives Diesel engines

SOURCE: Financial Post Corporation Service.

NOTES: [1] closed down in 1973   [4] disposed in 1979
       [2] dissolved in 1975   [5] disposed in 1983
       [3] disposed in 1976   [6] disposed in 1985

The Crunch for Snowmobiles

The early 1970s saw an increasing number of companies competing in the snow-mobile market. In addition to new American and Canadian firms, Bombardier saw the entry of Swedish, Italian, and Japanese manufacturers. Yet while the number of competitors was increasing, market growth in snowmobiles was slowing down.

Several reasons were advanced for the softening of snowmobile sales. The main blame was put on the stagnant economy, which was seen as the principal cause of the decline in demand. Snowmobiles constituted a type of purchase that was often postponed by consumers during a downturn in the economy. Other reasons were more peculiar to the snowmobile market. Poor winters, with late snow and unusually low precipitation, reduced the recreational use of snowmobiles. At the same time, newspaper stories of crashes and decapitated riders led to a mounting concern over the safety of snowmobiles. Finally, environmentalists were vocal in their criticism of the high noise levels generated by snowmobiles, particularly in wilderness areas.

There was growing awareness that stricter legislation covering the design and use of snowmobiles was likely to be forthcoming. For its part, Bombardier attempted to meet these concerns by trying to design better safety features and special mufflers for their upcoming snowmobile models. It also produced films, slides, and brochures on safety measures and the proper use of the snowmobile. Furthermore, a newly created public relations department tried to involve the various levels of government and different types of businesses in the creation of a system comparable to the one found in the ski industry. This was to include the development of snowmobile trails, snowmobile weekends, and snowmobile resorts.

Early in 1973, it looked like demand would increase again. But the sudden fuel crisis dampened the hopes of Bombardier. Its sales of snowmobiles continued to decline sharply, down from the high of 195,000 units sold during the winter of 1970–1971 (see Exhibit 28.1). This downturn was accompanied by consecutive losses of $5.8 million in 1973 and $7.3 million in 1974.

Beaudoin initially attributed the poor performance of Bombardier to the general state of the snowmobile industry, but eventually he acknowledged that Bombardier's position in the depressed snowmobile market had also been slipping. From a 40% share in 1970, based on the Ski-Doo alone, the company's share had declined to about 25% for the combined Ski-Doo and Moto-Ski brands. The competition had been closing in on Bombardier's leadership, causing it to have second thoughts about the merits of the industry which it had pioneered.

MOVING AWAY FROM SNOWMOBILES

In 1974, Bombardier seized upon an opportunity to bid on a four-year, $118-million contract to build 423 new cars for the proposed extension of the Montreal subway system. The bid represented a major departure from the core business of the company. It was not, however, the first time that Bombardier had ventured away from snowmobiles.

Early Moves

Even before the snowmobile market was developed, Bombardier had been producing all-terrain tracked and wheeled vehicles for different kinds of industrial use. The company had continuously developed and marketed many basic types or sizes of vehicles for work in swamps, forests, and snow. The earliest of these were the Muskeg series of carriers, tractors, and brushcutters that were used in logging, construction, petroleum, and mining. Later developments included the SW series for urban snow removal, the Skidozer line for grooming snowmobile trails and ski slopes, and the Bombi carrier for transporting people over snowy or marshy terrain.

A further departure from snowmobiles came as a result of Bombardier's acquisition of suppliers (see Exhibit 28.3). Originally, the acquisitions were undertaken in order to consolidate the company's position in the snowmobile market. Once made, they presented attractive opportunities. For example, Rotax-Werk was acquired in 1970 because it supplied the engines that were used on Ski-Doos. But it also manufactured engines for boats and motorcycles. Another acquired subsidiary proceeded to develop and introduce a new type of fiberglass sailboat, followed by a canoe and a catamaran.

In addition, the success of the snowmobile created other ancillary markets. For instance, travelling on snowmobiles at 40 miles per hour in subfreezing temperatures required specialized clothing. Beaudoin saw this new type of market as a promising opportunity:

> Someone was going to have to supply wet-proof clothing that was warm enough to prevent our customers from freezing to death on our machines. We decided it might as well be us.[6]

Consequently, Bombardier acquired an apparel manufacturer in order to introduce snowmobile clothing. This led the company into the sportswear market because the acquired manufacturer was already engaged in the production and marketing of several other types of sportswear. Said Beaudoin: "We are in the leisure business."[7]

In other instances, Bombardier sought to enter markets not directly related to its core snowmobile business. In 1970, the company introduced a new product called the Sea-Doo, which was a kind of snowmobile on water. It was marketed most heavily in Florida and California. Unfortunately, the Sea-Doo was found to rust in salt water, and production was suspended after a couple of years. A more technically successful product was the Can-Am motorcycle, which was test marketed by Bombardier in 1973. The idea for the motorcycle originated with the development of a new engine by Bombardier's new Rotax subsidiary in Austria. The result was a light, high-performance motorcycle that quickly gained recognition after it won several races in Canada, the United States, and Europe.

New Thrust

It was around this time that Bombardier began to see mass transit as a potentially lucrative market. As Beaudoin put it some time later, the company had already entered into this line of business when it had purchased Rotax-Werk in 1970:

> We acquired Rotax-Werk . . . and its parent company, Lohnerwerke, which made tramways for the city of Vienna, came along with it. We didn't intend to stay in the mass transit business, but at first sign of the energy crisis, that changed.[8]

The move was facilitated by overtures to Bombardier from the French-based Compagnie Industrielle de Matériel de Transport (CIMT). CIMT had been involved in a partnership with Canadian Vickers Limited on a previous subway car order. Charles Leblanc, who at the time was Vice-President, Administration, for the company stated:

> CIMT came to us. They said don't be afraid of it. They pointed out that the same manufacturing steps were needed for subway cars as for snowmobiles. So we went ahead and bid.[9]

Although Vickers had underbid them by $140,000, Bombardier won the contract. It was stated that Vickers had been disqualified because their bid did not include a specified Swedish coupling device.

EXHIBIT 28.4 **Mass Transit Orders, Bombardier, Inc.**

YEAR	TYPE OF VEHICLE	QUANTITY	CUSTOMER	DELIVERY
1974	Rubber-tired Subway Cars	423	Montreal Urban Community	1976–79
1976	Self-propelled Commuter Cars	36	Chicago South Suburban Transit	1978–79
1978	LRC Coaches	50	Via Rail Canada	1981–82
1980	Push-Pull Commuter Cars	117	New Jersey Transit	1982–83
1981	Rubber-tired Subway Cars	180	Mexico City	1982–83
1981	Light Rail Vehicles	26	Portland, Oregon	1984–85
1981	Push-Pull Commuter Cars	9	Metropolitan Authority of New York	1983
1982	LRC Coaches	50	Via Rail Canada	1984
1982	Steel-wheeled Subway Cars	825	Metropolitan Authority of New York	1984–87
1983	Push-Pull Commuter Cars	19	Metro-North Commuter of New York	1985
1984	Push-Pull Commuter Cars	20	Connecticut Department of Transportation	1986
1985	Push-Pull Commuter Cars	15	Metro-North Commuter of New York	1987

SOURCE: Fred Schilling, Nesbitt Research, 1986.

The award of this substantial contract represented Bombardier's entry into the mass transit market. The company moved to convert the Moto-Ski plant at La Pocatiere to handle production of subway cars. There were strong doubts about whether Bombardier had the necessary capabilities to complete the order. Up to this point, the company's involvement in mass transit products had been limited to trams and streetcars produced by its Austrian subsidiary. But trams and streetcars are classified as light rail vehicles and are substantially different in design from subway cars.

Bombardier did experience some problems in production, due in part to a labour strike in its newly converted plant. Nevertheless, the company began to make deliveries of subway cars to the city of Montreal late in 1976. By this time, Bombardier had also received its first order from outside Canada for 36 electric-powered double-decker commuter cars that were to be built at a cost of $27 million for the South Chicago Transit Authority.

In the following years, Bombardier began to receive larger orders from all parts of North America (see Exhibit 28.4). It received an order for 117 push-pull commuter cars from the New Jersey Transit Corporation. This was followed by an even larger order for 180 subway cars for Mexico City. A senior marketing official subsequently described the manner in which Bombardier had been developing its mass transit business:

> We progressed in terms of both regional expansion and product expansion in a logical, structured fashion. It's more a question of corporate policy or strategy. We started off in Canada in Montreal, then we went to the U.S. Now, we've broadened it into Mexico. There are no wild leaps into blue sky and the glorious beyond because that's the way companies go out of business.[10]

Spreading Out

Shortly after its entry into mass transit, Bombardier was trying to find new acquisitions that would help it to become a significant competitor in the transportation business. In 1976, Bombardier eventually succeeded in purchasing the Montreal Locomotive Works (MLW) from its U.S. parent for a cash payment of $16.8 million. Bombardier was given much needed financial help from the Quebec government in finalizing this deal. The province's holding company, Société Générale de Financement, contributed about 40% of the purchase price of MLW, in exchange for a block of Bombardier's shares.

MLW had previously made subway cars for Toronto, but its main products were diesel-electric locomotives and diesel engines for locomotives, ships, and power plants. The locomotives produced by the MLW plant were mostly in the lighter category, ranging from 1,000 to 2,000 horsepower. Because of this, their appeal was largely restricted to the railways in the developing countries. Bombardier was subsequently able to generate sales of diesel-engine locomotives to customers in several of these countries, including Venezuela, Jamaica, Cuba, Mexico, Guatemela, Pakistan, Bangladesh, Cameroon, Tanzania, and Malawi.

However, Bombardier's purchase of MLW had been largely motivated by its growing interest in the design and development of a Light, Rapid and Comfortable (LRC) passenger train. Its partners in this project were Alcan and Dofasco. The Canadian government also contributed development grants through its program for the advancement of industrial technology. The new train was meant to run at constant high speeds on existing North American tracks. Bombardier Vice-President Henry Valle, who had previously headed MLW, talked about the distinctive features of the LRC: "We think the LRC is as good or better than anything comparable on the market anywhere. And we don't think anyone anywhere knows any more about high-speed trains than we do."[11]

One of the first LRC contracts that Bombardier managed to obtain was a $10-million lease-purchase contract with Amtrack for two trains. The Amtrack contract was followed shortly thereafter by a $70-million order for 21 locomotives and 50 coaches for Via Rail in Canada (see Exhibit 28.4). The locomotives went into production at the MLW facility in Montreal, while the cars were slated for assembly at the La Pocatiere plant for mass transit products. Upon obtaining the contract from Via Rail, a senior marketing official at Bombardier declared: "Now that we have a home base, we can really begin to sell actively internationally."[12]

Thus far, according to Beaudoin, Bombardier's move into mass transit and rail products had done much to ameliorate the company's dependence on recreational products such as the snowmobile. He summed up his company's goal in the following terms:

> Our goal is to develop some equilibrium between transportation and recreation. The transportation and recreation cycles are different. Recreational products are strong when the economy is strong. It's the reverse for transportation because of energy problems.[13]

CURRENT SITUATION

The change in Bombardier during the 1970s was seen by Beaudoin as more than merely a shift in the company's products and markets. It represented a strong desire for an expansion of the company's scope of activities that would allow it to better spread out its risk. During the 1980s, Bombardier was trying to push for the further development of its several different types of products (see Exhibits 28.5 and 28.6 for distribution of sales and profits). In addition to the original line of recreational and utility products, the company was now engaged in new lines of mass transit and rail and diesel products.

Recreational Products

The bulk of sales in recreational products continued to come from snowmobiles. Bombardier offered about fifteen models of snowmobiles that were geared toward different uses. These included family models that were developed for

EXHIBIT 28.5

Sales by Class of Business, Bombardier, Inc.

(Canadian Dollar Amounts in Millions; Year Ended January 31)

	1981	1982	1983	1984	1985	1986
Recreation and Utility Products	216.0	215.4	234.4	260.2	198.4	252.3
Mass Transit Products	34.0	67.6	178.4	134.2	202.3	296.4
Rail and Diesel Products	144.4	165.8	138.3	96.6	114.8	107.9
Total	$394.4	$448.8	$551.1	$491.0	$515.5	$656.6

SOURCE: Bombardier Annual Reports.

EXHIBIT 28.6

Profit from Operations by Class of Business, Bombardier, Inc.

(Canadian Dollar Amounts in Millions; Year Ended January 31)

	1981	1982	1983	1984	1985	1986
Recreational and Utility Products	(5.5)	(24.2)	0.1	7.5	16.2	12.1
Mass Transit Products	5.0	1.4	17.4	17.6	9.3	3.6
Rail and Diesel Products	4.2	8.6	7.6	(13.7)	(13.1)	5.7
Total	$3.7	($14.2)	$25.1	$11.4	$12.4	$21.4

SOURCE: Bombardier Annual Reports.

better comfort and more safety as well as sporty models which were designed for higher speed and better performance.

The market for snowmobiles had picked up in the late 1970s, but declined again in the early 1980s. This had resulted in lower profits for Bombardier from its lines of snowmobiles. Beaudoin, however, believed that good snowfalls and an improving economy would bring about a growth in sales as well as greater profits. As he saw it, snowmobiles still had an important role to play in the future of Bombardier: "We see it as a cash cow. The shakeout has taken place and, with around 40% of the market, it could be a very profitable business for us in the future even on lower volume."[14]

In order to adjust to these lower levels of sales, the company sold off the various firms which were producing parts and accessories for snowmobiles (see Exhibit 28.3). Now, apart from assembling the snowmobiles, Bombardier's actual manufacture of the vehicle is limited to the engine, which is made by the Rotax division in Gunskirchen, Austria.

Bombardier was among the five remaining competitors in snowmobiles. Its share of the market had recently risen to as much as 35 percent (see Exhibit 28.1). But this position was under attack from Yamaha, a Japanese competitor with strong technological and manufacturing advantages. Other firms in the industry posed less of a threat since they were struggling with the downturn in snowmobile sales. In fact, Bombardier had at one point expressed interest in the purchase of Polaris, a U.S. based firm that was experiencing some financial difficulties. But the negotiations were dropped when the U.S. Justice Department threatened to block the sale on anti-trust grounds.

Apart from snowmobiles, the company had experienced limited success with its other recreational products. Its only other notable offering was its line of Can-Am off-road racing bikes. These appealed to specialized sectors of the market because of their technical performance attributes. Bombardier had received several orders for military versions of these motorcycles from certain NATO countries, such as Britain and Belgium. In 1981, a license was purchased from an Austrian company for the assembly and distribution of moped bicycles in Canada. "Our long-term strategy is to develop other recreational products,"[15] said Beaudoin.

Mass Transit Products

The greatest push for sales was being given to mass transit products. Bombardier was able to offer a wide variety of heavy, conventional and light rail vehicles as a result of licensing to gain access to the different technologies (see Exhibit 28.7). Beaudoin was confident that this wide range of products placed his company in the best possible position to exploit the mass transit business. He also

---

EXHIBIT 28.7 **Mass Transit Technology Capability, Bombardier, Inc.**

Heavy Rail	
Rubber-tired subway cars	Licence from CIMT France
Steel-wheeled subway cars	Licence from Kawasaki
Conventional Rail	
Commuter cars	Licence from Pullman
LRC cars	Developed with Alcan & Dofasco
Light Rail	
Light rail vehicles	Licence from BN Belgium
Monorail	Licence from Disney
PeopleMover	Licence from Disney

SOURCE: Tony Hine, McLeod Young Weir Equity Research, 1986.

felt that an energy-conserving society will in the future rely more heavily upon mass transit: "We're forecasting a North American mass transit market of $1 billion annually . . . and we aim to get a good part of it."[16]

Such a strong and sustained demand for mass transit products did appear to be likely. It had recently been estimated that of the close to 20,000 mass transit cars currently in operation all over North America, over 20% had already exceeded their normal useful life (see Exhibit 28.8). These cars would have to be replaced or refurbished. Refurbishing is usually cheaper, costing only about a third or a half of the $1-million purchase price of a new car.

In 1982, Bombardier was able to win a large and prestigious order worth about $1 billion for subway cars from the Metropolitan Transportation Authority of New York (see Exhibit 28.4). The company had recently started to make its first deliveries of the 825 steel-wheeled subway cars that had been ordered. However, the company was still searching for other orders of significant size that would allow it to maintain sufficient production activity after the deliveries to New York were completed in 1987.

Bombardier was experiencing severe difficulties in trying to break into large Canadian markets outside of Quebec because of the declared commitment of various provincial governments to award mass transit jobs to companies that are locally based. For example, Bombardier had just experienced a major setback when it lost out on a bid to acquire UDTC, a significant competitor located in Toronto with a $1.3 billion backlog of orders from the city.

It was also feared that cuts in mass transit funding by the Federal Government would make future sales in the United States even harder to come by. In fact, several large U.S. firms, such as Pullman, Rohr, and General Electric, had recently pulled out of the mass transit business because of uncertainty of orders and problems with contracts. Futhermore, competition for mass transit orders in the United States and in other export markets was coming from large firms that included Budd in United States, Kawasaki in Japan, FrancoRail in France, Breda Ferroviaria in Italy, and Siemens-Duwag in West Germany.

EXHIBIT 28.8   **Mass Transit Cars Currently in Use in North America**

TYPE OF CAR	UNITS IN OPERATION	EXCEEDING NORMAL USEFUL LIFE
Steel-wheeled subway cars	10,200	2,324
Rubber-tired subway cars	792	
Commuter cars	1,282	487
Light rail vehicles	4,502	568
Intercity rail cars	2,589	837
Total	19,365	4,216

SOURCE: Fred Schilling, Nesbitt Research, 1986.

Since 1981, Bombardier had begun to put much more emphasis upon light rail vehicles due to their cheaper construction and maintenance costs. Toward this end, the company had acquired the rights to build, market, and operate its own versions of elevated and automated monorail systems from the Disney organization. It had also just completed a $13.5-million acquisition of a 45% interest in a Belgian mass transit company that had supplied the technology to develop and build the streetcars that it had already delivered to Portland, Oregon. Nevertheless, Vice-President Poitras stated recently: "We don't want to depend completely on mass transit, because transit could also have cycles of good and bad years."[17]

Rail and Diesel Products

Bombardier had made substantial investments to upgrade the MLW facilities for the production of diesel locomotives. Besides manufacturing the locomotives, the plant also produced diesel engines which were used in locomotives, ships, and turbines. In 1984, the company attempted to expand its capacity and to obtain new customers through the $30-million acquisition of Alco Power, located in Auburn, New York. Alco produced diesel locomotives and diesel engines similar to those offered by MLW.

But sales of locomotives had begun to drop off in recent years, primarily due to a decline in orders from the various developing countries. Furthermore, the company increasingly began to feel that there was little likelihood of substantial improvement in sales unless it could become more competitive in the development and production of locomotives with greater horsepower, such as those presently produced by General Electric and General Motors.

Bombardier did manage to secure orders for as many as 30 higher-powered diesel locomotives from Canadian National, but serious problems with their performance after production resulted in the eventual delivery of only four of the locomotives that had been ordered. Efforts were made to convince Canadian National to increase the size of its order in order to justify further development work on a higher-powered locomotive. The company also explored the possibility of linking up with existing large competitors such as General Electric or Kawasaki in order to gain better access to technology as well as markets.

Ultimately, Bombardier was forced to terminate the production of new locomotives in 1985 and to focus primarily upon the manufacturing of diesel engines and the servicing of existing locomotives. Most of this work was subsequently channeled into the Alco facility in New York state. Raymond Royer, soon to become the company's President, stated: "It has been very painful to us. It's a major decision to make, but if we can't make a profit, we have to act as good managers."[18]

At the same time, Bombardier was also being forced to reevaluate its potential orders for passenger locomotives that would result from the sales of its LRC train. The company had believed that it would eventually make worldwide sales of 150 locomotives and 750 coaches. But by 1986, after the sales of only

31 locomotives and 100 coaches to Canadian-based Via Rail, there were no more orders on hand. Even Via Rail had declined to exercise its options for further orders because of mechanical and electrical problems that it had experienced with the equipment that it had already received. Company officials had recently been trying to generate sales of the LRC outside North America. Said Poitras: "We've had discussions on the LRC in other countries, but it takes time. Up to now, we have not succeeded."[19]

Utility Products

The industrial products of the company were constantly being expanded to include new kinds of vehicles for different types of markets. In recent years, Bombardier had introduced a new hydrostatic drive vehicle for ski slope maintenance. It had also started to offer wheeled carriers and skidders that were specifically aimed at the forestry industry. These were being manufactured under license from companies in the United States and Finland.

Industrial products were currently experiencing a period of slow demand. In part, this was attributed by the company to poor snow conditions, which had affected demand for vehicles designed for snow removal as well as for ski and snowmobile trail grooming. At the same time, depressed conditions in the construction and forestry industry were being blamed for decline in sales of other industrial products.

But this decline in demand for industrial products has been offset by Bombardier's recent push into the area of logistic support equipment for the military. The company had already been adapting some of its snowmobiles, motorcycles, and industrial-tracked vehicles to the needs of the military. In 1981, this activity was given a considerable boost when Bombardier was awarded a $150-million contract to build 2,700 trucks for the Canadian Armed Forces. These two-and-a-half ton trucks were built using a design of the AM General Corporation, a subsidiary of American Motors.

In 1982, Bombardier also acquired worldwide rights for the production of the Iltis, a four-wheel-drive military vehicle designed by Volkswagenwerk of West Germany. The license led to an initial order for 1,900 Iltis vehicles for the Canadian Armed Forces. This was followed by the sale of 2,500 vehicles to Belgium and 350 vehicles to West Germany. A senior official in the logistics division explained: "Our principle in developing the logistic division is pretty similar to Bombardier's thinking with any other product—first sell into Canada, build a base in Canada, then go offshore."[20]

Bombardier is counting on the current worldwide shift away from traditional Jeeps as army vehicles to create a major potential market for the Iltis. More orders for these vehicles are expected not only from Canada, but also from the Netherlands, Turkey, and Saudi Arabia.

Finally, the company has just signed an agreement with Oshkosh Truck Corporation of Wisconsin to produce and sell an 8.5-ton military truck known as the Oshkosh. The Oshkosh is a six-wheel-drive vehicle designed to carry heavy equipment and ammunition in rough terrain and is already in use with the U.S. Army. Bombardier is hoping to sell 500 to 1,000 of these trucks to the Canadian Armed Forces. It has also obtained the rights to sell the vehicle in twenty-eight countries aside from Canada.

PROFILE OF OPERATIONS

Organization

Bombardier's rapid growth and diversification forced top management to seek a more formal and structured approach to the running of the business. Toward this end, the company had been engaged in a series of moves that were designed to better integrate its operations with those of its various acquisitions. Beaudoin had anticipated the need for this restructuring in the early 1970s: "As we diversify more and more, we shall need to ensure central control of the overall operation . . . . . Our management structure isn't finalized yet and will change with the needs of the business."[21]

By 1986, Bombardier was organized into seven different divisions or subsidiaries. These fell into three different sectors (see Exhibit 28.9). Total em-

EXHIBIT 28.9   **Organizational Chart, Bombardier, Inc.**

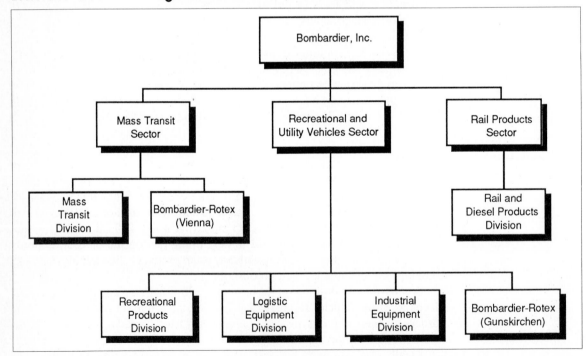

SOURCE: Bombardier Annual Reports.

ployment stood at between 5,000 and 6,000 employees. The largest number of divisions or subsidiaries were associated with the recreational and utility vehicles sector, which produced recreational products such as snowmobiles as well as certain types of industrial and logistic equipment. However, the main thrust of the company was oriented toward the mass transit sector that manufactured several forms of subway cars, train cars, and streetcars. Finally, the rail and diesel products sector had concentrated upon the production of locomotives but was now relying mainly on diesel engines for various industrial uses.

Although Bombardier moved to bring its various divisions and subsidiaries under centralized control, they remained separate administrative and financial entities. Each division or subsidiary was headed by a chief executive who possessed a considerable degree of autonomy. These chief executives were expected to submit on an annual basis a formal draft of a three- to five-year plan for their own divisions.

Research and Development

Bombardier's ability to produce and market such a diverse range of products hinged upon a policy of exploiting proven and tested technologies that were acquired through licensing agreements. As Vice-President Poitras explained, it was a policy that made a virtue of necessity:

> The risk that has been taken on the various contracts we've bid for has been minimal. It takes years to develop a technology. It takes years to prove the technology. Bombardier can't afford to do that. What we are trying to find is new products just before they reach the market. Then we would be an ideal manufacturer and marketing organization for those products.[22]

The reliance on licensing was particularly heavy in mass transit (see Exhibit 28.7). For Beaudoin, product reliability was crucial to success in mass transit. He felt that this reliability could be enhanced through the purchase of proven technology:

> Mass transit technology may not be as sophisticated as aerospace, but it has to be very, very reliable. It has to be in operation for at least five years before you know that you have a good product. Technology in mass transit has been developed for many years in Europe and Japan, and it's available.[23]

The recent push into logistic equipment was also dependent on the use of various licensing agreements with U.S. and European firms. But the company's moves in rail products were based on working in partnership with other companies. The LRC project had been undertaken as a joint venture with Alcan and Dofasco, in which Bombardier invested more than $30 million.

The only products which Bombardier had developed through its own extensive research and development were its original recreational products and industrial equipment. The company's primary research facilities had been established in Valcourt for the development of its early snowmobiles and all-terrain vehicles.

They included various kinds of laboratories and several different test tracks and chambers. These facilities had been expanded and renovated in 1979 and continue to be used for the early testing of most of the company's extensive range of products.

Production

Bombardier's diverse production activities are carried out in 3.0 million square feet of plants and warehouses scattered over Canada, the United States, and Austria (see Exhibits 28.10 and 28.11).

All of the company's recreational and utility products are manufactured in a large facility in Valcourt where the company was first started. An assembly line has been designed that is capable of producing several hundred snow-mobiles and motorcycles daily. Snowmobiles are manufactured for eight months

---

EXHIBIT 28.10

Capital Expenditures by Class of Business, Bombardier, Inc.

(Canadian Dollar Amounts in Millions; Year Ended January 31)

	1981	1982	1983	1984	1985	1986
Recreational and Utility Products	11.2	14.3	4.0	9.0	13.0	8.4
Mass Transit Products	5.5	8.0	4.4	8.7	5.4	1.0
Rail and Diesel Products	2.2	4.3	5.5	3.8	1.0	2.0
Total	$18.9	$26.6	$13.9	$21.5	$19.4	$11.4

SOURCE: Financial Post Corporation Service.

EXHIBIT 28.11

Capital Expenditures by Geographic Area, Bombardier, Inc.

(Canadian Dollar Amounts in Millions; Year Ended January 31)

	1981	1982	1983	1984	1985	1986
Canada	15.4	18.6	11.2	17.9	13.9	4.1
United States	0.2	4.7	0.7	1.3	1.7	2.8
Europe	3.3	3.3	2.0	2.3	3.8	4.5
Total	$18.9	$26.6	$13.9	$21.5	$19.4	$11.4

SOURCE: Financial Post Corporation Service.

of the year, from April to November. Part of the facilities have been expanded or adapted for the manufacturing of industrial and logistic equipment, with rates of production that can vary from three to six units per day.

The mass transit products are primarily constructed at La Pocatiere, in what had formerly been a Moto-Ski plant. The facilities, originally used for the manufacturing of snowmobiles, were converted in 1974 for the construction of subway cars. The complexity of a subway car is several orders of magnitude greater than that of a snowmobile. A subway car has 8,000 parts and 14 kilometers of electric wiring, compared with only 2,000 parts in a snowmobile. The shift to subway cars required considerable retraining of the labour force. It was also costly in terms of physical facilities. The estimated cost of conversion was about $5 million, of which $1 million was provided by a grant from the Canadian government.

The converted facility is now geared towards the production of a variety of mass transit vehicles and contains about 65 work stations. Currently, the plant is capable of producing two to five cars per week, based on a single, daily eight-hour shift. Bombardier had also recently completed an assembly plant in Barre, Vermont, to handle U.S. orders. Partly assembled transit cars are now shipped from La Pocatiere to this facility, where U.S.-made components are added.

Production of the diesel-electric locomotives and diesel engines is spread out over the old MLW facility in Montreal and the Alco plant in Auburn, New York. However, the MLW facility has not been utilizing its capacity for producing 100 locomotives and 50 diesel engines per year since the decision was made to withdraw from the manufacturing of locomotives.

Sales

Each of the categories of products offered by Bombardier represents a different type of sale and requires its own marketing effort. Most of the company's products, with the exception of its recreational line, are typically sold in bulk orders to industrial or governmental clients.

Mass transit equipment tends to require the most complex and extensive marketing effort. The average price for mass transit vehicles is about $1 million per unit. Sales are generated through the submission of competitive bids by the company as it vies for each potential order (see Exhibit 28.12). In order to be successful, a bid must be low in price, yet fulfill stringent technical requirements. In many cases, orders for mass transit equipment are accompanied by allegations that the choice was made on the basis of political and regional favoritism. The Montreal and New York orders were both legally contested by the companies that lost out to Bombardier.

Sales of logistic equipment and diesel products are similarly developed through a process of competitive bidding based upon price, specifications, and performance. Most of the military vehicles offered by Bombardier range in price

EXHIBIT 28.12   **Bidding Process**

Bids are very expensive to prepare, with the cost of preparing a complex bid often reaching six figures. Each component of the order must be analyzed and costed. Labor, overhead and toolings costs must also be evaluated. Working capital, maintenance, and warranty costs must all be factored in.

The process is further complicated by the customized nature of the work. Municipal transit authorities tend to retain consultants to define system and vehicle specifications in great detail. There are variations in tunnel construction and gauge which determine the width of the cars. Furthermore, there are differences in electrical voltages on which the different systems run.

The number of cars ordered is usually a key variable in costing as there are economies of scale and learning-curve developments which must be correctly calculated. Frequently, however, scale economies are impeded by the tendency of the customers to require a certain amount of parts that have been locally manufactured.

Parts usually make up 50–60% of the final cost, while direct labor accounts for around 10%. There is greater profit potential on repeat orders since tooling and start-up expenses are substantially reduced.

SOURCE: Adapted from Tony Hine, McLeod Young Weir Equity Research, 1986.

from $20,000 to $30,000 per unit. Export sales to the military may also depend on the ability of Bombardier to work in collaboration with a local firm.

Finally, sales of the company's original lines of recreational products and industrial equipment continue to be separately developed. Its snowmobiles and motorcycles are sold through a network of about 2,000 distributors and dealers throughout North America, as well as in select foreign markets. The list price of snowmobiles typically ranges from $1,500 to $7,000, with a good basic machine selling for around $3,000.

On the other hand, most industrial equipment is marketed directly by the company through its service centers. The various types of all-terrain tracked or wheeled vehicles usually cost between $125,000 and $150,000 per unit. The bulk of sales continue to be made in North America, but the company is presently concentrating on building up sales in overseas markets through its Rotax division in Austria.

Contracts

The sale and delivery of most of Bombardier's product lines, with the exclusion of snowmobiles, is highly dependent on the specific terms as laid out in carefully negotiated contracts. Though contracts tend to be very elaborate, they cannot anticipate all contingencies. Disputes tend to arise over technical specifications associated with the design, unforseen developments that may contribute to escalation of costs, and the rights of the customer to withdraw from the deal. These disputes are not only costly in the short run, but more importantly they can damage the reputation of the manufacturer in the long run.

Consequently, Beaudoin has frequently emphasized that special care must be taken to avoid the problems that have forced other companies to drop out of the mass transit business. To start with, Bombardier has tried to avoid technical problems with its designs by obtaining licenses on tried and tested technologies. This policy reduces the likelihood of expensive delays and repairs as well as the possibility of the customer moving to cancel a contract in midstream.

Additionally, Bombardier sought to negotiate contracts which stipulate precise conditions under which the customer can terminate a contract. In the event of disputes over quality or performance, the company attempted to avoid costly litigation by including provisions for specific arbitration procedures. The most serious problems were encountered with the early deliveries of subway cars to New York. Various mechanical and electrical problems led to the temporary suspension of production while the cars underwent some tests. It was speculated that failure on these tests could have led to a cancellation of the contract.

Finally, all contracts typically include a schedule for prepayments and progress payments to ensure sufficient financing for carrying out the order. Additional protection is provided through the specification of limits on penalties for delay in deliveries as well as through escalator clauses that index the price to the inflation rate. However, as Vice-President Poitras pointed out: "There is no protection against cost overruns. That is our risk."[24]

Labour

Most of Bombardier's products are fairly labour intensive because of their dependence upon manual assembly lines. When the company was essentially engaged in the production of snowmobiles and all-terrain vehicles at its facilities in Valcourt, the employees were administered by committees that set salary levels based on the average levels that prevailed in the area. Since then, the majority of the company's employees have become unionized and are covered by as many as ten separate agreements.

Furthermore, some of the agreements with labour were concluded only after long strikes that disrupted production in various plants. Bombardier had to deal with its first strike in 1975. The strike occurred at the La Pocatiere plant during the conversion to mass transit production. It lasted almost five months and resulted in considerable delays in the final delivery of subway cars to the City of Montreal. Recurrent and crippling strikes were also encountered at the MLW plant which underwent a five-month lockout in 1977 and a six-month strike in 1979.

However, Beaudoin believed that the relationship between management and labour had improved considerably over the past few years. This was due to changes in management personnel within the divisions and the introduction of new working arrangements. At the end of 1979, Bombardier also offered to all of its Quebec employees the opportunity to subscribe to a share purchasing plan. This plan was designed to allow employees to benefit from tax advantages that were recently introduced by the Quebec government, as well as to participate more directly in the growth of the company.

Top Management

Bombardier shifted its headquarters from Valcourt to Montreal in 1975. The move brought together in one location the chairman and chief executive officer of the company and seven vice-presidents responsible for different areas of the company's operations. Except for a brief period, the position of Chairman and Chief Executive Officer has been occupied by Laurent Beaudoin. Joseph-Armand's son, André Bombardier, and son-in-law, Jean-Louis Fontaine, are among the most senior of the group of Vice-Presidents.

In 1975, Beaudoin tried to bring in an outsider to help with the running of the company. Sixty-one-year-old Jean-Claude Hébert was appointed Chairman and Chief Executive Officer, with Beaudoin keeping the post of President. Beaudoin stated the reasons behind this move: "We really needed someone on the management end to guide the organization going into diversification."[25] It was under Hébert's direction that Bombardier mounted its aggressive search for possible acquisitions. But the poor performance of MLW subsequent to its acquisition led the family to question Hébert's plans for other major acquisitions. He was subsequently forced out in 1978, with the position returning to Beaudoin.

In 1979, Beaudoin appointed Louis Hollander as the President and Chief Operating Officer of the company. Hollander, who had previously been in charge of recreational and industrial products, remained in this position until the end of 1981. Recently, the position has been filled by Raymond Royer, who had been responsible for the company's mass transit products.

Financing

In 1986, the capital stock of Bombardier stood at 6.9 million class A, and 5.9 million class B shares. The shares represented close to $120 million of equity on the balance sheets of the company (see Exhibit 28.13). At the same time, long-term debt had dropped to $35 million, most of which was in the form of bonds, notes, and debentures.

Bombardier became a publicly owned organization in 1969. Its initial issue consisted of 2 million class A voting shares, representing about 15% of the company's equity. All of the 13 million class B nonvoting shares were kept by Les Enterprises de J. Armand Bombardier, a family-owned holding company. No dividends could be paid on the class B shares unless a dividend of a similar nature had been paid during the same fiscal year on the class A shares. But the

EXHIBIT 28.13   **Balance Sheets, Bombardier, Inc.**
(Canadian Dollar Amounts in Millions)

Year Ended January 31	1981	1982	1983	1984	1985	1986
Assets						
Current Assets						
Cash	$ 0.0	$ 0.0	$ 0.0	$ 0.0	$ 0.0	$ 6.9
Accounts receivable	67.8	73.2	56.9	77.3	90.6	103.3
Inventories	158.6	121.4	149.0	117.2	167.5	152.3
Deferred income taxes	0.0	18.7	15.9	13.5	10.3	8.0
Prepaid expenses	3.0	4.3	4.9	4.1	6.2	7.4
Total current assets	229.4	217.6	226.7	212.1	274.6	277.9
Investments	6.4	13.1	19.0	17.8	18.6	19.5
Fixed Assets						
Buildings & equipment	153.6	177.8	171.7	186.9	234.6	234.9
Less: accumulated depreciation	81.0	87.8	84.0	88.1	110.3	123.1
Total fixed assets	72.6	90.0	87.7	98.8	124.3	111.8
Other assets	5.0	5.7	4.7	8.6	9.7	10.8
Total assets	$313.4	$326.4	$338.1	$337.3	$427.2	$420.0
Liabilities & Shareholders' Equity						
Current Liabilities						
Bank loans	19.5	39.5	13.7	1.6	0.0	0.0
Accounts payable	80.6	91.1	95.9	73.3	107.4	134.7
Advances due	0.0	0.0	0.0	0.0	0.0	26.3
Income taxes	0.3	2.8	0.3	0.7	2.4	4.3
Maturing long-term debt	11.0	4.4	6.1	6.0	4.6	5.3
Total current liabilities	111.4	137.8	116.0	81.6	114.4	170.6
Contract advances	0.0	0.0	32.6	77.0	132.5	39.5
Long-term debt	65.7	73.0	66.9	49.0	39.8	35.2
Provisions for pensions	7.3	5.3	5.8	6.2	6.6	7.4
Shareholders' equity						
Capital stock	93.6	93.4	93.7	94.2	95.6	119.9
Retained earnings	35.4	16.9	23.1	29.3	38.3	47.4
Total liabilities & shareholders' equity	$313.4	$326.4	$338.1	$337.3	$427.2	$420.0

SOURCE: Bombardier Annual Reports.

class B shares were convertible at any time on a share-for-share basis into class A shares.

During 1976, all outstanding class A and B shares were exchanged for a total of 3.9 million class A shares. Since 1981, newly created class B shares have again been issued to the public, which have less voting rights, but which entitle their holders to dividends. As of early 1986, Les Enterprises de J. Armand Bombardier still held 71.9% of the class A shares, which gave it a 66.2% voting interest. Another 3% of the class A shares were held by directors, managers, and employees of the company.

DEVELOPING PROSPECTS

In the summer of 1986, Bombardier was taking steps to enter into two new areas of activity. One of these would move the company into aerospace, while the other would lead it into automobiles. Each of these would represent a major shift for the company, the first since its entry into mass transit. However, Laurent Beaudoin felt that the company had the financial, technical, and management capability to handle both of these moves.

Aerospace

Bombardier was making a serious bid for Canadair, an aerospace company located in Montreal. Canadair employed more than 4,000 people and had reported a profit of $19.6 million on sales of $430 million in the previous year. However, the company had only recently begun to show profitability and this had been largely based on sales of its newly developed Challenger business jet.

The Challenger executive jet has earned a reputation for being spacious, quiet, and fuel efficient. It was conceived and developed by Canadair following the acquisition of the company from General Dynamics by the Canadian government in 1975. But the design of the aircraft has taken longer than anticipated, resulting in development costs in excess of $1 billion. As a result, the company found itself unable to sell enough of these jets to cover its expenses until the government eventually decided to absorb the development costs.

Although it was now free of its debt, Canadair still has to contend with the inherent uncertainty of the business jet market. The total market for such aircraft is believed to be between 75 and 100 units per year. Canadair has already sold about 140 of its Challenger jets since they were first introduced in 1980. But the company has not yet found buyers midway into the year for the fifteen aircraft that it needs to build this year in order to break even. In fact, there were no outstanding orders for the Challenger business jet on the books of the company.

Apart from the business jet, the only other substantial offering of Canadair was a recent version of the CL-215 water bomber. The CL-215 had been the main drawing card for the company through the 1970s while the Challenger was being developed. The water bomber continues to offer excellent firefighting capabilities and can also be adapted to other uses. Although annual production stands at only ten units, demand for this type of aircraft is expected to pick up.

The recent decision to sell Canadair had been made by the newly elected Conservative government that was determined to privatize many of its business holdings. The book value of the company was estimated to be between $225 and $250 million. But it is considered to be quite likely that the government would settle for a lower price in exchange for some assurance that the company would remain intact and continue its operations.

Beaudoin was optimistic about his company's chances of winning the bid to acquire Canadair. He also believed that if successful the acquisition would provide Bombardier with a complementary business with a strong cash flow. At the same time, Bombardier will have to continue to make investments into its business jets and water bombers in the face of increasing competition from other U.S. and European firms. A greater push may also be needed to develop more subcontracting work with other aerospace companies and maintenance work for military aircraft.

Automobiles

Bombardier was also actively exploring the possibility of introducing into the North American market a small car designed to carry two people. The car would use a three-cylinder engine and would offer a maximum speed of about 55–65 miles per hour. It would be targeted as a second car that is mainly to be used for driving within the city.

The company has already concluded an agreement with Daihatsu Motor Company of Japan to obtain the technology that would be used in the design of the car. It is now negotiating a joint-venture agreement with the Japanese company under which these cars would be produced. Daihatsu, which is partly owned by Toyota, is the smallest producer of cars in Japan.

The joint-venture agreement could first result in the production of a new version of a Daihatsu three-cylinder car that is already being sold in Asia and Europe. Production on these could start as early as late 1987 or early 1988. A new front-wheel drive version of this car that is being designed by Bombardier would not be expected before 1991.

The cars would be produced by Bombardier at Valcourt, where the company has spare factory space. The facilities are initially expected to be able to handle about 200,000 cars being produced annually. It was believed that about 350 of Bombardier's snowmobile dealers in Canada and the United States could handle sales and service. The car was expected to retail for about $7,000.

The company was spending about $15 million, most of which was provided by various levels of government, to undertake various feasibility studies. Testing of four prototype cars has been going well, leading to speculation that a positive decision is forthcoming. Beaudoin had recently provided his own assessment about the possible move into the production of small cars: "We have the technical experience and the management depth to handle the job."[26] At the same time, it is widely speculated that Bombardier will take the final plunge only if it is able to develop a joint venture to get strong technical and financial backing for the move.

NOTES

1. "Bombardier: Making a Second Leap from Snowmobiles to Mass Transit," *Business Week*, February 23, 1981.

2. "Bombardier Skids to Success," *International Management*, January 1972.

3. "Snow Job?" *Forbes*, February 1, 1970.

4. *Ibid.*

5. "Bombardier Skids to Success."

6. *Ibid.*

7. *Ibid.*

8. "Snowmobiles to Subways: Bombardier Maps Out Its Route," *Financial Post*, September 13, 1980.

9. "Why Bombardier Is Trying Out Mass Transit," *Business Week*, March 10, 1975.

10. "Firms Looks to Commuter Vehicles as Gravy Train to Large Profits," *Financial Post*, December 12, 1981.

11. "Bombardier Looks to Amtrack to Open Doors to U.S. Inter-city Market," *Globe & Mail*, November 16, 1977.

12. "LRC Sale Considered Key to Foreign Market," *Globe & Mail*, November 4, 1977.

13. "Snowmobiles to Subways."

14. "Making the 'A' Train," *Forbes*, September 27, 1982.

15. "Snowmobiles to Subways."

16. *Ibid.*

17. "Bombardier's Formula for Growth," *Financial Times of Canada*, November 28, 1983.

18. "Locomotives to Be Dropped," *Globe & Mail*, July 13, 1985.

19. "Bombardier's Formula for Growth."

20. "Bombardier Has High Hopes in Military Vehicle Market," *Globe & Mail*, November 12, 1983.

21. "Bombardier Skids to Success."

22. "Bombardier's Formula for Growth."

23. "Making the 'A' Train."

24. "Bombardier's Formula for Growth."

25. "Why Bombardier Is Trying Out Mass Transit."

26. "Bombardier Plans Mini-car, Eyes Canadair," *Globe & Mail*, June 17, 1986.

CASE 29

Piper Aircraft Corporation

THOMAS L. WHEELEN • J. DAVID HUNGER • MOUSTAFA H. ABDELSAMAD

HISTORY

In 1928, William T. Piper and Ralph Lloyd were partners in the drilling and selling of crude oil in Bradford, Pennsylvania. During that year, Mr. Lloyd invested $400 in Piper's behalf (without Piper's knowledge) in a new venture and made a similar investment for himself. This new venture was the Taylor Aircraft Company of Bradford, Pennsylvania. At the time of the investment, Piper knew absolutely nothing about aircraft and in fact felt that they were unsafe. He was certainly unaware that this $400 investment would lead him into an era in which he would be known as the "Henry Ford of Aviation."[1]

For the next nine years, Taylor Aircraft struggled financially as its first airplane, the Chummy, fought to take a foothold in the light airplane market. To keep the company afloat, William Piper was forced to invest more and more money from his oil holdings. During this period the aviation industry was dominated by larger aircraft tailored for the airlines. With the flight of Charles Lindbergh in a light aircraft, the Spirit of St. Louis, Piper saw potential for an owner-flown, small aircraft market. As Piper saw it, the key was to make the airplane easy to operate and inexpensive to own. By the end of 1934 this philosophy had begun to pay off as Taylor Aircraft finally made a profit.

In 1935, Piper bought out the original founder of Taylor Aircraft, C. G. Taylor, and took complete control of the company. Piper renamed the Taylor Cub the J-2 Cub, an airplane that would eventually make the company the top manufacturer of light airplanes.

In 1937 the Bradford plant burned down. This growing aircraft manufacturing company needed a new site and a new name. In that same year the Taylor Aircraft Company ceased to exist, and Piper Aircraft Corporation began at a new site in Lock Haven, Pennsylvania, on the banks of the West Branch of the Susquehanna River. The new plant site, previously an old silk mill next to the airport, was still in use in 1983.

From the corporate headquarters in Lock Haven, the original plan of building an inexpensive airplane that was easy to fly continued to be the company's mission as the leadership of Piper Aircraft changed hands from father to sons. It was not until the mid-1950s that Piper Aircraft began to turn away from the

This case was prepared by Professor Thomas L. Wheelen of the University of South Florida, Professor J. David Hunger of Iowa State University, and Moustafa H. Abdelsamad, Dean, of Southeastern Massachusetts University with assistance of David Dunmore, Linda Montgomery, and John Westerman of the University of South Florida and Wayne Wylie of Piper Aircraft Corporation. Copyright © 1986 by Thomas L. Wheelen and J. David Hunger.

Source: Thomas L. Wheelen, J. David Hunger, and Moustafa H. Abdelsamad, "Piper Aircraft Corporation," *Case Research Journal* 1986, Vol. 6, pp. 32–59. Reprinted by permission of the authors and North American Case Research Association.

light, single-engine aircraft to its first twin-engine plane, the Apache. This was Piper's first attempt to break the Cub image of the company. But William Piper still believed that the light airplane market was the best niche for the company. Even though he had no knowledge of the aircraft business when he first started, William Piper's original idea had been to introduce flying to the ordinary individual through flying lessons. Piper hoped that, as people learned more about flying, they would eventually want to purchase their own airplanes.

THE GENERAL AVIATION INDUSTRY

General Aviation Aircraft in 1984 were basically divided into four categories. From the smallest to the largest they were (1) single-engine piston, (2) multi-engine piston, (3) turbo-prop, and (4) jets. (See Exhibit 29.1.) Each category was divided into classes. In the single-engine piston category the classes were the basic two-seater trainer, the narrow-body four-seat single, the wide-body six-seat single, and the wide-body cabin-class six-seat single. In the twin-engine piston category were the wide-body six-seat light twins and the wide-body six- to eight-seat cabin-class twins. Piper refers to multi-engine aircraft as twin-engine. All of the turbo-props were considered by Piper to be wide-body cabin-class, but seating varied from seven to eleven. The last category was the business (civil) jet.

The markets for these categories varied with price and usage. In the single-engine category, the classes up to the wide-body six-seat single were mostly used for training and sport flying. The cabin-class singles up to light twin-engine

EXHIBIT 29.1

U.S. General Aviation Aircraft
Shipments by Type of Aircraft

	TYPE OF AIRCRAFT					
YEAR	Single-Engine	Multi-Engine	Turbo-Prop	Jet	TOTAL	TOTAL FACTORY BILLINGS
1983	1,811	417	321	142	2,691	$1,469,504,000
1982	2,871	678	458	259	4,266	$1,999,463,689
1981	6,608	1,542	918	389	9,457	$2,919,947,000
1980	8,640	2,116	795	326	11,877	$2,486,182,900
1979	13,286	2,843	637	282	17,048	$2,164,973,000
1978	14,398	2,634	548	231	17,811	$1,781,245,400
1977	14,057	2,195	428	227	16,907	$1,488,114,000
1976	12,783	2,120	359	187	15,449	$1,225,483,000
1975	11,439	2,116	305	196	14,056	$1,032,900,000
1974	11,562	2,135	250	219	14,166	$ 909,400,000

SOURCE: *General Aviation Statistical Databook*, 1983 Edition.

aircraft were targeted for wealthy individuals and small companies. The cabin-class twins up to the turbo-props were primarily for the corporate market.

In the early 1970s the single-engine plane dominated the civil aviation market. However, by the mid-1970s the demand by business for a larger aircraft resulted in a shift in emphasis toward the cabin-class twin and turbo-prop airplanes. (See Exhibits 29.1–29.3.)

EXHIBIT 29.2 **Unit Shipment by Type, as Percentages of Total Unit Shipments[1]**

	SINGLE-ENGINE	MULTI-ENGINE	TURBO-PROP
1984E[2]	71.54%	16.26%	12.20%
1983	71.05	16.36	12.59
1982	71.65	16.92	11.43
1981	72.87	17.00	10.12
1980	74.80	18.23	6.88
1979	79.24	16.96	3.80
1978	81.90	14.98	3.12
1977	84.27	13.16	2.57
1976	83.76	13.89	2.35

SOURCE: Extrapolated from *General Aviation Statistical Databook*, 1983 Edition.
NOTES: [1] Excludes jets. [2] E means estimated.

EXHIBIT 29.3 **Market Trends[1]**

	SINGLE-ENGINE UNITS	% CHANGE	MULTI-ENGINE UNITS	% CHANGE	TURBO-PROP UNITS	% CHANGE
1984E[2]	2,200	+21.48%	500	+19.90%	375	+16.82%
1983	1,811	−36.92	417	−39.30	321	−29.91
1982	2,871	−56.55	678	−55.45	458	−50.11
1981	6,608	−23.52	1,542	−27.13	918	+15.47
1980	8,640	−34.97	2,116	−25.57	795	+24.80
1979	13,286	−7.72	2,843	+7.93	637	+16.24
1978	14,398	+2.43	2,634	+20.00	548	+28.04
1977	14,057	+9.97	2,195	+3.54	428	+19.22
1976	12,783	+11.75	2,120	+0.19	359	+17.70

SOURCE: Extrapolated from *General Aviation Statistical Databook*, 1983 Edition.
NOTES: [1] Excludes jets. [2] E means estimated.

Since the industry shifted to producing and selling more of the larger and more expensive corporate airplanes, its net billings (which represent dollar amounts invoiced from the factory to its distributors or directly to dealers) continued to grow for three years after total unit shipments began to decline in 1978. (See Exhibits 29.4 and 29.5.) Beginning in 1974, the average net billings per unit were $64,168 on 14,166 units shipped. By 1983 the average net billings per unit were $546,265 on 2,691 units shipped. Exhibits 29.1, 29.2, and 29.3 reflect the increasing role of twin-engine and turbo-prop aircraft during the late 1970s.

During the 1970s, private aircraft had become a major source of transportation for the business community. Since 1970 the general aviation fleet had almost doubled to 200,000 aircraft. By 1990 the fleet was projected to grow by 50% to 300,000. About 90% of general aviation sales were for business purposes.

Even though the corporate aircraft was becoming more popular, this asset was not income-producing for the purchaser. Planes were paid for typically with excess cash flow, which made the corporate aircraft sensitive to economic conditions, especially inflation and interest rates. Between 1979 and 1982 was

EXHIBIT 29.4   **General Aviation Unit Shipments/Billings**

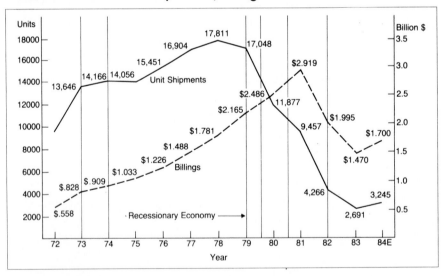

SOURCE: Adapted from General Aviation Manufacturer's Association presentation, January 1984.

NOTE: Data for 1984 (shown as 84E) was *forecast data* presented in January 1984. Forecast was later revised.

EXHIBIT 29.5

General Aviation Manufacturer's Association Domestic Billings and U.S. Corporate Profits

(In 1972 Dollars)

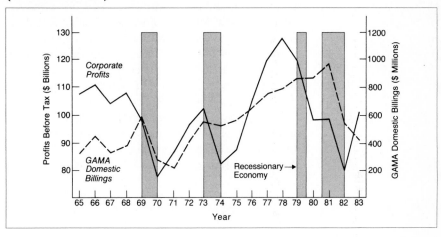

SOURCE: General Aviation Manufacturer's Association presentation, January 1984.

a period of high interest rates and inflation. The prime rate during this period went as high as 21%, while inflation reached a peak of 14%.

These factors had a pronounced effect on the general aviation manufacturers' pre-tax profits (as can be seen in Exhibit 29.5). These profits, as stated in 1972 dollars, dropped to less than $80 billion by 1982. Exhibit 29.4 shows that aircraft shipments from the factories declined sharply from an industry high of 17,811 units in 1978 to 2,691 units in 1983.

ORGANIZATIONAL STRUCTURE

Piper Management

From its inception through the 1960s, Piper Aircraft was run as a family business by Bill Piper, Sr.; Tony Piper; Bill Piper, Jr.; and Howard "Pug" Piper. Even though the Board of Directors typically consisted mainly of persons from outside the company, the direction of the company had been primarily set by Bill Piper, Sr.

In January 1969, when Bill Piper, Jr. was the President of the company, he received a call from Herbert J. Siegle, President of Chris-Craft Industries, who announced that Piper Aircraft was being targeted for takeover by Chris-Craft.[2] Neither had any knowledge that this conversation would start a fight for control of the company. A takeover battle for Piper soon erupted between Chris-Craft and Bangor Punta Corporation. During 1969, Bangor Punta was able to acquire an approximate 51% interest in Piper. Chris-Craft owned a lesser percentage of stock. The fight for control was not finally settled until 1977, when the United States Supreme Court awarded control of Piper Aircraft to Bangor Punta.

In 1969, Bill Piper, Sr. died. By this time, members of the Piper family were no longer affiliated with the company. Between 1969 and 1977, Piper's Board of Directors was evenly split between Bangor Punta and Chris-Craft. After 1977, Bangor Punta controlled the board.

Piper's new parent company, Bangor Punta Corporation, which had several other holdings, had a policy of decentralization. This meant that each of its divisions was allowed to operate almost independently. As quoted from the President of Bangor Punta, David W. Wallace:

> We must avoid like a plague having centralized headquarters. These divisions of ours are operated in most instances by the entrepreneurs who founded them and operated them successfully for many years.[3]

The 1983 Board of Directors of Piper Aircraft was made up of the following five people:

David W. Wallace: President of Bangor Punta Corporation. Mr. Wallace had been with Bangor Punta since 1967 with a background in law and a law degree from Harvard Law School.

David H. Street: Senior Vice-President and Treasurer of Bangor Punta Corporation. Mr. Street had come to Bangor Punta in 1978. His previous experience had been in the banking industry.

Max E. Bleck: President and Chief Executive Officer of Piper Aircraft. Mr. Bleck had come to Piper in 1976 as Senior Vice-President—Manufacturing Operations. He had been appointed President and Chief Operating Officer in 1979 and then promoted to President and Chief Executive Officer in 1980. Mr. Bleck's background prior to Piper had been in manufacturing and production with Cessna Aircraft.

Alfred J. Koontz, Jr.: Vice-President—Finance of Piper Aircraft. Mr. Koontz had come to Piper in 1975 from the accounting firm of Price Waterhouse and Co.

Dudley Phillips: Senior Vice-President and General Counsel of Bangor Punta Corporation.

Besides Max Bleck and Al Koontz, the top management of Piper included Robert Dickerson, Executive Vice-President and Chief Operations Officer. (See Exhibit 29.6.) Mr. Dickerson had been hired in 1980. His previous background had been in manufacturing and engineering at Cessna Aircraft.

EXHIBIT 29.6   **Summary Chart of Organization, Piper Aircraft Corporation**

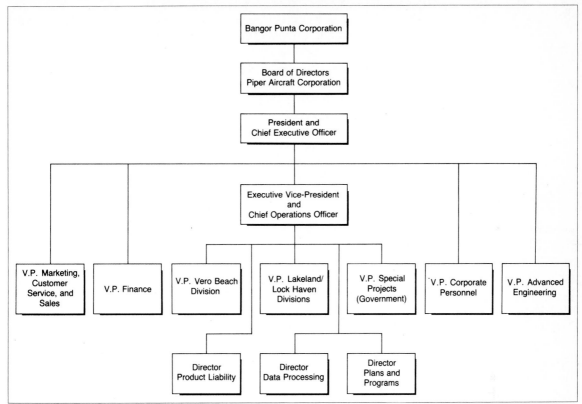

Bangor Punta Management

In 1983, Bangor Punta was a diversified company composed of the following four business segments in addition to Piper Aircraft:

Smith & Wesson: manufactured and marketed a line of quality handguns; law enforcement, military, and public-security equipment; shotguns; and knives. Smith & Wesson also conducted a training academy and an armorer's school for law enforcement agencies.

Recreational Products: manufactured and sold, in the United States, Canada, and Europe, a broad product line of marine products and recreational vehicles. Marine products included aluminum runabouts, cruisers, and fishing boats, as well as fiberglass powerboats. Recreational vehicles included van conversions and camping trailers. Jeanneau also manufactured the Microcar, a small, two-seat, powered vehicle.

Agriculture: served the agricultural market through Producers Cotton Oil Company, an integrated grower, processor, warehouser, and merchandiser of cotton and its related by-products.

Industrial Products: manufactured and marketed ovens and furnaces for the can manufacturing and building products industries.[4]

Bangor Punta's Board of Directors consisted of ten members, three of whom were outside the company.

EXHIBIT 29.7	**Market Share Trends[1]** (Percentage of Total Market)						
	1977	1978	1979	1980	1981	1982	1983
Single-Engine							
Piper Aircraft	26.70%	25.70%	30.80%	21.74%	22.99%	21.46%	25.83%
Beech Aircraft	5.25	4.80	5.12	6.72	7.50	7.80	8.50
Cessna Aircraft	57.34	56.93	51.59	62.06	59.73	60.74	52.95
Other Manufacturers	10.71	12.44	12.49	9.48	9.78	10.00	12.72
Twin-Engine							
Piper Aircraft	41.70	44.09	46.72	44.44	45.43	45.80	41.46
Beech Aircraft	15.51	13.61	18.44	18.80	20.13	16.55	21.73
Cessna Aircraft	29.76	35.53	31.54	36.63	34.38	36.53	35.03
Other Manufacturers	10.71	12.44	3.29	.13	.06	.11	1.77
Turbo-Prop							
Piper Aircraft	15.30	18.15	23.99	21.22	20.23	12.19	17.43
Beech Aircraft	48.34	44.46	46.70	46.15	45.34	47.08	42.51
Cessna Aircraft	—	9.26	7.73	9.81	15.34	18.02	18.35
Other Manufacturers	36.36	28.13	21.58	22.81	19.09	22.54	21.71
Total Share							
Piper Aircraft	28.43	28.10	33.26	25.82	26.53	24.77	27.36
Beech Aircraft	7.85	7.26	8.87	11.28	12.96	14.01	14.57
Cessna Aircraft	51.98	52.48	46.62	54.31	51.55	51.45	46.06
Other Manufacturers	11.74	12.16	11.25	8.59	8.96	9.77	12.01

SOURCE: Extrapolated from Bangor Punta Financial Statements and GAMA Handbook for 1983.

NOTE: [1] Based on fiscal year ending September 30.

MARKETING

Domestic Market

Piper's niche in the aircraft industry had traditionally been in the light, single-engine market. Nevertheless, in the mid-1970s the company began to emphasize the twin-engine piston market. Piper's marketing strategy was directed at the business community, where the airplane was beginning to become an important business tool. By the end of 1976, Piper had produced over 2,000 aircraft of its Navajo line (a cabin-class, twin-engine) and held a 70% share sales in the market.

A new marketing strategy was beginning to take hold in 1977. Piper was putting more emphasis on increasing the market share of its twin-engine, piston and turbo-prop lines. (See Exhibits 29.7 and 29.8.) Piper also introduced a new

EXHIBIT 29.8	Unit Shipments per Category[1]						
	1977	1978	1979	1980	1981	1982	1983
Single-Engine							
Piper Aircraft	3,619	3,760	4,249	2,065	1,707	762	526
Beech Aircraft	712	699	707	638	557	277	173
Cessna Aircraft	7,772	8,290	7,117	5,894	4,435	2,157	1,078
Other Manufacturers	1,452	1,812	1,723	900	726	355	259
Total units	13,555	14,561	13,796	9,497	7,425	3,551	2,036
Twin-Engine							
Piper Aircraft	922	1,066	1,376	1,007	765	410	187
Beech Aircraft	343	329	543	426	339	245	98
Cessna Aircraft	658	859	929	830	579	320	158
Other Manufacturers	288	164	97	3	1	1	8
Total units	2,211	2,418	2,945	2,266	1,684	976	451
Turbo-Prop							
Piper Aircraft	69	100	149	160	178	73	57
Beech Aircraft	218	245	290	348	399	282	139
Cessna Aircraft	0	51	48	74	135	109	60
Other Manufacturers	164	155	134	172	168	135	71
Total units	451	551	621	754	880	599	327
Total Share							
Piper Aircraft	4,610	4,926	5,774	3,232	2,650	1,245	770
Beech Aircraft	1,273	1,273	1,540	1,412	1,295	704	410
Cessna Aircraft	8,430	9,200	8,094	6,798	5,149	2,586	1,296
Other Manufacturers	1,940	2,131	1,954	1,075	895	491	338
Total units	16,253	17,530	17,362	12,517	9,989	5,026	2,814

SOURCE: Extrapolated from Bangor Punta Financial Statements and GAMA Handbook for 1983.

[1] Based on fiscal year ending September 30.

trainer airplane, the Tomahawk. As stated in the September 30, 1977, year-end financial statement of Bangor Punta:

> (A student pilot training program) is the foundation of effective general aviation marketing. One in every three student pilots will eventually buy a plane. A majority of these purchases will be from the manufacturer of the plane in which the student trained.

By 1979, Piper's emphasis was shifted to the twin-engine piston and turbo-prop planes, which provided higher margins. With the Cheyenne and cabin-class twin-engine lines, Piper had developed its new niche in the industry.

In the 1980s, Piper began developing new planes for the commercial aviation market, specifically the small commuter-aircraft segment. In 1981, Piper introduced two nine-passenger models, the T1020 and T1040. These aircraft were hybrids of Piper's cabin-class twin-engine, Chieftain, which was very popular with the commuter industry. By 1985, Piper held 25% of the commuter aircraft market for planes with nine seats or less, and thereby accounted for the largest portion of aircraft in the commuter industry.

Government Contracts

In the late 1970s, Piper began to submit bids for government contracts for the first time since World War II. In September 1981 the Department of Defense awarded Piper a $12 million contract for operational demonstration of the Enforcer aircraft, a lightweight turbo-prop, close-support aircraft. The first year's funding of $5.8 million initiated Piper to defense work. The aircraft was designed after the World War II P-51 Mustang and could reach speeds of over 350 knots.

Piper did not expect the U.S. Air Force to purchase many of the aircraft. The company did believe that many third-world countries still flying old P-51's would be very interested in the Enforcer. As predicted, many countries in South and Central America as well as the Middle East showed great interest in this plane.

Competition

Piper's main competition has always been Beech Aircraft and Cessna Aircraft. Exhibit 29.9 shows the billings of the fourteen largest manufacturers of general aviation aircraft. Like Piper, both Beech and Cessna had been founded in the early 1930s, but their orientation had always been with the higher-priced, big single- and twin-engine aircraft.

Exhibits 29.7 and 29.8 give sales data for the three aircraft manufacturers. Beech, which had always relied on larger, high-margin aircraft, introduced its

EXHIBIT 29.9   **Summary of Manufacturers' Net Billings for Shipments of General Aviation Aircraft**

(Dollar Amounts In Thousands)

	NET BILLINGS			
	1983	1982	1981	1980
Ayres Corporation	$ 2,247	$ 4,031	$ 8,654	$ 7,491
Beech Aircraft	250,228	320,188	619,727	514,604
Bellanca	NA	NA	NA	2,910
Cessna Aircraft	362,545	531,877	895,679	783,518
Fairchild Aircraft	77,486	87,602	NA	NA
Gates Learjet	198,130	423,053	436,070	298,557
Gulfstream Aerospace	436,353	446,442	303,818	156,018
Lake Aircraft	3,204	2,018	4,165	4,424
Maule Aircraft	1,647	1,895	1,805	2,052
Mooney Aircraft	NA	NA	NA	NA
Piper Aircraft	135,238	179,008	368,846	335,465
Rockwell International	NA	NA	150,765	252,589
Schweizer Aircraft	2,427	3,349	717	NA
Swearingen	NA	NA	129,783	108,652
Total	$1,469,504	$1,999,463	$2,919,947	$2,486,182

SOURCE: General Aviation Manufacturers Association, *Summary of Shipments of General Aviation Airplanes*, 1983.

first turbo-prop, the King Air, in 1965. Beech continued to dominate the turbo-prop market in 1983.

In contrast, Cessna was the overall dominant force in general aviation. Its dominant market niche was the single-engine market; it held at least a 50% share from 1976 through 1983. Nevertheless, it has also recently begun to emphasize the high-margin, turbo-prop line.

Even though both Beech and Cessna were strong in 1983 in both the single-engine and turbo-prop markets, Piper was committed to expand its market share in each of these categories. In 1983, Piper introduced six new models to its product line, more than any of its competitors. In its turbo-prop line, Piper introduced three models: Cheyenne 1A, Cheyenne IIIA, and Cheyenne IV. (See Exhibit 29.10.) Two models were phased out. In the single-engine, wide-body line, Piper added the new pressurized Malibu. The Mojave was added to the cabin-class, twin-engine line. The Aerostar 700P was introduced to the light twin-engine line.

EXHIBIT 29.10   **1984 Models by Class, Piper Aircraft Corporation**

	PLANT LOCATIONS		
	Lock Haven, PA	Vero Beach, FL	Lakeland, FL
Single-engine trainer	Tomahawk	Archer II Warrior Dakota	
Single-engine wide-body		Saratoga[1] Malibu	
Light twin-engine		Seneca III Aerostar	
Cabin-class			Navajo Navajo C/R Chieftain Mojave[3] T1020[2]
Turbo-prop	Cheyenne IA Cheyenne IIXL T1040[2,3]		Cheyenne IIIA Cheyenne IV T1040[2,3]

NOTES: [1] There are four variations in the Saratoga line.

[2] T1040—commuter model.

[3] Parts of the T1040 and Mojave are built in Lakeland, FL, and the aircraft are finished in Lock Haven, PA.

Distribution

Piper's distribution system was based on a combination of three-tier and two-tier systems. The three-tier system flowed from the factory to the wholesale distributor and then to the dealer. The two-tier system began at the factory and went directly to the dealer. The two-tier system was the most common one in the industry. Some of the dealerships were factory owned. The factory directly served four types of dealers: the basic single-engine dealer, the twin-engine dealer, the single- and twin-engine dealer, and the turbo-prop dealer. The distributor in the three-tier system was an independent business contracting with independent dealers. Dealers who were not under a distributor were contracted directly by the factory.

In 1983, Piper established the Piper Airline Division to sell commuter aircraft direct from the factory to the customers. Even though the Airline Division was set up as a factory dealer, it did not enjoy many of the benefits other Piper dealers had. Specifically, the Airline Division could not take trade-in aircraft or get subsidy financing from Piper Acceptance Corporation.

Dealers were contracted at the beginning of each model year, October 1. To stay at a certain dealer level, they had to commit to buy a certain number of airplanes through the model year to September 30. If a dealer failed to meet its commitment, it could be downgraded or have its dealership terminated.

EXHIBIT 29.11   **Domestic and Export Sales of General Aviation Aircraft**

	SALES BY UNITS		EXPORT % OF PRODUCTION	FACTORY NET BILLINGS ($ MILLIONS)	% OF TOTAL BILLINGS
	Domestic	Export			
1983[1]	2,158	533	19.8%	318.9	21.7%
1982	3,104	1,162	27.2	650.2	32.5
1981	7,187	2,270	24.0	749.0	25.6
1980	8,322	3,555	30.0	756.4	29.9
1979	13,053	3,995	25.5	600.9	27.9

SOURCE: *General Aviation Statistical Databook*, 1983 Edition.

NOTE: [1] Extrapolated from GAMA.

Foreign Distribution

There were thirty-six Piper piston distributors and twenty-four turbo-prop distributors outside the United States. These distributors also acted as dealers.
Piper's foreign unit sales and billings are shown here.

	1983	**1982**	**1981**	**1980**
Units	208	311	764	1,134
Billing	$34,037,267	$48,146,369	$85,837,053	$96,620,842

Export sales for the industry as a whole are provided in Exhibit 29.11.

PRODUCTION

Facilities

One very important variable that Piper used to determine production levels was the annual dealers' commitment. Between 1979 and 1983, when the economy went through two recessionary periods, dealers became backlogged with inventory. This situation affected Piper at all levels of production. During fiscal year 1979, Piper had six plants in operation. These were in Lock Haven, Pennsylvania; Lakeland, Florida; Vero Beach, Florida; Santa Maria, California; Quehanna, Pennsylvania; and Renovo, Pennsylvania. Exhibit 29.10 shows 1984 model production by plant location. The Quehanna and Renovo plants manufactured additional parts, which were supplied to the main manufacturing plants. The Santa Maria plant produced only the Aerostar line.

Piper began to lay off workers in 1981. By 1983, Piper had reduced the number of plants to four. The plants in Renovo and Santa Maria were closed down so as to better utilize space in Piper's other plants. Besides closing plants, Piper reduced production and employment at the remaining plants. Exhibit 29.12 shows the effect on average employment.

EXHIBIT 29.12   **Financial Information, Piper Aircraft**
(Dollar Amounts in Millions)

Information[1]	1976	1977	1978	1979	1980	1981	1982	1983
Net sales	$210.8	$267.6	$336.7	$446.7	$391.1	$409.5	$234.2	$161.2
Capital expenditures	6.8	7.8	15.9	14.5	15.5	5.1	12.2	8.9
Depreciation	2.4	2.9	6.1	8.3	9.4	8.5	8.1	9.2
Operating profit or (loss)	14.4	27.3	34.4	42.1	26.3	17.6	(22.4)	(38.5)
Average assets employed	93.3	197.7	143.1	172.8	194.1	183.2	182.1	161.7
Average employment	5,236.0	5,927.0	7,042.0	8,067.0	6,867.0	6,328.0	3,771.0	2,534.0

NOTE: [1] Fiscal year ending September 30.

DOLLARS SALES PER PRODUCT
(MILLIONS OF DOLLARS)

Product	1976	1977	1978	1979	1980	1981	1982	1983
Single-Engine	$ 80.8	$111.0	$127.2	$143.7	$ 87.7	$ 87.0	$ 45.4	$ 36.2
Twin-Engine	90.5	103.7	133.2	192.0	171.7	151.3	89.7	45.5
Turbo-Prop	24.0	34.2	53.1	85.0	102.4	143.8	69.4	52.5
Parts & Service	15.5	18.7	23.2	26.0	29.3	27.4	29.7	27.0

Piper's Lock Haven plant was unionized. Its two Florida plants were currently nonunion. Although Florida was a right-to-work state, unionization problems could occur if layoffs continued.

Technology

Piper Aircraft has made significant strides to keep up with technological changes in the general aviation industry. One key example was the new single-engine Malibu. This aircraft had been totally computer designed inside and out to give the passengers maximum comfort and the pilot the best handling characteristics. The Malibu was the world's first cabin-class pressurized single-engine aircraft in the industry. Production of the Malibu for 1984 was sold out before 1983 ended.

One important factor in Piper's favor was its emphasis on the use of engines specifically designed for its aircraft. Both the Malibu and the new Cheyenne IV (the industry's first 400-mph turbo-prop) had engines designed specifically for them. The new Cheyenne IV's engine not only produced speeds of 400 mph, a speed comparable to that of small jets, but it performed on 35% less fuel than did Cessna's Citation business jet.

The Cheyenne IV was the fastest prop jet in the world and had been designed as an alternative to the corporate jet. The Cheyenne 1A was the lowest priced prop jet on the market. The Cheyenne IIIA flew faster and farther than any comparable prop jet. The Aerostar 700P was the fastest piston twin in the world.

Piper has also been able to use the latest state of the air avionics. The Cheyenne IV could be equipped with an Electronic Flight Instrument System, similar to systems used on Boeing's new 757 and 767.

FINANCIAL INFORMATION	Piper

During the late 1970s Piper Aircraft had flourished, as sales between 1976 and 1979 increased an average of 30%. (See Exhibit 29.12.) Also during this period, net profits increased an average of 45%. In 1976, Piper boosted its company-wide machine-modernization and plant-expansion programs. These programs continued to 1980, with average annual increases in capital expenditures of 60% beginning in 1975. In 1978, Piper purchased Ted Smith Aerostar, Inc., including its plant in Santa Maria, California.

In 1981, Piper's sales still climbed, but the net profit margin declined from 6.7% in 1980 to 4.3%. For the next two years, sales dropped to a level not seen since 1975. The sales decreased from 1981 to 1983 by an annual average of 37%, while unit shipments declined by an average of 45% for the same period.

Besides the decline in sales, subsidy payments to Piper Acceptance Corporation (PAC), Piper's financing subsidiary, increased. Piper Acceptance had been formed in 1976 to finance aircraft for Piper's piston dealers and their retail

EXHIBIT 29.13 Selected Financial Information, Bangor Punta Corporation
(Dollar Amounts in Millions, Except Per Share Data)

Business Segment	1983 Net Operating Sales	1983 Net Operating Profit/Loss	1982 Net Operating Sales	1982 Net Operating Profit/Loss	1981 Net Operating Sales	1981 Net Operating Profit/Loss	1980 Net Operating Sales	1980 Net Operating Profit/Loss
Piper Aircraft	$161.2	($38.5)	$234.2	($22.4)	$409.5	$17.6	$391.1	$26.3
Smith & Wesson	126.2	7.2	152.5	23.7	145.0	23.6	124.3	22.3
Recreation products	172.0	20.6	124.9	8.8	101.0	4.3	101.5	2.8
Agriculture	88.3	8.9	97.4	10.4	118.2	13.9	115.4	13.6
Industrial products	—	—	13.3	0.2	25.8	0.1	26.6	2.5
Total	$547.7	($1.8)	$622.3	$20.7	$800.0	$59.5	$758.6	$67.5

Information	1983	1982	1981	1980
Net sales	$547.7	$622.3	$800.0	$758.6
Gross profit	76.5	100.1	129.0	128.2
Net income (loss)	(64.4)	3.1	44.2	33.8
Current assets	275.6	305.7	289.6	296.5
Current liabilities	106.4	124.9	118.6	124.5
Total assets	534.6	551.5	529.8	516.3
Long-term debt	143.2	145.5	157.5	173.0
EPS	($9.11)	$ 0.34	$ 6.06	$ 4.28
Net worth per share	$ 19.20	29.52	30.6	25.87
Common shares (000s)	7,149	7,027	7,160	7,250

SOURCE: Bangor Punta Corporation, *1983 Annual Report.*

customers. Piper Acceptance did not begin financing the turbo-prop line until 1983, and that service was only for retail customers. Piper's original investment in PAC became more important to the financing of Piper products, as high interest rates, a recessionary economy, and restrictive credit policies by banks and finance companies choked off sales. For PAC to acquire funds from banks, Piper had to maintain a minimum capital investment so that PAC could meet its defined net worth and fixed charges coverage tests. In addition, Piper had agreed to subsidize interest costs incurred by dealers and retail customers through PAC, under certain incentive programs. Piper made payments to PAC of $127,000 in 1979; $1,505,000 in 1980; $5,829,000 in 1981; $7,247,000 in 1982 and $4,965,000 in 1983.

Bangor Punta

Exhibit 29.13 contains relevant financial information on Bangor Punta Corporation.

LEAR SIEGLER ACQUIRES PIPER

On December 12, 1983, Bangor Punta and Lear Siegler top managements agreed on a merger of their two companies, and Bangor Punta was brought into Lear Siegler. According to its second-quarter report dated December 31, 1983, Lear Siegler stated that:

> Bangor Punta represented the right company at the right time. Our aerospace and defense contracting experience and our financial resources will allow Bangor Punta's businesses to accelerate product and marketing development programs. Each of the company's operations has demonstrated the ability to achieve leadership in the markets it serves and to maintain its tradition of excellence during the difficult economic times of the recent past.

Lear Siegler was organized into the following six business segments:

- Aerospace
- Material handling/machine tools
- Electronics
- Auto service products
- Auto/agricultural
- Commercial products

Exhibit 29.14 contains relevant financial information on Lear Siegler before the merger. Information about Lear Siegler's operations, objectives, strategic planning, acquisition strategy, management development, and productivity is provided in Exhibit 29.15.

Top executives of Piper Corporation wondered whether they would lose the autonomy that Bangor Punta had previously allowed them in managing the

EXHIBIT 29.14

Selected Financial Information, Lear Siegler, Inc.
(Dollar Amounts in Thousands, Except Per Share Data)

Business Segment	1983 Net Operating Sales	1983 Profit	1982 Net Operating Sales	1982 Profit	1981 Net Operating Sales	1981 Profit	1980 Net Operating Sales	1980 Profit
Aerospace	$ 488,978	$ 74,365	$ 419,575	$ 66,279	$ 384,304	$ 61,549	$ 350,235	$ 52,374
Material Handling/Machine Tool	267,352	12,022	327,596	32,092	369,605	49,175	287,193	44,589
Electronics	128,641	9,403	141,041	13,190	164,271	18,121	161,790	16,885
Auto Service Products	203,280	23,868	195,372	18,531	192,889	21,526	176,130	19,336
Auto/Agricultural	243,473	20,914	260,019	27,705	262,755	24,919	297,387	23,886
Commercial Products	132,466	11,717	143,902	15,882	156,875	21,811	150,662	18,763
Total	$1,464,190	$152,289	$1,487,505	$173,679	$1,530,699	$197,101	$1,423,397	$175,803

Information	1983	1982	1981	1980
Net sales	$1,464,190	$1,487,505	$1,530,699	$1,423,397
Gross profit	351,526	380,635	405,184	355,930
Net income (loss)	64,122	72,295	76,067	65,772
Total assets	894,898	909,697	864,641	841,067
Working capital	288,785	292,848	294,314	317,647
Government backlog	601,000	591,000	318,000	321,000
Long-term debt	108,295	157,544	148,124	204,176
EPS	$3.84	$4.36	$4.71	$4.23
Book value per share	$28.15	$25.74	$24.00	$20.80
Common Shares (000s)	16,483	16,371	15,896	15,129

EXHIBIT 29.15   **About Lear Siegler, Inc.**

OPERATIONS

Lear Siegler (LSI) is a broadly based manufacturer of components, assemblies and systems for consumer, industrial and military customers the world over. LSI's most important sales objective is to establish and maintain a leading market position for each product line.

Headquartered in Santa Monica, California, LSI operates 45 divisions and subsidiaries in 25 states and 10 foreign countries. For effective management and control of these diverse facilities, the Company's operations are divided into six major business segments, each under the direction of a corporate vice president.

LSI plays a vital role in upgrading American and allied defenses and in increasing the efficiency of commercial aircraft. The Company's aerospace activities are highly diversified among military and commercial programs, domestic and foreign sales and new and retrofit equipment.

Lear Siegler is the largest designer and manufacturer of material handling systems for industrial facilities, warehouses and distribution centers. It is also the leading manufacturer of gear cutting, honing and finishing machines.

The Company produces professional sound equipment and computer terminals and printers, and in telecommunications, it manufactures telephone line treatment equipment and test equipment.

LSI is a leading manufacturer, wholesaler and retailer of automotive replacement glass, and it makes and distributes the most complete line of replacement disc brake linings in North America.

The Company manufactures original equipment components, such as truck and trailer air suspension systems and brake products for heavy trucks, as well as automotive seating assemblies in the United States, Canada, Mexico, Germany, and France. Its principal agricultural products are grain handling equipment and specialized tillage equipment.

Lear Siegler's commercial products are directed toward specific markets influenced primarily by consumer spending and housing starts. They include heating and air conditioning units, furniture components and pre-engineered structural steel buildings.

OBJECTIVES

The key to successful management is the adoption and observance of certain fundamental principles. In the case of Lear Siegler, these have been stated in the following primary objectives:

To continually improve the quality and effectiveness of management through the selection, development and utilization of outstanding people.

To encourage, foster and stimulate the development and growth of new products and new markets to insure internal growth.

To satisfy customer needs with a marketing program, based on sound marketing research, that provides quality products, properly serviced and competitively priced.

(Continued)

EXHIBIT 29.15   (Continued)

To identify and pursue acquisitions in high-growth markets.

To maximize profitability and return on investment under any economic conditions through better utilization of resources, a constant surveillance of operations and strict financial controls.

To recognize changing economic conditions and to redeploy affected assets.
To achieve annual productivity improvement in all divisions.

STRATEGIC PLANNING

LSI's strategic planning program contributes significantly to the growth, competitive position and financial performance of the Company. An essential part of this program is an annual evaluation of the Company's more than 200 product lines by management at all levels of the organization. This analysis includes a review of the competitive standing of each product line, the economic conditions affecting its performance and other market and operational factors. Goals and strategies are then developed for each.

ACQUISITION STRATEGY

LSI's acquisition program is broad in interest and flexible in approach. It is designed to accelerate growth, improve earnings and complement the Company's product base.

Lear Siegler is interested in companies with strong profit, product and market positions; a record of growth and a favorable outlook; a demonstrated ability to generate earnings with an attractive return on investment, and capable management which will remain with an organization.

MANAGEMENT DEVELOPMENT

The Company's management development program provides regular assessment of LSI's overall management situation; realistic projections of the Company's anticipated management needs; procedures to adequately identify, motivate, monitor and reward management; formalized job rotation; techniques to identify and accommodate managers who demonstrate potential; and orderly and timely top management succession.

PRODUCTIVITY

Lear Siegler recognizes that increasing the Company's productivity significantly improves its competitive position in the marketplace. The corporate office provides leadership, motivation and encouragement and closely monitors the progress of the program at every Company facility.

LSI has proceeded on the premise that the people who know most about their jobs and how to improve them are the employees themselves. Numerous valuable and often ingenious suggestions on how to improve a process, add value to a product or simplify a task have been implemented.

SOURCE: *This Is LSI* (Santa Monica, CA: Lear Siegler, Inc., 1983), pp. 2–3. Reprinted by permission.

company. Given Lear Siegler's objectives, would Lear Siegler tolerate Piper's recent poor financial performance, especially the losses of the past two years? Piper's managers were also concerned that Piper's product identity and image might be lost within the dominant corporate identity of Lear Siegler.

NOTES

1. Francis Devon, *Mr. Piper and His Cubs* (Ames: The Iowa State University Press, 1973), p. 8

2. *Ibid.*, p. 219.

3. *Ibid.*, p. 228.

4. Bangor Punta Corporation, *1983 Annual Report*, p. 43.

Bally Manufacturing Corporation

SEXTON ADAMS • ADELAIDE GRIFFIN

The United States has always been a gambling society. Since the pilgrims landed at Plymouth rock, odds have been set, and lottery chances have been sold. The thirteen original colonies were "largely financed by lotteries, as were Harvard, Yale, Princeton, Brown, Dartmouth, and Columbia."[1] Thomas Jefferson described the lottery as a tax on the willing.[2] Gambling seems to be an American way of life. But what kind of life? "Public attitudes remain essentially judgmental and moralistic toward compulsive gambling and the compulsive gambler."[3] Dr. Scrully Blotnick, a research psychologist, found in a survey of lottery gamblers that 37% found something wrong with spending their money this way.[4] Forty-three percent said they would not play if giving their name and Social Security number was required.[5] It is not that they are naive, they know that the odds are against them; they have a deep passion for gambling. They love the "action." This is epitomized in the classic saying of the compulsive gambler: "Do you know what the next best thing to gambling and winning is? Gambling and losing."[6] Bally Manufacturing, by self definition, is in the gaming (which includes gambling) business.

HISTORY

Bally Manufacturing was incorporated in 1931 during the depths of the Great Depression. During the days of Prohibition, the owners and operators of "speak-easies" (illegal saloons) found that their clients wanted more entertainment than simply drinking illegally and dancing. These owners turned to two old ideas that were reborn during this time. The first of these was the invention from the mid-1800s called the nickel-in-the-slot machine. Today these are known as slot

This case was prepared by Jeff Chastain, Mike Ladd, Terry Byrne, Rick Bonczynski and Schuching Chuang under the supervision of Professor Sexton Adams, North Texas State University, and Professor Adelaide Griffin, Texas Woman's University. Copyright © 1988 by Sexton Adams and Adelaide Griffin.

machines. Owners of speakeasies found that these machines were instant successes in their establishments. A second machine also became popular in the nineteenth century. It was a French game called *Bagatelle* in which players used sticks to maneuver a ball around several pins and into a hole. During the 1920s, this game was modified into a game called *pinball*. With the advent of electricity, this game included flashing lights and electronic sounds. Again, owners of speakeasies found instant success. Bally Manufacturing began manufacturing and marketing these legal machines to various criminal establishments. It would be difficult for Bally to rid itself of this alleged alliance with organized crime.

THE COMPANY

In the 1980s Bally Manufacturing described itself as "a leader in the leisure and recreation market."[7] The basic goal of the company was to create game machines that "comprise a meaningful, attractive and enduring business."[8] Bally had continued to hold the idea that gaming and leisure were important elements of modern life. Bally Manufacturing was "organized in whole or in part, to develop, market or utilize games in one way or another."[9] For over fifty-five years, Bally has maintained a leadership position in this industry. The following is a description of a few of these games.

Pinball and Video Machines

William T. O'Donnell, founder of Bally Manufacturing, saw a rise in the sales of slot machines and pinball machines in the late 1920s. O'Donnell saw this as an opportunity to get into a growing business and founded Bally. Video machines were a late comer to the leisure market, but Bally had a major role in the business.

Surprisingly, pinball and video machines represented the rise of Bally and were the most solid business segment. But by 1987, pinball did not carry the weight it once did, although it was the product that Bally was perhaps best known for. In the 1969 landmark rock opera *Tommy* by The Who, there was a song entitled "Pinball Wizard." One line from the song emphasized Bally's presence in the pinball market: "I thought I was the Bally table king. But I just handed my pinball crown to him."[10]

Also in 1987, video machines were no longer a major segment of Bally's business because of economic conditions. Video represented about 7% of revenues and about 14% of operating income. According to industry observers, some of this performance could be attributed to the manufacture and sale of video machines, but, for the most part, the performance was due to the operation of arcades. The major advantage of video machine manufacture may have been in having the technology for use in the gaming equipment (e.g., slot machines) and for use in health and fitness equipment (e.g., Lifecircuit). These machines have utilized video technology in recent years and Bally's expertise in video technology probably made the transition into these areas easier.

Hotel Casinos

In 1979 Bally made a decision which would change the complexion of the company forever. Bally acquired 84% of the Park Place casino in Atlantic City, New Jersey (Atlantic City voted in casino gambling in 1978). This decision brought an adverse decision from the New Jersey Casino Control Commission when it came to license Bally's Park Place. The Commission refused to license Bally because William T. O'Donnell, Bally's founder, was found to have been allegedly "a partner with organized crime fronts and had tried to bribe the Kentucky legislature."[11] Mr. O'Donnell resigned his post and Robert Mullane took the helm.

However, this was not the last time some sort of legal scandal would hit Bally. In 1986, the purchase of the MGM Grand Hotels in Las Vegas and Reno was conditional upon Bally's Park Place Executive Vice-President Dorothy Attanasio taking a leave of absence to be investigated by the licensing board in Nevada.[12]

Lottery and Gaming Equipment

Bally was a relatively recent player in the lottery industry; however, the company's subsidiary Scientific Games, Inc., became one of the largest of the lottery servicing companies. In 1987, eleven state lotteries were being served by Bally.

The lottery was reinstated in 1964 in New Hampshire. Since then several states have followed suit. However, the fight against lotteries has not subsided. One senator from Minnesota said, "You can't run a successful lottery by telling the whole truth." He was alluding to the "take" by the state. It had been argued that if the average person knew how much a state makes from the lottery, the lottery would not prosper. The morality of gambling had not been the issue lately. The real question and the winning argument in the only state to defeat a lottery had been the political implications. Most lotteries were not efficiently operated according to industry observers.

Bally had not escaped the scandals of the lotteries. In the 1982 battle for the California lottery, Scientific Games, Inc. was the only bidder. It was alleged that "Bally lawyers wrote the lottery initiative and bankrolled the campaign to pass it. Their law required that lottery contractors reveal income tax returns of all owners, officers and directors—something that Bally happened to have done already to get a license for its casino in New Jersey."[13] When some legislators attempted to relax these requirements to encourage competition, a change was added to the amendment of the bill causing all Republicans to vote against the amendment. This brought on speculation that the House Speaker may have been "in cahoots with Bally, which had put at least $14,500 into his campaign fund."[14]

One of Bally's strongest segments was the production of slot machines. In 1987, Bally was the world's largest producer of slot machines and held a 50%

market share in the industry.[15] Bally has utilized its video machine expertise in this area to create new and innovative slot machines. One of the best things about these machines was that Bally could produce and sell some for a profit while operating some for a profit in its casinos. As discussion continued about Bally's future direction, one thing was clear: Bally would not dispose of its slot-machine-production facilities.[16]

Leisure and Entertainment

Chairman Mullane's strategic plan was to move away from Bally's dependence on slot machines and video games. Bally immediately began to make acquisitions in the leisure and entertainment industry. In 1982 Bally acquired Six Flags Corporation and became a leader in theme parks. In 1984, Bally acquired Health and Tennis Corporation and became the largest operator of fitness centers in America. Subsequently, Bally has tried to sell some of its holdings, including Health and Tennis, but has not been successful.

Bally's business was summarized by one word—games. It was the need for games that created Bally in the 1930s and it was the desire for gaming that sustained its existence.

THE GAMING INDUSTRY'S IMAGE PROBLEM

When Bally's founder William T. O'Donnell was asked to step down as Chairman of Bally Manufacturing Corporation because of his alleged ties with Mob officials, the gaming industry's reaction was one of "old news." Mob presence in the gaming industry had been suspected and fought for many years. Bally would not be the only company ever accused of unscrupulous activities. For example, in February, 1985, the New Jersey Casino Control Commission, which had earned a national reputation for policing Mob influence, refused to grant Hilton Hotels Corporation a gaming license for its new $308 million casino hotel in Atlantic City because of "allegations that the company continued to let reputed organized crime figures use the San Francisco Hilton for business meetings even after an internal company investigation in 1976 had identified them."[17] Also the Commission cited Hilton's ties since 1972 with Sidney Korshak, a Chicago labor lawyer believed to be the senior advisor to organized crime leaders throughout the country.

The industry's tarnished image was not entirely the result of Mob influence. Alleged bribery and cheating had also been mentioned. Resorts International, Inc., in February, 1985, was delayed the renewal of their gaming license because it was alleged that $341,000 of Resort's money ended up in the hands of the Prime Minister of the Bahamas, where the company had another casino. In a separate incident, Stuart and Clifford Perlman, co-founders of the Caesars Palace casino hotel, were denied a New Jersey gaming license because, "the jet-setting international high-rollers were gambling on credit and stiffing the house."[18] Finally, in April, 1986, Bally Manufacturing made the news when a federally protected witness, Vincent Ponzio, charged that in 1983, Bally Park Place Executive Vice-President Dorothy Attanasio had accepted a kickback from a cleaning service company given a contract with the casino in 1982. As a result, the Nevada Gaming Commission issued a dictum to both Attanasio, who was placed on leave of absence, and Park Place President Richard Gillman, to avoid any contact with the company's ongoing negotiations for the purchase of the Las Vegas and Reno MGM Grand casino hotels.

MANAGEMENT

Robert E. Mullane, (age 56 in 1988), President, Chairman and CEO of Bally Manufacturing Corporation, and Harvard Business School M.B.A., worked in the securities and vending machine business before joining Bally in 1971. He moved up through the company's arcade games business, and by 1974 was appointed to head Bally's Electronic Gaming business in Europe. In 1978, Mullane returned to the company's headquarters in Chicago and was asked by the Bally Board of Directors to replace the company's founder and Chairman William T. O'Donnell.[19]

By 1980, Mullane felt that Bally had made a strategic planning error by staying too long with the electromechanical generation of amusement arcade games (pinball machines) and "missing the boat" on the booming new video games craze. Although Bally did have tremendous success with two electronic games, *Space Invaders* and *PacMan*, Mullane was not satisfied and commented, "A game supplier needs a constant stream of new ideas, because a single game has a life span of only two years and a peak profit period of only ten months."[20] At this point in his career, Mullane's true underlying management style began to surface, and Bally's "new look" began to emerge.

Mullane had two single business management philosophies: (1) bigger is always better, and (2) it's better to be lucky than good. In keeping with the latter style, Mullane began to build Bally's arcade gaming business by hiring in-house staff designers who could create something new and entertaining for the customers and move away from the company's reliance on Japanese ideas. However, by 1981 it was apparent to Mullane that two factors threatened the company's survivability: (1) extreme competition and (2) an arcade boom that had, in reality, been nothing but a fad. If Bally was to survive through the 1980s, it would have to diversify away from the arcade gaming industry, and diversify it did. As *Business Week* noted, "The company began to act like the PacMan character that brought it success. Under Chairman Mullane Bally gobbled businesses at a dizzying pace: theme parks, health clubs, lottery services and casino properties."[21] Although Mullane's diversification mix seemed unusual to the outsider, he defended it with his belief that being bigger meant not being afraid of the competition. As Mullane put it, "it's the tier below us that is going to get hurt."[22] But when Bally's operating performance failed to respond to this diversification mix and as the company's balance sheet showed ever-increasing levels of debt, shareholders became restless and placed growing pressure on Mullane to perform, at one point demanding justification for his $1.8 million-per-year salary. As one shareholder stated, "It appears Mullane is managing Bally for himself."[23]

Richard Gillman, 52, Chairman of Bally's Park Place casino hotel in Alantic City, had considerable responsibilities over Bally's other casino hotel operations in New Jersey and Nevada. His expertise in casino hotel management went beyond the strategies that generated impressive earnings and market share. In 1985, Gillman served as President of the Atlantic City Casino Association and took on the responsibility of resolving the many problems that faced Atlantic City (lack of transportation facilities and a maturing market, among others) in addition to providing the leadership and direction for Bally's casinos in two markets, 1,800 miles apart. Gillman required of himself and his staff "excellence in innovation," and service to the customer. He stated if the customer was served at a level better than the competitors, they (the customers) would return to the Atlantic City, Las Vegas/Reno markets while providing new customers through referral. Gillman insists "the market is there, it's just a question of getting people here." Providing customers with what they need was the answer, while keeping costs, both to the company and the customer, at a minimum.

Exhibit 30.1 presents Bally Manufacturing's organizational chart. All corporate officers reported directly to Chairman Mullane, although they operated each subsidiary on their own with their respective staffs. However, all decisions were ultimately reviewed by Mullane within a very centralized environment. Business unit planning was the responsibility of each subsidiary's management while Mullane provided the final approval or rejection.

BUSINESS SEGMENTS

Bally Manufacturing Corporation underwent dramatic changes relating to its business unit mix, over the thirty months from June, 1985 to December, 1987. As Exhibit 30.2 indicates, as of December 31, 1985, Bally's revenues broke down into 26.6% from Casino Hotels, followed by Health and Fitness (38.5%), Amusement Gaming Services (18.1%), and Gaming Equipment and Services (16.8%). By December 31, 1987, the revenue emphasis had shifted to Casino Hotels (49.9%), Health and Fitness (32.8%), Gaming Equipment and Services (10.4%) and Amusement Gaming Services (6.9%). Bally experienced successful operations in each of its primary business segments but the operating emphasis had begun to shift from a stable health and fitness and gaming equipment and services to a heavier emphasis in the more competitive casino hotel market.

Casino Hotels

Bally Manufacturing Corporation through its subsidiary, Bally's Park Place Incorporated, operated four casino hotels, two in Atlantic City, N.J., one in Las Vegas, Nevada, and one in Reno, Nevada.

EXHIBIT 30.1   Key Executives, Bally Manufacturing Corporation

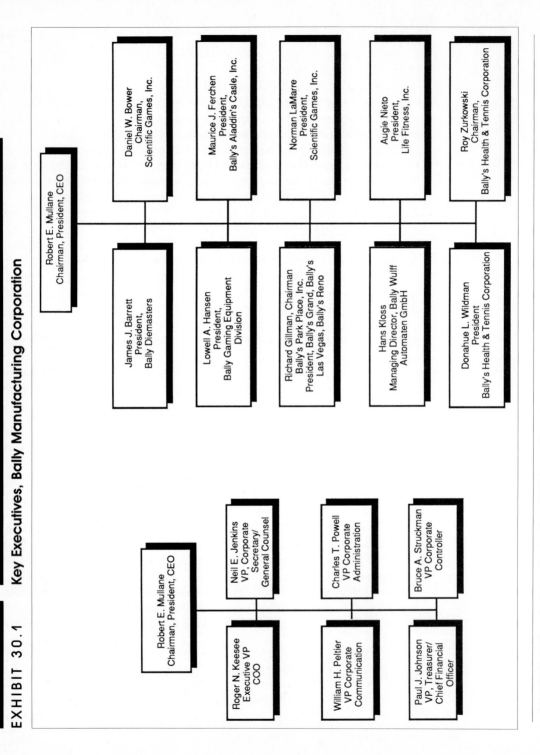

SOURCE: Bally Manufacturing Corporation, 1987 Annual Report.

EXHIBIT 30.2   **Revenue by Business Segment 1985–1987, Bally Manufacturing, Inc.**

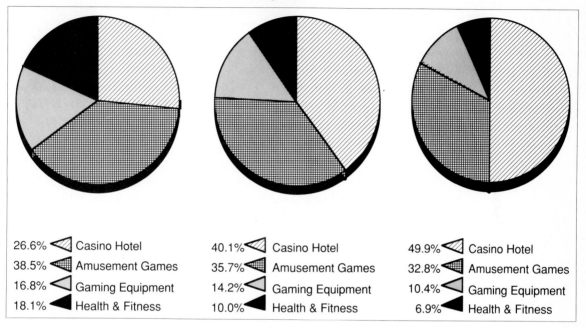

26.6% Casino Hotel	40.1% Casino Hotel	49.9% Casino Hotel
38.5% Amusement Games	35.7% Amusement Games	32.8% Amusement Games
16.8% Gaming Equipment	14.2% Gaming Equipment	10.4% Gaming Equipment
18.1% Health & Fitness	10.0% Health & Fitness	6.9% Health & Fitness

SOURCE: Bally Manufacturing, Inc., *1987 Annual Report.*

Atlantic City

Bally's Park Place, located in the heart of Atlantic City, encompassed 1.6 million square feet. The hotal offered 510 deluxe rooms while the casino included 60,000 square feet of gaming area. In addition, the facility offered a cabaret, cocktail lounges, restaurants, retail shops, and a 40,000-square-foot health spa. Citing a lack of convention and hotel space in Atlantic City, management embarked on the construction of an 800-room tower connected to the Bally's Park Place facility; completion was expected in late 1988. Management also intended to enlarge the casino and restaurant areas of the facility in the near future.

The Bally's Grand facility, located on the Boardwalk in Atlantic City, encompassed 1.2 million square feet. The hotel offered over 5,600 deluxe rooms and suites, a 43,500-square-foot casino, plus casino restaurants, retail shops, and a health facility. Bally's Grand was the newest casino hotel under Bally management, as it was purchased from Golden Nugget, Inc. in 1987. It launched Bally into a leadership role in the casino hotel marketplace.

Casino hotel operations in Atlantic City peaked during the summer months and tended to be less favorable during the winter. The two Bally facilities in Atlantic City employed more than 7,000 persons.

Bally's Park Place was the company's initial venture into casino hotel ownership and the establishment had performed well in the Atlantic City market. Park Place had a $22.3 million improvement in 1987 sales over 1986, an accomplishment during a period that saw the total casino hotel presence in Atlantic City grow to twelve. Park Place was one of only five Atlantic City casino hotels that earned a profit during the first quarter of 1988, a quarter in which the industry lost $17.8 million. During the second quarter of 1988, Park Place realized the highest profits of the twelve Atlantic City casino hotels: it earned $5.9 million on revenues of $69.8 million, or 9.8% of the market.

Bally's Grand, which was designed to attract the wealthy "high roller," contributed $230.5 million toward revenues during its ten months of operations in 1987, and was another of the five profitable casino hotels during the first quarter of 1988. The second quarter of 1988 saw profits of $1.1 million on revenues of $67.1 million (9.4% market share) compared to a $2.1 million loss a year earlier while under the Golden Nugget ownership.

Nevada

The Las Vegas casino hotel market included Bally's Las Vegas, a 3.2-million-square-foot facility with 2,800 rooms and suites, located on 43.3 acres on the busy "Vegas Strip". The facility also offered showrooms, restaurants, a motion picture theater, and 167,000 square feet of convention area.

The Bally's Reno facility included 2.6 million square feet of space, and was surrounded by 142 acres, which included a 32-acre lake. This casino was believed to be Reno's largest, at 100,000 square feet including 2,000 rooms and suites, convention space, restaurants, entertainment, movie theaters, bowling lanes, and a shopping area. Bally's Reno as well as Las Vegas facilities were situated very well to compete against the casino hotels in the Nevada market. Business in Las Vegas and Reno was also seasonal, peaking in the summer, while declining in the winter months. Bally's two Nevada facilities employed 7,400 persons.

The four months of operations of Bally's Las Vegas and Bally's Reno contributed an additional $117.4 million in revenues while improving operating income by $19.6 million during 1987.

Health and Fitness

In 1988, Bally Manufacturing's subsidiary, Bally Health and Tennis, was the largest operator of health clubs in the United States, in terms of revenue and membership. This business unit's health and fitness center included such popular clubs as Presidents, Jack Lalanne, Chicago Health Clubs, and Scandinavian.

Most of the clubs were located in large markets such as New York, Los Angeles, Chicago, Dallas, and Cleveland. Bally's Health and Tennis Clubs offered planned exercise programs and instruction stressing cardiovascular conditioning, strength development, and improved appearance. Most of the centers provided amenities such as indoor swimming pools, racquetball courts, whirlpools, steam rooms, and progressive-resistance exercise equipment. In addition, nutritional centers, restaurants, and bars could be found in some clubs.

Included within the Health and Fitness unit was the fitness equipment area of Bally Manufacturing, known as Life Fitness, Inc. This business segment manufactured many of the pieces of equipment found in health clubs throughout the country. Most notable was the Lifecycle stationary exercise bike. This product had gained market-wide acceptance and built a strong reputation in both the fitness club and home fitness market. Also, the Liferower stationary rowing machine was gaining the same kind of acceptance. Life Fitness, Inc.'s newest product was the Lifecircuit computerized strength training equipment. Life Fitness, Inc. marketed its products to both fitness centers and to homes. Life Fitness President Augie Nieto states, "We prove the success of the equipment in the health clubs, then we tailor it for the home."[24] Nieto believed the key to success in the highly competitive fitness industry was based upon the equipment's design and reliability, not to mention price. People wanted computerized exercise equipment with flashy graphics showing rpm's and number of calories burned. Bally would appear to be a natural for the manufacture of these products given in the company's success with video games.

Health and Fitness revenues totaled $575.6 million during 1987, an increase of $122 million (27%) over 1986. The improvement was due in part to an 18% increase in existing health club revenues and, to a lesser extent, an increase of nineteen new clubs during the year. Bally also closed fifteen unprofitable clubs that did not attract the minimum number of patrons (750 members for the average size club) during 1987. In addition, revenues during 1987 were positively impacted by a $27.4 million increase (127%) in Life Fitness, Inc. sales, due to the successful marketing of Life Fitness equipment for the home market. During the first quarter of 1988, Bally management was concerned with the state of the fitness movement in both the United States and world wide, and began to seriously question both Bally's Health and Tennis and Life Fitness, Inc. as viable components of the company's long-term plan, fearing that long-term earnings could be hurt if the fitness boom fizzled.

Gaming Equipment and Services

Through its Gaming Equipment and Services business unit, Bally manufactured slot machines for the casino hotels market throughout the United States and foreign locations. Bally considered itself a leading manufacturer of slot devices, which were built in its Benseville, Illinois, facility. The machines offered basic electronic-reel-type action along with electronic video slot and other video gaming models. All possessed variations in design, payout features, and coinage acceptance. Bally utilized internal sources as well as independent distributors and sales representatives to distribute its gaming equipment throughout the United States (Atlantic City, Reno and Las Vegas) and elsewhere in the world. Distributors were expected to keep an inventory of parts and to service and maintain the equipment. Management stressed the importance of product performance, service, and design along with competitive pricing. Bally continuously improved models and constructed new variations of models providing added security and accounting for income and payout.

Bally designed, produced, and supplied instant ticket lottery games to thirteen states that operated lotteries in the United States and to several foreign jurisdictions, as of 1987. In addition, its subsidiary, Scientific Games, Inc., developed, produced and supplied on-line lottery systems used in player-selected numbers games such as Lotto. The Gaming Equipment and Services business employed approximately 860 persons in the United States and 380 persons in its foreign operations in Berlin, Germany (Bally Wulff).

Revenues for the Gaming Equipment and Services segment increased $2.6 million (1%) during 1987 to $182.5 million. However, the improved performance was due almost entirely to better sales of German wall machines (slots) sold by Bally's foreign operations, Bally Wulff. Besides the greater demand for these wall machines by European nations, there was also a high average foreign exchange rate during 1987 compared to 1986 which translated to improved operating results. The improved revenue results created by better foreign sales were substantially offset in 1987 by disappointing lottery product and service revenues due to a reduction in the number and unit price of lottery tickets sold. But as Norman Lamarre (President of Scientific Games, Inc.) stated, "It is very difficult to keep a state's population interested in the lottery. Typically, the first year has exceptional sales with a gradual decline thereafter resulting from individuals' realization of the limited odds of winning."[25] For the first time since the birth of the modern lottery, price had become a leading competitive factor in obtaining business. As a result, in 1987, Scientific Games, Inc. began a cost reduction program involving staff reductions, consolidation of product related operations, and increased self-sufficiency in areas such as ink production and graphics for lottery ticket printing.

In 1987, the Gaming Equipment Division began shipment of the company's new System 5000 series slot machine to all casinos in New Jersey and Nevada. In addition, final touches were being made to the new V5000 line of slots that combined System 5000 technology with video and would be tested at U.S. Army and Air Force bases located in Europe and the Far East. Of the products that were included in Gaming Equipment and Services, Bally management was most impressed with the future prospects, both nationally and internationally, of slot machines. The reasons for management's high hopes were simple. First, as *Fortune* pointed out in March, 1987, "On average, a casino pays maybe $5,000 for a slot machine. The average casino in Atlantic City and Nevada had around 1,230 of the machines on its casino floor in 1986, and just standing there for a year, with essentially no human help, they won $124 million from the players—an average of $100,598 per machine. Try to name another piece of capital equipment yielding a return of over 1900%."[26] Second, the international prospects for Bally were as favorable as ever in 1987. Holland had recently approved the legalization of slots and in France, the use of slots outside of casinos was expected by 1988.

Amusement Games and Services

The Amusement Games and Services business unit owned and operated 300 family amusement centers under the Bally's Aladdin's Castle, Inc. subsidiary. The centers were located in various shopping malls throughout the United States and offered forty to sixty-five coin-operated amusement games within a 1,000 to 2,500 square foot facility. Perhaps Bally Manufacturing, Inc. had cemented its name and success as a result of its subsidiary, Bally Midway Sente, which had designed, manufactured, and sold "Pac Man," "Ms. Pac Man" and "Space Invaders," three highly successful Bally creations.

Bally manufactured one of the first truly successful pinball machines early in this century. "BallyHoo" sold 50,000 units in 1932, establishing a trend, a company and an industry. Chairman Mullane believed that success in the electronic video and pinball amusement game markets depended upon design and player appeal, not to mention increasing skill and difficulty levels. The pinball and video games were marketed throughout the United States and Canada, along with Europe, Japan and Australia, by a line of distributors who also handled other lines of coin-operated amusement games. The Amusement Games and Services business unit employed approximately 2,200 persons.

In July, 1988, citing economic realities, Bally's management sold Bally Midway Sente, the production facility of the division it had created in 1931, to WMS Industry, Inc. Chairman Mullane's hard line strategy of never fearing the competition caught up with him as management succumbed to the stiff competition of the Japanese. At its peak in 1982, the Amusement Games division brought in $600 million. By 1987, revenue had fallen to $24.3 million.

Total 1987 revenues for the Amusement Games and Services Division including Aladdin's Castles were $121.1 million while operating profits totalled $23.4 million. Revenues were down $6.6 million (5%) due primarily to the planned closing of business in this unit. The division was represented exclusively by Aladdin's Castle arcade operations as of January 1988.

BALLY VS. DONALD TRUMP

Soon after Robert Mullane accepted the position of President and Chairman of the Board of Bally Manufacturing, shareholders began to question his strategy of diversification. According to industry observers, Bally's success with its previous ventures was, at best, mediocre. But no decision created as much shareholder uproar as management's handling of the confrontation with real estate developer and casino hotel operator Donald Trump.

In early 1987 Trump began to buy shares of Bally stock, accumulating a 9.9% stake in the company, while, according to industry analysts, the stock was at a yearly low reflecting shareholders' disapproval with the company's performance. Trump saw Bally's casino holdings as a very attractive addition to his two casino hotels, Trump Plaza and Trump's Castle. Bally management, fearing a hostile takeover, began to search for a way of thwarting Trump's efforts. They found two ways: (1) the repurchase of Trump's 9.9% stake in the company, and (2) the use of New Jersey Gaming Commission (NJGC) law to their advantage. NJGC regulations allowed one company to operate up to three casino hotels in Atlantic City. If Bally purchased a second casino hotel in Atlantic City, they would then own two and therefore disqualify Trump, who owned two casino hotels, as a potential acquirer. Bally management immediately entered into negotiations with Steven Wynn of the Golden Nugget, Inc. Mr. Wynn had previously expressed an interest in leaving the Atlantic City market. At the same time, Bally management began negotiations with Trump to repurchase his 9.9% ownership in the company. In February, 1987, Bally reclaimed the shares at a substantial premium paying Trump $84.7 million ($24 million in profit for Trump, which was charged against Bally's 1987 operations). One week later, management approved the purchase of the Golden Nugget casino hotel for $440 million, a price many industry analysts believed could not be justified. Shareholders accused management of "trading away the health of the company for their jobs" and accused Trump of greenmail. The shareholders believed that Bally management purchased the Golden Nugget (renamed Bally's Grand) in an effort to avoid a Trump takeover and not to maximize the best interest of the company's owners. Bally officials admitted they had not considered a purchase of Golden Nugget until after Trump's 9.9% purchase but insisted they would have continued to pursue the purchase even if Trump was out of the picture. The Trump confrontation cost Bally $24 million in greenmail that would never provide a measurable return, in addition to $300 million in new long-term debt relative to the Golden Nugget mortgage.

LEGAL AND POLITICAL FACTORS: REGULATION

Gaming activities in Atlantic City were subject to the New Jersey Casino Control Act, regulations of the New Jersey Casino Control Commission, and other applicable laws.[27] Effective December 29, 1987, and September 21, 1987, the Casino licenses of Bally's subsidiaries that operate Bally's Park Place and Bally's Grand, respectively, were renewed for one year by unanimous vote of the Casino Control Commission. Both of the Casino hotels in Atlantic City would be subject to license renewal in September 1988, at which time each was expected to receive a two-year license.[28]

The ownership and operation of casino gaming facilities and slot machine routes in Nevada were subject to the licensing and regulatory control of the Nevada Gaming Commission, the Nevada Gaming Control Board, and various local, city, and county regulatory agencies.[29] Bally and its subsidiaries, which conducted gaming operations at Bally's Las Vegas and Bally's Reno, had been granted all required gaming licenses by the Nevada Gaming Authorities.[30]

Pursuant to Nevada law, neither Bally nor any subsidiary can engage in gaming activities in Nevada without the prior approval of the Commission. The Commission had previously granted approval to Bally to engage in gaming activities in Nevada as well as in Atlantic City.[31]

DEMOGRAPHICS OF GAMBLING

In 1984 gross wagering amounted to more than fifteen times the amount Americans donated to churches, twice as much as they spent on higher education, and over half of what they spent on food.[32] Legalized gambling was popular with voters because it promised revenues without raising taxes. In 1987, more than thirty states approved lotteries despite the fact that lotteries amounted to a regressive tax because minorities, those with low incomes, and older people were the heaviest ticket buyers. Gambling was strongly influenced by demographic variables such as age, sex, income, education, and religion.[33]

Four out of five lottery players were thirty-five years or older with incomes between $18,000 and $36,000 and some college education. Bigger jackpots attracted a more upscale player. "Shallow play" games such as bingo and slot machines, along with the lotteries, were the most profitable games for casinos and states because the chances of winning were much less than at the more complex games.[34] "Deep-play" gamblers, who prefer high-stakes games such as blackjack and craps, were mostly men, with the craps players being the oldest with the highest incomes and the blackjack players being the youngest, most educated, and having the second highest incomes. Although all groups gamble primarily for enjoyment and excitement, the "deep-play" gamblers were most likely to play to make money.[35]

MARKETING

Although in 1988 Bally's International Marketing Corporation was formed to attract convention business,[36] Bally's marketing strategy at the Park Place hotel casino was designed to attract "low rollers." The company aimed to attract the people who play the nickel slot machines and bet the minimum at the blackjack tables; people the industry not so affectionately calls the "grinds."[37]

Catering to low rollers had its advantages. Low rollers were predictable, plentiful, and provided the casino with a broad revenue base. They were also less costly, as it was not necessary to staff slot machines or maintain lavish suites. High rollers brought with them bigger risks. Because there were fewer of them and because they were more skilled, they stood a better chance of beating the house.[38]

Bally's Park Place's high percentage of low rollers was hardly unique. In 1987, more than 50% of Atlantic City's total casino revenues came from low bettors. However, Park Place's decision to focus almost exclusively on the small bettor while avoiding the costly warfare for high rollers made it an exception in the casino industry. Bally saw this strategy as successful: since its casinos posted an operating margin of 14% in 1987. Bally also viewed this approach as a non-gambling way to be in the gambling business. The risks associated with low rollers were lower than those affiliated with bettors who gambled large sums.[39]

Bally's management also kept close tabs on "comps"—complimentary inducements ranging from dinner to $250 per night luxury suites. In 1987, Bally's had the lowest "comp ratio" in Atlantic City; just 14.6% of revenues compared to the industry average of 22%. This tightfisted philosophy extended throughout the operation. Unlike many of its competitors, Bally's refused to treat food service and entertainment as loss leaders.[40]

Bally's Grand catered to the high rollers—the wealthy, more skilled gambler. These gamblers were interested in the "deep play" games and usually won more often than low rollers. Thus, Bally had conflicting marketing strategies within the Atlantic City market.

Marketing efforts in the health and fitness unit of Bally's involved the operation and promotion of over 250 fitness centers operated as either wholly or partially owned subsidiaries. Revenues were produced through the sale of memberships, either an initial fee plus month-to-month fees, or a term membership for a fixed length of time. In 1988, Bally expanded into the European market with a health club in London with expectations of a fast growing market.[41]

Management believed Bally had an advantage over its competition because of its ability to devote substantial resources to advertising, promotion, and construction of large, contemporary fitness centers offering more amenities. Bally's health and fitness chain targeted as its market women and men ages twenty-five to thirty-five with activities that included club expansion and continued development of promotional and television programs with acknowledged spokespeople such as Cher and Heather Locklear. Management believed that for this target market, carrying gym bags became typical. Since the mid-1970s, many people had been participating in the fitness lifestyle. Bally's management insisted that fitness was not a craze, but more a way of life in America.[42]

In July, 1988, the advertising agency of J. Walter Thompson U.S.A. was given the $6 million job of bringing Lifecycle, the computerized stationary bicycle, and Liferower, the computerized rowing machine, out of the health clubs and into the consumer market. Meanwhile, it created another campaign directed at health clubs for a new fitness machine, Lifecircuit strength training systems. Before being awarded this contract, Thompson had done campaigns for Bally's nationwide Health and Fitness Division.[43]

The chain of Aladdin's Castle amusement centers, located in shopping malls, utilized a management training program along with mall promotional activities and traffic builders to increase growth of this business segment.[44]

The Gaming Equipment and Service Division sold its products both internally and externally. It achieved vertical integration through the sale of slot and poker machines to Bally's casino division.

Overall, Bally management viewed market leadership as an important element in each business in which it chose to complete. Mullane stated, "Market leadership is important because I'm more confident if we are number one or number two and I don't want someone to beat up on us because we are small."

THE COMPETITION

Mid-1986 marked the end of the glory days for Atlantic City's casinos. The industry maturity that had been evident in Las Vegas and Reno for years had finally occurred in Atlantic City. Symptoms of that maturity included a pronounced slowdown in win (money taken in by the casinos), a proliferation in competition, a proliferation of weak sisters, marginal operators like the Atlantis and the Claridge, in Exhibit 30.3, and a pronounced pressure on profit margins and earnings.[45] Merrill Lynch Vice-President Harold Vogel commented that the industry's $2.8 billion investment returned only $2.1 billion in 1986, and win per square foot of casino space—a measure of productivity—had been dropping dramatically since 1984.[46]

Atlantic City

Steven Wynn, Chairman of Golden Nugget, Inc., stated that the symptoms of maturity in Atlantic City made Bally's $440 million purchase of the Golden

EXHIBIT 30.3   Composite Statistics: Hotel/Gaming Industry

	1986	1987	1988[1]	1989[1]
Sales ($mill)	12,703	14,266	15,700	17,700
Net profit ($mill)	513.9	652.0	755	855
Operating margin	17.2%	17.1%	17.0%	16.5%
Net profit margin	4.1%	4.6%	4.8%	4.8%

1987 Atlantic City Hotel/Gaming Industry Market Share

Caesars World	10.9%
Harrah's Marina	10.2
Bally's Park Place	10.0
Bally's Grand	9.8
Trump Plaza	9.8
Resorts International	9.5
Trump Castle	9.2
Tropicana	8.1
Showboat	7.6
Sands	6.9
Del Webb's Claridge	4.9
Elsinore's Atlantis	3.1

SOURCE: *Variety*, February, 1988.

NOTE:

[1] Values for 1988 and 1989 are *Value Line* Estimates.

Nugget's Boardwalk casino riskier. Bally, already steeply leveraged, was going deeper into debt with the Nugget purchase. If cash projections did not pan out, Bally's profit ratios could well turn out negative. This was especially alarming because Bally had been losing market share to Donald Trump's Plaza and his Castle hotel casinos, which had taken almost 20% of the win since their debuts in 1984.[47] The 1987 opening of the Showboat casino had also caused a loss in market share (for all Atlantic City casinos, not just Bally). According to industry observers such as Marvin Roffman of Janney Montgomery Scott, Inc., a consulting firm, the outlook for Atlantic City included a period of bloodletting followed by a consolidation, in which Bally and other big operators will push poorly financed casinos to the wall.

Nevada

The Las Vegas and Reno gaming markets were no less competitive and had no more momentum going for them than did Atlantic City. Thirty major casinos were battling for elbow room on the Las Vegas Strip. By Marvin Roffman's estimate only a dozen were profitable.[48] This had not stopped massive expansion efforts along the Strip. Circus Circus Enterprises was breaking ground on a $290 million hotel-casino, Golden Nugget was to open a $565 million resort in 1989, and Caesars Place, Inc. was building an 875,000 square foot Roman theme shopping center. Also, an unnamed Japanese company was reportedly planning a $600 million resort-casino-residential development. With every major property on the Strip adding or planning to add rooms and casino space, the room inventory would increase more than 10% by 1990.[49] Despite this massive expansion in Las Vegas, an economic slowdown or downturn just as all the new casinos and hotels come online in 1990–1992 could be disastrous. As Peter Thomas, President of Valky Bank of Nevada, noted in a *Forbes* interview, "The Las Vegas economy wasn't recession-resistant in the early eighties. The town was in an expansion phase at the time, and while growth didn't go negative, some hotels went under."

This could spell trouble for Bally, because except for Park Place, its casinos were not all that profitable. Bally's Grand's operating income fell 19% for the twelve months ending March 31, 1988, according to analyst Marvin Roffman. Excluding Park Place, Bally's casinos posted operating margins of 14% in 1987, compared with 27% by industry leader Circus Circus Enterprises, Inc.[50]

Investment advice given by *Value Line* stated that by the early 1990s, the expansion in Atlantic City and Las Vegas would be finished and demand would have had a chance to begin absorbing the new supply. Survivors of the intense competition of the late 1980s and early 1990s might experience faster earnings growth in three to five years. *Value Line* ranked four hotel gaming stocks to outperform the 1989 market: Bally Manufacturing, Caesars World, Circus Circus Enterprises, and Prime Motor Inns. Of the four, *Value Line* noted that Caesars carried more than an average degree of risk.[51]

FINANCE

After a loss of $100.4 million in 1984 due to the $122 million writeoff of amusement game assets, Bally rebounded. (See Exhibit 30.4.) In 1987, the Company reported a net income of $57.1 million compared to 1986 income of $23.7 million, an increase of $33.4 million.[52] This figure was influenced by two major events in this unusual year. First, the repurchase in 1987 of 3,057,000 shares of common stock (9.9%) from Donald Trump resulted in a 24.3 million charge against its operating income.[53] Second, Bally sold its Six Flags theme park subsidiary in May 1987 resulting in an after tax extraordinary gain of $76.3 million.[54] Without these events, the Company's operating income for 1987

EXHIBIT 30.4

Revenue and Net Income, 1983–1987

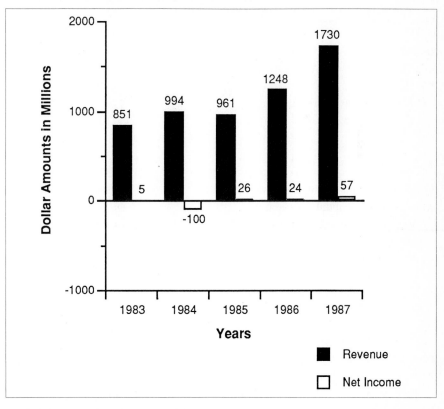

SOURCE: Bally Manufacturing, Inc., *1987 Annual Report.*

would have been $17.9 million with net income of $5.1 million. (See Exhibit 30.5 for consolidated income statements for 1987 and 1986.)

For Bally, 1987 revenues were $1,730.1 million, an increase of $482.6 million (38.69%) compared to 1986.[55] The increase came mostly from the Casino Hotels and the Health and Fitness units.[56] Revenues and operating income from Casino Hotels had been increasing since the company acquired Bally's Las Vegas and Bally's Reno in 1986, and Bally's Grand in Atlantic City in 1987.[57] Health and Fitness had increased revenues from the operating of new clubs and increased sales of Life Fitness equipment.[58] But operating income decreased $2.1 million because of the increase of expenses in health club operations, selling and promotion, and bad debts.[59] The Gaming Equipment and Services unit enjoyed increased revenues, but suffered a greater operating loss of $8.9 million

EXHIBIT 30.5   **Consolidated Statements of Income, Bally Manufacturing Corporation**

(Dollar Amounts in Thousands)

Years ended December 31	1987	1986	1985
Revenues:			
Services	$1,436,601	$987,119	$669,388
Sales	239,659	221,654	252,164
Other, principally interest income	53,868	38,771	39,228
Total revenues;	1,730,128	1,247,544	960,780
Cost and expenses:			
Cost of services	1,001,373	694,387	478,391
Cost of sales	195,337	175,615	191,182
Selling, general and administrative	267,305	180,931	138,055
Provision for doubtful receivables	69,754	49,802	47,839
Common stock purchase expense	24,275	—	—
Interest	172,123	112,621	52,072
Interest capitalized	(6,463)	(6,743)	(3,021)
Total expenses	1,723,704	1,206,613	904,358
Income from continuing operations before income taxes and minority interests	6,424	40,931	56,422
Provision for income taxes	12,295	21,793	29,362
Minority interests in net income of subsidiaries	488	1,759	4,040
Income (loss) from continuing operations	(6,359)	17,379	23,020
Income from discontinuing operations	63,497	6,322	2,617
Net income	$ 57,138	$ 23,701	25,637

SOURCE: Bally Manufacturing, Inc., *1987 10-K*, p. 20.

due to the lower price and higher operating expenses of the lottery business.[60] The Amusement Games and Services subsidiary suffered a decrease in revenue due to poorer economic conditions. Revenues and operating incomes of each segment for 1987 and 1986 are shown in Exhibit 30.6.

Chairman Mullane stated, "If I want to sleep at night, I need a little stability."[61] Bally's further involvement in the gaming industry seemed to give the company stability. Revenues and operating income from Casino Hotels continued to grow for the first six months of 1988. The other segments also showed improvement. (See Exhibit 30.7 for revenue and operating income for the first six-month period of 1988 and 1987.) For the first half of 1988, total revenues increased by $129.3 million (15.91%), but net income decreased $31 million compared to the same period in 1987. The high net income of 1987 was due principally to the sale of Six Flags. Without such extraordinary events, net income would have increased by $16.2 million in 1988. According to an estimate by *Value Line*, the increase should continue into the second half of 1988 and into 1989.[62] (Comparative income statements for six months of 1988 and 1987 are shown in Exhibit 30.8.)

Chairman Mullane stated, "Bally's future is gaming."[63] Bank financing and liability assumption produced a high debt ratio of 77.42% in 1987, up from 75.93% in 1986.[64] The acquisition of U.S. Health, Inc. (merged into the Health and Fitness segment) in April 1988 resulted in a liability assumption of approximately $53.6 million, causing a further increase to 79.31% at June 30, 1988. According to the *New York Times*, Bally Manufacturing Corporation's debt rating was under review by Standard & Poor's for possible downgrading.[65] (Consolidated Balance Sheets at December 31, 1986 and 1987, and at June 30, 1988, are presented in Exhibit 30.9.)

EXHIBIT 30.6

Business Segments, Bally Manufacturing Corporation
(Dollar Amounts in Millions)

Years Ended December 31	1987	1986	1985
Revenues:			
Casino Hotels	$874.9	$509.7	$260.3
Health and Fitness	575.7	453.6	376.2
Gaming Equipment and Services	182.5	179.9	164.1
Amusement Games and Services	121.1	127.7	177.0
Operating income (loss):			
Casino Hotels	$148.1	$ 92.6	$ 56.6
Health and Fitness	66.4	68.5	49.1
Gaming Equipment and Services	(18.8)	(9.8)	20.1
Amusement Games and Services	23.4	19.7	(1.2)

SOURCE: Bally Manufacturing, Inc., 1987 10-K, p. 34

EXHIBIT 30.7

Business Segments, Bally Manufacturing Corporation
(Dollar Amounts in Millions)

Six Months Ended June 30	1988	1987
Revenues:		
Casino Hotels	$452.6	$403.4
Health and Fitness	338.6	272.9
Gaming Equipment and Services	102.0	93.4
Amusement Games and Services	62.7	56.1
Operating income (loss):		
Casino Hotels	$ 70.1	$ 65.6
Health and Fitness	51.0	35.9
Gaming Equipment and Services	6.2	(4.5)
Amusement Games and Services	12.8	8.8

SOURCE: Bally Manufacturing, Inc., *1988 10-Q*.

EXHIBIT 30.8

Consolidated Statements of Income, Bally Manufacturing Corporation
(Dollar Amounts in Thousands)

Six Months Ended June 30	1988	1987
Revenues:	$940,462	$811,193
Cost and expenses:		
Cost of services and sales	636,796	567,496
Selling, general and administrative	141,200	118,755
Provision for doubtful receivables	34,996	32,784
Common stock purchase expense	—	24,273
Interest	8,628	80,078
Total expense	899.282	823,386
Income from continuing operations before income taxes and minority interests	41,190	(12,193)
Provision for income taxes	17,539	4,832
Minority interests in net income of subsidiaries	423	176
Income (loss) from continuing operations	23,228	(17,201)
Income from discontinuing operations	—	71,658
Net income	$ 23,228	$ 54,457

SOURCE: Bally Manufacturing, Inc., *1988 10-Q*.

EXHIBIT 30.9   **Consolidated Balance Sheets, Bally Manufacturing Corporation**

(Dollar Amounts in Thousands)

	JUN. 30 1988	DEC. 31 1987	DEC. 31 1986
Assets			
Current assets			
Cash and equivalents	$ 89,331	$ 76,306	$ 50,353
Receivables	435,975	356,140	270,973
Inventories	39,122	38,934	26,551
Other current assets	57,929	44,240	37,318
Total current assets	622,357	515,620	385,195
Property, plant and equipment, at cost less accumulated depreciation	1,711,221	1,604,609	1,189,056
Other assets	91,200	97,925	271,884
Intangible assets	334,504	306,979	201,583
Total assets	$2,759,282	$2,525,133	$2,047,718
Liabilities and stockholders' equity			
Current liabilities			
Accounts receivable	$ 67,772	$ 66,310	$ 75,013
Income taxes payable	33,373	66,715	4,015
Deferred income taxes	59,747	35,212	44,637
Deferred revenues	92,288	65,199	54,587
Accrued liabilities	227,711	222,834	179,460
Current maturities of long-term debt	11,005	24,149	6,159
Total current liabilities	491,896	480,419	363,871
Total long-term debt	1,589,933	1,387,471	1,096,174
Other long-term liabilities	27,883	12,884	21,573
Deferred income taxes	78,805	74,072	73,144
Total liabilities	2,188,517	1,954,846	1,554,762
Stockholders' equity			
Preferred stock, $1 par value	2,013	2,013	13
Common stock, $0.67 par value	21,246	21,206	21,006
Capital in excess of par value	285,170	288,900	185,477
Retained earnings	347,097	334,142	294,131
Cumulative translation adjustment	7,235	11,472	4,933
Less: Common stock in treasury	(91,996)	(87,446)	(12,604)
Total stockholders' equity	570,765	570,287	492,956
Total Liabilities and stockholders' equity	$2,759,282	$2,525,133	$2,047,718

SOURCE: Bally Manufacturing, Inc., *1988 10-K* and *1987 10-Q*.

Since 1983 Bally has paid a consistent dividend of $.20 per share per year.[66] Despite this, Bally's stock price had lagged in recent years, primarily because of Bally's spotty record with new ventures and the internal disputes over the long-term direction of the company. Some financial analysts have stated that Bally's stock was undervalued. The company was facing added pressure from investors to improve its financial performance.[67]

FINAL THOUGHTS

In the August 8, 1988, edition of *Business Week*, Gene G. Marcial wrote an article entitled, "What's in the Cards for Bally."[68] Rumors were circulating throughout the gaming industry and on Wall Street that Bally was a potential takeover target. The company's stock had fluctuated in a range from $10\frac{1}{2}$ to $27\frac{1}{2}$ in 1987 and from $12\frac{7}{8}$ to $24\frac{1}{8}$ during the first eight months of 1988. "Investors were confused as to Bally's diversification strategy", stated Marcial, "a strategy that appeared to be a case of mixing apples and oranges."[69] After all, can one company manage business units as different as health clubs and equipment, lottery companies, video games, and hotel casinos? Chairman Mullane had always felt that bigger meant better as well as not having to fear your competition. However, as one industry analyst stated, "the competition doesn't feel that way and Bob Mullane better not either."

NOTES

1. Pasquale A. Carone, editor, *Addictive Disorders Update* (New York: Human Sciences Press, Inc., 1982).

2. Bally Manufacturing, Inc., *1987 Annual Report*, p. 17.

3. Carone, 1982.

4. *Forbes*, January 13, 1986.

5. *Ibid.*

6. Carone, 1982.

7. Bally, *1987 Annual Report*, Introduction.

8. *Ibid*, p. 19.

9. *Ibid*, p. 10.

10. *Ibid*, p. 12

11. *The New Republic*, "Postcard Los Angeles," July 1, 1985.

12. *Variety*, April 23, 1986, p. 4.

13. *The Christian Century*, April 29, 1987.

14. *The New Republic*, July 1, 1985, p. 12.

15. *Ibid.*

16. *The Insider Chronicle*, January 19, 1987, back page.

17. Christopher S. Eklund, "Atlantic City Is No Longer On a Hot Streak," *Fortune*, March 18, 1985, pp. 124–128.

18. Ellen Paris, "It's Just Like the Manufacturing Business," *Fortune*, November 14, 1988, pp. 124, 128.

19. Maurice Barnfather, "Luck Has Nothing to Do with It," *Forbes*, October 1981, pp. 34–35.

20. *Ibid.*, p. 35.

21. Michael Oneal, "Can Bally Live Down Its High-Rolling Past?" *Business Week*, August 1, 1988, pp. 94–95.

22. Richard Phalen, "Zero-Sum Game," *Forbes*, March 19, 1986, pp. 110–112.

23. Oneal, "Can Bally Live Down Its High-Rolling Past?" pp. 94–95.

24. Susan Caminiti, "On the Rise," *Fortune*, December 21, 1987, p. 167.

25. Francis J. Flaherty, "Going for Broke," *The Progressive*, March 1988, pp. 31–33.

26. "Turmoil Time in the Casino Business," *Fortune*, March 2, 1987, pp. 102–116.

27. Bally Manufacturing, Inc., *1987 Form 10-K*, p. 2.

28. *Ibid.*

29. *Ibid.*

30. *Ibid*, p. 4.

31. *Ibid.*

32. Brad Edmindsun, "Demographics of Gambling," *American Demographics*, July 1986, p. 39.

33. *Ibid.*

34. *Ibid*, p. 41.

35. *Ibid*, p. 42.

36. Bally, *1987 Annual Report*, p. 5.

37. Christopher S. Eklund, "Bally's: Living High off Low Rollers," *Business Week*, May 27, 1985, pp. 118–119.

38. *Ibid.*

39. *Ibid.*

40. *Ibid.*

41. "Conspicuous Waist," *The Economist*, February 20, 1988.

42. Bally, *1987 Annual Report*, p. 6.

43. "Thompson U.S.A. Wins $10 Million in Business," *New York Times*, July 27, 1988, p. D18.

44. Bally, *1987 Annual Report*, pp. 7–8.

45. Richard Phalon, "The Black and the Red," *Forbes*, March 19, 1986, p. 94.

46. *Ibid*, p. 98.

47. Phalon, "Zero-Sum Game," *Forbes*, March 23, 1987, p. 110.

48. *Ibid*, p. 111.

49. Mark Beauchamp, "On a Roll," *Forbes*, October 3, 1988, p. 130.

50. Oneal, "Can Bally Live Down Its High-Rolling Past?" p. 92.

51. *Value Line*, September 9, 1988.

52. Bally, *1987 Annual Report*, p. 23.

53. Bally, *1987 Form 10-K*, p. 30.

54. Bally, *1987 Annual Report*, p. 2.

55. *Ibid.*, p. 20.

56. Bally, *1987 Form 10-K*, p. 12.

57. Bally, *1987 Annual Report*, p. 23.

58. Bally, *1987 Form 10-K*, p. 12.

59. *Ibid.*

60. *Ibid.*

61. Kathleen Deveny, "Bally Is on a Winning Streak," *Business Week*, December 2, 1985, p. 31.

62. *Value Line*, September 8, 1988, p. 1774.

63. Michael Oneal, "Dumping Trump," *Business Week*, March 9, 1987, p. 45.

64. Bally, 1987 *Form 10-K*, p. 18.

65. "Briefs," *New York Times*, May 12, 1988, p. D16.

66. Bally, *1987 Annual Report*, p. 23.

67. Julia Flynn Siler, "Bally Sets a Spinoff to Holders," *New York Times*, August 12, 1988, p. D1.

68. Gene G. Marcial, "What's In the Cards for Bally," *Business Week*, August 8, 1988, p. 67.

69. *Ibid.*

Harcourt, Brace, Jovanovich

VIRGINIA L. BACKBURN • CHARLES B. SHRADER

In late 1987, William Jovanovich, CEO of Harcourt, Brace, Jovanovich (HBJ), found himself at the helm of a firm whose future could best be described as uncertain. Jovanovich had fended off unwanted suitors, but at the same time had saddled his firm with an enormous debt burden. HBJ's financial worries were exacerbated by a trend toward the increasing globalization and consolidation of the book publishing industry. HBJ faced some tough choices as it finished the 1980s and entered the 1990s.

COMPANY BACKGROUND AND DESCRIPTION

Originally incorporated as Harcourt, Brace & Co. in 1919, the company adopted its current name in 1970. Acquisitions played a major role in HBJ's growth. Historically, HBJ's strength had been the publishing of textbooks, professional books, and journals; it was the fifth largest book publisher. During the 1980s however, HBJ retreated somewhat from its publishing emphasis. In 1980, book publishing accounted for 52.4% of sales and 61.5% of operating profit. In 1985 publishing's contribution to sales and profit declined to 39.4% and 35%, respectively.[1]

HBJ consisted of three business segments: Publishing, Sea World Enterprises, and Communications and Services. Primary publications included textbooks, professional journals, and general fiction and nonfiction books. In addition, HBJ had operations in the publication and scoring of aptitude tests and the manufacture and sale of school and office graphic supplies.

Sea World Enterprises operated three marine theme parks in Cleveland, San Diego, and Orlando. It also owned and operated Cypress Gardens, a botanical garden in Winter Haven, Florida. A fourth Sea World was scheduled to open in San Antonio in 1988.

HBJ Communications and Services Division operated two ABC affiliated VHF TV stations; published farm, business, and professional periodicals; sold accident, health, and life-insurance, and operated book clubs.

RECENT DEVELOPMENTS

In 1986, HBJ reversed its recent trend away from book publishing and purchased for $500 million, CBS' Educational and Professional publishing division. The acquisition, including Holt, Rinehart, and Winston and W. B. Saunders, made HBJ the largest U.S. publisher of elementary and high school textbooks and the largest medical publisher.[2] Analysts who noted HBJ's recent concen-

This case was prepared by Professors Virginia L. Backburn and Charles B. Shrader of Iowa State University. It was presented at the 1988 Workshop of the Midwest Society for Case Research. Copyright © 1988 by V. L. Blackburn and C. B. Shrader. It also appears in *Annual Advances, 1988*, pp. 202–215, edited by Susan L. Wiley. Reprinted by permission.

trations in theme parks and insurance, characterized the acquisition—to the chagrin of Peter Jovanovich—as a "strategic about-face." Jovanovich maintained that HBJ had internally developed its book publishing segments all along and suggested that "analysts only look at what you buy, not what you do."[3]

In early 1987, HBJ made a $50 per share bid for Harper and Row, that topped Theodore L. Cross' bid of $34 per share. Eventually, Rupert Murdoch was also drawn into the battle, and the spoils finally went to his company, News Corp. Ltd. Rumors abounded, in the face of HBJ's offer for Harper and Row and its acquisition of CBS, that HBJ had attempted to take on debt to make itself a less likely takeover target.

MANAGEMENT

William Jovanovich had held the position of HBJ's CEO for over thirty-two years. He joined the company as a salesman in 1947 and by 1955 had been promoted to his current position. Jovanovich's tenure saw a succession of Number Two people come and go, which prompted questions regarding Jovanovich's management style and potential successor. As to the question of whether his management style was too autocratic, Jovanovich replied that the suggestion was "a *People* magazine notion that has nothing to do with corporate structure. There's no communal way to run a company. If there's a strong number two man he goes out and becomes number one elsewhere."[4]

Jovanovich, the son of an immigrant coal miner, surrounded himself with the trappings of his position. A *Forbes* columnist reported seeing in Mr. Jovanovich's office: five briefcases with the CEO's initials, a Tiffany desk set, and a facsimile set of Leonardo drawings. By way of justification for multiple office locations, Jovanovich observed "I like edifices."

Jovanovich managed HBJ much the same as a lord would rule a manor. He reputedly would not hesitate to deride or remove anyone in management he was not pleased with. Therefore, no Number Two executive stayed very long at HBJ. Robert Hillebrecht, an Executive Vice-President and head of Sea World, who left HBJ once said, "Jovanovich makes and breaks executives and fast."[5]

With no clear successor in sight, analysts believed that Jovanovich hoped to pass the reins to his son Peter who had been named President and held a seat on HBJ's board. Both William and Peter attempted to quash any such rumors. William Jovanovich went so far as to say that there was no question of succession since "I'm not retiring."[6] His current contract was planned to run through 1989. (Exhibit 31.1 details the remainder of HBJ's officers and directors along with their corporate affiliations.)

GENERAL TRENDS IN THE PUBLISHING INDUSTRY

In 1987, the book publishing industry generated approximately $10 billion in sales and the top six firms accounted for approximately 30% of the industry revenues. Although the industry had historically been fairly fragmented, it faced increasing consolidation in the 1980s. 1986 was a banner year with book publishing acquisitions that totalled more than $2 billion.[7] (The largest of these

EXHIBIT 31.1 **Directors (Showing Principal Corporate Affiliations), HBJ**

Theodore M. Black, President, Walter J. Black, Inc.

J. William Brandner, Executive Vice-President, Office of President, and Treasurer, Harcourt Brace Jovanovich, Inc.

Ralph D. Caulo, Executive Vice-President, Office of President, Harcourt Brace Jovanovich, Inc.

Trammell Crow, founder of Trammell Crow Co.; Director, Fidelity Union Life Insurance Co., Dallas

Robert L. Edgell, Vice-Chairman, Harcourt Brace Jovanovich, Inc.

Paul Gitlin, Partner, Ernst, Cane, Berner & Gitlin, Attorneys

Maria C. Istomin, Artistic Director, John F. Kennedy Center for the Performing Arts, Washington, D.C.

Walter J. Johnson, President, Walter J. Johnson, Inc.

Peter Jovanovich, Executive Vice-President, Office of President, Harcourt Brace Jovanovich, Inc.

William Jovanovich, Chairman and CEO, Harcourt Brace Jovanovich, Inc.

Eugene J. McCarthy, Senator from Minnesota (1958–1970); Writer and Lecturer

Peter J. Ryan, Partner, Fried, Frank, Harris, Shriver & Jacobson, Attorneys

Virginia B. Smith, Former President, Vassar College; Director, Marine Midland Banks, Inc. and Marine Midland Bank, N.A.

Jack O. Snyder, Executive Vice-Presidents, Office of President, Harcourt Brace Jovanovich, Inc.

Michael R. Winston, Vice-President for Academic Affairs, Howard University

acquisitions are shown in Exhibit 31.2.) Even though acquisitions and consolidation were expected to continue, analysts expected the industry to continue to be characterized by fragmented specialty publishing even if six or seven firms in aggregate held a significant portion of the market.[8]

Explanations for the acquisition fever in the publishing industry were numerous. The most controversial explanation cast publishing acquisitions in terms

EXHIBIT 31.2 **Largest Book Publishing Acquisitions of 1986**

PROPERTY	BUYER	PRICE (In millions of dollars)
Scott, Foresman	Time	$520
CBS book publishing operations	Harcourt Brace Jovanovich	500
Doubleday & Co.	Bertelsmann AG	475
South-Western Publishing	International Thomson	270
Silver Burdett	Gulf & Western	125

of ego gratification. Publishing executives desired to have acclaimed literary artists under contract because these enhanced their own importance. The value of backlists, however, provided probably the most compelling justification for acquisitions. Backlist books by well known authors such as Hemingway and Fitzgerald sold well (in predictable quantities) year after year with little advertising or sales support. Also, by combining manufacturing, distribution, and sales force efforts, some publishers were able through merger to increase revenues without realizing commensurate cost increases. Finally, mergers provided a means of jumping traditional entry barriers and expanding the acquiring firm's scope of publishing interests.[9]

A related trend in the 1980s in publishing was the gradual globalization of the industry, characterized primarily by foreign entry into the U.S. markets through both internal expansion and acquisition. Reasons for European expansion into U.S. markets included saturation of the European market, value of the dollar relative to foreign currency, and the internationalization of literary artistry.[10] Bertelsmann and International Thomson were incorporated in West Germany and Britain, respectively. In addition, News Corp. Ltd., a British firm, won the hotly contested battle for Harper and Row in 1987.

In early 1987, Harcourt Brace was rumored, along with Addison Wesley, Macmillan, Houghton Mifflin, and McGraw Hill, to be a potential target for takeover.[11] At this time the consensus seemed to be that European firms represented the most likely and viable takeover threats to these firms.

THE BATTLE FOR CONTROL OF HBJ

On May 18, 1987, British Printing and Communications Corporation (BPCC) made a $44/share offer for HBJ. This $2 billion offer officially launched the battle for control of HBJ and pitted Robert Maxwell, the Czechoslovak-born, socialist CEO of BPCC, against William Jovanovich.[12] Jovanovich immediately characterized the "sudden, unsolicited offer" as "preposterous, both as to intent and value."[13]

The offer represented the largest bid ever in the very active publishing acquisition market. Most analysts, however, believed that the bid was too low and that additional suitors offering between $50 and $60 per share might be enticed to enter the fray. In reaction to the offer and in anticipation of a bidding war, HBJ's share price rose $16.125 the day after the announcement, closing at $46.63. Analysts speculated that Jovanovich would rely on the low bid price and Robert Maxwell's background to justify any defensive moves.

After World War II, Robert Maxwell held the position of CEO of Pergamon Press. In an attempted takeover bid, Saul Steinberg found that Pergamon's profits had been significantly overstated. The ensuing investigation by the British government concluded with Mr. Maxwell being stripped of his board position. Maxwell subsequently regained his board position in 1974 and claimed that he was cleared of all previous charges.[14]

In fact, at the time of the bid for HBJ, Jovanovich made reference to Maxwell's background, saying that "Maxwell's dealings since he emerged from the mists of Ruthenia after World War II have not always favored shareholders—as Mr. Saul Steinberg can attest."[15] Jovanovich also seemed offended by the fact that the bid was being made by a much smaller company. In 1986 HBJ, including theme parks and insurance, earned $70.48 million on revenues of $1.3 billion and BPCC earned $135 million on $775 million in revenues, making BPCC approximately 60% the size of HBJ in terms of sales.

THE DEFENSE

In defense against the hostile bid by BPCC Jovanovich took immediate, drastic action to ensure his continued control of HBJ. A complicated recapitalization plan, which increased HBJ debt to nearly $3 billion, was announced. The plan entailed paying a special dividend of $40/share at a total cost of $1.6 billion on July 31. In addition to the cash payment shareholders received a fraction of a share of new preferred issue with a face value of $13.50. The market value of the preferred share, however, was estimated at closer to $10.00 and the value of the existing common stock was expected to drop.[16] HBJ also began a share repurchase and by the last week in May had bought back 4.8 million shares at a cost of $265.2 million.[17]

Like all recapitalization plans, HBJ's plan basically resulted in a great deal of equity being replaced by debt. Also, the combined effect of HBJ's share repurchases and issuance of new super voting preferred stock placed approximately 30% of the voting rights in the friendly hands of management, directors, employees, and First Boston Corporation.

Maxwell reacted to the recapitalization plan by filing suit as a shareholder to block the plan. At the time of the takeover bid and filing of the suit BPCC owned 460,600 shares or almost 2% of HBJ's outstanding common stock. BPCC also held $9,490,000 in HBJ convertible subordinate debentures. In the suit, Maxwell charged that the planned dividend was illegal under New York (HBJ's state of incorporation) state law, because it exceeded by $1 billion HBJ's surplus available for dividends. The law cited precludes paying dividends in excess of surplus. The suit claimed that HBJ ended 1986 with a $500 million surplus, lost $34 million in the first quarter of 1987, and spent $330 million for share repurchases. In addition, Maxwell charged that the issuance of new equity classes and common stock share repurchases relegated common stockholders to a minority position when control was effectively shifted to management. The net result according to Maxwell did not differ substantially from a leveraged buyout.

At 8:30 A.M., June 8, Maxwell also attempted to win an injunction to prevent that day from serving as the day of record for dividend payments. The injunction also would have prevented setting another record date. Under HBJ's indenture contract, convertible subordinate debentures were convertible into common stock at the price in effect at the time of conversion.[18] Maxwell filed this injunction as a debenture holder seeking to prevent the dividend payment until HBJ provided full disclosure to holders of convertible debentures (totalling $200 million) issued in March 1986.

The judge in the Manhattan district court denied Maxwell's request, indicating that the filing had not been made in a timely manner and that disputes regarding debenture conversion were already being handled in Florida State Court. In Florida, Sun Bank, the trustee for debenture holders, was simultaneously involved in litigation with HBJ in an attempt to clarify the conversion price. The Manhattan judge suggested that any further claims Maxwell had as a debenture holder should be handled in conjunction with the Sun Bank case.[19]

In June, BPCC themselves made a $1.03 billion rights issue. (A right entitles the buyer to purchase shares for a given amount at a future time.) Robert Maxwell indicated at the time of the offer that the proceeds could be used to make a further offer for HBJ if the Florida courts blocked the recapitalization plan. Even if the plan succeeded, however, British analysts believed that BPCC's new financing would allow them to top HBJ's offer. If not, the proceeds from the sale of rights gave BPCC the "resources and flexibility to pursue other opportunities for international expansion."[20]

On July 27, 1986 Robert Maxwell announced that BPCC was ending all litigation against HBJ and would soon be bidding for a different U.S. publishing company. In conceding defeat, Maxwell stated that although "BPCC did not achieve its ultimate goal of acquiring HBJ we are pleased that our efforts have greatly benefitted the shareholders of HBJ which included BPCC."[21] On the day of the announcement Houghton Mifflin, Macmillan, and McGraw-Hill stock prices rose in anticipation of possible bids from Maxwell. William Jovanovich did not have a public response to BPCC's withdrawal announcement.[22]

ANALYSTS' EVALUATION

The recapitalization plan announced by HBJ was one of the first of its kind. Analysts immediately began to discuss the implications of such bold defensive tactics. American corporations became increasingly assertive in their reactions to hostile takeover attempts. (Exhibit 31.3 gives a brief description of some of the more widely used takeover defenses.)

EXHIBIT 31.3

Descriptions of Takeover Defenses

POISON PILL   The issuance of securities that can be converted to cash, notes or equity of the acquirer.

PAC MAN   The target firm defends itself by attempting to acquire threatening firm.

LEVERAGED BUYOUT   Usually implemented by management, this defense entails taking the firm private using loans secured by the firm's assets and future cash flows.

SALE OF VALUED ASSETS   The target firm sells off those assets that are of the most interest to the acquiring firm, thereby reducing the firm's value as a target.

SELF-TENDER   Share repurchase reduces the number (percent) of shares available for purchase by the potential acquirer.

One of the more popular defenses was the leveraged buyout. Usually implemented by executives of the target firm, this defense entailed taking the firm private using debt secured by the future cash flows and assets of the firm. This type of defense was criticized by William Jovanovich and others as posing conflicts of interest for managers,[23] since as the company was taken private, management was thereafter not subjected to public scrutiny regarding the performance of the firm. Leveraged buyouts, however, legally put the firm "into play," (up for sale) and so obligated the officers and board to sell to the highest bidder.

The defense used by HBJ was termed the *leveraged recapitalization*. Like the leveraged buyout, the leveraged recapitalization required the incurring of enormous debt loads. In addition, those characteristics that make a firm a favorable leveraged buyout candidate also make a firm a likely leveraged recapitalization candidate. These characteristics included a strong market position, steady cash flows that can be used to service and pay down debt, a low debt position prior to the buyout or recapitalization, and undervalued assets that can be sold at a profit to pay down debt. Unlike buyouts, recaps, however, did not legally put the firm into play, absolving management of its responsibility to sell to the highest bidder. Critics maintained that as a result, management was able to gain control of the firm's equity for bargain prices without making a personal investment.[24]

Analysts also criticized leveraged recapitalizations, however, as adding to shareholder risk. Shareholders had fared well in the recent recapitalization trend. Harcourt's share price increased $9.00 immediately following the plan's announcement. Investment analysts feared, however, that shareholders would become overly optimistic in light of these early successes and fail to recognize the potential for disaster. As long as operating earnings met expectations, stockholders would continue to reap the benefits of recapitalization. When operating margins fell even slightly below expectations, however, stock prices fell dramatically. Even the slightest economic downturn precipitated heavy losses for such highly leveraged firms. In addition, recap firms put themselves at risk of rising interest rates and reduced financial and competitive flexibility.

The ability of all recap firms to survive was contingent on meeting sales and profit expectations. Any shortfall spelled disaster for shareholders and creditors. Management, on the other hand, had relatively little to lose from a financial standpoint.

HARCOURT'S FUTURE

Ivan Obolensky, a partner with Sterling, Grace, and Company, an investment firm, expressed concern for HBJ's future. "I don't understand where all the euphoria is coming from. Jovanovich has succeeded, but there's no room for error in meeting his projections,"[25]

For the second quarter of 1987, Harcourt, Brace, Jovanovich reported a net loss of $70.8 million versus a net income of $10.9 for the same quarter of 1986.

Revenues increased 31% to $408.7 million for the second quarter of 1987 from $312 million for the second quarter of 1986. For the total first six months of 1987, HBJ suffered a loss of $98.5 million versus a profit of $3.5 million for the preceding year. (See Exhibits 31.4–31.7 for HBJ's financial statements for the years 1982–1986.)

EXHIBIT 31.4 Consolidated Balance Sheets, Harcourt, Brace, Jovanovich

Year Ended December 31	1986	1985
Assets		
Current Assets:		
Cash	$ 12,884,174	$ 2,627,360
Marketable securities, at cost, which approximates market	3,800,000	—
Accounts receivable (less allowances for doubtful accounts of $9,655,171 in 1986 and $7,229,085 in 1985)	189,527,191	142,997,748
Inventories, at lower of cost or market	228,566,863	120,955,336
Prepaid expenses	17,272,452	11,829,228
Future tax benefits	6,544,899	7,562,027
Total current assets	458,595,579	285,971,699
Equity in net assets of HBJ Insurance	182,558,072	161,810,096
Property and Equipment, at cost:		
Land and improvements	115,076,076	86,304,457
Buildings	231,185,822	132,620,127
Furniture, machinery, and equipment	202,680,981	133,263,496
Other	6,637,041	2,759,202
Total property and equipment	555,579,920	354,947,282
Less: accumulated depreciation	131,321,559	105,665,981
	424,258,361	249,281,301
Plates, less accumulated amortization	118,727,343	35,697,102
Leasehold improvements, less accumulated amortization	12,604,122	9,371,526
Net property and equipment	555,589,826	294,349,929
Other Assets:		
Publishing rights	181,944,000	—
Other intangibles	266,528,313	18,177,656
Notes receivable	24,633,730	14,118,878
Royalty advances to authors	15,325,702	11,487,527
Other	24,320,201	16,839,297
Total other assets	512,751,946	60,623,358
Total assets	$1,709,495,423	$802,755,082

(*Continued*)

EXHIBIT 31.4   (Continued)

Year Ended December 31	1986	1985
Liabilities		
Current Liabilities:		
Notes payable	$ 1,815,012	$ —
Accounts payable	62,876,249	40,528,643
Accrued liabilities	79,734,921	15,331,693
Accrued compensation	13,444,097	8,206,715
Royalties payable	35,047,906	17,637,023
Federal, state, and local income taxes payable	32,467,540	29,056,147
Current portion of long-term debt	21,256,727	18,106,536
Total current liabilities	246,642,452	128,866,757
Noncurrent Liabilities and Other:		
$6\frac{3}{8}\%$ convertible subordinated debentures	199,995,000	—
Other long-term debt	590,282,858	222,302,939
ESOP debt guarantee	6,950,000	36,000,000
Unearned subscription income and other	80,487,238	49,975,552
Deferred income taxes	47,563,390	24,698,581
Noncurrent Federal income taxes payable	872,634	1,308,950
Royalties payable after one year	2,224,675	2,695,686
Deferred pension plan gain	3,000,000	31,000,000
Total noncurrent liabilities	931,375,795	367,981,708
Shareholders' Equity		
Common stock, $1.00 par value:		
Authorized 50,000,000 shares—outstanding 39,418,557 and 11,391,413 shares	39,418,557	11,391,413
Capital in excess of par value	218,098,145	104,501,446
Unearned ESOP compensation	(6,950,000)	(36,000,000)
Retained earnings	282,998,780	229,006,132
Cumulative translation adjustments	(2,088,306)	(2,992,374)
Total shareholders' equity	531,477,176	305,906,617
Total liabilities and stockholders' equity	$1,709,495,423	$802,755,082

The success of HBJ's recapitalization plan was contingent on HBJ's ability to achieve its extremely ambitious sales and profit projections. Estimates included in the plan called for 1987 net income of $23 million (before preferred dividends) and $33 million in 1988. Revenue projections of $2.2 billion by 1989 were more than double those of 1986. Harcourt officials hastened to point out in SEC

EXHIBIT 31.5 Consolidated Statements of Income, Harcourt, Brace, Jovanovich

Year Ended December 31	1986	1985	1984	1983	1982	1981
Sales and revenues	$968,554,926	$818,908,999	$712,544,413	$648,827,041	$575,254,594	$539,296,454
Costs and expenses:						
Cost of sales	431,093,075	373,097,973	324,651,146	297,820,715	271,261,955	251,160,186
Selling and editorial	274,068,904	236,427,716	200,008,650	181,336,740	163,653,634	143,369,330
General and administrative	143,640,104	120,993,166	111,859,452	108,035,640	102,248,290	92,283,937
Relocation costs[1]	—	—	6,624,678	—	27,700,000	—
Total costs and expenses	848,802,083	730,518,855	643,143,926	587,193,095	564,863,879	486,813,453
Income from operations, excluding HBJ Insurance[2]	119,752,843	88,300,144	69,400,487	—	—	—
Income from HBJ Insurance[2]	31,754,313	18,870,150	4,461,871	—	—	—
Income from operations	151,507,156	107,260,294	73,862,358	61,633,946	10,390,715	52,483,001
Interest Expense	21,718,605	18,544,415	13,326,603	10,276,507	12,647,026	12,839,113
Income (loss) before taxes	129,788,551	88,715,879	60,535,755	51,357,439	(2,256,311)	39,643,888
Income taxes (credit):						
Federal	47,632,000	29,926,863	19,225,150	17,570,000	(6,811,000)	11,893,000
State and local	11,681,000	8,242,000	6,831,140	6,311,000	1,261,000	3,996,000
Total taxes	59,313,000	38,168,863	26,056,290	23,881,000	(5,550,000)	15,889,000
Net income	$ 70,475,551	$ 50,547,016	$ 34,479,465	$ 27,476,439	$ 3,293,689	$ 23,754,888
Net income per share of common stock	$ 1.91	$ 1.62	$ 1.23	$ 3.03	$ 0.36	$ 2.70

NOTES:

[1] In 1982, the Company charged to income $27,700,000 as the estimated cost of relocating its headquarters during the years 1982, 1983, and 1984. The Company's relocation to Orlando, Florida, was completed during 1984. The actual costs of relocation exceeded the original estimates by $6,624,678.
[2] HBJ Insurance listed separately only after 1983.

EXHIBIT 31.6 Consolidated Sales and Revenues, Harcourt, Brace, Jovanovich

By Sources

	1986		1985		1984		1983		1982	
	AMOUNT	%	AMOUNT	%	AMOUNT	%	AMOUNT	%	AMOUNT	%
Educational	$ 450,013,149	34.6%	$400,585,206	40.5%	$355,780,595	47.1%	$227,315,275	49.4%	$273,774,531	46.9%
Informational Publishing & Services	$ 278,412,316	21.4	247,935,638	25.0	213,581,836	28.3	177,901,179	26.9	168,101,646	28.8
Publishing	728,425,465	56.0	648,520,844	65.5	569,362,431	75.4	505,216,454	76.3	441,876,177	75.7
Parks	223,239,856	17.2	170,388,155	17.2	143,181,982	19.0	129,366,819	19.5	118,980,621	20.4
Insurance	331,549,863	25.5	171,576,097	17.3	42,226,887	5.6	28,093,385	4.2	22,758,135	3.9
Corporate	16,889,605	1.3	0	0.0	0	0.0	0	0.0	0	0.0
	$1,300,104,789	100.0%	$990,485,096	100.0%	$754,771,300	100.0%	$662,676,658	100.0%	$583,614,933	100.0%

EXHIBIT 31.7 — Consolidated Income from Operations, Harcourt, Brace, Jovanovich
By Sources

	1986		1985		1984		1983		1982	
	AMOUNT	%	AMOUNT	%	AMOUNT	%	AMOUNT	%	AMOUNT	%
Educational	$ 53,935,046	35.6%	$ 35,746,372	33.3%	$36,719,971	49.7%	$26,128,447	41.7%	$14,038,775	128.0%
Informational Publishing & Services	$ 37,953,557	25.0	31,903,349	29.7	27,587,668	37.4	21,574,211	34.4	14,398,610	131.3
Publishing	91,888,603	60.6	67,649,721	63.0	64,307,639	87.1	47,702,658	76.1	28,437,385	259.3
Parks	40,089,435	26.5	34,240,931	31.9	24,033,525	32.5	19,207,692	30.7	18,148,471	165.5
Insurance	31,754,313	21.0	18,870,150	17.6	4,461,871	6.0	4,707,578	7.5	98,560	0.9
Corporate	(12,225,195)	(8.1)	(13,500,508)	(12.5)	(12,315,999)	(14.3)	(8,975,747)	(14.3)	(8,018,753)	(73.1)
Relocation Costs	0	0.0	0	0.0	(6,624,678)	(8.9)	0	0.0	(27,700,000)	(256.6)
	$151,507,156	100.0%	$107,260,294	100.0%	$73,862,358	100.0%	$62,642,181	100.0%	$10,965,663	100.0%

filings of second quarter losses that the majority of HBJ's sales and income were realized during the third quarter of the year.[26]

Additional documents filed with the SEC in August 1987 outlined specific plans to reduce costs. The plans called for a 5% to 10% reduction in staff over the next year, which translated into a loss of 800–1,600 positions. This announcement came on the heels of a July cut of thirty-eight positions in the trade division, eighteen of which were in customer service. HBJ also planned to cancel all philanthropic activities through 1988, freeze some wages, and sell executive perquisites, including company owned planes and condominiums.

In late 1987, the top management of Harcourt, Brace, Jovanovich faced some difficult decisions regarding the company's future. HBJ might now be safe from a takeover, but does it have the ability not only to survive the next few years, but to do so profitably?

NOTES

1. Peter W. Barnes and Roger Lowenstein, "Harcourt Brace to Buy CBS's Book Division," *The Wall Street Journal*, October 27, 1986, p. 4.

2. *Ibid.*

3. "HBJ to Buy CBS Text Unit for $500 Million," *Publishers Weekly*, November 7, 1986, p. 12.

4. Barbara Rudolph, "The Day You Retire You're Finished," *Forbes*, April 22, 1985, p. 107.

5. *Ibid.*

6. *Ibid.*

7. Robert J. Cole, "Bids for Harper & Row Spur Publishing Stocks," *The Wall Street Journal*, March 13, 1987, p. D2.

8. *Ibid.*

9. Katherine Bishop, "The Battle of the Booksellers," *New York Times*, March 17, 1987, p. D1.

10. *Standard & Poor's Industry Survey*, October 1987.

11. Cole, "Bids for Harper & Row Spur Publishing Stocks," p. D2.

12. Edwin McDowell, "Maxwell's Harcourt Bid Ends," *New York Times*, May 29, 1987, p. D1.

13. "HBJ Rejects Maxwell's $1.7 Billion Bid," *Publishers Weekly*, May 29, 1987, p. 18.

14. *Ibid.*

15. *Ibid.*

16. John Marcom, Jr., and Clifford Krauss, "British Printing Drops Its Offer for Harcourt," *The Wall Street Journal*, May 29, 1987, p. 4.

17. "Maxwell Sues to Block HBJ's $3 Billion Plan," *Publishers Weekly*, June 12, 1987, p. 23.

18. "Judge Rules Against Maxwell, Clearing HBJ Proposal," *Publishers Weekly*, June 19, 1987, p. 25.

19. *Ibid.*

20. Barbara Toman, "British Printing Sets $1.03 Billion Issue; Maxwell Sees New Harcourt Bid Possible," *The Wall Street Journal*, June 17, 1987, p. 12.

21. "Maxwell Concedes Defeat in HBJ Takeover, Aims at Other U.S. Firms," *Publishers Weekly*, August 7, 1987, p. 309.

22. *Ibid.*

23. Marcom and Krauss, "British Printing Drops Its Offer for Harcourt," p. 4.

24. McDowell, "Maxwell's Harcourt Bid Ends," p. D1.

25. *Ibid.*

26. Charles F. McDoy, "Harcourt Posts 2nd-Period Loss of $70.8 Million," *The Wall Street Journal*, August 17, 1987, p. 7.

DEVELOPING CONCEPTUAL SKILLS: THE CASE METHOD AND THE STRATEGIC AUDIT

STRATEGIC MANAGEMENT MODEL

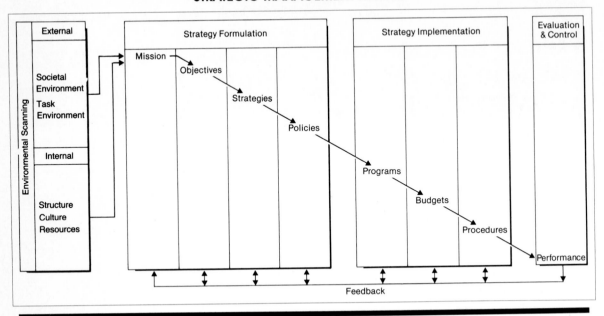

An analysis of a corporation's strategic management calls for a top-down view of the organization. In our analysis we view the corporation as an entity composed of interrelated units and systems, such as accounting, marketing, and finance. We examine the interrelationships of these units in light of the opportunities and threats in the corporation's environment. We carry out analysis through the use of complex cases or management simulations. These techniques will give you the opportunity to move from a narrow, specialized view to a broader, less precise analysis of the overall corporate picture. Consequently, the emphasis in case analysis is on developing and refining conceptual skills, which are different from the skills you developed in your technical and function-oriented courses. As you will see, conceptual skills are vital to successful performance in the business world.

IMPORTANCE OF CONCEPTUAL SKILLS IN BUSINESS

Many have attempted to specify the characteristics necessary for a person to successfully advance from an entry-level position to one in top management. Few of these studies have been successful.[1] But Robert L. Katz has suggested one interesting approach. He focused on the skills successful managers exhibit in performing their jobs; this approach negates the need to identify specific personality traits.[2] These skills imply abilities that can be developed and are manifested in performance.

Katz suggests that effective administration rests on three basic skills: technical, human, and conceptual. He defines them as follows:[3]

- **Technical skills** pertain to *what* is done and to working with *things*. They comprise one's ability to use technology to perform an organizational task.
- **Human skills** pertain to *how* something is done and to working with *people*. They comprise one's ability to work with people in the achievement of goals.
- **Conceptual skills** pertain to *why* something is done and to one's view of the corporation as a *whole*. They comprise one's ability to understand the complexities of the corporation as it affects and is affected by its environment.

Katz further suggests that the optimal mix of these three skills varies at the different corporate levels:

> At lower levels, the major need is for technical and human skills. At higher levels, the administrator's effectiveness depends largely on human and conceptual skills. At the top, conceptual skill becomes the most important of all for successful administration.[4]

Results of a survey of 300 presidents of *Fortune*'s list of the top fifty banking, industrial, insurance, public utility, retailing, and transportation firms support Katz's conclusion regarding the different skill mixes needed at the different organizational levels.[5] As shown in Figure 1, the need for technical skills decreases and the need for conceptual skills increases as a person moves from first-line supervision to top management.

In addition, when executives were asked, "Are there certain skills necessary to move from one organizational level to another?", 55% reported conceptual skills to be the most crucial in movement from middle to top management.[6] Similar results concerning accountants in CPA firms have been reported.[7] Most theorists therefore agree that conceptual work carried out by an organization's leaders is the heart of strategy-making.[8]

The strategic management and business policy course attempts to develop conceptual skills through the use of comprehensive cases or complex simulations. Or course, you also need technical skills in order to analyze various aspects of each case. And you will use human skills in team presentations, study groups, or team projects. But in this course, by focusing on strategic issues, you will primarily develop and refine your conceptual skills. Concentrating on strategic management processes forces you to develop a better understanding of the political, social, and economic environment of business, and to appreciate the interactions of the functional specialties required for corporate success.

FIGURE 1

Optimal Skill Mix of a Manager by Hierarchical Level

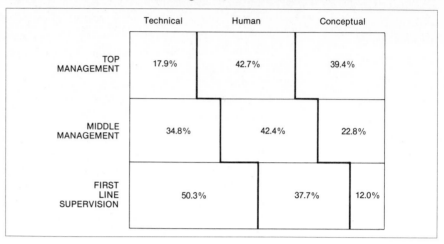

	Technical	Human	Conceptual
TOP MANAGEMENT	17.9%	42.7%	39.4%
MIDDLE MANAGEMENT	34.8%	42.4%	22.8%
FIRST LINE SUPERVISION	50.3%	37.7%	12.0%

SOURCE: T. L. Wheelen, G. K. Rakes, and J. D. Hunger, "Skills of an Executive," a paper presented to the Academy of Management, Kansas City, Mo., August 1976.

AUDITS

Consulting firms, management scholars, boards of directors, and practicing managers suggest the use of audits of corporate activities.[9] An audit provides a checklist of questions, by area or issue, that enables a systematic analysis of various corporate activities to be made. It is extremely useful as a diagnostic tool to pinpoint problem areas and to highlight strengths and weaknesses.

Management Audit

The National Association of Regulatory Utility Commissioners analyzed thirty-one management audits that had been completed or were in progress. The report concluded that the regulatory agencies using management audits were pleased with the results and intended to continue using them. In general, these audits recommended changes in the operating practices of management and suggested areas where substantial reductions in operating costs could be made. The audits gave the boards of directors and management the opportunity to establish new priorities in their objectives and planning, and provided specific recommendations that had impact on the "bottom line."[10]

Typically, the term **management audit** is used to describe a list of questions that forms the basis for an in-depth analysis of a particular area of importance to the corporation. Examples are the sales-force management audit, the social audit, the stakeholder audit, the forecasting audit, the technology audit, the strategic-marketing audit, the culture audit, and the human-resource-management audit.[11] Rarely, however, does it include consideration of more than one issue or functional area. The **strategic audit** is, in comparison, a *type of management audit* that takes a corporate-wide perspective and provides a comprehensive assessment of a corporation's strategic situation. Most business analysts predict that the use of management audits of all kinds will increase. As corporate boards of directors become more aware of their expanding duties and responsibilities, they should call for more corporate-wide management audits to be conducted.

Strategic Audit

As contrasted with the typically more specialized management audit, the strategic audit considers external as well as internal factors and includes alternative selection, implementation, and evaluation and control. It therefore covers the key aspects of the strategic management process and places them within a decision-making framework. This framework is composed of the following eight interrelated steps:

1. **Evaluation of a corporation's current performance results**, in terms of (a) return on investment, profitability, etc., and (b) the current mission, objectives, strategies, and policies.

2. **Examination and evaluation of a corporation's strategic managers**—its board of directors and top management.

3. **A scan of the external environment**, to locate strategic factors that pose opportunities and threats.

4. **A scan of the internal corporate environment**, to determine strategic factors that are strengths and weaknesses.

5. **Analysis of the strategic factors**, to (a) pinpoint problem areas, and (b) review and revise the corporate mission and objectives as necessary.

6. **Generation, evaluation, and selection of the best alternative strategy** in light of the analysis conducted in step 5.

7. **Implementation** of selected strategies, via programs, budgets, and procedures.

8. **Evaluation** of the implemented strategies via feedback systems, and the **control** of activities to ensure their minimum deviation from plans.

This strategic decision-making process, depicted in Figure 2, basically reflects the approach to strategic management being used successfully by corporations such as Warner-Lambert, Dayton Hudson, Avon Products, and Bechtel Group, Inc.[12] Although some research suggests that this type of "normative" approach might not work so well for firms in very unstable environments,[13] a recent survey of 956 corporate long-range planners reveals that actual business practice agrees generally with the model presented in Figure 2.[14] This strategic decision-making process is made operational through the strategic audit.

The audit presents an integrated view of strategic management in action. It describes not only how objectives, strategies, and policies are formulated as

FIGURE 2   **Strategic Decision-making Process**

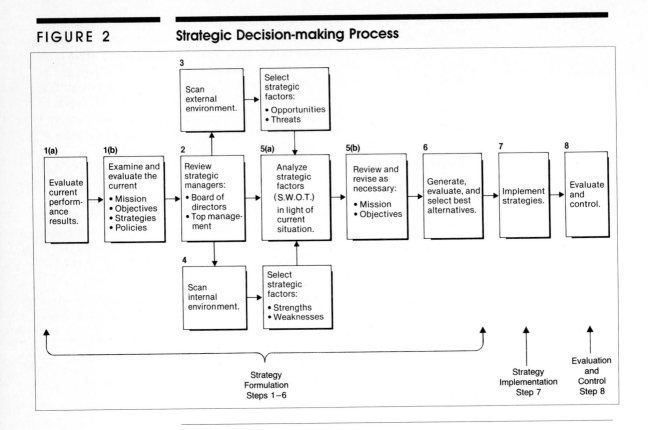

long-range decisions, but also how they are implemented, evaluated, and controlled by programs, budgets, and procedures. The strategic audit, therefore, enables a person to better understand the *ways* in which various functional areas are interrelated and interdependent, as well as the *manner* in which they contribute to the achievement of the corporate mission. Consequently, the strategic audit is very useful to those people, such as boards of directors, whose jobs are to evaluate the overall performance of a corporation and its management.

Exhibit A at the end of this Appendix is an example of a strategic audit proposed for use in the analysis of complex business policy cases and for strategic decision-making. The questions in the audit parallel the eight steps depicted in Figure 2, the strategic decision-making process. It is *not* an all-inclusive list, but it presents many of the critical questions needed for the strategic analysis of any business corporation. You should consider the audit as a guide for analysis. Some questions or even some areas might be inappropriate for a particular case; in other cases, the questions may be insufficient for a complete analysis. However, each question in a particular area of the strategic audit can be broken down into an additional series of subquestions. It is up to you to develop these subquestions when they are needed.

A strategic audit fulfills three major *functions* in a case-oriented strategy and policy course:

1. It serves to highlight and review important concepts from previously studied subject areas.
2. It provides a systematic framework for the analysis of complex cases. (It is especially useful if you are unfamiliar with the case method.)
3. It generally improves the quality of case analysis and reduces the amount of time you might spend in learning how to analyze a case.

Students also find the audit helpful in their organizing a case for written or oral presentation and in seeing that all areas have been considered. The strategic audit thus enables both students and teachers to maximize their efficiency, both in analyzing why a certain area is creating problems for a corporation, and in considering solutions to the problems.

Strategic Audit Worksheet

THE STRATEGIC AUDIT WORKSHEET (as shown in Figure 3) is provided as a systematic method to organize a student's strategic audit (see Appendix A). The strategic audit worksheet is part of the software, *STrategic and Financial ANalyzer* (ST. FAN™), which is attached to the back cover of this book. This computerized worksheet will allow the student to organize information from the case by topic headings of the strategic audit.

CASE METHOD

The analysis and discussion of case problems has been the most popular method of teaching strategy and policy for many years.[15] Cases present actual business situations and enable you to examine both successful and unsuccessful corporations. For example, you might be asked to critically analyze a situation in which a manager had to make a decision of long-run corporate importance. This approach gives you a feel for what it is like to work in a large corporation and to be faced with making a business decision.

Case Analysis and Presentation

There is no one best way to analyze or present a case report. Each instructor has personal preferences for format and approach. Nevertheless, we present one suggested approach for both written and oral reports in Exhibit B, at the end of the Appendix. This approach provides a systematic method for successfully attacking a case.

The presentation of case analysis can be organized on the basis of a number of frameworks. One obvious framework to follow is the strategic audit as detailed in Exhibit A. Another is the McKinsey 7-S Framework, composed of the

FIGURE 3   **Strategic Audit Worksheet**

Audit Pages	Text Pages	AUDIT HEADING	ANALYSIS		COMMENTS
			(+) Factors	(-) Factors	
I	681	**CURRENT SITUATION**			
IA	681	A. Past Corporate Performance Indexes			
IB	681	B. Corporate Mission, Objectives, Strategies, & Policies			
		S.W.O.T. ANALYSIS BEGINS			
II	681	**STRATEGIC MANAGERS**			
IIA	681	A. Board of Directors			
IIB	681	B. Top Management			
III	681-682	**EXTERNAL ENVIRONMENT:** Opportunities and Threats (S.W.O.T.)			
IIIA	681	A. Societal Environment			
IIIB	681	B. Task Environment (Industry Analysis)			
IV	682-684	**INTERNAL ENVIRONMENT:** Strength and Weaknesses (S.W.O.T.)			
IVA	682	A. Corporate Structure			
IVB	682	B. Corporate Culture			
IVC	682	C. Corporate Resources			
	682	1. Marketing			
	682	2. Finance			
	683	3. Research and Development			
	683	4. Operations (Manufacturing/Service)			
	684	5. Human Resources			
	684	6.Information Systems			
V	684	**ANALYSIS OF STRATEGIC FACTORS**			
VA	684	A. Key Internal and External Strategic Factors (S.W.O.T.)			
VB	684	B. Review of Mission and Objectives			
		S.W.O.T. ANALYSIS ENDS	(PROS)	(CONS)	(COMMENTS)
VI	684	**STRATEGIC ALTERNATIVES**			
VII	685	**RECOMMENDATION**			
VIII	685	**IMPLEMENTATION**			
IX	685	**EVALUATION AND CONTROL**			

SOURCE: T. L. Wheelen and J. D. Hunger, "Strategic Audit Worksheet," Copyright © 1989 by Wheelen and Hunger Associates. Reprinted by permission.

seven organizational variables of *structure, strategy, staff, management style, systems and procedures, skills,* and *shared values.*[16] Regardless of the framework chosen, be especially careful to include a complete analysis of key environmental variables—especially of trends in the industry and of the competitors' activity.

The focus in case discussion is on critical analysis and logical development of thought. A solution is satisfactory if it resolves important problems and is likely to be implemented successfully. How the corporation actually dealt with the case problems has no real bearing on the analysis, because its management might have analyzed its problems incorrectly and implemented a series of flawed solutions.

Researching the Case

You should undertake outside research into the environmental setting of the case. Check each case to find out when the case situation occurred and then screen the business periodicals for that time. This background will give you an appreciation for the situation as it was experienced by the people in the case. A company's annual report from that year can be very helpful.[17] An understanding of the economy during that period will help you avoid making a serious error in your analysis—for example, suggesting a sale of stock when the stock market is at an all-time low or taking on more debt when the prime interest rate is over 15%. Information on the industry will provide insights on its competitive activities. Some resources available for research into the economy and a corporation's industry are suggested in Exhibit C at the end of the Appendix.

If you are unfamiliar with these business resources we urge you to read *How to Use the Business Library: With Sources of Business Information,* 5th ed., by H. W. Johnson, A. J. Faria, and E. L. Maier (Cincinnati: South-Western Publishing Co., 1984).

Financial Analysis: A Place To Begin

A review of key financial ratios can help you assess the company's overall situation and pinpoint some problem areas. Table 1 lists some of the most important financial ratios. Included are (1) **liquidity ratios,** which measure the corporation's ability to meet its financial obligations, (2) **profitability ratios,** which measure the degree of the corporation's success in achieving desired profit levels, (3) **activity ratios,** which measure the effectiveness of the corporation's use of resources, and (4) **leverage ratios,** which measure the contributions of owners' financing compared with creditors' financing.

In your analysis do *not* simply make an exhibit including all the ratios, but select and discuss only those ratios that have an impact on the company's problems. For instance, external resources, accounts receivable, and inventory may provide a source of funds. If receivables and inventories are double the industry average, reducing them may provide needed cash. In this situation, the case

TABLE 1 Financial Ratios

	FORMULA	HOW EXPRESSED	MEANING
1. Liquidity Ratios			
Current ratio	$\dfrac{\text{Current assets}}{\text{Current liabilities}}$	Decimal	A short-term indicator of the company's ability to pay its short-term liabilities from short-term assets; how much of current assets are available to cover each dollar of current liabilities.
Quick (acid test) ratio	$\dfrac{\text{Current assets} - \text{Inventory}}{\text{Current liabilities}}$	Decimal	Measures the company's ability to pay off its short-term obligations from current assets, excluding inventories.
Inventory to net working capital	$\dfrac{\text{Inventory}}{\text{Current assets} - \text{Current liabilities}}$	Decimal	A measure of inventory balance; measures the extent to which the cushion of excess current assets over current liabilities may be threatened by unfavorable changes in inventory.
Cash ratio	$\dfrac{\text{Cash} + \text{Cash equivalents}}{\text{Current liabilities}}$	Decimal	Measures the extent to which the company's capital is in cash or cash equivalents; shows how much of the current obligations can be paid from cash or near-cash assets.
2. Profitability Ratios			
Net profit margin	$\dfrac{\text{Net profit after taxes}}{\text{Net sales}}$	Percentage	Shows how much after-tax profits are generated by each dollar of sales.
Gross profit margin	$\dfrac{\text{Sales} - \text{Cost of goods sold}}{\text{Net sales}}$	Percentage	Indicates the total margin available to cover other expenses beyond cost of goods sold, and still yield a profit.
Return on investment (ROI)	$\dfrac{\text{Net profit after taxes}}{\text{Total assets}}$	Percentage	Measures the rate of return on the total assets utilized in the company; a measure of management's efficiency, it shows the return on all the assets under its control regardless of source of financing.
Return on equity (ROE)	$\dfrac{\text{Net profit after taxes}}{\text{Stockholders' equity}}$	Percentage	Measures the rate of return on the book value of stockholders' total investment in the company.

Ratio	Formula	Unit	Description
Earnings Per Share (EPS)	$\dfrac{\text{Net profit after taxes} - \text{Preferred stock dividends}}{\text{Average number of common shares}}$	Dollar per share	Shows the after-tax earnings generated for each share of common stock.

3. Activity Ratios

Ratio	Formula	Unit	Description
Inventory turnover	$\dfrac{\text{Net sales}}{\text{Inventory}}$	Decimal	Measures the number of times that average inventory of finished goods was turned over or sold during a period of time, usually a year.
Days of inventory	$\dfrac{\text{Inventory}}{\text{Cost of goods sold} \div 365}$	Days	Measures the number of one day's worth of inventory that a company has on-hand at any given time.
Net working capital turnover	$\dfrac{\text{Net sales}}{\text{Net working capital}}$	Decimal	Measures how effectively the net working capital is used to generate sales.
Asset turnover	$\dfrac{\text{Sales}}{\text{Total assets}}$	Decimal	Measures the utilization of all the company's assets; measures how many sales are generated by each dollar of assets.
Fixed asset turnover	$\dfrac{\text{Sales}}{\text{Fixed assets}}$	Decimal	Measures the utilization of the company's fixed assets (i.e., plant and equipment); measures how many sales are generated by each dollar of fixed assets.
Average collection period	$\dfrac{\text{Accounts receivable}}{\text{Sales for year} \div 365}$	Days	Indicates the average length of time in days that a company must wait to collect a sale after making it; may be compared to the credit terms offered by the company to its customers.
Accounts receivable turnover	$\dfrac{\text{Annual credit sales}}{\text{Accounts receivable}}$	Decimal	Indicates the number of times that accounts receivable are cycled during the period (usually a year).
Accounts payable period	$\dfrac{\text{Accounts Payable}}{\text{Purchases for year} \div 365}$	Days	Indicates the average length of time in days that the company takes to pay its credit purchases.
Days of cash	$\dfrac{\text{Cash}}{\text{Net sales for year} \div 365}$	Days	Indicates the number of days of cash on hand, at present sales levels.

(Continued)

TABLE 1 (Continued)

	FORMULA	HOW EXPRESSED	MEANING
4. Leverage Ratios			
Debt to asset ratio	$\dfrac{\text{Total debt}}{\text{Total assets}}$	Percentage	Measures the extent to which borrowed funds have been used to finance the company's assets.
Debt to equity ratio	$\dfrac{\text{Total debt}}{\text{Stockholders' equity}}$	Percentage	Measures the funds provided by creditors versus the funds provided by owners.
Long-term debt to capital structure	$\dfrac{\text{Long-term debt}}{\text{Stockholders' equity}}$	Percentage	Measures the long-term component of capital structure.
Times interest earned	$\dfrac{\text{Profit before taxes} + \text{Interest charges}}{\text{Interest charges}}$	Decimal	Indicates the ability of the company to meet its annual interest costs.
Coverage of fixed charges	$\dfrac{\text{Profit before taxes} + \text{Interest charges} + \text{Lease charges}}{\text{Interest charges} + \text{Lease obligations}}$	Decimal	A measure of the company's ability to meet all of its fixed-charge obligations.
Current liabilities to equity	$\dfrac{\text{Current liabilities}}{\text{Stockholders' equity}}$	Percentage	Measures the short-term financing portion versus that provided by owners.
5. Other Ratios			
Price/Earning ratio	$\dfrac{\text{Market price per share}}{\text{Earnings per share}}$	Decimal	Shows the current market's evaluation of a stock, based on its earnings; shows how much the investor is willing to pay for each dollar of earnings.
Dividend payout ratio	$\dfrac{\text{Annual dividends per share}}{\text{Annual earnings per share}}$	Percentage	Indicates the percentage of profit that is paid out as dividends.
Dividend yield on common stock	$\dfrac{\text{Annual dividends per share}}{\text{Current market price per share}}$	Percentage	Indicates the dividend rate of return to common stockholders at the current market price.

NOTE: In using ratios for analysis, calculate ratios for the corporation and compare them to the average ratios for the particular industry. Refer to Standard and Poor's and Robert Morris Associates for average industry data. For an in-depth discussion of ratios and their use, refer to J. F. Weston and E. F. Brigham, *Essentials of Managerial Finance*, 8th ed. (Chicago, Ill.: Dryden Press, 1987), pp. 240–259. Special thanks to Dr. Moustafa H. Abdelsamad, Dean of Southeastern Massachusetts University, for his writing of the meanings of these ratios.

report should include not only sources of funds, but also the number of dollars freed for use.

A typical financial analysis of a firm would include a study of the operating statements for five or ten years, including a trend analysis of sales, profits, earnings per share, debt/equity ratio, return on investment, etc., plus a ratio study comparing the firm under study with industry standards. To begin, scrutinize historical income statements and balance sheets. These two basic statements provide most of the data needed for analysis. Compare the statements over time if a series of statements is available. Calculate changes that occur in individual categories from year to year, as well as the total change over the years. Determine the change as a percentage as well as an absolute amount, and determine the amount *adjusted for inflation* (constant dollars). Examination of this information may reveal developing trends. Compare trends in one category with trends in related categories. For example, an increase in sales of 15% over three years may appear to be satisfactory until you note an increase of 20% in the cost of goods sold during the same period. The outcome of this comparison might suggest that further investigation into the manufacturing process is necessary.

Another approach to the analysis of financial statements is to convert them into **common-size statements**. Convert every category from dollar terms to percentages. For the balance sheet, give the total assets or liabilities a value of 100%, and calculate all other categories as percentages of the total assets or liabilities. For the income statement, net sales represent 100%: calculate the percentage of each category so that the categories sum to the net sales percentage (100%). When you convert statements to this form, it is relatively easy to note the percentage that each category represents of the total. Comparisons of these percentages over the years can point out areas for additional analysis. To get a proper picture, however, make comparisons with industry data, if available, to see if fluctuations are merely reflecting industry-wide trends. If a firm's trends are generally in line with those of the rest of the industry, there is a lower likelihood of problems than if the firm's trends are worse than industry averages. These statements are especially helpful *in developing scenarios and pro forma statements*, since they provide a series of historical relationships (for example, cost of goods sold to sales, interest to sales, and inventories as a percent of assets).

If the corporation being studied appears to be in poor financial condition, calculate its "Z-value." Developed by Edward Altman, the formula combines five ratios by weighting them according to their importance to a corporation's financial strength (see Illustrative Example 1). The formula predicts the likelihood of the company going bankrupt. Firms in serious trouble have Z values below 1.81.

Adjusting for Inflation

Many of the cases in business policy/strategy textbooks take place during a period of inflation. When analyzing these cases, you should calculate sales and profits in constant dollars in order to perceive the "true" performance of the cor-

ILLUSTRATIVE EXAMPLE 1

The Altman Bankruptcy Formula

Edward I. Altman developed a formula to predict a company's likelihood of going bankrupt. His system of multiple discriminate analysis is used by stockholders to determine if the corporation is a good investment. The formula was developed from a study of thirty-three manufacturing companies with assets averaging $6.4 million that had filed Chapter X bankruptcies. These were paired with thirty-three similar but profitable firms with assets between $1 million and $25 million. The formula is:

$$Z = 1.2x_1 + 1.4x_2 + 3.3x_3 + 0.6x_4 + 1.0x_5$$

where

x_1 = Working capital divided by total assets.

x_2 = Retained earnings divided by total assets.

x_3 = Earnings before interest and taxes divided by total assets.

x_4 = Market value of equity divided by book value of total debt.

x_5 = Sales divided by total assets.

Z = Overall index of corporate fiscal health.

The range of the Z-value for most corporations is -4 to $+8$. According to Altman:

- Financially strong corporations have Z values above 2.99.

- Corporations in serious trouble have Z values below 1.81.

- Corporations between 1.81 and 2.99 are question marks that could go either way.

The closer a firm gets to bankruptcy, the more accurate is the Z value as a predictor.

SOURCE: M. Ball, "Z Factor: Rescue by the Numbers," *INC.* (December 1980), p. 48. Reprinted with permission, *INC.* magazine, (December, 1980). Copyright © 1980 by INC. Publishing Company, 38 Commercial Wharf, Boston, MA 02110.

poration in comparison with that of the industry, or of the economy in general. Remember that chief executive officers wish to keep their jobs and that some will tend to bias the figures in their favor. Sales stated in current dollars may seem to show substantial growth, but when they're converted to constant dollars, they may show a steady decline.

The return-on-investment ratio is doubly susceptible to distortion. Because net income is generally measured in current dollars, it rises with inflation. Meanwhile, investment (generally valued in historical dollars) effectively falls. Thus ROI may appear to be rising when it is actually stable, or appear to be stable when it is actually falling.[18]

To adjust for general inflation, most firms use the Consumer Price Index (CPI), as given in Table 2. The simplest way to adjust financial statements for inflation is to divide each item by the CPI for that year. This changes each figure

TABLE 2

Consumer Price Index for All Items (1967 = 100.0)

YEAR	CPI	YEAR	CPI
1975	161.2	1982	289.1
1976	170.5	1983	298.4
1977	181.5	1984	311.1
1978	195.4	1985	322.2
1979	217.4	1986	328.4
1980	246.8	1987	340.4
1981	272.4	1988	354.3

SOURCE: U.S. Department of Commerce, *1988 Statistical Abstract of the United States,* 108th edition, Chart no. 740, p. 451. *Monthly Labor Review* (May, 1989), p. 94.

to 1967 constant dollars. The CPI uses 1967 as the base year (with a CPI of 100.0) against which all other years' prices are compared. Remember that the CPI for each year is a percentage. For example, to convert 1985 reported sales of $950,000 to constant (1967) dollars, divide 950,000 by the CPI for 1985 (3.222); 1985 sales are thus converted to constant (1967) dollars of $294,848. This conversion displays the fact that, in terms of general purchasing power, a U.S. dollar in 1985 was worth only 32 cents in 1967 dollars.

TABLE 3

General Price Level Adjustment for Inflation Using Consumer Price Index

(Dollar Amounts in Millions[1])

	1984	1983	1982
Operating Revenue, as reported	$7,934	$5,891	$4,909
% increase (decrease) over 1982	62%	20%	—
Operating Revenue			
Constant (1982) dollars	7,374	5,708	4,909
% increase over 1982	50%	16%	—
Net Earnings, as reported	465	272	414
% increase (decrease) over 1982	12%	(66%)	—
Net Earnings			
Constant (1982) dollars	432	263	414
% increase (decrease) over 1982	4%	(63%)	—
CPI Adjustment Factor (1982 = 100%)	1.076	1.032	1.000
$\frac{198x \text{ CPI}}{1982 \text{ CPI}}$	$\left(\frac{311.1}{289.1}\right)$	$\left(\frac{298.4}{289.1}\right)$	$\left(\frac{289.1}{289.1}\right)$

NOTE: [1] Selected figures taken from CSX Corporation, *1984 Annual Report,* p. 20.

TABLE 4

Changes in Prime Interest Rates*

YEAR	LOW	HIGH	YEAR	LOW	HIGH
1975	7	$10\frac{1}{2}$	1982	$11\frac{1}{2}$	17
1976	$6\frac{1}{4}$	$7\frac{1}{4}$	1983	$10\frac{1}{2}$	$11\frac{1}{2}$
1977	$6\frac{1}{2}$	$7\frac{3}{4}$	1984	$10\frac{3}{4}$	$12\frac{3}{4}$
1978	6	$11\frac{3}{4}$	1985	$9\frac{1}{2}$	$10\frac{3}{4}$
1979	$11\frac{1}{2}$	$15\frac{3}{4}$	1986	$7\frac{1}{2}$	9
1980	11	$21\frac{1}{2}$	1987	$7\frac{3}{4}$	$9\frac{3}{4}$
1981	$15\frac{3}{4}$	$20\frac{1}{2}$	1988	$8\frac{1}{2}$	10

SOURCE: D. S. Benton, "Banking and Financial Information," Table 1.1, p. 2 in *Thorndike Encyclopedia of Banking and Financial Tables,* 3rd Edition, *1989 Yearbook* (Boston, Mass.: Warren, Gorham & Lamont, 1989).

* The rate of interest that banks charge on the lowest-risk loans they make.

For a comparison of recent financial statements, it might help to use a more recent base year than 1967 in the adjustment for inflation. For example, in Table 3 selected figures are taken from CSX Corporation's annual reports for 1982 through 1984. Instead of using 1967 as the base year for these comparisons, one may use 1982. To do so, divide the CPIs for 1983 and 1984 (as provided in Table 2) by the CPI for 1982; the appropriate adjustment factors are found to be 1.032 for 1983 and 1.076 for 1984. Table 3 shows operating revenue and net earnings figures first as reported (in 1983 and 1984 dollars) and second, divided by each year's adjustment factor, to result in 1982 constant dollars. Once this conversion is done, the impact of inflation on a firm's revenues and earnings can be clearly seen. Note, for example, that reported operating revenue increased by 62% from 1982 to 1984. In constant 1982 dollars, however, they increased only 50%. Although net earnings as reported in 1984 increased 12% from 1982, they increased only 4% when they are considered in constant dollar terms.

Another helpful aid in the analysis of cases in business policy is the chart on prime interest rates given in Table 4. For better assessments of strategic decisions, it can be useful to note the level of the prime interest rate at the time of the case. A decision to borrow money to build a new plant would have been a good one in 1977, but somewhat foolhardy in 1981.

SUMMARY AND CONCLUSION

The strategic management/business policy course is concerned with developing the conceptual skills that successful top management needs. The emphasis is therefore on improving your analytical and problem-solving abilities. The case method develops those skills and gives you an appreciation of environmental issues and the interdependencies among the functional units of a large corporation. The strategic audit is one recommended technique for the systematization of the analysis of fairly long and complex policy cases. It also provides a basic checklist for the investigation of any large corporation. Nevertheless, the strategic audit is only one of many techniques with which you can analyze and diagnose case problems. We expect consultants, managers, and boards of directors to increasingly employ the audit as an analytical technique.

DISCUSSION QUESTIONS

1. Should people be selected for top management positions primarily on the basis of their having a particular combination of skills? Explain.

2. What are the strengths and weaknesses of the strategic audit as a technique for assessing corporate performance?

3. What value does the case method hold for the study of strategic management/business policy?

4. Why should one begin a case analysis with a financial analysis? When are other approaches appropriate?

NOTES

1. B. M. Bass, *Stogdill's Handbook of Leadership* (New York: Free Press, 1981), p. 73.

2. R. L. Katz, "Skills of an Effective Administrator," *Harvard Business Review* (January–February 1955), p. 33.

3. Katz, pp. 33–42. These definitions were adapted from the material in this article.

4. Katz, p. 42.

5. T. L. Wheelen, G. K. Rakes, and J. D. Hunger, "Skills of an Executive" (Paper presented at the Thirty-Sixth Annual Meeting of the Academy of Management, Kansas City, Mo., August 1976).

6. Wheelen, Rakes, and Hunger, p. 7.

7. W. G. Shenkir, T. L. Wheelen, and R. H. Strawser, "The Making of an Accountant," *CPA Journal* (March 1973), p. 219.

8. E. E. Chaffee, "Three Models of Strategy," *Academy of Management Review* (January 1985), pp. 89–90.

D. Norburn, "GOGOs, YOYOs and DODOs: Company Directors and Industry Performance," *Strategic Management Journal* (March–April 1986), p. 112.

B. C. Reimann, "Doers as Planners," *Planning Review* (September 1986), p. 45.

9. T. L. Wheelen and J. D. Hunger, "Using the Strategic Audit," *SAM Advanced Management Journal* (Winter 1987), pp. 4–12.

R. B. Buchele, "How to Evaluate a Firm," *California Management Review* (Fall 1962), pp. 5–16.

J. Martindell, *The Appraisal of Management* (New York: Harper & Row, 1962).

R. Bauer, L. T. Cauthorn, and R. P. Warner, "Management Audit Process Guide," (Boston: Intercollegiate Case Clearing House, no. 9-375-336, 1975).

J. D. Hunger and T. L. Wheelen, "The Strategic Audit: An Integrative Approach To Teaching Business Policy" (Paper presented at the Forty-Third Annual Meeting of the Academy of Management, Dallas, Texas, August 1983).

M. Lauenstein, "The Strategy Audit," *Journal of Business Strategy* (Winter 1984), pp. 87–91.

10. T. Barry, "What a Management Audit Can Do for You," *Management Review* (June 1977), p. 43.

11. A. J. Dubinsky and R. W. Hansen, "The Sales Force Management Audit," *California Management Review* (Winter 1981), pp. 86–95.

A. B. Carroll and G. W. Beiler, "Landmarks in the Evolution of the Social Audit," *Academy of Management Journal* (September 1975), pp. 589–599.

R. E. Freeman, *Strategic Management: A Stakeholder Approach* (Boston: Pitman Publishing, 1984), p. 111.

J. S. Armstrong, "The Forecasting Audit," in S. Makridakis and S. C. Wheelwright (eds.), *The Handbook of Forecasting* (New York: Wiley and Sons, 1982), pp. 535–552.

D. Ford, "The Management and Marketing of Technology," in *Advances in Strategic Management, Vol. 3,* edited by R. Lamb and P. Shrivastava (Greenwich, Conn.: Jai Press, 1985), pp. 107–109.

M. P. Mokwa, "The Strategic Marketing Audit: An Adoption/Utilization Perspective," *Journal of Business Strategy* (Spring 1986), pp. 88–95.

J. W. Lorsch, "Strategic Myopia: Culture as an Invisible Barrier to Change," in *Gaining Control of the Corporate Culture*, edited by R. H. Kilmann, M. J. Saxton, and R. Serpa (San Francisco: Jossey Bass, 1985), pp. 97–98.

C. J. Fombrun, M. A. Devanna, and N. M. Tichy, in *Strategic Human Resources Management*, edited by C. J. Fombrun, N. M. Tichy, and M. A. Devanna (New York: John Wiley and Sons, 1984), pp. 235–248.

12. E. E. Tallett, "Repositioning Warnet-Lambert as a High-Tech Health Care Company," *Planning Review* (May 1984), pp. 12–16, 41.

K. A. Macke, "Managing Change: How Dayton Hudson Meets the Challenge," *Journal of Business Strategy* (Summer 1983), pp. 78–81.

D. M. Slavick, "Planning at Bechtel: End of the Megaproject Era," *Planning Review* (September 1986), pp. 16–22.

H. Waldron, "Putting a New Face On Avon," *Planning Review* (July 1985), pp. 18–23.

13. J. W. Fredrickson, "The Comprehensiveness of Strategic Decision Processes: Extension, Observation, Future Directions," *Academy of Management Journal* (September 1984), pp. 445–466.

14. P. M. Ginter and A. C. Rucks, "Relative Emphasis Placed on the Steps of the Normative Model of Strategic Planning by Practitioners," *Proceedings, Southern Management Association* (November 1983), pp. 19–21.

15. C. Boyd, D. Kopp, and L. Shufelt, "Evaluative Criteria in Business Policy Case Analysis: An Exploratory Study," *Proceedings, Midwest Academy of Management* (April 1984), pp. 287–292.

16. T. J. Peters and R. W. Waterman, Jr., *In Search of Excellence* (New York: Harper & Row, 1982), pp. 9–12.

17. A survey of 6,000 investors and analysts in the United States, United Kingdom, and New Zealand, revealed a strong belief in the importance of annual reports, especially the financial statement sections, for investment decisions. Sec. L. S. Chang and K. S. Most, "An International Study of the Importance of Financial Statements," *International Journal of Management* (December 1985), pp. 76–85.

18. M. J. Chussil, "Inflation and ROI," *The Pimsletter on Business Strategy, Number 22* (Cambridge, Mass.: The Strategic Planning Institute, 1980), p. 1.

AIDS FOR CASE ANALYSIS AND PRESENTATION

EXHIBIT A
STRATEGIC AUDIT OF A CORPORATION

Special Note: Terms underlined appear as headings in *Strategic Audit Worksheet* in ST. FAN™ SOFTWARE accompanying this textbook.

I. Current Situation

A. How is the corporation performing in terms of return on investment, overall market share, profitability trends, earnings per share, etc.?

B. What are the corporation's current mission, objectives, strategies, and policies?

   1. Are they clearly stated or are they merely implied from performance?

   2. *Mission* (purpose or reason for the company's existence): What business(es) is the corporation in? Why?

   3. *Objectives* (quantified statements telling what is to be accomplished by a particular date): What are the corporate, business, and functional objectives? Are they consistent with each other, with the mission, and with the internal and external environments?

   4. *Strategies* (comprehensive master plan stating *how* a company will achieve its mission and objectives): What strategy or mix of strategies is the corporation following? Are they consistent with each other, with the mission and objectives, and with the internal and external environments?

   5. *Policies* (broad guidelines for decision making to link strategy formulation with its implementation): What are they? Are they consistent with each other, with the mission, objectives, and strategies, and with the internal and external environments?

II. Strategic Managers

A. Board of Directors

   1. Who are they? Are they internal or external?

   2. Do they own significant shares of stock?

   3. Is the stock privately held or publicly traded?

   4. What do they contribute to the corporation in terms of knowledge, skills, background, and connections?

   5. How long have they served on the board?

   6. What is their level of involvement in strategic management? Do they merely rubber-stamp top management's proposals or do they actively participate and suggest future directions?

B. Top Management

   1. What person or group constitutes top management?

   2. What are top management's chief characteristics in terms of knowledge, skills, background, and style?

   3. Has top management been responsible for the corporation's performance over the past few years?

   4. Has it established a systematic approach to the formulation, implementation, and evaluation and control of strategic management?

   5. What is its level of involvement in the strategic management process?

   6. How well does top management interact with lower-level management?

   7. How well does top management interact with the board of directors?

   8. Is top management sufficiently skilled to cope with likely future challenges?

III. External Environment: Opportunities and Threats (S.W.O.T.)

A. Societal Environment

   1. What general environmental factors among the sociocultural, economic, political-legal, and technological forces are currently affecting both the corporation and the industries in which it competes? Which present current or future threats? Opportunities?

   2. Which of these are currently the most important (that is, are **strategic factors**) to the corporation and to the industries in which it competes? Which will be important in the future?

SOURCE: T. L. Wheelen and J. D. Hunger, "Strategic Audit of a Corporation." Copyright © 1982 by Wheelen and Hunger Associates. Reprinted by permission. Revised 1989.

B. Task Environment

1. What forces in the immediate environment (that is, threat of new entrants, bargaining power of buyers, threat of substitute products or services, bargaining power of suppliers, rivalry among competing firms, and the relative power of unions, governments, etc.) are currently affecting the level of competitive intensity within the industries in which the corporation offers products or services?

2. What key factors in the immediate environment (that is, customers, competitors, suppliers, creditors, labor unions, governments, trade associations, interest groups, local communities, and stockholders) are currently affecting the corporation? Which present current or future threats? Opportunities?

3. Which of these forces and factors are the most important (that is, are **strategic factors**) at the present time? Which will be important in the future?

IV.   Internal Environment: Strengths and Weaknesses (S.W.O.T.)

A Corporate Structure

1. How is the corporation presently structured?
   a) Is decision-making authority centralized around one group or decentralized to many groups or units?
   b) Is it organized on the basis of functions, projects, geography, or some combination of these?

2. Is the structure clearly understood by everyone in the corporation?

3. Is the present structure consistent with current corporate objectives, strategies, policies, and programs?

4. In what ways does this structure compare with those of similar corporations?

B. Corporate Culture

1. Is there a well-defined or emerging culture composed of shared beliefs, expectations, and values?

2. Is the culture consistent with the current objectives, strategies, policies, and programs?

3. What is the culture's position on important issues facing the corporation (that is, on productivity, quality of performance, adaptability to changing conditions)?

C. Corporate Resources

1. Marketing
   a) What are the corporation's current marketing objectives, strategies, policies, and programs?
      i) Are they clearly stated, or merely implied from performance and/or budgets?
      ii) Are they consistent with the corporation's mission, objectives, strategies, policies, and with internal and external environments?
   b) How well is the corporation performing in terms of analysis of market position and marketing mix (that is, of product, price, place, and promotion)?
      i) What trends emerge from this analysis?
      ii) What impact have these trends had on past performance and how will they probably affect future performance?
      iii) Does this analysis support the corporation's past and pending strategic decisions?
   c) How well does this corporation's marketing performance compare with those of similar corporations?
   d) Are marketing managers using accepted marketing concepts and techniques to evaluate and improve product performance? (Consider product life cycle, market segmentation, market research, and product portfolios.)
   e) What is the role of the marketing manager in the strategic management process?

2. Finance
   a) What are the corporation's current financial objectives, strategies, policies, and programs?
      i) Are they clearly stated or merely implied from performance and/or budgets?
      ii) Are they consistent with the corporation's mission, objectives, strategies, policies, and with internal and external environments?
   b) How well is the corporation performing in terms of financial analysis? (Consider liquidity ratios, profitability ratios, activity ratios, leverage ratios, capitalization structure, and constant dollars.)
      i) What trends emerge from this analysis?
      ii) Are there any significant differences when statements are calculated in constant versus reported dollars?

iii) What impact have these trends had on past performance and how will they probably affect future performance?

iv) Does this analysis support the corporation's past and pending strategic decisions?

c) How well does this corporation's financial performance compare with that of similar corporations?

d) Are financial managers using accepted financial concepts and techniques to evaluate and improve current corporate and divisional performance? (Consider financial leverage, capital budgeting, and ratio analysis.)

e) What is the role of the financial manager in the strategic management process?

3. Research and Development (R&D)

a) What are the corporation's current R&D objectives, strategies, policies, and programs?

i) Are they clearly stated, or implied from performance and/or budgets?

ii) Are they consistent with the corporation's mission, objectives, strategies, policies, and with internal and external environments?

iii) What is the role of technology in corporate performance?

iv) Is the mix of basic, applied, and engineering research appropriate given the corporate mission and strategies?

b) What return is the corporation receiving from its investment in R&D?

c) Is the corporation technologically competent?

d) How well does the corporation's investment in R&D compare with the investments of similar corporations?

e) What is the role of the R&D manager in the strategic management process?

4. Operations (Manufacturing/Service)*

a) What are the corporation's current manufacturing/service objectives, strategies, policies, and programs?

---

* Research suggests that the strategic approach developed for manufacturing companies is very useful for service firms. See H. M. O'Neill, "Do Strategic Paradigms Work in Service Industries?" in *Handbook of Business Strategy, 1986/87 Yearbook,* edited by W. D. Guth (Boston: Warren, Forham, and Lamont, 1986), pp. 19.1–19.14.

i) Are they clearly stated, or merely implied from performance and/or budgets?

ii) Are they consistent with the corporation's mission, objectives, strategies, policies, and with internal and external environments?

b) What is the type and extent of operations capabilities of the corporation?

i) If product-oriented, consider plant facilities, type of manufacturing system (continuous mass production or intermittent job shop), age and type of equipment, degree and role of automation and/or robots, plant capacities and utilization, productivity ratings, availability and type of transportation.

ii) If service-oriented, consider service facilities (e.g., hospital, theater, or school buildings), type of operations systems (continuous service over time to same clientele or intermittent service over time to varied clientele), age and type of supporting equipment, degree and role of automation and/or use of mass communication devices (e.g., diagnostic machinery, videotape machines), facility capacities and utilization rates, efficiency ratings of professional/service personnel, availability and type of transportation to bring service staff and clientele together.

c) Are manufacturing or service facilities vulnerable to natural disasters, local or national strikes, reduction or limitation of resources from suppliers, substantial cost increases of materials, or nationalization by governments?

d) Is operating leverage being used successfully with an appropriate mix of people and machines, in manufacturing firms, or of support staff to professionals, in service firms?

e) How well does the corporation perform relative to the competition? Consider costs per unit of labor, material, and overhead; downtime; inventory control management and/or scheduling of service staff; production ratings; facility utilization percentages; and number of clients successfully treated by category (if service firm), or percentage of orders shipped on time (if product firm).

i) What trends emerge from this analysis?

ii) What impact have these trends had on past

performance and how will they probably affect future performance?

iii) Does this analysis support the corporation's past and pending strategic decisions?

f) Are operations managers using appropriate concepts and techniques to evaluate and improve current performance? Consider cost systems, quality control and reliability systems, inventory control management, personnel scheduling, learning curves, safety programs, engineering programs, that can improve efficiency of manufacturing or of service.

g) What is the role of the operations manager in the strategic management process?

5. Human Resources Management (HRM)

a) What are the corporation's current HRM objectives, strategies, policies, and programs?

i) Are they clearly stated, or merely implied from performance and/or budgets?

ii) Are they consistent with the corporation's mission, objectives, strategies, policies, and with internal and external environments?

b) How well is the corporation's HRM performing in terms of improving the fit between the individual employee and the job? Consider turnover, grievances, strikes, layoffs, employee training, quality of work life.

i) What trends emerge from this analysis?

ii) What impact have these trends had on past performance and how will they probably affect future performance?

iii) Does this analysis support the corporation's past and pending strategic decisions?

c) How does this corporation's HRM performance compare with that of similar corporations?

d) Are HRM managers using appropriate concepts and techniques to evaluate and improve corporate performance? Consider the job analysis program, performance appraisal system, up-to-date job descriptions, training and development programs, attitude surveys, job design programs, quality of relationship with unions.

e) What is the role of the HRM manager in the strategic management process?

6. Information Systems (IS)

a) What are the corporation's current IS objectives, strategies, policies, and programs?

i) Are they clearly stated, or merely implied from performance and/or budgets?

ii) Are they consistent with the conporation's mission, objectives, strategies, policies, and with internal and external environments?

b) How well is the corporation's IS performing in terms of providing a useful database, automating routine clerical operations, assisting managers in making routine decisions, and providing information necessary for strategic decisions?

i) What trends emerge from this analysis?

ii) What impact have these trends had on past performance and how will they probably affect future performance?

iii) Does this analysis support the corporation's past and pending strategic decisions?

c) How does this corporation's IS performance and stage of development compare with that of similar corporations?

d) Are IS managers using appropriate concepts and techniques to evaluate and improve corporate performance? Do they know how to build and manage a complex data-base, conduct system analyses, and implement interactive decision-support systems?

e) What is the role of the IS manager in the strategic management process?

V.   Analysis of Strategic Factors

A. What are the key internal and external factors (S.W.O.T.) that strongly affect the corporation's present and future performance?

1. What have been the key historical strategic factors for this corporation?

2. What are the key short-term (0–1 year) strategic factors for this corporation?

3. What are the key intermediate-term (1–3 year) strategic factors for this corporation?

4. What are the key long-term (3–10 year) strategic factors for this corporation?

B. Are the current mission and objectives appropriate in light of the key strategic factors and problems?

1. Should the mission and objectives be changed? If so, how?

2. If changed, what will the effects on the firm be?

VI.   Strategic Alternatives

A. Can the current or revised objectives be met by the simple, more careful implementing of those strategies presently in use (for example, fine tuning the strategies)?

B. What are the major feasible alternative strategies available to this corporation? What are the pros and cons of each? Can *scenarios* be developed and agreed upon?

1. Consider stability, growth, and retrenchment as corporate strategies.

2. Consider cost leadership, differentiation, and focus as business strategies.

3. Consider any functional strategic alternatives that might be needed for reinforcement of an important corporate or business strategic alternative.

VII.   Recommendation

A. Specify which of the strategic alternatives you are recommending for the corporate, business, and functional levels of the corporation. Do you recommend different business or functional strategies for different units of the corporation?

B. Justify your recommendation in terms of its ability to resolve both long- and short-term problems and effectively deal with the key strategic factors.

C. What policies should be developed or revised to guide effective implementation?

VIII.   Implementation

A. What kinds of programs (for example, restructuring the corporation) should be developed to implement the recommended strategy?

1. Who should develop these programs?

2. Who should be in charge of these programs?

B. Are the programs financially feasible? Can *pro forma* budgets be developed and agreed upon? Are priorities and timetables appropriate to individual programs?

C. Will new standard operating procedures need to be developed?

IX.   Evaluation and Control

A. Is the current information system capable of providing sufficient feedback on implementation activities and performance?

1. Can performance results be pinpointed by area, unit, project, or function?

2. Is the information timely?

B. Are adequate control measures, to ensure conformance with the recommended strategic plan, in place?

1. Are appropriate standards and measures being used?

2. Are reward systems capable of recognizing and rewarding good performance?

EXHIBIT B
SUGGESTED TECHNIQUES FOR CASE ANALYSIS AND PRESENTATION

A. Case Analysis

1. Read the case rapidly, to get an overview of the nature of the corporation and its environment. Note the date on which the case was written so that you can put it into the proper time context of the decision issue.

2. Read the case a second time, and give it a detailed analysis according to the strategic audit (*see Exhibit A*) when appropriate. The audit will provide a conceptual framework for the examination of the corporation's objectives, mission, policies, strategies, problems, symptoms of problems, and issues. You should end up with a list of the salient issues and problems in the case. Perform a financial analysis.

3. Undertake outside research, when appropriate, to uncover economic and industrial information. *Exhibit C* suggests possible sources for outside research. These data should provide the environmental setting for the corporation. Conduct an in-depth analysis of the industry. Analyze the important competitors. Consider the bargaining power of suppliers, as well as buyers that might affect the firm's situation. Consider also the possible threats of future competitors in the industry, as well as the likelihood of new or different products or services that might substitute for the company's present ones.

4. Marshal facts and evidence to support selected issues and problems. Develop a framework or outline to organize the analysis. Your method of organization could be one of the following:

   a) The case as organized around the strategic audit.

   b) The case as organized around the key individual(s) in the case.

   c) The case as organized around the corporation's functional areas: production, management, finance, marketing, and R&D.

   d) The case as organized around the decision-making process.

   e) The case as organized around the seven variables (McKinsey 7-S Framework) of structure, strategy, staff, management style, systems and procedures, skills, and shared values.

5. Clearly identify and state the central problem(s) as supported by the information in the case. Use the S.W.O.T. format to sum up the key **strategic factors** facing the corporation: Strengths and Weaknesses of the company; Opportunities and Threats in the environment.

6. Develop a logical series of alternatives that evolve from the analysis to resolve the problem(s) or issue(s) in the case.

7. Evaluate each of the alternatives in light of the company's environment (both external and internal), mission, objectives, strategies, and policies. For each alternative, consider both the possible obstacles to its implementation and its financial implications.

8. Make recommendations on the basis of the fact that action must be taken. (Don't say, "I don't have enough information." The individuals in the case may have had the same or even less information than is given by the case.)

   a) Base your recommendations on a total analysis of the case.

   b) Provide the evidence gathered in step A4 (p. 685) to justify suggested changes.

   c) List the recommendations in order of priority—those to be done immediately and those to be done in the future.

   d) Show clearly how your recommendations deal with each of the *strategic factors* that were mentioned earlier in step A5. How do they build upon corporate *Strengths* to take advantage of environmental *Opportunities*? How do they deal with environmental *Threats* and corporate *Weaknesses*?

   e) Explain how each recommendation will be implemented. How will the plan(s) deal with anticipated resistance?

   f) Suggest feedback and control systems, to ensure that the recommendations are carried out as planned and to give advance warning of needed adjustments.

B. Written Presentation

1. Use the outline from step A4 (p. 685) to write the first draft of the case analysis. Follow steps A5 through A8.

   a) Don't rehash the case material; rather, supply the salient evidence and data to support your recommendations.

   b) Develop exhibits on financial ratios and other data for inclusion in your report. The exhibits should provide meaningful information. Mention key elements of an exhibit in the text of the written analysis. If you include a ratio analysis as an exhibit, explain the meaning of the ratios in the text and cite only the critical ones in your analysis.

2. After it is written, review your case analysis for content and grammar. Remember to compare the outline (step A4) with the final product. Make sure you've presented sufficient data or evidence to support your problem analysis and recommendations. If the final product requires rewriting, do so. Keep in mind that the written report is going to be judged not only on *what* is said but also on the *manner* in which it is said.

3. If your written or oral presentation requires *pro forma* statements, you may wish to develop a scenario for each quarter and/or year in your forecast. A well-constructed scenario will help improve the accuracy of your forecast.

C. Oral Presentation by Teams

1. The team should first decide upon a framework or outline for analysis, as mentioned in step A4. Although teams often divide the analysis work among team members, it is helpful if each team member also follows steps A5 through A8 in developing a preliminary analysis of the entire case to share and compare with team members.

EXHIBIT C **687**

2. The team should combine member input into one consolidated team audit, including S.W.O.T. analysis, alternatives, and recommendation(s). Gain agreement on the strategic factors and the best alternative(s) to support.

3. Divide among the team's members the further development and presentation of the case analysis and recommendation(s). Agree upon responsibilities for the preparation of visual aids and handouts.

4. Modify the team outline, if necessary, and have one or two rehearsals of the presentation. If there is a time constraint for the final presentation, apply it to the practice presentation. If exhibits are used, make sure to allow sufficient time for their explanation. Critique one another's presentations and make the necessary modifications to the analysis.

5. During the class presentation, if a presenter misses a key fact, either slip a note to him or her, or deal with it in the summary speech.

6. Answer the specific questions raised by the instructor or classmates. If one person acts as a moderator for the questions and refers the questions to the appropriate team member, the presentation runs more smoothly than it will if everyone (or no one!) tries to deal with each question.

EXHIBIT C
RESOURCES FOR CASE RESEARCH

A. Company Information
  1. Annual Reports
  2. *Moody's Manuals on Investment* (a listing of companies within certain industries, that contains a brief history and a five-year financial statement of each company)
  3. Securities and Exchange Commission Annual Report Form 10-K
  4. *Standard and Poor's Register of Corporations, Directors, and Executives*
  5. *Value Line Investment Survey*

B. Economic Information
  1. Regional statistics and local forecasts from large banks
  2. *Business Cycle Development* (Department of Commerce)
  3. Chase Econometric Associates' publications
  4. Census Bureau publications on population, transportation, and housing
  5. *Current Business Reports* (Department of Commerce)
  6. *Economic Indicators* (Joint Economic Committee)
  7. *Economic Report of the President to Congress*
  8. *Long-Term Economic Growth* (Department of Commerce)
  9. *Monthly Labor Review* (Department of Labor)
  10. *Monthly Bulletin of Statistics* (United Nations)
  11. "Survey of Buying Power," *Sales Management*
  12. Standard and Poor's Statistical Service
  13. *Statistical Abstract of the United States* (Department of Commerce)
  14. *Statistical Yearbook* (United Nations)
  15. *Survey of Current Business* (Department of Commerce)
  16. *U.S. Industrial Outlook* (Department of Defense)
  17. *World Trade Annual* (United Nations)
  18. *Overseas Business Reports* (published by country, by U.S. Department of Commerce)

C. Industry Information
  1. Analyses of companies and industries by investment brokerage firms
  2. *Annual Report of American Industry* (a compilation of statistics by industry and company, published by *Fortune*)
  3. *Business Week* (provides weekly economic and business information, and quarterly profit and sales rankings of corporations)
  4. *Fortune Magazine* (publishes listings of financial information on corporations within certain industries)
  5. *Industry Survey* (published quarterly by Standard and Poor Corporation)
  6. *Value Line Investment Survey.*

D. Directory and Index Information
  1. *Business Information: How to Find and Use It*
  2. *Business Periodical Index*
  3. *Directory of National Trade Associations*
  4. *Encyclopedia of Associations*
  5. *Funk and Scott Index of Corporations and Industries*
  6. *Thomas Register of American Manufacturers*

7. *Wall Street Journal Index*
8. *Where to Find Business Information*

E. Ratio Analysis Information
1. *Almanac of Business and Industrial Ratios* (Prentice-Hall)
2. *Annual Statement Studies* (Robert Morris Associates)
3. *Dun's Review* (Dun and Bradstreet: published annually in September-December issues)
4. *Industry Norms and Key Business Ratios* (Dun and Bradstreet)
5. *How to Read a Financial Report* (Merrill Lynch, Pierce, Fenner and Smith, Inc.)
6. *Quality of Earnings: The Investor's Guide to How Much Money a Company Is Really Making* (T. L. O'Glove, Free Press, 1987)

F. General Sources
1. *Commodity Yearbook*
2. *U.S. Census of Business*
3. *U.S. Census of Manufacturers*
4. *World Almanac and Book of Facts*

G. Business Periodicals
1. *Business Week*
2. *Forbes*
3. *Wall Street Journal*
4. *Fortune*
5. Industry-specific periodicals (e.g., *Oil and Gas Journal*)

H. Academic/Practitioner Journals
1. *Harvard Business Review*
2. *Journal of Business Strategy*
3. *Long-Range Planning*
4. *Strategic Management Journal*
5. *Planning Review*
6. *Academy of Management Review*
7. *SAM Advanced Management Journal*